Welcome to ACT Premier!

In this Quick Start Guide, we'll walk you through everything you'll need to know to take advantage of the book, CD-ROM, and online resources. We'll help you prep smarter and score higher.

You've taken the first steps toward maximizing your ACT score—now what?

Kaplan's *ACT Premier* gives you everything you'll need for test day. Here's a handy checklist to get your studying on track:

- ❏ **Register your online companion** for extra practice; Live Online classroom event; chapter-specific tutorial videos; sample essays for the Writing section; and more.

- ❏ **Take the online Diagnostic Quiz** to figure out your strong and weak areas.

- ❏ **Build your study plan.**

- ❏ **Review English, Reading, Math, and Science** concepts.

- ❏ **Practice, practice, practice** with our full-length tests in the book and on the CD-ROM.

▶ Your ACT Premier Book

Kaplan's *ACT Premier* is packed with resources to help you get ready for test day.

It's got:

- a targeted review of key ACT terms and concepts

- tips and strategies for each exam section and question type

- lots of test practice (including 4 full-length exams in the book, and 2 on the CD-ROM)

▶ Take Advantage of Kaplan Exclusives

These powerful tools will help you score higher on test day!

ACT Expert Tutor Tips

Inside each you'll find proven test tips provided by Kaplan's expert ACT instructors.

ACT Perfect Score Tips

Inside each of these you'll find advice and strategies from a Kaplan student who earned a perfect score on the ACT.

▶ SmartPoints™

SmartPoints rank the skills and topics that are tested most often on the ACT. They help you focus your test prep on the areas that will earn you the most points on test day.

How does it work? We ranked the most tested topics and crucial ACT skills using our exclusive SmartPoints bars system. The more SmartPoint bars an item has (from 1 bar to 5 bars), the more important it likely will be on test day.

As you go through this book, you'll see SmartPoints skills and topics discussed throughout.

Look for the SmartPoints bars as you study:

Use SmartPoints to prioritize your ACT studies:

- ■ Customize your study plan according to your strengths and weaknesses, giving extra time to items with higher SmartPoints rankings.

- ■ If you're short on time, focus your study on items with higher SmartPoints rankings first, and review items with lesser rankings as time allows.

▶ Practice on the Go!

Don't forget to use your *ACT Premier* CD-ROM for extra practice— anywhere you have access to a computer. This bonus CD-ROM contains section-length practice tests for each question type on the ACT, and 2 full-length practice tests.

System Requirements

WINDOWS®:

- Windows® 98SE, NT 4.0 (with Service Pack 6), 2000, ME, XP

- Pentium® II 300 MHz or faster, 15 MB free hard disk space, 640 × 480–thousands of colors (millions recommended), SoundBlaster-compatible sound card, 4x CD-ROM or higher.

  Note: An Internet connection is required for the Web features of the program.

MACINTOSH®:

- Macintosh® OS 8.6, OS 9.1, 9.2.2, OS 10.1.3, 10.1.5, 10.2.4, 10.2.8, 10.3, 10.3.7, 10.3.8, 10.4

- 400 MHz Power PC®, G3, G4 or faster, 15 MB free hard disk space, 640 × 480–thousands of colors (millions recommended), 4x CD-ROM or higher.

  Note: An Internet connection is required for the Web features of the program.

Installation

WINDOWS®:

1. Exit all open applications; make sure you have no applications running.

2. Insert the Higher Score CD into your CD-ROM drive. The installation window opens automatically if Autorun is enabled on your system.

3. If you have Autorun disabled, from the Start Menu choose Run and type (or browse for) d:\setup.exe (where d: is your CD-ROM drive). Press OK and follow the prompts.

4. To launch the program, go to the Start Menu, choose Programs, then Kaplan, or double-click the ACT icon on your desktop.

MACINTOSH®:

1. Exit all open applications; make sure you have no applications running.

2. Insert the Higher Score CD into your CD-ROM drive.

3. Double-click the Kaplan install icon. Follow the prompts.

4. To launch the program, double-click the Higher Score on the ACT icon.

If you are experiencing any problems installing this program, please visit our website, kaptest.com/support.

▶ Tips for Customizing Your Study Plan

The most effective study plan will adapt to your individual needs. Here are some helpful tips:

○ Start with a review of the content you're weakest in and include quizzes on these weaker topics to boost your skills and understanding.

○ Devote time to reinforcing content strengths through lesson reviews and practice quizzes.

○ Use full-length practice tests as milestones. There are 6 full-length practice tests in the program—don't plan on saving them all for the final weeks. Test yourself periodically and chart your progress.

○ Think about the topics on which you need to focus. Plan to read those lessons in the book, take practice sets, and review answer explanations.

○ As time permits, go back to the question types that you aced so you can keep the material sharp.

○ Take time to practice your essay writing. Understanding the essay requirements and practicing your writing will help you deliver a great essay on test day.

○ Reevaluate your strengths and weaknesses regularly. If they change, adjust your plan accordingly.

Your Online Companion

Using Your ACT Online Companion

DOUBLE CHECK!

The serial number on the inside back cover of your book is your key to the online companion. *Enter it carefully* and make sure all of the numbers and letters match exactly!

1 REGISTER YOUR ONLINE COMPANION

2 TAKE THE ONLINE DIAGNOSTIC QUIZ

3 CREATE YOUR STUDY PLAN

4 JOIN A LIVE ONLINE
STUDY GROUP SESSON

5 WATCH THE FAST
FACT VIDEOS

① REGISTER YOUR ONLINE COMPANION

The online companion gives you access to even more test prep, including 2 full-length practice tests; the Fast Fact videos; registration for a Live Online event, a Diagnostic Quiz; fresh new quizzes every month; and more!

Register your online companion using these simple steps:

1. **Locate your serial number** on the inside back cover of this book.

2. **Go to Kaptest.com/ACTbooksonline.**

3. **Enter your serial number.** Make sure to enter it exactly as it appears inside the back cover of the book. Example:

74NDA-WU35W-ZHW8L-SJSET-9TDXE

2 TAKE THE ONLINE DIAGNOSTIC QUIZ

The Diagnostic Quiz will help you to do the following:

- **Identify your strengths and weaknesses.** This will help you target your practice time, so you can work on the areas where you need help.

- **Develop your ACT study plan.** Once you review the results of your Diagnostic Quiz, you know where you went wrong. Build your study plan based on your needs and schedule.

  - Check your answers carefully, noting how many questions you got right and wrong.

  - Look for patterns.

- **Know what to expect on test day.** The diagnostic quiz provides you with a sample of each question type, so you'll know just what's waiting for you on test day.

- **Reinforce key concepts and sharpen your skills.**

3 GET TO KNOW THE ACT AND CREATE YOUR STUDY PLAN

Remember, your ACT Premier program is designed to meet your individual needs.

What does that mean?

- **You're in control.** Study how and when it works best for you.

- **You can customize your study.** We've made your ACT program interactive—you get to mix things up by jumping between the book and the online resources.

Take some time to familiarize yourself with some of the key components of your ACT Premier book. It's got all the tools you'll need to conquer the ACT exam on test day.

4 JOIN A LIVE ONLINE SESSION

Kaplan's ACT Live Online sessions are interactive, instructor-led ACT prep lessons that you can participate in from anywhere you can access the Internet.

ACT Live Online sessions are held in a state-of-the-art virtual classroom—actual lessons in real time, just like a physical classroom experience. Interact with your teacher and other classmates using audio, instant chat, whiteboard, polling, and screen-sharing functionality. And just like courses at Kaplan centers, an ACT Live Online Session is led by an experienced Kaplan instructor.

To register for an ACT Live Online event:

1. Once you've signed in to your student home page, open your Syllabus.

2. In the Syllabus window, go to the "Live Online Registration" menu option.

3. Click on the link. A separate window will appear with registration instructions.

There are four ACT Live Online events available. These events are scheduled to take place throughout 2010.

Please check your online companion for dates and times!

Please note: Registration begins one month before the session date. Be sure to sign-up early, since spaces are reserved on a first-come, first serve basis.

 WATCH THE FAST FACT VIDEOS

In Fast Fact videos, one of Kaplan's highly rated ACT tutors explains and reinforces the most important concepts from each chapter.

Fast Fact videos can only be accessed through your online companion. Here's how:

1. Once you've signed into your student home page, open your Syllabus.

2. In the Syllabus window, go to the "Fast Fact Videos" menu option.

3. Click on the link for the video you'd like to see. A separate window will appear with your video.

GOOD LUCK!

ACT®

Premier

2010 Edition

RELATED TITLES FOR COLLEGE-BOUND STUDENTS

ACT Strategies for Super Busy Students, Third Edition

Spotlight ACT

Spotlight SAT

SAT Premier, 2010 Edition

SAT Strategies, Practice, and Review, 2010 Edition

12 Practice Tests for the SAT

SAT Strategies for Super Busy Students

Inside the SAT: 10 Strategies to Help You Score Higher

SAT Advanced, Second Edition

SAT Critical Reading Workbook

SAT Math Workbook

SAT Writing Workbook

SAT in a Box Flashcards

SAT Vocabulary Flashcards Flip-O-Matic, Third Edition

Extreme SAT Vocabulary Flashcards Flip-O-Matic, Second Edition

The Ring of McAllister: A Score-Raising Mystery Featuring 1,046 Must-Know SAT Vocabulary Words

Frankenstein: A Kaplan New SAT Score-Raising Classic

The Tales of Edgar Allan Poe: A Kaplan New SAT Score-Raising Classic

Dr. Jekyll and Mr. Hyde: A Kaplan New SAT Score-Raising Classic

War of the Worlds: A Kaplan New SAT Score-Raising Classic

Wuthering Heights: A Kaplan New SAT Score-Raising Classic

Domina El SAT: Prepárate para Tomar el Examen para Ingresar a la Universidad

AP Biology

AP Calculus AB & BC

AP Chemistry

AP English Language & Composition

AP English Literature & Composition

AP Environmental Science

AP European History

AP Human Geography

AP Macroeconomics/Microeconomics

AP Physics B & C

AP Psychology

AP Statistics

AP U.S. Government & Politics

AP U.S. History

AP U.S. History in a Box

AP World History

SAT Subject Test: Biology E/M

SAT Subject Test: Chemistry

SAT Subject Test: Literature

SAT Subject Test: Mathematics Level 1

SAT Subject Test: Mathematics Level 2

SAT Subject Test: Physics

SAT Subject Test: Spanish

SAT Subject Test: U.S. History

SAT Subject Test: World History

ACT®

Premier

2010 Edition

KAPLAN PUBLISHING

New York

This publication is designed to provide accurate and authoritative information in regard to the subject matter covered. It is sold with the understanding that the publisher is not engaged in rendering legal, accounting, or other professional service. If legal advice or other expert assistance is required, the services of a competent professional should be sought.

© 2010 by Kaplan, Inc.

Published by Kaplan Publishing, a division of Kaplan, Inc.
1 Liberty Plaza, 24th Floor
New York, NY 10006

Printed in the United States of America

10 9 8 7 6 5 4 3 2

ISBN-13: 978-1-4195-5327-1

Kaplan Publishing books are available at special quantity discounts to use for sales promotions, employee premiums, or educational purposes. For more information or to order books, please call the Simon & Schuster special sales department at 866-506-1949.

Table of Contents

NOTE FOR INTERNATIONAL STUDENTS

If you are an international student considering attending an American university, you are not alone. Over 600,000 international students pursued academic degrees at the undergraduate, graduate, or professional school level at U.S. universities during the 2004–2005 academic year, according to the Institute of International Education's Open Doors report. Almost 50 percent of these students were studying for a bachelor's or first university degree. This number of international students pursuing higher education in the United States is expected to continue to grow. Business, management, engineering, and the physical and life sciences are particularly popular majors for students coming to the United States from other countries.

If you are not a U.S. citizen and you are interested in attending college or university in the United States, here is what you'll need to get started.

- **If English is not your first language, you'll probably need to take the TOEFL® (Test of English as a Foreign Language) or provide some other evidence that you are proficient in English.** Colleges and universities in the United States will differ on what they consider to be an acceptable TOEFL score. Because American undergraduate programs require all students to take a certain number of general education courses, all students—even math and computer science students—need to be able to communicate well in spoken and written English.

- **You may also need to take the SAT® or the ACT®.** Many undergraduate institutions in the United States require both the SAT and TOEFL for international students.

- There are over 3,400 accredited colleges and universities in the United States, so selecting the correct undergraduate school can be a confusing task for anyone. **You will need to get help from a good advisor or at least a good college guide that gives you detailed information on the different schools available.** Since admission to many undergraduate programs is quite competitive, you may want to select three or four colleges and complete applications for each school.

- **You should begin the application process at least a year in advance.** An increasing number of schools accept applications year round. In any case, find out the application deadlines and plan accordingly. Although September (the fall semester) is the traditional time to begin university study in the United States, you can begin your studies at many schools in January (the spring semester).

- **In addition, you will need to obtain an I-20 Certificate of Eligibility from the school you plan to attend if you intend to apply for an F-1 Student Visa to study in the United States.**

KAPLAN ENGLISH PROGRAMS*

If you need more help navigating the complex process of university admissions, preparing for the SAT, ACT, or TOEFL, or building your English language skills in general, you may be interested in Kaplan's programs for international students.

Kaplan English Programs were designed to help students and professionals from outside the United States meet their educational and career goals. At locations throughout the United States, international students take advantage of Kaplan's programs to help them improve their academic and conversational English skills, raise their scores on the TOEFL, SAT, ACT, and other standardized exams, and gain admission to the schools of their choice. Our staff and instructors give international students the individualized attention they need to succeed. Here is a brief description of some of Kaplan's programs for international students:

GENERAL INTENSIVE ENGLISH

Kaplan's General Intensive English course is the fastest and most effective way for students to improve their English. This full-time program integrates the four key elements of language learning—listening, speaking, reading, and writing. The challenging curriculum and intensive schedule are designed for both the general language learner and the academically bound student.

TOEFL AND ACADEMIC ENGLISH

Our world-famous TOEFL course prepares you for the TOEFL and also teaches you the academic language and skills needed to succeed in a university. Designed for high-intermediate to advanced-level English speakers, our course includes TOEFL-focused reading, writing, listening, speaking, vocabulary, and grammar instruction.

GENERAL ENGLISH

Our General English course is a semi-intensive program designed for students who want to improve their listening and speaking skills without the time commitment of an intensive program. With morning class time and flexible computer lab hours throughout the week, our General English course is perfect for every schedule.

*Kaplan is authorized under federal law to enroll nonimmigrant alien students. Kaplan is accredited by ACCET (Accrediting Council for Continuing Education and Training).

OTHER KAPLAN PROGRAMS

Since 1938, more than three million students have come to Kaplan to advance their studies, prepare for entry to American universities, and further their careers. In addition to the above programs, Kaplan offers courses to prepare for the ACT, GMAT®, GRE®, MCAT®, DAT®, USMLE®, NCLEX-RN®, and other standardized exams at locations throughout the United States.

APPLYING TO KAPLAN ENGLISH PROGRAMS

To get more information or to apply for admission to any of Kaplan's programs for international students and professionals, contact us at:

KAPLAN ENGLISH PROGRAMS

700 South Flower, Suite 2900

Los Angeles, CA 90017, USA

Phone (if calling from within the United States): 800-818-9128

Phone (if calling from outside the United States): (213) 452-5800

Fax: (213) 892-1364

Website: www.kaplanenglish.com

Email: world@kaplan.com

FREE Services for International Students

Kaplan now offers international students many services online—*free of charge*! Students may assess their TOEFL skills and gain valuable feedback on their English language proficiency in just a few hours with Kaplan's TOEFL Skills Assessment. Log onto www.kaplanenglish.com today.

Part One

ACT BASICS

CHAPTER 1: INTRODUCTION TO THE ACT

Before you plunge into studying for the ACT, let's take a step back and look at the big picture. What's the ACT all about? How can you prepare for it? How's it scored? This chapter will answer these questions and more.

The ACT is an opportunity, not a barrier. In fact, you should be grateful that you have to take it. Really. Because a strong ACT score is one credential that doesn't depend on things you can't control. It doesn't depend on how good or bad your high school is. It doesn't depend on how many academic luminaries you know, or how rich and famous your family is, or whether any of your teachers are gullible enough to swear in a letter of recommendation that you're the greatest scientific mind since Isaac Newton. No, your ACT score depends on only you.

Granted, the ACT is a tough exam. It's probably one of the toughest exams you'll ever take. But you should be grateful for that too. Really. If the ACT were easy, everyone would do well. A good score wouldn't mean much. But because it's such a bear of a test, the ACT can be your single best opportunity to show what you can do, to prove to colleges that you are the candidate of choice—for admission, for advanced placement, for scholarships.

It's important, though, that you take the test in the right spirit. Don't be timid in the face of the ACT. Don't let it bully you. You've got to take control of the test. Our mission in this book is to show you exactly how to do that.

It helps to think of the ACT challenge as a contest—not only between you and the test, but also between you and that other person trying to get your spot in college. The ACT, after all, is meant to provide a way for all college applicants to compete on an even playing field. How do you compete successfully in a fair academic fight? You train—harder and smarter than the next person. First, you learn whatever knowledge and skills you need to know. But then, just as importantly, you learn how

> **EXPERT TUTOR TIP**
>
> " If you have two weeks or fewer to prep for the ACT, don't panic. The first thing you should do is become familiar with the test. This chapter is the place to start. "

> **PERFECT SCORE TIP**
>
> " The best thing you can do for yourself is really get to know the test. The ACT is a very predictable test, and being familiar with it will help you with both time and nerves on test day. "

to show what you know, in ways that the test is designed to reward. You learn how to be a savvy test taker.

FOUR KEYS TO ACT SUCCESS

There are four basic commandments for achieving ACT success. Following any of these by itself will improve your score. Following all four together will make you nothing less than awesome.

1. THOU SHALT LEARN THE TEST

The ACT is very predictable. You'd think the test makers would get bored after a while, but they don't. The same kinds of questions, testing the same skills and concepts, appear every time the ACT is given.

Because the test specifications rarely change, you should know in advance what to expect on every section. Just a little familiarity can make an enormous difference on the ACT. Here are a few ways in which learning the test will boost your score:

- **You'll learn the directions.** Why waste valuable time reading directions when you can have them down pat beforehand? You need every second during the test to answer questions and get points.

- **You'll learn the difficulty range of questions.** It's a fact that a typical ACT test taker gets only about half the questions right. Knowing this will stop you from panicking when you hit an impossible science passage or trigonometry question. Relax! You can skip many tough questions on the ACT and still get a great score! And once you know that the questions aren't arranged in order of difficulty, you'll know that just beyond that awful question will be one, two, or even three easy questions that you can score on with no sweat at all.

- **You'll learn how to get extra points by guessing.** Unlike some other standardized tests, the ACT has no wrong-answer penalty. Knowing that simple fact can boost your score significantly. If you can't answer a question, guess.

- **You'll learn what makes a high-scoring essay.** If you are taking the optional Writing test, learning how it is scored will help you craft a good essay.

We'll help you get a better understanding of the ACT in the chapter following this one, entitled "The Subject Tests: A Preview."

PERFECT SCORE TIP

" The ACT will not penalize you for a wrong answer. So answer every question, and don't lose possible points by leaving questions blank. "

2. Thou Shalt Learn the Strategies

The ACT isn't a normal exam. Most normal exams test your memory. The ACT tests problem-solving skills rather than memory, and it does so in a standardized-test format. That makes the test highly vulnerable to test-smart strategies and techniques.

Most students miss a lot of ACT questions for no good reason. They see a tough-looking question, say to themselves, "Uh-oh, I don't remember how to do that," and then they start to gnaw on their No. 2 pencils.

But many ACT questions can be answered without perfect knowledge of the material being tested. Often, all you need to do to succeed on the ACT is to think strategically and creatively. We call this kind of strategic, creative frame of mind "The ACT Mind-set."

How do you put yourself into the ACT Mind-set? You continually ask yourself questions like: "What does this mean? How can I put this into a form I can understand and use? How can I do this faster?" Once you develop some savvy test-taking skills, you'll find yourself capable of working out problems that at first reading might have scared you half to death! In fact, we'll show you how you can sometimes get right answers when you don't even understand the question or the passage it's attached to!

There are many, many specific strategies you can use to boost your score. For instance, here are just a couple of things you'll learn:

- **You'll learn the peculiarities of the ACT format.** Except for the Writing test, the ACT is a multiple-choice test. The correct answer is **always** right there in front of you. We'll show you how to develop specific tactics for each question type to maximize the chances of selecting the correct answer. The wrong answers are often predictable. For example, in English the shortest answer is the correct answer with surprising frequency. Strange, but true. Knowing statistical information like this can give you an important edge.

- **You'll learn a plan of attack for each subject test.** We'll show you some really useful ways of attacking each subject test. You'll learn how to do "question triage"—deciding which questions to do now and which to save for later. You'll learn a strategic method for each subject test designed to get you points quickly and systematically. You'll learn gridding techniques to avoid any answer-sheet disasters.

- **You'll learn "unofficial" ways of getting right answers fast.** On the ACT, nobody cares how you decide which choice to select. The only thing that matters is picking the right answer. That's different from the way it works on most high school tests, where you get credit for showing that you've done the questions the "right" way (that is, the way you were taught to do them by

PERFECT SCORE TIP

Don't let tough questions scare you. The Kaplan strategies will help teach you how to tackle them. And remember: you don't need to know every question to do well.

PERFECT SCORE TIP

Test taking tips can only take you so far if you don't know the material. Figure out which topics you need the most help on, and make sure to focus time on learning or refreshing those topics.

Mrs. Crabapple in high school). We'll show you how to find creative shortcuts to the correct answers— "unofficial" methods that will save you precious time and net you extra points.

The basic test-smart techniques and strategies for the whole test are covered in the chapter called "Taking Control: The Top Ten Strategies." General strategies for each subject test, plus specific hints, techniques, and strategies for individual question types, are found in the Skill-Building Workouts. These are then summarized in the Strategic Summaries.

3. THOU SHALT LEARN THE MATERIAL TESTED

The ACT is designed to test skills and concepts learned in high school and needed for college. Familiarity with the test, coupled with smart test-taking strategies, will take you only so far. For your best score you need to sharpen up the skills and knowledge that the ACT rewards. Sometimes, in other words, you've just got to eat your spinach.

The good news is that most of the content on the ACT is pretty basic. You've probably already learned most of what the ACT expects you to know. But you may need help remembering. That's partly what this book is for—to remind you of the knowledge you already have and to build and refine the specific skills you've developed in high school. Here are just a few of the things we'll "remind" you of:

- **You'll learn how to read graphs and tables.** Many Science questions rely on your ability to use data presented in the form of graphs and tables. (We'll teach you how to read graphs and tables in Science Workout 1.)

- **Have you met any FANBOYS lately?** Don't know? Well, this is the acronym for the conjunctions that connect two independent clauses in a run-on sentence. We know you want to know more about this, so here's a sneak preview: FANBOYS help you remember **F**or, **A**nd, **N**or, **B**ut, **O**r, **Y**et, **S**o. For more grammar rules, check out English Workout 3.

- **If your math "engine" is rusty when it comes to triangles, probabilities, algebraic expressions**, and more, we'll get you up and running. The three Math Workout chapters and the 100 Key Math Concepts for the ACT will have that engine purring again in no time.

- **You'll learn how to do trigonometry problems.** Do you remember exactly what a cotangent is? A cosine? We didn't think so. But there are four trig problems on every ACT. (You can learn about trigonometry problems in 100 Key Math Concepts for the ACT, items 96–100.)

- **You'll learn the difference between *lie* and *lay*.** Is it "I lay down on the couch" or "I lie down on the couch"? You may want to lie down yourself if you encounter such issues on the ACT. But don't fret. We'll remind you of the common grammar traps the test lays for you (or is it lies for you ???). (For a discussion of this conundrum, see Classic Grammar Error #9 in English Workout 3.)

4. THOU SHALT PRACTICE, PRACTICE, PRACTICE

Practice creates confidence. On test day you need to have all the strategies and concepts in your brain and to be relaxed and ready to go. Reading and understanding the contents of this book is key. But there's one more step. For Kaplan's methods to be most effective on test day, you need to make them part of your everyday routine. The best way to do that is to practice as much as possible.

Test day often becomes THE DAY. You're in a room full of people, all in a state of anticipation and nervousness—it's contagious. Don't let the moment take over and make you forget your methods. Your best ally in this excitement is the confidence that practice gives you.

Note: If you don't have time to practice with all of the sections, you *can* (and should!) practice in the areas you feel weakest.

Specifics like those mentioned above comprise what we call the ACT "knowledge base." The components of this knowledge base are reviewed along the way throughout this book. The ACT Resources in this book and online summarize this information for the two sections of the ACT that explicitly test knowledge: English and Math.

In sum, then, follow these four commandments:

1. **Thou shalt learn the test.**
2. **Thou shalt learn the strategies.**
3. **Thou shalt learn the material tested.**
4. **Thou shalt practice, practice, practice.**

If you do, you'll find yourself just where you should be on 4: in full command of your ACT test-taking experience. Count on it.

WHAT IS THE ACT?

It was Attila the Hun who first coined this epigram: knowing the enemy is the first step in conquering the enemy. Attila, of course, was talking about waging wars on the steppes of Central Asia, but his advice also works for taking standardized tests in central Illinois. In fact, that's probably why Attila got a Composite Score of 30 on the ACT.

Well, to be honest, we haven't fact-checked Attila the Hun's ACT score, but the point remains valid. To succeed on the ACT, you've got to know the ACT.

PERFECT SCORE TIP

" Don't be tricked into thinking the ACT is a test based solely on intelligence. Anyone can do well on this test if they really do study for it. "

But is the ACT really your enemy? Only in a manner of speaking. The test is more like an adversary in a game of chess. If you know your adversary's entire repertoire of moves and clever stratagems, you'll find it that much easier to beat him. Myths about the ACT are common. Even high school teachers and guidance counselors sometimes give out inaccurate information (we know you're shocked to hear this). To earn your best score, you need to know how the ACT is really put together.

OVERVIEW OF THE ACT

- The ACT is about three hours long (three and a half with the Writing test).

- There will be a short break between the second and third subtests.

- The ACT consists of a total of 215 scored multiple-choice questions, and one optional essay.

- The exam is comprised of four subject tests and an optional Writing test:

  — English (45 minutes, 75 questions)

  — Math (60 minutes, 60 questions)

  — Reading (35 minutes, 40 questions)

  — Science (35 minutes, 40 questions)

  — Writing (30 minutes, 1 essay question)

EXPERT TUTOR TIP

Speaking of myths, you may have heard that the ACT is really the only thing colleges look at when deciding whether to admit you. Untrue. Most admissions officers say the ACT is only one of several factors.

So, before anything, take some time and get to know this so-called adversary. Let's start with the basics. The ACT is a three-hour exam (three and a half hours if you take the optional Writing test) taken by high school juniors and seniors for admission to college. It is not an IQ test; it's a test of problem-solving skills—which means that you can improve your performance by preparing for it.

But let's be realistic about ACT scores. Here's this neat and easy way of comparing all students numerically, no matter what their academic backgrounds and no matter how much grade inflation exists at their high schools. You know the admissions people are going to take a serious look at your test scores.

The ACT consists of four subject tests: English, Math, Reading, and Science, as well as the optional Writing test. All the subject tests are primarily designed to test skills rather than knowledge, though some knowledge is required—particularly in

English, for which a familiarity with grammar and writing mechanics is important, and in Math, for which you need to know the basic math concepts taught in a regular high school curriculum. The Writing test tests your ability to communicate clearly your position on an issue.

ACT FAQS

Here are some quick answers to the questions students ask most frequently about the ACT.

HOW IS THE ACT SCORED?

No, your ACT score is not merely the sum total of questions you get right. That would be too simple. Instead, what the test makers do is add up all of your correct answers to get what they call a "raw score." Then they put that raw score into a very large computer, which proceeds to shake, rattle, smoke, and wheeze before spitting out an official score at the other end. That score—which has been put through what they call a *scoring formula*—is your "scaled score."

ACT scaled scores range from 1 to 36. Nearly half of all test takers score within a much narrower range: 17–23. Tests at different dates vary slightly, but the following data is based on a recent administration of the test and can be considered typical.

ACT Approximate Percentile Rank*	Scaled (or Composite) Score	Percentage of Questions Correct
99%	31	90%
90%	26	75%
76%	23	63%
54%	20	53%
28%	17	43%

* Percentage of ACT takers scoring at or below given score

Notice that to earn a score of 20 (the national average), you need to answer only about 53 percent of the questions correctly. On most tests, getting only a bit more than half the questions right would be terrible. Not so on the ACT. Getting about half of the ACT questions correct and earning a score of 20 won't earn you a lifetime membership in the Academy of Arts and Sciences, but it's nothing to be ashamed of.

The score data above includes two very strong scores: 26 and 31. Either score would impress almost any college admissions officer. A 26 would put you in the top 10 percent of the students who take the exam, and a 31 would put you in the top 1 percent. Even a 31 requires getting only about 90 percent of the questions right.

PERFECT SCORE TIP

"" Be realistic about your goals for scores. Take a diagnostic test, and use this to create appropriate goals as well as determine what sections you need to work on. ""

EXPERT TUTOR TIP

"" Most ACT test takers score between 17 and 23. A score below 17 will seriously limit your choice of colleges. But any score above 23 will be an asset in your quest for admission to a competitive college. ""

EXPERT TUTOR TIP

"" Just a few questions right or wrong on the ACT can make a big difference. Answering only five extra questions correctly on each subject test can move you from the bottom of the applicant pool into the middle from the middle up to the top. ""

EXPERT TUTOR TIP

" By the end of each subject test, you should have answered every question, even if you had to take a random guess on some. A lucky guess will raise your score, and an unlucky guess will leave you no worse off. There's no penalty for a wrong answer. None. Zippo. "

The best student in your high school will probably get at least a dozen questions wrong. There are questions that even your smartest teachers would get wrong.

If you earn a score of 23, you'll be in about the 76th percentile. That means that 76 percent of the test takers did as well as, or worse than, you did—in other words, that only 24 percent did better than you. It means you're in the "top quarter" of the people who take the ACT. That's a good score. But notice that to earn this score, you need only about 63 percent of the questions correct. On most tests, a score of 63 is probably a D or an F. But on the ACT, it's about a B+.

How Many ACT Scores Will You Get?

The "ACT scaled score" we've talked about so far is technically called the "composite score." It's the really important one. But when you take the ACT, you actually receive 12 (or 13) different scores: the composite score, 4 (or 5) subject scores, and 7 (or 8) subscores. Though the subject scores can play a role in decisions at some schools, the subscores usually aren't important for most people, so feel free to ignore the chart below if you don't feel like looking at it.

Here's the full battery of ACT scores (1–36) you'll receive. Few people (except your parents, maybe) will care about anything except your composite score for college admissions, though some schools use subscores for course placement.

EXPERT TUTOR TIP

" When you sign up for the ACT, you can choose colleges to receive your score. Unless time is of the essence, don't do it, even though the first four score reports are sent for free. Wait until you get your score, then send it out (for a small additional fee) if you're happy. If you hate your score, you can take the test again and send only the new, improved score. "

English Score (1–36)	Usage/Mechanics subscore (1–18); Rhetorical Skills subscore (1–18); (Optional) Writing subscore (2–12)
Math Score (1–36)	Prealgebra/Elementary Algebra subscore (1–18); Algebra/Coordinate Geometry subscore (1–18); Plane Geometry/ Trigonometry subscore (1–18)
Reading Score (1–36)	Social Sciences/Sciences subscore (1–18); Arts/Literature subscore (1–18)
Science Score (1–36)	There are no subscores in Science.
(Optional) Combined English-Writing Score (1–36)	Does not count toward your composite score, but colleges will see it.

How Do Colleges Use Your ACT Score?

The most important score for most test takers is the composite score (which is an average of the four major subject scores). This is the score used by most colleges and universities in the admissions process and the one that you'll want to mention casually at parties during your freshman year of college. The subject scores and subscores may be used for advanced placement or occasionally for scholarships, but are primarily used by college advisors to help students select majors and first-year courses.

Although many schools deny that they use benchmark scores as cutoffs, we're not sure we really believe them. Big Ten universities and colleges with similarly competitive admissions generally decline to accept students with composite scores below 22 or 23. For less competitive schools, the benchmark score may be lower than that; for some very selective schools, the cutoff may be higher.

To be fair, no school uses the ACT as an absolute bar to admission, no matter how low it is. But for most applicants, a low ACT score is decisive. As a rule, only students whose backgrounds are extremely unusual or who have overcome enormous disadvantages are accepted if their ACT scores are below the benchmark. It also sometimes helps if you can convince your parents to donate a gymnasium to the school you're aiming for.

Should You Take the Optional Writing Test?

You should decide whether to take the ACT Writing test based on the admissions policies of the schools you will apply to and on the advice of your high school guidance counselors. A list of colleges requiring the test is maintained on the ACT website, www.act.org/aap/writing. If you are unsure about what schools you will apply to, you should plan to take the Writing test. However, testing will be available later if you decide not to take the Writing test and discover later that you need it.

How Do Schools Use the Optional Writing Test?

The ACT Writing test may be used for either admissions or course placement purposes, or both. Students who take the Writing test will receive an English score, a Writing subscore, and a combined English-Writing score on a 1–36 scale. (The combined English-Writing score is not averaged into the composite score.) Copies of the essay (with the graders' comments) will also be available online for downloading. Schools that do not require the Writing test will also receive the Combined English-Writing score for students who have taken the Writing test, unless the school specifically asks *not* to receive those results.

PERFECT SCORE TIP

" Many schools prefer that you take the ACT Writing test. If you don't know yet where you will be applying, consider taking this optional test to reduce the chances you will have to take this long test again. "

SHOULD YOU GUESS ON THE ACT?

The short answer? Yes! The long answer? Yes, of course!

As we saw, ACT scores are based on the number of correct answers only. This means that questions that you leave blank and questions you answer incorrectly simply don't count. Unlike some other standardized tests, the ACT has no "wrong-answer penalty." That's why you should **always** take a guess on every ACT question you can't answer, even if you don't have time to read it. Though the questions vary enormously in difficulty, harder questions are worth exactly the same as easier ones, so it pays to guess on the really hard questions and spend your time breezing through the really easy ones.

CAN YOU RETAKE THE TEST?

You can take the ACT as many times as you like. You can then select whichever test score you prefer to be sent to colleges when you apply. However, you cannot take advantage of this option if, at the time you register for the test, you designate certain colleges to receive your scores. Thus, it is crucial that you not designate any colleges at the time you register for the test. You can (for a small additional fee) have ACT scores sent to colleges at any time you desire after the scores are reported.

Unless you don't have enough money for that small extra fee or if you're taking the ACT under the wire and you need your scores to reach the schools you're applying to ASAP, give yourself the freedom to retake the test. What this means, of course, is that even if you blow the ACT once, you can give yourself another chance without the schools of your choice knowing about it. The ACT is one of the few areas of your academic life in which you get a second chance.

ACT REGISTRATION OVERVIEW

- **To get a registration packet, see your guidance counselor, or contact:**

  ACT Registration
  P.O. Box 144
  Iowa City, IA 52243-0414
  Phone: (319) 337-1270
  Web: www.act.org

- **You can also register online at www.actstudent.org.**

- **Students with disabilities or with other special circumstances can call (319) 337-1332.**

- **The basic fee at press time for the ACT is $29 without the Writing test and $43 with the Writing test, in the United States.** (For students testing outside the 50 United States, the fee is $49 ($63 for the ACT with Writing test). Call (319) (337)-1448 for more information on taking the test outside the United States.

  This price includes reports for you, your high school, and up to four college choices. There are additional fees for late registration, standby testing, changing test centers or test dates, and for additional services and products.

- **In the United States, the ACT is administered in October, December, February, April, and June.** (The February date is not available in the state of New York.) In selected states, the ACT is also offered in late September. Register early to secure the time you want at the test center of your choice and to avoid late registration fees.

- **You may take the ACT Assessment as often as you wish.** Many students take it twice, once as a junior and again as a senior. There are no limitations on how many times you can take the ACT, but there are some restrictions on how often you can test. For example, you can test only once per national test date.

- **Be sure you take your test center admission ticket and acceptable identification with you to the test center.** Acceptable forms of identification are a photo ID or a recent published photo with your full name printed. Unacceptable forms of identification are a birth certificate, Social Security card, or any other ID without photo. You will not be admitted without acceptable identification.

- **Check with ACT, Inc., for all the latest information on the test.** Every effort is made to keep the information in this book up-to-date, but changes may occur after the book is published.

- **Go online (act.org) to make sure you know ALL the ACT regulations for test day.** For example, all electronic devices (including cell phones) must be turned off from the time you're admitted to the test until you're dismissed after testing concludes.

Note: Violations of these rules, such as an alarm going off or a phone ringing in the test room, may result in your dismissal from the room and the nonscoring of your answer sheet.

- **You might be considering whether to take the ACT, the SAT, or both.** For more information on the SAT, go to the College Board's website at www.collegeboard.com.

GO ONLINE

" Visit the test maker's website at www.act.org for the latest information on test registration, fees, and content. "

PERFECT SCORE TIP

" The ACT and SAT are very different tests. Many people have an affinity for one over the other. Try some sample questions from each, and decide which one works best for you. "

TAKING THE PLAN EXAM

Students should also be aware of the PLAN exam, which offers a preview of the format and content of the material found on the ACT. A student's success on this exam is often an accurate predictor of success on the ACT. PLAN scores help students decide which courses to take their junior and senior years of high school in addition to helping students consider certain career paths prior to college, based on their strengths or weaknesses as indicated by their scores. The PLAN is generally offered to students in the fall of their sophomore year. To learn more, visit PLAN's website for student information at www.actstudent.org/plan.

IF YOU LEARNED ONLY FIVE THINGS IN THIS CHAPTER . . .

1. The ACT consists of four required subject tests (English, Math, Reading, and Science) plus an optional Writing test.

2. Total testing time is about three hours, plus half an hour for Writing.

3. All questions are multiple choice except on the Writing test (one essay question).

4. There is no penalty for a wrong answer, so you should guess.

5. ACT composite scores range from 1–36.

CHAPTER 2: THE SUBJECT TESTS: A PREVIEW

Okay, you've seen how the ACT is set up. But to really know your adversary, you've got to know something about the ACT subject tests.

As we'll see, the questions in every subject test vary widely in difficulty. Some are so easy that most elementary school students could answer them. Others would give even Einstein a little trouble. But, again: **The questions are not arranged in order of difficulty.** That's different from some other tests, in which easier questions come first. Skipping past hard questions is very important, since otherwise you may **never** reach easy ones toward the end of the exam.

Here's a preview of the types of questions you'll see on the subject tests. We'll keep them toward the easy end of the difficulty scale here, but later, in the Skill-Building Workouts, we'll be less kind.

After we look at the four required subject tests, we'll give you a preview of the optional Writing test.

ENGLISH

The English test lasts 45 minutes and includes 75 questions. That works out to about 30 seconds per question. When it comes down to it, though, you should spend less time on easier questions and more on harder questions. The test is divided into five passages, each with about 15 questions.

Note: You're not tested on spelling or vocabulary here. Rather, the ACT is designed to test your understanding of the conventions of English—punctuation, grammar, sentence structure—and of rhetorical skills. Rhetorical skills are more strategic things like organizing the text and making sure it's styled clearly.

PERFECT SCORE TIP

The structure of the ACT is very predictable. Know the order, number of questions, and time for each section cold by the time you get to test day.

PERFECT SCORE TIP

Kaplan will teach you to save time by marking the questions you know will take extra time and doing them last.

EXPERT TUTOR TIP

If you have two weeks or less to prep for the ACT, you should spend time getting familiar with the test.

Students nearly **always** get more questions correct in English than in any other section. That tends to make them think that English is a lot easier than the rest of the ACT. But, alas, it's not that simple. Because most students do well, the test makers have much higher expectations for English than for other parts of the test. They know that it's generally easier to get English questions right than, say, Science questions. They have a whole department of little statistician elves who keep track of things like this. That's why, to earn an average English subscore (a 20, say), you have to get almost two-thirds of the questions right, while on the rest of the test you need to get only about half right.

THE FORMAT

Almost all of the English questions follow a standard format. A word, phrase, or sentence in a passage is underlined. You're given four options: to leave the underlined portion alone (NO CHANGE, which is **always** the first choice), or to replace it with one of three alternatives.

Example

. . . Pike's Peak in Southwest Colorado

is named before Zebulon Pike, an
         37

early explorer. He traveled through
    37

the area, exploring . . .

37.   A.   NO CHANGE
      B.   before Zebulon Pike
             became an explorer,
      C.   after Zebulon Pike, when,
      D.   after Zebulon Pike.

The best answer for number 37 above is D. The other choices all have various problems: grammatical, stylistic, logical. They make the passage look and sound like it was written by your baby brother. Only D makes the sentence sensible and correct. That's why it's the answer.

Notice that a single question can test several kinds of writing errors. We find that about a third of the English questions test your ability to write concisely (we call them Economy Questions), about another third test for logic and sense (Sense Questions), and only the remaining third test hard-and-fast rules of grammar (Technicality Questions). There's a lot of overlap between these question types, so don't worry too much about categories. We provide them simply to give you an idea of the kinds of errors you'll be expected to correct.

TO OMIT OR NOT TO OMIT

Some English questions offer, as one of the alternatives, the chance to completely omit the underlined portion, usually as the last of the four choices.

EXPERT TUTOR TIP

" ACT questions are not arranged in order of ascending difficulty. Skip past the tough questions and spend your first minutes on the test piling up some easy points. "

PERFECT SCORE TIP

" In English passages, always read the options in context, pretending you are saying them out loud. Often, the mistake will become clear to you when you sound it out. "

Example

Later, Pike fell while valiantly defending

America in the War of 1812.

It goes without saying that this took
                    40
place after he discovered Pike's Peak. He
              40
actually died near York (now called

Toronto) . . .

40. F.   NO CHANGE
    G.   Clearly, this must have
         occurred subsequent to his
         discovering Pike's Peak.
    H.   This was after he found
         Pike's Peak.
    J.   OMIT the underlined
         portion.

In this case, J is correct. The idea really does "go without saying." For that reason, it shouldn't be stated. On recent ACTs, when OMIT has appeared as an answer choice, it's been correct more than half of the time (As you can see, the ACT makers aren't the only ones with a department of little statistician elves . . .). This doesn't mean you should **always** select OMIT, however, since it's also been wrong almost half of the time.

THE DIRECTIONS

The directions on the English test illustrate why there's an advantage to knowing the directions beforehand. The directions are long and complicated. Here's what they'll look like, but take our advice—don't bother reading them. We'll show you what you'll need to do. Then, while everyone else is reading the directions on test day, you'll be racking up points.

Directions: In the following five passages, certain words and phrases have been underlined and numbered. You will find alternatives for each underlined portion in the right-hand column. Select the one that best expresses the idea, that makes the statement acceptable in standard written English, or that is phrased most consistently with the style and tone of the entire passage. If you feel that the original version is best, select NO CHANGE. You will also find questions asking about a section of the passage or about the entire passage. For these questions decide which choice gives the most appropriate response to the given question. For each question on the test, select the best choice and fill in the corresponding space on the answer folder. You may wish to read each passage through before you begin to answer the questions associated with it. Most answers cannot be determined without reading several sentences around the phrases in question. Make sure to read far enough ahead each time you choose an alternative.

PERFECT SCORE TIP

Answer A in many English questions is NO CHANGE. Remember that this is sometimes the answer. If you are sure the sentence is completely correct, select this answer instead of making up nonexistent grammar problems.

PERFECT SCORE TIP

The same goes for the option to OMIT. This is often the answer, so don't be scared to think part of the passage is unnecessary. There will be more tips about this in the first English workout.

PERFECT SCORE TIP

Don't waste valuable time reading the directions on test day, or miss valuable points by not following them. Most directions are not that complicated—so make sure you know them cold before test day.

NONSTANDARD-FORMAT QUESTIONS

Some ACT English questions—usually about ten per exam—don't follow this standard format. These items pose a question and offer four possible responses. In many cases, the responses are either "yes" or "no," with an explanation. Pay attention to the reasoning. Question 40 could have appeared in a nonstandard format as follows:

Example

... Later, Pike fell while valiantly

defending America in the War of 1812. 40

He actually died near York (now called

Toronto) ...

40. Suppose the author considered adding the following sentence at this point: "It goes without saying that this occurred after he discovered Pike's Peak." Given the overall purpose of the passage, would this sentence be appropriate?

F. No, because the sentence adds nothing to the meaning of the passage.

G. No, because the passage is not concerned with Pike's achievements.

H. Yes, because otherwise the sequence of events would be unclear.

J. Yes; though the sentence is not needed, the author recognizes this fact by using the phrase *it goes without saying*.

The correct answer for this question is F. Though G correctly states that the sentence doesn't belong in the passage, it offers a pretty inappropriate reason. The passage is concerned with Pike's achievements. Choices H and J are wrong because they recommend including a sentence that is clearly redundant.

Many of the nonstandard questions occur at the end of a passage. Some ask about the meaning, purpose, or tone of individual paragraphs or of the passage as a whole. Others ask you to evaluate the passage. And still others ask you to determine the proper order of words, sentences, or paragraphs that have been scrambled in the passage.

We think you'll like the English subject test. It can actually be fun, which is probably why the test makers put it first. We'll cover strategies for the English question types in the English Workouts.

MATH

The Math test is 60 minutes long and includes 60 questions. That works out to one minute per question, but you'll want to spend less time on easy questions and more on the tough ones.

THE FORMAT

All of the Math questions have the same basic multiple-choice format. They ask a question and offer five possible choices (unlike questions on the other subject tests, which have only four choices each). Why the Math test has five choices while the other tests have only four is one of those mysteries that only the ACT makers understand.

The questions cover a full range of math topics, from pre-algebra and elementary algebra to plane geometry and even a little bit of trigonometry. If you have specific weaknesses in any of these areas, the 100 Key Math Concepts for the ACT section at the end of this book will help.

Although the Math questions, like those in other sections, aren't ordered in terms of difficulty, questions drawn from elementary school or junior high tend to come earlier in the section, while those from high school math curricula tend to come later. But this doesn't mean that the easy questions come first and the hardest ones come later. We've found that high school subjects tend to be fresher in most students' minds than things they were taught years ago, so you may actually find the later questions easier. (Do *you* remember the math you learned in seventh grade?)

THE DIRECTIONS

Here's what the Math directions will look like:

> **Directions:** Solve each of the following problems, select the correct answer, and then fill in the corresponding space on your answer sheet.

Don't linger over problems that are too time-consuming. Do as many as you can, then come back to the others in the time you have remaining.

Calculator use is permitted, but some problems can best be solved without a calculator.

Note: Unless otherwise noted, all of the following should be assumed:

1. Illustrative figures are *not* necessarily drawn to scale.

2. All geometric figures lie in a plane.

3. The term *line* indicates a straight line.

PERFECT SCORE TIP

" If you come across any questions for which you do not know or remember the material, review it! Especially in math, tricks can only get you so far if you don't remember the math behind it. "

EXPERT TUTOR TIP

" We'll tell you the exact number of questions in each area later, in Math Workout 1. "

EXPERT TUTOR TIP

" Do not waste any time on test day reading the directions. "

4. The term *average* indicates arithmetic mean.

Again, when it comes to directions on the ACT, the golden rule is: ***Don't read them on test day!*** You'll already know what they say by the time you take the test.

The Math directions don't really tell you much anyway. Of the four special notes at the end of the Math directions, #2, #3, and #4 almost go without saying. Note #1—that figures are *not* necessarily drawn to scale—seems pretty scary, but in fact the vast majority of ACT figures *are* drawn to scale, a fact that, as we'll see, has significant implications for how to guess on geometry questions.

READING AND DRAWING DIAGRAMS

We find that about a third of the Math questions either give you a diagram or describe a situation that should be diagrammed. For these questions, the diagrams are crucial.

Example

1. The figure below contains five congruent triangles. The longest side of each triangle is 4 meters long. What is the area of the whole figure?

A. 12.5 square meters
B. 15 square meters
C. 20 square meters
D. 30 square meters
E. Cannot be determined from the given information

The key to this question is to let the diagram tell you what you need to know: that each triangle represents one-quarter of the area of the square and that the sides of the *square* are 4 meters (you can figure this out because the top side of the square is the hypotenuse—or longest side—of the triangle that makes the "roof"). Since the area of a square can be found by squaring the side, the area of the square is 16 square meters. Thus, each triangle has an area one-fourth as much—4 square meters. Since the whole figure consists of *five* triangles, each with area 4, the total area is $5 \times 4 = 20$. The answer is C.

How to Approach That Story

We find that about another third of the Math questions are story problems like the following:

Example

2. Evan drove halfway home at 20 miles per hour, then sped up and drove the rest of the way at 30 miles per hour. What was his average speed for the entire trip?

   F.   20 miles per hour

   G.   22 miles per hour

   H.   24 miles per hour

   J.   25 miles per hour

   K.   28 miles per hour

A good way to comprehend—and resolve—a story problem like this is to think of a real situation just like the one in the story. For example, what if Evan had 120 miles to drive? (You should pick a distance that's easily divisible by both rates). He would go 60 miles at 30 mph, then 60 miles at 20 mph. How long would it take? Well, 60 miles at 30 mph is 2 hours; 60 miles at 20 mph is 3 hours. That's a total of 120 miles in 5 hours; 120 divided by 5 gives an average speed of 24 mph. The correct answer is thus H. (Note: We'll show you alternative ways to answer questions like this later on.)

Getting the Concept

Finally, we find that about a third of the questions directly ask you to demonstrate your knowledge of specific math concepts.

Example

3. If angles A and B are supplementary, and the measure of angle A is 57°, what is the measure, in degrees, of angle B?

   A.   33

   B.   43

   C.   47

   D.   123

   E.   147

This question simply requires that you know the concept of supplementary angles. Two angles are *supplementary* when they form a straight line—in other words, when they add up to 180°. Thus, question 3 boils down to this: What number, added to 57, makes 180? The answer is D.

These three types of Math questions, of course, will be discussed more fully in the Math Workouts.

READING

The Reading test is 35 minutes long and includes 40 questions. It contains four passages, each followed by ten questions. You should allow three minutes (or less) to read and mark up the passage. You will then have about 30 seconds per question.

THE FORMAT

There are four categories of reading passages: Social Studies, Natural Sciences, Humanities, and Prose Fiction. You'll get one passage in each category. The passages are about 1,000 words long and are written at about the same difficulty level as college textbooks and readings. After each passage, you'll find ten questions.

The Social Studies, Natural Sciences, and Humanities passages are usually well-organized essays. Each has a very specific theme. Questions expect you to recognize this theme, to comprehend specific facts contained in the passage, and to understand the structure of the essay. Prose Fiction passages require you to understand the thoughts, feelings, and motivations of fictional characters, even when these are not explicitly stated in the passage (we'll have a special section on Prose Fiction passages in Reading Workout 3).

There are really only three different categories of Reading questions:

- Specific Detail Questions (What does the author say?)
- Inference Questions (Why is this included? What conclusions can you make?)
- Big Picture Questions (What's the overall topic?)

THE DIRECTIONS

The Reading directions are general:

Directions: This test contains four passages, each followed by several questions. After reading a passage, select the best answer to each question and fill in the corresponding oval on your answer sheet. You are allowed to refer to the passages while answering the questions.

Nothing stupefying here. But nothing very substantive either. We'll be a little more specific and strategic than the test makers when we suggest a plan of attack in the three Reading Workouts.

PERFECT SCORE TIP

" Unlike the SATs, ACT Reading will always have the same format. You will always have four passages, and they will always appear in this order: Prose, Social Science, History, Natural Science. "

PERFECT SCORE TIP

" You do not have to do the readings in order. For example, if you always have trouble with Prose but are very good at Natural Science, do Natural Science first to make sure you don't run out of time to get those easy points. Especially if you have trouble with time, develop a personal order that works for you. "

NAILING DOWN THE DETAILS

Specific Detail Questions ask about things stated explicitly in the passage. Your challenge is to:

1. Find the exact place in the passage where the answer can be found. If the question doesn't give line references to help, you will be glad you marked up the passage (Remember: **A**bbreviating margin notes, **B**racketing key sentences, and **C**ircling key words and phrases).

2. Match the text in the passage with the correct answer (by locating either similar words or antonyms).

Note: Many wrong choices will be designed to trip you up by including details from other parts of the passage or by using the same wording as the passage while distorting the meaning.

Two important points to keep in mind:

1. There is a "best" answer, which means there may be other tempting answers.

2. "Refer to the passage" in the Reading directions means that it's a good idea to look at the text before you try to answer the question.

Example

When we say "Bach" we almost **always** refer to Johann Sebastian Bach (1685–1750), but in fact the name "Bach" belongs to a whole family of Baroque German musicians . . .

(7 paragraphs and 950 words omitted)

The works of Johann Christian Bach, J. S. Bach's son, clearly prefigure the rich musical developments that followed the Baroque period. Thus, it is both surprising and unfortunate that the rest of J. S. Bach's family isn't more well known.

6. According to the author, J. S. Bach is the best-known:
   F. German Baroque musician.
   G. member of a musical family.
   H. organist in German history.
   J. composer of Lutheran hymns.

7. Johann Christian Bach was:
   A. born earlier than Johann Sebastian Bach.
   B. a composer of the "Romantic" school of music.
   C. a composer whose works are transitional in style.
   D. well known during his own lifetime.

PERFECT SCORE TIP

❝ Always make sure you read the entire question and answer. The incorrect answers are made to look tempting on purpose, so avoid picking them based on "key words." ❞

The answer for question 6 is G. Both the first and last sentences in the passage refer to J. S. Bach as the most famous member of a whole family of musicians. You might think J. S. Bach is the best-known "German Baroque musician" (choice F), but that's not what the passage says, so it's wrong.

The answer for question 7 is C. At the end of the passage the author says that Johann Christian's work "prefigure[d]" the music that followed the Baroque. Thus, it must have had some Baroque characteristics and some new aspects. In other words, it was transitional.

MAKING AN INFERENCE

Most Reading passages also include a large number of Inference Questions, which require you to make an inference from the passage (to "read between the lines"). They differ somewhat from Specific Detail Questions. For one thing, students usually consider them harder. An example of each can be found on the next page.

Example

. . . though schizophrenia and multiple personality disorder (M.P.D.) may be related, and are often confused by laymen, the two terms have radically different meanings . . .

32. Which of the following best expresses the relationship between schizophrenia and multiple personality disorder?

    F. They are two terms that describe essentially the same phenomenon.

    G. The two disorders have nothing in common.

    H. Though the two have some similarities, they are fundamentally different.

    J. The two are not exactly alike, but are very close.

33. Suppose that a patient has been diagnosed with schizophrenia. Based on the passage, which of the following is least likely?

    A. The patient's doctors immediately assume that the patient also suffers from M.P.D.

    B. The patient is a layman.

    C. The patient denies that he has M.P.D.

    D. The patient is related to someone with M.P.D.

Note the differences between Specific Detail and Inference Questions: Question 32, a Specific Detail Question, requires that you understand the explicitly stated idea that schizophrenia and M.P.D. have some connection, but are not the same. That's what choice H says. Question 33, on the other hand, requires you to apply the idea that the two disorders are different. If they are, it's highly unlikely that doctors would simply assume that a patient suffering from one disorder must suffer from the other. Therefore, choice A is least likely—and therefore correct. The other choices may or may not be true, and nothing in the passage leads us to think one way or the other about them. Question 33 is what we'd call a garden-variety Inference Question.

GETTING THE BIG PICTURE

Although the majority of Reading questions are Specific Detail and Inference Questions, the Reading subtest also includes another type of question that we call Big Picture Questions. Some Big Picture Questions ask about the passage as a whole, requiring you to find the theme, tone, or structure of the passage. Others ask you to evaluate the writing. Here's a typical Big Picture Question that might have appeared with the Bach family passage we talked about earlier.

Example

9. The author's main point in the passage is to:
   A. show that many of the lesser-known members of the Bach family also influenced music history.
   B. argue that J. C. Bach was actually a greater composer than his father, J. S. Bach.
   C. demonstrate that musical talent **always** runs in families.
   D. dispute the claim that the Bach family was the best-known family of German Baroque musicians.

In order to answer this kind of question, you've got to have a good sense of the Big Picture—of the shape and flow of the whole passage. Of course, we printed only a few selected lines from the passage, but that should have been enough to lead you to A as the answer. The first line definitely indicates that the subject of the passage is going to be the entire Bach family, with a focus on the ones who aren't as well known as the big cheese, J. S. himself.

SCIENCE

The Science test is 35 minutes long and includes 40 questions. It has seven passages, each with five to seven questions. This breaks down to approximately five minutes per passage.

PERFECT SCORE TIP

"Even when the test asks you to infer an answer, the answer will be based on the passage and what the author says. Do not make unsubstantiated judgments on the reading."

No, you don't have to be a scientist to succeed on the ACT Science test. You don't have to know the atomic number of cadmium or the preferred mating habits of the monarch butterfly. All that's required is common sense (though a knowledge of standard scientific processes and procedures sure does help). You'll be given passages containing various kinds of scientific information—drawn from the fields of biology, chemistry, physics, geology, astronomy, and meteorology—which you'll have to understand and use as a basis for inferences.

THE FORMAT

On the Science section of the test, the seven passages are broken down as follows:

- Three passages about tables and graphs
- Three passages about experiments
- One passage that presents opposing viewpoints on the same issue

Each passage will generate between five and seven questions. A warning: some passages will be very difficult to understand, but they'll usually make up for that fact by having many easy questions attached to them. The test makers do show some mercy once in a while.

THE DIRECTIONS

Here's what the Science directions will look like:

Directions: There are seven passages in this test. Each passage is followed by several questions. After reading each passage, decide on the best answer to each question and fill in the corresponding oval on your answer sheet. You may refer to the passages as often as necessary. You are NOT permitted to use a calculator on this test.

Sounds a lot like the set of directions for Reading, doesn't it? Not much substance here, either.

ANALYZING DATA

About two-thirds of the questions on the Science subtest require you to read data from graphs or tables. In easier questions, you need only report the information. In harder questions, you may need to draw inferences or note patterns in the data. For example:

Example

1. A test taker who scores in approximately the 40th percentile has correctly answered about what fraction of the questions?

A. $\dfrac{9}{10}$

B. $\dfrac{2}{3}$

C. $\dfrac{1}{2}$

D. $\dfrac{1}{5}$

2. Which of the following best describes the relationship between percentile rank and percent of questions correct?

F. As percentile rank increases, percent of correct questions also increases.

G. Percentile rank is inversely proportional to the percent of correct questions.

H. As percentile rank increases, the percent of correct questions decreases.

J. As percentile rank decreases, percent of correct questions usually, but not always, also decreases.

The correct answer to question 1 is C. The point for the 40th percentile is slightly above the 50 percent point on the horizontal axis (percent correct). Fifty percent is the same as $\dfrac{1}{2}$. Note that this question involves a little simple arithmetic (translating a percent into a fraction)—not uncommon for Science questions.

In question 2, the correct answer is F. The points that are higher on the graph (higher percentile) are always farther to the right (higher percentage of correct questions). Note that answers G and H say essentially the same thing (we'll discuss direct and inverse proportionality in Science Workout 1), and thus are wrong for the same reason: they get the relationship backwards. J is wrong because it says that the percent of correct questions does not **always** decrease as percentile rank decreases.

CONDUCTING EXPERIMENTS

Other Science questions require that you understand the way experiments are designed and what they prove. For example, part of a passage might describe an experiment as follows:

Example

Experiment 1

A scientist adds one drop of nitric acid to Beakers A, B, and C. Each Beaker contains water from a different stream. The water in Beaker A came from Stream A, that in Beaker B came from Stream B, and that in Beaker C came from Stream C. Precipitates form in Beakers B and C, but not in Beaker A.

12. Which of the following could properly be inferred on the basis of Experiment 1?

    F. Stream A is more polluted than Streams B and C.

    G. Streams B and C are more polluted than A.

    H. Stream A contains material that neutralizes nitric acid.

    J. Streams B and C contain some substance that reacts in the presence of nitric acid.

The correct answer is J. Since a precipitate forms when nitric acid is added to Beakers B and C, which contain water from Streams B and C, something in these streams must be involved. However, we don't know that it is pollution, so answers F and G are unwarranted. We also don't know exactly *why* no precipitate formed in Beaker A, so H is also an unwarranted conclusion. Scientists *hate* unwarranted conclusions.

THE PRINCIPLE OF THE THING

The remaining Science questions require you either to logically apply a principle or to identify ways of defending or attacking a principle. Often, the question will involve two scientists stating opposing views on the same subject. But this is not **always** the case. A passage might describe a theory that most "V-shaped" valleys are typically formed on Earth—by water erosion through soft rock.

Example

16. Which of the following is most likely to be a V-shaped valley?

    F. A valley formed by glaciers

    G. A river valley which is cut into very hard basalt

    H. A valley formed by wind erosion

    J. A river valley in a region of soft shale rocks

17. Which of the following discoveries would most weaken the theory of V-shaped valley formation given in the passage?

   A. Certain parts of many valleys formed by water that are U-shaped
   B. A group of V-shaped valleys almost certainly formed by wind erosion
   C. A group of U-shaped valleys formed by water erosion in hard rock
   D. A group of valleys on Mars that appear to be V-shaped but that are not near any running water

In question 16, the correct answer is J, since this is consistent with the passage as described. The correct answer in question 17 is B. Finding V-shaped valleys not formed by water erosion would tend to weaken the theory that they are formed this way. The other answers do not offer evidence about V-shaped valleys on Earth, and thus are irrelevant to a theory about them.

We'll be showing you strategies for each kind of Science question in the three Science Workouts.

WRITING

The Writing test is 30 minutes long and includes one essay. You'll be given a topic or issue and expected to take a position on it, supporting your point of view with examples and evidence.

You don't have to be a great creative writer to succeed on the ACT Writing test. Instead, you have to show that you can focus on an issue and argue your point of view in a coherent, direct way with concrete examples. Furthermore, the essay graders are not primarily concerned with your grammar and punctuation skills. In terms of writing, clarity is what they are looking for. You are being tested on your ability to communicate in writing.

One of the biggest challenges of the Writing test is the time frame. With only 30 minutes to read about the issue, plan your response, draft the essay, and proofread it, you have to work quickly and efficiently. Coming up with a plan and sticking to it are key to succeeding on the Writing test.

THE FORMAT

The Writing test consists of one prompt that lays out the issue and gives directions for your response. There are no choices of topic; you have to respond to the topic that's there. Don't worry too much about not knowing anything about the issue you have to write about. Test makers try to craft topics that will be relevant to high school students and about which they can be expected to have a point of view.

> **PERFECT SCORE TIP**
>
> " Organization is the key to success on the Writing section. Get used to reading a question and immediately developing three body paragraphs and a thesis. This will not only make for a better essay, but will let you finish it in the allowed time. "

> **PERFECT SCORE TIP**
>
> " ACT essay topics always deal with "high school situations," so don't worry about not understanding the topics. Read the entire prompt and feel free to use the background info they give you. "

THE DIRECTIONS

Here's what the Writing test directions will look like:

In many high schools, the administration has provided guidelines for the publication of student newspapers. These guidelines often determine which topics can and cannot be discussed in the newspaper and prohibit what the administration deems inappropriate language. Many administrators and teachers feel that these restrictions enable them to provide a safe learning environment for students. Others feel that any restriction on the student newspaper is a violation of freedom of speech. In your opinion, should high schools place restrictions on student newspapers?

In your essay, take a position on this question. You may write about either one of the two points of view given, or you may present a different point of view on this question. Use specific reasons and examples to support your position.

The first paragraph gives some background on the issue about which you must write. The final paragraph giving directions is **always** the same. Notice that there are two distinct parts to the assignment: (1) state a position and (2) provide support for your position.

WRITING TEST SKILLS

The readers realize you're writing under time pressure and expect you to make some mistakes. **The content of your essay is not relevant; readers are not checking your facts. Nor will they judge you on your opinions. What they want is to see how well you can communicate a relevant, coherent point of view.**

The test makers identify the following as the skills tested on the Writing test:

- **Stating a clear perspective on an issue.** This means answering the question in the prompt.

- **Providing supporting evidence and logical reasoning.** This means offering relevant support for your opinion, building an argument based on concrete details and examples.

- **Maintaining focus and organizing ideas logically.** You've got to be organized, avoid digressions, and tie all your ideas together in a sensible way.

- **Writing clearly.** This is the only skill addressing your ability to write directly, and it's limited to clarity.

The Writing test is not principally a test of your grammar and punctuation (which are tested on the English test)—colleges want a chance to see your reasoning and communication skills. To learn more about doing well on the Writing test, review the Writing Workout.

PERFECT SCORE TIP

" The questions will always ask you to take a position. Don't try to argue both opinions, or feel tied to the one you agree with. For example, on my essay I argued a stance I do not agree with personally, but found it an easier topic for an organized and complete essay. "

DON'T WORRY

" In the Writing Workout, we'll show you how to plan and draft a high-scoring essay. You'll learn what the essay readers will be looking for and how to give it to them. "

GO ONLINE

" Try writing an ACT-style essay using one of the sample prompts and model essays in the online companion. "

IF YOU LEARNED ONLY FIVE THINGS IN THIS CHAPTER . . .

1. The ACT English test includes 75 questions to be answered in 45 minutes. It tests your knowledge of grammar and usage. You'll be asked to fix errors in passages and sometimes to comment on the passage as a whole.

2. The ACT Math test consists of 60 questions to be answered in 60 minutes. Topics include pre-algebra, elementary and intermediate algebra, coordinate and plane geometry, and trigonometry. Questions are not given in order of difficulty.

3. The ACT Reading test includes 40 questions to be answered in 35 minutes. The questions refer to four passages: Prose Fiction, Humanities, Social Sciences, and Natural Sciences.

4. The ACT Science test is comprised of 40 questions to be answered in 35 minutes. There are seven passages with related questions which ask you to analyze and interpret experiments, figures, and scientists' viewpoints. There will only be one to three questions which call on you to use your existing science knowledge.

5. The ACT Writing test consists of one essay prompt that asks you to take a stand on an issue. You have 30 minutes to write a clear and persuasive essay, supported with evidence from your experience, reading, current events, or other sources.

CHAPTER 3: TAKING CONTROL: THE TOP TEN STRATEGIES

Now that you've got some idea of the kind of adversary you face in the ACT, it's time to start developing strategies for dealing with this adversary. In other words, you've got to start developing your ACT Mind-set.

The ACT, as we've just seen, isn't a normal test. A normal test requires that you rely almost exclusively on your memory. On a normal test, you'd see questions like this:

The "golden spike," which joined the Union Pacific and Central Pacific Railroads, was driven in Ogden, Utah, in May 1869. Who was president of the United States at the time?

To answer this question, you have to resort to memory dredging. Either you know the answer is Ulysses S. Grant or else you don't. No matter how hard you think, you'll **never** be able to answer this question if you can't remember your history.

But the ACT doesn't test your long-term memory. The answer to every ACT question can be found on the test. Theoretically, if you read carefully and understand the words and concepts the test uses, you can get almost any ACT question right. Notice the difference between the regular-test question above and the ACT-type question below:

Example

1. What is the product of n and m^2, where n is an odd number and m is an even number?
   A. An odd number
   B. A multiple of four
   C. A noninteger
   D. An irrational number
   E. The square of an integer

EXPERT TUTOR TIP

" Be sure to take plenty of breaks while studying! It keeps your brain fresh and prevents you from getting overwhelmed. "

EXPERT TUTOR TIP

" The mind-set for the ACT is "creative problem-solving mode." Don't rely too heavily on your memory. Instead, use your brain's creative thinking cells. The ACT Mind-set isn't too different from the one you'd use to play chess, work a crossword, or run a maze. (You run mazes all the time, don't you?) "

EXPERT TUTOR TIP

" ACT questions are puzzles to solve. Don't think: "Can I remember?" Think: "Let me figure this thing out!" "

Aside from the obvious difference (this question has answer choices, while the other one does not), there's another difference: the ACT question mostly tests your ability to understand a situation rather than your ability to passively remember a fact. Nobody expects you to know off the top of your head what the product of an odd number and the square of an even number is. But the ACT test makers do expect you to be able to roll up your sleeves and figure it out (as we'll do below).

THE ACT MIND-SET

Most students take the ACT with the same mind-set that they use for normal tests. Their brains are on "memory mode." Students often panic and give up because they can't seem to remember enough. **But you don't need to remember a ton of picky little rules for the ACT. Don't give up on an ACT question just because your memory fails.**

On the ACT, if you understand what a question is really asking on the test, you can almost always answer it. For instance, take the math problem on the previous page. You might have been thrown by the way it was phrased. "How can I solve this problem?" you may have asked yourself. "It doesn't even have numbers in it!"

The key here, as in all ACT questions, is taking control. Take the question (by the throat, if necessary) and wrestle it into a form you can understand. Ask yourself: What's really being asked here? What does it mean when they say something like "the product of n and m^2"?

Well, you might start by putting it into words you might use. You might say something like this: "I've got to take one number times another. One of the numbers is odd and the other is an even number squared. Then I've got to see what kind of number I get as an answer." Once you put the question in your own terms like this, it becomes much less intimidating—and much easier to get right. You'll realize that you don't have to do complex algebraic computations with variables. All you have to do is substitute numbers.

So do it! Try picking some easy-to-use numbers. Say that n is 3 (an odd number) and m is 2 (an even number). Then m^2 would be 4, because 2^2 is 4. And $n \times m$ would be 3×4, which is 12—a multiple of four, but not odd, not a noninteger, not an irrational number, and not a perfect square. The only answer that can be right, then, is B.

See what we mean about figuring out the answer creatively rather than passively remembering it? True, there are some things you had to remember here—what even and odd numbers are, how variables and exponents work, and maybe what integers and irrational numbers are. But these are very basic concepts. Most of what you're expected to know on the ACT is like that: basic.

Of course, basic doesn't always mean easy. Many ACT questions are built on basic concepts, but are tough nonetheless. The problem above, for instance, is difficult because it requires some thought to figure out what's being asked. This isn't only true in Math. It's the same for every part of the ACT.

The creative, take-control kind of thinking we call the ACT Mind-set is something you want to bring to virtually every ACT question you encounter. As we'll see, being in the ACT Mind-set means reshaping the test-taking experience so that you are in the driver's seat.

It means:

- Answering questions **if** you want to (by guessing on the impossible questions rather than wasting time on them).

- Answering questions **when** you want to (by skipping tough but "doable" questions and coming back to them after you've gotten all of the easy questions done).

- Answering questions **how** you want to (by using "unofficial" ways of getting correct answers fast).

And that's really what the ACT Mind-set boils down to: Taking control. Being creative. Solving specific problems to get points as quickly and easily as you can.

What follows are the top ten strategies you need to do just that.

TEN STRATEGIES FOR MASTERING THE ACT

1. Do Question Triage

In a hospital emergency room, the triage nurse is the person who evaluates each patient and decides which ones get attention first and which ones should be treated later. You should do the same thing on the ACT.

Practicing triage is one of the most important ways of controlling your test-taking experience. It's a fact that there are some questions on the ACT that most students could **never** answer correctly, no matter how much time or effort they spent on them.

EXPERT TUTOR TIP

" You'll find basic concepts gathered together in the very attractive 100 Key Math Concepts for the ACT section at the end of this book. "

GO ONLINE

" With two full-length practice tests and eight section-length practice tests online, you'll get plenty of opportunities to practice the strategies in this chapter. "

PERFECT SCORE TIP

" If you encounter a hard problem, don't let it demoralize you. On the test, I had some problems I found extremely difficult, yet the key to scoring well was to not let them worry me. Instead I kept going in order to get as many other points as possible. "

Example

57. If $\sec^2 x = 4$, which of the following could be $\sin x$?
    A. 1.73205
    B. 3.14159
    C. $\sqrt{3}$
    D. $\dfrac{\sqrt{3}}{2}$
    E. Cannot be determined from the given information.

Clearly, even if you could manage to come up with an answer to this question, it would take some time (if you insist on doing so, refer to the explanation below). But would it be worth the time? We think not.

This question clearly illustrates our point: do question triage on the ACT. The first time you look at a question, make a quick decision about how hard and time-consuming it looks. Then decide whether to answer it now or skip it and do it later.

- If the question looks comprehensible and reasonably doable, do it right away.
- If the question looks tough and time-consuming, but ultimately doable, skip it, circle the question number in your test booklet, and come back to it later.
- If the question looks impossible, forget about it. Guess and move on, **never** to return.

This triage method will ensure you spend the time needed to do all the easy questions before getting bogged down with a tough problem. Remember, every question on a subject test is worth the same number of points. You get no extra credit for test machismo.

Answering easier questions first has another benefit: it gives you confidence to answer harder ones later. Doing problems in the order you choose rather than in the order imposed by the test makers gives you control over the test. Most students don't have time to do all of the problems, so you've got to make sure you do all of the ones you can easily score on!

DO YOU KNOW YOUR TRIG?

Okay, since you're reading this, it's obvious that you want to know the answer to the trig question we just looked at. The answer is D. Here's how we got it:

$$\sec^2 x = 4 \qquad \text{given}$$

$$\sec x = 2 \text{ or } -2 \qquad \text{square root both sides}$$

$$\cos x = \frac{1}{2} \text{ or } -\frac{1}{2} \qquad \cos x = \frac{1}{\sec x}$$

$$\cos^2 x = \frac{1}{4} \qquad \text{square both sides}$$

$$\sin^2 x = 1 - \frac{1}{4} \qquad \sin^2 x + \cos^2 x = 1$$

$$\sin^2 x = 1 - \cos^2 x$$

$$\sin^2 x = \frac{3}{4}$$

$$\sin x = \sqrt{\frac{3}{4}} \text{ or } -\sqrt{\frac{3}{4}} \qquad \text{square root both sides}$$

$$\sin x = \sqrt{\frac{3}{2}} \text{ or } -\sqrt{\frac{3}{2}} \qquad \sqrt{4} = 2$$

So answer choice D is correct. But if you got it right, don't congratulate yourself quite yet. How long did it take you to get it right? So long that you could have gotten the answers to two easy questions in the same amount of time?

DEVELOP A PLAN OF ATTACK

For the English, Reading, and Science sections, the best plan of attack is to do each passage as a block. Make a longish first pass through the questions (call it the "triage pass"), doing the easy ones, guessing on the impossible ones, and skipping any that look like they might cause trouble. Then make a second pass (call it the "cleanup pass"), and do those questions you think you can solve with some elbow grease.

For Math, you use the same two-pass strategy, except that you move through the whole subject test twice. Work through the doable questions first. Most of these will probably be toward the beginning, but not all. Then come back and attack the questions that look possible but tough or time-consuming.

No matter what subject test you're working on, **you should take pains to grid your answers in the right place.** It's easy to misgrid when you're skipping around, so be careful. And of course: *Make sure you have an answer gridded for every question by the time the subject test is over!*

2. PUT THE MATERIAL INTO A FORM YOU CAN UNDERSTAND

ACT questions are rarely presented in the simplest, most helpful way. In fact, your main job for many questions is to figure out what the question means so you can solve it.

EXPERT TUTOR TIP

Let's say you took three minutes to get a tough question right. That might feel good, but you would actually be better off if you had skipped the tough question and, in the same amount of time, answered two or three easier questions correctly.

PERFECT SCORE TIP

In Reading and Science, try to finish each passage before moving on as you will waste time rereading the passage if you skip between readings.

EXPERT TUTOR TIP

Write all over your test booklet. Crossing out wrong answers eliminates confusion and helps you to see clearly which answer is correct. Underlining key points when reading passages helps you to determine the main idea.

Since the material is presented in such an intimidating way, one of your best strategies for taking control is to recast (reword) the material into a form you can handle better. This is what we did in the math problem about "the product of n and m^2." We took the question and reworded it in a way we could understand.

MARK UP YOUR TEST BOOKLET

This strategy should be employed on all four subject tests. For example, in Reading, many students find the passages overwhelming: 85 to 90 lines of dense verbiage for each one! But the secret is to put the passages into a form you can understand and use. Circle or underline the main idea, for one thing. And make yourself a road map of the passage, labeling each paragraph so you understand how it all fits together. That way, you'll also know—later, when you're doing the questions—where in the passage to find certain types of information you need.

REWORD THE QUESTIONS

You'll find that you also need to do some recasting of the *questions*. For instance, take this question from a Science passage:

Example

Figure 1

15. According to Figure 1, at approximately what latitude would calculations using an estimated value at sea level of $g = 9.80$ m/sec^2 produce the least error?

A.   0°

B.   20°

C.   40°

D.   80°

At what latitude would the calculations using a value of $g = 9.80$ m/sec^2 produce the least error? Yikes! What does that mean?

Take a deep breath. Ask yourself: where would an estimate for g of 9.80 m/sec^2 produce the least error? In a latitude where 9.80 m/sec^2 is the real value of g. If you find the latitude at which the real value of g is 9.80 m/sec^2, then using 9.80 m/sec^2 as an estimate there would produce no error at all!

So, in other words, what this question is asking is: at what latitude does $g = 9.80$ m/sec^2? Now that's a form of the question you can understand. In that form, you can answer it easily: choice C, which you can get just by reading the chart.

DRAW DIAGRAMS

Sometimes putting the material into usable form involves drawing with your pencil. For instance, take a look at the following math problem.

Example

2. Jason bought a painting with a frame 1 inch wide. If the dimensions of the outside of the frame are 5 inches by 7 inches, which of the following could be the length of one of the sides of the painting inside the frame?

    F. 3 inches

    G. 4 inches

    H. $5 \dfrac{1}{2}$ inches

    J. $6 \dfrac{1}{2}$ inches

    K. 7 inches

Just looking at the question the first time, you might be tempted simply to subtract 1 from the outside dimensions and think that the inside dimensions are 4 by 6 (and pick G). Why isn't this correct? Because the frame goes all the way around—both above and below the painting, both to the right and to the left. This would have been clear if you had put the problem in a form you could understand and use.

For instance, you might have made the situation graphic by actually sketching out the painting frame (who says you don't have to be an artist to succeed at the ACT?):

When you draw the picture frame like this, you realize that if the outside dimensions are 5 by 7, the inside dimensions must be 3 by 5. Thus, the correct answer is F.

So remember: on the ACT, you've got to put everything into a form that you can understand and use.

3. IGNORE IRRELEVANT ISSUES

It's easy to waste time on ACT questions by considering irrelevant issues. Just because an issue looks interesting, or just because you're worried about something, doesn't make it important.

Example

. . . China was certainly one of the cradles

of civilization. <u>It's obvious that, China</u>
                           14
<u>has a long history</u>. As is the case with
     14
other ancient cultures, the early history

of China is lost in mythology . . .

14. F. NO CHANGE

G. It's obvious that China has a long history.

H. Obviously; China has a long history.

J. OMIT the underlined portion.

In this question, the test makers are counting on you to waste time worrying about punctuation. Does that comma belong? Can you use a semicolon here? These issues might be worrisome, but there's a bigger issue here—namely, does the sentence belong in the passage at all? No, it doesn't. If China has an ancient culture and was a cradle of civilization, it must have a long history, so the sentence really is "obvious." Redundancy is the relevant issue here, not punctuation. Choice J is correct.

Remember, you've got limited time, so don't get caught up in issues that won't get you a point.

4. CHECK BACK

Remember, the ACT is not a test of your memory, so don't make it one. All of the information you need is in the test itself. Don't be afraid to refer to it. Much of the information is too complex to accurately remember anyway.

In Reading and Science, always refer to the place in the passage where the answer to a question can be found (the question stem will often contain a line reference or a reference to a specific table, graph, or experiment to help you out). Your chosen answer should match the passage—not in exact vocabulary or units of measurement, perhaps, but in meaning.

Example

Isaac Newton was born in 1642 in the hamlet of Woolsthorpe in Lincolnshire, England. But he is more famous as a man of Cambridge, where he studied and taught . . .

7. Which of the following does the author imply is a fact about Newton's birth?
    A. It occurred in Lincoln, a small hamlet in England.
    B. It took place in a part of England known for raising sheep.
    C. It did not occur in a large metropolitan setting.
    D. It caused Newton to seek his education at Cambridge.

You might expect the right answer to be that Newton was born in a hamlet, or in Woolsthorpe, or in Lincolnshire. But none of those is offered as a choice. Choice A is tempting, but wrong. Newton was born in Lincolnshire, not Lincoln. Choice B is actually true, but it's wrong here. As its name suggests, Woolsthorpe was once known for its wool—which comes from sheep. But the question asks for something implied in the passage.

The correct answer here is C, because a hamlet is a small village. That's not a large metropolitan setting. (It's also a famous play, but that's not among the choices.)

Checking back is especially important in Reading and Science because the passages leave many people feeling adrift in a sea of details. Often, the wrong answers will be "misplaced details"—details taken from different parts of the passage. They are things that don't answer the question properly but that might sound good to you if you aren't careful. By checking back with the passage, you can avoid choosing such devilishly clever wrong choices.

There's another important lesson here: **don't pick a choice just because it contains "key words" you remember from the passage.** Many wrong choices, like D in the question above, are distortions—they use the right words but say the wrong things about them. Look for answer choices that contain the same ideas you find in the passage.

One of the best ways to avoid choosing misplaced details and distortions is to check back with the passage.

5. Answer the Right Question

This strategy is a natural extension of the last. As we said, **the ACT test makers often include among the wrong choices for a question the correct answer to a different question.** Under time pressure, it's easy to fall for one of these red herrings, thinking that you know what's being asked for when really you don't.

PERFECT SCORE TIP

" Even if you have the best memory in the world, don't waste points by trusting your memory of the passage. Always refer to where each answer was said in the passage. "

EXPERT TUTOR TIP

" Researching Reading questions is important because the correct answer directly relates to the passage. Incorrect answers, **even if true,** don't relate well to either the passage OR the question. "

PERFECT SCORE TIP

" Many words are put in answers purely to tempt you. Make sure your answers are based on knowledge of the passage. "

Example

7. What is the value of $3x$ if $9x = 5y + 2$ and $y + 4 = 2y - 10$?
   A.   5
   B.   8
   C.   14
   D.   24
   E.   72

To solve this problem, we need to find y first, even though the question asks about x (because x here is given only in terms of y). You could solve the second equation like this:

$y + 4 = 2y - 10$	given
$4 = y - 10$	by subtracting y from both sides
$14 = y$	by adding 10 to both sides

But choice C, 14, isn't the right answer here, because the question doesn't ask for the value of y—it asks about x. We can use the value of y to find x, however, by plugging the calculated value of y into the first equation:

$9x = 5y + 2$	given
$9x = 5(14) + 2$	because $y = 14$
$9x = 70 + 2$	
$9x = 72$	

But E, 72, isn't the answer either, because the question doesn't ask for $9x$. It doesn't ask for x either, so if you picked B, 8, you'd be wrong as well. Remember to refer to the question! The question asks for $3x$. So we need to divide $9x$ by 3:

$9x = 72$	from above
$3x = 24$	dividing by 3

Thus, the answer is D.

Always check the question again before choosing your answer. Doing all the right work but then getting the wrong answer can be seriously depressing. So make sure you're answering the right question.

6. LOOK FOR THE HIDDEN ANSWER

On many ACT questions, the right answer is hidden in one way or another. An answer can be hidden by being written in a way that you aren't likely to expect. For example, you might work out a problem and get .5 as your answer, but then find that .5 isn't among the answer choices. Then you notice that one choice reads "$\frac{1}{2}$." Congratulations, Sherlock. You've found the hidden answer.

There's another way the ACT can hide answers. **Many ACT questions have more than one possible right solution, though only one correct answer choice is given. The ACT will hide that answer by offering one of the less obvious possible answers to a question.**

Example

2. If $3x^2 + 5 = 17$, which of the following could be the value of x?

    A. −3
    B. −2
    C. 0
    D. 1
    E. 4

You quickly solve this very straightforward problem like so:

$$3x^2 + 5 = 17 \qquad \text{given}$$
$$3x^2 = 12 \qquad \text{by subtracting 5}$$
$$x^2 = 4 \qquad \text{dividing by 3}$$
$$x = 2 \qquad \text{taking square root of both sides}$$

Having gotten an answer, you confidently look for it among the choices. But 2 isn't a choice. The explanation? This question has two possible solutions, not just one. The square root of 4 can be either 2 or −2. B is thus the answer.

Keep in mind that though there's only one right answer choice for each question, that right answer may not be the one that occurs to you first. A common mistake is to pick an answer that seems "sort of" like the answer you're looking for even when you know it's wrong. Don't settle for second best. If you don't find your answer, don't assume that you're wrong. Try to think of another right way to answer the question.

> **EXPERT TUTOR TIP**
>
> " If you guess blindly, you have one chance in four (or one in five, on the Math) of getting the question right. But if you can eliminate one or two choices as definitely wrong, you can improve those odds. "

> **EXPERT TUTOR TIP**
>
> " Get the points you deserve on the questions you can answer. But don't worry about the ones you have to guess on. Odds are good that you'll guess some correctly. And those correct guesses will increase your score just as much as if you'd figured out the answers. "

7. GUESS INTELLIGENTLY

An unanswered question is always wrong, but even a wild guess may be right.
On the ACT, a guess can't hurt you, but it can help. In fact, smart guessing can make
a big difference in your score. **Always** guess on every ACT question you can't answer.
Never leave a question blank.

You'll be doing two different kinds of guessing during your two sweeps through any
subject test:

- Blind guessing (which you do mostly on questions you deem too hard or
  time-consuming even to try).

- Considered guessing (which you do mostly on questions that you do some
  work on, but can't make headway with).

When you guess blindly, you just choose any letter you feel like choosing (many
students like to choose B for Bart; few choose H for Homer). When you guess in a
considered way, on the other hand, you've usually done enough work on a question
to eliminate at least one or two choices. If you can eliminate any choices, you'll up
the odds that you'll guess correctly.

Here are some fun facts about guessing: If you were to work on only half of the
questions on the ACT but get them all right, then guess blindly on the other half
of the questions, you would probably earn a composite ACT score of around 23
(assuming you had a statistically reasonable success rate on your guesses). A 23
would put you in roughly the top quarter of all those who take the ACT. It's a good
score. And all you had to do was answer half the questions correctly.

On the other hand, if you were to hurry and finish all the questions, but get only
half of them right, you'd probably earn only a 19, which is below average.

How? Why are you better off answering half and getting them all right instead of
answering all and getting only half right?

Here's the trick. The student who answers half the questions right and skips the
others can still take guesses on the unanswered questions—and odds are this student
will have enough correct guesses to move up 4 points, from a 19 to a 23. But the
student who answers all the questions and gets half wrong doesn't have the luxury of
taking guesses.

In short: **guess if you can't figure out an answer for any question!**

PERFECT SCORE TIP

❝ Focus your time on
questions you know you
can answer. Remember that
spending time to get one
right answer is better than
two wrong ones. ❞

PERFECT SCORE TIP

❝ When gridding,
don't be a hero and
try to remember eight
answers in your head and
transfer to your grid. Work
deliberately, but one place
you cannot afford to lose
points is in gridding your
answers. ❞

8. BE CAREFUL WITH THE ANSWER GRID

Your ACT score is based on the answers you select on your answer grid. Even if you work out every question correctly, you'll get a low score if you misgrid your answers. So be careful! Don't disdain the process of filling in those little "bubbles" on the grid. Sure, it's mindless, but under time pressure it's easy to lose control and make mistakes.

It's important to **develop a disciplined strategy for filling in the answer grid.** We find that it's smart to grid the answers in groups rather than one question at a time. What this means is this: As you figure out each question in the test booklet, circle the answer choice you come up with. Then transfer those answers to the answer grid in groups of five or more (until you get close to the end of the section, when you start gridding answers one by one).

Gridding in groups like this cuts down on errors because you can focus on this one task and do it right. It also saves time you'd otherwise spend moving papers around, finding your place, and redirecting your mind. Answering ACT questions takes deep, hard thinking. Filling out answer grids is easy, but you have to be careful, especially if you do a lot of skipping around. Shifting between "hard thinking" and "careful bookkeeping" takes time and effort.

In English, Reading, and Science, the test is divided naturally into groups of questions—the passages. For most students, it makes sense to circle your answers in your test booklet as you work them out. Then, when you're finished with each passage and its questions, grid the answers as a group.

In Math, the strategy has to be different because the Math test isn't broken up into natural groups. Mark your answers in the test booklet and then grid them when you reach the end of each page or two. Since there are usually about five math questions per page, you'll probably be gridding five or ten math answers at a time.

No matter what subject test you're working on, though, if you're near the end of a subject test, start gridding your answers one at a time. You don't want to be caught with ungridded answers when time is called.

During the test, the proctor should warn you when you have about five minutes left on each subject test. But don't depend on proctors! Yes, they're usually nice people, but they can mess up once in a while. **Rely on your own watch.** When there are five minutes left on a subject test, start gridding your answers one by one. With a minute or two left, start filling in everything you've left blank. Remember: even one question left blank could cut your score.

> **PERFECT SCORE TIP**
>
> "I found it helpful to grid after each Reading passage and after every two pages of Math. Gridding too often can be distracting to your concentration, but there is nothing worse than running out of time to grid your answers."

PERFECT SCORE TIP

" Especially if you have time problems, realize that gridding does take time. Actually grid answer sheets when doing practice tests to get a feel for whether you will have trouble finishing the actual test. "

EXPERT TUTOR TIP

" Spend your test time wisely! English, Reading passages: about nine minutes each (including questions), Science passages: about five minutes each (including questions), Math questions: about 30–60 seconds each, depending on the difficulty. "

9. USE THE LETTERS OF THE CHOICES TO STAY ON TRACK

One oddity about the ACT is that even-numbered questions have F, G, H, J (and, in Math, K) as answer choices, rather than A, B, C, D (and, again, E in Math). This might be confusing at first, but you can make it work for you. **A common mistake with the answer grid is to accidentally enter an answer one row up or down. On the ACT, that won't happen if you pay attention to the letter in the answer.** If you're looking for an A and you see only F, G, H, J, and K, you'll know you're in the wrong row on the answer grid.

Another advantage of having answers F through K for even-numbered questions is that it makes you less nervous about patterns in the answers. It's common to start worrying if you've picked the same letter twice or three times in a row. Since the questions have different letters, this can't happen on the ACT. Of course, you could pick the first choice (A or F) for several questions in a row. This shouldn't worry you. It's common for the answers in the same position to be correct three times in a row, and even four times in a row isn't unheard of.

10. KEEP TRACK OF TIME

During each subject test, you really have to pace yourself. On average, English, Reading, and Science questions should take about 30 seconds each. Math questions should average less than one minute each. Remember to take into account the fact that you'll probably be taking two passes through the questions.

Set your watch to 12:00 at the beginning of each subject test, so it will be easy to check your time. Again, don't rely on proctors, even if they promise that they will dutifully call out the time every 15 minutes. Proctors get distracted once in a while.

More basic questions should take less time, and harder ones will probably take more. In Math, for instance, you need to go much faster than one per minute during your first sweep. But at the end, you may spend two or three minutes on each of the harder problems you work out.

TAKE CONTROL

You are the master of the test-taking experience. A common thread in all ten strategies above is: take control. That's Kaplan's ACT Mind-set. Do the questions in the order you want and in the way you want. Don't get bogged down or agonize. Remember, you don't earn points for suffering, but you do earn points for moving on to the next question and getting it right.

THE ACT IS NOT SCHOOL

You have spent at least 11 years in school at this point. There, you learned some techniques that won't help you on the ACT. (Want two good examples? "Don't guess on a test" and "If you show your work on math problems, you'll get partial credit.") Many of these school-driven methods don't work well on the ACT. In fact, they work *against* you.

Don't fall into the trap of familiar school habits on ACT test day. Test day is an exciting and stressful event. We strongly suggest that you practice using the ten strategies in this chapter so that you're rehearsed and confident for test day.

Just reading and understanding these strategies before the test doesn't mean you'll remember to do them effectively on test day. These techniques will only work if you use them, so practice!

As you practice, time yourself. Buy or borrow a digital watch, and get used to working with it so it doesn't beep at the wrong moment. Your cell phone will be turned off during the test, so you won't be able to use that as a timekeeper.

Practicing the various sections of the test at home and taking at least one entire practice test in one sitting are the best ways to make sure you're comfortable with the test and ready to get your highest scores on test day.

BASIC STRATEGY REFERENCE SHEET

THE FOUR COMMANDMENTS

1. THOU SHALT LEARN THE TEST

- Learn the directions before test day.
- Become familiar with all the subject tests.
- Get a sense of the range of difficulty of the questions.

2. THOU SHALT LEARN THE STRATEGIES

- Develop a plan of attack for each subject test.
- Develop a guessing strategy that works for you.
- Find "unofficial" ways of finding answers fast.

> **GO ONLINE**
>
> " Before going on to the subject-specific Workouts, take the online Diagnostic Quiz if you haven't already. You'll learn where to focus your study time. "

3. THOU SHALT LEARN THE MATERIAL

- Bone up on weak areas.
- Find out what is and isn't part of the ACT knowledge base.
- Use the ACT Resources section to review important Math and English concepts.

4. THOU SHALT PRACTICE, PRACTICE, PRACTICE

THE TOP TEN STRATEGIES

1. Do question triage.
2. Put the material into a form you can understand and use.
3. Ignore irrelevant issues.
4. Check back.
5. Answer the right question.
6. Look for the hidden answer.
7. Guess intelligently.
8. Be careful with the answer grid.
9. Use the letters of the choices to stay on track.
10. Keep track of time.

IF YOU LEARNED ONLY TWO THINGS IN THIS CHAPTER . . .

1. Remember the ACT Mind-set: take control of your test experience.
2. Know the four commandments and the top ten strategies.

Part Two

SKILL-BUILDING WORKOUTS

CHAPTER 4: ENGLISH WORKOUT 1: WHEN IN DOUBT, TAKE IT OUT

SMARTPOINTS COVERED IN THIS CHAPTER

CONNECTIONS	
VERB TENSE	
PUNCTUATION	
WORD CHOICE	
WORDINESS	
WRITING STRATEGY	
SENTENCE SENSE	
ORGANIZATION	

EXPERT TUTOR TIP

" The ACT English test includes:

- 10 punctuation questions
- 12 grammar and usage questions
- 18 sentence structure questions
- 12 strategy questions
- 11 organization questions
- 12 style questions "

Think back to the last paper you had to write. Maybe your teacher assigned something like ten pages. You wrote and you wrote and ended up with six pages. It was the night before the paper had to be turned in. You were out of research and ideas. But you knew what to do: pad it.

You're not alone. Almost all of us have padded papers at one time or another. The recipe for padding, in fact, is practically universal: You repeat yourself a few times. You trade short phrases for long-winded verbiage. You add a few offbeat ideas that don't really belong. And presto! Your six-page paper is transformed into a ten-page paper.

The ACT test makers know that most students pad. And they know how to punish you for it. In fact, almost a third of the English questions on the ACT are testing for the very same bad writing habits—long-windedness, repetitiousness, irrelevance— that padders tend to cultivate.

But there's hope. Once you know what ACT English is testing for, you can easily avoid making these common English mistakes. More than any other part of the exam, the ACT English subject test is predictable.

ECONOMY QUESTIONS

On the ACT, more than 20 questions—almost a third of all the English items—test your awareness of redundancy, verbosity, relevance, and similar issues. We call these Economy Questions. Take a look.

Example

On recent ACTs, the shortest answer has been <u>correct,</u>
₁
<u>and absolutely right,</u> for about half of all English
₁
questions. Because this is <u>true</u>, a student who knows no
₂
English at all could earn <u>—and justly so—</u>an English
₃
subject score of about 15. Such a student could

compare the choices carefully and choose the <u>single</u>
₄
<u>shortest one</u> every time. Where the answers are the
₄
same length, the student could pick at random. On

recently published ACTs, guessing in this way would have

yielded between 35 and 38 correct answers out of 75

questions. Of course, you're going to <u>be doing</u> much
₅
better than that. You actually <u>are capable of speaking</u>
₆
<u>the English language.</u> You may not know every little
₆
rule of English usage, but you certainly know some-

thing. Obviously, getting the question right because

you know the <u>right answer</u> is better than getting it
₇
right because you guessed well.

1. A. NO CHANGE
   B. correct
   C. right, that is, correct,
   D. correct, absolutely, and right,

2. F. NO CHANGE
   G. truthfully factual
   H. factually correct
   J. factual—and true too—

3. A. NO CHANGE
   B. , and justly so,
   C. and justify
   D. OMIT the underlined portion.

4. F. NO CHANGE
   G. singularly shortest one
   H. uniquely short item
   J. shortest one

5. A. NO CHANGE
   B. do
   C. achieve
   D. be, achieving,

6. F. NO CHANGE
   G. possess the capability of speaking that wonderful language called the language of England
   H. possess the capability of speaking in the land called England
   J. speak English

7. A. NO CHANGE
   B. best choice to select
   C. most correct answer of the choices given
   D. answer considered as correct

But you should **always** remember that the ACT test

makers <u>like</u> the shortest answers. Why? Why should the
8
ACT make life so easy for you? <u>Why can't history or
9
science classes in high school be so easy?</u> Because
9
usually, the best way to write something really is the

shortest way to write it. The ACT can't help that, <u>any
10
more than you can help the fact that you must take the
10
ACT to get into college.</u> Good writing is concise and
10
<u>clear.</u> There are many rules of English, but many of
11
them grow from one dominant principle: use only the

words you need to say what you mean. 12

8. F. NO CHANGE
   G. have a habit of liking
   H. habitually tend to like
   J. are in the habit of liking

9. A. NO CHANGE
   B. Why isn't history or science?
   C. History and science aren't so easy, either!
   D. OMIT the underlined portion.

10. F. NO CHANGE
    G. just as you are helpless to avoid the requirement of taking the ACT
    H. whether or not they'd want to
    J. OMIT the underlined portion and end the sentence with a period after "that."

11. A. NO CHANGE
    B. clearly better
    C. translucent, like clear water
    D. clear. Thus it is short and to the point.

12. Suppose the author considers adding this final sentence: "Thus, if you can't say something nice, don't say anything at all." Would this be an effective conclusion for the paragraph?
    F. Yes, because this concept is needed to explain the meaning of the previous sentence.
    G. Yes, because it adds an uplifting moral tone to an otherwise depressing, amoral text.
    H. Yes, because this thought is relevant to the next paragraph.
    J. No, because the paragraph is not concerned with being nice.

ANSWERS

1. B
2. F
3. D
4. J
5. B
6. J
7. A
8. F
9. D
10. J
11. A
12. J

The shortest answer happens to be correct in all 12 of the questions above. Note that OMIT, where it is an option, is the shortest answer, since taking the material out leaves a shorter text than leaving anything in. In question 12, answer J is the shortest answer, since it leaves the proposed final sentence off entirely.

REDUNDANCY

In questions 1–4 above, the wrong (long) answers are redundant. This means that they make the passage say the same thing twice. **The ACT is very strict about redundancy: never let the text in a sentence repeat itself.**

VERBOSITY

In questions 5–8, the wrong (long) answers are verbose. They force the reader to read more words, but they are no clearer than the short answers and don't add meaning. **This is another rule the ACT is very strict about: the best way to write something is the shortest way, as long as it doesn't violate any rules of writing mechanics (like grammar or punctuation) or contain vulgarities inappropriate to civilized discourse.**

IRRELEVANCE

Questions 9–12 test relevance. The wrong (long) answers introduce irrelevant concepts. The paragraph is about ACT English questions and how to answer them—it's not about history or science classes, the necessity of taking the ACT, or that lovely translucence of clear water. **Omit the ideas that are not directly and logically tied in with the purpose of the passage.**

> **EXPERT TUTOR TIP**
>
> On recent ACTs, the shortest answer has been correct on about half of all English questions.

PERFECT SCORE TIP

❝ In English, every single word and sentence should have a unique purpose. If the underlined portion is not absolutely necessary, it is probably redundant. ❞

AVAILABLE ONLINE

❝ The online companion includes two section-length ACT English practice tests. Hone your skills with these before tackling a full-length practice test. ❞

PERFECT SCORE TIP

❝ Different people work better with different strategies for completing the English section. Personally, I never have time issues, so I prefer to read the entire passage and answer questions as I get to them, as the context helps me. Learn what amount of reading the passage works for you. ❞

With Economy Questions, the shortest answer is correct with great frequency. What that means is:

- If you're not sure whether an idea is redundant, it probably is, so take it out.
- If you're not sure whether a certain way to say something is too verbose, it probably is, so take it out.
- If you're not sure whether an idea is relevant, it probably isn't, so take it out.

In other words: **when in doubt, take it out**.

KEEP IT SHORT—ON ALL ENGLISH QUESTIONS

Questions on which the lengths of the answers vary greatly, or questions that contain the answer choice OMIT, are usually Economy Questions. For these questions, you should be especially inclined to choose the shortest choice. For the other questions, the shortest answer is not nearly as often correct.

As we'll see in later workouts, the other English questions mostly test your ability to spot nonsense, bad grammar, and bad punctuation. But even in these cases, the rule "when in doubt, take it out" still holds. Most grammatical mistakes can be solved by removing the offending words.

Because these issues of writing economy are so important to English questions of all kinds, we've made them the linchpin for our recommended approach to the English subject test. **When approaching English questions, the very first question you should ask yourself is: "Does this stuff belong here? Can the passage or sentence work without it?"**

READING AS YOU GO

Read the passage as far as you find necessary to answer each question, and then answer each one in turn. *Don't skip over sentences without questions in them*—you'll need to understand the whole passage when you answer the questions at the end.

THE KAPLAN THREE-STEP METHOD FOR ACT ENGLISH

Here's our three-step (or really, three-question) approach to ACT English questions. (Note: Steps 2 and 3 will be covered more thoroughly in English Workouts 2 and 3.)

1. DO THESE WORDS BELONG HERE?

As we've seen, writing economy is very near to the hearts of ACT test makers. So ask yourself: Does the underlined section belong? Is it expressed as succinctly as possible? If the answer is no, choose the answer that gets rid of the stuff that doesn't belong. If the answer is yes, move on to . . .

2. DO THESE WORDS MAKE SENSE?

The ACT test makers want simple, easy-to-understand prose. They expect everything to fit together logically. Does the underlined part of the passage make logical sense? If the answer is no, select the choice that turns nonsense into sense. If the answer is yes, go on to . . .

3. DO I HEAR OR SEE AN ERROR?

Many grammar errors will sound wrong to your ear. Even the ones that don't will be recognizable to you if you study our 19 Classic Grammar Errors in English Workout 3 and create a "flag list" of the ones you're shaky on. Choose the answer that corrects the error and makes the sentence sound right.

Most ACT English test takers are so worried about grammar and punctuation that they don't think about anything else. That's the wrong mind-set. Don't think too much about technical rules. As indicated in the approach above, the first thing to think about is getting rid of unnecessary or irrelevant words. Only after you've decided that the underlined selection is concise and relevant do you go on to Steps 2 and 3. Note that this means you won't necessarily be going through all three steps on any English question. The answer can come at any point in the three-step method.

> **PERFECT SCORE TIP**
>
> " Get into a "grammar mind-set." For the weeks before I took the ACT, I got used to noticing all the grammar mistakes in my life. While sometimes annoying to my family, immediately noticing agreement and other mistakes really helped me notice these mistakes on test day. "

PRACTICE BEING ECONOMICAL

Now try the next practice passage, keeping in mind the approach you just learned:

Example

The Phoenix Cardinals are the <u>oldest, most long-</u>

<u>established, longest-playing</u> football club in the
        1

National Football League (NFL). They began as the

Racine Avenue Cardinals on Chicago's South Side

sometime in the 1870s or <u>1880s, during the nineteenth</u>
                       2

<u>century.</u> At that time, the Cardinals were an amateur
 2

team <u>that did not play for money.</u>
         3

There was <u>nothing in the world which so much as</u>
              4

<u>resembled</u> pro football in those days. The Racine
  4

Avenue Cardinals played amateur ball all through the

late 1800s and <u>the game they played was football, no</u>
                5

<u>doubt about it.</u>
   5

None of the other clubs in the NFL was formed before

the league itself was established in 1919. When the NFL

was first established, the Cardinals remained <u>aloof and</u>
                  6

<u>thumbed their noses at it.</u> Professional football had a
   6

1. A.   NO CHANGE
    B.   oldest
    C.   most long-established
    D.   longest-playing

2. F.   NO CHANGE
    G.   1880s
    H.   the nineteenth century
    J.   during the 1880s

3. A.   NO CHANGE
    B.   that played for the pure joy of the sport
    C.   that played on a nonprofessional level
    D.   OMIT the underlined portion and end the
         sentence with a period.

4. F.   NO CHANGE
    G.   nothing anything like
    H.   no such thing as
    J.   not even a dream of

5. A.   NO CHANGE
    B.   no doubt about it
    C.   to be assured it was football
    D.   OMIT the underlined portion and end the
         sentence with a period.

6. F.   NO CHANGE
    G.   aloof.
    H.   aloof and tried to ignore it.
    J.   off in their own corner.

bad reputation, and the Cardinals were greatly prideful
                                                    7
of their record as amateurs. But in 1921, the Cardinals

decided to join the NFL. They were required to play a

"game to the death" with the Chicago Tigers (the
                                                 8
Detroit Tigers are a baseball team). Whichever team
              8
won would be allowed to stay in Chicago; the other

team would have to move. The Cardinals won. The
              9
Tigers moved away and soon went bankrupt. The

Cardinals are thus the only NFL team that won their

franchise on the football field.

Ironically, the team that fought to stay in Chicago

eventually moved away. The Cardinals were rarely as

successfully able to win games or make money as the
                    10
Chicago Bears, their crosstown rivals. Fans gradually

deserted the Cardinals, so the team moved—to St.

Louis in 1958 and to Phoenix in 1986, seeking a more

profitable market. Maybe Phoenix is the place in which
                                                    11
the Cardinals are destined to stay. Some people say that

the name "Cardinal" was a nineteenth-century

name for a mythical bird that arose from its own ashes

in the fireplace, and that the Cardinals date back to
12

7. A. NO CHANGE
    B. full of great pride
    C. proud
    D. gratefully proud

8. F. NO CHANGE
    G. (not to be confused with the Detroit
        Tigers, a baseball team)
    H. (not the more famous modern-day
        Detroit Tigers baseball team)
    J. OMIT the underlined portion and end
        the sentence with a period.

9. A. NO CHANGE
    B. be forced to move along
    C. be legally obliged, by injunction, to relo-
        cate their franchise
    D. be obligated to be moving out

10. F. NO CHANGE
    G. successful at winning
    H. winning or profitable, a team,
    J. successful

11. A. NO CHANGE
    B. is the place at which
    C. is where
    D. OMIT the underlined portion.

12. F. NO CHANGE
    G. that had consumed it
    H. created by the fire that had consumed it
    J. OMIT the underlined portion.

1871, the year of the great Chicago fire—which may

have begun on Racine Avenue (or maybe not). Chicago

<u>13</u>

was proud to rise from its ashes like the mythical

Cardinal. The <u>name that is more common</u> for that

14

mythical firebird is—the Phoenix. 15

13. A. NO CHANGE
    B. according to ironic legend
    C. resulting from violations of the fire code and a cow in a barn
    D. OMIT the underlined portion and end the sentence with a period.

14. F. NO CHANGE
    G. common name
    H. name that is famous
    J. common way of speaking

15. Suppose the author wishes to add a new paragraph at the end of the existing passage quickly summarizing the history of Canadian football. Would this be appropriate, in light of the content and style of the rest of the passage?
    A. Yes, because it is only fair to mention Canadian football at least once in the passage.
    B. Yes, because the Phoenix Cardinals now play Canadian football.
    C. No, because the passage does not focus on sports history.
    D. No, because the passage has nothing to do with Canadian football.

ANSWERS

1.	B	9.	A
2.	G	10.	J
3.	D	11.	C
4.	H	12.	J
5.	D	13.	D
6.	G	14.	G
7.	C	15.	D
8.	J		

> **EXPERT TUTOR TIP**
>
> " Remember that OMIT is **always** the shortest answer. For instance, D is "shorter" than A and B in question 15 because not including a new paragraph makes the passage shorter than including it. "

Did you see the point? On every regular format question except number 11, you shouldn't have gotten past the first step of the three-step method, because all of the questions test economy errors. In fact, the shortest answers are correct on every question here except that one. In 11, if you omit the phrase "is the place in which," the sentence doesn't make any sense, meaning that you'd correct it in Step 2 of the three-step approach. (Note: This passage is not typical—most ACT passages don't consist exclusively of Economy Questions—but we used this passage to drive home the point about choosing concise answers on the English subject test.)

Many students might object to answer J in question 10, because the word *successful* alone does not indicate the kind of success meant. But use common sense. What would make a professional football team successful? Winning and making money. Thus, the concepts of "winning" and "profitability" are implicit in the notion that the Cardinals are (now) a successful team. **The ACT expects you to cut anything that isn't absolutely needed.**

> **PERFECT SCORE TIP**
>
> " Do not defend something if the passage could make sense without it. The ACT will never ask you to add any unnecessary details or description. "

IF YOU LEARNED ONLY THREE THINGS IN THIS CHAPTER . . .

1. Many English questions test redundancy, verbosity, and irrelevance. Start with the shortest answer.

2. When approaching questions, ask yourself, "Do these words belong here? Do these words make sense? Is there an error in grammar here? How does this idea (or these words) sound in context?"

3. Read the passage as far as you find necessary to answer each question, and then answer each one in turn.

CHAPTER 5: MATH WORKOUT 1: THE END JUSTIFIES THE MEANS

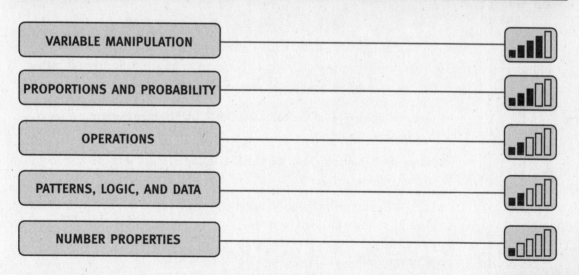

SMARTPOINTS COVERED IN THIS CHAPTER

- VARIABLE MANIPULATION
- PROPORTIONS AND PROBABILITY
- OPERATIONS
- PATTERNS, LOGIC, AND DATA
- NUMBER PROPERTIES

Your goal on the Math subject test is to get as many correct answers as you can in 60 minutes. It doesn't matter what you do (short of cheating, naturally) to get those correct answers.

You don't have to do every problem the way your math teacher would. **Be open to clever and original solution methods.** All that matters is that your methods be quick and that they get you a solid number of correct answers. How many correct answers you need depends on what kind of score you're aiming for, but chances are you don't have to get so many right as you might think to get a good score. Yes, it's a tough test, but it's graded "on a curve."

As we've pointed out, the ACT is different from the typical high school test. On a typical high school math test, you get a series of problems just like the ones you've

EXPERT TUTOR TIP

" Here's how to use this chapter if you don't have much time. Learn the Kaplan Method for ACT Math, trying the sample questions that follow. Read the sidebars throughout the whole chapter for quick ACT strategy tips. "

PERFECT SCORE TIP

"Remember that no one will be checking your method of doing problems. Don't feel compelled to do unnecessary algebra when you know a simpler way to solve the problem."

EXPERT TUTOR TIP

"The ACT Math test includes:

- 24 pre-algebra and elementary algebra questions (corresponding roughly to the 100 Key Math Concepts for the ACT, #1–65)

- 10 intermediate algebra questions (100 Key Math Concepts for the ACT, #66–70)

- 8 coordinate geometry questions (100 Key Math Concepts for the ACT, #71–77)

- 14 plane geometry questions (100 Key Math Concepts for the ACT, #78–95)

- 4 trigonometry questions (100 Key Math Concepts for the ACT, #96–100)"

been doing in class. Since you're being tested on a relatively narrow scope of topics, you're expected to get almost every question right.

ACT Math is different. The scope of what's tested is deliberately wide so that every student will get an opportunity to demonstrate his or her strengths, wherever they may lie.

The average ACT student gets fewer than half of the Math questions right. **You need only about 40 correct answers to get your Math score over 25—just two right out of every three questions gets you a great score!**

THE ACT MATH MIND-SET

According to an old legend at MIT, a physics professor once asked the following question on a final exam: *How could a barometer be used to determine the height of a tower?*

To answer the question, most students worked out complex equations based on the fact that air pressure (which is what a barometer measures) decreases at higher altitudes. But one student made three suggestions instead:

1. Measure the length of the barometer, then use the barometer as a ruler and measure the tower.

2. Drop the barometer and time its fall, keeping in mind that the acceleration of falling objects is about 32 ft/sec^2.

3. Find the person who built the tower and say, "I'll give you a nice barometer if you tell me how tall your tower is."

Guess which student got an A . . .

On the ACT, as in college and beyond, you'll sometimes be called upon to do more than merely regurgitate memorized facts and unquestioningly follow prepackaged procedures. True, some ACT Math questions are straightforward: as soon as you understand what the question's asking, you know what to do. But more challenging—and more fun (really)—are the ACT Math questions that aren't what they seem at first glance. These are the questions that call for creative solutions.

DON'T BE OBEDIENT

On the ACT, there's no partial credit. All that matters is the right answer. It makes no difference how you find it. In fact, as we'll see, it's sometimes safer and faster if you don't do ACT problems the "right" way—the way you've been taught in school. For a lot of ACT Math problems there's more than one way to find the answer. And many of these other ways are faster than the so-called right way.

If you do every problem the way your algebra teacher would want you to, you may earn his or her undying gratitude, but you won't achieve your goal of getting as many correct answers as possible. **You don't have time to use the textbook approach on every question.** You don't have time to write out every step.

PICK NUMBERS

Sometimes you can get stuck on an algebra problem because it's too general or abstract. A good way to get a handle on such a problem is to make it more explicit by temporarily substituting numbers for the variables.

Example

1. If a is an odd integer and b is an even integer, which of the following must be odd?

    A. $2a + b$
    B. $a + 2b$
    C. ab
    D. a^2b
    E. ab^2

> **PERFECT SCORE TIP**
>
> " Learn the correct amount of work to write down on math problems. Writing down some steps will help lessen your confusion, but writing too much will make it harder for you to find the right answer. "

Rather than try to think this one through abstractly, it's easier to pick numbers for a and b. There are rules that predict the evenness or oddness of sums, differences, and products, but there's no need to memorize those rules. When it comes to adding, subtracting, and multiplying evens and odds, what happens with one pair of numbers generally happens with all similar pairs.

Just say, for the time being, that $a = 1$ and $b = 2$. Plug those values into the answer choices, and there's a good chance only one choice will be odd:

    A. $2a + b = 2(1) + 2 = 4$
    B. $a + 2b = 1 + 2(2) = 5$
    C. $ab = (1)(2) = 2$
    D. $a^2b = (1)^2(2) = 2$
    E. $ab^2 = (1)(2)^2 = 4$

Choice B was the only odd one for $a = 1$ and $b = 2$, so it *must* be the one that's odd no matter *what* odd number a actually stands for and even number b actually stands for.

BACK-SOLVE

With some ACT Math problems, it may actually be easier to try out each answer choice until you find the one that works, rather than attempt to solve the problem and then look among the choices for the answer. Since this approach involves working backwards from the answer choices to the question stem, it's called "back-solving."

Example

2. All 200 tickets were sold for a particular concert. Some tickets cost $10 apiece, and the others cost $5 apiece. If total ticket sales were $1,750, how many of the more expensive tickets were sold?

    F.   20
    G.   75
    H.   100
    J.   150
    K.   175

There are ways to solve this problem by setting up an equation or two, but if you're not comfortable with the algebraic approach to this one, why not just try out each answer choice?

Start with choice H. If 100 tickets went for $10, then the other 100 went for $5. 100 at $10 is $1,000, and 100 tickets at $5 is $500, for a total of $1,500—too small. There must have been more than 100 $10 tickets.

Try choice J next. If 150 tickets went for $10, then the other 50 went for $5. So 150 tickets at $10 is $1,500, and 50 tickets at $5 is $250, for a total of $1,750—that's it! The answer is J.

Back-solving your way to the answer may not be a method you'd show your algebra teacher with pride—but your algebra teacher won't be watching on test day. Remember, all that matters is right answers—it doesn't matter how you get them.

BE A THINKER—NOT A NUMBER CRUNCHER

One reason you're given limited time for the Math subject test is that the ACT is testing your ability to think, not your willingness to do a lot of mindless calculations. So one of your guiding principles for ACT Math should be: **work less, but think harder.**

If you want to get the best score you can, be on the lookout for quicker ways to solve problems. Here's an example that could take a lot more time than it needs to.

Example

3. When $\frac{4}{11}$ is converted to a decimal, the 50th digit after the decimal point is

   A. 2

   B. 3

   C. 4

   D. 5

   E. 6

It seems that when you convert $\frac{4}{11}$ to a decimal, there are at least 50 digits after the decimal point. The question asks for the 50th. One way to answer this question would be to divide 11 into 4, carrying the division out to 50 decimal places. That method would work, but it would take forever. It's not worth spending that much time on one question.

No ACT Math question should take more than a minute to solve. There has to be a faster way to solve this problem. There must be some kind of pattern you can take advantage of. And what kind of pattern might there be with a decimal? How about a *repeating* decimal?!

In fact, that's exactly what you have here. The decimal equivalent of $\frac{4}{11}$ is a repeating decimal: $\frac{4}{11} = .3636363636\ldots$

The 1st, 3rd, 5th, 7th, and 9th digits are each 3. The 2nd, 4th, 6th, 8th, and 10th digits are each 6. Put simply, odd-numbered digits are 3s and even-numbered digits are 6s. The 50th digit is an even-numbered digit, so it's a 6 and the answer is E.

What looked at first glance like a "fractions and decimals" problem turned out to be something of an "odds and evens" problem. If you don't use creative shortcuts on problems like this one, you'll get bogged down, you'll run out of time, and you won't get a lot of correct answers.

Question 3 demonstrates how the ACT designs problems to reward clever thinking and to punish students who blindly "go through the motions." But how do you get yourself into a creative mind-set on the Math test? For one thing, you have to take the time to understand thoroughly each problem you decide to work on. Most students are so nervous about time that they skim each math problem and almost immediately start computing with their pencils. But that's the wrong way of thinking. **Sometimes you have to *take* time to *save* time.** A few extra moments spent understanding a math problem can save many extra moments of computation or other drudgery.

EXPERT TUTOR TIP

" You will not get credit for anything you write under "DO YOUR FIGURING HERE." You get credit only for correct answers correctly gridded into the "bubbles" on your answer sheet. "

EXPERT TUTOR TIP

" Underlining what the question is asking will help you to make sure you choose the correct answer. "

PERFECT SCORE TIP

" As will be discussed later, a calculator can be your biggest aid or your greatest weakness. Use it to eliminate timely and costly calculation mistakes but not as a substitute for thinking about a problem. "

THE KAPLAN THREE-STEP METHOD FOR ACT MATH

At Kaplan, we've developed this take-time-to-save-time philosophy into a three-step method for ACT Math problems. The approach is designed to help you find the fast, inventive solutions that the ACT rewards. The steps are:

Step 1. Understand

Focus first on the question stem (the part before the answer choices), and make sure you understand the problem. Sometimes you'll want to read the stem twice, or rephrase it in a way you can better understand. Think to yourself: "What kind of problem is this? What am I looking for? What am I given?" Don't pay too much attention to the answer choices yet, though you may want to give them a quick glance just to see what form they're in.

To understand an ACT Math problem, you first have to understand the language. Mathematicians are generally very precise in their use of language. They choose their words carefully and mean exactly what they say.

In everyday life we can be a little loose with math terminology. It doesn't really matter that Harvard Square is not a square or that a batting average is not an average.

In an ACT Math problem, however, words have precise meanings. You don't need to memorize definitions (you'll **never** have to recite one on the ACT), but you do need to understand what the question writer means.

Step 2. Analyze

Think for a moment and decide on a plan of attack. Don't start crunching numbers until you've given the problem a little thought. There are three ways to solve the problem:

1. Use your math skills. If you know what to do, go for it!
2. Picking numbers. Are there variables in the answer choices that you can pick numbers for?
3. Back-solving. Are there numbers in the answer choices that you can use to figure out which one has to be the correct answer?

Step 3. Select

Once you get an answer, check the answer choices. If your answer matches one of the answer choices, double-check that it answered what the question was asking, and then circle the answer in your test book and fill in the answer grid.

If you are stuck: skip the problem on the first pass through the test. Go get all your "easy" points first! When you come back, if you still don't know how to approach the problem, try guessing strategically. In other words, are there any answer choices that you know there is no way could possibly be the answer? Eliminate as many as you can before you choose an answer. Each answer choice you eliminate gets you one step closer to the correct answer!

Each of these steps can happen in a matter of seconds. And it may not always be clear when you've finished with one step and moved on to the next. Sometimes you'll know how to attack a problem the instant you read and understand it.

USING THE KAPLAN METHOD

Here's how the three-step method could be applied to Question 1 above.

STEP 1: UNDERSTAND

First, we made sure we understood what the problem was asking for: the 50th digit after the decimal point in the decimal equivalent of a certain fraction. Because we knew what digit and decimal equivalent mean, it took only a second to understand what the problem was asking.

STEP 2: ANALYZE

Second, and most crucially, we analyzed the situation and thought about a plan of attack before we tried to solve the problem. We realized that the "obvious" method would take too long, so we figured out a creative approach that got us an answer of 6 in just a few seconds.

STEP 3: SELECT

Third, we looked at the answer choices, found 6, and selected choice E.

The three-step method isn't a rigid procedure; it's a set of guidelines that will keep you on track, moving quickly, and evading pitfalls.

Example

4. If the sum of five consecutive even integers is equal to their product, what is the greatest of the five integers?

    F.   4
    G.   10
    H.   14
    J.   16
    K.   20

> **GO ONLINE**
>
> " You can find Kaplan's Three-Step Method for ACT Math on your downloadable study sheet, for review on the go. "

STEP 1: UNDERSTAND

Before you can begin to solve this problem, you have to figure out what it's asking, and to do that you need to know the meanings of *sum, product, consecutive, even,* and *integer*. Put the question stem into words you can understand. What the question stem is really saying here is that when you add up these five consecutive even integers you get the same thing as when you multiply them.

STEP 2: ANALYZE

How are we going to figure out what these five numbers are? We could set up an equation:

$$x + (x - 2) + (x - 4) + (x - 6) + (x - 8) = x(x - 2)(x - 4)(x - 6)(x - 8)$$

But there's no way you'll have time to solve an equation like this! So don't even try. Come up with a better way.

Let's stop and think logically about this one for a moment. When we think about sums and products, it's natural to think mostly of positive integers. With positive integers, we would generally expect the product to be *greater* than the sum.

But what about negative integers? Hmm. Well, the sum of five negatives is negative, and the product of five negatives is also negative, and generally the product will be "more negative" than the sum, so with negative integers the product will be less than the sum.

So when will the product and sum be the same? How about right at the boundary of positive and negative—that is, around 0? The five consecutive even integers with equal product and sum are: −4, −2, 0, 2, and 4.

$$(-4) \times (-2) \times 0 \times 2 \times 4 = (-4) + (-2) + 0 + 2 + 4$$

The product and sum are both 0. Ha! We've done it!

How to back-solve: The question asks about which is the greatest of the integers, so you start with the greatest answer choice: K. If the largest number is 20, then the other numbers must be 18, 16, 14, 12. Their sum is 20 + 18 + 16 + 14 + 12 = 80. 20 times 18 is already 360, so we know that K is not correct and that it is WAY too big! Let's try choice H (14). We want to add: 14 + 12 + 10 + 8 + 6 = 50. Still too big, because 10 times 6 is already 60. So let's try 4, choice F. 4 + 2 + 0 + (−2) + (−4) = 4 × 2 × 0 × (−2) × (−4) = 0. It works!

STEP 3: SELECT

The question asks for the greatest of the five integers, which is 4, choice F.

EXPERT TUTOR TIP

" If you don't have any idea how to solve this problem, ask yourself, "Can I pick numbers? Can I back-solve?" There are numbers in the answer choices, so you should back-solve. "

You've probably encountered every math term that appears on the ACT sometime in your high school math career, but you may not remember exactly what every one of them means. The Math Glossary in the ACT Resources section of your online syllabus is a complete but compact list of the terminology you need for ACT Math problems. Look it over. Jot down the ones you're not sure of for future reference. And be sure to use the Glossary to look up any unfamiliar term you encounter while practicing with ACT Math questions.

DEFINITION ALERT

As you refresh your memory of key terminology, watch out for technicalities. Here are a few examples of such technicalities (by the way, these are great for stumping your know-it-all friends):

- *"Integers" include 0 and negative whole numbers.* If a question says "x and y are integers," it's not ruling out numbers like 0 and −1.

- *"Evens and odds" include 0 and negative whole numbers.* Zero and −2 are even numbers; −1 is an odd number.

- *"Prime numbers" do not include 1.* The technical definition of a prime number is: "a positive integer with exactly two distinct positive integer factors." Two is prime because it has exactly two positive factors: 1 and 2. Four is not prime because it has three positive factors (1, 2, and 4)—too many! And 1 is not prime because it has only one positive factor (1)—too few!

- *"Remainders" are integers.* If a question asks for the remainder when 15 is divided by 2, don't say "15 divided by 2 is 7.5, so the remainder is .5." What you should say is: "15 divided by 2 is 7 with a remainder of 1."

- *The $\sqrt{}$ symbol represents the positive square root only.* The equation $x^2 = 9$ has two solutions: 3 and −3. But when you see $\sqrt{9}$, it means positive 3 only.

- *"Rectangles" include squares.* The definition of a rectangle is a four-sided figure with four right angles. It doesn't matter if the length and width are the same or not—if it has four right angles, it's a rectangle. When a question refers to "rectangle ABCD," it's not ruling out a square.

PERFECT SCORE TIP

❝ Math is one section where actual knowledge of material is necessary. If any terms you read here are unfamiliar to you, learn them! Don't waste precious easy points because you don't know the definition of basic terms. ❞

Example

5. What is the value of $x^2 + 3x - 9$ when $x = -3$?

   A. −27
   B. −9
   C. −6
   D. 0
   E. 9

EXPERT TUTOR TIP

" Whenever plugging negative numbers into your calculator, always make sure to put them in parentheses. Not using them will lead to a wrong answer! "

EXPERT TUTOR TIP

" Use your calculator to fly right through Example 6. If you don't use a calculator all the time in school, start practicing so you are familiar with it by test day. "

KAPLAN'S TARGET STRATEGY

" Step 2: "Analyze" is where you'll be doing most of your serious thinking. The other two Math Workouts will address this step in greater detail. "

STEP 1: UNDERSTAND

You've probably seen dozens of problems just like this. If so, then you realize right away that what it's asking is, "What do you get when you plug $x = -3$ into $x^2 + 3x - 9$?"

STEP 2: ANALYZE

So that's what you do—plug it in and solve:

$$x^2 + 3x - 9 = (-3)^2 + 3(-3) - 9$$
$$= 9 + (-9) - 9$$
$$= -9$$

STEP 3: SELECT

The answer is B.

So this is a case where you knew exactly what to do as soon as you understood what the question was asking. Sometimes you're not so lucky. Let's look at a case where the method of solution is not so obvious, even after you "understand" the stem:

 NUMBER PROPERTIES

Example

6. What is the greatest of the numbers $1^{50}, 50^1, 2^{25}, 25^2, 4^{10}$?

    F. 1^{50}
    G. 50^1
    H. 2^{25}
    J. 25^2
    K. 4^{10}

STEP 1: UNDERSTAND

It's not hard to figure out what the question is asking: which of five numbers is the greatest? But the five numbers are all written as powers, some of which we don't have time to calculate. Yikes! How are we going to compare them?

STEP 2: ANALYZE

If all the powers had the same base or the same exponent, or if they could all be rewritten with a common base or exponent, we could compare all five at once. As it is, though, we should take two at a time.

Compare 1^{50} and 50^1 to start: $1^{50} = 1$, while $50^1 = 50$, so there's no way choice F could be the biggest.

Next, compare 50^1 and 2^{25}. We don't have time to calculate 2^{25}, but we can see that it doesn't take anywhere near 25 factors of 2 to get over 50. In fact, 2^6 is 64, already more than 50, so 2^{25} is much more than 50. That eliminates G.

Choice J, 25^2, doesn't take too long to calculate: $25 \times 25 = 625$. How does that compare to 2^{25}? Once again, with a little thought, we realize that it doesn't take 25 factors of 2 to get over 625. That eliminates J.

The last comparison is easy because choice K, 4^{10}, can be rewritten as $(2^2)^{10} = 2^{20}$, in that form clearly less than 2^{25}. That eliminates K.

STEP 3: SELECT

So the answer is H.

KNOW WHEN TO SKIP

At any time during the three-step process, you could choose to cut bait and skip the question. **Almost everyone should skip at least some questions the first time through.**

If you know your own strengths and weaknesses, you can sometimes choose to skip a question while still in Step 1: "Understand." For example, suppose you **never** studied trigonometry. Maybe you think that a secant is something that sailors sing while climbing up the yardarms. Well, the ACT includes exactly four trigonometry questions, and it's not hard to spot them. Why waste a second on such a question? Skip it! You don't need those four measly questions to get a great score. And since you know a second visit later won't help any, you might as well go ahead and make some random guesses.

> **EXPERT TUTOR TIP**
>
> " The fastest way to a higher score on the ACT is to get all your easy points first—skip those hard problems, and go back to them later if you have time. "

> **EXPERT TUTOR TIP**
>
> " If you need to take a random guess, guess the same letter for every question you need to guess on throughout the ACT. This will increase your chance of getting some points off of those guesses. "

KAPLAN'S TWO-PASS PLAN FOR ACT MATH

We recommend that you plan two "passes" through the Math test.

- **First Pass:** Examine each problem in order. Do every problem you understand. Don't skip too hastily—sometimes it takes a few seconds of thought to see how to do something—but don't get bogged down. Never spend more than a minute on any question in the first pass. This first pass should take about 45 minutes.

- **Second Pass:** Use the last 15 minutes to go back to the questions that stumped you the first time. Sometimes a fresh look is all you need—after going away and then coming back, you'll sometimes suddenly see what to do. In most cases, though, you'll still be stumped by the question stem, so it's time to give the answer choices a try. Work by process of elimination, and guess. Be sure to select an answer for every question, even if it's just a blind guess.

It can be harder to decide when to skip a question if you understand it, but then get stuck in Step 2: "Analyze." Suppose you just don't see how to solve it. Don't give up too quickly. Sometimes it takes 30 seconds or so before you see the light. But don't get bogged down either. Never spend more than a minute on a question the first time through the section. No single question is worth it. Be prepared to leave a question and come back to it later. Often, on the second try, you'll see something you didn't see before. That old lightbulb will light up over your head and you'll be on your way.

Of course, eventually you're going to grid in an answer choice for every question, even the ones you don't understand. **The first time through the section, you should concentrate on the questions you understand.**

Don't plan on visiting a question a third time; it's inefficient to go back and forth that much. Every time you leave a question and come back to it, you have to take at least a few seconds to refamiliarize yourself with the problem. **Always** grid in an answer choice on the second pass—even if it's just a wild guess. At the end of the second pass, every question should be answered.

Don't worry if you don't work on every question in the section. The average ACT test taker gets fewer than half of the problems right. You can score in the top quarter of all ACT test takers if you can do just half of the problems on the test, get every single one of them right, and guess blindly on the other half. If you did just one-third of the problems and got every one right, then guessed blindly on the other 40 problems, you would still earn an average score.

DON'T MAKE CARELESS MISTAKES

Most students don't worry much about careless errors. Since in school (where you show your work) you can earn partial credit, many students think that careless errors somehow "don't count." Not so on the ACT. There are only so many problems you'll know how to do. Some of the problems will be impossible for you, so you'll make or break your score on the problems you can do. You can't afford to miss one easy problem!

Unless math is a very strong area for you, the best way to maximize your score is to work on the questions you deserve to get correct. Don't worry about getting to every problem (though, of course, you should mark an answer for every problem on your answer grid, even if it's a blind guess).

Even if math is a strong area for you, don't get complacent on easy problems—that causes careless errors. For strong students, the easy problems may be the most challenging. You have to find a way to answer them quickly and accurately in order to have time for the tougher ones. You won't have time for the hard problems unless you save some time on the easy ones.

EXPERT TUTOR TIP

Making two passes through the Math test means you'll never run out of time before seeing every question.

PERFECT SCORE TIP

I skipped multiple questions on my first time through. When I returned to them the second time, I found that they often became clearer to me. It is possible to get a very good score even if the solution to every problem does not pop out to you.

Here's a question that's not hard to understand but is hard to solve if you don't remember the rules for simplifying and adding radicals:

 NUMBER PROPERTIES

Example

7. $\dfrac{\sqrt{32} + \sqrt{24}}{\sqrt{8}} = ?$

3.78205

~~A.~~ $\sqrt{7}$

B. $\sqrt{2} + \sqrt{3}$

C. $2 + \sqrt{3}$

D. $\sqrt{2} + 3$

E. 7

STEP 1: UNDERSTAND

The question wants you to simplify the given expression, which includes three radicals. In other words, turn the radicals into numbers you can use, then work out the fraction.

STEP 2: ANALYZE

The best way to solve this problem would be to apply the rules of radicals—but what if you don't remember them? Don't give up; you can still guesstimate. In the question stem, the numbers under the radicals are not too far away from perfect squares. You could round $\sqrt{32}$ off to $\sqrt{36}$, which is 6. You could round $\sqrt{24}$ to $\sqrt{25}$, which is 5. And you could round $\sqrt{8}$ off to $\sqrt{9}$, which is 3. So the expression is now $\dfrac{6+5}{3}$, which is $3\dfrac{2}{3}$. That's just a guesstimate, of course—the actual value might be something a bit less or a bit more than that.

STEP 3: SELECT

Now look at the answer choices. Choice A—$\sqrt{7}$—is less than 3, so it's too small. Choice B—$\sqrt{2} + \sqrt{3}$—is about $1.4 + 1.7$, or just barely more than 3, so it seems a little small, too. Choice C—$2 + \sqrt{3}$—is about $2 + 1.7$, or about 3.7—that's very close to our guesstimate! We still have to check the other choices. Choice D—$\sqrt{2} + 3$—is about $1.4 + 3$, or 4.4—too big. And choice E, 7, is obviously way too big. Looks like our best bet is C—and C in fact is the correct answer.

TO CALCULATE OR NOT TO CALCULATE

You are permitted to use a calculator on the Math section. The good news is that you never *absolutely need* to use a calculator on the ACT. No Math question requires

PERFECT SCORE TIP

❝ Sometimes radicals can be intimidating. Remember that even if you forget the rules, there are simpler ways to deal with them such as using known radicals to estimate, or if worse comes to worst use your calculator to get estimates. ❞

messy or tedious calculations. But while the calculator can't answer questions for you, it can keep you from making computational errors on questions you know how to solve. The bad news, however, is that a calculator can actually cost you time if you overuse it. Take a look at this example:

Example

8. The sum of all the integers from 1 to 44, inclusive, is subtracted from the sum of all the integers from 7 to 50, inclusive. What is the result?

    A.   6
    B.   44
    C.   50
    D. 264
    E. 300

You could . . . add all the integers from 1 through 44, and then all the integers from 7 through 50, and then subtract the first sum from the second. And then punch in all the numbers into the calculator. And then hope you didn't hit any wrong buttons.

But that's the long way . . . and the wrong way. That way involves hitting over 250 keys on your calculator. It'll take too long, and you're too likely to make a mistake. The amount of computation involved in solving this problem tells you that there must be an easier way. Remember, no ACT problem absolutely requires the use of a calculator.

Look at the problem again: a calculator *can* help you on this question, but you have to think first. Both sums contain the same number of consecutive integers, and each integer in the first sum has a corresponding integer 6 greater than it in the second sum. Here's the scratchwork:

1	7
+2	+8
+3	+9
.	.
.	.
.	.
+42	+48
+43	+49
+44	+50

PERFECT SCORE TIP

❝ One of my biggest weaknesses is simple arithmetic, so my calculator was very helpful in eliminating these mistakes. Still, I had to be sure that I had a plan for how to do most problems without a calculator, and then use it just to check my math. ❞

This means there are 44 pairs of integers which are each 6 apart. So the total difference between the two sums will be the difference between each pair of integers, times the number of pairs. Now you can pull out your calculator, punch in "6 × 44 =" and get the correct answer of 264 with little or no time wasted. Mark D in your test booklet and move on.

Of course, there will be many situations on the ACT in which using a calculator can save you time. Here's a trig question that's much easier with a calculator:

Example

8. $\sin 495° =$

~~F.~~ $-\dfrac{\sqrt{2}}{2}$

~~G.~~ $-\dfrac{1}{2}$

~~H.~~ $\dfrac{1}{2}$

J. $\dfrac{\sqrt{2}}{2}$

K. $\dfrac{3\sqrt{2}}{2}$

Without a calculator this is a very difficult problem. To find a trigonometric function of an angle greater than or equal to 90°, sketch a circle of radius 1 and centered at the origin of the coordinate grid. Start from the point (1, 0) and rotate the appropriate number of degrees counterclockwise. When you rotate counterclockwise 495°, you rotate 360° (which brings you back to where you started), and then an additional 135°. That puts you midway into the second quadrant. Now you need to know whether sine is positive or negative in the second quadrant. Pretty scary, huh?

With a calculator this problem becomes simple. Just punch in "sin 495°" and you get 0.7071067811865. Choices F and G are negative, so they're out, and 0.7071067811865 is clearly not equal to $\dfrac{1}{2}$, so H is also wrong. That leaves only J or K. Now, with respect to choice K: $\sqrt{2}$ is greater than 1, so if you multiply it by another number greater than 1 (namely $\dfrac{3}{2}$), the result is obviously greater than 1. So you can eliminate K, leaving J as the correct answer. With a calculator, you can get this question right without really understanding it.

The key to effective calculator use is practice, so don't run out the night before the test to buy a fancy new calculator. If you don't already have a calculator (and intend to use one on the test), buy one now. Unless you're studying math or science in

> **EXPERT TUTOR TIP**
>
> If a problem seems to involve a lot of calculation, look for a quicker way. Try to spot a pattern that will help you save some time.

> **EXPERT TUTOR TIP**
>
> When doing trig functions, make sure that your calculator is in degree mode—unless the answers contain π, in which case you have to use radians.

college, you won't need anything more complex than trig functions. You're better off bringing a straightforward model you're familiar with than an esoteric model you don't know how to use.

Practicing with your calculator is the best way to get a sense of where it can help and save time. Here's a brief guide to spotting those calculator-friendly Math questions.

Example

10. $(7.3 + 0.8) - 3(1.98 + 0.69) =$

   A.   −0.99
   B.   −0.09
   C.   0
   D.   0.09
   E.   0.99

This problem basically involves straightforward computation, so you'd be right if you reached for your calculator. However, if you just start punching the numbers in as they appear in the question, you will come up with the wrong answer. When you're performing a string of computations, you know that you need to follow the right order of operations. The problem is, your calculator might not know this. Some calculators have parentheses keys and do follow the order of operations, so it's important to know your calculator and what its capabilities are. See 100 Key Math Concepts for the ACT, #7 for further explanation of PEMDAS.

If your calculator doesn't follow the order of operations, you'd need to perform the operations within parentheses separately and proceed carefully from there. You'd get $8.1 - 3(2.67)$. Multiplication comes before subtraction, so you'd get $8.1 - 8.01$, and then finally 0.09, choice D.

Example

11. A certain bank issues three-letter identification codes to its customers. If each letter can be used only once per code, how many different codes are possible?

   F.   26
   G.   78
   H.   326
   J.   15,600
   K.   17,576

Just manipulating the numbers in this problem will get you nowhere, but once you arrive at the setup, a calculator is very useful.

For the first letter in the code, you can choose any of the 26 letters in the alphabet. For the second letter, you can choose from all the letters in the alphabet except the one you used in the first spot, so there are $26 - 1 = 25$ possibilities. For the third, there are $26 - 2 = 24$ possibilities. So the total number of different codes possible is equal to $26 \times 25 \times 24$. Using your calculator you find that there are 15,600 codes—choice J.

Example

12. Which of the following fractions is greater than 0.68 and less than 0.72 ?

A. $\dfrac{5}{9}$

B. $\dfrac{3}{4}$

C. $\dfrac{7}{11}$

D. $\dfrac{2}{3}$

E. $\dfrac{5}{7}$

GO ONLINE

Your downloadable study sheet contains key math formulas and concepts.

Here you have to convert the fractions to decimals and see which one falls in the range of values given in the question. If you're familiar with common decimal/fraction conversions you might know that choice B, $\dfrac{3}{4}$, is equal to 0.75 (too large) and choice D, $\dfrac{2}{3}$, is approximately 0.67 (too small). But you'd still have to check out the other three choices. Your calculator can make short work of this, showing you that choice A, $\dfrac{5}{9}$, equals $0.\overline{55}$, choice C, $\dfrac{7}{11}$, equals $.\overline{63}$, and choice E, $\dfrac{5}{7}$, is approximately 0.71. Only 0.71 falls between 0.68 and 0.72, so E is correct.

IF YOU LEARNED ONLY FOUR THINGS IN THIS CHAPTER . . .

1. Look for the quickest ways to solve problems. Sometimes this requires creative thinking.

2. Use the answer choices to help you. If you are stuck, can you plug numbers in for the variables or use the numbers in the answer choices to get to the correct answer?

3. Follow Kaplan's Two-Pass Plan: skip problems that are more difficult, and come back to them after you've finished the easy ones.

4. Practice with your calculator so you are comfortable using it—and understand when it is faster not to use it.

CHAPTER 6: READING WORKOUT 1: KNOW WHERE YOU'RE GOING

Reading skills are crucial on every part of the ACT, not just on the Reading test. Savvy ACT-style reading is certainly useful for the English and Science tests, and even your work on many of the Math problems will benefit from the skills discussed below. So don't ignore the Reading Workouts, even if you think you're an ace reader.

The kind of reading rewarded by the ACT is special. You probably know how to do it already, but you may be reluctant to do it on a standardized test. You may think that success on a test like this requires that you read very slowly and deliberately, making sure you remember everything. Well, we at Kaplan have found that this kind of reading won't work on the ACT. In fact, it is a sure way to run out of time halfway through the Reading test.

THE KEY TO ACTIVE ACT READING

The real key to ACT reading is to read quickly but actively, getting a sense of the gist or "main idea" of the passage and seeing how everything fits together to support that main idea. You should constantly try to think ahead. Look for the general outline of the passage—determine how it's structured. Don't worry about the details. You'll come back for those later.

Fast, active reading, of course, requires a little more mental energy than slow, passive reading. But it pays off. Those who dwell on details—who passively let the passage reveal itself at its own pace—are sure to run out of time. Don't be that kind of reader! Make the passage reveal itself to you on your schedule, by skimming the passage with an eye to structure rather than detail. Look for key words that tell you what the author is doing so that you can save yourself time. For instance, read examples very quickly, just glancing over the words. When an author says "for example," you know that what follows is an example of a general point. Do you need to understand that specific example? Maybe, maybe not. If you do, you can come

> **EXPERT TUTOR TIP**
>
> " The ACT Reading test includes:
> - One Prose Fiction passage with ten questions
> - One Humanities passage with ten questions
> - One Social Sciences passage with ten questions
> - One Natural Sciences passage with ten questions "

> **PERFECT SCORE TIP**
>
> " Remember that on the ACT the goal of reading is very different than English class. No one is looking for original ideas or deep reading—just for you to get the main ideas. "

EXPERT TUTOR TIP

" Here's how to use this chapter if you don't have much time. Learn the Kaplan Method for ACT Reading. Try the sample passage that follows. Check your answers. If you need more help, go back and read the whole chapter. "

PERFECT SCORE TIP

" The key to ACT reading is main ideas. At the end of every paragraph and passage you should be able to give a very brief summary of what it was about. This will really help with the questions. "

EXPERT TUTOR TIP

" Read actively, with an eye toward where the author is going. **Don't** worry about remembering the details. You can (and should) always refer to them later. "

back and read the verbiage when you're attacking the questions. You'll know exactly where the author gave an example of general point *x* (or whatever). If you *don't* need to know the example for any of the questions, great! You haven't wasted much time on something that won't get you a point.

You actually do this kind of "reading" all the time, and not just when you're reading a book or newspaper. When you watch TV or see a movie, for instance, you can often figure out much of what's going to happen in advance. You see the bad guys run out of a bank with bags of money in their hands, and you can guess that the next thing they'll do is get into a car and drive away in excess of the speed limit. You see a character in an old sitcom bragging to his friends about how great a driver he is, and you know that he's bound to get into a fender bender before the next commercial. **This ability to know where something is going is very valuable. Use it on the ACT.**

To help you know where an author is going, pay careful attention to "structural clues." Words like *but, nevertheless,* and *moreover* help you get a sense of where a piece of writing is going. Look for signal phrases (like *clearly, as a result,* or *no one can deny that*) to determine the logic of the passage. The details, remember, you can come back for later, when you're doing the questions. **What's important in reading the passage is getting a sense of how those details fit together to express the point or points of the passage.**

PRACTICE KNOWING WHERE YOU'RE GOING

In the following exercise, try to fill in the word or phrase that should come next. For most, there are many possible answers, so don't worry about getting the "right" answer.

1. You'd think that the recipe for a strawberry soufflé would be complicated, but my friend's version was _____.

2. I can't believe my good luck! The one time in my life I buy a lottery ticket, I _____.

3. A parked car burns no fuel and causes no pollution. Once the ignition is turned on, however, _____.

4. As their habitat is destroyed, wild animals _____

5. The new word-processing program was far easier to use than the old one. Moreover, the accompanying instruction booklet explained the commands in a _____ way.

6. The new word-processing program was far easier to use than the old one. On the other hand, the accompanying instruction booklet explained the commands in a _____ way.

ANSWERS

- In Sentence 1, the active reader would probably complete the sentence by saying that the friend's version was "actually quite simple" or something similar. How do you know what's coming next here? The structural clue *but* tips you off. *But* tells you that a contrast is coming up. You'd think the recipe would be complicated, *BUT* it's "actually quite simple."

- In Sentence 2, on the other hand, there's no real structural clue to help you out, but the *meaning* of the sentence should make clear what's coming up. The speaker here is marveling at his good luck, right? That means that he must have won some money. So a likely completion would be something like: The one time in my life I buy a lottery ticket, I "win the jackpot."

- In Sentence 3, we have another contrast, signaled by the clue *however*. A parked car doesn't burn fuel or pollute. *HOWEVER*, once you turn on the ignition . . . The answer has to be something like "the car starts burning gas and polluting." That's the clear contrast that was anticipated by the structural clue *however*.

- Sentence 4 demonstrates again that you don't need explicit structural clues to stay ahead. Sometimes all you need is common sense. What do you think would happen to animals whose habitat had been destroyed? Would they thrive? Celebrate? Buy a condo in Florida? No, they'd probably "start dying out." They might even "become extinct."

- Sentences 5 and 6 show clearly how you can use an author's language to anticipate what point he or she is going to make next. Here, we have identical sentences, except for one small (but very important) difference. The sentences in #5 include the word *moreover*, indicating continuation or addition of similar information. The blank should be something close to "in a clear and easy-to-understand" way. It makes sense that, "The program was easy to use; moreover, the instructions were easy to understand." The sentences in #6 have an *On the other hand* connection, indicating contrast. So the sentences make sense only if you fill the blank with "a confusing and unclear" way.

CREATE A PASSAGE MAP

The best way to read actively is to take quick notes, marking up the passage as you go. You don't have time to write extensively in the margin, nor do you want to underline too many sentences. After all, *if you underline everything, nothing stands out on the page*. Your goal is to create flags that wave at you when you are looking for the answers to the questions in the passage.

The fastest way to create your passage map is to follow the ABCs of Active Reading:

    Abbreviate margin notes.

    Bracket key sentences.

    Circle key words and phrases.

Abbreviate margin notes. Develop your own shorthand notes, such as *opin* (opinion), *contr* (contrast or comparison), *hist* (history), *bio* (early years). You must be able to understand what you've written. Otherwise, the notes won't be helpful.

Bracket key sentences. These may (or may not) be the first and last sentences of a paragraph. You are looking for any sentences that express key themes, conclusions, or opinions (of either the author or of the characters in the passage). If you string these bracketed sentences together, you will have highlighted the author's train of thought.

Circle key words and phrases. These are the structural clues or flags (*however, therefore, on one hand . . . on the other hand*), as well as proper names, dates, key actions, etc.—the signposts of each paragraph. For example, if a passage were about child development, you'd want to circle the key ages discussed in each paragraph. Thus, circling *six months, one year, age two through five* would help you know where to look for the answers to questions about those ages.

THE KAPLAN FIVE-STEP METHOD FOR ACT READING

These steps are tried-and-true. If you learn and practice them, you'll be able to read all four passages successfully and have time to answer all the questions. This is your goal, and when test day rolls around, you'll be glad you've got these steps to follow.

The key to this section is being in control of timing—meaning how much time you spend reading the passage (about three minutes) and answering the questions (an average of 30 seconds per question).

If you divide 40 questions into 35 minutes, you'll see that you have 8¾ minutes per passage. As you practice, it will be clear that one or two passages take more (or less) time than the others. So your goal is an average of just under 9 minutes per passage. How do you learn to do this? Practice. Practice. Practice.

For the ACT, however, you have a special purpose: to answer specific multiple-choice questions. And we've found that the best way to do that is initially to read a passage quickly and actively for general understanding, then refer to the passage to answer individual questions. Not everybody should use the exact same strategy, but we find that almost every ACT test taker can succeed by following these basic steps:

1. **Preread the passage.**

2. **Consider the question stem.**

3. **Refer to the passage** (before looking at the choices).

4. **Answer questions in your own words.**

5. **Match your answer with one of the choices.**

For most students, these five tasks should together take up about nine minutes per passage. Less than three of those nine minutes should be spent prereading. The remaining time should be devoted to considering the questions and referring to the passage to check your answers. As we mentioned in the ACT Basics section, you'll probably want to take two sweeps through the questions for each passage, getting the doable ones the first time around, coming back for the harder ones.

STEP 1: PREREAD THE PASSAGE

Prereading means quickly working through the passage before trying to answer the questions. Remember to "know where you're going," anticipating how the parts of the passage fit together. In this preread, the main goals are to:

- Understand the "gist" of the passage (the main idea).
- Create a road map of the passage, using the ABCs of Active Reading: **A**bbreviate margin notes, **B**racket key sentences, and **C**ircle key words.

You may want to underline key points, jot down notes, circle structural clues— whatever it takes to accomplish the two goals above. You may even want to label each paragraph, to fix in your mind how the paragraphs relate to one another and what aspect of the main idea is discussed in each. That could be your road map.

Two important reminders: ***Don't*** read slowly, and ***don't*** get bogged down in individual details. Most of the details in the passage aren't required for answering the questions, so why waste time worrying about them?

STEP 2: CONSIDER THE QUESTION STEM

Approaching the questions requires self-discipline in Reading. Most test takers have an almost irresistible urge to immediately jump to the answer choices to see what "looks okay." That's not a good idea. Don't peek at the answer choices.

Read the question stem to identify what the test maker is asking. Is it about:

A detail (what happened)

The passage as a whole (the Big Idea)

A conclusion (reading between the lines)

A specific word or phrase used in the passage

Analyzing what the question stem is asking is very important because the test maker will offer you answers that don't answer the question at hand. These wrong answers

EXPERT TUTOR TIP

Mark up the passages! Have a system worked out where you use different symbols to mean different things. For example, circle names, box numbers, and dates, underline key sentences, and draw arrows to lists of details. Once you know your system, you can find the facts you are looking for faster.

GO ONLINE

" Refer to your downloadable study sheet to review the Kaplan Five-Step Method for ACT Reading—anywhere, anytime. "

are tempting—but only to someone who hasn't taken time to predict an answer. It is easy to get the right answer—if you know what you are looking for.

In Reading, think about the question stem without looking at the choices. In most questions, you won't be able to remember exactly what the passage said about the matter in question. That's okay. In fact, even if you do think you remember, don't trust your memory. Instead . . .

STEP 3: REFER TO THE PASSAGE

Now's the time when your marked-up passage comes to your aid. You have **A**bbreviated margin notes, **B**racketed key sentences, and **C**ircled key words and phrases—these are all waiting to help you find the answers to ten questions.

In Step 3, these become the flags which catch your eye as you look to the passage for help with answers. This road map is especially helpful when the question doesn't give you any specific line references.

STEP 4: ANSWER THE QUESTION IN YOUR OWN WORDS

It's extremely important in Reading to **make a habit of answering the question in your own words** (based on your checking of the passage) *before* looking at the answer choices. Most students waste enormous amounts of time thinking about answer choices in Reading. If you do that, you'll **never** finish, and you'll get so confused you'll probably get many questions wrong.

STEP 5: MATCH YOUR ANSWER WITH ONE OF THE CHOICES

PERFECT SCORE TIP

" Make sure to pay attention to trick words in answer choices. ACT writers try to put tempting words from the passage in incorrect answer choices. "

When you look at answer choices in Reading, your mental process should be "matching." You've got an answer in your head based on what you've read and rechecked in the passage. You need to match it to one of the answer choices. Avoid trying to see if they "look right." **You don't want to think very hard about the choices if you can help it.** They're intended to confuse you, after all, so don't think about them any more than you absolutely have to.

Now practice the Kaplan Method on the full-length ACT passage that follows. We're going to give you added incentive to use it by first showing you the questions *without* answer choices. That way you can't give in to the temptation to look at the choices before you think about the questions. The same questions in ACT style, *with* answer choices, will follow the passage. But try to answer them in "fill-in-the-blank" format first.

Example

Questions	**Your Answers**

1. The description of the near starvation of the oxen (lines 70–74) serves to:

2. According to the passage, the fact that the peasants' individual strips of land were unfenced subdivisions of larger fields required each peasant to:

3. According to the second paragraph (lines 4–31), the **fallow** part of the arable had to be plowed a total of how many times in any given calendar year?

4. The passage suggests that the practice of peasants owning strips "scattered through the three fields in different parts" (lines 37–38) was instituted in order to:

5. On the basis of the information in the passage, it may be inferred that people in medieval times did not think of sowing hay because:

6. As it is used in line 53, the word *garnered* means:

7. According to the passage, if one of the arable's three great fields were left fallow one year, it would be:

8. Which of the following conclusions is suggested by the fourth paragraph (lines 41–58)?

9. According to the passage, a manor's value might be judged according to the number of its plows because:

10. According to the passage, summer pasture for a manor's geese would be provided:

PASSAGE I

By the tenth century most of northern Europe
was divided into farming units known as
manors . . . .

Line   Almost always a manor comprised four parts:
(5)   arable, meadow, waste, and the village area itself.
The arable was of course the land which grew the
crops on which the inhabitants of the manor sub-
sisted. To maintain fertility and keep down weeds
it was necessary to fallow a part of the cultivated
(10)   land each year. It was, therefore, usual (though not
universal) to divide the arable into three fields.
One such field was planted with winter grain, a
second with spring grain, and the third left fallow;
the following year, the fallow field would be planted
(15)   with winter grain, the field in which winter grain
had been raised was planted with spring grain,
and the third field left fallow. By following such a
rotation, the cycle was completed every three
years. Since the fallow field had to be plowed twice
(20)   in the year in order to keep down the weeds, and
the others had to be plowed once, work for the
plow teams extended almost throughout the year.
Plowing stopped only at times when all hands
were needed to bring in the harvest, or when the
(25)   soil was too wet to be plowed, or was frozen. The
amount of land that could be tilled was fixed fairly
definitely by the number of plows and plow teams
which the manor could muster; and official docu-
ments sometimes estimated the wealth and value
(30)   of a manor in terms of the number of plows it
possessed.

The three great fields lay open, without fences,
but were subdivided into numerous small strips
(often one acre in size, i.e., the amount of one
(35)   day's plowing) which individual peasants "owned."
The strips belonging to any one individual were
scattered through the three fields in different
parts, perhaps in order to assure that each peasant
would have strips plowed early and late, in fertile
(40)   and infertile parts of the arable land.
Custom severely restricted the individual's
rights over his land. The time for plowing and
planting was fixed by custom and each peasant
had to conform, since he needed his neighbor's
(45)   help to plow his strips and they needed his.

Uniform cropping was imperative, since on a
given day the village animals were turned into the
fields to graze after the harvest had been gathered,
and if some individual planted a crop which did
(50)   not ripen as early as that of his neighbors, he had
no means of defending his field from the hungry
animals. If his crop ripened sooner, on the other
hand, it could not be garnered without trampling
neighboring fields. Moreover, the very idea of
(55)   innovation was lacking: men did what custom
prescribed, cooperated in the plowing and to
some extent in the harvesting, and for many generations did not dream of trying to change.

The meadow was almost as important as the
(60)   arable for the economy of the village. Hay from
the meadow supported the indispensable draught
animals through the winter. The idea that hay
might be sown did not occur to men in medieval
times; consequently they were compelled to rely
(65)   on natural meadows alone. One result was that in
many manors shortage of winter fodder for the
plow teams was a constant danger. It was common
practice to feed oxen on leaves picked from trees,
and on straw from the grain harvest; but despite
(70)   such supplements the draught animals often
nearly starved in winter. In some cases oxen actually had to be carried out from their winter stalls
to spring pastures until some of their strength was
recovered and plowing could begin. Thus on
(75)   many manors meadow land was even more valuable than the arable and was divided into much
smaller strips (often the width of a scythe stroke).

The waste provided summer pasture for various animals of the manor: pigs, geese, cattle, and
(80)   sheep. The animals of the whole manor normally
grazed together under the watchful eyes of some
young children or other attendants who could
keep them from wandering too far afield, and
bring them back to the village at night. The waste
(85)   also was the source of wood for fuel and for building purposes, and helped to supplement the food
supply with such things as nuts, berries, honey,
and rabbits. . . .

The fourth segment of the manor was the vil-
(90)   lage itself, usually located in the center of the
arable near a source of drinking water, and perhaps along a road or path or footpath leading to

the outside world. The cottages of medieval peasants were extremely humble, usually consisting of
(95) a single room, with earthen floor and thatched
roof. Around each cottage normally lay a small
garden in which various vegetables and sometimes
fruit trees were planted. In the village streets
chickens, ducks, and dogs picked up a precarious
(100) living.

From *History of Western Civilization, A Handbook*, Sixth
Edition, copyright ©1986 by William H. McNeill. Reprinted by
permission of the University of Chicago Press.

1. The description of the near starvation of the
   oxen (lines 70–74) serves to:

   A. demonstrate how difficult life on the
       manor was in tenth century northern
       Europe;

   B. showcase how important work animals
       were to medieval manors.

   C. emphasize how important natural mead-
       ows were to feeding the work animals.

   D. explain why uniform cropping was a
       critical practice that ensured survival on
       the medieval manor.

2. According to the passage, the fact that the
   peasants' individual strips of land were
   unfenced subdivisions of larger fields required
   each peasant to:

   F. follow a fixed planting schedule so as to
       be able to harvest crops at the same time
       as the other peasants.

   G. harvest crops independently of his
       neighbors.

   H. limit the size of strips to what could be
       plowed in a single day.

   J. maintain small garden plots in order to
       provide his family with enough food.

3. According to the second paragraph
   (lines 4–31), the fallow part of the arable had
   to be plowed a total of how many times in any
   given calendar year?

   A. one

   B. two

   C. four

   D. six

4. The passage suggests that the practice of
   peasants owning strips "scattered through the
   three fields in different parts" (lines 37–38) was
   instituted in order to:

   F. divide resources fairly evenly.

   G. preserve the wealth of elite landowners.

   H. protect the three fields from overuse.

   J. force neighbors to work only their own
       lands.

5. On the basis of the information in the passage,
   it may be inferred that people in medieval
   times did not think of sowing hay because:

   A. hay sowing had not been done in
       the past.

   B. the need for more hay was not great
       enough to warrant the extra work.

   C. northern Europeans did not yet have the
       necessary farming techniques for suc-
       cessful hay cultivation.

   D. the tight schedule of cultivating the ara-
       ble meant that the peasants had no time
       to cultivate extra crops.

6. As it is used in line 53, the word *garnered*
   means:

   F. planted

   G. watered

   H. gathered

   J. plowed

7. According to the passage, if one of the arable's three great fields were left fallow one year, it would be:

   A. left fallow for two more years in succession.

   B. planted the next year with winter grain only.

   C. planted the next year with spring grain only.

   D. planted with either winter or spring grain the next year.

8. Which of the following conclusions is suggested by the fourth paragraph (lines 41–58)?

   I. An individual was free to cultivate his own land in any way he wished.

   II. The manor was run according to tradition.

   III. Successful farming required cooperative methods.

   F. I and II only

   G. I and III only

   H. II and III only

   J. I, II, and III

9. According to the passage, a manor's value might be judged according to the number of its plows because:

   A. the more plows a manor had, the less land had to be left fallow.

   B. plows, while not in themselves valuable, symbolized great wealth.

   C. manors with sufficient plows could continue plowing throughout the year.

   D. the number of plows a manor owned determined how much land could be cultivated.

10. According to the passage, summer pasture for a manor's geese would be provided:

    F. next to cottages, within the village.

    G. on the fallow field of the arable.

    H. on the communal ground of the waste.

    J. on the whole of the meadow.

THE LAY OF THE LAND

Well, how'd you do? Did you remember to refer to the passage? You probably found that you had to do a more thorough check for some questions than for others.

This passage, like most nonfiction passages on the ACT, is organized in a fairly logical way around the main idea, which you might have expressed as "the structure and common practices of the medieval manor." Here's one possible road map you might have come up with:

- Paragraph 1 (just a single sentence, really): Intro to the topic of medieval manors (divided, as cited in the first line of next paragraph, into arable, meadow, waste, and village)

- Paragraphs 2, 3, and 4: Discussion of the arable and the practices associated with it

- Paragraph 5: Discussion of the meadow

- Paragraph 6: Discussion of the waste

- Paragraph 7: Discussion of the village

It should be obvious why, in your prereading step, you really need to get some sense of the layout of the passage like this. **Many questions don't contain specific line references to help you locate information, and if you don't have a road map of the passage in your head or on paper, you might get lost.**

Following is a key to the ten questions attached to this passage.

KEY TO PASSAGE I

(Nonfiction—Social Studies)

	Answer	Refer to	Type	Comments
1.	C	Lines 59–77	Function	The entire paragraph supports this claim.
2.	F	Lines 46–52	Detail	"Uniform cropping was imperative . . ."
3.	B	Lines 19–21	Detail	Don't confuse fallow with planted fields.
4.	F	Lines 36–40	Inference	Every peasant got some fertile and some infertile land—inferably, to be fair to each.
5.	A	Lines 54–58, 62–64	Inference	No line reference, so you had to have a sense of the structure to find this.
6.	H	Lines 52–54	Vocab-in-Context	Use context. The crop is ripe, and so must be ready to be gathered.
7.	B	Lines 14–15	Detail	No line reference; otherwise no problem.
8.	H	Lines 41–58	Inference	I: lines 42–44 say the opposite II: lines 41–46 III: lines 49–54 Statement I is false, so that means F, G, and J are wrong. That means H must be the answer.
9.	D	Lines 26–28	Detail	No line reference; number of plows = amount of land.
10.	H	Lines 78–80	Detail	Whole paragraph devoted to describing waste.

EXPERT TUTOR TIP

A few ACT questions—like question 8 in this passage—are Roman numeral questions. You're given three or four statements, each labeled with a Roman numeral. The idea is to treat each one as a true/false statement. Decide which statements are true, and then select the choice that includes only those statements. Often, you can save yourself some time on these questions. For instance, in question 8: Once you decide that Statement I is false, you can eliminate choices F, G, and J, all of which include Statement I. Thus, you can get your answer, choice H, without even looking at Statements II and III.

IF YOU LEARNED ONLY THREE THINGS IN THIS CHAPTER . . .

1. Follow structural clues and content to figure out the overall passage using the ABCs of Active Reading:

   Abbreviate margin notes, **B**racket key sentences, and **C**ircle key words and phrases.

2. Carefully read the question stems (*only*) to determine the type of question being asked.

3. Look for the correct answer in the passage—don't try to answer from memory. Predict an answer, and look for the answer that best matches your prediction.

CHAPTER 7: SCIENCE WORKOUT 1: LOOK FOR PATTERNS

SMARTPOINTS COVERED IN THIS CHAPTER

- FIGURE INTERPRETATION
- PATTERNS
- SCIENTIFIC REASONING

The Science subject test causes a lot of unnecessary anxiety among ACT takers. Many people get so overwhelmed by the terminology and technicality of the passages that they just give up. What they fail to realize is that **Science is a little like the reverse of Math.** In Math, you'll remember, we said that many of the questions are difficult problems based on elementary principles. In Science, on the other hand, many of the questions are elementary problems based on difficult material. So it's important not to panic if you don't understand the passage in Science. You can often get many of the questions right on a passage, even if you find it virtually incomprehensible!

Many ACT takers also tend to rely too heavily on what they've learned in school when approaching the Science subject test. But as we've said, "remembering" is not the mind-set the ACT will reward. You couldn't possibly know the answers to ACT Science questions in advance: you have to pull them out of the passages. **All the information you need to answer the questions is right on the page.**

Worrying about science knowledge can be a problem no matter how good or bad your science background is. Students who have done poorly in science tend to panic because they think they don't know enough. Students who have done well in science

EXPERT TUTOR TIP

The ACT Science test covers biology, chemistry, earth/space sciences, and physics. It includes:

- Three Data Representation passages with Five questions each

- Three Experiment passages with six questions each

- One Conflicting Viewpoints passage with seven questions

EXPERT TUTOR TIP

" Here's how to use this chapter if you don't have much time. Learn the Kaplan Method for ACT Science on the next page. Try the sample passage that follows. Then read the section called Reading Tables and Graphs. "

PERFECT SCORE TIP

" A common myth is that the ACT Science section is based on science knowledge. It is really another reading comprehension section, not a test of your scientific knowledge. "

PERFECT SCORE TIP

" I know many people are scared about the fact that a calculator is not allowed on Science. This is really not an issue, as you will not need one. "

might know **too** much. Some questions include wrong choices that are scientifically correct but don't relate to the passages. Choosing such answers will not earn you points on the ACT. So try not to rely primarily on your knowledge of science. Instead, use your ability to refer to the passages.

ACT Science requires many of the same skills that ACT Reading does. The strategies discussed in Reading Workout I will therefore also work well for many Science passages. The most important difference between Reading and Science is that the "details" you have to find in the Science passages almost all relate to numbers or scientific processes, and they are often contained in graphs and tables rather than in paragraph form.

- **Reading graphs, tables, and research summaries.** Many questions involve only accurately retrieving data from a single graph or table. Others involve combining knowledge from two different graphs or tables. Still others involve understanding experimental methods well enough to evaluate information contained in summaries of experiments.

- **Looking for patterns in the numbers that appear.** Do these numbers get bigger or smaller? Where are the highest numbers? the lowest? At what point do the numbers change? A little calculation is sometimes required, but not much. In Science, you won't be computing with numbers so much as thinking about what they mean.

In Science, as in Reading, it's crucial to consider the questions and at least try to answer them before looking at the answer choices. Refer to the passage to find the answer, and try to match it with one of the choices. **Use the process of elimination** as a fallback strategy for hard questions—but don't make it your main approach.

THE KAPLAN FIVE-STEP METHOD FOR ACT SCIENCE

The same Kaplan Method for Reading is also useful in Science. The steps, you'll remember, are:

1. Preread the passage (one minute).

2. Consider the question stem.

3. Refer to the passage (before looking at the choices).

4. Answer the question in your own words.

5. Match your answer with one of the choices.

In Science, you have seven shorter passages to do instead of the four longer ones in Reading. Each passage should average five minutes. We recommend using just about one minute or so to preread the passage, and then a total of about four minutes to consider the questions and refer to the passage (that's about 40 seconds per question). Notice that this is less time prereading than in the Reading test.

STEP 1: PREREAD THE PASSAGE

Don't get bogged down in details (we'll see that this is also critical in the Natural Sciences passage in Reading). Some of the material covered is extremely technical, and you'll just get frustrated trying to understand it completely. So it's crucial that you skim, to get a general idea of what's going on and—just as important—to get a sense of where certain types of data can be found.

Almost all Science passages have the same general structure. They begin with an introduction. **Always** read the introduction first to orient yourself. Some passages relate to material you may have already studied in high school. If you're familiar with the concepts, you may not need to do more than skim the introduction. If not, you'll want to read the introduction more carefully. But remember, don't focus on details. In the introduction, mark the purpose of the experiment. Whether you bracket it, circle it, or put a "P" next to it doesn't really matter. The only important thing is that somehow you note where it is in case a question refers to it. The purpose will answer the question, "Why was this experiment performed?"

After reviewing the introduction, quickly scan the rest of the passage. Take note of the method of the experiment(s). The method will answer the question "How was the experiment set up?" How is the information presented? Graphs? Diagrams? Are there experiments? What seems to be important? Size? Shape? Temperature? Speed? Chemical composition? Don't worry about details and don't try to remember it all. Plan to refer to the passage just as you would in Reading.

Example

   Scientists researching the relationship between birds and dinosaurs have chosen to carefully examine three fossils dating from the Jurassic period: an *archaeopteryx* (the oldest known bird) at the British Museum in London, a *compsognathus* (a dinosaur) at the Field Museum in Chicago, and a *teleosaurus* (a crocodile) at the National Museum in Beijing. All three creatures were about the same size as a turkey.

Remember to read actively. Ask yourself: why would the scientists choose these three creatures? Since the scientists are studying birds and dinosaurs, the first two choices seem natural. But why should they include a crocodile? Maybe the National Museum in Beijing had a special deal on crocodile bones? More likely it's because crocodiles are somewhat like dinosaurs, but not extinct.

PERFECT SCORE TIP

" I often find the intro is the most useful part of the whole reading. Don't try to understand everything in them, but definitely make sure to read all the intros as they will give you background for the rest of the passage. "

KAPLAN'S STRATEGY FOR ACT SCIENCE

" 1. Preread the Passage

2. Consider the Question Stem

3. Refer to the Passage

4. Answer the Question in Your Own Words

5. Match Your Answer with One of the Choices "

As you preread the passage, you also want to make sure you know what any tables and graphs in the passage are meant to represent. Feel free to take notes, mark up the test booklet, or circle important information. Get a sense of what kind of data is contained in each graph and table, but don't read the data carefully yet! You may want to take note of general trends in the data, but don't waste time taking in information that may not be relevant to the questions. **Remember, your goal is to answer questions, not to learn and remember everything that goes on in the passage.**

STEP 2: CONSIDER THE QUESTION STEM

Most of your time in Science will be spent considering questions and referring to the passage to find the answers. Here's where you should do most of your really careful reading. **It's essential that you understand exactly what the question is asking.** Then, go back to the passage and get a sense of what the answer should be before looking at the choices.

There are three basic kinds of Science questions:

- **Figure Interpretation Questions.** For these questions, you'll almost certainly be going back to the graphs. They are usually among the easiest on the Science test. Knowing the headings of each figure will help make these questions that much easier.

- **Patterns Questions.** These are usually medium difficulty. You have to look beyond just the data that is presented in the figures to see what the patterns are in the data.

- **Scientific Interpretation Questions.** These questions are usually among the hardest on the test, because they are based on what is in the text versus what is in the figures. Here you must apply a scientific principle or identify ways of defending or attacking a principle. This includes making predictions based on a given theory or showing how a hypothesis might be strengthened or weakened by particular findings. (These questions will be especially important for the Conflicting Viewpoints passage, discussed in Science Workout 3.)

As we mentioned, one possible pitfall in answering the questions is relying too heavily on your own knowledge of science. In answering questions, use your knowledge of scientific *methods* and *procedures*. But don't rely heavily on any knowledge of specific facts. For example, the following question might have appeared with the passage excerpted above:

SCIENTIFIC REASONING

Example

1. The dinosaur studied by the scientists, *compsognathus*, was:

   A.   definitely a reptile.
   B.   definitely a bird.
   C.   about the size of a turkey.
   D.   larger than *archaeopteryx* or *teleosaurus*.

If you know that dinosaurs are usually classified as reptiles, choice A would be very tempting. But it's wrong. The passage doesn't say that. In fact, if we had seen the rest of this passage, we would have learned that the researchers were questioning whether dinosaurs should be classified as reptiles or birds. What the passage *does* say is that all three of the creatures tested are turkey sized, making the correct choice C.

STEP 3: REFER TO THE PASSAGE

As in Reading, you have to be diligent about referring to the passage. Your prereading of the passage should have given you an idea of where particular kinds of data can be found. Sometimes the questions themselves will direct you to the right place.

Be careful not to mix up units when taking information from graphs, tables, and summaries. Don't confuse *decreases* and *increases*: Many questions will hinge on whether you can correctly identify the factors that decrease and the ones that increase. The difference between a correct and an incorrect answer will often be a *decrease* where an *increase* should be. **Read the questions carefully!**

STEP 4: ANSWER THE QUESTION IN YOUR OWN WORDS

The answers to the Science questions are there in the passage. As we mentioned in Step 2 above, don't rely too much on your own knowledge of science. Instead think of paraphrasing the information in the passage.

STEP 5: MATCH YOUR ANSWER WITH ONE OF THE CHOICES

Once you've paraphrased the information and matched it to an answer choice, double-check the question to make sure that you've actually answered the question asked. **Many of the questions in Science are reversal questions. Always look for words like *not* and *except* in the questions.**

EXPERT TUTOR TIP

" Reading the question carefully is the most important step. If you miss a little word like *not*, you will get the question wrong. "

EXPERT TUTOR TIP

" If the answer that you want is not there, eliminate answer choices that you know are wrong, and then pick the best answer that remains. "

PERFECT SCORE TIP

" The words *not* and *except* will show up in question stems, and missing them is an easy way to get a question wrong. Pay attention to these words and circle them when you see them. "

READING TABLES AND GRAPHS

Most of the information in ACT Science passages is presented in tables or graphs, usually accompanied by explanatory material. Knowing how to read data from tables and graphs is critical to success on the Science subject test! In order to read most graphs and tables, ask yourself:

- **What does the figure show?**
- **What are the units of measurement?**
- **What is the pattern in the data?**

Let's say you saw the following graph in a Science passage:

AIR TEMPERATURE AT VARIOUS
ALTITUDES AT TEST SITE #3

- **What does the figure show?** Most graphs and tables have titles that tell you what they represent. For some, though, you may have to get that information from the introduction. Here, the graph is representing how cold or hot the air is at various altitudes above a certain Test Site #3.

- **What are the units of measurement?** Note that distance here is measured in *kilometers*, not miles or feet. Temperature is measured in degrees *Celsius*, not Fahrenheit.

- **What is the pattern in the data?** The pattern of the data in this graph is pretty clear. As you rise in altitude, the temperature drops—the higher the altitude, the lower the temperature. (As we'll see later, this kind of trend is called an *inverse variation*.)

The sloping line on the graph represents the various temperatures measured at the various altitudes. To find what the measured temperature was at, say, 2 km above sea level, find the 2 km point on the *x*-axis and trace your finger directly up from it until it hits the line. It does so at about the level of 3° C. In other words, at an altitude of 2 km above sea level at Test Site #3, the air temperature was about 3° C.

Be careful with units of measurement! Most passages use the metric system, but a few may use traditional or British units of measure. You won't be expected to remember oddball unit conversions like 8 furlongs = 1 mile or 2.54 cm = 1 in, and passages that use special units of measure such as microns or parsecs will define these units if necessary. But don't assume that all the units in the graphs match the units in the questions. For instance, try the following question:

 FIGURE INTERPRETATION

Example

2. At what altitude did the meteorologists measure an air temperature of 10° C?

   F. 1.4 m
   G. 140 m
   H. 1,400 m
   J. 14 km

Many test takers solving the problem above would find the point on the line at the level of 10° C on the *y*-axis, trace their fingers down to the *x*-axis, see that the altitude would be about halfway between 1 and 2 (a little closer to 1, maybe), and then quickly choose F. But F is wrong, since F gives you 1.4 *meters*, while the graph figures are given in *kilometers*. Remember to translate the data! A kilometer is 1,000 meters, so 1.4 kilometers would be 1.4 times 1,000 meters = 1,400 meters. That's choice H.

You should follow a similar procedure with tables of information. For instance, in the introduction to the passage in which the following table might have appeared, you would have learned that scientists were trying to determine the effects of two pollutants (Pb and Hg, lead and mercury) on the trout population of a particular river.

Table 1

Location	Water Temperature (°C)	Presence of Pb (parts per million)	Presence of Hg (parts per million)	Population Density of Speckled Trout (# per 100 m³)
1	15.4	0	3	7.9
2	16.1	0	1	3.5
3	16.3	1	67	0
4	15.8	54	3	5.7
5	16.0	2	4	9.5

- **What does the figure show?** Here, each row represents the data from a different numbered location on the river. Each column represents different data: water temperature, presence of the first pollutant, presence of the second pollutant, population of one kind of trout.

- **What are the units of measurement?** Temperature is measured in degrees Celsius. The two pollutants are measured in parts per million (or ppm). The trout populations are measured in average number per 100 cubic meters of river.

- **What is the pattern in the data?** Glancing at the table, it looks like locations where the Hg concentration is high (as in Location 3), the trout population is virtually nonexistent. This would seem to indicate that trout find a high Hg concentration incompatible. But notice the location where the other pollutant is abundant—in Location 4. Here, the trout population seems to be more in line with other locations. That would seem to indicate that this other pollutant—Pb—is NOT quite so detrimental to trout populations (though we'd have to do more studies if it turned out that all of the trout in that location had three eyes).

HOW TABLES AND GRAPHS RELATE

To really understand tables and graphs, it helps to see how the same information can be represented in both. For instance, look at the next table and graph:

Concentration of *E. coli* in Cooling Pool B	
DISTANCE FROM EFFLUENT PIPE 3	1000s OF *E. COLI* PER CENTILITRE
zero m	.4
5 m	5.6
10 m	27.6
15 m	14.0
20 m	7.5

Concentration of *E. coli* in Cooling Pool B

The table and graph above represent the exact same data. And here's yet another way of depicting the same data, in a bar chart:

Concentration of *E. coli* in Cooling Pool B

Remember that data can be represented in many different ways. But however it appears in the passage, whether it be in tables, graphs, or charts, you'll have to read and translate it to answer the questions.

LOOK FOR PATTERNS AND TRENDS

When you first examine a graph or table, don't focus on exact numbers. **Look for *patterns* in the numbers. But don't assume that there is *always* a pattern or trend:** finding that there isn't a pattern is just as important as finding that there is one. When looking for patterns and trends, you should keep three things in mind:

1. EXTREMES

Extremes—or maximums and minimums—are merely the highest and lowest points that things reach. In tables, the minimums and maximums will be represented by relatively high and low numbers. In graphs, they will be represented by highs and lows on the *x*- and *y*-axes. In bar charts, they will be represented by the tallest and shortest bars.

Look back at Table 1. What location on the river has the maximum concentration of Hg? Of Pb? A glance at the numbers tells you that Location 3—with 67 ppm—represents the maximum for Hg, while Location 4—with 54 ppm—represents the maximum for Pb.

How can taking note of maximums and minimums help you spot patterns in the data? Look again at Table 1. Notice that the maximum concentration of Hg, 67 ppm, just happens to coincide with the *minimum* for trout population—0 per 100 m^3. That's a good indication that there's some cause and effect going on here. Somehow, a maximum of Hg concentration correlates with a minimum of trout population. The obvious (though not airtight) conclusion is that a high concentration of Hg is detrimental to trout populations. And this kind of finding is much more evident when you look at maximums and minimums.

2. CRITICAL POINTS

To find out how critical points can help you evaluate data, take another look at the graph representing the concentration of *E. coli* (a common type of bacterium) in Cooling Pool B.

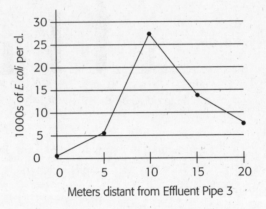

Notice how the concentration is low very near Effluent Pipe 3. From there, it rises until about 10 meters away from the pipe, then it falls again, tapering off as you get farther from the pipe. There's a critical point, then, right around 10 meters from Effluent Pipe 3. Somehow, that vicinity is most conducive to the growth of *E. coli*. As you move closer to or farther away from that point, the concentration falls off. So, in looking to explain the data, you'd want to focus on that location—10 meters from the pipe. What is it about that location that's so special? What makes it the hot new place for *E. coli* to see and be seen?

3. RELATIONSHIPS

Being able to recognize relationships within a figure will lead directly to earning more points on test day. Look at the figure below.

Hours of Sunlight	Air Temperature (Fahrenheit)		
	Chamber 1	Chamber 2	Chamber 3
2	73.23	75.67	78.87
4	71.23	75.79	79.78
6	69.23	74.76	81.34
8	67.23	79.87	82.12
10	65.23	80.65	83.06

What happens in Chamber 1? What do you think the temperature is going to be after 12 hours of sunlight? Do you notice the pattern? The temperature goes down by two degrees for every two hours of sunlight. The temperature is going to be 63.23 degrees.

As the number of hours of sunlight increases, what happens to the temperature in Chamber 2? When you look at the data, there doesn't appear to be a relationship! This is a valid answer.

Based on the data, what do you think the temperature will be after one hour of sunlight in Chamber 3? Well, as the number of hours of sunlight increase, the temperature in the chamber increases. So if you had to predict what would happen after only one hour of sunlight, then according to the table, it is going to be less than 78.87 degrees.

Before you tackle a "real" Science passage, let's review the Kaplan Method for the Science section. Note how similar it is to the steps for the Reading section. However, here you spend only one minute prereading (actively reading) the passage.

THE REAL THING: PRACTICE PASSAGE

Let's take a look at a full-fledged Science passage that requires these skills. Give yourself about seven minutes to do the passage and the questions (on the actual test, you'll want to move a bit faster).

PASSAGE I

Although the effective acceleration due to gravity at the earth's surface is often treated as a constant ($g = 9.80$ m/sec^2), its actual value varies from place to place because of several factors.

First, a body on the surface of any rotating spheroid experiences an effective force perpendicular to the rotational axis and proportional to the speed of rotation. This centrifugal force, which counteracts gravity, varies with latitude, increasing from zero at the poles to a maximum at the equator. In addition, because the earth "bulges" at the equator, a body at equatorial sea level is farther from the center of the earth than is a body at polar sea level. Figure 1 shows the variation of mean values of g at sea level resulting from both effects; the contribution from "bulging" is about half that from rotation.

> **EXPERT TUTOR TIP**
>
> " If the terminology in the passage scares you, just concentrate on the figures to answer the questions. "

Figure 1

Measurements of g also vary depending on local rock density and altitude. Table 1 shows the effect of altitude on g at various points above sea level.

Table 1

Altitude above Sea Level (km)	g (m/sec²)
1	−0.0031
5	−0.0154
10	−0.0309
25	−0.0772
30	−0.1543

 FIGURE INTERPRETATION

Example

3. If the earth's density were uniform, at approximately what latitude would calculations using an estimated value at sea level of $g = 9.80$ m/sec² produce the least error?

   A. 0°

   B. 20°

   C. 40°

   D. 80°

4. According to Table 1, what would the change in gravity (in m/s²) be at 2 km above sea level?

   F. −0.0001

   G. −0.0030

   H. −0.0081

   J. −0.0165

PATTERNS

5. Given the information in the passage, which of the following figures most closely approximates the value of g at a point 10 km high along the equator?

   A. 9.75 m/sec^2

   B. 9.80 m/sec^2

   C. 9.81 m/sec^2

   D. 9.87 m/sec^2

6. Suppose that the earth stopped rotating but still "bulged." Based on information from the passage, the value of g at sea level at the equator would be:

   F. exactly 9.80 m/sec^2.

   G. greater than 9.78 m/sec^2.

   H. exactly 9.78 m/sec^2.

   J. less than 9.78 m/sec^2.

7. According to the information in Figure 1, the value of g:

   A. changes by a greater average amount per degree latitude between 30° and 60° than it does near the equator or poles.

   B. changes by a greater average amount per degree latitude near the equator or poles than it does between 30° and 60°.

   C. increases by an average of 5.8 m/sec^2 per degree latitude from the equator to the poles.

   D. decreases by an average of 3.1×10^{-3} m/sec^2 per degree latitude from the equator to the poles.

ANSWERS

1. **C**
2. **H**
3. **C**
4. **J**
5. **A**
6. **H**
7. **B**

ANSWERS AND EXPLANATIONS

This was actually a relatively simple, straightforward Science passage, but the terminology may have been intimidating nonetheless. The introduction tells you that the issue here is gravity, and how its pull (in other words, the acceleration due to gravity) changes because of several factors. Those factors—and the changes they cause—are represented in Figure 1 (which deals with the factor of latitude) and Table 1 (which deals with the factor of altitude).

Analyzing Figure 1 as described above, you should have seen that the graph is supposed to show how g (the acceleration due to gravity) is affected by latitude (i.e., north-south location on the globe). The higher the latitude (the greater the distance from the equator), the greater the value of g. As the curves at the beginning and ending of the line in Figure 1 tell you, the increase in g is "slower" near the equator and near the poles.

Notice how you could have answered **Question 3** just by understanding Figure 1. Question 3 asks, assuming the earth's density were uniform, "at what latitude would calculations using an estimated value at sea level of $g = 9.80$ m/sec^2 produce the least error?" First, figure out what that question is asking. You remember this question; we mentioned it in ACT Basics. It's simply asking you: Where would you get an actual value of g closest to 9.80 m/sec^2? Find 9.80 on the y-axis of the graph, follow across until you intersect with the curved line, and see where you are on the x-axis. That turns out to be about a third of the way from 30° to 60° latitude. In other words, choice C, 40°, is the answer.

Question 4 is simply asking you to figure out the pattern in Table 2. To find out what the change in g at 2 km is, you would need to look at the table between 1 km and 5 km. There is only one answer choice that falls between the values of −0.0031 and −0.0154, and that is answer H, −0.0081.

We'll get to **Question 5** below.

Question 6 requires more applications of principles, and is yet another question that can be answered by simply reading Figure 1. It asks you to suppose that rotation effects (one of the two factors affected by latitude) ceased, but that the earth still bulged at the equator. What would be the value of g? Well, again, rotation tends to "counteract" gravity, so it would have a depressing effect on g. Without rotation, then, g would be less depressed—it would go up, in other words. That means (reading from Figure 1 again) that g at 0° latitude (the equator) would, in the absence of rotation, go up from its current value of 9.78. That's why B is correct.

Question 7 (not to get monotonous) is still another that can be answered just by a proper reading of Figure 1. It asks you to describe what the graph tells you about the value of g. As we saw, the value rises slowly as you head away from 0° latitude (the equator), rises more rapidly in the middle latitudes, and slows down again near 90° latitude (the poles). That's best described by choice F. (Choice G gets it backwards—remember to read the choices carefully!) Choices H and J would involve you in some extensive calculations, at the end of which you'd realize that they were not true. But there's no reason to get that far. If you find yourself doing extensive calculation, you should know that you're on the wrong track. ACT Science will involve simple calculation only.

Notice how you could have answered four of the five questions with just a rudimentary grasp of the introduction and an understanding of how to "read" Figure 1 and Table 1.

The other question, **Question 5,** requires that you read both Figure 1 and Table 1 properly. It asks for the value of g at the equator (that information comes from Figure 1), but at an altitude of 10 km above sea level (that information comes from Table 1). Figure 1 tells you that the value of g at the equator at sea level would be 9.78 m/sec^2. But at 10 km above sea level, according to Table 1, g would be slightly lower—0.0309 m/sec^2 lower, to be precise. So 9.78 minus 0.0309 would be about 9.75 m/sec^2. That's choice A.

LOOK FOR PATTERNS

The passage and questions above should convince you of one thing: to do well on Science, you have to be able to read graphs and tables, paying special attention to trends and patterns in the data. Sometimes that's all you need to do to get most of the points on a passage.

IF YOU LEARNED ONLY THREE THINGS IN THIS CHAPTER . . .

1. The information you need is given in the passages—don't rely on your outside knowledge of science.

2. Approach Science passages like Reading passages: preread to get the sense of a passage, focus on the question stem, and find the answer in the data or scenario given.

3. When reading graphs and tables, determine what's being represented, the units of measurement, and any patterns or trends.

CHAPTER 8: ENGLISH WORKOUT 2: MAKE IT MAKE SENSE

SMARTPOINTS COVERED IN THIS CHAPTER

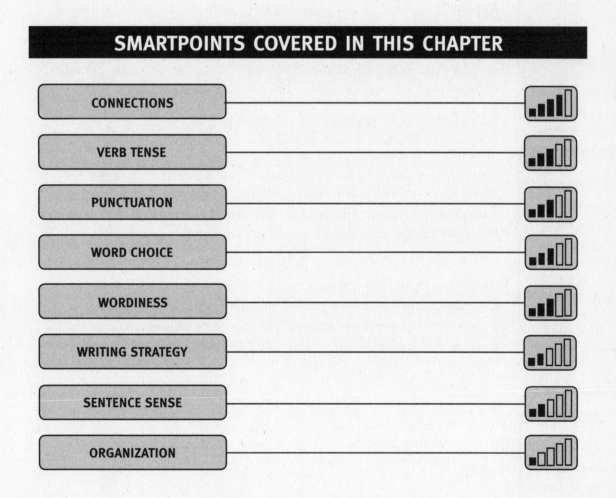

CONNECTIONS

VERB TENSE

PUNCTUATION

WORD CHOICE

WORDINESS

WRITING STRATEGY

SENTENCE SENSE

ORGANIZATION

EXPERT TUTOR TIP

" What you read **always** has two possible meanings: an intended meaning and a literal meaning. The intended meaning is what the writer was trying to say. The literal meaning is what the author actually did say. The ACT demands that the intended and literal meanings of every passage be exactly the same. "

PERFECT SCORE TIP

" If you can't find the mistake in an underlined sentence, consider logic. A sentence may sound like English, but actually have a logical inconsistency, which makes it not make sense. "

PERFECT SCORE TIP

" In the Reading section, skimming and not noting small problems is a good thing. In English, you must pay close attention to all words in the underlined region. "

In English Workout 1, we saw that the ACT expects you to use your words efficiently, and that, in fact, the shortest answer is correct remarkably often. But, obviously, the shortest answer is often wrong. What could make it wrong? It may not mean what it says.

Take this example: "Abraham Lincoln's father was a model of hardworking self-sufficiency. He was born in a log cabin he built with his own hands." Well, that's a cute trick, being born in a cabin you built yourself. Presumably the writer means that Abe was born in a cabin that his father built. But the literal meaning of the example is that the father somehow managed to be born in a cabin that he himself had built.

It's possible, of course, to analyze this example in terms of the rules of apostrophe use and pronoun reference. But that's not practical for the ACT, even for a student who has good grammar skills. There isn't time to carefully analyze every question, consider all the rules involved, and decide on an answer. You have to do 75 English questions in only 45 minutes—that's almost two questions per minute.

But there *is* plenty of time to approach examples like this one in a more pragmatic way. Ask yourself, *Do these words make sense?*

For the ACT, it's important to care. You need to adjust your mind-set. After deciding whether or not the selection in a question is concise and relevant (Step 1 in the Three-Step Method), the next step is to make sure that the sentence *says* exactly what it's supposed to *mean*. If it doesn't, your job is to make it so. In other words, make it make sense.

We at Kaplan have a name for questions that test errors of meaning—**Sense Questions.** Once you get the hang of them, these questions can actually be fun. They're often funny once you see them. The following passage gives examples of the most common kinds of Sense Questions you'll find on the ACT.

Example

PASSAGE I

Most people—even those who've never read Daniel Defoe's *Robinson Crusoe*—are familiar with the strange story of the sailor shipwrecked on a far-flung Pacific island. Relatively few of them, however, know that Crusoe's story. It was actually based on the real-life
$$1$$
adventures of a Scottish seaman, Alexander Selkirk. Selkirk came to the Pacific as a member of a 1703 privateering expedition led by a captain named William Dampier. During the voyage, Selkirk became dissatisfied with conditions aboard ship. After a bitter
$$2$$
quarrel with his captain, he put Selkirk ashore on tiny
$$2$$
Mas a Tierra, one of the islands of Juan Fernandez, off the coast of Chile. Stranded, Selkirk lived there alone— in much the same manner as Defoe's Crusoe—until
$$3$$
1709, when he was finally rescued by another English privateer. Upon his return to England, Selkirk found himself a celebrity, his strange tale had already become
$$4$$
the talk of pubs and coffeehouses throughout the British Isles. The story even reached the ears of Richard Steele, who featured it in his periodical, *The Tatler*. Eventually, he became the subject of a
$$5$$

1. A. NO CHANGE
   B. story: was
   C. story, was
   D. story was

2. F. NO CHANGE
   G. Quarreling with his captain, the boat was put ashore
   H. Having quarreled with his captain, Selkirk was put ashore
   J. Having quarreled with his captain, they put Selkirk ashore

3. A. NO CHANGE
   B. same manner that
   C. identical manner that
   D. identical way as

4. F. NO CHANGE
   G. celebrity, but his
   H. celebrity. His
   J. celebrity his

5. A. NO CHANGE
   B. Selkirk became
   C. his became
   D. he becomes

best-selling book, *A Cruizing Voyage Round the World*, by

Woodes Rogers. And while there is some evidence that
                   6

Defoe, a journalist, may actually have interviewed

Selkirk personally, most literary historians believe

that it was the reprinting of the Rogers book in 1718

that served as the real stimulus for Defoe's novel.

In *Crusoe*, which has been published in 1719,
                        7

Defoe took substantial liberties with the Selkirk story.

For example, while Selkirk's presence on the island was

of course known for many people (certainly everyone
              8

in the crew that stranded him there), no one in the

novel is aware of Crusoe's survival of the wreck and

presence on the island. Moreover, while Selkirk's exile

lasted just six years, Crusoe's goes on for a much more

dramatic, though less credible, twenty-eight (over four
                                                  9

times as long). But Defoe's most blatant embellishment
       9

of the tale is the invention of the character of Friday,

for whom there was no counterpart whatsoever in the

real-life story.

Because of its basis in fact, Robinson Crusoe is
    10

often regarded as the first major novel in English

6. F. NO CHANGE
   G. But since
   H. And therefore
   J. OMIT the underlined portion and start the sentence with *There*.

7. A. NO CHANGE
   B. was published
   C. had been published
   D. will have been published

8. F. NO CHANGE
   G. widely known among people
   H. known about many people
   J. known to many people

9. A. NO CHANGE
   B. (much longer)
   C. (a much longer time, of course)
   D. OMIT the underlined portion

10. F. NO CHANGE
    G. Despite
    H. Resulting from
    J. As a consequence of

literature. Still popular today, contemporary audiences
                                    11
enjoyed the book as well. In fact, two sequels, in which
                11
Crusoe returns to the island after his rescue, were

eventually published. Though to little acclaim.
                    12
Meanwhile, Selkirk himself never gave a hoot
                                    13
about returning to the island that had made him
        13
famous. Legend has it that he never gave up his

eccentric living habits, spending his last years in a cave

teaching alley cats to dance in his spare time. One

wonders if even Defoe himself could have invented a

more fitting end to the bizarre story of his shipwrecked

sailor.

11. A. NO CHANGE
    B. Still read today, Defoe's contemporaries
        also enjoyed it.
    C. Viewed by many even then as a classic, the
        book is still popular to this day.
    D. Much read in its day, modern audiences
        still find the book compelling.

12. F. NO CHANGE
    G. published, though
    H. published although
    J. published; although

13. A. NO CHANGE
    B. evinced himself as desirous of returning
    C. could whip up a head of steam to return
    D. expressed any desire to return

Items 14–15 ask about the passage as a whole.

---

14. Considering the tone and subject matter of
    the preceding paragraphs, is the last sentence an
    appropriate way to end the essay?

    F. Yes, because it is necessary to shed some
        doubt on Defoe's creativity.
    G. Yes, because the essay is about the rela-
        tionship between the real Selkirk and
        Defoe's fictionalized version of him.
    H. No, because there is nothing "bizarre"
        about Selkirk's story as it is related in the
        essay.
    J. No, because the focus of the essay is more
        on Selkirk himself than on Defoe's fic-
        tionalized version of him.

15. This essay would be most appropriate as part of a:

    A. scholarly study of 18th-century maritime
        history.
    B. study of the geography of the islands off
        of Chile.
    C. history of privateering in the Pacific.
    D. popular history of English literature.

Sense Questions vs. Economy Questions

Most of the time, we don't usually care much if an author isn't clear. We have learned to interpret what the writer meant to say and move on. On the ACT test takers *must* care and make sure that what is written is the same as what the author meant. Sense Questions may seem harder than the Economy Questions—the shortest answers aren't necessarily right.

Step 1 is all you needed in question numbers 1, 3, 7, 8, 9, 10, and 13. When in doubt, take it out worked for these. As we saw in English Workout 1, questions that include an OMIT option, and those in which some of the answers are much longer than others, are usually testing writing economy.

In the rest of the questions in this passage, the answers differ in other ways. They may join or fragment sentences, rearrange things, or add words that affect the meaning of the sentences. When the answers are all about the same length, as in most of the questions here, the question is more likely to test sense. Consider the shortest answer first, but don't be as quick to select it and move on. Think about the effect each choice has on the *meaning* of the sentence and pick longer answers if the shortest one doesn't make sense.

ANSWERS

1. D
2. H
3. A
4. H
5. B
6. F
7. B
8. J
9. D
10. G
11. C
12. G
13. D
14. G
15. D

GRAMMAR RULES AND SENSE QUESTIONS

 SENTENCE SENSE

 CONNECTIONS

The ACT test makers include questions like those in Passage I to test many different rules of writing mechanics. Though it's *not necessary* to think about rules to answer the questions, being familiar with them will help. **The more ways to think about a question you have, the more likely you are to find the right answer.**

We'll discuss some of these examples in groups based on what they're designed to test. That way we can briefly discuss the rules, but also show you how the basic strategic approach of "make it make sense" can get you the answers without a lot of technical analysis. Let's start with **Question 1.**

COMPLETENESS

 CONNECTIONS

 SENTENCE SENSE

 PUNCTUATION

Rule at work: Every sentence must stand alone as a complete thought.

. . . Relatively few of them, however,

know that Crusoe's <u>story. It was</u> actually
₁
based on the real-life adventures of a

Scottish seaman, Alexander Selkirk.

1. A. NO CHANGE
   B. story: was
   C. story, was
   D. story was

If the underlined section for Question 1 were left as it is, the second sentence of the passage would be incomplete. It wouldn't make sense. "Relatively few people know that Crusoe's story" what? To make it make sense, you've got to continue the sentence so that it can tell us what it is that few people know about Crusoe's story. The three alternatives all do that, but B introduces a nonsensical colon, while C adds a comma when there's no pause in the sentence. D, however, continues the sentence—adding nothing unnecessary, but making it complete.

When you are testing a sentence for completeness, don't just look to see if it has a subject and verb.

Question 12 tests the same concept:

. . . In fact, two

sequels, in which Crusoe returns to the

island after his rescue, were eventually

published. Though to little acclaim.
    12

12. F. NO CHANGE
     G. published, though
     H. published although
     J. published; although

Here, the fragment should be more obvious, since the clause that's trying to pass itself off as a sentence—"Though to little acclaim"—contains neither a subject nor a verb. That's the technical reason it's wrong, and if you recognized this, great. But on a more intuitive level, it just doesn't make sense to say, as a complete thought: "Though to little acclaim."

Clearly, that fragment has to be connected to the sentence before it, so F and J are wrong, since both would leave the fragment isolated. H goes too far in the other direction, omitting any punctuation at all between the fragment and the main body of the sentence, and that's no good. But the correct choice, G, does just what we need it to do: it connects the fragment logically to the main sentence, but it provides a comma to represent the pause between the two.

SENTENCE STRUCTURE

Rule at work: A sentence can have two thoughts, but they must be combined correctly (see below). If none of the answer choices does this, select the choice that creates two separate sentences.

…Upon his return to England, Selkirk

found himself a celebrity, his strange
                        4
tale had already become the talk of

pubs and coffeehouses throughout the

British Isles.

4. F. NO CHANGE
    G. celebrity, but his
    H. celebrity. His
    J. celebrity his

Here we have two complete thoughts: (1) Selkirk found himself a celebrity upon his return, and (2) his tale was bandied about the pubs and coffeehouses. You can't just

> **PERFECT SCORE TIP**
>
> " If considering independent versus dependent clauses seems too confusing for you, just think, "If I put a period in the middle of this sentence and did not change any words, would the two new sentences make sense?" If the answer is yes, the sentence is run-on. "

run these two complete thoughts together with a comma, as the underlined portion does. And you certainly can't just run them together *without* a comma or anything else, as choice J does. You can relate the two thoughts with a comma and a linking word (*and*, for instance), but choice G's inclusion of the word *but* makes no sense. It implies a contrast, while the two complete thoughts are actually very similar. Thus, you should create two sentences, one for each thought. That's what correct choice H does.

Rule at work: There are three ways to connect complete thoughts.

1. Use a semicolon.

2. Use a comma with a FANBOY (For, And, Nor, But, Or, Yet, So) conjunction.

3. Make one of the two thoughts *IN*complete (or dependent).

Working with these three possibilities for Question 4, you might have seen any of these correct answer choices:

1) Selkirk found himself a celebrity**;** his strange tale had already…

2) Selkirk found himself a celebrity**,** *for* his strange tale had already…

3) Selkirk found himself a celebrity *because* his strange tale had already…

MODIFIERS

 SENTENCE SENSE

Question 2 tests modifier problems:

… After a bitter quarrel with his captain,
              2

he put Selkirk ashore on tiny Mas a
    2

Tierra, one of the islands of Juan

Fernandez …

2.
F. NO CHANGE
G. Quarreling with his captain, the boat was put ashore
H. Having quarreled with his captain, Selkirk was put ashore
J. Having quarreled with his captain, they put Selkirk ashore

Rule at work: A modifier, or "describer," is any word or *group of words* that describes another. Any and all describers must clearly relate to (be close to) whatever they are referring to.

> **PERFECT SCORE TIP**
>
> ❝ Misplaced modifiers are a common ACT trick. If multiple answers sound right to you, consider, "Is every adjective/verb modifying the right noun or pronoun?" ❞

Sentences become confused if a descriptive word, phrase, or clause is separated from the verb, noun, pronoun, etc. that it should be connected to. In the underlined portion of Question 2, the clause "after a bitter quarrel with his captain" should describe the person (or pronoun) that follows next. It doesn't.

The *he* who put Selkirk ashore must be the captain, but it can't be the captain who had "a bitter quarrel with his captain." That doesn't make sense (unless the captain quarrels with himself). So put the thing modified next to the thing modifying it. The person who quarreled with his captain was Selkirk—not the boat and not "they," whoever they are—so H is correct.

If you recognized the problem with Question 2 as a "misplaced modifier," that's great. Fantastic, even. But you didn't have to know the technicalities to get the right answer here. You just had to make the sentence make sense.

Question 11 tests a similar problem:

. . . <u>Still popular today, contemporary</u>
               11
<u>audiences enjoyed the book as well.</u>
     11

11. A. NO CHANGE
    B. Still read today, Defoe's contemporaries also enjoyed it.
    C. Viewed by many even then as a classic, the book is still popular to this day.
    D. Much read in its day, modern audiences still find the book compelling.

The way the sentence is written, it basically means that contemporary audiences are "still popular today." That doesn't make sense. The *intended* meaning is that the *book* is still popular today, as it was then. Choice C fixes the sense problem by putting its modifier—"viewed by many even then as a classic"—next to the thing it modifies—"the book." Notice that the other choices all misplace their modifiers in the same way, making them modify "Defoe's contemporaries" (in B) and "modern audiences" (in D).

As a rule of thumb, you should **always** make sure that modifiers are as close as possible to the things they describe.

Idiom (Accepted Word Form and Choice)

 Word Choice

Rule at work: The correct preposition can vary depending on the sense of the sentence. Many other phrases in English are correct because people have agreed to

---

use them in a certain way. No overall rules apply. To master these, listen to what sounds right or if English is not your native language, remember them one by one.

Question 3 tests idiom, or unusual but accepted uses of English words. Many words have special rules.

. . . Stranded, Selkirk lived there alone—

in much the <u>same manner as</u> Defoe's
                    3

Crusoe—until 1709, when he was

finally rescued by another . . .

3. A. NO CHANGE
   B. same manner that
   C. identical manner that
   D. identical way as

The sentence as written actually makes sense. Selkirk lived in "much the same manner as" Defoe's Crusoe. The idiom "much the same" calls for *as* to complete the comparison between Selkirk's and Crusoe's ways of life. Note how B and C would create completeness problems—in much the same (or identical) manner as Defoe's Crusoe what? Choice D, meanwhile, sounds strange. In English, we just don't say "in much the identical way as," because the word *identical* is an absolute. You can't be more or partially identical; you either are or aren't identical to something else. But even if you didn't analyze D this carefully, it should have just sounded wrong to your ear. (In English Workout 3 we'll show you how "trusting your ear" can be a great way to get correct answers on the English subject test.)

Question 8 tests another idiom problem:

. . . For example, while Selkirk's presence

on the island was of course <u>known for</u>
                                    8

<u>many people</u> (certainly everyone in the
     8

crew that stranded him there), no one

in the novel is aware of Crusoe's survival

of the wreck and presence on the island.

8. F. NO CHANGE
   G. widely known among people
   H. known about many people
   J. known to many people

The underlined portion as written is unidiomatic. Selkirk's presence wasn't known *for* many people—it was known *by*, or known *to*, many people. When you're known *for* something, that means you have a reputation for doing such and such. That makes no sense in this context. But J *does* make sense, since it points out that Selkirk's presence on the island was known *to* many people—that is, it was

PERFECT SCORE TIP

❝ If you are a native English speaker, the key to idioms is really trusting your ear. Chances are incorrect idioms will jump out to you if you trust what you hear. ❞

something that many people knew about. G is unidiomatic; we just wouldn't say "among people" here, since it's not specific enough. That sounds as if we're talking about people as a species. H would have been acceptable if it had read "known about *by* many people," but without the *by,* the correction just wouldn't make sense.

Idiom is a tough topic if you're not a native speaker. You have to think very carefully about the meaning of every word. But if you *are* a native speaker, **use your many years of hearing English as a guide.** Choose the correction that makes sense and doesn't sound weird.

PRONOUNS

 WORD CHOICE

 SENTENCE SENSE

 ORGANIZATION

Rule at work: A pronoun must agree with the person or thing it is referring to, in person, gender, and number (singular or plural). The reference must be clear; if there is *any* confusion, the sentence must be fixed.

Sometimes, the test will throw you a sentence in which the meaning of a pronoun is unclear. You won't be sure to whom or what the pronoun is referring. That's the kind of problem you were given in **Question 5**:

. . . The story even reached the ears of

Richard Steele, who featured it in his

periodical, *The Tatler.* Eventually, <u>he</u>
              5

<u>became</u> the subject of a best-selling
  5

book . . .

5. A. NO CHANGE
   B. Selkirk became
   C. his became
   D. he becomes

> **PERFECT SCORE TIP**
>
> " Ambiguous pronouns are never right. If *he* or *they* are used, make sure it is obvious whom these pronouns are describing. "

The *intended* meaning of the pronoun *he* here is "Selkirk." But what's the closest male name to the pronoun? Richard Steele, the publisher of *The Tatler.* Your job is to make it clear whom the pronoun is returning to. Make it clear! Choice B takes care of the problem by naming Selkirk explicitly. C would create a sense problem—his *what* became the subject of a book? Meanwhile, D shifts the verb tense into the present, which makes no sense since this book was written over 250 years ago!

Mistakes of sense often involve pronouns. Make a habit of checking every underlined pronoun as you go along. What does the pronoun stand for? Can you tell? If not, there's an error. Does it make sense? If not, there's an error. Make sure it's perfectly clear to what or to whom all pronouns refer.

LOGIC

 WORD CHOICE

 SENTENCE SENSE

 ORGANIZATION

Remember when we talked about structural clues back in Reading Workout 1? (C'mon, it wasn't *that* long ago!) Structural clues are words that signal where an author is going in a piece of writing. They show how all of the pieces logically fit together. If the author uses the structural clue *on the other hand*, that means a contrast is coming up; if he or she uses the clue *moreover*, that means that a continuation is coming up—an addition that is more or less in the same vein as what came before.

Many ACT English questions mix up the logic of a piece of writing by giving you the wrong structural clue or other logic word. That's what happened in **Question 10:**

> . . . <u>Because of</u> its basis in fact,
>   10
> *Robinson Crusoe* is often regarded as
>
> the first major novel in English literature.

10. F.   NO CHANGE
    G.   Despite
    H.   Resulting from
    J.   As a consequence of

> **EXPERT TUTOR TIP**
>
> " The ACT test makers love to include questions about transitions between clauses, sentences, and paragraphs. Learn to recognize the logic and direction of a piece of writing—this will help you on the English and Reading tests. "

As written, this sentence means that *Crusoe* was regarded as the first major novel because it was based on fact. But that makes no sense. If it was based on fact, that would work against its being regarded as a novel. There's a contrast between "basis in fact" (which implies nonfiction) and "first major novel" (which implies fiction). To show that contrast logically, you need a contrast word like *despite*. That's why G is correct here.

Question 6 also tests logic:

. . . the subject of a best-selling book, *A*

Cruizing Voyage Round the World, by

Woodes Rogers. <u>And while</u> there is
                        6
some evidence that Defoe, a journalist,

may actually have interviewed Selkirk

personally, most literary historians

believe that it was the reprinting of the

Rogers book in 1718 that served as the

real stimulus for Defoe's novel.

6. F.   NO CHANGE
   G.   But since
   H.   And therefore
   J.   OMIT the underlined portion
        and start the sentence with
        There.

The structural clue should convey a sense of continuation from the preceding sentence (since we're still talking about the book *A Cruizing Voyage*) and a sense of contrast with the latter part of the sentence. Even though Defoe may have interviewed Selkirk, many believe Defoe's main source was the book by Rogers. *And* provides the continuation; *while* provides the needed contrast, making NO CHANGE the correct answer.

Answers G and H have *since* and *therefore* which are cause-and-effect words, which make no sense in context. Answer J omits key words and creates a run-on sentence—two independent clauses that are combined improperly. Remember, don't pick OMIT simply because it's there!

> **PERFECT SCORE TIP**
>
> ❝ Take out surrounding words and just say the subject and the verb. Other words can hide verb mistakes, but a verb that doesn't match its subject will become clearer if you just say it after its subject. ❞

VERB USAGE

 VERB TENSE

 WORD CHOICE

 SENTENCE SENSE

Rules at work:

1. Use the simplest tense possible. In most cases, the present, past, and future tenses are all you need.

2.   Change tenses only if the sentence doesn't make sense as written.

3.   Make sure the verb is singular if it has a singular subject and plural if the subject is plural.

Verbs have an annoying habit of changing form depending on who's doing the action and when that person is doing it. Example: "I *hate* verbs; he hates verbs; and we both have hated verbs ever since we were kids." **You have to be very careful to make sure verbs match their subject and the tense of the surrounding context.**

. . . In *Crusoe*, which <u>has been published</u>
                                    7
in 1719, Defoe took substantial liberties

with the Selkirk story.

7. A.   NO CHANGE
    B.   was published
    C.   had been published
    D.   will have been published

The publication of *Robinson Crusoe* is something that took place in 1719—the past, in other words. So the underlined portion, which puts the verb in the present perfect tense, is flawed. Choices C and D, meanwhile, would put the verb into bizarre tenses normally used to convey a complex time relationship. C makes it seem as if publication of the book happened before Defoe took his liberties with the story. But that's nonsensical. The liberties were taken in the writing of the book. D, meanwhile, does strange things with the time sequence. The book was published in the past; Defoe also took his substantial liberties in the same past. So just use the simple past tense, choice B.

TONE

 WORD CHOICE

 WRITING STRATEGY

Rule at work: Every writer of an ACT English passage has a voice, or tone. This voice is usually either casual (conversational) or factual (informational). Be sure to make choices that fit the author's voice.

As we said earlier, the passages in the English subject test vary in tone. Some are formal; others are informal. Usually, you'll know which is which without having to think about it. If a passage contains slang, a few exclamation points, and a joke or two, the tone is informal; if it sounds like something a Latin instructor would say, it's probably formal.

Good style requires that the tone of a piece of writing be at the same level throughout. Sometimes the underlined portion might not fit the tone of the rest of the passage. If so, it's up to you to correct it. Look at **Question 13:**

. . . Meanwhile, Selkirk himself never <u>gave</u>

13

<u>a hoot about returning</u> to the island

13

that had made him famous.

13. A. NO CHANGE

    B. evinced himself as desirous of returning

    C. could whip up a head of steam to return

    D. expressed any desire to return

Selkirk "never gave a hoot" about going back? No way! Slang doesn't belong in this passage. Choose answer D because it uses a straightforward, factual tone that fits the passage. The NO CHANGE choice is silly; Choice B is too wordy and formal. Choice C is also slang.

NONSTANDARD-FORMAT QUESTIONS

 WRITING STRATEGY

 ORGANIZATION

The Nonstandard-Format Questions ask about the passage as a whole. Keep in mind the main point of the passage—the "gist"—as well as the overall tone and style. For an entire passage to "make sense," it has to be consistent throughout, both in content and in tone and style.

JUDGING THE PASSAGE

Question 14 asks you to judge the passage. Was the last sentence an appropriate ending or not?

14. Considering the tone and subject matter of the preceding paragraphs, is the last sentence an appropriate way to end the essay?

    F. Yes, because it is necessary to shed some doubt on Defoe's creativity.

    G. Yes, because the essay is about the relationship between the real Selkirk and Defoe's fictionalized version of him.

    H. No, because there is nothing "bizarre" about Selkirk's story as it is related in the essay.

    J. No, because the focus of the essay is more on Selkirk himself than on Defoe's fictionalized version of him.

Think of the passage as a whole. It has been comparing Selkirk's real life with the one that Defoe made up for the character of Robinson Crusoe. Therefore, ending in this way, with an ironic reference wondering whether Defoe could have written a more fitting end to Selkirk's life, is perfectly appropriate. The answer to the question is yes (eliminating choices H and J). Choice G restates the point of the passage and is the best answer.

READING COMPREHENSION QUESTIONS

If you thought Question 15 looked like a Reading question hiding in the English part of the exam, you were right. As mentioned in ACT Basics, one reason that you should keep thinking about what the passage means—rather than focusing on picky rules of grammar or punctuation—is that **the English section includes Reading Comprehension Questions.**

15. This essay would be most appropriate as part of a:

    A. scholarly study of 18th-century maritime history.

    B. study of the geography of the islands off of Chile.

    C. history of privateering in the Pacific.

    D. popular history of English literature.

What was this passage principally about? How Defoe's *Robinson Crusoe* was loosely based on the life of a real shipwrecked sailor, Alexander Selkirk. Would that kind of thing belong in a study of geography (choice B)? No. The focus is on the fictionalization of a historical life, not on the physical features of the islands off Chile. The passage isn't principally about privateering or maritime history either, so C and A are wrong as well. This passage is about the relationship between a true story and a famous fictionalized story. And its tone isn't overly scholarly either. So it probably belongs in a popular history of English literature (choice D).

STRUCTURE AND PURPOSE

The English section will also have questions that test your grasp of overall structure and purpose in a piece of prose. The test makers scramble the order of the sentences

> **PERFECT SCORE TIP**
>
> " As I don't have time problems, I like to skim the entire English passage as I go as opposed to just focusing on the questions. This is very helpful when it is time for Nonstandard-Format English questions. "

in a paragraph (or of the paragraphs in a passage). The question then asks you to decide on the best order for the scrambled parts. Take a look at **Question 16:**

[1] Only recently has new evidence led many scientists to question the accepted division between birds and dinosaurs. [2] Traditionally, they have been placed in entirely separate classes within the subphylum *Vertebrata*. [3] Birds and dinosaurs don't have many obvious similarities. [4] Birds formed the class *Aves*, while dinosaurs constituted two orders, *Saurischia* and *Ornithischia*, within the class *Reptilia*.

16. To best fulfill the author's purpose, the order of the sentences in the paragraph above should be:

F. 1, 2, 3, 4

G. 2, 3, 4, 1

H. 3, 2, 4, 1

J. 3, 2, 1, 4

Here again, the goal is to make it make sense. All of the sentences in this paragraph relate to the differences between birds and dinosaurs. Sentence 3 best introduces this idea. Notice that two of the answer choices begin with Sentence 3—H and J. The other two can be eliminated.

Look again at the logic of the sentences. Since Sentence 4 elaborates on the distinction introduced in Sentence 2, Sentence 4 should immediately follow Sentence 2. Only H has them in that order, so H looks like the answer.

Just to check, you'll want to read the entire paragraph in the order suggested by H. And if you do, you'll notice that the paragraph makes perfect sense, with Sentence 3 introducing the topic, Sentences 2 and 4 showing how that topic has been traditionally viewed, and Sentence 1 coming in naturally to show how that traditional view is no longer valid.

For questions like this, it's usually a good idea to start by trying to figure out the first (and sometimes the last) sentence, because first and last sentences usually have the most obvious functions in an ACT-style paragraph.

EXPERT TUTOR TIP

" Don't know where to start on an organization question? Look at the answers that begin with the same number (H and J), compare the two, and eliminate one or both answers. "

IF YOU LEARNED ONLY TWO THINGS IN THIS CHAPTER . . .

1. Consider the meaning of a sentence. If it doesn't make sense, there's probably a grammatical mistake. The correct answer will make sense.

2. Nonstandard-Format Questions ask you to judge the passage and consider it as a whole. You may be asked about paragraph structure and function.

CHAPTER 9: MATH WORKOUT 2: SHAKE IT UP!

SMARTPOINTS COVERED IN THIS CHAPTER

VARIABLE MANIPULATION	
PLANE GEOMETRY	
COORDINATE GEOMETRY	
PROPORTIONS AND PROBABILITY	
OPERATIONS	
NUMBER PROPERTIES	

The main idea of Math Workout 1 was: don't jump in headfirst and start crunching numbers until you've given a problem some thought. Make sure you know what you're doing—*and* that what you're doing won't take too long.

As we saw in Math Workout 1, sometimes you'll know how to proceed as soon as you understand the question. A good number of ACT algebra and coordinate geometry questions are straightforward textbook questions you may already be prepared for.

GO ONLINE

❝ Get more coordinate geometry practice with the online workshop and quiz available through your online syllabus. ❞

TEN TEXTBOOK ALGEBRA AND COORDINATE GEOMETRY QUESTIONS

 VARIABLE MANIPULATION

 COORDINATE GEOMETRY

When you take the ACT, you can be sure you'll see some of the following questions with only slight variations. You'll find answers and explanations for these questions in the 100 Key Math Concepts for the ACT section.

1. **Evaluate an algebraic expression.** (*See 100 Key Math Concepts for the ACT, #52*)

   Example: If $x = -2$, then $x^2 + 5x - 6 = ?$

2. **Multiply binomials.** (*See 100 Key Math Concepts for the ACT, #56*)

   Example: $(x + 3)(x + 4) = ?$

3. **Factor a polynomial.** (*See 100 Key Math Concepts for the ACT, #61*)

   Example: What is the complete factorization of $x^2 - 5x + 6$?

4. **Simplify an algebraic fraction.** (*See 100 Key Math Concepts for the ACT, #62*)

   Example: For all $x \neq \pm 63$, $\dfrac{x^2 - x - 12}{x^2 - 9} = ?$

5. **Solve a linear equation.** (*See 100 Key Math Concepts for the ACT, #63*)

   Example: If $5x - 12 = -2x + 9$, then $x = ?$

6. **Solve a quadratic equation.** (*See 100 Key Math Concepts for the ACT, #66*)

   Example: If $x^2 + 12 = 7x$, what are the two possible values of x?

7. **Solve a system of equations.** (*See 100 Key Math Concepts for the ACT, #67*)

   Example: If $4x + 3y = 8$, and $x + y = 3$, what is the value of x?

8. **Solve an inequality.** (*See 100 Key Math Concepts for the ACT, #69*)

   Example: What are all the values of x for which $-5x + 7 < -3$?

9. **Find the distance between two points in the (x, y) coordinate plane.** (*See 100 Key Math Concepts for the ACT, #71*)

   Example: What is the distance between the points with (x, y) coordinates $(-2, 2)$ and $(1, -2)$?

PERFECT SCORE TIP

❝ Basic algebra is a must-know for ACT Math. If any of these concepts seem unfamiliar to you, be sure to read about them in the 100 Key Math Concepts. ❞

10. **Find the slope of a line from its equation.** (*See 100 Key Math Concepts for the ACT, #73*)
    Example: What is the slope of the line with the equation $2x + 3y = 4$?

These questions are all so straightforward and traditional they could have come out of a high school algebra textbook. Do these questions the way you were taught. In case you'd like to review them, you'll find all the standard approaches succinctly summarized in *100 Key Math Concepts for the ACT*. We're not so concerned in these workouts with problems you may already know how to solve. Here we're going to focus on several situations where the quick and reliable solution method is not so obvious.

THREE WAYS TO SHAKE IT UP

It's bound to happen at some point on test day. You look at a math problem and you don't see what to do. Don't freak out. Think about the problem for a few seconds before you give up. **When you don't see the quick and reliable approach right away, shake the problem up a little.** Try one of these "shake-it-up" techniques:

1. **Restate.**

2. **Remove the disguise.**

3. **Try eyeballing.**

1. RESTATE THE PROBLEM

Often, the way to get over that stymied feeling is to change your perspective. Have you ever watched people playing Scrabble®? In their search to form high-scoring words with the letters on their seven tiles, they continually move the tiles around in their racks. Sometimes a good word becomes apparent only after rearranging the tiles. One might not see the seven-letter word in this arrangement:

REBAGLA

But reverse the tiles and a word almost reveals itself:

ALGABER

The tiles can spell ALGEBRA.

The same gimmick works on the ACT too. **When you get stuck, try looking at the problem from a different angle.** Try rearranging the numbers, or changing fractions to decimals, or factoring, or multiplying out, or redrawing the diagram, or anything that might give you the fresh perspective you need to uncover a good solution method.

Here's a question you might not know what to do with at first glance:

OPERATIONS

Example

1. Which of the following is equivalent to $7^{77} - 7^{76}$?

    A. 7
    B. 7^{77-76}
    C. $7^{77 \div 76}$
    D. $7(77 - 76)$
    E. $7^{76}(6)$

Here's a hint: *Think of an easier problem testing the same principles.* The important thing to look for is the basic relationships involved—here, we have exponents and subtraction. That subtraction sign causes trouble, because none of the ordinary rules of exponents (see 100 Key Math Concepts for the ACT, #47–48) seem to apply when there is subtraction of "unlike" terms.

Another hint: How would you work with $x^2 - x$? Most test takers could come up with another expression for $x^2 - x$: they'd factor to $x(x - 1)$. Or if the problem asked for $x^{77} - x^{76}$, they'd factor to $x^{76}(x - 1)$. The rule is no different for 7 than for x. Factoring out the 7^{76} gives you: $7^{76}(7 - 1)$, which is $7^{76}(6)$, or choice E.

Sometimes an ACT algebra question will include an expression that isn't of much use in its given form. The breakthrough in such a case may be to restate the expression by either simplifying it or factoring it.

 NUMBER PROPERTIES

Example

2. If $\dfrac{x}{2} - \dfrac{x}{6}$ is an integer, which of the following statements must be true?

    F. x is positive.
    G. x is odd.
    H. x is even.
    J. x is a multiple of 3.
    K. x is a multiple of 6.

Re-express: $\dfrac{x}{2} - \dfrac{x}{6} = \dfrac{3x}{6} - \dfrac{x}{6} = \dfrac{2x}{6} = \dfrac{x}{3}$

This form of the expression tells us a lot more. If $\dfrac{x}{3}$ is an integer, then x is equal to 3 times an integer:

$$\frac{x}{3} = \text{an integer}$$

$$x = 3 \times (\text{an integer})$$

In other words, x is a multiple of 3, choice J.

2. Remove the Disguise

Sometimes it's hard to see the quick and reliable method immediately because the true nature of the problem is hidden behind a disguise. Look at this example:

 Variable Manipulation

Example

3. What are the (x, y) coordinates of the point of intersection of the line representing the equation $5x + 2y = 4$ and the line representing the equation $x - 2y = 8$?

   A. (2, 3)
   B. (−2, 3)
   C. (2, −3)
   D. (−3, 2)
   E. (3, −2)

$2y = -5x + 4 \qquad y = \frac{-5}{2}x + 4$

$-2y = -x + 8$

$y = \frac{x - 8}{2}$

This may look like a coordinate geometry question, but do you really have to graph the lines to find the point of intersection? Remember, the ACT is looking for creative thinkers, not mindless calculators! Think about it for a moment—what's the special significance of the point of intersection, the one point that the two lines have in common? That's the one point whose coordinates will satisfy *both* equations.

So what we realize now is that this is not a coordinate geometry question at all, but a "system-of-equations" question. All it's really asking you to do is solve the pair of equations for x and y. The question has nothing to do with slopes, intercepts, axes, or quadrants. It's a pure algebra question in disguise.

Now that we know we're looking at a system of equations, the method of solution presents itself more clearly. The first equation has $a + 2y$, and the second equation has $a - 2y$. If we just add the equations, the y terms cancel:

$$\begin{array}{r} 5x + 2y = 4 \\ \underline{x - 2y = 8} \\ 6x \quad\;\; = 12 \end{array}$$

If $6x = 12$, then $x = 2$. Plug that back into either of the original equations and you'll find that $y = -3$. The point of intersection is (2, −3), and the answer is C.

> **EXPERT TUTOR TIP**
>
> " Although this question turned out not to be a real coordinate geometry problem, the test makers do have a soft spot in their hearts for coordinate geometry. Typically 8 or more of the 60 Math questions involve coordinate geometry. It's hard to get a top score without getting at least some of these geometry questions right. Use 100 Key Math Concepts for the ACT #71–77 to review the relevant rules and formulas. "

> **EXPERT TUTOR TIP**
>
> " When you have a system of equations, you can solve it by:
> - Combination
> - Substitution
> - Graphing
>
> This example demonstrates combination. "

VARIABLE MANIPULATION

Example

4. A geometer uses the following formula to estimate the area A of the shaded portion of a circle as shown in the figure below when only the height h and the length of the chord c are known:

$$A = \frac{2ch}{3} + \frac{h^3}{2c}$$

What is the geometer's estimate of the area, in square inches, of the shaded region if the height is 2 inches and the length of the chord is 6 inches?

F. 6

G. $6\frac{2}{3}$

H. $7\frac{1}{2}$

J. $8\frac{2}{3}$

K. 12

At first glance, this looks like a horrendously esoteric geometry question. Who ever heard of such a formula? But when you think about the question a bit, you realize that you don't really have to understand the formula. You certainly don't have to remember it—it's right there in the question.

In fact, this is not really a geometry question at all. It's just an "evaluate the algebraic expression" question in disguise. All you have to do is plug the given values $h = 2$ and $c = 6$ into the formula:

$$A = \frac{2ch}{3} + \frac{h^3}{2c}$$

$$= \frac{2(6)(2)}{3} + \frac{(2)^3}{2(6)}$$

$$= 8 + \frac{2}{3} = 8\frac{2}{3}$$

Choice J is correct.

The people who wrote this question wanted you to freak out at first sight and give up. Don't give up on a question too quickly just because it looks like it's testing something you never saw before. In many such cases, it's really a familiar problem in disguise.

3. Stuck? Try Eyeballing

There is another simple but powerful strategy that should give you at least a 50-50 chance on almost any diagram question: **When in doubt, use your eyes. Trust common sense and careful thinking; don't worry if you've forgotten most of the geometry you ever knew.** For almost half of all diagram questions, you can get a reasonable answer without solving anything: just eyeball it.

The Math directions say, "Illustrative figures are NOT necessarily drawn to scale," but in fact they almost **always** are. You're never really *supposed* to just eyeball the figure, but it makes a lot more sense than random guessing. Occasionally, eyeballing can help you narrow down the choices.

Here's a difficult geometry question that you might just decide to eyeball:

 PLANE GEOMETRY

Example

6. In the figure below, points *A*, *B*, and *C* lie on a circle centered at *O*. Triangle *AOC* is equilateral, and the length of *OC* is 3 inches. What is the length, in inches, of arc *ABC* ?

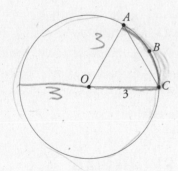

   F.   3
   G.   π
   H.   2π
   J.   3π
   K.   6π

STEP 1: UNDERSTAND

There's an "equilateral" triangle that connects the center and two points on the circumference of a circle. You're looking for the length of the arc that goes from A to C.

STEP 2: ANALYZE

What you're "supposed" to do to answer this question is recall and apply the formula for the length of an arc. But suppose you don't remember that formula (most people don't). Should you give up and take a wild guess?

No. You can eyeball it. If you understand the question well enough to realize that "equilateral" means all sides are equal, then you know immediately that side $\overline{AC}$ is 3 inches long. Now look at arc ABC compared to side $\overline{AC}$. Suppose you were an ant, and you had to walk from A to C. If you walked along line segment $\overline{AC}$, it would be a 3-inch trip. About how long a walk would it be along arc ABC? Clearly more, but not much more, than 3 inches.

STEP 3: SELECT

Now look at the answer choices. Choice F is no good: you know the arc is more than 3 inches. All the other choices are in terms of π. Just think of π as "a bit more than 3," and you will quickly see that only one answer choice is in the right ballpark. Choice G—π—would be "a bit more than 3," which sounds pretty good. Choice H—2π—would be "something more than 6." Already that's way too big. Choices J and K are even bigger. It sure looks like the answer has to be G—and it is.

Not many ACT students would be able to solve question 6 the textbook way. If you could, great! Solving the problem is **always** more reliable than eyeballing. But when you *don't* know how to solve a diagram problem, or if you think it would take forever to get an answer, eyeballing and eliminating answer choices sure beat wild guessing. Sometimes, as with question 6, you might even be able to narrow the choices down to the one that's probably correct.

TYPICAL STORY PROBLEMS

We find that about one-third of the questions on the Math test are Story Problems. Though some Story Problems present unique situations that must be analyzed on the spot, others are just variations on familiar themes.

GO ONLINE

If you have forgotten any of the geometry terms discussed in this workout, look them up in the Math Glossary of your online syllabus.

EXPERT TUTOR TIP

Answer choices are in order. If the first number you try doesn't work, the process of plugging in that first number might tell you whether you'll need a smaller or a larger number. So when back-solving, start with the middle choice (C or H) to be safe.

PERCENT PROBLEMS

In Percent Problems, you're usually given two numbers and asked to find a third. The key is to identify what you have and what you're looking for. In other words identify the part, the percent, and the whole.

Put the numbers and the unknown into the general form:

Part = Percent × Whole

Usually the part is associated with the word *is*, and the whole is associated with the word *of*.

 PROPORTIONS AND PROBABILITY

Example

6. In a group of 250 students, 40 are seniors. What percentage of the group is seniors?

   A. 1.6%
   B. 6.25%
   C. 10%
   D. 16%
   E. 40%

The percent is what we're looking for ("What percentage . . ."); the whole is 250 (". . . of the group . . ."); and the part is 40 (". . . are seniors"). Plug these into the general formula:

Part = Percent × Whole

$$40 = 250x$$
$$x = \frac{40}{250} = .16 = 16\%$$

The answer is D.

Many ACT Percent Problems concern percent change. To increase a number by a certain percent, calculate that percent of the original number and add it on. To decrease a number by a certain percent, calculate that percent of the original number and then subtract. For example, to answer the question, "What number is 30 percent greater than 80?" first find 30 percent of 80—that's 24—and add that on to 80: 80 + 24 = 104.

The ACT has ways of complicating percent change problems. Especially tricky are problems with multiple changes, such as a percent increase followed by another percent increase, or a percent increase followed by a percent decrease.

PROPORTIONS AND PROBABILITY

Example

7. If a positive number is increased by 70 percent, and then the result is decreased by 50 percent, which of the following accurately describes the net change?

    F.   a 20 percent decrease

    G.   a 15 percent decrease

    H.   a 12 percent increase

    J.   a 20 percent increase

    K.   a 120 percent increase

To get a handle on this one, pick a number. Suppose the original number is 100. After a 70 percent increase it rises to 170. That number, 170, is decreased by 50 percent, which means it's reduced by half to 85. The net change from 100 to 85 is a 15 percent decrease—choice G.

AVERAGE PROBLEMS

Instead of giving you a list of values to plug into the average formula, ACT Average Problems often put a slight spin on the question. They tell you the average of a group of terms and ask you to find the value of the missing term. Here's a classic example:

 PROPORTIONS AND PROBABILITY

Example

8. To earn a B for the semester, Linda needs an average of at least 80 on the five tests. Her average for the first four test scores is 79. What is the minimum score she must get on the fifth test to earn a B for the semester?

    A.   80

    B.   81

    C.   82

    D.   83

    E.   84

The key to almost every Average Problem is to use the sum. Sums can be combined much more readily than averages. An average of 80 on five tests is more usefully thought of as a combined score of 400. To get a B for the semester, Linda's five test scores have to add up to 400 or more. The first four scores add up to $4 \times 79 = 316$. She needs another 84 to get that 316 up to 400. The answer is E.

> **PERFECT SCORE TIP**
>
> ❝ One of the most common mistakes on percentages is thinking that taking 25 percent off twice is the same as taking 50 percent off—it is not. To avoid this, try pretending you began with 100 dollars and then doing the percentage manipulations in the question. ❞

WEIGHTED AVERAGE PROBLEMS

Another spin ACT test makers put on Average Problems is to give you an average for part of a group and an average for the rest of the group and then ask for the combined average.

 PROPORTIONS AND PROBABILITY

Example

9. In a class of 10 boys and 15 girls, the boys' average score on the final exam was 80 and the girls' average score was 90. What was the average score for the whole class?

    F. 83

    G. 84

    H. 85

    J. 86

    K. 87

(handwritten: 800, 1350)

Don't just average 80 and 90 to get 85. That would work only if the class had exactly the same number of girls as boys. In this case, there are more girls, so they carry more "weight" in the overall class average. In other words, the class average should be somewhat closer to 90 (the girls' average) than to 80 (the boys' average).

As usual with averages, the key is to use the sum. The average score for the whole class is the total of the 25 individual scores divided by 25. We don't have 25 scores to add up, but we can use the boys' average and the girls' average to get two subtotals.

If 10 boys average 80, then their 10 scores add up to 10×80, or 800. If 15 girls average 90, then their 15 scores add up to 15×90, or 1,350. Add the boys' total to the girls' total: $800 + 1,350 = 2,150$. That's the class total, which can be divided by 25 to get the class average: $\frac{2,150}{25} = 86$. The answer is J.

PROBABILITY PROBLEMS

Probabilities are part-to-whole ratios. The whole is the total number of possible outcomes. The part is the number of "favorable" outcomes. For example, if a drawer contains two black ties and five other ties, and you want a black tie, the total number of possible outcomes is 7 (the total number of ties), and the number of "favorable" outcomes is 2 (the number of black ties). The probability of choosing a black tie at random is $\frac{2}{7}$.

WHAT TO DO NEXT

Because more than half the Math questions on the ACT involve algebra, it's a good idea to solidify your understanding of the basics before test day. Focus on #52–70 in 100 Key Math Concepts for the ACT. Keep things in perspective. **Geometry questions are important, too, but algebra questions are more important.**

IF YOU LEARNED ONLY THREE THINGS IN THIS CHAPTER . . .

1. You should be familiar with the ten textbook algebra and coordinate geometry problems.

2. Some ACT Math problems will be disguised so that their method of solution isn't obvious.

3. Be familiar with the formulas for calculating percentages and averages.

CHAPTER 10: READING WORKOUT 2: LOOK IT UP!

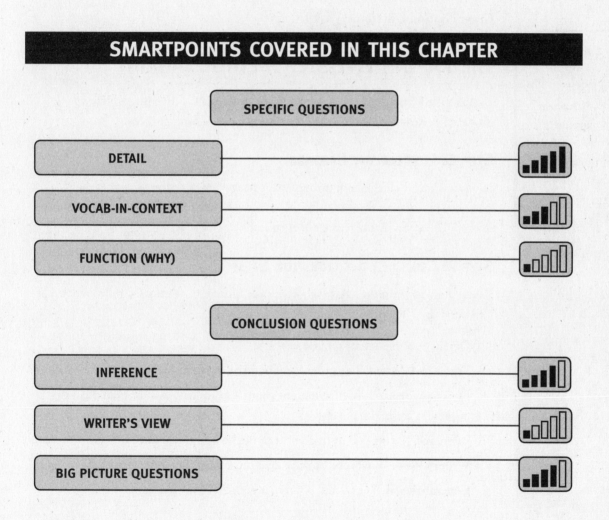

SMARTPOINTS COVERED IN THIS CHAPTER

SPECIFIC QUESTIONS

DETAIL

VOCAB-IN-CONTEXT

FUNCTION (WHY)

CONCLUSION QUESTIONS

INFERENCE

WRITER'S VIEW

BIG PICTURE QUESTIONS

In Reading Workout 1, we discussed general strategies for approaching ACT Reading. Now let's look more closely at the types of questions you'll encounter.

The three main types of Reading questions are:

Specific Questions

Detail

Vocab-in-Context

Function (Why)

Conclusion Questions

Inference

Writer's View

Generalization Questions

THE KAPLAN FIVE-STEP METHOD (AGAIN)

Don't forget to use the Kaplan Five-Step Method for ACT Reading which we discussed in Reading Workout 1. Here's a reminder of how it works:

STEP 1: PREREAD THE PASSAGE

In other words, quickly work through the passage before trying to answer the questions in less than three minutes. Read actively, and assemble a mental road map or overall idea of how the passage is organized.

STEP 2: CONSIDER THE QUESTION STEM

Before plunging into the answer choices, take a moment to understand what kind of question it is. They are:

Detail: Specific "what" questions

Vocab-in-Context: The meaning of word or words in context

Function: Specific "why" questions about a word, sentence, or example—the purpose it has in the passage

Inference: Asking you to read between the lines of the passage

Writer's View: What tone of voice does the author use?

Generalization: The overall point or argument of the passage

STEP 3: REFER TO THE PASSAGE

You don't need to refer to the whole passage. Just refer to the passage by finding the place where the answer to a question can be found. Sometimes a line reference will be included in the question; otherwise, rely on your road map of the passage.

STEP 4: ANSWER THE QUESTION IN YOUR OWN WORDS

Do this before looking at the answer choices.

STEP 5: MATCH YOUR ANSWER WITH ONE OF THE CHOICES

With an answer in mind, it'll be easier to spot the best choice.

IMPORTANT QUESTION TYPES

Try the following typical ACT nonfiction passage, this one from the Humanities. Afterward, we'll discuss selected questions from this set as examples of Specific Detail, Inference, and Big Picture Questions.

PASSAGE II

Tragedy was the invention of the Greeks. In their Golden Age, the fifth century before Christ, they produced the world's greatest dramatists, new forms
Line of tragedy and comedy that have been models ever
(5) since, and a theatre that every age goes back to for rediscovery of some basic principles . . . .

Since it derived from primitive religious rites, with masks and ceremonial costumes, and made use of music, dance, and poetry, the Greek drama was at
(10) the opposite pole from the modern realistic stage. In fact, probably no other theatre in history has made fuller use of the intensities of art. The masks, made of painted linen, wood, and plaster, brought down from primitive days the atmosphere of gods, heroes,
(15) and demons. Our nineteenth- and twentieth-century grandfathers thought masks must have been very artificial. Today, however, we appreciate their exciting intensity and can see that in a large theatre they were indispensable. If they allowed no fleeting
(20) change of expression during a single episode, they could give for each episode in turn more intense expression than any human face could. When Oedipus comes back with bleeding eyes, the new mask could be more terrible than any facial makeup
(25) the audience could endure, yet in its sculpted intensity more beautiful than a real face.

Most essential of all intensities, and hardest for us to understand, was the chorus. Yet many playwrights today are trying to find some equivalent to do for a
(30) modern play what the chorus did for the Greeks. During the episodes played by the actors, the chorus would only provide a background of group response, enlarging and reverberating the emotions of the actors, sometimes protesting and opposing
(35) but in general serving as ideal spectators to stir and lead the reactions of the audience. But between episodes, with the actors out of the way, the chorus took over. We have only the words, not the music or dance, and some translations of the odes are in such
(40) formal, old-fashioned language that it is hard to guess that they were accompanied by vigorous, sometimes even wild dances and symbolic actions that filled an orchestra which in some cities was sixty to ninety feet in diameter. Sometimes the cho-
(45) rus expressed simple horror or lament. Sometimes it chanted and acted out, in unison and in precise formations of rows and lines, the acts of violence the characters were enacting offstage. When Phaedra rushes offstage in *Hippolytus* to hang herself from
(50) the rafters, the members of the chorus, all fifteen of them, perform in mime and chant the act of tying the rope and swinging from the rafters. Sometimes the chorus tells or reenacts an incident of history or legend that throws light on the situation in the play.
(55) Sometimes the chorus puts into specific action what is a general intention in the mind of the main character. When Oedipus resolves to hunt out the guilty person and cleanse the city, he is speaking metaphorically, but the chorus invokes the gods of
(60) vengeance and dances a wild pursuit.

On the printed page, the choral odes seem static and formal, lyric and philosophical, emotional letdowns that punctuate the series of episodes, like

(65) intermissions between two acts of a play. The reader
who skips the odes can get the main points of the
play. A few are worth reading as independent poems,
notably the famous one in *Antigone* beginning,
"Many are the wonders of the world, but none is
(70) more wonderful than man." Some modern acting
versions omit the chorus or reduce it to a few background figures. Yet to the Greeks the odes were certainly more than mere poetic interludes: the wild
Dionysian words and movements evoked primitive
(75) levels of the subconscious and at the same time
served to transform primitive violence into charm
and beauty and to add philosophical reflections on
the meaning of human destiny.

For production today, we can only improvise
(80) some partial equivalent. In Athens the entire population was familiar with choral performances. Every
year each of the tribes entered a dithyramb in a
contest, rehearsing five hundred men and boys for
weeks. Some modern composers have tried to write

(85) dramatic music for choruses: the most notable
examples are the French composer Darius Milhaud,
in the primitive rhythms, shouts, and chants of his
operatic version of the *Oresteia*; George Gershwin, in
the Negro funeral scenes of *Porgy and Bess*; and Kurt
(90) Weill, in the African choruses for *Lost in the Stars*,
the musical dramatization of Alan Paton's novel,
Cry, the Beloved Country. For revivals of Greek
tragedies we have not dared use much music beyond
a few phrases half shouted, half sung, and drum-
(95) beats and suggestive melodies in the background.

From *Invitation to the Theatre*, Third Edition, copyright © 1985
by George Kernodle. Reprinted by permission of Wadsworth, a
division of Thomson Learning: www.thomsonlearning.com.

Fax 800-730-2215.

A quick preread of the passage should have given you a sense of its general organization:

- First paragraph: introduces the topic of Greek tragedy
- Second paragraph: discusses use of masks (artificial but intense)
- Third paragraph: discusses use of chorus (also artificial but intense)
- Fourth paragraph: expands discussion to choral odes
- Fifth paragraph: concludes with discussion of how Greek tragedy is performed today, and how it has influenced some modern art

That's really all the road map you need going into the questions. Aside from that, you should take away the author's main point: Greek tragedy included many artificial devices, but these devices allowed it to rise to a high level of intensity.

1. Combined with the passage's additional information, the fact that some Greek orchestras were sixty to ninety feet across suggests that:

   A. few spectators were able to see the stage.

   B. no one performer could dominate a performance.

   C. choruses and masks helped overcome the distance between actors and audience.

   D. Greek tragedies lacked the emotional force of modern theatrical productions.

2. The phrase "fuller use of the intensities of art" (line 12) most nearly means:

   F. employment of brightly illuminated effects.

   G. good use of powerful, dramatic effects of music, dance, and poetry.

   H. the enjoyment of strong elements of effects on stage.

   J. the utilization of dramatic interactions.

3. The description of the chorus's enactment of Phaedra's offstage suicide (lines 48–52) shows that, in contrast to modern theater, ancient Greek theater was:

   A. more violent.

   B. more concerned with satisfying an audience.

   C. more apt to be historically accurate.

   D. less concerned with a realistic portrayal of events.

4. It can be inferred that one consequence of the Greeks' use of masks was that:

   F. the actors often had to change masks between episodes.

   G. the characters in the play could not convey emotion.

   H. the actors wearing masks played non-speaking roles.

   J. good acting ability was not important to the Greeks.

5. Which of the following is supported by the information in the second paragraph (lines 7–26)?

A. Masks in Greek drama combined artistic beauty with emotional intensity.

B. The use of masks in Greek drama was better appreciated in the nineteenth century than it is now.

C. Masks in Greek drama were used to portray gods but never human beings.

D. Contemporary scholars seriously doubt the importance of masks to Greek theater.

6. The author indicates in lines 57–58 that Oedipus's resolution "to hunt out the guilty person and cleanse the city" was:

F. at odds with what he actually does later in the performance.

G. misinterpreted by the chorus.

H. dramatized by the actions of the chorus.

J. angrily condemned by the chorus.

7. According to the passage, when actors were present on stage, the chorus would:

A. look on silently as spectators.

B. inevitably agree with the actors' actions.

C. communicate to the audience solely through mime.

D. react to the performance as an audience might.

8. The main point of the fifth paragraph (lines 61–77) is that choral odes:

F. should not be performed by modern choruses.

G. have a meaning and beauty that are lost in modern adaptations.

H. can be safely ignored by a modern-day reader.

J. are only worthwhile in *Antigone*.

9. The passage suggests that modern revivals of Greek tragedies "have not dared use much music" (line 93) because:

A. modern instruments would appear out of place.

B. to do so would require a greater understanding of how choral odes were performed.

C. music would distract the audience from listening to the words of choral odes.

D. such music is considered far too primitive for modern audiences.

10. The author discusses *Porgy and Bess* and *Lost in the Stars* in order to:

F. show how two modern plays reenact ancient Greek tragedies.

G. demonstrate the use of music in modern plays.

H. give examples of two modern-day playwrights who used musical choruses in their dramas.

J. illustrate how music evokes subconscious emotions in modern-day plays.

Now let's take a look at selected questions, which fall into three categories.

SPECIFIC QUESTIONS

 DETAIL

 VOCAB-IN-CONTEXT

 FUNCTION

Questions 2, 6, 7, and 10 above are typical Specific Questions. Some Specific Questions give you a line reference to help you out; others don't, forcing you either to start tearing your hair out (if you're an unprepared test taker) or else to seek out the answer based on your sense of how the passage is laid out (one of the two key reasons to preread the passage).

Question 2 is a Vocab-in-Context Question. This stem refers to a word or phrase in the passage and asks you to select the answer that is closest to the meaning in *context*.

Note: The best answer is not a direct definition of the words. Look instead for the answer that would make the most sense. To check your answer, plug it into the sentence.

Question 6 provides a line reference (lines 57–58), but to answer the question confidently, you should have also read a few lines *before* and a few lines *after* the cited lines. There you would have read: "Sometimes the chorus puts into action what is a general intention in the mind of the main character. When Oedipus resolves . . ." Clearly, the Oedipus example is meant to illustrate the point about the chorus acting out a character's intentions. So H is correct—they are "dramatizing" (or acting out) Oedipus's resolution. (By the way, G might have been tempting, but there's no evidence that the chorus is "misinterpreting," just that they're "putting a general intention into specific action.")

Question 7 is a Specific Question *without* a line reference. Such questions are common on the ACT, and they require that you have a good sense of the structure of the passage as a whole, so that you can locate the place where the question is answered. The mention of the chorus in the question should send you to paragraph 3. We have marked this paragraph with the ABC method we've discussed. A quick glance over the marked-up version leads you to the sentence that begins on line 31, where the author claims that the chorus serves to "lead the reactions of the audience"—captured by correct choice D.

Question 10 is another type of Specific Question: Function. These questions ask why an author uses a word, phrase, or detail in the passage. You can spot these

BE SMART!

❝ The answers are in the passage. Focus your attention on locating them. Your mind-set should be: "Find the answer," not "Remember the answer." Locate them using your trusty road map. ❞

questions because you'll see phrases like, "is used to," "is meant to," and "in order to" in the question stem.

Question 10 asks why the author mentions the modern plays *Porgy and Bess* and *Lost in the Stars* in the passage. It is important to remember that WHY something is discussed is different from WHAT is discussed. Choice H is the right answer.

Note: While G and J may be true, they are not the reason why the author mentions these plays. F is false—they are not reenactments of Greek tragedies.

INFERENCE QUESTIONS

INFERENCE

With Inference Questions, your job is to combine ideas logically to make an inference—something that's not stated explicitly in the passage but that is definitely said implicitly. Often, you'll see a word like *suggest, infer, inference,* or *imply* in the question stem to tip you off.

To succeed on Inference Questions, you have to "read between the lines." Common sense is your best tool here. You use various bits of information in the passage as evidence for your own logical conclusion.

Questions 1, 3, and **5** require that you combine information from more than one place in the passage. **Question 1** has no line references to help; a quick survey of the passage tells you that C is the only answer compatible with the passage. **Question 3** research might lead to a prediction of "the chorus emphasizes what's happening on stage," pointing you to answer D. **Question 5** research leads you to the key word *intensity*, which you examined previously for Question 2.

Note: The relationship between Question 2 and 5 is a good example of how answering one question can help you with the answer to another. Thus, you may find that if you skip a question the first time, you can answer it during a second pass.

Question 4 provides no line reference, but the mention of masks should have sent you to the second paragraph of the passage. Lines 19–20 explain that masks "allowed no fleeting change of expression during a single episode." Treat that as your first piece of evidence. Your second comes in lines 20–22: "they [the masks] could give for each episode in turn more intense expression than any human face could." Put those two pieces of evidence together—masks can't change expression *during* a single episode, but they can give expression for each episode in *turn*.

Clearly, the actors must have changed masks between episodes, so that they could express the different emotions that different episodes required. Choice F is correct.

PERFECT SCORE TIP

While Inference Questions will ask you to read between the lines, remember that they will never ask you to make conclusions outside the scope of the passage, so be sure all your answers have a basis in the reading.

EXPERT TUTOR TIP

Making inferences often requires that you combine bits of information from different parts of the passage. Common sense will then lead you to an appropriate inference—one that's not too extreme.

One warning: Keep your inferences as close to the passage as possible. Don't make wild inferential leaps. An inference should follow naturally and inevitably from the evidence provided in the passage.

BIG PICTURE QUESTIONS

 ### GENERALIZATION QUESTIONS

About one-third of the ACT Reading questions are Detail Questions and most of the rest are Inference Questions. But there are also a few questions that test your understanding of the theme, purpose, and organization of the passage as a whole. **Big Picture Questions tend to look for:**

- **Main point or purpose of a passage or part of a passage**
- **Author's attitude or tone**
- **Logic underlying the author's argument**
- **How ideas in different parts of the passage relate to each other**
- **Difference between fact and opinion**

One way to see the Big Picture is to read actively. As you read, ask yourself, "What's this all about? What's the point of this? Why is the author saying this?"

Question 8 asks for the main idea of a particular paragraph—namely, the fifth, which our general outline indicates is the paragraph about choral odes. Skimming that paragraph, you find reference to how the odes seem to us modern people—"static and formal" (lines 61–62), "like intermissions between two acts of a play" (lines 63–64). Later, the author states, by way of contrast (note the use of the clue word *yet*): "Yet to the Greeks the odes were certainly more than mere poetic interludes." Clearly, the author wants to contrast our modern static view of the odes with the Greeks' view of them as something more. That idea is best captured by choice G.

FIND AND PARAPHRASE . . . AND OTHER TIPS

The examples above show that your real task in Reading is not what you might expect. **Your main job is to find the answers.** Perhaps a better name for the Reading subtest would be "find and paraphrase." But students tend to think that their task in Reading is to "comprehend and remember." That's the wrong mind-set.

DON'T BE AFRAID TO SKIP

Now that you've done a couple full-length passages and questions, you've probably encountered at least a few questions that you found unanswerable. **What do you do**

EXPERT TUTOR TIP

"If you're still stumped on a Big Picture Question after reading the passage, try doing the Detail and Inference Questions first. They can help you fill in the Big Picture."

EXPERT TUTOR TIP

"A good way to distinguish fact from opinion is to picture yourself as a fact-checker for a newspaper. Is the point in question something you could verify in a book or with an expert? If not, it's probably not a fact."

PERFECT SCORE TIP

"I found skipping questions during the first pass the most useful in Reading. Don't spend too much time on one question the first time through."

if you can't find the answer in the passage, or if you can find it but don't understand, or if you do understand but can't see an answer choice that makes sense? Skip the question. Skipping is probably more important in Reading than in any other ACT subject test. Many students find it useful to skip as many as half of the questions on the first pass through a set of Reading questions. That's fine.

When you come back to a Reading question the second time, it usually makes sense to use the process of elimination. The first time around, you tried to find the *right* answer but you couldn't. So, now try to identify the three *wrong* answers. Eliminating three choices is slower than finding one right choice, so don't make it your main strategy for Reading. But it is a good way to try a second attack on a question.

Another thing to consider when attacking a question for a second time is that the right answer may have been hidden. Maybe it's written in an unexpected way, with different vocabulary. Or maybe there is another good way that you haven't thought of to answer the question. But remember that it's still important to avoid getting bogged down when you come back to a question. **Be willing to admit that there are some problems you just can't answer. Guess if you have to.**

Here's a key to the Greek tragedy passage so that you can check the answers to the questions not discussed above.

KEY TO PASSAGE II
(Nonfiction—Humanities)

	Answer	Refer to	Type	Comments
1.	C	Lines 17–19, 29–44	Inference	Q-stem emphasizes distance between audience and stage; masks and choruses help to "enlarge" the action so that it can be understood from a distance.
2.	G	Lines 7–22	Vocab-in-Context	Must make sense in context.
3.	D	Lines 48–52	Inference	Combine info from lines 7–10, 48–52, 72–77.
4.	F	Lines 19–22	Inference	Discussed above.
5.	A	Lines 7–26	Inference	Combine info from lines 10–12, 22–27.
6.	H	Lines 57–60	Detail	Don't overthink the answer.
7.	D	Lines 31–36	Detail	No line reference. Be careful.
8.	G	Lines 61–77	Big Picture	Which answer echoes the passage?
9.	B	Lines 91–94	Inference	Be sure to consult all your notes for the last paragraph.
10.	H	Lines 83–91	Function	"Some modern composers have tried to write dramatic music for choruses."

IF YOU LEARNED ONLY THREE THINGS IN THIS CHAPTER . . .

1. Preread the passage and make a road map: know what each paragraph is saying.

2. Refer to your road map when you attack the questions, and **always** refer back to the passage to find the answer.

3. Reading questions can ask about specific details of a passage, what a passage implies, and its overall structure and argument.

CHAPTER 11: SCIENCE WORKOUT 2: THINK LIKE A SCIENTIST

SMARTPOINTS COVERED IN THIS CHAPTER

FIGURE INTERPRETATION

SCIENTIFIC REASONING

In Science Workout 1, you learned that to succeed on the ACT Science subtest, you've got to be able to spot trends and patterns in the data of graphs and tables. But that's not all you need to do well. You've also got to learn how to think like a scientist. You don't have to know very much science (though it certainly helps), but you should at least be familiar with how scientists go about getting and testing knowledge.

HOW SCIENTISTS THINK

Scientists use two very different kinds of logic, which (to keep things nontechnical) we'll call:

- **General-to-Specific Thinking**
- **Specific-to-General Thinking**

GENERAL-TO-SPECIFIC

In some cases, scientists have already discovered a law of nature and wish to apply their knowledge to a specific case. For example, a scientist may wish to know how fast a pebble (call it Pebble A) will be falling when it hits the ground three seconds after being dropped. There is a law of physics from which it can be determined that on earth, falling objects accelerate at a rate of about 9.8 m/sec^2. The scientist could use this known general principle to calculate the specific information she needs:

PERFECT SCORE TIP

" Most Science questions will give you data and ask you for conclusions, so focus on these skills. "

after three seconds, the object would be falling at a rate of about 3 sec $\times$ 9.8 m/sec^2, or roughly 30 m/sec. You could think of this kind of logic as *general-to-specific*. The scientist uses a *general* principle (the acceleration of any object falling on earth) to find a *specific* fact (the speed of Pebble A).

SPECIFIC-TO-GENERAL

But scientists use a different kind of thinking in order to discover a new law of nature. In this case, they examine many specific facts and then draw a general conclusion about what they've seen. For example, a scientist might watch hundreds of different kinds of frogs live and die and might notice that all of them developed from tadpoles. She might then announce a conclusion: all frogs develop from tadpoles. You could think of this kind of logic as *specific-to-general*. The scientist looks at many *specific* frogs to find a *general* rule about all frogs.

This conclusion is called a hypothesis, not a fact or a truth, because the scientist has not checked every single frog in the universe. She knows that there theoretically *could* be a frog somewhere that grows from pond scum or from a Dalmatian puppy. But until she finds such a frog, it is reasonable to think that her hypothesis is correct. Many hypotheses, in fact, are so well documented that they become the equivalent of laws of nature.

In your science classes in school, you mostly learn about general-to-specific thinking. Your teachers explain general rules of science to you and then expect you to apply these rules to answer questions and solve problems. Some ACT Science questions are like that as well. But a majority are not. **Most ACT Science questions test specific-to-general thinking.** The questions test your ability to see the kinds of patterns in specific data that, as a scientist, you would use to formulate your own general hypotheses. We did something like this in Science Workout 1, when we theorized—based on the trends we found in a table of data—that the pollutant Hg was in some way detrimental to trout populations.

EXPERT TUTOR TIP

" Only one to three questions on the entire test will be based on your science knowledge. Everything else is based on what's in the passage. "

HOW EXPERIMENTS WORK

Many ACT passages describe experiments and expect you to understand how they're designed. Experiments help scientists do specific-to-general thinking in a reliable and efficient way. Consider the tadpole researcher above. In a real-world situation, what would probably happen is that she would notice some of the frogs develop from tadpoles and wonder if maybe they all did. Then she'd know what to look for and could check all the frogs systematically. This process contains the two basic steps of any experiment:

1. **Forming a hypothesis** (guessing that all frogs come from tadpoles)

2. **Testing a hypothesis** (checking the frogs to see if this guess was right)

Scientists are often interested in cause-and-effect relationships. Having formed her hypothesis about tadpoles, a scientist might wonder what *causes* a tadpole to become a frog. To test causal relationships, a special kind of experiment is needed. She must test one possible cause at a time in order to isolate which one actually produces the effect in question. For example, the scientist might inject tadpoles with several different kinds of hormones. Some of these tadpoles might die. Others might turn into frogs normally. But a few—those injected with Hormone X, say—might remain tadpoles for an indefinite time. One reasonable explanation is that Hormone X in some way inhibited whatever causes normal frog development. In other words, the scientist would hypothesize a causal relationship between Hormone X and frog development.

METHOD

The relationship between Hormone X and frog development, however, would not be demonstrated very well if the scientist also fed different diets to different tadpoles, kept some in warmer water, or allowed some to have more room to swim than others—or if she didn't also watch tadpoles who were injected with no hormones at all but who otherwise were kept under the same conditions as the treated tadpoles. Why? Because if the "eternal tadpoles" had diets that differed from that of the others, the scientist wouldn't know whether it was Hormone X or the special diet that kept the eternal tadpoles from becoming frogs. Moreover, if their water was warmer than that of the others, maybe it was the warmth that somehow kept the tadpoles from developing. And if she didn't watch untreated tadpoles (a control group), she couldn't be sure whether under the same conditions a normal, untreated tadpole would also remain undeveloped.

Thus, a scientist creating a well-designed experiment will:

- **Ensure that there's a single variable (like Hormone X) that varies from test to test or group to group**

- **Ensure that all other factors (diet, temperature, space, etc.) remain the same**

- **Ensure that there is a control group (tadpoles who don't get any Hormone X at all) for comparison purposes**

EXPERT TUTOR TIP

Many ACT Science questions ask you to determine the purpose of an experiment or to design one yourself. To figure out the purpose of an experiment, look to see what factor was allowed to change: that's what's being tested. To design an experiment yourself, keep everything constant except the factor you must investigate.

RESULTS

One of the advantages to knowing how experiments work is that you can tell what a researcher is trying to find out about by seeing what she allows to vary. That's what is being researched—in this case, Hormone X. Data about things other than hormones and tadpole-to-frog development would be outside the design of the experiment. Information about other factors might be interesting, but could not be part of a scientific proof.

For example, if some of the injected tadpoles that did grow into frogs later actually turned into princes, the data from experiments about the hormone they were given would not prove what causes frogs to become princes, though the data *could* be used to design another experiment intended to explore what could make a frog become a prince.

Therefore, whenever you see an experiment in Science, you should ask yourself:

1. **What's the factor that's being varied?** That is what is being tested.

2. **What's the control group?** It's the group that has nothing special done to it.

3. **What do the results show?** What differences exist between the results for the control group and those for the other group(s)? Or between the results for one treated group and those for another, differently treated group?

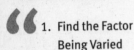

KAPLAN'S STRATEGY FOR EXPERIMENTS

1. Find the Factor Being Varied
2. Identify the Control Group
3. Analyze the Results

HANDLING EXPERIMENT QUESTIONS

On the next page is a full-fledged Science passage organized around two experiments. Use the Kaplan Method, but this time, ask yourself the three questions above. Take about five or six minutes to do the passage and its questions.

EXPERT TUTOR TIP

Don't forget . . . ask yourself:
1. What does the figure show?
2. What are the units of measurement?
3. What is the pattern in the data?

PASSAGE II

A *mutualistic* relationship between two species increases the chances of growth or survival for both of them. Several species of fungi called *mycorrhizae* form mutualistic relationships with the roots of plants. The benefits to each species are shown in the figure below.

Figure 1

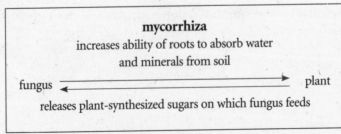

mycorrhiza
increases ability of roots to absorb water and minerals from soil

fungus ⟵————————————⟶ plant

releases plant-synthesized sugars on which fungus feeds

Some of the plant species that require or benefit from the presence of mycorrhizal fungi are noted below.

Cannot survive without mycorrhizae	Grow better with mycorrhizae
All conifers	Citrus trees
Some deciduous trees (e.g., birch, beech)	Ericaceae (heath, rhododendrons, azaleas)
	Grapes
Orchids	Soybeans

Agronomists investigated the effects of mycorrhizae on plant growth and survival in the following studies.

STUDY 1

Three four-acre plots were prepared with soil from a pine forest. The soil for Plot A was mixed with substantial quantities of cultured mycorrhizal fungi. The soil for Plot B contained only naturally occurring mycorrhizal fungi. The soil for Plot C was sterilized in order to kill any mycorrhizal fungi. Additionally, Plot C was lined with concrete. After planting, Plot C was covered with a fabric that filtered out microorganisms while permitting air and light to penetrate. 250 pine seedlings were planted in each of the three plots. All plots received the same amount of water. The six-month survival rates were recorded in the following table.

Table 1

	Number of seedlings alive after 6 months	Utilization of available K (average)	Utilization of available P (average)
Plot A	107	18%	62%
Plot B	34	10%	13%
Plot C	0	N/A	N/A

N/A = not applicable

STUDY 2

The roots of surviving seedlings from Plots A and B were analyzed to determine how efficiently they absorbed potassium (K) and phosphorus (P) from the soil. The results were added to Table 1.

1. The most likely purpose of the concrete liner was:

    A. to block the seedlings from sending out taproots to water below the plot.

    B. to prevent mycorrhizal fungi in the surrounding soil from colonizing the plot.

    C. to absorb potassium and phosphorus from the soil for later analysis.

    D. to provide a firm foundation for mycorrhizal fungi in the plot.

2. Mycorrhizae are highly susceptible to acid rain. Given the information from the passage, acid rain is probably most harmful to:

    F. wheat fields.

    G. birch forests.

    H. orange groves.

    J. grape vines.

3. In a third study, pine seedlings were planted in soil from a different location. The soil was prepared as in Study 1. This time, the survival rates for seedlings planted in Plot A and Plot B were almost identical to each other. Which of the following theories would NOT help to explain these results?

    A. Sterilization killed all the naturally occurring mycorrhizal fungi in the new soil.

    B. The new soil was so mineral-deficient that it could not sustain life.

    C. The new soil was naturally more fertile for pine seedlings than that used in Study 1.

    D. Large quantities of mycorrhizal fungi occurred naturally in the new soil.

4. According to the passage, in which of the following ways do plants benefit from mycorrhizal associations?

    I. More efficient sugar production

    II. Enhanced ability to survive drought

    III. Increased mineral absorption

    F. I only

    G. III only

    H. II and III only

    J. I, II, and III

5. Which of the following generalizations is supported by the results of Study 2?

    A. Mycorrhizal fungi are essential for the survival of pine seedlings.

    B. Growth rates for pine seedlings may be improved by adding mycorrhizal fungi to the soil.

    C. Mycorrhizal fungi contain minerals that are not normally found in pine forest soil.

    D. Pine seedlings cannot absorb all the potassium that is present in the soil.

ANSWERS

1. B
2. G
3. A
4. H
5. D

ANSWERS AND EXPLANATIONS

Notice how many diagrams and tables were used here. That's common in experiment passages, where information is given to you in a wide variety of forms. Typically, though, the experiments themselves are clearly labeled, as Study 1 and Study 2 were here.

A quick preread of the introduction would have revealed the topic of the experiments here—the "mutualistic relationship" between some fungi and some plant roots, the fungi called mycorrhizae ("myco" for short). The first diagram just shows you who gets what out of this relationship. The benefit accruing to the plant (the arrow pointing to the word *plant*) is an increased ability to absorb water and minerals. The benefit accruing to the *fungus* (the other arrow) is the plant-synthesized sugars on which the fungus feeds. That's the mutual benefit that the myco association creates.

Notice, by the way, that reading this first diagram alone is enough to answer **Question 4.** The question is asking: what do the plants get out of the association? And we just answered that—increased ability to absorb water and minerals. Statement III is obviously correct, but so is Statement II, since increased water absorption would indeed enhance the plant's ability to survive drought (a drought is a shortage of water, after all). Statement I, though, is a distortion. We know that the *fungi* benefit from sugars produced by the plants, but we don't have any evidence that the association actually causes plants to produce sugar more efficiently. So I is out; II and III are in, making H the answer.

CAN'T LIVE WITHOUT THOSE FUNGI

Let's get back to the passage. We've just learned who gets what out of the myco association. Now we get a table that shows what *kinds* of plants enter into such associations. Some (those in the first column) are so dependent on myco associations that they can't live without them. Others (those in the second column) merely grow better with them; presumably, they could live without them.

Here again, is a question we can answer based solely on information in this one table. **Question 2** tells us that mycos are highly susceptible to acid rain, and then asks what kind of plant communities would be most harmed by acid rain. Well, if acid rain hurts mycos, then the plants that are most dependent on myco fungi (that is, the ones listed in the first column) would be the most harmed by acid rain. Of the four choices, only birch forests—choice G—correspond to something in column 1 of the table. Birch trees can't even *survive* without myco fungi, so anything that hurts myco fungi would inferably hurt birch forests. (Grapevines and orange groves—which are citrus trees—would also be hurt by acid rain, but not as much, since they *can* survive without myco fungi; meanwhile, we're told nothing about wheat in the passage.)

> **EXPERT TUTOR TIP**
>
> " Every Science passage will have easy and hard questions. Make sure you do the easy questions first to get all of the easy points that you can! "

STUDY 1

Now look at the first experiment. Three plots, each with differently treated soil, are planted with pine seedlings. Plot A gets soil with cultivated myco fungi; Plot B gets untreated soil with only naturally occurring myco fungi; and Plot C gets no myco fungi at all, since the soil has been sterilized and isolated (via the concrete lining and the fabric covering). Now ask yourself the three important experiment questions:

1. **Find the factor being varied.** The factor being varied is the amount of myco fungi in the soil. Plot A gets lots; Plot B gets just the normal amount; Plot C gets none at all. It's clear, then, that the scientists are testing the effects of myco fungi on the growth of pine seedlings.

2. **Identify the control group.** The plants in Plot B, since they get untreated soil. To learn the effects of the fungi, the scientists will then compare the results from fungi-rich Plot A with the control, and the results from fungi-poor Plot C with the same control.

3. **Analyze the results.** The results are listed in the first column of the table. And they are decisive: no seedlings at all survived in Plot C; 34 did in Plot B; and 107 did in Plot A. The minimums and maximums coincide. Minimum fungi = minimum number of surviving seedlings; maximum fungi = maximum number of surviving seedlings. Clearly there's a cause-and-effect relationship here. Myco fungi probably help pine seedlings survive.

Questions 1 and 3 can be answered solely on the basis of Study 1. **Question 1** is merely a procedural question: why the concrete liner in Plot C? Well, in the analysis of the experiment above, we saw that the factor being varied was the amount of myco fungi. Plot C was designed to have none at all. Thus, one can safely assume that the concrete liner was probably there to prevent any stray myco fungi from entering the sterilized soil—choice B.

Question 3 actually sets up an extra experiment based on Study 1. The soils were prepared in the exact same way, except that the soil came from a different location. The results? The number of surviving seedlings from Plots A and B were almost identical. What can that mean? Well, Plot A was supposed to be the fungi-rich plot, whereas Plot B (the control) was supposed to be the fungi-normal plot. But here they have the same results. However, notice that we're *not* told what those results are; it could be that no seedlings survived in any plots this time around.

The question—a reversal question—is phrased so that the three wrong choices are things that *could* explain the results; the correct choice will be the one that *can't*. Choices B, C, and D all *can* explain the results, since they all show how similar results could have been obtained from Plots A and B. If the new soil just couldn't support life—fungi or no fungi—well, Plots A and B would have gotten similar results; namely, no seedlings survive. On the other end of the spectrum, choices C and D show how the two plots might have gotten similar *high* survival rates. If there were lots of myco fungi naturally in this soil (that's choice D), then there wouldn't be all that much difference between the soils in Plots A and B. And if the soil were naturally extremely fertile for the pine seedlings (that's choice C), there must have been lots of fungi naturally present in the soil because pine tress (conifers) don't grow without fungi. So all three of these answers would help to explain similar results in Plots A and B.

Choice A, however, wouldn't help, since it talks about the sterilized soil that's in Plot C. The soil in Plot C won't affect the results in Plots A and B, so choice A is the answer here—the factor that *doesn't* help to explain the results.

STUDY 2

This study takes the surviving seedlings from Plots A and B in Study 1 and just tests how much potassium (K) and phosphorus (P) the roots have used. The results are listed in the second and third columns of the table. (Notice the N/A—not applicable—for Plot C in these columns, since there were no surviving seedlings to test in Plot C!) The data shows much better utilization of both substances in the Plot A seedlings, the seedlings that grew in a fungi-rich soil. This data would tend to support a theory that the myco fungi aid in the utilization of K and P, and that this in turn aids survival in pine seedlings.

The only question that hinges on Study 2 is **Question 5.** It asks what generalization would be supported by the specific results of Study 2. Notice that Study 2 involved only measuring K and P. It did not involve survival rates (that was Study 1), so Choice A can't be right. And *neither* study measured growth rates, so B is out. The minerals K and P were in the control group's soil, which was natural, untreated pine forest soil, so choice C is clearly unsupported.

But the *data* did show that not all of the potassium (K) could be absorbed by pine seedlings. Only 18 percent was absorbed in Plot A, while only 10 percent was absorbed in Plot B. That's a long way from 100 percent, so choice D seems a safe generalization to make.

> ### EXPERT TUTOR TIP
>
> " Many questions on experiment passages will be answerable based solely on the data contained in a single graph or table. You can get these points with relative ease, even if you don't have time for, or don't fully understand, the experiments. "

THE REAL THING: PRACTICE PASSAGE

Now that we've taken you step by step through a Science passage based on an experiment, it's time to try one on your own. Give yourself about six minutes for the next passage and questions. This time the explanations at the end will be very short:

PASSAGE III

The following flowchart shows the steps used by a chemist in testing sample solutions for positive ions of silver (Ag), lead (Pb), and mercury (Hg).

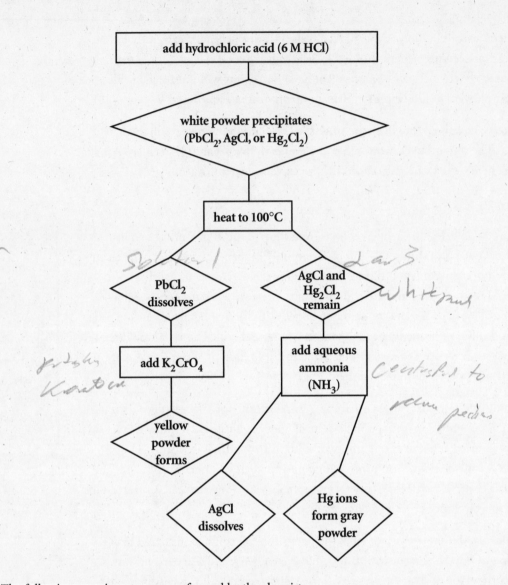

The following experiments were performed by the chemist:

Experiment 1

Hydrochloric acid (6 M HCl) was added to samples of four unknown solutions labeled 1, 2, 3, and 4. A white powder precipitated out of solutions 1, 2, and 3; no precipitate formed in solution 4.

Experiment 2

Each of the sample solutions from Experiment 1 was placed in a 100°C water bath for 15 minutes. The precipitate in solution 1 redissolved completely; solutions 2 and 3 still contained a white powder; solution 4 was unchanged. Solutions 2 and 3 were centrifuged to remove the precipitates, which were retained for further testing. Potassium chromate (K_2CrO_4) was then added to each sample. A bright yellow precipitate formed in solutions 1 and 2; none formed in solutions 3 or 4.

Experiment 3

The white powder centrifuged from solutions 2 and 3 in Experiment 2 was treated with aqueous ammonia (NH_3). The precipitate from solution 2 returned into solution, while that from solution 3 produced a gray powder.

 SCIENTIFIC REASONING

6. Which conclusion is best supported by the results of Experiment 1 alone?

F. Silver ions are present only in solution 3.

G. No ions are present in solution 4.

H. Lead ions are present in solutions 1, 2, and 3.

J. No positive ions of silver, mercury, or lead are present in solution 4.

 SCIENTIFIC REASONING

7. Based on the experimental results, which ions did solution 2 contain?

A. Lead ions only

B. Lead and silver ions only

C. Silver and mercury ions only

D. Silver ions only

 SCIENTIFIC REASONING

8. The yellow precipitate that formed in Experiment 2 was most likely:

F. AgCl

G. Hg_2Cl_2

H. $PbCrO_4$

J. Ag_2CrO_4

 FIGURE INTERPRETATION

9. The experimental results suggest that if lead chloride ($PbCl_2$) were treated with aqueous ammonia (NH_3), the results would be:

A. a bright yellow precipitate.

B. a light gray precipitate.

C. a powdery white precipitate.

D. impossible to determine from the information given.

 FIGURE INTERPRETATION

10. A student proposed that the analysis could be carried out more efficiently by heating the samples to 100° C before adding the 6 M HCl. This suggestion is:

F. a bad idea; since PbCl2 will not precipitate out of solution at this temperature, lead ions would be undetectable.

G. a bad idea; the hot solutions could not be safely centrifuged.

H. a good idea; the number of steps would be reduced from 3 to 2, saving much time and effort.

J. a good idea; the chloride-forming reaction would proceed faster, eliminating the necessity for a 15-minute water bath.

ANSWERS

6. **J**
7. **B**
8. **H**
9. **D**
10. **F**

ANSWERS AND EXPLANATIONS

This experiment passage was somewhat different from the preceding one. In the mycorrhiza experiment, the scientists were thinking in specific-to-general terms (observing the growth of *specific* pine seedlings to come to a conclusion about the general effect of myco fungi on pine seedlings). In this series of experiments, the general principle is known—silver, lead, and mercury will precipitate or dissolve when certain things are done to them—and the scientists are using this principle to test certain substances in order to identify them. In fact, this is more like a procedure than an experiment, since there's no control group. But the same kind of experimental thinking—using the results of varying procedures to make reasonable inferences about what's happening—will get you your answers.

This passage also introduces the idea of a flowchart. Basically, the flowchart indicates an order of procedures. You follow the flowchart from top to bottom. The things in squares indicate what's done to a specimen; the things in diamonds indicate possible results.

Let's say you have an unknown substance. Following the flowchart, the first thing you do is add hydrochloric acid. If a white powder precipitates, that means there are positive ions of silver, lead, and/or mercury. (If nothing precipitates, the experiment is over; the substance is not of interest here.)

But, assuming you do get a white powder, how do you identify exactly which kind of white powder you have? You do the next procedure—heat it to 100°C. When you do this, any lead ions will dissolve, but any silver or mercury ions will remain as a powder. So the flowchart has to divide here.

If part of your specimen dissolved when heated, that doesn't necessarily mean you have lead ions. To test for that, you add K_2CrO_4. If a yellow powder forms, then you know you've got lead; if not, you've got something else.

But what about the other branch? That tells you what has to be done if you *do* have some powder remaining after heating. And what you do is add NH_3. If the powder dissolves, you've got silver ions. If it forms a gray powder, on the other hand, what you've got are mercury (Hg) ions.

The three experiments here are actually three parts of a single experiment or procedure, each one using the results of the former in the way outlined in the flowchart. The questions ask for results at various points in the procedure, so let's look at them briefly now.

KEY TO PASSAGE III

	Answer	Refer to	Comments
6.	J	Experiment 1 only	If any Ag, Pb, or Hg ions were present, they would have precipitated out as powder. Note that G is too extreme (could be ions of a fourth type not within scope of the experiment). Not enough testing in Exp. 1 to determine F or H.
7.	B	All 3 experiments	Heating left powder, so has to have Ag or Hg or both, so cut A. Addition of K_2CrO_4 left yellow precipitate, so must contain Pb (cut C and D).
8.	H	Experiment 2	Must be lead-based, because Ag and Hg precipitates were already removed (cut F, G, and J).
9.	D	Flowchart	No evidence for what would happen— two different branches of the flowchart.
10.	F	Flowchart	If the solutions were heated first, and then the HCl was added, the $PbCl_2$ would **never** form, and the chemist would not know whether lead ions were present.

As you've seen, not all experiments on the ACT Science subject test are specific-to-general experiments; some are general-to-specific procedures. But the same kind of strict thinking—manipulating factors to narrow down possibilities—can get you points, no matter what direction you're thinking in.

GO ONLINE

Review Science strategies on your downloadable study sheet.

EXPERT TUTOR TIP

If you get stuck on a problem, see what answer choices you can eliminate. The more you eliminate, the closer you are to the correct answer.

IF YOU LEARNED ONLY THREE THINGS IN THIS CHAPTER . . .

1. When you encounter experiment questions, identify the factor being varied, the control group (if any), and how results vary between groups.

2. Look for Figure Interpretation Questions first—they'll get you the quickest points.

3. Some scenarios ask you to make inferences about data (specific-to-general); others ask you to use general ideas to determine what will happen in a particular case (general-to-specific).

CHAPTER 12: ENGLISH WORKOUT 3: LOOK AND LISTEN

In the first two English Workouts, we discussed English questions that hinged mostly on common sense. But there are also some English questions—we call them Technicality Questions—that may seem harder because they test for the technical rules of grammar, requiring you to correct errors that don't necessarily harm the economy or sense of the sentence. But don't worry. You don't have to be a grammar whiz to get these questions right. Luckily, you can often detect these errors because they "sound funny." **Most of the time on the ACT, it's safe to trust your ear.**

LISTEN TO THE CHOICES

Which of the following "sounds right" and which "sounds funny"?

- Bob doesn't know the value of the house he lives in.
- Bob don't know the value of the house he lives in.

The first sounds a lot better, right? For many of these questions, all you need to do is "listen" carefully in this way.

Your ear can help you determine the tone of a passage. For example, if the passage starts off "You'll just love Bermuda—great beaches, good living . . ." it won't end like this: "and an infinitely fascinating array of flora and fauna which may conceivably exceed, in range and scope, that of any alternative . . ." It's too formal. Pick something like this: "You'll just love Bermuda—great beaches, good living, and lots of awesome plants and animals."

Although ACT passages differ in level of formality, they all are designed to test "standard" English—the kind used by people in most of America. Test takers who speak regional or ethnic dialects may therefore find it more difficult to follow their ears on some ACT questions. In much of the South, for instance, it's common to use

PERFECT SCORE TIP

" The best preparation for the English sections is really to enter a grammar "hyper mode" where you recognize grammar mistakes around you. If you are used to doing this in everyday life, common verb or agreement errors will pop out to you on the test. "

the word *in* with the word *rate*, like this: "Mortality declined *in* a rate of almost 2 percent per year." Most speakers of English, however, use the word *at* with *rate*, like this: "Mortality declined *at* a rate of . . ." Fortunately, ACT questions testing issues like this are rare. And even if you do speak a "nonstandard" dialect, you probably know what standard English sounds like. The dialect used on most television and radio programs would be considered "standard."

In the following short passage, use your eyes and ears.

Example

PASSAGE II

Halloween was first celebrated <u>among various</u> Celtic
1
tribes in Ireland in the fifth century B.C. It traditionally

took place on the official last day of summer—October

<u>31, and</u> was named "All-Hallows' Eve." It was believed
2
that all persons who had died during the previous year

returned on this day to select persons or animals to

inhabit for the next twelve months, until they could

<u>pass peaceful</u> into the afterlife.
3

On All-Hallows' Eve, the Celts <u>were dressing</u> up as
4
demons and monsters to frighten the spirits away, and tried

to make their homes <u>as coldest</u> as possible to prevent any
5
stray ghosts from crossing their thresholds. Late at night,

the townspeople typically gathered outside the village,

where a druidic priest would light a huge bonfire to

frighten away ghosts and to honor the sun god for the

past summer's harvest. Any villager <u>whom was</u> suspected of
6

1. A. NO CHANGE
   B. among varied
   C. between the various
   D. between various

2. F. NO CHANGE
   G. 31—and
   H. 31. And
   J. 31; and

3. A. NO CHANGE
   B. pass peacefully
   C. passed peacefully
   D. be passing peaceful

4. F. NO CHANGE
   G. were dressed
   H. dressed
   J. are dressed

5. A. NO CHANGE
   B. colder
   C. coldest
   D. as cold

6. F. NO CHANGE
   G. whom were
   H. who was
   J. who were

being possessed would be captured, after which they
₇
might be sacrificed in the bonfire as a warning to other

spirits seeking to possess the living. When the Romans

invaded the British Isles, they adopted Celtic—not

Saxon—Halloween rituals, but outlawed human sacrifice

in A.D. 61. Instead, they used effigies for their sacrifices.

In time, as belief in spirit possession waned, Halloween
₈
rituals lost their serious aspect and had been instead
₉
performed for amusement.

Irish immigrants, fleeing from the potato famine in

the 1840s, brought there Halloween customs to the
₁₀
United States.

In New England, Halloween became a night of costumes and

practical jokes. Some favorite pranks included unhinging
₁₁
front gates and overturning outhouses. The Irish also

introduced the custom of carving jack-o'-lanterns. The

ancient Celts probably began the tradition by hollowing

out a large turnip, carving it with a demon's face, and

lighting it from inside with a candle. Since there were

far less turnips in New England than in Ireland, the
₁₂
Irish immigrants were forced to settle for pumpkins.

Gradually, Halloween celebrations spread to other

regions of the United States. Halloween has been a

popular holiday ever since, although these days it's
₁₃
principal celebrants are children rather than adults.
₁₄

7. A. NO CHANGE
   B. it
   C. he or she
   D. those

8. F. NO CHANGE
   G. belief for
   H. believing about
   J. belief of

9. A. NO CHANGE
   B. having been
   C. have been
   D. were

10. F. NO CHANGE
    G. brought they're
    H. brought their
    J. their brought-in

11. A. NO CHANGE
    B. include unhinging
    C. had included unhinged
    D. includes unhinged

12. F. NO CHANGE
    G. lots less
    H. not as much
    J. far fewer

13. A. NO CHANGE
    B. although these days its
    C. while now it's
    D. while not it is

14. F. NO CHANGE
    G. rather then
    H. rather
    J. else then

KEY TO PASSAGE II

Answer		Issue
1.	A	*among/between* distinction
2.	G	commas and dashes mixed
3.	B	use of adjectives and adverbs
4.	H	unnecessary *-ing* ending
5.	D	comparative/superlative
6.	H	*who/whom* confusion
7.	C	pronoun usage error
8.	F	preposition usage
9.	D	tense problem with *to be*
10.	H	*they're/there/their* mix-up
11.	A	verb tense usage
12.	J	*less/fewer* confusion
13.	B	*it's/its* confusion
14.	F	*then/than* confusion

GRAMMAR RULES TO KNOW

The rest of this workout is designed to help you build your own "flag list" of common errors on the ACT that your ear might not catch. Consider each classic error. If it seems like common sense to you (or, better, if the error just sounds like bad English to you, while the correction sounds like good English), you probably don't have to add it to your flag list. On the other hand, if it doesn't seem obvious, add it to your list.

As we'll see, making things match works in two ways. Some rules force you to match one part of the sentence with another part. Other rules force you to match the right word or word form with the intended meaning.

ERROR 1: PROBLEM SENTENCES

The most tested "matching" rule on the ACT is this: singular nouns must match with singular verbs and pronouns, and plural nouns must match with plural

> **PERFECT SCORE TIP**
>
> " The overarching grammar principle on the ACT really is "does it all match?" Make sure every word matches the word it is modifying, and the English section will be a breeze. "

> **PERFECT SCORE TIP**
>
> " Depending on if the people around you use correct grammar, your ear may or may not give you correct answers. Even if you generally have correct grammar, knowing the rules will help make you more confident in yourself. So be sure to review the grammar rules in this section. "

PERFECT SCORE TIP

" I found knowing the rules of direct vs. indirect objects helped make me more confident when choosing the correct pronoun. "

verbs and pronouns. The most common error in this area involves the use of the word *they*. It's plural, but in everyday speech, we often use it as a singular.

Wrong:	"If a student won't study, they won't do well."
Problem:	A *student* (singular) and *they* (plural) don't match.
Correction:	"If students won't study, they won't do well," or "If a student won't study, he or she won't do well."

ERROR 2: AND (COMPOUND PHRASES)

Another common matching error concerns "compound subjects" (lists).

Wrong:	"The fool gave the wrong tickets to Bob and I."
Problem:	*I* is a subject; it can't be the object of the preposition *to*.
Correction:	"The fool gave the wrong tickets to Bob and me."

HINT: Try dropping the rest of the list (Bob and). "The fool gave the wrong tickets to I" should sound funny to you.

ERROR 3: COMMAS OR DASHES (PARENTHETICAL PHRASES)

Parenthetical phrases must begin and end with the same punctuation mark. Such phrases can be recognized because without them the sentence would still be complete. For instance: "Bob, on his way to the store, saw a large lizard in the street." If you dropped the phrase "on his way to the store," the sentence would still be complete. Thus, this phrase is parenthetical. It could be marked off with commas, parentheses, or dashes. But the same mark is needed at both ends of the phrase.

Wrong:	"Bob—on his way to the store, saw a lizard."
Problem:	The parenthetical phrase starts with a dash but finishes with a comma.
Correction:	"Bob, on his way to the store, saw a lizard."

ERROR 4: COMMAS (RUN-ONS AND COMMA SPLICES)

You can't combine two sentences into one with a comma (though you can with a semicolon or conjunction).

Wrong:	"Ed's a slacker, Sara isn't."
Problem:	Two sentences are spliced together with a comma.
Correction:	"Ed's a slacker, but Sara isn't." Or "Ed's a slacker; Sara isn't." Or "Ed, unlike Sara, is a slacker."

ERROR 5: FRAGMENT

This rule goes hand in hand with the one above. **A sentence must have at least one "major event."** A "fragment" is writing that could be a subordinate part of a sentence, but not a whole sentence itself.

Wrong:	"Emily listened to music. While she studied."
Problem:	"She studied" would be a sentence, but *while* makes this a fragment.
Correction:	"Emily listened to music while she studied."

ERROR 6: ANY PUNCTUATION MARK

The ACT doesn't test tricky rules of punctuation. But it does expect you to know what the punctuation marks mean and to match their use to their meanings. Here are some common punctuation marks and their meanings:

Period (.):	means "full stop" or "end of sentence."
Question mark (?):	serves the same purpose, but for questions.
Exclamation mark (!):	can be used instead of a period, but is generally inappropriate for all but very informal writing because it indicates extreme emotion.
Comma (,):	sets off items in a list of three or more items; separates two independent clauses with a FANBOY conjunction (For, And, Nor, But, Or, Yet, So); separates an introductory phrase from the rest of the sentence; separates nonessential information from the rest of the sentence, called a parenthetical phrase.
Semicolon (;):	joins two independent clauses (another option for run-on sentences); separates items in a series or list if those items already include commas.
Colon (:):	introduces an important short phrase, quotation, explanation, example, or list.
Dash (—):	sets off an explanatory element in a sentence; indicates a hesitation or a break in thought.
Apostrophe ('):	indicates the possessive form of a noun; stands in for a letter or letters in a contraction (don't = do not; can't = cannot).

> **PERFECT SCORE TIP**
>
> " Knowing the meaning of different punctuation marks is vital. Refresh your memory on any of these if you forget how to use them. For example, I find many people don't know how to use a semicolon and have trouble with it on the ACT. "

> **EXPERT TUTOR TIP**
>
> " Most test takers need some review of punctuation. Brush up on your skills with English Review for the ACT on your online syllabus. "

ERROR 7: -LY ENDINGS (ADVERBS AND ADJECTIVES)

The ACT expects you to understand the difference between adverbs (the -ly words) and adjectives. The two are similar because they're both "modifiers." They modify, or refer to, or describe, another word or phrase in the sentence. The trick is that nouns and pronouns must be modified by adjectives, while other words, especially verbs and adjectives themselves, must be modified by adverbs.

Wrong: "Anna is an extreme gifted child, and she speaks beautiful too."

Problem: *Extreme* and *beautiful* are adjectives, but they're supposed to modify an adjective (*gifted*) and a verb (*speaks*) here, so they should be adverbs.

Correction: "Anna is an extremely gifted child, and she speaks beautifully too."

ERROR 8: GOOD OR WELL

In everyday speech, we often confuse the words *good* and *well*. But *good* is an adjective (it modifies a noun or pronoun); *well* is an adverb (it can modify verbs and adjectives).

Wrong: "Joe did good on the ACT."

Problem: *Good* is an adjective, but here it's modifying a verb (*did*), so use an adverb.

Correction: "Joe did well on the ACT."

One exception: *well* can also be used as an adjective, when it means "healthy." So: "Joe was well again by the morning of the ACT" is correct, even though *well* is modifying the noun *Joe*.

ERROR 9: LIE, LAY, LAID, LAIN

The words *lay* and *lie* are easy to confuse because they look alike and have similar meanings. The key difference in meaning is point of view. If the speaker is doing something without a direct object, he is "lying." If the speaker is doing it to something else, he is "laying." So, for example, "I will go lie down" (not *lay* down), but "I will lay this pencil on the desk" (not *lie* it).

It gets worse. The past tense of *lay* is *laid*. That's not too hard. The confusing word is *lie*. The past tense of *lie* is *lay*; when used for special tenses (with the words *had*, *have*, or *been*, for example), the form is *lain*. Thus, you'd say, "I lay down" (meaning you, yourself, took a rest at some time in the past), or "I have lain down for a nap every afternoon for years now." But you'd say, "I laid that pencil on the desk yesterday, just as I have laid it on the desk every day for years now."

Don't confuse *lie* with the word *lie* that relates to dishonesty. The past tense of *lie* (meaning to tell an untruth) is *lied*.

Wrong:	"I lied. I said that I had lain down, but I hadn't. In fact, I had just laid the pencil down. After I lied, though, I lay down to repent for having lied."
Problem:	None. All uses of *lie*, *lied*, *lay*, *laid*, and *lain* above are correct.

Try not to get bogged down with *lie* and *lay*. If you don't get it, don't sweat it. It will account for one point if it appears at all.

ERROR 10: *IN, OF, TO, FOR* (IDIOMATIC PREPOSITION USE)

Whenever you see a preposition, double-check to make sure it makes sense and that it "matches" the other words. Many words require particular prepositions.

Wrong:	"She tried to instill on me a respect to the law." "I want to protect you in all dangers."
Problem:	The prepositions don't match the verbs.
Corrections:	"She tried to instill in me a respect for the law." "I want to protect you from all dangers."

ERROR 11: *WHO* OR *WHOM*

Many students fear the words *who* and *whom* more than any other grammatical conundrum. Fear no more. There's an easy way to remember when to use them: they work the same way *he* and *him* work. Turn the sentence into a question as we've done in the example below. If the answer to the question is *he*, the form should be *who*. If the answer is *him*, the form should be *whom*. Notice that the *m*s go together.

Wrong:	"Always remember who you're speaking to."
Problem:	*Who* is wrong. Ask: Speaking to who? Speaking to him, not to he. So it should be *whom*.
Correction:	"Always remember whom you're speaking to."

> **PERFECT SCORE TIP**
>
> 66 The Kaplan method for distinguishing between *who* and *whom* was very helpful for me. I substituted *he* and *him*, and a difficult grammar concept became manageable. 99

Some students try to avoid the who/whom problem by using the word *which* instead. Nope. It's not nice to call people "whiches." **Never** use the word *which* for a person.

ERROR 12: *ITS* OR *IT'S* (APOSTROPHE USE)

Probably the trickiest rule on the ACT is the proper use of apostrophes. Apostrophes are used primarily for two purposes: possessives and contractions. When you make a *noun* (not a pronoun) possessive by adding an *s*, you use an apostrophe. Examples: *Bob's, the water's, a noodle's*. You **NEVER** use an apostrophe to make a pronoun possessive—pronouns have special possessive forms. You'd never write *her's*. When you run two words together to form a single word, you use an apostrophe to join them. For example: *you'd, he's, they're*.

Apostrophes also have a few unusual uses, but luckily they're almost **never** tested on the ACT. So master the basics and you're in good shape. The most common apostrophe issue on the ACT is usage of the words *its* and *it's*. A good way to remember which is which is that *its* and *it's* follow the same rule as do *his* and *he's*. Both *its* and *his* are possessive pronouns: so they have *no* apostrophes. Both *it's* and *he's* are contractions—so they *do* have apostrophes.

> Wrong: "The company claims its illegal to use it's name that way."
>
> Problem: *It's* is a contraction of *it is*; *its* is the possessive form of *it*.
>
> Correction: "The company claims it's illegal to use its name that way."

ERROR 13: *THERE, THEIR,* OR *THEY'RE* AND *ARE* OR *OUR* (PROPER WORD USAGE)

Some students confuse the words *there, their,* and *they're*. **A good way to remember which is *they're* is to remember that contractions use apostrophes—so *they're* is the contraction for *they are*.** You can tell which is *there* because it's spelled like *here*, and the words *here* and *there* match. (*Their* means "of or belonging to them"; you'll just have to remember that one the old-fashioned way.)

Students also frequently confuse the words *are* (a verb) and *our* (a possessive). You can remember that *our* is spelled like *your*, another, less confusing possessive.

ERROR 14: *SANG, SUNG, BRANG, BRUNG,* ETC. (VERB FORMS)

When the answers differ because of different forms of the same or similar verbs (for example, *live, lives, lived*), ask yourself *who* did it and *when* did they do it? We would say "I now live" but "he now lives." In these sentences, the *who* is different—and so the verb changes. Similarly, we would say "I now live" but "I lived in the past." In these sentences, the *when* is different—so the verb changes.

Most verbs are "regular" in this way, with only the endings *s* and *d* to worry about. You use the *s* when the point of view is "he," "she," or "it" and the time is now (present tense). You use the *d* for times in the past. For times in the future, or several steps backward in time, there are no special endings. You use the words *will, will have, have,* and *had* for these time sequences. "I *will* live. I *will* have lived for 25 years by the time the next century begins. I *had* lived in Nebraska, but we moved. I *have* lived in Indiana since then."

But a few verbs are irregular. They have special forms. For example, we say *sang* rather than *singed* and *have sung* rather than *have singed* or *have sang*. Each of these verbs must be learned separately.

One irregular verb commonly tested on the ACT is *bring*.

Wrong:	"I've brung my umbrella to work."
Problem:	*Brang* and *brung* aren't used in standard English.
Correction:	"I've brought my umbrella to work."

ERROR 15: *BE* AND *WAS* (FORMS OF THE VERB *TO BE*)

The ACT tests the use of proper verb forms, especially of the verb *to be*. You must use the following forms. Memorize them if you have to:

Present Tense:	I *am*, we *are*, you *are*, they *are*, he *is*, she *is*, it *is*
Past Tense:	I *was*, we *were*, you *were*, they *were*, he/she/it *was*
Future Tense:	I/we/you/they/he/she/it *will be*
Perfect Tense:	I/we/you *have been*, he/she/it *has been*
Past Perfect:	I/we/you/he/she/it *had been*
Future Perfect:	I/we/you/he/she/it *will have been*

Notice that different forms of the verb (*am, are, is, were, was, will be, have been, had been, will have been*) are used depending on point of view (called "case" in grammar) and whether the action is now, in the past, or in the future (called "tense" in grammar). In many dialects, the words *be* and *was* are used instead of the special forms given. For example, many speakers might say, "They *be* going home" or "They *was* going home." But the ACT would require you to write, "They *are* (or *were*) going home."

ERROR 16: *-ING* ENDINGS (UNIDIOMATIC VERB USE)

Don't use *-ing* endings where they aren't needed. They are used to indicate repeated or continuous action and shouldn't be used for a single action that occurs once.

> **PERFECT SCORE TIP**
>
> " The verb *to be* is so commonly conjugated incorrectly in everyday life, and the writers know this. Review the rules and make a concerted effort to use them correctly when speaking, and I guarantee it will pay off on test day. "

Wrong:	"When I left for the store, I was forgetting my list."
Problem:	The -ing ending isn't necessary.
Correction:	"When I left for the store, I forgot my list."

ERROR 17: -ER AND -EST, MORE, AND MOST (COMPARATIVES AND SUPERLATIVES)

Whenever you see the endings -er or -est, or the words *more* or *most*, double-check to make sure they're used logically. Words with -er or with *more* should be used to compare only two things. If there are more than two things involved, use -est or *most*.

Wrong:	"Bob is the fastest of the two runners."
Problem:	The comparison is between just two things, so -est is inappropriate.
Correction:	"Bob is the faster of the two runners."

Don't use the words *more* or *most* if you can use the endings instead. Say "I think vanilla is tastier than chocolate," not "I think vanilla is more tasty than chocolate." Never use both *more* or *most* **and** an ending. Don't say "Of the five flavors of frozen yogurt I've eaten, strawberry delight is the most tastiest." Just say it's "the tastiest."

A note on *than* and *then*: *Than* is used in comparisons such as "Bob is faster than Jim." *Then* refers to time, as in "Bob ran and then stopped."

ERROR 18: BETWEEN OR AMONG

Make sure that you use the word *between* only when there are two things involved. When there are more than two things, or an unknown number of things, use *among*.

Wrong:	"I will walk among the two halves of the class." "I will walk between the many students in class."
Problem:	Use *between* for two things and *among* for more than two.
Correction:	"I will walk between the two halves of the class." "I will walk among the many students in class."

ERROR 19: *LESS* OR *FEWER*

Make sure that you use the word *less* only for uncountable things. When things can be counted, they are *fewer*.

Wrong: "I have fewer water than I thought, so I can fill less buckets."

Problem: You can count buckets; you can't count water.

Correction: "I have less water than I thought, so I can fill fewer buckets."

HINT: People are **always** countable, so use *fewer* when writing about them.

GO ONLINE

" For a more thorough account of the grammar points you should know for the ACT, refer to the English Review for the ACT section of your online syllabus. "

IF YOU LEARNED ONLY THREE THINGS IN THIS CHAPTER . . .

1. You can recognize some grammar mistakes because they sound strange. Listening is a great tool in the English section.

2. Other grammar mistakes break rules in context. To find these, you must read the sentence carefully to determine the correct punctuation, word, phrase, or clause.

3. Grammar rules tested by the ACT are relatively few. Refer to the quick outline provided in this chapter to learn them.

CHAPTER 13: MATH WORKOUT 3: FIGURING IT OUT

SMARTPOINTS COVERED IN THIS CHAPTER

PLANE GEOMETRY

COORDINATE GEOMETRY

Every ACT Math subject test has about 14 geometry questions and exactly 4 trigonometry questions. Depending on what kind of score you're aiming for, you don't need to spend too much time working on trigonometry problems, but you definitely want to spend some time brushing up on your geometry skills.

Fortunately, a good number of the geometry questions are straightforward. Nothing is distorted or disguised. With these questions, you know what to do—if you know your geometry—the instant you understand them.

TEN TEXTBOOK GEOMETRY QUESTIONS

PLANE GEOMETRY

COORDINATE GEOMETRY

Here's a set of ten such questions. When you take the ACT you will see quite a few questions just like these—possibly reworded and certainly with different numbers and figures. Use these questions to find out how well you remember your geometry.

Example

1. In the figure below, line *t* crosses parallel lines *m* and *n*. What is the degree measure of ∠*x* ?

A. 40
B. 50
C. 60
D. 130
E. 140

2. What is the slope of the line perpendicular to the equation $4x + 3y = 9$?

F. $-\dfrac{4}{3}$

G. $-\dfrac{3}{4}$

H. $\dfrac{4}{3}$

J. $\dfrac{3}{4}$

K. 3

3. In the figure below, ∠B is a right angle and the lengths of $\overline{AB}$, $\overline{BC}$, and $\overline{CD}$ are given in units. What is the area of △ACD, in square units?

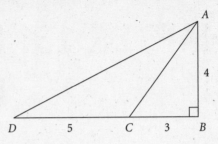

A. 10
B. 12
C. 16
D. 20
E. 32

4. In the figure below, △ABC is similar to △DEF. ∠A corresponds to ∠D, ∠B corresponds to ∠E, and ∠C corresponds to ∠F. If the given lengths are of the same unit of measure, what is the value of *x* ?

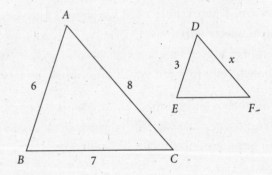

F. 3
G. 3.5
H. 4
J. 5
K. 6

5. In △ABC below, ∠B is a right angle. If $\overline{AB}$ is
    1 unit long and $\overline{BC}$ is 2 units long, how many
    units long is $\overline{AC}$?

A. $\sqrt{2}$
B. $\sqrt{3}$
C. 2
D. $\sqrt{5}$
E. 3

6. Point P (−3, 5) and point Q (0, 1) are points
    on the x-y coordinate plane. What is the
    distance between points P and Q?

F. 4
G. 5
H. 6
J. 7
K. 8

7. In the figure below, $\overline{BE}$ is perpendicular to
    $\overline{AD}$, and the lengths of $\overline{AB}$, $\overline{BC}$, $\overline{CD}$, and $\overline{BE}$
    are given in inches. What is the area, in square
    inches, of trapezoid ABCD?

A. 24
B. 30
C. 32
D. 34
E. 36

8. What is the area, in square inches, of a circle
    with a diameter of 8 inches?

F. 4π
G. 8π
H. 16π
J. 32π
K. 64π

9. In the circle centered at O in the figure below, the measure of $\angle AOB$ is 40°. If $\overline{OA}$ is 9 units long, how many units long is minor arc AB?

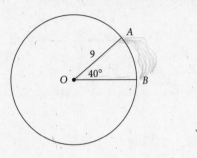

A. π
B. 2π
C. 9
D. 9π
E. 40

$$\frac{\pi s^2}{2}$$

$$\frac{25\pi}{2}$$

10. In the figure below, $ABCD$ is a square and $\overline{AB}$ is a diameter of the circle centered at O. If $\overline{AD}$ is 10 units long, what is the area, in square units, of the shaded region?

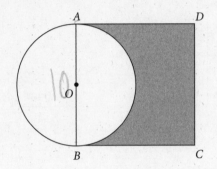

F. $100 - 50\pi$
G. $100 - 25\pi$
H. $100 - \dfrac{25\pi}{2}$
J. $100 - 10\pi$
K. $100 - 5\pi$

SCORING

10 correct: You have a solid grounding in geometry. Straightforward textbook geometry questions are no problem for you. Skip ahead to the section called Tackling More Complex Geometry Questions.

8–9 correct: You have a pretty good grasp of the geometry you need to know for the ACT. Before moving on to the discussion of more complex geometry, read the explanations below of the questions you got wrong, and study the appropriate pages of the 100 Key Math Concepts for the ACT section at the back of this book.

0–7 correct: You have gaps in your knowledge of geometry. Before you can hope to get much out of our discussion of more complex geometry, you had better solidify your geometry foundations. Look at the explanations below and study the corresponding pages of the 100 Key Math Concepts for the ACT section at the back of this book.

ANSWERS

1. E
2. J
3. A
4. H
5. D
6. G
7. E
8. H
9. B
10. H

ANSWERS AND EXPLANATIONS

1. When a transversal crosses parallel lines, the four acute angles formed are all equal, the four obtuse angles formed are all equal, and any angles that are not equal are supplementary. The angle marked x is obtuse, so it's supplementary to the given 40° angle. $180 - 40 = 140$. The answer is E. (*100 Key Math Concepts for the ACT, #79*)

2. First you need to put the equation you are given into $y = mx + b$ form. When you do this, you can see that the slope of this line is $-\frac{4}{3}$. We are looking for the slope of the line perpendicular to this line. That means that we need the opposite reciprocal slope, which is $\frac{3}{4}$, J.

3. The formula for the area of a triangle is $A = \frac{1}{2}bh$. To apply this formula, you need the base and the height. Here you can use $\overline{CD}$ for the base and $\overline{AB}$ for the height. So: Area $= \frac{1}{2}(CD)(AB) = \frac{1}{2}(5)(4) = 10$. The answer is A. (*100 Key Math Concepts for the ACT, #83*)

4. In similar triangles, corresponding sides are proportional. $\overline{DE}$ corresponds to $\overline{AB}$, and $\overline{DF}$ corresponds to $\overline{AC}$, so we can set up this proportion:

$$\frac{AB}{DE} = \frac{AC}{DF}$$

$$\frac{6}{3} = \frac{8}{x}$$

$$6x = 3 \times 8$$

$$6x = 24$$

$$x = 4$$

The answer is H. (*100 Key Math Concepts for the ACT, #82*)

5. The Pythagorean theorem says: $(\text{leg}_1)^2 + (\text{leg}_2)^2 = (\text{hypotenuse})^2$. Here the legs have lengths of 1 and 2, so plug them into the formula:

$$(1)^2 + (2)^2 = (\text{hypotenuse})^2$$

$$1 + 4 = x^2$$

$$x^2 = 5$$

$$x = \sqrt{5}$$

The answer is D. (*100 Key Math Concepts for the ACT, #84*)

6. There are a couple of ways to solve a distance problem. If you can remember the formula, great! If you can't, you can still get this problem correct. Draw a quick graph and plot the two points that you are given. See if you can make a triangle once you draw the points, and then determine the lengths of the two legs. You will need to solve for the hypotenuse, but you know how to do this—the Pythagorean theorem! You might also recognize the Pythagorean triplet (3-4-5). Any way you solve it, you will get 5, G.

7. The formula for the area of a trapezoid is $A = \left(\dfrac{b_1 + b_2}{2} \right) h$, where b_1 and b_2 are the lengths of the parallel sides. You could think of it as the height times the average of the bases. You're given the height (3 inches), one base (8 inches), and enough information to figure out the other base. Notice that $\triangle ABE$ is a 3-4-5 triangle, so $AE = 4$ inches. And if you were to drop an altitude down from point C, you'd get another 3-4-5 triangle on the right:

EXPERT TUTOR TIP

" If you don't remember the formula for the area of a trapezoid, break it into shapes that you do know the area formulas for—triangles and a rectangle. "

Now you can see that the bottom base is 16 inches. Plug these numbers into the formula:

$$A = \left(\frac{b_1 + b_2}{2}\right)h$$

$$= \left(\frac{8 + 16}{2}\right) \times 3$$

$$= 12 \times 3 = 36$$

The answer is E. (*100 Key Math Concepts for the ACT*, #87)

8. The formula for the area of a circle is $A = \pi r^2$, where r is the radius. If the diameter is 8 inches, then the radius is 4 inches, which we plug into the formula:

$$A = \pi r^2$$

$$= \pi(4)^2$$

$$= 16\pi$$

The answer is H. (*100 Key Math Concepts for the ACT*, #91)

9. The central angle of minor arc *AB* is 40°, which is $\frac{1}{9}$ of the whole circle's 360°. The length of minor arc *AB*, therefore, is $\frac{1}{9}$ of the whole circle's circumference.

$$C = 2\pi r = 2\pi(9) = 18\pi$$

$$\frac{1}{9}C = \frac{1}{9}(18\pi) = 2\pi$$

The answer is B. (*100 Key Math Concepts for the ACT*, #90)

10. The shaded region is equal to the area of the square minus the area of the semicircle. The area of the square is $10 \times 10 = 100$. The radius of the circle is half of 10, or 5, so the area of the whole circle is $\pi(5)^2 = 25\pi$, and the area of the semicircle is $\frac{25\pi}{2}$. The square minus the semicircle, then, is: $100 - \frac{25\pi}{2}$.

The answer is H. (*100 Key Math Concepts for the ACT*, #87, #91)

> **EXPERT TUTOR TIP**
>
> " The length of an arc is only a fraction of the length around the circle (the circumference). The fraction is the angle divided by 360. "

TACKLING MORE COMPLEX GEOMETRY QUESTIONS

Not all ACT geometry questions are straightforward. The test writers have ways of further complicating them. It's not **always** obvious at first what the question is getting at. Sometimes you really have to think about the figure and the given information before that lightbulb goes on in your head. Often, the inspiration that brings illumination is finding the hidden information.

PLANE GEOMETRY

Example

1. In the figure below, $\triangle ABC$ is a right triangle and $\overline{AC}$ is perpendicular to $\overline{BD}$. If $\overline{AB}$ is 6 units long, and $\overline{AC}$ is 10 units long, how many units long is $\overline{AD}$?

A. 3
B. $2\sqrt{3}$
C. 3.6
D. 4
E. $3\sqrt{2}$

At first this looks like a Pythagorean theorem question. In fact, the two given sides of $\triangle ABC$ identify it as the 6-8-10 version of the 3-4-5 special right triangle. (*100 Key Math Concepts for the ACT*, #85) So we know that $BC = 8$. So what? How's that going to help us find $\overline{AD}$?

The inspiration here is to realize that this is a "similar triangles" problem. We don't see the word *similar* anywhere in the question stem, but the stem and the figure combined actually tell us that all three triangles in the figure—$\triangle ABC$, $\triangle ADB$, and $\triangle BDC$—are similar. We know the triangles are similar because they all have the same three angles. Here are the three triangles separated and oriented to show the correspondences:

In this orientation it's easy to see the proportion setup that will solve the problem:

$$\frac{10}{6} = \frac{6}{x}$$

$$10x = 36$$

$$x = 3.6$$

The answer is C.

 PLANE GEOMETRY

Example

2. In the figure below, the area of the circle centered at O is 25π, and $\overline{AC}$ is perpendicular to $\overline{OB}$. If $\overline{AC}$ is 8 units long, how many units long is $\overline{BD}$?

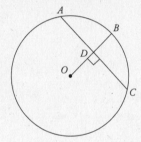

   F. 2
   G. 2.5
   H. 3
   J. 3.125
   K. 4

This is a tough one. It's not easy to see how to get $\overline{BD}$ from the given information. You can use the area—25π—to figure out the radius, and then you'd know the length of $\overline{OB}$:

$$Area = \pi r^2$$
$$25\pi = \pi r^2$$
$$25 = r^2$$
$$r = 5$$

So you know $\overline{OB} = 5$, but what about $\overline{BD}$? If you knew $\overline{OD}$, you could subtract that from $\overline{OB}$ to get what you want. But do you know $\overline{OD}$? This is the place where most people get stuck.

The inspiration that will lead to a solution is that you can take advantage of the right angle at D. Look what happens when you take a pencil and physically add $\overline{OA}$ and $\overline{OC}$ to the figure:

$\triangle OAD$ and $\triangle OCD$ are right triangles. And when we write in the lengths, we discover some special right triangles:

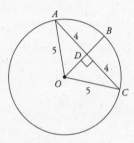

Now it's apparent that $\overline{OD} = 3$. Since $\overline{OB} = 5$, $\overline{BD}$ is $5 - 3 = 2$. The answer is F.

FIGURELESS PROBLEMS

Some ACT geometry problems present an extra challenge because they don't provide a figure. You have to "figure it out" for yourself. Try this one:

 PLANE GEOMETRY

Example

3. If one side of a right triangle is 3 units long, and a second side is 4 units long, which of the following could be the length, in units, of the third side?

   A. 1
   B. 2
   C. $\sqrt{7}$
   D. $3\sqrt{2}$
   E. $3\sqrt{3}$

The key to solving most figureless problems is to sketch a diagram, but sometimes that's not so easy because the test makers deliberately give you less information than you might like. Question 3 is the perfect example. It gives you two sides of a right triangle and asks for the third. Sounds familiar. And the two sides it gives you—3 and 4—*really* sound familiar. It's a 3-4-5, right?

So the answer's 5 . . .

Whoops! There's no 5 among the answer choices! What's going on?!

Better check back. Notice that the question asks, "Which of the following *could* be the length . . ." That *could* is crucial. It suggests that there's more than one possibility. Our answer of 5 was too obvious. There's another one somewhere.

Can you think of another way of sketching the figure with the same given information? Who says that the 3 and 4 have to be the two legs? Look at what happens when you make one of them—the larger one, of course—the *hypotenuse*:

This is not a 3-4-5 triangle, because in a 3-4-5, the 3 and the 4 are the legs. This is no special right triangle; to figure out the length of the third side, resort to the Pythagorean theorem:

$$(\text{leg}_1)^2 + (\text{leg}_2)^2 = (\text{hypotenuse})^2$$
$$3^2 + x^2 = 4^2$$
$$9 + x^2 = 16$$
$$x^2 = 7$$
$$x = \sqrt{7}$$

The answer is C.

> **PERFECT SCORE TIP**
>
> " Remember that there are multiple ways to draw diagrams. If the one you picked isn't working, try another instead of trying to do weird manipulations to an incorrect picture. "

MANY STEPS AND MANY CONCEPTS

Some of the toughest ACT geometry questions are ones that take many steps to solve and combine many different geometry concepts. The following is an example.

 PLANE GEOMETRY

Example

4. In the figure below, $\overline{AB}$ is tangent to the circle at A. If the circumference of the circle is 12π units and $\overline{OB}$ is 12 units long, what is the area, in square units, of the shaded region?

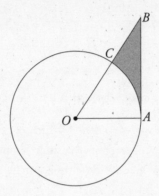

F. $18\sqrt{3} - 6\pi$

G. $24\sqrt{3} - 6\pi$

H. $18\sqrt{3} - 2\pi$

J. $12\pi - 12$

K. $243 - 2\pi$

This is about as hard as they come on the ACT. It is by no means clear how the given information—the circumference of the circle and the length of $\overline{OB}$—will lead you to the area of the shaded region.

So what do you do? Give up? No. *Don't* give up immediately unless you're really short on time or you know for sure you can't do the problem.

So then should you just plow ahead blindly and figure out every length, angle, and area you can and see where that leads you? *Well, not exactly.* It would be better to be more systematic.

The key to success with a circuitous problem like this is to focus on your destination—what you're looking for—and think about what you need to get there. Then go back to the given information and see what you can do to get you going in the right direction. Think about where you're headed before you take even one step; otherwise you may just have to backtrack.

Your destination in question 4 is "the area of the shaded region." That region is a shape that has no name, let alone an area formula. Like most shaded regions, this one is in fact the difference between two familiar shapes with names and area formulas. Think of the shaded region in question 4 as:

$$(\text{the area of } \Delta AOB) - (\text{the area of sector } AOC)$$

So now you know you need to figure out the area of the triangle and the area of the sector.

First, the triangle. You are explicitly given $\overline{OB} = 12$. You are also given that $\overline{AB}$ is tangent to the circle at A, which tells you that $\overline{OA}$ is a radius and that $\angle OAB$ is a right angle. So if you can figure out the radius of the circle, you'll have two sides of a right triangle, which will enable you to figure out the third side, and then figure out the area.

You can get the radius from the given circumference. Plug what you know into the formula and solve for r:

$$\text{Circumference} = 2\pi r$$
$$12\pi = 2\pi r$$
$$r = \frac{12\pi}{2\pi} = 6$$
$$\overline{OA} = 6$$

Aha! So it turns out that ΔAOB is no ordinary right triangle. Since one leg—6—is exactly half the hypotenuse—12—you're looking at a 30°-60°-90° triangle. By applying the well-known side ratios $(1 : \sqrt{3} : 2)$ for a 30°-60°-90° triangle (*100 Key Math Concepts for the ACT,* #85), you determine that $\overline{AB} = 6\sqrt{3}$. Now plug the lengths of the legs in for the base and altitude in the formula for the area of a triangle, and you'll get:

$$\text{Area} = \frac{1}{2}bh$$
$$= \frac{1}{2}(6\sqrt{3})(6)$$
$$= 18\sqrt{3}$$

Already it looks like the answer is going to be F or H—they're the choices that begin with $18\sqrt{3}$. You could just guess F or H and move on, but if you've come this far, you might as well go all the way.

Next, you need to determine the area of the sector. Fortunately, while working on the triangle, you figured out the two things you need to get the area of the sector:

GO ONLINE

" Brush up on your trig. Try the online trigonometry workshop and test yourself with the online quiz. "

the radius of the circle (6) and the measure of the central angle (60°). The radius tells you that the area of the whole circle (πr^2) is 36π. And the central angle tells you that the sector is $\dfrac{60}{360}$ or $\dfrac{1}{6}$ of the circle. One sixth of 36π is 6π. So the area of the shaded region is $18\sqrt{3} - 6\pi$, choice F.

IF YOU LEARNED ONLY THREE THINGS IN THIS CHAPTER . . .

1. You should be familiar with the ten textbook geometry questions.

2. When dealing with "disguised" geometry questions, use the figure and the question stem to find the information you need. It may not be stated directly.

3. If a geometry question doesn't have a figure, it usually helps to draw one.

CHAPTER 14: READING WORKOUT 3: SUBJECT MATTERS

Now that you've learned the general approach to ACT Reading and the approach for each of the specific question-types, let's look more closely at the two passage types that give students the most trouble—the Prose Fiction passage and the Natural Sciences passage.

The passage breakdown for the ACT Reading test is as follows:

Prose Fiction—one passage per test

Nonfiction—three passages per test, one each in:

- Social Studies
- Natural Sciences
- Humanities

Your approach will be essentially the same for all three nonfiction passages, since they're all well-organized essays. Your approach to the Prose Fiction passage, however, will be somewhat different.

What follows are two full ACT Reading passages—one Prose Fiction passage and one Natural Sciences passage (which, for convenience, we'll call just Science)—complete with questions. We'll talk about specific strategies for each, but just as importantly, we'll talk about how you can bring together everything you've learned so far and combine this knowledge into a plan of attack for *all* Reading passages. At the end of the workout, we'll also show you how to salvage a few extra points if you find yourself near the end of the test with not enough time to read the final passage.

THE PROSE FICTION PASSAGE

The Prose Fiction passage differs from the three nonfiction passages in that it is not a well-structured essay designed to communicate ideas in a logical, orderly way.

> **PERFECT SCORE TIP**
>
> " You do not have to read the four Reading passages in order! Figure out your best and start there. If prose is hard for you and takes a while, do it last even though it is first in the test book. "

EXPERT TUTOR TIP

" Fiction passages focus on the characters. Who are they? What are they like? What do they think about each other? So watch what they say and do in the passages. "

PERFECT SCORE TIP

" I found imagining the prose passage as a movie very helpful. It helped keep me awake and engaged while reading it so I was more prepared for the questions. "

EXPERT TUTOR TIP

" Once you've finished reading a passage and its questions, put it out of your mind. There's no connection at all between passages, so don't carry your stress or doubt to the next one. Approach each passage as if it were the only one. Stay active and confident—you're doing great! "

It is, usually, a story in which characters fully equipped with their own motivations and emotions interact with each other in revealing ways. For that reason, the Prose Fiction passage won't break down into an orderly outline or road map, so don't even try to characterize the function of each paragraph. Pay attention instead to the *story*.

In the Prose Fiction passage, almost all of the questions relate to the characters. Your job is to find the answers to the following questions:

- **Who are these people?** What are they like? How are they related to each other?

- **What is their state of mind?** Are they angry? Sad? Reflective? Excited?

- **What's going on?** What's happening on the surface? What's happening beneath the surface?

- **What's the author's attitude toward the characters?**

Most of the passages focus on one person or are written from the point of view of one of the characters. Figure out who this main character is and pay special attention to what he or she is like. **Read between the lines to determine unspoken emotions and attitudes. Little hints—a momentary frown, a pointed or sarcastic comment—are sometimes all you have to go on, so *pay attention*.** In fact, you'll probably want to spend more time prereading the Prose Fiction passage than you do any of the other three passages. It's important to get a good feel for the tone and style of the passage as a whole before going to the questions.

Fortunately, the questions that accompany these passages tend to go more quickly than those for the other passages, so you'll be able to make up some of that time you lose reading the passage.

MAKE IT A MOVIE IN YOUR HEAD

Try to make the passage into a movie! Imagine the scenes, the characters, the events. In the Prose Fiction passage, it should be easy to imagine the story unfolding like a movie. Pay careful attention not only to what the characters say but how they say it as well.

And don't forget to read actively, as always. Don't just read and then react. Once you have an idea of the personality of the characters, you should be able to respond to the questions. What should you do if you are struggling to understand what's going on? Go to the questions and let the line and paragraph references guide you to important words, phrases, and sentences. One or two questions should help you discover the meaning of the passage. And don't forget to guess.

THE REAL THING: PRACTICE PASSAGE

What follows is a typical ACT Prose Fiction passage, complete with questions. Before trying it, you might want to glance back at the techniques discussed in our first Reading Workout. Review the Kaplan Reading Method. **Recall that you should probably plan to spend about three minutes prereading (a little more, actually, since this is the Prose Fiction passage). Then do whichever questions you can figure out quickly. Skip any hard or time-consuming problems and come back to them later.**

When you work on the questions, constantly refer to the passage. Plan to spend much more time with your eyeballs pointed at the passage than at the questions. And don't forget to answer the questions in your own words (based on what you've preread and reread in the passage) *before* you look at the answers.

PASSAGE III

I recall a mist starting in as I crossed the lawn that afternoon. I was making my way up to the summer house for the purpose of clearing away
Line the remains of his lordship's taking tea there with
(5) some guest a little while earlier. I can recall spotting from some distance . . . . Miss Kenton's figure moving about inside the summerhouse. When I entered she had seated herself on one of the wicker chairs scattered around its interior, evidently
(10) engaged in some needlework. On closer inspection, I saw she was performing repairs to a cushion. I went about gathering up the various items of crockery from amidst the plants and the cane furniture, and as I did so, I believe we exchanged a
(15) few pleasantries, perhaps discussed one or two professional matters. For the truth was, it was extremely refreshing to be out in the summerhouse after many continuous days in the main building and neither of us was inclined to hurry
(20) with our tasks . . . . In fact, I was looking out over the lawn to where the mist was thickening down around the poplar trees planted along the cart-track, when I finally introduced the topic of the previous year's dismissals. Perhaps a little pre-
(25) dictably, I did so by saying:

"I was just thinking earlier, Miss Kenton. It's rather funny to remember now, but you know, only this time a year ago, you were still insisting you were going to resign. It rather amused me to
(30) think of it." When I finally turned to look at her,

she was gazing through the glass at the great expanse of fog outside.

"You probably have no idea, Mr. Stevens," she said eventually, "how seriously I really thought of
(35) leaving this house. I felt so strongly about what happened. Had I been anyone worthy of any respect at all, I dare say I would have left Darlington Hall long ago." She paused for a while, and I turned my gaze back out to the poplar trees
(40) down in the distance. Then she continued in a tired voice: "It was cowardice, Mr. Stevens. Simple cowardice. Where could I have gone? I have no family. Only my aunt. I love her dearly, but I can't live with her for a day without feeling my whole
(45) life is wasting away. I did tell myself, of course, I would soon find some situation.

"But I was so frightened, Mr. Stevens. Whenever I thought of leaving, I just saw myself going out there and finding nobody who knew or
(50) cared about me. There, that's all my high principles amount to. I feel so ashamed of myself. But I just couldn't leave, Mr. Stevens. I just couldn't bring myself to leave."

Miss Kenton paused again and seemed to be
(55) deep in thought. I thus thought it opportune to relate at this point, as precisely as possible, what had taken place earlier between myself and Lord Darlington. I proceeded to do so and concluded by saying:
(60) "What's done can hardly be undone. But it is at least a great comfort to hear his lordship declare

so unequivocally that it was all a terrible misunderstanding. I just thought you'd like to know, Miss Kenton, since I recall you were as distressed
(65) by the episode as I was."

"I'm sorry, Mr. Stevens," Miss Kenton said behind me in an entirely new voice, as though she had just been jolted from a dream, "I don't understand you." Then as I turned to her, she went on:
(70) "As I recall, you thought it was only right and proper that Ruth and Sarah be sent packing. You were positively cheerful about it."

"Now really, Miss Kenton, that is quite incorrect and unfair. The whole matter caused me great
(75) concern, great concern indeed. It is hardly the sort of thing I like to see happen in this house."

"Then why, Mr. Stevens, did you not tell me so at the time?"

I gave a laugh, but for a moment was rather at
(80) a loss for an answer. Before I could formulate one, Miss Kenton put down her sewing and said:

"Do you realize, Mr. Stevens, how much it would have meant to me if you had thought to share your feelings last year? You knew how upset
(85) I was when my girls were dismissed. Do you realize how much it would have helped me? Why, Mr. Stevens, why, why, why do you always have to pretend?"

I gave another laugh at the ridiculous turn the
(90) conversation had suddenly taken. "Really, Miss Kenton," I said, "I'm not sure I know what you mean. Pretend? Why, really . . . ."

"I suffered so much over Ruth and Sarah leaving us. And I suffered all the more because I
(95) believed I suffered alone."

1. According to the passage, the author thinks Mr. Stevens is:

   A. worthy of respect.

   B. not an admirable person.

   C. too formal in his demeanor.

   D. disloyal to his friends.

2. The statement "Had I been anyone worthy of any respect at all, I dare say I would have left Darlington Hall long ago" (lines 36–38) can be interpreted to mean:

   F. no one at Darlington Hall truly respects Miss Kenton.

   G. Miss Kenton has little respect for Mr. Stevens.

   H. Miss Kenton feels she betrayed her principles by staying.

   J. Miss Kenton senses that Mr. Stevens feels superior to her.

3. According to the passage, the intent of Mr. Stevens's recollection of Miss Kenton's desire to resign (lines 26–30) is most likely to:

   A. open up a discussion of an event that had upset Miss Kenton.

   B. turn the conversation to the professional topic of furniture repair.

   C. indulge in nostalgic reminiscences of happier days.

   D. irritate Miss Kenton by mocking the seriousness of that desire.

4. Mr. Stevens gives "a laugh" (line 79) because he is suddenly:

   F. amused.

   G. insecure.

   H. suspicious.

   J. sarcastic.

5. The main point of Miss Kenton's references to her own family (lines 42–45) is that:

   A. she would have nowhere to turn if she left her job.

   B. children often reject those they should love.

   C. she was afraid of discovering that she did not love her aunt.

   D. life becomes very tedious when one visits relatives.

6. What is it that Mr. Stevens describes as "done" (line 60)?

     F. Lord Darlington's earlier conversation with him

   G. Miss Kenton's talk of leaving Darlington Hall

   H. Ruth and Sarah's dismissal

   J. Any talk of Miss Kenton's dismissal

7. As he is revealed in the passage, Mr. Stevens is:

   A. bored with their conversation in the summer house.

   B. increasingly hostile to Miss Kenton's depiction of his actions.

   C. uncomfortable with expressing his deep affection for Miss Kenton.

   D. unaware of how his past behavior had affected Miss Kenton.

8. Which of the following would be out of character for the narrator?

   I. Pointing out to Miss Kenton why she was unfairly characterizing his actions

   II. Spending time thinking about Miss Kenton's accusations

   III. Ridiculing Miss Kenton for poorly repairing the cushion

   F. I only

   G. II only

   H. I and II only

   J. III only

9. Miss Kenton interacts with Mr. Stevens in a way that can best be described as:

   A. sincere but formal.

   B. indifferent but polite.

   C. timid but angry.

   D. patronizing but kindly.

10. At the end of the passage, Miss Kenton asks, "Why, Mr. Stevens, why, why, why do you always have to pretend?" (lines 86–88) What specific action of Mr. Stevens does she have in mind?

    F. His apparent cheerfulness at Ruth and Sarah's dismissal

    G. His simulation of great affection for her

    H. His phony concern for her own future employment

    J. His empty expressions of sympathy for her own suffering

ANSWERS AND EXPLANATIONS

Paragraphs in the Prose Fiction passage move the story forward. Your prereading road map should center on answers to four main questions about character, actions, and attitudes. They are:

- **Who are these people?** The first paragraphs are peppered with hints about who these people are. Lines 3–4 discuss Mr. Stevens "clearing away the remains of his lordship's taking tea." Lines 11–12 describe Miss Kenton "performing repairs to a cushion." Lines 28–29 discuss her previous plans for resigning. Clearly, Mr. Stevens and Miss Kenton are servants (we later learn—in lines 57–58—that their employer is Lord Darlington). Notice how, by answering this basic question, you've already answered Question 1.

- **What is their state of mind?** We read of "the previous year's dismissals" (lines 23–24) and Miss Kenton's intentions to leave the house (lines 34–36) as a result of them. She "felt so strongly about what happened" (lines 35–36), but she was afraid to take the step of actually leaving in protest ("It was cowardice," she admits in line 41). It sounds like some other servants were dismissed unfairly last year and that this upset Miss Kenton. Apparently, Mr. Stevens also found the incident distressing (lines 64–65), but Miss Kenton hadn't realized this at the time.

- **What's going on?** These are obviously very formal people, but there are strong emotions rumbling beneath the surface. It's clear that Miss Kenton is very upset because she didn't realize that Mr. Stevens disapproved of the dismissals too ("Do you realize, Mr. Stevens, how much it would have meant to me if you had thought to share your feelings last year?"—lines 82–84. And later: "Why, Mr. Stevens, why, why, why do you always have to pretend?"—lines 86–88). We get the impression that Mr. Stevens is not a man who very readily shows his feelings and emotions—as Miss Kenton puts it, he always *pretends*.

- **What is the author's attitude toward the characters?** Often, there will be a question asking about the author's point of view. Be careful here—don't confuse what the characters think about each other with what the author thinks. The two may not be the same.

Note: The first question here is about Writer's View. Your best bet is to skip the question and leave it to last.

Notice how many inference-type questions there are. This is typical of the Prose Fiction passage, where so much information is conveyed implicitly—"between the lines." In most cases, you have to read around the specific line references in order to find your answer. If you've done your preread properly, however, you should be able to knock off most of the questions quickly.

KEY TO PASSAGE III

(PROSE FICTION)

 INFERENCE

BIG PICTURE

DETAIL

	Answer	Refer to	Type	Comments
1.	D	First two paragraphs	Inference	Stevens says he was "amused" and thought it "funny" that she wanted to resign her position. Miss Kenton replies very seriously to his words, saying she doesn't understand him and how he could be so cheerful if he disapproved of the two firings. Miss Kenton has plainly suffered, and Mr. Stevens has not reacted kindly to her pain. The author's sympathy is with Miss Kenton, not Mr. Stevens.
2.	H	Lines 36–38, 50–51	Inference	"There, that's all my high principles amount to," she says.
3.	A	Lines 26–30, 55–58	Inference	Lines 55–58 show that Mr. Stevens has just been discussing this subject with Lord Darlington, and now wants to discuss it with Miss Kenton.
4.	G	Lines 79–80	Inference	He is "at a loss for an answer," and clearly not laughing out of amusement.
5.	A	Lines 42–45	Detail	"Where could I have gone? I have no family."
6.	H	Lines 60–65	Detail	Refers to "the previous year's dismissals," first mentioned in lines 23–24.
7.	D	Throughout	Big Picture	Mr. Stevens's nervous laughs hint that he had no idea how deeply Miss Kenton was affected.
8.	J	Throughout	Inference	I—He does this in lines 73–76. II—He wishes to respond to the accusations in lines 70–72. III—This kind of blatant harshness would be uncharacteristic of so discreet and proper a man.

| 9. | A | Throughout | Big Picture | Miss Kenton freely expresses her feelings to him throughout, so she is sincere. But she **never** loses her formal language and demeanor. |
| 10. | F | Lines 82–86, 66–72 | Inference | She wishes that he "had thought to share [his] feelings"; she was under the impression that he was "positively cheerful about [the dismissals]." |

THE NATURAL SCIENCES PASSAGE

The Science passage in the Reading subject test emphasizes reading. Here, it is more important understanding ideas than analyzing experiments and data.

Approaching the Science passage is really not any different from approaching the other nonfiction passages, since all are well-organized essays that lay out ideas in a straightforward, logical way. But you may be more likely to find unfamiliar vocabulary in Science passages. *Don't panic.* **Any unfamiliar terms will usually be defined in the passage, or else will have definitions inferable from context.**

DON'T GET LOST!

In the Science passage, it's easy to lose yourself in complex details. Don't do it. **It's *especially* important not to get bogged down in the Science passage!** Many students try to understand and remember everything as they read. But that's not the right ACT mind-set. In your preread of the passage, just get the "gist" and the outline; don't sweat the details. As always, use line references in the questions when possible. They will lead you back to the details that are important. You'd be surprised how many questions you can answer on a passage you don't really understand.

THE REAL THING: PRACTICE PASSAGE

The next passage is a typical ACT-style Science passage with questions. Try to attack it with the same Kaplan Method you use for other passages. Don't worry if you don't understand everything. Your only goal is to get a sense of the passage and its outline.

PERFECT SCORE TIP

" Often, the Natural Science passage will be difficult and have a lot of unknown scientific knowledge in it. Just remind yourself that you don't have to understand all the science behind it. The answer to every question is found in the passage and is within your grasp. "

PASSAGE IV

Atoms can be excited in many ways other than by absorbing a photon. The element phosphorous spontaneously combines with oxygen when
Line exposed to air. There is a transfer of energy to the
(5) phosphorous electrons during this chemical reaction which excites them to sufficiently high energy states that they can subsequently emit light when dropping into a lower state. This is an example of what is termed chemiluminescence, the emission
(10) of light as a result of chemical reaction.

A related effect is bioluminescence, when light is produced by chemical reactions associated with biological activity. Bioluminescence occurs in a variety of life forms and is more common in
(15) marine organisms than in terrestrial or freshwater life. Examples include certain bacteria, jellyfish, clams, fungi, worms, ants, and fireflies. There is considerable diversity in how light is produced. Most processes involve the reaction of a protein
(20) with oxygen, catalyzed by an enzyme. The protein varies from one organism to another, but all are grouped under the generic name luciferin. The enzymes are known as luciferase. Both words stem from the Latin lucifer meaning light-bearing. The
(25) various chemical steps leading to bioluminescence are yet to be explained in detail, but in some higher organisms the process is known to be activated by the nervous system.

The firefly is best understood. Its light organ is
(30) located near the end of the abdomen. Within it luciferin is combined with other atomic groups in a series of processes in which oxygen is converted into carbon dioxide. The sequence culminates when the luciferin is split off from the rest, leaving
(35) it in an excited state. The excess energy is released as a photon. The peak in the emission spectrum lies between 550 and 600 nm depending on the type of luciferase. This flash produced by the simultaneous emission of many photons serves to
(40) attract mates, and females also use it to attract males of other species, which they devour.

Certain bacteria also produce light when stimulated by motion. This is why the breaking sea or

a passing boat generate the greenish light seen in
(45) some bodies of water such as Phosphorescent Bay in Puerto Rico. Some fish have a symbiotic relationship with bacteria. The "flashlight fish" takes advantage of the light created by bacteria lodged beneath each eye. Certain other fish produce their
(50) own bioluminescence, which serves as identification. However, the biological advantage if any of bioluminescence in some other organisms such as fungi remains a mystery.

Triboluminescence is the emission of light
(55) when one hard object is sharply struck against another. This contact, when atom scrapes against atom, excites electrons and disrupts electrical bonds. Light is then created when the electrons find their way to lower states. Triboluminescence
(60) is not to be confused with the glow of small particles that may be broken off by the impact. Such "sparks" are seen as a result of their high temperature. Light given off by hot objects is known as thermoluminescence, or incandescence.

(65) Another form of thermoluminescence is the basis for dating ancient ceramic objects. Quartz and other constituents of clay are continually irradiated by naturally occurring radioactive elements (e.g., uranium and thorium) and by cosmic rays.
(70) This produces defects in the material where electrons may be trapped. Heating pottery to 500°C releases the trapped electrons, which can then migrate back to their original atoms, where on returning to an atomic orbit they then emit a pho-
(75) ton. The intensity of thermoluminescence is therefore a measure of the duration of irradiation since the time when the pottery had been previously fired.

Excitation is also possible by other means. The
(80) passage of an electrical current (electroluminescence) is one. The impact of high energy particles is another. The *aurora borealis* and its southern counterpart the *aurora australis* arise when a stream of high energy particles from the sun
(85) enters the earth's upper atmosphere and literally shatters some of the molecules of the air. This leaves their atoms in excited states, and the light

subsequently given off is characteristic of the atoms. Although the oxygen molecule, a major (90) constituent of our atmosphere, has no emission in the visible, the oxygen atom can emit photons in either the red or green portions of the spectrum. Other atoms contribute to light at other wavelengths.

From *Light and Color in Nature and Art*, copyright © 1983 by Samuel J. Williamson. Reprinted by permission of John Wiley & Sons, Inc.

11. According to the information in the sixth paragraph (lines 65–78), the brighter the thermoluminescence of a heated piece of ancient pottery:

A. the younger the piece is.

B. the older the piece is.

C. the less irradiation has occurred within the piece's clay.

D. the fewer electrons have become trapped within the clay.

12. If an ancient ceramic bowl is heated to 500°C, light is emitted when certain electrons:

F. release radioactive elements found in the clay.

G. scrape against other electrons.

H. become superheated.

J. return to their former atoms.

13. Compared to bioluminescence, chemiluminescence is NOT produced by:

A. organic proteins that have been catalyzed.

B. a chemical reaction.

C. any reaction involving oxygen.

D. a change in energy states.

14. It can be inferred from the passage that the description of the firefly's production of light is a good example of the degree to which researchers understand:

F. why light attracts fireflies.

G. how a chemical process can trigger bioluminescence.

H. how female fireflies attack male fireflies.

J. how to measure the intensity of a firefly's bioluminescence.

15. In both chemiluminescence and bioluminescence, photons are emitted:

A. as excess energy.

B. only by certain marine organisms.

C. only when luciferase is present.

D. only when phosphorous is present.

16. Based on details in the passage, the word *excited* as used in line 1 means:

F. split off from a molecule.

G. agitated until glowing.

H. raised to a higher energy level.

J. heated to the point of disintegration.

17. In discussing the creation of the two kinds of aurora, the passage asserts that the oxygen molecule "has no emission in the visible [spectrum]" (line 90–91) but also states that "the oxygen atom can emit photons in either the red or the green portions of the spectrum" (lines 91–92). Is the passage logically consistent?

   A. Yes, because visible light is emitted after the oxygen molecules have been broken apart into oxygen atoms.

   B. Yes, because the passage presents factual information and therefore cannot be illogical.

   C. No, because the oxygen molecule forms the largest part of the atmosphere and scientific theories must account for its invisible emissions.

   D. No, because the writer has failed to adequately differentiate between the oxygen molecule's behavior and that of the oxygen atom.

18. Assume that two meteors have collided and shattered. Astronomers see both a burst of light and then a subsequent glow. Such a visual phenomenon could best be explained as the result of:

   I. chemiluminescence

   II. triboluminescence

   III. thermoluminescence

   F. II only

   G. II and III only

   H. I and III only

   J. I, II, and III

19. Based on information presented in the passage, which of the following is a hypothesis, rather than a fact?

   A. Fireflies use bioluminescence to attract mates.

   B. Thermoluminescence and triboluminescence are two distinctly different kinds of light emission.

   C. A firefly's type of luciferase determines the peak of its light emission's intensity.

   D. All organisms that produce bioluminescence do so for some biological advantage.

20. According to the last paragraph (lines 79–94), both the *aurora borealis* and the *aurora australis*:

   F. demonstrate the effects on atoms of high energy particles.

   G. occur without the presence of oxygen.

   H. emit light due to the presence of electrical currents.

   J. are visible from the surface of the earth.

ANSWERS AND EXPLANATIONS

Feeling a little numb? Unless you're a real science buff, you probably found this passage a lot less exciting than the atoms did. And you may have found yourself adrift in a sea of bewildering terms—*chemiluminescence, luciferin, aurora australis.*

We hope, though, that you didn't panic. You could still get points—and lots of them—from this passage even if all that you took away from your preread was a sense that the passage was mainly about things in nature glowing when their atoms are excited. That, and a sense of a road map, was really all you needed. Most of the questions were answerable by referring to the appropriate lines in the passage and paraphrasing what you read there.

Here's a possible road map for the passage:

- **First paragraph:** Introduction of idea of excited atoms releasing photons (i.e., luminescence). Discusses *chemiluminescence* (resulting from a chemical reaction).

- **Second paragraph:** Discusses *bioluminescence* (associated with biological activity—that is, with things that are alive).

- **Third paragraph:** Example of *bioluminescence*—fireflies.

- **Fourth paragraph:** More examples of *bioluminescence*—sea life.

- **Fifth paragraph:** Discusses *triboluminescence* (things hitting each other) and *thermoluminescence* (hot objects).

- **Sixth paragraph:** Example of *thermoluminescence*—refired ceramic objects.

- **Seventh paragraph:** Concludes with discussion of *electroluminescence* (associated with electrical currents).

Basically, the author is giving us a rundown on the various kinds of luminescence in nature. When the questions ask about one kind or another, you simply refer to the appropriate paragraph and lines.

Following is a key to the answers for this passage. Notice how you could have gotten an answer to number 12, for instance, *even if you were totally confused.* If you found "500°" in the passage (line 71), the sentence more or less spelled out the answer for you, requiring a minimum of paraphrasing.

KEY TO PASSAGE IV

(NONFICTION—NATURAL SCIENCES)

 INFERENCE

 DETAIL

 BIG PICTURE

Answer		Refer to	Type	Comments
11.	B	Lines 65–78	Inference	More time since last firing to trap more electrons, creating brighter glow.
12.	J	Lines 65–75	Detail	"migrate back to their original atoms"
13.	A	Paragraph 2	Detail	Be careful with the reversal word *NOT* in the question. Organic means "having to do with life."
14.	G	Lines 19–28, 29–41	Inference	Remember, passage is about luminescence, not fireflies.
15.	A	Lines 4–10, 38–40	Inference	B and C aren't chemi-; D isn't bio-. Only A is both.
16.	H	Lines 2–10, 56–66	Detail	Lines 4–8 say it all.
17.	A	Lines 79–93	Detail	Note difference between oxygen molecule and oxygen atom.
18.	G	Lines 54–64	Inference	I—No, since no chemical reaction; II—Yes, since impact reaction; III—Yes, since "subsequent glow" (probably a heat reaction)
19.	D	Throughout	Big Picture	Any statement about "all organisms" is probably a hypothesis, since no one can verify what's true of every organism in existence.
20.	F	Lines 79–94	Detail	"a stream of high energy particles from the sun"

EMERGENCY STRATEGY FOR TEST DAY

If you have less than four minutes left and you've still got an entire passage untouched, you need to shift to last-minute strategies. Don't try to preread the passage; you'll just run out of time before you answer any questions. Instead, scan the questions without reading the passage and look first for the ones that mention line numbers or specific paragraphs. You can often get quick points on these questions by referring back to the passage as the question stem directs, reading a few lines around the reference, and taking your best shot.

Of course, the most important thing is to make sure you have gridded in at least a random guess on every question. If some of your blind guesses are right (as some of them statistically *should* be), they'll boost your score just as much as well-reasoned, thought-out answers would!

IF YOU LEARNED ONLY TWO THINGS IN THIS CHAPTER . . .

1. In the Prose Fiction passage, concentrate on who the characters are and what they are doing. What are the characters' attitudes toward each other? What is the author's attitude toward his characters?

2. For Natural Sciences passages, ask yourself, "What's new?" in each paragraph. Don't get bogged down in details or terminology. All you need is the general idea of how the paragraphs fit together.

CHAPTER 15: SCIENCE WORKOUT 3: KEEP YOUR VIEWPOINTS STRAIGHT

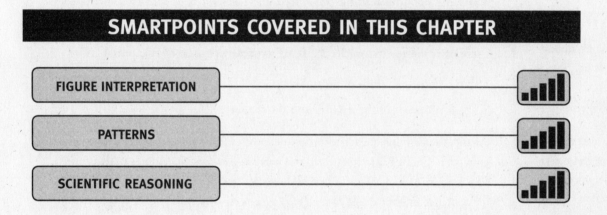

SMARTPOINTS COVERED IN THIS CHAPTER

FIGURE INTERPRETATION

PATTERNS

SCIENTIFIC REASONING

On the Science test, you'll find one Conflicting Viewpoints passage, in which two scientists propose different theories about a particular scientific phenomenon. Often, the two theories are just differing interpretations of the same data; other times, each scientist offers his own data to support his own opinion. In either case, it's essential that you know more or less what theory each scientist is proposing, and that you pay careful attention to how and where their theories differ.

In Science Workout 2, we talked about how scientists think, and you should bring all of that information to bear on the Conflicting Viewpoints passage. Since the scientists are disagreeing on interpretation, it's usually the case that they're engaging in specific-to-general thinking. They're each using specific data, sometimes the *same* specific data, but they're coming to very different general conclusions.

Your job is *not* to figure out which scientist is right and which is wrong. Instead, you'll be tested on whether you *understand* each scientist's position and the thinking behind it.

> **PERFECT SCORE TIP**
>
> " On the Conflicting Viewpoints passages, I found it helpful to briefly summarize each one—just like a Reading passage. This helped keep me focused and engaged in the passage. "

PREREADING THE CONFLICTING VIEWPOINTS PASSAGE

When tackling the Conflicting Viewpoints passage, you'll probably want to spend a little more time than usual on the prereading step of the Kaplan Reading Method. As we saw on other Science passages, your goal in prereading is to get a general idea of what's going on so that you can focus when you do the questions. But we find that **it pays to spend a little extra time with the Conflicting Viewpoints passage in order to get a clearer idea of the opposing theories and the data behind them.**

The passage will usually consist of a short introduction laying out the scientific issue in question, followed by the different viewpoints. Sometimes these viewpoints are presented under the headings Scientist 1 and Scientist 2, or Theory 1 and Theory 2, or Hypothesis 1 and Hypothesis 2.

A scientific viewpoint on the ACT will typically consist of two parts:

- A statement of the general theory
- A summary of the data behind the theory

Usually, the first line of each viewpoint expresses the general theory. Scientist 1's first sentence might be something like: *The universe will continue to expand indefinitely.* This is Scientist 1's viewpoint boiled down to a single statement. Scientist 2's first sentence might be: *The force of gravity will eventually force the universe to stop expanding and to begin contracting.* This is Scientist 2's viewpoint, and it clearly contradicts Scientist 1's opinion.

While it's important that you understand these basic statements of theory, it is just as important that you see how they oppose each other. In fact, you might want to circle the theory statement for each viewpoint, right there in the test booklet, to fix the two positions in your mind.

After each statement of theory will come the data that's behind it. As we said, sometimes the scientists are just drawing different interpretations from the same data. But usually, each will have different supporting data. There are two different kinds of data:

- Data that supports the scientist's own theory
- Data that weakens the opposing scientist's theory

It's normally a good idea to identify the major points of data for each theory. You might underline a phrase or sentence that crystallizes each, or even take note of whether it primarily supports the scientist's own theory or shoots holes in the opposing theory.

Once you understand each scientist's theory and the data behind it, you'll be ready to move on to the questions. Remember that some of the questions will refer to only one of the viewpoints. **Whatever you do, *don't mix up the two viewpoints*!** A question asking about the data supporting Theory 2 may have wrong answers that perfectly describe the data for Theory 1. If you're careless, you can easily fall for one of these wrong answers.

THE REAL THING: PRACTICE PASSAGE

What follows is a full-fledged, ACT-style Conflicting Viewpoints passage. Give yourself six minutes or so to read the passage and do all seven questions.

PASSAGE V

Tektites are natural, glassy objects that range in size from the diameter of a grain of sand to that of a human fist. They are found in only a few well-defined areas, called strewn fields. Two theories about the origin of tektites are presented below.

Scientist 1

Tektites almost certainly are extraterrestrial, probably lunar, in origin. Their forms show the characteristics of air-friction melting. In one study, flanged, "flying saucer" shapes similar to those of australites (a common tektite form) were produced by ablating lenses of tektite glass in a heated airstream that simulated atmospheric entry.

Atmospheric forces also make terrestrial origin extremely improbable. Aerodynamic studies have shown that because of atmospheric density, tektite-like material ejected from the earth's surface would never attain a velocity much higher than that of the surrounding air, and therefore would not be shaped by atmospheric friction. Most likely, tektites were formed either from meteorites or from lunar material ejected in volcanic eruptions.

Analysis of specimen #14425 from the *Apollo 12* lunar mission shows that the sample strongly resembles some of the tektites from the Australasian strewn field. Also, tektites contain only a small fraction of the water that is locked into the structure of terrestrial volcanic glass. And tektites never contain unmelted crystalline material; the otherwise similar terrestrial glass produced by some meteorite impacts **always** does.

Scientist 2

Nonlocal origin is extremely unlikely, given the narrow distribution of tektite strewn fields. Even if a tightly focused jet of lunar matter were to strike the earth, whatever was deflected by the atmosphere would remain in a solar orbit. The next time its orbit coincided with that of the earth, some of the matter would be captured by earth's gravity and fall over a wide area.

There are striking similarities not only between the composition of the earth's crust and that of most tektites but between the proportions of various gases found in the earth's atmosphere and in the vesicles of certain tektites.

Tektites were probably formed by meteorite impacts. The shock wave produced by a major collision could temporarily displace the atmosphere above. Terrestrial material might then splatter to suborbital heights and undergo air-friction melting upon reentry. And tektite fields in the Ivory Coast and Ghana can be correlated with known impact craters.

MENTAL NOTE

" In the heat of the moment, it's easy to confuse the two opposing theories. **Always** double-check to make sure you haven't assigned the ideas of Scientist 1 to Scientist 2, and vice versa. "

EXPERT TUTOR TIP

" Keep viewpoints straight:

1. Read the intro and Scientist 1 passage.
2. Answer questions that say "Scientist 1."
3. Read Scientist 2 paragraph.
4. Answer "Scientist 2" questions.
5. Answer any other questions. "

EXPERT TUTOR TIP

" Marking up the intro and the Scientist 1 and 2 paragraphs is critical. Bracket and circle key phrases and sentences as you go. "

SCIENTIFIC REASONING

1. The discovery that many tektites contain unmelted, crystalline material would:

   A. tend to weaken Scientist 1's argument.

   B. tend to weaken Scientist 2's argument.

   C. be incompatible with both scientists' views.

   D. be irrelevant to the controversy.

2. Which of the following is a reason given by Scientist 2 for believing that tektites originate on the earth?

   F. The density of the earth's atmosphere would prevent any similar lunar or extraterrestrial material from reaching the earth's surface.

   G. Tektites have a composition totally unlike that of any material ever brought back from the moon.

   H. Extraterrestrial material could not have been as widely dispersed as tektites are.

   J. Material ejected from the moon or beyond would eventually have been much more widely distributed on Earth.

3. Scientist 1 could best answer the point that some tektites have vesicles filled with gases in the same proportion as the earth's atmosphere by:

   A. countering that not all tektites have such gas-filled vesicles.

   B. demonstrating that molten material would be likely to trap some gases while falling through the terrestrial atmosphere.

   C. suggesting that those gases might occur in the same proportions in the moon's atmosphere.

   D. showing that similar vesicles, filled with these gases in the same proportions, are also found in some terrestrial volcanic glass.

4. How did Scientist 2 answer the argument that tektite-like material ejected from the earth could not reach a high enough velocity relative to the atmosphere to undergo air-friction melting?

   F. By asserting that a shock wave might cause a momentary change in atmosphere density, permitting subsequent aerodynamic heating

   G. By pointing out that periodic meteorite impacts have caused gradual changes in atmospheric density over the eons

   H. By attacking the validity of the aerodynamic studies cited by Scientist 1

   J. By referring to the correlation between tektite fields and known impact craters in the Ivory Coast and Ghana

5. The point of subjecting lenses of tektite glass to a heated airstream was to:

   A. determine their water content.

   B. see if gases became trapped in their vesicles.

   C. reproduce the effects of atmospheric entry.

   D. simulate the mechanism of meteorite formation.

6. Researchers could best counter the objections of Scientist 2 to Scientist 1's argument by:

   F. discovering some phenomenon that would quickly remove tektite-sized objects from orbit.

   G. proving that most common tektite shapes can be produced by aerodynamic heating.

   H. confirming that active volcanoes once existed on the moon.

   J. mapping the locations of all known tektite fields and impact craters.

7. Which of the following characteristics of tektites is LEAST consistent with the theory that tektites are of extraterrestrial origin?

    A. Low water content

    B. "Flying saucer" shapes

    C. Narrow distribution

    D. Absence of unmelted material

ANSWERS AND EXPLANATIONS

Your preread of the introduction should have revealed the issue at hand—namely, tektites, which are small glassy objects found in certain areas known as strewn fields. The conflict is about the *origin* of these objects: in other words, where did they come from?

Scientist 1's theory is expressed in his first sentence: "Tektites almost certainly are extraterrestrial, probably lunar, in origin." Put that into a form you can understand: in other words, Scientist 1 believes that tektites come from space, probably the moon. Scientist 2, on the other hand, has an opposing theory, also expressed in her first sentence: "Nonlocal origin is extremely unlikely." In other words, it's unlikely that tektites came from a nonlocal source; instead, they probably came from a *local* source, i.e., right here on Earth. The conflict is clear. One says that tektites come from space; the other says they come from Earth. You might have even labeled the two positions: "space origin" and "Earth origin."

Scientist 1 presents three points of data:

1. Tektite shapes show characteristics of "air-friction melting" (supporting the theory of space origin).

2. "Atmospheric forces" wouldn't be great enough to shape tektite-like material ejected from Earth's surface (weakening the theory of Earth origin).

3. Tektites resemble moon rocks gathered by *Apollo 12*, but not Earth rocks (strengthening the theory of space origin).

Scientist 2 also presents three points of data:

1. Any matter coming from space would "fall over a wide area" instead of being concentrated in strewn fields (weakening the theory of space origin).

2. There are "striking similarities" between tektites and the composition of the earth's crust (strengthening the theory of Earth origin).

ANSWERS

1. A
2. J
3. B
4. F
5. C
6. F
7. C

GO ONLINE

 The Diagnostic Quiz in your online companion includes a practice Conflicting Viewpoints passage.

3. "Meteorite impacts" could create shock waves, explaining how terrestrial material could undergo air-friction melting (strengthening the theory of Earth origin by counteracting Scientist 1's first point).

Obviously, you won't have time to write out the supporting data for each theory the way we've done above. But it is important to circle or bracket the key phrases in the data descriptions ("air-friction melting," "*Apollo 12*," etc.) and number them. **What's important is that you have an idea of what data supports which theory.** The questions, once you get to them, will then force you to focus.

Question 1 asks how it would affect the scientists' arguments if it were discovered that many tektites contain unmelted crystalline material. Well, Scientist 1 says that tektites never contain unmelted crystalline material, and that the terrestrial glass produced by some meteorite impacts *always* does. Therefore, by showing a resemblance between tektites and Earth materials, this discovery would weaken Scientist 1's argument for extraterrestrial origin. **Choice A is correct.**

For **Question 2,** you had to identify which answer choice was used by Scientist 2 to support the argument that tektites are terrestrial in origin. You should have been immediately drawn to choice J, which expresses what we've identified above as Scientist 2's first data point. Notice how choice F is a piece of evidence that Scientist 1 cites. (Remember not to confuse the viewpoints!) As for G, Scientist 2 says that tektites *do* resemble Earth materials, but never says that they *don't* resemble lunar materials. And choice H gets it backwards; Scientist 2 says that extraterrestrial material *would* be widely dispersed and that the tektites are *not* widely dispersed, rather than vice versa.

For **Question 3,** you need to find the best way for Scientist 1 to counter the point that some tektites have vesicles filled with gases in the same proportion as the earth's atmosphere. First, make sure you understand the meaning of that point. The idea that these gases must have been trapped in the vesicles (little holes) while the rock was actually being formed is being used by Scientist 2 to suggest that tektites are of terrestrial origin. Scientist 1 *could* say that not all tektites have such gas-filled vesicles—choice A—but that's not a great argument. If any reasonable number of them *do*, Scientist 1 would have to come up with an alternative explanation (Scientist 2 **never** claimed that *all* tektites contained these vesicles). But if, as B suggests, Scientist 1 could demonstrate that molten material would be likely to trap some terrestrial gases while falling through Earth's atmosphere, this would explain how tektites might have come from beyond Earth and still contain vesicles filled with Earthlike gases. Choice C is easy to eliminate if you know that the moon's atmosphere is extremely thin and totally different in composition from Earth's atmosphere, so it doesn't make much sense to suggest that those gases might occur in the same proportions as in the moon's atmosphere. Finally, since it's Scientist 2 who

---

EXPERT TUTOR TIP

" Active Reading in the Conflicting Viewpoints passage will make it easier to find the information you need to answer questions correctly. "

EXPERT TUTOR TIP

" Many Conflicting Viewpoints questions relate to *evidence* (or *data*). You may be asked:

What was presented?

Why?

Would it help or hurt a scientist's claim? "

claims that tektites are terrestrial in origin, choice D, showing that similar gas-filled vesicles occur in some terrestrial volcanic glass, this wouldn't help Scientist 1 at all.

In **Question 4,** you're asked how Scientist 2 answered the argument that tektite-like material ejected from the earth could not reach a high enough velocity to undergo air-friction melting. Well, that was Scientist 2's third data point. The shock wave produced by a major meteorite collision could momentarily displace the atmosphere right above the impact site (meaning the air moved out of the way for a brief time). So when the splattered material reentered the atmosphere, it would undergo air-friction melting. That's basically what choice F says, so F is correct.

In **Question 5,** the concept of subjecting lenses of tektite glass to a heated airstream was mentioned toward the beginning of Scientist 1's argument. The point was to simulate the entry of extraterrestrial tektite material through Earth's atmosphere, and that's closest to choice C.

Question 6 shows again why it pays to keep each scientist's viewpoint straight. You can't counter the objections of Scientist 2 to Scientist 1's argument unless you know what Scientist 2 was objecting to. Scientist 2's first data point is the only one designed to shoot holes in the opposing viewpoint. There, Scientist 2 takes issue with the idea that lunar material could strike the earth without being dispersed over a far wider area than the known strewn fields. But if, as correct choice F says, researchers found some force capable of removing tektite-sized objects from orbit *quickly*, it would demolish the objection that Scientist 2 raises in her first paragraph. The tektite material would strike the earth or be pulled away quickly, instead of remaining in a solar orbit long enough to be captured by the earth's gravity and subsequently be distributed over a wide area of the earth.

Question 7 wasn't too tough if you read the question stem carefully. You want to find the tektite characteristic that is LEAST consistent with the theory that tektites came from the moon or beyond. This is Scientist 1's theory, so you want to pick the answer choice that doesn't go with his argument. Scientist 1's evidence *does* include tektites' low water content, "flying saucer" shapes, and absence of unmelted material. The only answer choice that she didn't mention was the narrow distribution of the strewn fields. And with good reason. That's part of Scientist 2's argument *against* an extraterrestrial origin. So the correct answer is choice C.

> **EXPERT TUTOR TIP**
>
> " If a passage looks very difficult for you, skip it. Do the easy passages first, then come back to the passages that look like they are harder. "

THE DEEP END: FACING TOUGH SCIENCE PASSAGES

Now we're going to do something very cruel. We're going to throw you a Science passage of such technical difficulty that you will want to go screaming for the exit before you finish reading it.

We're doing this for a reason. Sometimes on the ACT Science test, you'll find yourself encountering a bear of a passage—one that seems entirely incomprehensible. **The secret to success with these passages is: *don't panic.*** As we'll show you, you can get points on even the most difficult Science passage in the entire history of the ACT—as long as you keep your cool and approach it in a savvy, practical way. Here's the passage:

PASSAGE VI

Neutrinos (n) are subatomic particles that travel at approximately the speed of light. They can penetrate most matter, because they are electrically neutral and effectively massless.

Generally accepted theory holds that the nuclear reactions that power the Sun create vast quantities of neutrinos as byproducts. Three proposed stages (PPI, PPII, and PPIII) of the most important solar reaction are shown in Figure 1, along with their neutrino-producing subpaths. Equations for the subpaths are shown in Table 1, as are the predicted neutrino energies and fluxes.

Figure 1

Table 1

Subpath name	Subpath equation	Neutrino energy (MeV)	Expected flux on Earth ($10^{10} cm^{-2} sec^{-1}$)
p-p	$_1H^1 + {}_1H^1 \longrightarrow {}_1H^2 + \beta^+ + n$	0.42	6.06781
p-e-p	$_1H^1 + \beta^- + {}_1H^1 \longrightarrow {}_1H^2 + n$	1.44	0.01524
Be^7†	$_4Be^7 + \beta^- \longrightarrow {}_3Li^7 + n$	0.87	0.43924
Be^7††	$_4Be^7 + \beta^- \longrightarrow {}_3Li^7 + n$	0.38	0.04880
B^8	$_5B^8 \longrightarrow {}_4Be^8 + \beta^+ + n$	14.05*	0.00054

†Be^7 subpath 1
††Be^7 subpath 2

*Maximum

FIGURE INTERPRETATION

8. According to the information presented in the passage, which of the following stages or subpaths should contribute the smallest portion of the total solar neutrino flux on Earth?

   F.   p-p
   G.   PPI
   H.   PPII
   J.   PPIII

FIGURE INTERPRETATION

9. Of the neutrinos that are produced in the subpaths described in the passage, which type can have the greatest energy?

   A. n_1
   B. n_2
   C. n_3
   D. n_4

PATTERNS

10. Based on the information presented in the passage, the percentage of solar neutrinos produced by Be^7 subpath 2 is approximately:

   F.   1.2%
   G.   10%
   H.   12%
   J.   90%

FIGURE INTERPRETATION

11. Solar neutrinos are detected through a reaction with $_{37}Cl$ for which the minimum neutrino energy is approximately 0.8 MeV. Of the neutrinos discussed in the passage, this method would detect:

   A.   all of the neutrinos produced in PPI and PPII.

   B.   some of the neutrinos produced in PPI, PPII, and PPIII.

   C.   only neutrinos produced in Be^7 subpath 1 of PPII.

   D.   only neutrinos produced in PPIII.

ANSWERS

8. J
9. D
10. F
11. B
12. G

 SCIENTIFIC REASONING

12. The symbol β represents a beta particle, a particle emitted during nuclear decay. Beta particles may be positively or negatively charged. During which of the following subpaths are beta particles emitted?

    I.   p-p

    II. p-e-p

    III. B^8

    F. II only
    G. I and III only
    H. II and III only
    J. I, II, and III

ANSWERS AND EXPLANATIONS

Confused? If you aren't, you should stick close to your phone, because the Nobel Prize committee will probably be calling sometime soon! On the other hand, if you *are* confused, don't sweat it. **As we said in ACT Basics, some ACT questions are so hard that even your *teachers* would have a hard time getting them correct.**

The good news is that you don't have to understand a passage to get a few questions right. Here's how you might have approached the passage above:

GETTING POINTS EVEN IF YOU DON'T GET THE POINT

Your preread of the introduction should have told you that the passage is about neutrinos coming from the sun. But that may be all you were able to get from this gibberish. You may have been in a total fog looking at Figure 1 and Table 1. But if you didn't panic, you might have noticed a few things: First, that whatever Figure 1 illustrates, there are some really big parts and some really small parts. If you look at the *x*-axis of the chart, you'll see that, whatever PPI, PPII, and PPIII are, the first is 88 percent, the second only 12 percent, and the third only .01 percent.

Is that tiny, vague insight enough to get a point? Yes! Look at **Question 8.** It asks which stage or subpath contributes the *smallest* portion of flux. Well, look for a small portion. PPIII's figure of 0.01 percent is a very small number, whatever it's supposed to be referring to, so PPIII would be a good guess here. And indeed, choice J is correct for Question 8.

What about Table 1? This is a little easier to understand, especially if you ignore the column about subpath equations. But "neutrino energy" sounds like something we can comprehend. Apparently, each subpath produces a different level of neutrino energy. Some have high energy (like B^8, with 14.06) and some have low energy (like B^{7++}, with only 0.38). Energy is mentioned in **Question 9.** Which type of neutrinos can have the greatest energy? Well, if B^8 were a choice, we'd pick that. But the choices are ns, not Bs. Well, try to find B^8 somewhere in the other chart—Figure 1. There we find it somehow associated with n_4 neutrinos. So take a gamble; choose n_4—which is choice D—for this question. If you did that, you'd still have gotten another point, still without really understanding much more than before.

You're hot; keep it going. **Question 10** refers to Be^7 subpath 2. You may have noticed in the note under Table 1 that the Be^7 with two little dagger marks signifies subpath 2. So far, so good. Notice that the choices are all percentages. Where are percentages mentioned? In Figure 1. So find Be^7 with two dagger marks in Figure 1. You find it in the area of PPII, which is 12 percent of the x-axis in that chart. But notice that Be^7 with two dagger marks represents only *part* of that part of the figure—10 percent, to be exact. So 10 percent of 12 percent would be 1.2 percent. That's choice F. It's also the correct answer.

Things get a little harder with **Question 11,** but you still might have gotten the answer if you used common sense. Here we get some mumbo jumbo about $_{37}Cl$, but the part of the question that should have caught your eye was the bit about a minimum neutrino energy of 0.8 MeV. Neutrino energy was represented in the third column of Table 1. According to that table, only three subpaths have an energy greater than 0.8—p-e-p (with 1.44), Be^7 with one dagger mark (with 0.87), and B^8 (the champion, with 14.06). Unfortunately, the answer choices aren't expressed in those terms; they're expressed in terms of PPI, II, and III, so we're going to have to translate from table to figure again, just as we did with Question 9.

Take p-e-p first. That's part (but not all) of the PPI portion of Figure 1. Be^7 with one dagger mark, similarly, is part (but not all) of the PPII portion. And B^8 is all of the PPIII portion. So there are at least parts of PPI, PPII, and PPIII implicated here. That should have led you to choice B, which would have gotten you yet another point. Notice that choice A is inaccurate because it talks about *all* of something in PPI and PPII, and doesn't mention PPIII at all. Choices C and D, meanwhile, seem too limited, since they only mention one of the PP areas (whatever they are). So B was definitely the closest answer choice.

Finally, **Question 12** talks about beta particles. Well, that little beta symbol appears only in the subpath column of Table 1. There we find beta symbols in the equations for *all* of the subpaths in the table. That may have led you to believe that

> **EXPERT TUTOR TIP**
>
> " Don't spend too long on any one question. They are all worth the same, so if you have no idea on a question, guess and move on. "

all three Roman numerals should be included, and no one would have blamed you for choosing choice J (I, II, and III). You would have been wrong, but you can't win them all when you're winging questions you don't really understand.

Of course, if you noticed that the question was asking for beta particles *emitted*, and if you knew that in the subpath equations everything *before* the arrow is what you start with while everything *after* the arrow is what you finish with, you might have been able to make a better guess. You would have realized that those equations with a beta symbol *before* the arrow were ones in which a beta particle was *absorbed*, while those with a beta symbol *after* the arrow were ones in which a beta particle was *emitted*. In that case, then, you would have seen that the equations for p-p and B[8] do have beta particles emitted, while the equation for p-e-p does not. That might have led you to choice G—I and III only—which is the correct answer.

Six questions, six points—and all without understanding the passage in any deep or thorough way. Of course, if you understand the mysteries of neutrino flux and p-e-p subpaths, congratulations. You're probably enough of a science whiz to ace the subject test anyway. But if you're like most ACT test takers, you won't understand everything the passages talk about. Sometimes you'll even find yourself totally lost.

The moral of the story, of course, is **don't give up on a passage just because you don't understand it.** You may not be able to get *every* point associated with the passage, but you may be able to get at least one or two (or three or four). Remember: the test is designed in such a way that you can *figure out* many of the questions, even if you don't know the subject area.

Let's conclude now with another quick point about getting quick points. If you're nearly out of time and you've still got a whole Science passage left, you need to shift to last-minute strategies. As in Reading, don't try to preread the passage, or you'll just run out of time before you answer any questions. Instead, scan the questions without reading the passage and look first for the ones that require only reading data off of a graph or table. You can often get a couple of quick points just by knowing how to find data quickly.

Again, the most important thing is to make sure you have gridded in at least a random guess on every question.

EXPERT TUTOR TIP

" If you run out of time, guess the same letter on every problem. This will give you a higher chance of increasing your score purely on guessing. "

PERFECT SCORE TIP

" The advice that cannot be repeated enough times is to answer every question. If you are running out of time, be sure to guess on every answer. Even one lucky guess could boost your score. "

IF YOU LEARNED ONLY THREE THINGS IN THIS CHAPTER . . .

1. Each ACT Science test has one Conflicting Viewpoints passage in which two scientists debate an issue.

2. Spend more time prereading Conflicting Viewpoints passages. Determine each scientist's view and identify the supporting and undermining evidence.

3. You can get many Science questions right even when you don't understand the entire passage. Don't panic when faced with a tough passage.

CHAPTER 16: WRITING WORKOUT: WRITE WHAT COUNTS

A growing number of colleges want an assessment of your written communication skills. If you consider yourself a good writer and are accustomed to scoring well on essays, there may be a temptation to skip this chapter. Don't. Top scores are not given out easily, and writing a scored first draft in under a half hour is unlike most of your past writing experiences.

In addition, the ACT essay is not a typical essay that you are used to writing in school. For example: You are allowed (even encouraged) to use the first person *I* and *we* in your argument. Personal experiences are excellent ways to back up your position. If you need to embroider the facts a little to make your point, no one is going to fact-check your essay.

Let's start with the facts.

JUST THE FACTS

Writing has **always** been an essential skill for college success. An optional Writing test will be available when you take the ACT. Some colleges require it; others do not. **Before registering for the ACT, find out if the schools to which you're applying want applicants to take the Writing test.**

The ACT English test already measures knowledge of effective writing skills, including grammar, punctuation, organization, and style. The Writing test complements that evaluation of technical skill with an example of your simple, direct writing.

GO ONLINE

❝ Your online companion contains two practice essay prompts (in addition to the one in this chapter). After you test yourself, evaluate your essays by comparing them to the model essays provided. ❞

PERFECT SCORE TIP

" I suggest taking the Writing section if you think there is any chance a college you want to go to might want it. Personally, the thought of being forced to retake such a long test sounds more painful than just preparing for Writing in the first place. "

PERFECT SCORE TIP

" The key to the ACT essay really is clarity. The graders want to see if you can logically put together an argument and are not going to waste their time trying to decode cryptic language, so make your points clear and obvious. "

HOW THE ACT ESSAY IS SCORED

Your essay will be graded on a holistic scale of 1–6 (6 being the best). Graders will be looking for an overall sense of your essay, not assigning separate scores for specific elements like grammar or organization. Two readers read and score each essay; then those scores are added together to arrive at your Writing subscore (from 2–12). If there's a difference of more than a point between the two readers' scores, your essay will be read by a third reader.

Statistically speaking, there will be few essays that score 6. If each grader gives your essay a 4 or 5, that will place you at the upper range of those taking the exam.

WHAT SHOULD I DO?

The readers realize you're writing under time pressure and expect you to make some mistakes. **The facts in your essay are not important, readers are not checking your facts. Nor will they judge you on your opinions. What they want is to see how well you can communicate a relevant, coherent point of view.**

The test makers identify the following as the skills tested in the Writing test:

- **Answer the question in the prompt.** State a clear perspective on an issue.

- **Build an argument.** Assemble supporting evidence logically with relevant, specific points.

- **Maintain focus and organize your specific points logically.** Avoid digressions and be sure to draw everything together in a concluding paragraph.

- **Address the complexity of the issue.** Discuss BOTH sides of the argument. Don't ignore the opposite side.

- **Write clearly.** Make sure your argument is easy to follow. Grammar rules are not the point of the essay; however, many errors that interfere with the essay's argument will hurt your score.

CAN I PREPARE FOR THE ESSAY?

The underlying skill in the Writing test is speed. On the ACT, you have only 30 minutes, and you must accomplish a lot in that time. It takes practice (and more practice) to read the prompt, organize your position with relevant ideas and facts, write a concluding paragraph—and proofread the whole.

DO YOU NEED TO PREPARE FOR THE ESSAY?

The ACT essay is not like other writing experiences. It's a first draft that will be graded. Not only must it be complete and well organized, but it must also be easy for a grader to see that it is complete and well organized (and the grader may spend as little as a minute reading your essay). That's a lot to do in 30 minutes, so preparation and practice are a good idea.

THE KAPLAN FOUR-STEP METHOD FOR THE ACT ESSAY

Step 1: Pause to Know the Prompt

Step 2: Plan

Step 3: Produce

Step 4: Proofread

TEST TIP

By the way, practicing the ACT essay also reinforces what you've learned for the English test and strengthens your Reading test skills: in Reading, you take an argument apart; in Writing, you put together an argument.

If you plan your essay and adhere to your plan when you write, the result will be solidly organized. Between now and test day, you can't drastically change your overall writing skills—and you probably don't need to. **If your plan is good, all you need to do in the writing and proofreading steps is draw on your strengths and avoid your weaknesses.** Get to know what those are as you practice.

Write what counts: to maximize your score, use the Kaplan Method to help you focus on writing what the scorers will look for—*and nothing else.*

Step:	A high-scoring essay:	A low-scoring essay:
Prompt	clearly develops a position on the prompt	does not clearly state a position
Plan	supports with concrete, relevant examples	is general, repetitious, or overly simplistic
Produce	maintains clear focus and organization	digresses or has weak organization
Proofread	shows competent use of language	contains errors that reduce clarity

Kaplan has found this approach useful in its many years of experience with hundreds of sample essay statements on a wide range of tests. Let's look at what the test makers tell you about how the essays are scored.

To score Level 4, you must:

- **Answer the question.**
- **Support ideas with examples.**
- **Show logical thought and organization.**
- **Avoid major or frequent errors that make your writing unclear.**

Organization and clarity are key to an above-average essay. If the reader can't follow your train of thought—if ideas aren't clearly organized or if grammatical errors, misspellings, and incorrect word choices make your writing unclear—you can't do well.

To score Level 5, all you have to add to a 4 is:

- **Address the topic in depth.**

That is, offer more examples and details. The test makers' graders love specific examples, and the more concrete your examples are the more they clarify your thinking and keep you focused.

To score Level 6, all you have to add to a 5 is:

- **Make transitions smoother and show variety in syntax and vocabulary.**

Use words from the prompt to tie paragraphs together, rather than relying exclusively on connectors like *however* and *therefore*. Vary your sentence structure, sometimes using simple sentences and other times using compound and complex ones. Adding a few college-level vocabulary words will also boost your score.

Now let's apply the Kaplan Method to a practice prompt:

STEP 1: PAUSE TO KNOW THE PROMPT

The ACT Writing prompt usually relates to a topic that is familiar to high school students. It will outline an issue that teenagers are likely to have an opinion on, or can devise one fairly easily.

If, by chance, the prompt describes a situation you feel strongly about, be sure to present your argument in a careful, thoughtful manner. Do NOT write an overly emotional response.

Spend less than a minute reading the prompt on test day.

EXPERT TUTOR TIP

" Note that you can't earn a 5 or 6 (10 or 12) if you haven't met the basic requirements for a 4 (8). Think of the requirements as building blocks to higher scores. "

PERFECT SCORE TIP

" You must take a position on the Writing section. Graders like to see decisiveness no matter what the opinion may be. In other words, don't try to toe the line and support both pro and con—pick one. "

EXPERT TUTOR TIP

" The assignment is not to write something vaguely inspired by the information given—that's where many good, creative writers go wrong. "

STEP 2: PLAN

Take five or six minutes to build a plan before you write. This step is critical—a successful plan leads directly to a high-scoring essay. Focus on what kinds of reasoning and examples you can use to support your position.

Note: If you find you have more examples for a position different from the one you thought you would take originally, *change your position*.

There is no one way to plan an essay. One method is to draw a large "T" on the page and align examples and ideas on either side of the line. So you might have the following notes on the prompt we started with in Step 1:

NEWSPAPERS IN SCHOOL

• Safe learning environment (more control)	• Freedom of speech (less control)
Can have faculty advisor monitor coverage to make sure issues are clearly, fairly, and *tastefully* presented.	Add coverage of state, local elections, & discussion of school issues imp't to students
Administration can get its side heard too.	Help prepare students to be adults who know how to think and to vote
Promotes safe discussion, improves student morale, and avoids protests.	Air debates about student rights ex. dress code ex. off-campus lunch privileges
	Students have rights and should be acknowledged

CONCLUSION: Everyone benefits from freedom of speech in a school newspaper.

Information Banks: Don't wait until test day to think of examples you can use to support your ideas. Regardless of what question is raised in the prompt, you will draw your support from the things you know best and are most comfortable writing about—things that you know a fair amount of concrete detail about.

Refresh your memory about your favorite or most memorable books, school subjects, historical events, personal experiences, activities—anything. By doing so, you strengthen mental connections to those ideas and details—that will make it easier to connect to the right examples on test day.

> **PERFECT SCORE TIP**
>
> " Organization is the biggest gift you can give yourself on the essay. "Clever ideas" are nowhere near as important as having a solid road map that is obvious to the readers. Make sure you do not start writing without knowing your three points and how you will support them, as you will end up wasting time. "

> **PERFECT SCORE TIP**
>
> " When you read the prompt, immediately decide a position and three major points. You don't have to pick the position you believe in; so if you have more points for the other side, write that essay. Don't feel as if you morally have to defend your opinion. "

Structure Your Essay: Plan a clear introduction, a distinct middle section, and a strong conclusion. **Choose your best examples, decide in what order you'll handle them, and plan your paragraphs.**

With that in mind, we suggest:

- **Use an effective *hook* to bring the reader in.**
- **Use regular *transitions* to provide the glue that holds your ideas together.**
- **End with a *bang* to make your essay memorable.**

A "hook" means avoiding an essay that opens (as thousands of other essays will): "In my opinion, …, because …" Try a more general statement that introduces one or more of the key words you will use from the prompt.

Using the "T" model presented earlier, you might use the following sentence: *A student newspaper should help students learn to think and express themselves.*

A "bang" means a closing that ties the three paragraphs together. Good choices can be a clear, succinct statement of your thesis in the essay or a vivid example that's right on point.

To conclude the planned "T" essay you might finish with:

Both students and the administration *would benefit from a school newspaper that covers a broad array of topics.*

Plan for our prompt using a paragraph-by-paragraph method. The answer we've chosen is this:

> I agree that restrictions on student newspapers violate freedom of speech and I also believe restrictions impede student learning.

This position clearly responds to the assignment, and adding some reasoning not taken directly from the prompt immediately tells the reader "I have ideas of my own."

Next, working with our proposed response, comb your memory or your imagination for supporting reasons and examples to use. We'll use:

> Point: student newspapers should mimic real life newspapers.
>
> Point: not being in the school paper doesn't mean it's not discussed.
>
> Point: students can avoid "harming" others as well as adults.
>
> Point: censorship is anti-democratic.

PERFECT SCORE TIP

" Every reader is going to read thousands of essays, so make yours memorable. A good hook and interesting writing will help wake up your reader and hopefully boost your score. "

Fill in the details. Jot down any notes you need to ensure that you use the details you've developed, but don't take the time to write full sentences. When you have enough ideas for a few supporting paragraphs, decide what your introduction and conclusion will be and the order in which you'll discuss each supporting idea.

Here's our sample plan:

> Para 1:   I agree with "free speech." Student newspapers should prepare for real life.
>
> Para 2:   Press is treated specially in real life.
>
> Para 3:   Potential harm not a good argument.
>
> Para 4:   Censorship vs. democracy.
>
> Para 5:   Better to have discussion out in the open.
>
> Para 6:   Restate thesis.

If you take our advice and use examples that are very familiar to you, you won't have to write much in your plan in order to remember the point being made. **Learn how brief you can make your notes and still not lose sight of what you mean to say.**

A good plan:

- **Responds to the prompt**
- **Has an introduction**
- **Has strong examples, usually one per paragraph**
- **Has a strong conclusion**

In addition to writing practice essays, practice just making plans on your own whenever you have a few spare minutes, using ideas for changes in high school curriculum, events, lifestyle, and activities such as: longer vs. shorter class sessions; students should/should not be allowed off campus during the school day; study halls should/should not be eliminated; vocational options vs. all college prep. The more you do this, the easier it will become.

STEP 3: PRODUCE

Appearances Count: In purely physical terms, your essay will make a better impression if you fill a significant portion of the space provided and if it is clearly divided into three to five reasonably equal paragraphs (except that the final paragraph can be short). **Use one paragraph for your introduction, one for each**

> **EXPERT TUTOR TIP**
>
> " Save your best example for last and stress its relative importance. "

> **PERFECT SCORE TIP**
>
> " To practice for the Writing section, think of "school scenarios" they might ask and make outlines. Practice thinking of body paragraph topics and theses and be able to do it fast. This will help you have an organized essay as well as help save you time. "

EXPERT TUTOR TIP

On test day, use 6–7 minutes for planning and 23–24 minutes for writing and proofreading. Try writing practice essays in 20 minutes to make the "real" essay seem easier.

EXPERT TUTOR TIP

The ACT essay isn't the place for creative writing. Make your writing direct, persuasive, and error-free. Give the graders what they are looking for.

PERFECT SCORE TIP

Topic sentences are very important in ACT essays. The reader should be able to read just the topic sentences of each paragraph and get your major arguments, so make sure they are existent and clear.

example or line of reasoning, and one for your conclusion so your essay will be easy for readers to follow.

Write neatly: graders will give you a zero if your essay is hard to read—and negative feelings affect holistic scoring. If your handwriting is a problem, print.

Stick with the Plan: Resist any urge to introduce new ideas—no matter how good you think they are—or to digress from the central focus or organization of each paragraph.

Think Twice, Write Once: Write mentally before you write on paper. If your essays are littered with misspellings and grammatical mistakes, you may get a low score simply because the reader cannot follow what you are trying to say.

Use Topic Sentences: Each paragraph should be organized around a topic sentence that you should finish in your mind before you start to write:

- *I believe…*
- *One example…*
- *Another example…*
- *Another example…*
- *Therefore, we can conclude…*

You don't have to write it this way in the essay, but completing these sentences in your mind ensures that you focus on what idea organizes each paragraph.

Choose Words Carefully: Use vocabulary that you know well. Inserting new or fancy words that you have learned recently often sticks out. The result of unfamiliar words in an essay is the opposite of what you want: awkward, confusing thoughts. Instead of impressing the graders, you have made a mess. Two more points here:

- Avoid using "I" excessively.
- Avoid slang.

Use Transitions: Think about the relationship between ideas as you write, and spell them out clearly. This makes it easy for the readers to follow your reasoning, and they'll appreciate it. **Use key words from the prompt as well as the kinds of words you've learned about in Reading that indicate contrast, opinion, relative importance, and support.**

Essay Length: While many poor essays can be quite long, there will be few 6 essays under about 300 words, so take this into consideration as you practice. The length of an essay is no assurance of its quality. However, it's hard to develop an argument in depth—something the graders look for—in one or two short paragraphs. **Don't ramble, digress, or write off topic just to make your essay longer.** Practice writing organized essays with developed examples, and you'll find yourself writing more naturally.

Don't Sweat the Small Stuff: Do not obsess over every little thing. If you cannot remember how to spell a word, do your best and just **keep going.** Even the top scoring essays can have minor errors. The essay readers understand that you are writing first drafts and have no time for research or revision.

STEP 4: PROOFREAD

Always leave yourself two or three minutes to review your work—the time spent will definitely pay off. Very few of us can avoid the occasional confused sentence or omitted word when writing under pressure. Quickly review your essay to be sure your ideas are on the page, not just in your head.

Don't hesitate to make corrections on your essay—these are timed first drafts, not term papers. But keep it clear: use a single line through deletions and an asterisk to mark where text should be inserted.

You don't have time to look for every minor error or to revise substantially. Learn the types of mistakes you tend to make and look for them. Some of the most common mistakes in students' essays are those found in the English test questions.

Common Errors

- Omitted words
- Sentence fragments
- Subject-verb agreement or verb tense errors
- Misplaced modifiers
- Pronoun agreement errors
- Misused words—especially homonyms like *their* for *there* or *they're*
- Spelling errors

Common Style Problems

- Choppy sentences (combine some)
- Too many long, complex sentences (break some up)
- Too many stuffy-sounding words (replace some with simple words)
- Too many simple words (add a few college-level words)

PERFECT SCORE TIP

" Do you notice that most of your sentences tend to be relatively simple and begin with a subject followed by a passive verb? This is a problem. Varying sentence structure and writing in active voice will not only make your essay more enjoyable, but can be the difference between a 5 and a 6. "

EXPERT TUTOR TIP

" Use a caret ^ or an asterisk * to insert a word or words. Write a backward P to create a new paragraph, and cross words out with one line. Don't make a mess! "

KNOW THE SCORE: SAMPLE ESSAYS

The best way to be sure you've learned what the readers will look for is to try scoring some essays yourself.

The graders will be scoring holistically, not checking off "points"—but to learn what makes a good essay, it may help to consider these questions, based on the test makers' scoring criteria:

- Does the author answer the question?
- Is the author's position clearly stated?
- Does the body of the essay support and develop the position taken?
- Are there at least three supporting paragraphs?
- Is the relevance of each supporting paragraph clear?
- Does the writer address the other side of the argument?
- Is the essay organized, with a clear introduction, middle, and end?
- Did the author use one paragraph for each new idea?
- Is each sentence in a paragraph relevant to the point made in that paragraph?
- Are transitions clear?
- Is the essay easy to read? Is it engaging?
- Are sentences varied?
- Is good vocabulary used effectively?

Let's look at a sample essay based on the prompt and plan we've been looking at.

Here's the prompt:

In many high schools, the administration has provided guidelines for the publication of student newspapers. These guidelines often determine which topics can and cannot be discussed in the newspaper and prohibit what the administration deems inappropriate language. Many administrators and teachers feel that these restrictions enable them to provide a safe learning environment for students. Others feel that any restriction on the student newspaper is a violation of freedom of speech. In your opinion, should high schools place restrictions on student newspapers?

In your essay, take a position on this question. You may write about either one of the two points of view given, or you may present a different point of view on this question. Use specific reasons and examples to support your position.

EXPERT TUTOR TIP

" Don't cheat yourself by reading our explanation without first deciding what holistic grade you would give the sample essay. "

PERFECT SCORE TIP

" I know it is tempting to copy the prompt in your essay. The readers will notice and you will be penalized! There is nothing worse than copying the prompt in your essay, as it is not only painfully obvious that you don't have your own ideas, but it wastes time and space as readers will simply disregard it. Do not copy the prompt! "

SAMPLE ESSAY 1

In many high schools, the administration has provided guidelines for the publication of student newspapers. These guidelines often determine which topics can and cannot be discussed in the newspaper, and prohibit what the administration deems inappropriate language. Many administrators and teachers feel that these restrictions enable them to provide a safe, appropriate learning environment for students. Others feel that any restriction on the student newspaper is a violation of freedom of speech. In my opinion, students should be free to write on any topic.

Firstly, restrictions will not stop certain topics being talked about. Students will always discuss topics that they are interested in. Second, students are more aware of what is or is not appropriate than the administration might think. A newspaper is there to tell news and students will therefore write about the news.

Finally and most importantly, a right such as freedom of speech should not be checked at the school door. Students not being able to cognizant and value rights such as these if they are not taught their importance in school. So high schools should not place restrictions on student newspapers.

Score: _____/6

It should have been fairly easy to see that this isn't a strong essay. The author does state a clear opinion, but half of the essay is a direct copy of the prompt—something the graders will notice and, if anything, be annoyed by. The time and space spent just quoting the prompt was completely wasted—it earned the writer zero points.

The rest of the essay is organized and uses transition words (*firstly* and *finally*). The author states her thesis, follows with three supporting reasons, and then a conclusion. However, none of this is discussed fully enough—no concrete detail or examples are given. In the second paragraph, for instance, the author should have added an example demonstrating that students are aware of what is appropriate or an example of topics that students will discuss.

The language is understandable but there are significant errors affecting clarity. For instance, the second sentence of paragraph 3 is a fragment—there is no verb. Some vocabulary words are clearly plugged in without a clear understanding of their meaning: In paragraph 3 "not being able to cognizant" is incorrect; perhaps the student meant, "not being able to understand."

This essay looks like the writer couldn't think of "good" ideas, waited too long, and had to write in a hurry.

Let's try another, better essay. Read quickly and select a score before reading our evaluation.

SAMPLE ESSAY 2

Many high schools place restrictions on appropriate topics and language for student newspapers. Many people disagree with these restrictions. While arguments can be made for either side, I believe that newspapers, as part of the school, should be placed under guidelines of the school.

First, a high school necessarily has stricter rules than normal society. These rules are not in place to punish students. They protect them and providing a suitable learning environment. In this way, when students leave high school they will have grown from children to adults, ready to succeed in the larger world. For example, the strict time schedule, with exactly three or four minutes given between classes, prepares students for strict schedules in the broader world.

Second, students interested in journalism should have instruction in how to write and publish newspaper articles. A student newspaper, which for obvious reasons has limited scope, is a perfect laboratory for students to experiment with journalistic writing. The administration and faculty dedicated to the newspaper can guide students in choosing appropriate topics, such as student elections. Then they can write articles on politics in the future. Imagine a student whose high school teacher taught the proper techniques for reporting on the race for student council president, joining a major news organization and reporting on the United States Presidential election.

Lastly, students may not realize the harm which their writing may cause. In my school, a student discovered a teacher's affair and "reported" on it in a story on the student's TV network, before the school could interfere. The teacher's career was destroyed and his marriage fell apart. Perhaps he deserved it, but student television should not have been the vehicle that ruined his life. The student reporter felt terribly in the end, as she had not thought through the consequences of her story. The same consequences could occur in a student newspaper that was restricted by no guidelines from the school.

Therefore, while many people argue that freedom of speech is a right too precious to give up, it is more important to provide guidelines for young people.

Score: _____/6

Okay, now do you want to revise the score you gave this essay?

Actually, this sample exceeds the basic requirements for a 4; it's a 5.

This essay addresses the assignment. The writer's position is clear and the personal example in the fourth paragraph provides good support. The organization is good and the author uses transition words. Each paragraph discusses a different aspect of the writer's argument. Let's look at why it doesn't rate a 6.

Some of the support isn't explained enough. The second paragraph, for example, doesn't show the connection between strict schedules and restrictions on newspaper reporting—the subject of the essay. The idea, in paragraph 3, of a student growing up to be a presidential reporter is interesting, but it doesn't particularly address the idea of restrictions. The final paragraph doesn't tie back to the main argument about newspapers; it only generally mentions "guidelines for young people."

The author's writing is good, but unexceptional. There are a few examples of complex sentences. For example, in paragraph 2: "A student newspaper, which for obvious reasons has limited scope, is a perfect laboratory for students to experiment with journalistic writing." The essay includes grammar mistakes, however—such as, in paragraph 2: "They protect them and providing a suitable learning environment." In paragraph 3, the sentence "Then they can write articles on politics in the future" includes the ambiguous *they*, which could refer to the administration and teachers or the students.

Let's look at another essay. Read it quickly and decide how you would score it.

SAMPLE ESSAY 3

School administrations and teachers who support restrictions believe that these restrictions are needed to form an appropriate learning environment. But I agree with those who oppose such restrictions because they violate freedom of speech and these limits impede student progress and success after high school.

Despite the true need for rules in high schools, newspapers should be exempt. Students need discipline in the form of detention for misbehavior or demerits for poor study, but the student newspaper should not be a part of that system. Rather, it should mimic "real world" journalism.

Student editors, usually seniors aged seventeen or eighteen, are well aware of the overall environment in which they publish, and understand what is or is not appropriate. High school should give students

> **EXPERT TUTOR TIP**
>
> " To get from a 4 to a 5, you need fully developed examples and logic. To get to a 6, you need lively, mostly error-free writing. "

practice at being cognizant of the larger arena in which they act. The few negative incidents that free press will admittedly cause will teach students that in life, one must take responsibility for one's actions.

Therefore, the argument for freedom of speech in student newspapers advances substantial educational goals for students, as well as our unalienable right of freedom of speech. This right, however, is paramount. The American public school is an extension of the American government and community, and censorship is inconsistent with American democracy. Again, students need to be prepared for the world they will live in; depriving them of rights that are promoted in the greater community prepares students poorly for life after high school.

Finally, censoring information in the student newspaper will not remove the subject from student discussion. Rather, it will remove a balanced, informative viewpoint, and often make the "inappropriate" action more desirable and "cool." Placing restrictions on student newspapers would be a serious mistake that would hinder students from learning what it is to participate in a free society.

Score: _____/6

Did you recognize this as an essay similar to the plan we did earlier?

Para 1:   I agree with "free speech." Student newspapers should
           prepare for real life.

Para 2:   Press is treated specially in real life.

Para 3:   Potential harm not a good argument.

Para 4:   Censorship vs. democracy.

Para 5:   Not discussing in press doesn't mean not discussing in school.

This essay is pretty good—it would earn a 4. The position is clearly stated, and some supporting reasoning is given.

However, the reasoning is too general and the writing is too ordinary to earn the top score. Let's see how it could be improved.

TURNING A 4 INTO A 6

The essay plunges right into the two points of view offered in the prompt. It could be improved by introducing the issue with a general statement, like:

Many students, parents, and school administrators are debating the proper role of student newspapers. Should their language and content be restricted?

In the last sentence of the first paragraph, the writer introduces some additional reasoning *not* included in the prompt. That's excellent, but it would be better to make it clear where the position from the prompt ends and the author's position begins, perhaps like this:

> But I agree with those who oppose such restrictions because they violate freedom of speech. <u>I would further argue that</u> these limits impede student progress and success after high school.

The second paragraph is relevant and organized—it covers one of the two positions offered in the prompt. But it would be better if the writer tied this argument more clearly to something specific in the prompt, perhaps with an opening sentence using language from the prompt, like:

> Some people claim that high school students need strict guidelines in order to prepare for life after school.

Moreover, at the end of the paragraph, the reference to mimicking "real world" journalism would be improved by telling the reader what "real world" journalism is:

> Rather, it should mimic "real world" journalism, which strives to provide valid, balanced reporting on events important to the public, or in this case the student body.

The third paragraph addresses the view in the prompt that students can cause harm by printing inappropriate articles. But, again, it should be made clearer what part of the prompt this paragraph is responding to, with a first sentence like:

> Others believe that students may cause unintended harm with newspaper articles written on controversial subjects. I think that is laughable.

Paragraph four is pretty good, as is. It states clearly what the author considers the most important argument. The fifth paragraph raises good arguments, but leaves them undeveloped. It would be best to provide an example of what type of story would help promote "balanced, informative" discussion to counteract "inappropriate…cool" actions, like:

> For instance, a reporter for my high school paper researched and wrote an in-depth story on the increasing drug problem among students. The administration quickly intervened and stopped the story, declaring that drugs were an inappropriate topic for student discussion. This story, however, would have focused discussion on a crucial issue for students, so that they can make the right choice when offered drugs or when they see friends using drugs. Unfortunately, this is a situation most students will face, and they need to be prepared. Suppressing the story made drugs seem even more rebellious and mysterious and most importantly did not give students facts with which they could prepare.

This makes it clear why the writer saved this argument for the last—an important, detailed example.

Finally, since this writer offers a fair number of supporting ideas, it would also be a good idea to add some transitions that establish the relative importance of those ideas. For example, in the third paragraph:

> First of all, student editors, usually seniors aged seventeen or eighteen, are well aware of the overall environment in which they publish, and understand what is or is not appropriate. But even more importantly, high school should give students practice at being cognizant of the larger arena in which they act.

Here's how this essay would look with the improvements we've suggested.

> Many students, parents, and school administrators are debating the proper role of student newspapers. Should their language and content be restricted? School administrations and teachers who support restrictions believe that these restrictions are needed to form an appropriate learning environment. But I agree with those who oppose such restrictions because they violate freedom of speech. I would further argue that these limits impede student progress and success after high school.
>
> Some people claim that high school students need strict guidelines in order to prepare for life after school. Despite the true need for rules in high schools, newspapers should be exempt. Students need discipline in the form of detention for misbehavior or demerits for poor study, but the student newspaper should not be a part of that system. Rather, it should mimic "real world" journalism, which strives to provide valid, balanced reporting on events important to the public, or in this case the student body.
>
> Others believe that students may cause unintended harm with newspaper articles written on controversial subjects. I think that is laughable. First of all, student editors, usually seniors aged seventeen or eighteen, are well aware of the overall environment in which they publish, and understand what is or is not appropriate. But even more importantly, high school should give students practice at being cognizant of the larger arena in which they act. The few negative incidents that free press will admittedly cause will teach students that in life, one must take responsibility for one's actions.
>
> Therefore, the argument for freedom of speech in student newspapers advances substantial educational goals for students, as well as our unalienable right of freedom of speech. This right, however, is paramount. The American public school is an extension of the

American government and community, and censorship is inconsistent with American democracy. Again, students need to be prepared for the world they will live in; depriving them of rights that are promoted in the greater community prepares students poorly for life after high school.

Finally, censoring information in the student newspaper will not remove the subject from student discussion. Rather, it will remove a balanced, informative viewpoint, and often make the "inappropriate" action more desirable and "cool." For instance, a reporter for my high school paper researched and wrote an in-depth story on the increasing drug problem among students. The administration quickly intervened and stopped the story, declaring that drugs were an inappropriate topic for student discussion. This story, however, would have focused discussion on a crucial issue for students, so that they can make the right choice when offered drugs or when they see friends using drugs. Unfortunately, this is a situation most students will face, and they need to be prepared. Suppressing the story made drugs seem even more rebellious and mysterious and most importantly did not give students facts with which they could prepare.

Placing restrictions on student newspapers would be a serious mistake that would hinder students from learning what it is to participate in a free society.

> **EXPERT TUTOR TIP**
>
> " There are no right or wrong opinions. You can earn a 6 with an essay for or against the issue raised in the prompt. "

This is now a 6 essay. It addresses the task both fully and concretely. It addresses both sides of the argument, refutes two opposing arguments, and then moves to the bulk of the author's own reasoning. The first paragraph introduces all the lines of reasoning that will be used, demonstrating to the reader that the writer knew right from the start where this essay was headed. The development of ideas is clear and logical and the paragraphs reflect this organization.

The author shows a high level of skill with language. The transitions between paragraphs are clear and guide the reader through the reasoning. The sentence structure varies throughout the passage and is at times complex.

So what did we do to our 4 to make it a 6?

- We added examples and detail.

- We varied sentence structure and added stronger vocabulary (*strives, laughable, intervened,* and *suppressing*).

- While length alone doesn't make a 6, we've added detail to our original essay.

- The conclusion, rather than being lost in the fifth paragraph, is now a strong, independent statement that concisely sums up the writer's point of view.

Remember that your graders will be reading *holistically*. They will not be grading you by assigning points to particular aspects of your writing. However, as you practice essay writing, you can build an otherwise humdrum essay into a 6 by working on specific elements, with the net effect of giving your essay that 6 glow.

PREPARING FOR THE ESSAY

INFORMATION BANKS

Don't wait until test day to think about what subjects you can draw on for your examples to create animated and engaging essays. Examples can be drawn from anywhere: your life experience, a story you saw on the news, etc. So prepare yourself by refreshing your memory about your favorite subjects—collect examples that can be used for a variety of topics.

Don't hesitate to use your examples broadly. If the topic is about school, that doesn't mean you have to use school-based examples. It's better to write about things that you are comfortable with and know a lot about—but be sure to make it clear how they are relevant to the topic.

READ OP-ED ESSAYS

Newspapers and blogs have op-ed essays (stands for opinion-editorial) articles. These present arguments and opinions, which present authors' opinions on a wide range of topics. Some will present their arguments well, others will not. Make a point of reading and evaluating them. Ask yourself:

- What is the author's point?
- How is it supported?
- Is the argument convincing? If not, why?

FOLLOW A PRACTICE REGIMEN

Don't try to cut corners. Learn the Kaplan Method and practice writing at least one essay a week; last minute cramming will not be effective. If you intend to maximize your score, you must establish and adhere to a practice schedule. And practice at the same time of day that you will be writing on test day.

Be hard on yourself. **Always** time yourself to internalize the necessary pacing. Don't allow yourself any extra minutes to complete an essay.

Never start to write until you have a complete plan, and then adhere to your plan.

Always reserve two minutes to look over the essay and make needed additions or corrections.

PERFECT SCORE TIP

" Writing an essay fast can be very challenging if you are not used to it. If this scares you, practice! Go to a quiet place and give yourself 25 minutes to write a sample essay. Make sure you handwrite it as you will have to on the test. "

SELF-EVALUATION

After each practice essay, score yourself based on the guidelines provided. As part of your self-evaluation, determine which types of example are most useful to you and what types of error you make most often. Then analyze how well you followed the Kaplan Method in constructing your essay, and what you might focus on to improve. Do you have a tendency to rush your plan, or do you find that you haven't left two minutes to proofread at the end? **Practice to make your pacing reliable.**

GET A SECOND OPINION

Ask someone else to read and critique your practice essays. If you know someone else who's taking the ACT, you might agree to assist each other in this way. Knowing whether another person can follow your reasoning is the single most important learning aid you can have for the essay.

IF YOU'RE NOT A "WRITER"

While the essay is optional, many colleges require the ACT essay. Remember that the essay is set up so that *everyone* can do well on it. You don't have to be a writer to formulate a good argument and support it well. Plain, clear language will go a long way toward getting a good score.

IF ENGLISH IS YOUR SECOND LANGUAGE

The ACT essay can be a special challenge for the international student or ESL student here in the United States. On the ACT, you will be taking a position on the prompt, something that sometimes, but not **always,** happens on the TOEFL® (Test of English as a Foreign Language). However, plan your essay using all the tools in this chapter and write according to your plan. Make a special point of spending time proofreading your practice essays when you finish them, and edit anything that makes your writing unclear. There's a strong connection between your English reading skills and your writing skills, so keep reading as well (and don't forget to look for material for your Information Banks as well).

PRACTICE ESSAY

Try out the Kaplan Method on the following essay prompt. After you're finished, read over your essay and if possible, have someone else read it as well. You can compare it to the model essay that follows the lined pages. Good luck!

Many city councils have introduced proposals that would give them the power to ban certain books from the children's and young adult sections of local public libraries. Some citizens support such proposals because they hope to limit young

> **PERFECT SCORE TIP**
>
> " I really recommend getting a second opinion on practice essays. I know many things I write that I believe are clear others cannot understand. If you are not good at judging your own clarity and logic, have someone else help you. "

> **EXPERT TUTOR TIP**
>
> " If you're down to the wire, allow yourself a few minutes to plan and then write, based on that plan, no matter how much you wish you could think of other ideas. Remember that the essay tests your ability to convey those ideas—not the ideas themselves. "

people's exposure to inappropriate materials. However, other people believe that these measures are equivalent to censorship. In your opinion, should the government have the right to restrict the materials available to young people in libraries?

In your essay, take a position on this question. You may write about either one of the two points of view given, or you may present a different point of view on this question. Use specific reasons and examples to support your position.

_____

_____

_____

_____

_____

_____

_____

_____

_____

_____

_____

_____

_____

_____

_____

_____

_____

_____

_____

MODEL ESSAY

Here's one possible way to approach this essay prompt. Remember that the opinion you express is less important than the way you present it. Notice how this response includes a logically arranged argument with specific examples.

In some districts, city councils and other governing bodies have suggested that they be given the power to ban certain teen and children's books from public libraries. While some citizens believe that it would be beneficial for an outside party to screen the books that are available to young people, others are upset at what they see as censorship of the library's offerings.

Leaving the question of censorship aside, I believe that decisions about which books are appropriate for young people should be left to the young people themselves and their parents, not to city councils or librarians. Young people's reading levels and maturity levels can vary dramatically even within the same age group, and parents are the best judges of what kinds of books are suitable for their children. The proposal to have the city council make these decisions also fails to take into account the huge variations in parents' own preferences for their children; the idea of inappropriateness is a very subjective one. While some parents may agree with the city council's decisions, others may feel that the city council bans too many books, or even too few. In the end, parents must be responsible for knowing what books their children are reading and making their own decisions about those books' appropriateness within the context of their own values.

Additionally, whether certain books are appropriate or not, it's unrealistic to think that removing "objectionable" material from public libraries will keep young people from ever encountering that kind of material. Between television, the Internet, and interactions with friends and classmates, young people encounter all sorts of situations that may not necessarily be age appropriate. It's understandable that adults are concerned, but trying to keep potentially objectionable books away from young readers doesn't ensure that they won't encounter the language or situations used in those books elsewhere. To my mind, the best solution is for adults to encourage young people to analyze these situations thoughtfully, ask questions, and form their own opinions, rather than trying to shield them from the realities of the world.

Finally, although certain books contain elements that some people may find offensive or upsetting, those elements don't necessarily outweigh the literary merits of the books in question. One example of this is *Huckleberry Finn*, which all of the students at my school read as a requirement in English classes. It is widely recognized as a classic of American literature, even though it also includes portrayals of

African-American characters that many people find offensive. The historical context that is necessary to understand *The Diary of Anne Frank* may be upsetting to younger readers, but the diary is still a significant historical document. Many books with controversial content are still worth reading, and a policy that screens out books based on their potential to offend may exclude important works of literature from libraries.

In conclusion, I believe that the power to make determinations about a book's appropriateness should lie not with a city council or a librarian, but with young readers and their parents. The role of a library is to make information available, not to make or enforce judgments about what its patrons should or should not be reading.

IF YOU LEARNED ONLY FOUR THINGS IN THIS CHAPTER . . .

1. You should be familiar with Kaplan's Four-Step Method for the ACT Essay: pause to know the prompt, plan, produce, and proofread.

2. The Writing test asks you to take a position on the issue in the prompt. The best essays knock down the opposing arguments and positively support the side you take.

3. Support your view with relevant and clearly organized evidence. Examples will come from your own experiences.

4. Pacing is crucial to getting all your ideas on paper. Be sure to leave yourself two or three minutes to proofread.

| Part Three |

READY, SET, GO

CHAPTER 17: STRATEGIC SUMMARIES

SMARTPOINTS COVERED IN THIS CHAPTER

CONNECTIONS	
VERB TENSE	
PUNCTUATION	
WORD CHOICE	
WORDINESS	
WRITING STRATEGY	
SENTENCE SENSE	
ORGANIZATION	

ENGLISH TEST

The English subject test:

- Is 45 minutes long

- Includes five passages, representing a range of writing styles and levels of formality

- Consists of 75 questions, divided among the five passages. They test many points of grammar, punctuation, writing mechanics, usage, and rhetorical skills, by proposing ways of expressing information underlined at various points in the passages. We divide the questions strategically into three groups:

  1. **Economy Questions**

  2. **Sense Questions**

  3. **Technicality Questions**

There are also a few Nonstandard-Format Questions that require different strategies, as outlined in Special Strategies below.

The questions **do *not*** get harder as you proceed through the section.

MIND-SET

- **When in doubt, take it out.** Make sure that everything is written as concisely as possible. If you think something doesn't belong in a sentence, it probably doesn't, so choose an answer that leaves it out.

- **Make it make sense.** Grammar allows language to communicate meaning clearly. Most grammatically faulty sentences on the ACT don't say what the author intended to say. If a sentence has more than one possible meaning, figure out what the author intended to say, and fix the sentence so it conveys that meaning properly.

- **Trust your eyes and ear.** Mistakes in grammar often sound or look bad to your ear. Trust that instinct. Don't choose the answer that "sounds fancy," choose the one that "sounds right." Review the Grammar Rules to Know in English Workout 3.

THE KAPLAN METHOD

For each question, ask yourself three things. Note that you may actually have your answer before getting to all three questions:

1. **Do these words belong here?** Is it redundant? Is it relevant? Is this a long way to say a short idea? If so, choose an answer that gets rid of the stuff that doesn't belong.

2. **Do these words make sense?** The ACT test makers want short, simple, easy-to-understand prose. They expect everything to fit together logically. Choose the answer that turns nonsense into sense.

3. **Do I hear or see an error?** If so, choose the answer that fixes the problem. Recognize the issues discussed in English Workout 3 and let them help out when your ear isn't sure. These errors appear again and again on ACT English subject tests.

SPECIAL STRATEGIES

A few questions will require you to rearrange the words in a sentence, the sentences in a paragraph, or even the paragraphs in a passage. Others may ask questions about the meaning of all or part of the passage, or about its structure. Your approach to these Nonstandard-Format Questions should be:

1. **Determine your task.** What are you being asked to do?

2. **Consider the passage as a whole.** Read the sentences without a numbered question. You need to know the various points made there. Most passages will have a well-defined theme, laid out in a logical way. Choose the answer that expresses this theme or the arrangement of elements that best continues the logical "flow" of the passage.

3. **Predict your answer.** As in Reading, you should have an idea of what the answer is before looking at the choices.

Note: Grammar "fixes" cannot be predicted. There are many ways to make a sentence correct grammatically.

TIMING

We recommend that you *not* skip around in the English subject test. Although you can certainly use the usual Two-Pass Approach, you might prefer to go straight from beginning to end, answering all of the questions as you go. Unlike in other sections, in English you'll usually have at least a sense of what the right answer should be rather quickly. Remember, even the correct answer will start to sound wrong if you think about it too much!

Set your watch to 12:00 at the beginning of the subject test. Although you should go faster if you can, here's roughly where you should be at the following checkpoints.

12:09 . . . . . One passage finished and answers gridded in

12:18 . . . . . Two passages finished and answers gridded in

12:27 . . . . . Three passages finished and answers gridded in

12:36 . . . . . Four passages finished and answers gridded in

12:45 . . . . . Five passages finished and answers for the entire section gridded in

Note that you should do at least some work on all 75 English questions, and make sure you have at least one guess gridded in for every question when time is called.

WHEN YOU'RE RUNNING OUT OF TIME

If you have no time left even to read the last few questions, choose the shortest answer for each one. Remember that OMIT, when it appears, counts as the shortest answer.

SCORING

Your performance on the English subject test will be averaged into your ACT Composite Score, weighted equally with your scores on the other three major subject tests. You will also receive:

- English subject score—from 1 to 36—for the entire English subject test
- Usage/Mechanics subscore—from 1 to 18—based on your performance on the questions testing grammar, usage, punctuation, and sentence structure
- Rhetorical Skills subscore—from 1 to 18—based on your performance on the questions testing strategy, organization, and style
- Writing subscore—from 2 to 12—based on the optional Writing test
- Combined English-Writing score—from 1 to 36—if you take the optional Writing test

MATH TEST

The Math subject test:

- Is 60 minutes long.
- Consists of 60 questions, which test your grasp of prealgebra, algebra, coordinate geometry, plane geometry, and trigonometry. We break down the questions into the following strategic categories:

    1. **Diagram Questions**
    2. **Story Questions**
    3. **Concept Questions**

The questions **do get** more advanced math concepts as you proceed through the section.

MIND-SET

- **The end justifies the means.** That means getting as many correct answers as quickly as possible. If that means doing straightforward questions in a straightforward way, that's fine. But many questions can be solved faster by unorthodox methods.

- **Take time to save time.** It sounds paradoxical, but to go your fastest on the Math test you've got to slow down. Never dive in headlong, wildly crunching numbers or manipulating equations without first giving the problem some thought.

- **When in doubt, shake it up.** ACT Math questions are not always what they seem at first glance. Sometimes all you need is a new perspective to break through the disguise.

THE KAPLAN METHOD

1. **Understand.** First focus on the question stem and make sure you understand the problem. Underlining what the question is asking might help you. If it is a word problem and you are completely lost, try taking notes. You will pull out the information that is necessary to solve the problem. Think to yourself: "What kind of problem is this? What am I looking for? What am I given?"

2. **Analyze.** Think for a moment and decide on a plan of attack.

   - **Math skills.** Do you know how to solve the problem using your math knowledge? Go for it!

   - **Picking numbers.** Are there variables in the answer choices? If so, is there a way to pick numbers for the variable to help you get to the right answer?

   - **Back-solving.** Are there numbers in the answer choices? What is the question asking for? That is what the numbers in the answer choices represent. Is there are way to use the answers to get to the right answer?

3. **Select.** Once you get an answer, does it match one of the answer choices? If so, circle the answer in your test book and fill in the appropriate bubble on your answer grid. If you are stuck, circle the problem in your test book and move on to get all your "easy" points first! Come back to this problem after you have gone through the entire test.

SPECIAL STRATEGIES

We offer several recommendations for what to do when you get stuck. If after a few moments of thought you find you still can't come up with a reasonable way of doing the problem, try one of these techniques:

1. **Restate.** When you get stuck, try looking at the problem from a different angle. Try rearranging the numbers, changing decimals to fractions, fractions to decimals, multiplying out numbers, factoring problems, redrawing a diagram, or anything that might help you to look at the problem a bit differently.

GO ONLINE

" Find the Kaplan Method for approaching each section of the ACT on your downloadable study sheet. "

PERFECT SCORE TIP

" Remember that the textbook way to solve a problem is not always the best in Math. Try to simplify problems by plugging in numbers for variables and restating difficult problems. "

2. **Remove the disguise.** A problem might look like a different problem sometimes! Find out what the question is really asking, and it might not be what the problem looks like it would be asking. See Math Workout 2 for some examples!

3. **Try Eyeballing.** Even though the directions warn you that diagrams are "not necessarily" drawn to scale, eyeballing is a surprisingly effective guessing strategy. Unless a problem says "Note: Not drawn to scale," you can assume that it is drawn to scale! Use that to help you eliminate answer choices that you know are wrong!

TIMING

Remember the Two-Pass Approach. **Spend about 45 minutes on your first pass through the Math subject test: do the easier questions, guess on the questions you know you'll never get, and mark the tough ones that you'll want to come back to.** Spend the last 15 minutes picking up those questions that you skipped on the first pass.

We recommend that you grid your answers at the end of every page or two. In the last five minutes or so, start gridding your answers one by one. And make sure that you have an answer (even if it's a blind guess) gridded for every question by the time the test is over.

Don't worry if you have to guess on a lot of the Math questions. You can miss a lot of questions on the subject test and still get a great score. **Remember that the average ACT test taker gets less than half the Math questions right!**

WHEN YOU'RE RUNNING OUT OF TIME

If at some point you realize you have more questions left than you have time for, be willing to skip around, looking for questions you understand right away. Pick your spots. Concentrate on the questions you have the best chance of correctly answering. Just be sure to grid an answer—even if it's just a wild guess—for every question.

SCORING

Your performance on the Math subject test will be averaged into your ACT Composite Score, equally weighted with your scores on the other three major subject tests. You will also receive:

- Math subject score—from 1 to 36—for the entire Math subject test

- Prealgebra/Elementary Algebra subscore—from 1 to 18

- Intermediate Algebra/Coordinate Geometry subscore—from 1 to 18

- Plane Geometry/Trigonometry subscore—from 1 to 18

READING TEST

The Reading subject test:

- Is 35 minutes long.

- Includes four passages:

    — Three Nonfiction passages (one each in Social Studies, Natural Sciences, and Humanities, though there is no significant difference among them except subject matter)

    — One Prose Fiction passage (an excerpt from a short story or novel)

- Consists of 40 questions, 10 on each passage. They include:

    1. Specific Questions

        a. Detail

        b. Vocab-in-Context

        c. Function (Why)

    2. Conclusion Questions

        a. Inference

        b. Writer's View

    3. Generalization Questions

The questions do *not* get harder as you go through the section.

MIND-SET

- **Know where the passage is going.** Read the passages actively, and pay attention to structural clues and key words and sentences. The easiest way to do this is to create a road-map using the ABCs of Active Reading:

    — **A**bbreviate margin notes.

    — **B**racket key sentences.

    — **C**ircle key words and phrases.

- **Conquer the questions.** Look up the answers; don't remember them.

THE KAPLAN METHOD

1. **Preread the passage.** Try to understand the "gist" of the passage. Get a sense of the overall structure of the passage. Create a road map to make referring back easier.

2. **Consider the question stem.** Understand the question first, without looking at the array of answer choices. Remember that many wrong choices are

> **PERFECT SCORE TIP**
>
> " On the Reading section, remember to be able to summarize each paragraph and passage after prereading so you have a road-map to help you with answering questions. "

designed to mislead test takers who just jump past the question stem and start comparing choices to each other.

3. **Refer to the passage before looking at the choices. Always** refer to the passage before answering the question. If the question includes line references, read around them. Only then look at the choices. Make sure your answer matches the passage in meaning.

4. **Answer the question in your own words** before looking at the choices.

5. **Match your answer with one of the choices.** Having an answer in mind will keep you from getting bogged down.

SPECIAL STRATEGIES

THE PROSE FICTION PASSAGE

When you preread the passage, pay attention to the characters, especially the main character. Read between the lines to determine unspoken emotions and attitudes. Ask yourself:

- **Who are these people?** What are they like? How do the characters relate to each other?

- **What is their state of mind?** Are they angry, sad, reflective, excited?

- **What's going on?** What's happening on the surface? What's happening beneath the surface?

NONFICTION PASSAGES

Don't be thrown by unfamiliar vocabulary or topics. The Natural Science passage may enter strange territory. Everything you need to know will be covered in the passage. If you find a difficult term, odds are the definition will be given to you in context (or else it simply might not matter what the word means). You can still get lots of questions right, even if you don't fully understand the passage. Remember, you can find all the answers in the passage.

TIMING

You might want to take a few seconds at the beginning of the subject test to page through the passages, gauging the difficulty of each one. At first glance, you may wish to skip an entire passage if it seems very difficult.

We recommend that you treat each passage and its questions as a block. Take two passes through each block before moving on to the next (skip around if you like, but watch your answer grid if you do!). Get the easy questions on the first pass through and save the tougher ones for the second pass. Just make sure to keep track of time.

Note: The last passage is the eight-minute one.

Set your watch to 12:00 at the beginning of the subject test. Although you should go faster if you can, here's roughly where you should be at the following checkpoints.

12:09 . . . . . One passage finished and answers gridded in

12:18 . . . . . Two passages finished and answers gridded in

12:27 . . . . . Three passages finished and answers gridded in

12:35 . . . . . Four passages finished and answers for entire section gridded in

Three minutes to read; about 30 seconds (average) per question. Some questions take more time than others (ones with Roman numerals in them and ones that have EXCEPT are examples). If you feel the need to spend a lot of time to get the right answer, don't. Either guess or skip and come back. (Don't forget to do so.)

Do the best you can to finish all four passages, but don't panic if you don't. Develop a fallback position to use, if you fall short (see below). If, during practice, you often don't get to *many* of the questions, approach all the passages this way:

1. Learn to spot the easier questions and answer these quickly.

2. Address the ones you might be able to get with more research.

3. Guess randomly on the ones you would need lots of time for.

Note: If you are a slow reader and have trouble with the ABCs of Active Reading, this method may help.

Don't panic if you can't finish all four passages. Make sure you do a good job on at least three passages—and remember to grid answers (even if they're blind guesses) for all questions by the end. Even if you try all four passages, you probably won't really work on all 40 questions. For many questions, you'll just have to guess. Just make sure you guess on the tough ones and actually work on the easy ones!

When You're Running Out of Time

If you have less than five minutes left for the last passage, do the following:

1. **Skip the prereading step.**

2. **Look for questions with specific line references and do them.**

3. **Refer to the cited location in the passage and answer the question as best you can, based on what you see there.**

4. **Make sure you have gridded in an answer for every question before time is called.**

Scoring

Your performance on the Reading subject test will be averaged into your ACT Composite Score, weighted equally with your scores on the other three major subject tests. You will also receive:

- Reading subject score—from 1 to 36—for the entire Reading subject test

- Social Science/Sciences subscore—from 1 to 18—based on your performance on the nonfiction passages drawn from Social Studies and Natural Sciences

- Arts/Literature subscore—from 1 to 18—based on your performance on the Nonfiction passage (drawn from the Humanities) and on the Prose Fiction passage

SCIENCE TEST

The Science subject test:

- Is 35 minutes long.

- Includes seven passages or sets of scientific information, involving graphs, tables, and research summaries. Typically, one of the passages involves two conflicting viewpoints on a single scientific issue.

- Consists of 40 questions, divided among the seven passages. We divide the questions strategically into three categories:

  1. Figure Interpretation Questions

  2. Patterns Questions

  3. Scientific Reasoning Questions

The questions **do not** get harder as you proceed through the section.

MIND-SET

- **Look for patterns.** Usually, the exact data contained in Science passages are not as important as are changes in the data. Look for extremes (maximums and minimums), critical points (points of change), and variation (direct and inverse).

- **Know your direction.** There are two kinds of scientific reasoning—general-to-specific and specific-to-general. **Always** be aware of when scientists are inferring a specific case from a general rule and when they are using specific data to form a (general) hypothesis.

- **Refer, don't remember.** Don't even think of trying to remember data. It's **always** there, right on the page, for you to refer to when needed.

THE KAPLAN METHOD

1. **Preread the passage.** Actively read the passage looking for and marking the purpose, method, and results. What is being researched? What are the scientists varying? What are the scientists keeping constant? Don't get bogged down in the details, and don't worry about understanding everything.

2. **Consider the question stem.** Make sure you understand exactly what the question is asking. Get a sense of what the answer should be without looking at the choices, many of which are designed to mislead you if you're indecisive.

3. **Refer to the passage before looking at the choices. Always** refer back to the passage before looking at the choices and selecting one. Make sure you read charts and graphs accurately, and that you do not confuse different kinds of units.

4. **Answer the question in your own words.** Don't rely too much on your knowledge of science. Paraphrase the information in the passage.

5. **Match your answer with one of the choices.** Having an answer in mind will help you to avoid falling for a wrong answer.

> **PERFECT SCORE TIP**
>
> " Remember that you do not have to understand all the science in the Science section to do well, so don't let difficult concepts throw you. "

SPECIAL STRATEGIES

READING TABLES AND GRAPHS

When reading tables and graphs, you should ask yourself:

- **What does the figure show?**
- **What are the units of measurement?**
- **What is the pattern in the data?**

EXPERIMENTS

Remember how experiments work. There is typically (though not always) a control group plus an experimental group or groups. In a well-designed experiment, the only difference between the groups will be a variation in the factor that's being tested. Ask yourself:

- **What's the factor that's being varied?**
- **What's the control group, if any?**
- **What do the results show? What differences exist between the results for one group and those for another?**

CONFLICTING VIEWPOINTS PASSAGE

Spend a little more time than usual on the prereading step of this passage. Focus on the two points of view. What are the scientists arguing about? What do they agree on, if anything? What do they differ on? Identify the following for each scientist:

- **Basic theory statement** (usually the first sentence of each scientist's presentation)

- Major pieces of data behind the theory (keeping in mind whether each supports the scientist's own theory or weakens the opposing scientist's theory)

TIMING

Some Science passages are a lot harder than others, and they're not arranged in order of difficulty, so you might want to **take a few seconds at the beginning of the subject test to page through the passages, gauging the difficulty of each one.** You may wish to skip an entire passage if it seems very difficult (but remember that a very difficult passage may have very easy questions).

As in Reading, treat each passage and its questions as a block, taking two passes through each block before moving on to the next. Get the easy questions on the first pass through and save the tougher ones for the second pass. Some questions will probably be impossible for you to answer; take an intuitive guess on these.

Set your watch to 12:00 at the beginning of the subject test. Although you should go faster if you can, here's where you should be at the following checkpoints:

12:05 . . . . One passage finished and answers gridded in

12:10 . . . . Two passages finished and answers gridded in

12:15 . . . . Three passages finished and answers gridded in

12:20 . . . . Four passages finished and answers gridded in

12:25 . . . . Five passages finished and answers gridded in

12:30 . . . . Six passages finished and answers gridded in

12:35 . . . . Seven passages finished and answers for the entire section gridded in

Don't spend time agonizing over specific questions. Avoid thinking long and hard about the answer choices. If you've spent a minute or so on a question and don't seem to be making any headway, make your best guess and move on.

Don't panic if you can't finish all seven passages, but try to do a good job on at least five of them. And make sure you remember to grid answers (even if they're blind guesses) for all questions by the end.

WHEN YOU'RE RUNNING OUT OF TIME

If you have fewer than three minutes left for the last passage, do the following:

1. **Skip the prereading step.**

2. **Look for questions that refer to specific experiments or to specific graphs or tables.**

3. **Refer to the cited location in the passage and answer the question as best you can, based on what you see there.**

4. **Make sure you have gridded in an answer for every question before time is called.**

SCORING

Your performance on the Science subject test will be averaged into your ACT Composite Score, weighted equally with your scores on the other three major subject tests. You will also receive:

- A Science subject score—from 1 to 36—for the entire Science subject test

Unlike the other three subject scores, the Science score is not divided into subscores.

WRITING TEST

The Writing test:

- Is optional (check with the schools to which you are applying and with your guidance counselor about whether you should take the test)
- Is 30 minutes long
- Includes just one prompt about which you must write an essay. The essay must:
    1. State a point of view on the issue.
    2. Support the point of view with concrete, detailed examples.
    3. Provide a clear and coherent argument, which includes a discussion of the opposite point of view.

MIND-SET

Don't wait until test day to think of examples you can use to support your ideas. Regardless of what question is raised in the prompt, you will draw your support from the things you know best and are most comfortable writing about—things that you know a fair amount of concrete detail about.

Refresh your memory about school subjects, current events, personal experiences, and activities—anything. By doing so, you strengthen mental connections to those ideas and details—that will make it easier to connect to the right examples on test day.

THE KAPLAN METHOD

1. **Pause to know the prompt.** Read about the issue and take a position on it. There is no right or wrong answer, but make sure you address the issue. In other words, answer the question.

> **PERFECT SCORE TIP**
>
> " Remember to write a "textbook essay" with a clear structure, topic sentences, well developed examples, and sentence variation. "

2. **Plan.** Take six or seven minutes or less to plan the essay before you write. Focus on what kinds of reasoning and examples you can use to support your position. If you find you have more examples for a position different from the one you thought you would take, *change your position*.

3. **Produce.** Write your draft, sticking closely to your plan. The essay should have three to five well-developed paragraphs with topic sentences and supporting details. Include an introductory paragraph stating your position and a concluding paragraph. Write neatly.

4. **Proofread. Always** leave yourself two minutes to review your work—the time spent will definitely pay off. Very few of us can avoid the occasional confused sentence or omitted word when writing under pressure. Quickly review your essay to be sure your ideas are on the page, not just in your head.

HELPFUL STRATEGIES

You must be very focused in order to write a complete, coherent essay in 30 minutes. During the planning stage, use one of the two following strategies.

1. **Draw a "T" and list your argument on either side of it** (your stance on one side, and your arguments addressing the other side on the other). See page 225. This method will help you decide if you have enough to back up your stance. You may find you need to take the opposite point of view!

OR

2. **List the topic of each paragraph** you plan to write, noting the segments of the argument that you want to make.

Stick to the plan as you write the essay. Don't change the plan in midstream if another idea suddenly comes to you; it might derail the essay. Keep your focus on the issue and don't digress.

Make the structure of your essay very easy to for the reader to see. Have an introductory paragraph, two or three middle paragraphs, each focused on one example or bit of evidence, and a concluding paragraph.

Write neatly: graders will give you a poor grade if it's hard to decipher. If your handwriting is a problem, print.

TIMING

With only 30 minutes, efficient use of time is critical. Divide your time as follows:

6–7 minutes—Read the prompt and plan the essay.

20–21 minutes—Draft the essay, sticking to the plan.

3 minutes—Proofread and correct any errors.

WHEN YOU'RE RUNNING OUT OF TIME

Try not to. Running out of time doesn't just mean guessing the last few questions as it does on the other tests; it means your essay won't be as complete and coherent as it should be. If you do start running out of time, forget the proofreading stage. If absolutely necessary, leave out one of your example paragraphs and go on to the concluding paragraph.

SCORING

Your essay will be graded on a holistic scale of 1–6 or 2–12 (6/12 being the best). Graders will be looking for an overall sense of your essay, not assigning separate scores for specific elements like grammar or organization. Two readers read and score each essay; then those scores are added together to arrive at your Writing subscore (from 2–12), which is reported as part of your English score. If there's a difference of more than a point between the two readers' scores, your essay will be read by a third reader. A combined English-Writing score also will be recorded. Two-thirds of this score is based on your English score and one-third is based on your writing subscore. The combined English-Writing score does not count toward your composite score.

Statistically speaking, there will be few essays that score 6/12. If each grader gives your essay a 4 or 5 (8 or 10), that will place you at the upper range of those taking the exam.

CHAPTER 18: LAST-MINUTE TIPS

Is it starting to feel like your whole life is a buildup to the ACT? You've known about it for years, you've worried about it for months, and now you've spent at least a few hours in solid preparation for it. As the test gets closer, you may find your anxiety is on the rise. But you really shouldn't worry. After the preparation you've received from this book, you're in good shape for test day.

To calm any pretest jitters you may have (and assuming you've left yourself at least some breathing time before your ACT), let's go over a few last-minute strategies for the couple of days before and after the test.

THREE DAYS BEFORE THE TEST

- If you haven't already done so, take one of the the full-length Practice Tests in this book under timed conditions. If you have already worked through all the tests in the book, try an actual published ACT (your guidance counselor might have one).

- Try to use all of the techniques and tips you've learned in this book. Take control. Approach the test strategically and creatively.

WARNING: Don't take a full practice ACT unless you have at least 48 hours left before the test! Doing so will probably exhaust you, hurting your scoring potential on the actual test! You wouldn't run a marathon the day before the real thing, would you?

TWO DAYS BEFORE THE TEST

- **Go over the results of your Practice Test.** Don't worry too much about your score or whether you got a specific question right or wrong. Remember the Practice Tests doesn't count. But do examine your performance on specific questions with an eye to how you might get through each one faster and with greater accuracy on the actual test to come.

- **After reviewing your test, look over the Strategic Summaries.** If you feel a little shaky about any of the areas mentioned, quickly read the relevant workouts.

- **This is the day to do your last studying—review a couple of the more difficult principles we've covered, do a few more practice problems, and call it quits.** It doesn't pay to make yourself crazy right before the test. Besides, you've prepared. You'll do well.

THE DAY BEFORE THE TEST

- **Don't study.**
- **Get together an "ACT survival kit" containing the following items:**
  — Watch (preferably digital)
  — At least three sharpened No. 2 pencils
  — Pencil sharpener
  — Two erasers
  — Photo ID card (if you're not taking the test at your high school, make sure your ID is official)
  — An approved calculator
  — Your admission ticket
  — Snack and a bottle of water—there's a break, and you'll probably get hungry
  — Confidence!

- **Know exactly where you're going and how you're getting there.** It's probably a good idea to visit your test center sometime before test day so that you know what expect on the big day.

- **Relax!** Read a good book, take a bubble bath, watch TV. Exercise can be a good idea early in the afternoon. Working out makes it easier to sleep when you're nervous, and it also makes many people feel better. Of course, don't work so hard that you can't get up the next day!

- **Get a good night's sleep.** Go to bed early and allow for some extra time to get ready in the morning.

EXPERT TUTOR TIP

Guard against being easily distracted during the test—by traffic outside or a sniffling neighbor. Try practicing in a coffee shop or with the door to your room open.

PERFECT SCORE TIP

Make sure you prepare the things you will need the day before. It is not worth getting stressed the morning of because you cannot find your calculator or pencils.

PERFECT SCORE TIP

You have worked too hard for this test to give it all up by going out the night before. Relax the night before and get a good night's sleep so you are ready for the next morning.

THE MORNING OF THE TEST

- **Eat breakfast.** Protein is brain food, but don't eat anything too heavy or greasy. Don't drink a lot of coffee if you're not used to it; bathroom breaks cut into your time, and too much caffeine—or any other kind of drug—is a bad idea.

- **Dress in layers** so that you can adjust to the temperature of the test room.

- **Read something.** Warm up your brain with a newspaper or a magazine. Don't let the ACT be the first thing you read that day.

- **Be sure to get there early.** Allow yourself extra time for traffic, mass-transit delays, and any other possible problems.

- **If you can, go to the test with a friend** (even if he or she isn't taking the test). It's nice to have somebody supporting you right up to the last minute.

DURING THE TEST

- **Don't get rattled.** If you find your confidence slipping, remind yourself how well you've prepared. You've followed the Four Commandments of ACT Success, and you have practiced. You know the test; you know the strategies; you know the material tested. You're in great shape, as long as you relax!

- **Even if something goes really wrong, don't panic.** If the test booklet is defective—two pages are stuck together or the ink has run—try to stay calm. Raise your hand, and tell the proctor you need a new book. If you accidentally misgrid your answer page or put the answers in the wrong section, again don't panic. Raise your hand, and tell the proctor. He or she might be able to arrange for you to regrid your test after it's over, when it won't cost you any time.

Good luck! with all of your practice and Kaplan's strategies under your belt, we know you'll do great on the ACT.

AFTER THE TEST

Once the test is over, put it out of your mind. If you don't plan to take the ACT again, shelve this book and start thinking about more interesting things.

You might walk out of the ACT thinking that you blew it. This is a normal reaction. Lots of people—even the highest scorers—feel that way. You tend to remember the questions that stumped you, not the many that you knew. If you're really concerned, call us for advice. Also call us if you had any problems with your test experience—a

---

PERFECT SCORE TIP

"Be sure to bring food for breaks and eat a sufficient breakfast. I find foods such as peanut butter and raisins give me the lasting energy needed for such a grueling test. Be careful of eating sugar, as it only gives short-term energy."

GO ONLINE

"Feeling nervous? The online stress management workshop and quiz on your syllabus will help calm any pretest jitters."

PERFECT SCORE TIP

"Calm down during the test. Take a deep breath if you are getting stressed and remember that you are prepared and have an arsenal of tools to help increase your chances of answering even the toughest problems."

PERFECT SCORE TIP

❝ Congratulations! You're done! Schedule something fun to do after the test as a reward for your hard work—and don't fret about score reports. I certainly did not expect my score after Test Day, so don't beat yourself up if you don't think you did your best. ❞

proctor who called time early, a testing room whose temperature hovered just below freezing. We'll do everything we can to make sure that your rights as a test taker are preserved!

However, we're positive that you performed well and scored your best on the exam because you followed our ACT Premier Program. Be confident that you were prepared, and celebrate in the fact that the ACT is a distant memory.

If you want more help or just want to know more about the ACT, college admissions, or Kaplan prep courses for the ACT, give us a call at 800-KAP-TEST or visit us at www.kaptest.com. We're here to answer your questions and to help you in any way we can. Also, be sure to return one last time to your online syllabus and complete our survey. We're only as good as our successful students.

Part Four

PRACTICE TESTS AND EXPLANATIONS

PRACTICE TEST ONE

HOW TO TAKE THESE PRACTICE TESTS

Practice Tests One and Two are Kaplan-created tests, similar to the actual ACT test booklet. Before taking a practice test, find a quiet room where you can work uninterrupted for three hours. Make sure you have a comfortable desk, your calculator, and several No. 2 pencils. Use the answer sheet to record your answers. Once you start a Practice Test, don't stop until you've finished. Remember: You can review any questions within a section, but you may not jump from one section to another.

You'll find the answers and explanations to the test questions immediately following each test.

ACT Practice Test One
Answer Sheet

English Test

10. Ⓕ Ⓖ Ⓗ Ⓙ 20. Ⓕ Ⓖ Ⓗ Ⓙ 30. Ⓕ Ⓖ Ⓗ Ⓙ 40. Ⓕ Ⓖ Ⓗ Ⓙ 50. Ⓕ Ⓖ Ⓗ Ⓙ 60. Ⓕ Ⓖ Ⓗ Ⓙ 70. Ⓕ Ⓖ Ⓗ Ⓙ
1. Ⓐ Ⓑ Ⓒ Ⓓ 11. Ⓐ Ⓑ Ⓒ Ⓓ 21. Ⓐ Ⓑ Ⓒ Ⓓ 31. Ⓐ Ⓑ Ⓒ Ⓓ 41. Ⓐ Ⓑ Ⓒ Ⓓ 51. Ⓐ Ⓑ Ⓒ Ⓓ 61. Ⓐ Ⓑ Ⓒ Ⓓ 71. Ⓐ Ⓑ Ⓒ Ⓓ
2. Ⓕ Ⓖ Ⓗ Ⓙ 12. Ⓕ Ⓖ Ⓗ Ⓙ 22. Ⓕ Ⓖ Ⓗ Ⓙ 32. Ⓕ Ⓖ Ⓗ Ⓙ 42. Ⓕ Ⓖ Ⓗ Ⓙ 52. Ⓕ Ⓖ Ⓗ Ⓙ 62. Ⓕ Ⓖ Ⓗ Ⓙ 72. Ⓕ Ⓖ Ⓗ Ⓙ
3. Ⓐ Ⓑ Ⓒ Ⓓ 13. Ⓐ Ⓑ Ⓒ Ⓓ 23. Ⓐ Ⓑ Ⓒ Ⓓ 33. Ⓐ Ⓑ Ⓒ Ⓓ 43. Ⓐ Ⓑ Ⓒ Ⓓ 53. Ⓐ Ⓑ Ⓒ Ⓓ 63. Ⓐ Ⓑ Ⓒ Ⓓ 73. Ⓐ Ⓑ Ⓒ Ⓓ
4. Ⓕ Ⓖ Ⓗ Ⓙ 14. Ⓕ Ⓖ Ⓗ Ⓙ 24. Ⓕ Ⓖ Ⓗ Ⓙ 34. Ⓕ Ⓖ Ⓗ Ⓙ 44. Ⓕ Ⓖ Ⓗ Ⓙ 54. Ⓕ Ⓖ Ⓗ Ⓙ 64. Ⓕ Ⓖ Ⓗ Ⓙ 74. Ⓕ Ⓖ Ⓗ Ⓙ
5. Ⓐ Ⓑ Ⓒ Ⓓ 15. Ⓐ Ⓑ Ⓒ Ⓓ 25. Ⓐ Ⓑ Ⓒ Ⓓ 35. Ⓐ Ⓑ Ⓒ Ⓓ 45. Ⓐ Ⓑ Ⓒ Ⓓ 55. Ⓐ Ⓑ Ⓒ Ⓓ 65. Ⓐ Ⓑ Ⓒ Ⓓ 75. Ⓐ Ⓑ Ⓒ Ⓓ
6. Ⓕ Ⓖ Ⓗ Ⓙ 16. Ⓕ Ⓖ Ⓗ Ⓙ 26. Ⓕ Ⓖ Ⓗ Ⓙ 36. Ⓕ Ⓖ Ⓗ Ⓙ 46. Ⓕ Ⓖ Ⓗ Ⓙ 56. Ⓕ Ⓖ Ⓗ Ⓙ 66. Ⓕ Ⓖ Ⓗ Ⓙ
7. Ⓐ Ⓑ Ⓒ Ⓓ 17. Ⓐ Ⓑ Ⓒ Ⓓ 27. Ⓐ Ⓑ Ⓒ Ⓓ 37. Ⓐ Ⓑ Ⓒ Ⓓ 47. Ⓐ Ⓑ Ⓒ Ⓓ 57. Ⓐ Ⓑ Ⓒ Ⓓ 67. Ⓐ Ⓑ Ⓒ Ⓓ
8. Ⓕ Ⓖ Ⓗ Ⓙ 18. Ⓕ Ⓖ Ⓗ Ⓙ 28. Ⓕ Ⓖ Ⓗ Ⓙ 38. Ⓕ Ⓖ Ⓗ Ⓙ 48. Ⓕ Ⓖ Ⓗ Ⓙ 58. Ⓕ Ⓖ Ⓗ Ⓙ 68. Ⓕ Ⓖ Ⓗ Ⓙ
9. Ⓐ Ⓑ Ⓒ Ⓓ 19. Ⓐ Ⓑ Ⓒ Ⓓ 29. Ⓐ Ⓑ Ⓒ Ⓓ 39. Ⓐ Ⓑ Ⓒ Ⓓ 49. Ⓐ Ⓑ Ⓒ Ⓓ 59. Ⓐ Ⓑ Ⓒ Ⓓ 69. Ⓐ Ⓑ Ⓒ Ⓓ

Math Test

9. Ⓐ Ⓑ Ⓒ Ⓓ Ⓔ 18. Ⓕ Ⓖ Ⓗ Ⓙ Ⓚ 27. Ⓐ Ⓑ Ⓒ Ⓓ Ⓔ 36. Ⓕ Ⓖ Ⓗ Ⓙ Ⓚ 45. Ⓐ Ⓑ Ⓒ Ⓓ Ⓔ 54. Ⓕ Ⓖ Ⓗ Ⓙ Ⓚ
1. Ⓐ Ⓑ Ⓒ Ⓓ Ⓔ 10. Ⓕ Ⓖ Ⓗ Ⓙ Ⓚ 19. Ⓐ Ⓑ Ⓒ Ⓓ Ⓔ 28. Ⓕ Ⓖ Ⓗ Ⓙ Ⓚ 37. Ⓐ Ⓑ Ⓒ Ⓓ Ⓔ 46. Ⓕ Ⓖ Ⓗ Ⓙ Ⓚ 55. Ⓐ Ⓑ Ⓒ Ⓓ Ⓔ
2. Ⓕ Ⓖ Ⓗ Ⓙ Ⓚ 11. Ⓐ Ⓑ Ⓒ Ⓓ Ⓔ 20. Ⓕ Ⓖ Ⓗ Ⓙ Ⓚ 29. Ⓐ Ⓑ Ⓒ Ⓓ Ⓔ 38. Ⓕ Ⓖ Ⓗ Ⓙ Ⓚ 47. Ⓐ Ⓑ Ⓒ Ⓓ Ⓔ 56. Ⓕ Ⓖ Ⓗ Ⓙ Ⓚ
3. Ⓐ Ⓑ Ⓒ Ⓓ Ⓔ 12. Ⓕ Ⓖ Ⓗ Ⓙ Ⓚ 21. Ⓐ Ⓑ Ⓒ Ⓓ Ⓔ 30. Ⓕ Ⓖ Ⓗ Ⓙ Ⓚ 39. Ⓐ Ⓑ Ⓒ Ⓓ Ⓔ 48. Ⓕ Ⓖ Ⓗ Ⓙ Ⓚ 57. Ⓐ Ⓑ Ⓒ Ⓓ Ⓔ
4. Ⓕ Ⓖ Ⓗ Ⓙ Ⓚ 13. Ⓐ Ⓑ Ⓒ Ⓓ Ⓔ 22. Ⓕ Ⓖ Ⓗ Ⓙ Ⓚ 31. Ⓐ Ⓑ Ⓒ Ⓓ Ⓔ 40. Ⓕ Ⓖ Ⓗ Ⓙ Ⓚ 49. Ⓐ Ⓑ Ⓒ Ⓓ Ⓔ 58. Ⓕ Ⓖ Ⓗ Ⓙ Ⓚ
5. Ⓐ Ⓑ Ⓒ Ⓓ Ⓔ 14. Ⓕ Ⓖ Ⓗ Ⓙ Ⓚ 23. Ⓐ Ⓑ Ⓒ Ⓓ Ⓔ 32. Ⓕ Ⓖ Ⓗ Ⓙ Ⓚ 41. Ⓐ Ⓑ Ⓒ Ⓓ Ⓔ 50. Ⓕ Ⓖ Ⓗ Ⓙ Ⓚ 59. Ⓐ Ⓑ Ⓒ Ⓓ Ⓔ
6. Ⓕ Ⓖ Ⓗ Ⓙ Ⓚ 15. Ⓐ Ⓑ Ⓒ Ⓓ Ⓔ 24. Ⓕ Ⓖ Ⓗ Ⓙ Ⓚ 33. Ⓐ Ⓑ Ⓒ Ⓓ Ⓔ 42. Ⓕ Ⓖ Ⓗ Ⓙ Ⓚ 51. Ⓐ Ⓑ Ⓒ Ⓓ Ⓔ 60. Ⓕ Ⓖ Ⓗ Ⓙ Ⓚ
7. Ⓐ Ⓑ Ⓒ Ⓓ Ⓔ 16. Ⓕ Ⓖ Ⓗ Ⓙ Ⓚ 25. Ⓐ Ⓑ Ⓒ Ⓓ Ⓔ 34. Ⓕ Ⓖ Ⓗ Ⓙ Ⓚ 43. Ⓐ Ⓑ Ⓒ Ⓓ Ⓔ 52. Ⓕ Ⓖ Ⓗ Ⓙ Ⓚ
8. Ⓕ Ⓖ Ⓗ Ⓙ Ⓚ 17. Ⓐ Ⓑ Ⓒ Ⓓ Ⓔ 26. Ⓕ Ⓖ Ⓗ Ⓙ Ⓚ 35. Ⓐ Ⓑ Ⓒ Ⓓ Ⓔ 44. Ⓕ Ⓖ Ⓗ Ⓙ Ⓚ 53. Ⓐ Ⓑ Ⓒ Ⓓ Ⓔ

Reading Test

6. Ⓕ Ⓖ Ⓗ Ⓙ 12. Ⓕ Ⓖ Ⓗ Ⓙ 18. Ⓕ Ⓖ Ⓗ Ⓙ 24. Ⓕ Ⓖ Ⓗ Ⓙ 30. Ⓕ Ⓖ Ⓗ Ⓙ 36. Ⓕ Ⓖ Ⓗ Ⓙ
1. Ⓐ Ⓑ Ⓒ Ⓓ 7. Ⓐ Ⓑ Ⓒ Ⓓ 13. Ⓐ Ⓑ Ⓒ Ⓓ 19. Ⓐ Ⓑ Ⓒ Ⓓ 25. Ⓐ Ⓑ Ⓒ Ⓓ 31. Ⓐ Ⓑ Ⓒ Ⓓ 37. Ⓐ Ⓑ Ⓒ Ⓓ
2. Ⓕ Ⓖ Ⓗ Ⓙ 8. Ⓕ Ⓖ Ⓗ Ⓙ 14. Ⓕ Ⓖ Ⓗ Ⓙ 20. Ⓕ Ⓖ Ⓗ Ⓙ 26. Ⓕ Ⓖ Ⓗ Ⓙ 32. Ⓕ Ⓖ Ⓗ Ⓙ 38. Ⓕ Ⓖ Ⓗ Ⓙ
3. Ⓐ Ⓑ Ⓒ Ⓓ 9. Ⓐ Ⓑ Ⓒ Ⓓ 15. Ⓐ Ⓑ Ⓒ Ⓓ 21. Ⓐ Ⓑ Ⓒ Ⓓ 27. Ⓐ Ⓑ Ⓒ Ⓓ 33. Ⓐ Ⓑ Ⓒ Ⓓ 39. Ⓐ Ⓑ Ⓒ Ⓓ
4. Ⓕ Ⓖ Ⓗ Ⓙ 10. Ⓕ Ⓖ Ⓗ Ⓙ 16. Ⓕ Ⓖ Ⓗ Ⓙ 22. Ⓕ Ⓖ Ⓗ Ⓙ 28. Ⓕ Ⓖ Ⓗ Ⓙ 34. Ⓕ Ⓖ Ⓗ Ⓙ 40. Ⓕ Ⓖ Ⓗ Ⓙ
5. Ⓐ Ⓑ Ⓒ Ⓓ 11. Ⓐ Ⓑ Ⓒ Ⓓ 17. Ⓐ Ⓑ Ⓒ Ⓓ 23. Ⓐ Ⓑ Ⓒ Ⓓ 29. Ⓐ Ⓑ Ⓒ Ⓓ 35. Ⓐ Ⓑ Ⓒ Ⓓ

Science Test

6. Ⓕ Ⓖ Ⓗ Ⓙ 12. Ⓕ Ⓖ Ⓗ Ⓙ 18. Ⓕ Ⓖ Ⓗ Ⓙ 24. Ⓕ Ⓖ Ⓗ Ⓙ 30. Ⓕ Ⓖ Ⓗ Ⓙ 36. Ⓕ Ⓖ Ⓗ Ⓙ
1. Ⓐ Ⓑ Ⓒ Ⓓ 7. Ⓐ Ⓑ Ⓒ Ⓓ 13. Ⓐ Ⓑ Ⓒ Ⓓ 19. Ⓐ Ⓑ Ⓒ Ⓓ 25. Ⓐ Ⓑ Ⓒ Ⓓ 31. Ⓐ Ⓑ Ⓒ Ⓓ 37. Ⓐ Ⓑ Ⓒ Ⓓ
2. Ⓕ Ⓖ Ⓗ Ⓙ 8. Ⓕ Ⓖ Ⓗ Ⓙ 14. Ⓕ Ⓖ Ⓗ Ⓙ 20. Ⓕ Ⓖ Ⓗ Ⓙ 26. Ⓕ Ⓖ Ⓗ Ⓙ 32. Ⓕ Ⓖ Ⓗ Ⓙ 38. Ⓕ Ⓖ Ⓗ Ⓙ
3. Ⓐ Ⓑ Ⓒ Ⓓ 9. Ⓐ Ⓑ Ⓒ Ⓓ 15. Ⓐ Ⓑ Ⓒ Ⓓ 21. Ⓐ Ⓑ Ⓒ Ⓓ 27. Ⓐ Ⓑ Ⓒ Ⓓ 33. Ⓐ Ⓑ Ⓒ Ⓓ 39. Ⓐ Ⓑ Ⓒ Ⓓ
4. Ⓕ Ⓖ Ⓗ Ⓙ 10. Ⓕ Ⓖ Ⓗ Ⓙ 16. Ⓕ Ⓖ Ⓗ Ⓙ 22. Ⓕ Ⓖ Ⓗ Ⓙ 28. Ⓕ Ⓖ Ⓗ Ⓙ 34. Ⓕ Ⓖ Ⓗ Ⓙ 40. Ⓕ Ⓖ Ⓗ Ⓙ
5. Ⓐ Ⓑ Ⓒ Ⓓ 11. Ⓐ Ⓑ Ⓒ Ⓓ 17. Ⓐ Ⓑ Ⓒ Ⓓ 23. Ⓐ Ⓑ Ⓒ Ⓓ 29. Ⓐ Ⓑ Ⓒ Ⓓ 35. Ⓐ Ⓑ Ⓒ Ⓓ

ENGLISH TEST
45 Minutes—75 Questions

5 Wrong

Directions: In the following five passages, certain words and phrases have been underlined and numbered. You will find alternatives for each underlined portion in the right-hand column. Select the one that best expresses the idea, that makes the statement acceptable in standard written English, or that is phrased most consistently with the style and tone of the entire passage. If you feel that the original version is best, select "NO CHANGE." You will also find questions asking about a section of the passage or about the entire passage. For these questions, decide which choice gives the most appropriate response to the given question. For each question in the test, select the best choice, and fill in the corresponding space on the answer sheet. You may wish to read each passage through before you begin to answer the questions associated with it. Most answers cannot be determined without reading several sentences around the phrases in question. Make sure to read far enough ahead each time you choose an alternative.

PASSAGE I

[1]

Since primitive times, societies have created, and
                                                    1
told legends. Even before the development of written
1
language, cultures would orally pass down these

popular stories.

[2]

2 These stories served the dual purpose of

entertaining audiences and of transmitting values and

beliefs from generation to generation. Indeed today we
                                            3
have many more permanent ways of handing down our

beliefs to future generations, we continue to create and

tell legends. In our technological society, a new form of

1. A. NO CHANGE
   B. created then subsequently told
   C. created and told
   D. created, and told original

2. Suppose that the author wants to insert a sentence here to describe the different kinds of oral stories told by these societies. Which of the following sentences would best serve that purpose?

   F. These myths and tales varied in substance, from the humorous to the heroic.
   G. These myths and tales were often recited by paid storytellers.
   H. Unfortunately, no recording of the original myths and tales exists.
   J. Sometimes it took several evenings for the full story to be recited.

3. A. NO CHANGE
   B. However,
   C. Indeed,
   D. Although

GO ON TO THE NEXT PAGE ⟹

folk tale has emerged: <u>the</u> urban legend.
4

[2]

Urban legends are stories we all have heard; they are supposed to have really happened, but are never <u>verifiable however.</u> It seems that the people involved can
5
never be found. Researchers of the urban legend call the elusive participant in such supposed "real-life" events a FOAF—a Friend of a Friend.

[3]

Urban legends have some characteristic features. They are often humorous in nature with a surprise <u>ending and a conclusion.</u> One such legend is the tale of
6
the hunter who was returning home from an unsuccessful hunting trip. On his way home, he accidentally hit and killed a deer on a deserted highway. Even though he knew it was illegal, he decided to keep the deer, and he <u>loads it in</u> the back of his station wagon.
7

As the hunter continued driving, the deer, <u>he was</u>
8
only temporarily knocked unconscious by the car, woke up and began thrashing around. The hunter panicked, stopped the car, ran to the ditch, and watched the enraged deer destroy his car.

4. F. NO CHANGE
    G. it is called the
    H. it being the
    J. known as the

5. A. NO CHANGE
    B. verifiable, however.
    C. verifiable, furthermore.
    D. verifiable.

6. F. NO CHANGE
    G. ending.
    H. ending, which is a conclusion.
    J. ending or conclusion.

7. A. NO CHANGE
    B. loaded it in
    C. is loading it in
    D. had loaded it in

8. F. NO CHANGE
    G. which being
    H. that is
    J. which was

GO ON TO THE NEXT PAGE

[4]

One legend involves alligators in the sewer systems

of major metropolitan areas. According to the story,

before alligators were a protected <u>species, people</u>
                                            9
vacationing in Florida purchased baby alligators to take

home as souvenirs. <u>Between 1930 and 1940, nearly a</u>
                                    10
<u>million alligators in Florida were killed for the value of</u>
                              10
<u>their skin, used to make expensive leather products such</u>
                        10
<u>as boots and wallets.</u> After the novelty of having a pet
        10
alligator wore off, many people flushed their baby

souvenirs down toilets. Legend has it that the baby

alligators found a perfect growing and breeding

environment in city sewer systems, where they thrive to

this day on the ample supply of rats.

[5]

In addition to urban legends that are told from

friend to friend, a growing number of urban legends are

passed along through the Internet and e-mail. One of

the more popular stories <u>are about</u> a woman who was
                              11
unwittingly charged $100 for a cookie recipe she

requested at an upscale restaurant. To get her money's

9. A. NO CHANGE
   B. species; people
   C. species. People
   D. species people

10. F. NO CHANGE
    G. Because their skin is used to make
       expensive leather products such as boots
       and wallets, nearly a million alligators
       in Florida were killed between 1930
       and 1940.
    H. Killed between 1930 and 1940, the
       skin of nearly a million alligators from
       Florida was used to make expensive
       leather products such as boots and
       wallets.
    J. OMIT the underlined portion.

11. A. NO CHANGE
    B. would be about
    C. is about
    D. is dealing with

GO ON TO THE NEXT PAGE

worth, this <u>woman supposed</u> copied the recipe for
12

the delicious cookies and forwarded it via e-mail to

everyone she knew.

[6]

Although today's technology enhances our ability

to tell and retell urban legends, the Internet can also

serve as a monitor of urban legends. <u>Dedicated to</u>
13

<u>commonly told urban legends, research is done by many</u>
13

<u>websites.</u> According to those websites, most legends,
13

including the ones told here, have no basis in reality.

12. F. NO CHANGE
G. woman supposedly
H. women supposedly
J. women supposed to

13. A. NO CHANGE
B. Many websites are dedicated to research-ing the validity of commonly told urban legends.
C. Researching the validity of commonly told urban legends, many websites are dedicated.
D. OMIT the underlined portion.

Items 14–15 ask about the passage as a whole.

---

14. The author wants to insert the following sentence:

Other urban legends seem to be designed to instill fear.

What would be the most logical placement for this sentence?

F. After the last sentence of paragraph 2
G. After the second sentence of paragraph 3
H. Before the first sentence of paragraph 4
J. After the last sentence of paragraph 4

15. Suppose that the author had been assigned to write an essay comparing the purposes and topics of myths and legends in primitive societies and in our modern society. Would this essay fulfill that assignment?

A. Yes, because the essay describes myths and legends from primitive societies and modern society.

B. Yes, because the essay provides explanations of possible purposes and topics for myths and legends from primitive societies and modern society.

C. No, because the essay does not provide enough information about the topics of the myths and legends in primitive societies to make a valid comparison.

D. No, because the essay doesn't provide any information on the myths and legends of primitive societies.

GO ON TO THE NEXT PAGE ➤

PASSAGE II

What does it mean to be successful? Do one
                                        16
measure success by money? If I told you about a man:
                                                  17
working as a teacher, a land surveyor, and a factory

worker (never holding any of these jobs for more than

a few years), would that man sound like a success to

you? If I told you that he spent two solitary years living
                                                     18
alone in a small cabin that he built for himself, and that
 18
he spent those years looking at plants and writing in a

diary—would you think of him as a celebrity or an

important figure? What if I told you that he rarely
                                               19
ventured far from the town where he was born, that he
 19
was thrown in jail for refusing to pay his taxes, and that

he died at the age of forty-five? Do any of these facts

seem to point to a man whose life should be studied

and emulated?

You may already know about this man. You may

even have read some of his writings. His name was:
                                              20
Henry David Thoreau, and he was, in addition to the
        20
jobs listed above, a poet, an essayist, a naturalist, and a

social critic. Although the facts listed about him may

16. F. NO CHANGE
    G. Does we
    H. Does one
    J. Did you

17. A. NO CHANGE
    B. man who worked
    C. man and worked
    D. man, which working

18. F. NO CHANGE
    G. two years living alone
    H. two solitary years all by himself
    J. a couple of lonely years living in solitude

19. A. NO CHANGE
    B. he ventured rarely
    C. he has rare ventures
    D. this person was to venture rarely

20. F. NO CHANGE
    G. was Henry David Thoreau and he
    H. was: Henry David Thoreau, who
    J. was Henry David Thoreau, and he

GO ON TO THE NEXT PAGE

not seem to add up to much, he <u>was, in fact a</u>
                                            21

tremendously influential person. Along with writers

such as Ralph Waldo Emerson, Mark Twain, and Walt

Whitman, Thoreau helped to create the first literature

and philosophy that most people identify as <u>unique</u>
                                                    22

"American."

In 1845, Thoreau built a <u>cabin. Near</u> Walden Pond
                                23

and remained there for more than two years, living

alone, fending for himself, and observing the nature

around him. He kept scrupulous notes in his diary,

notes that he later distilled into his most famous work

titled *Walden*. <u>*Walden* is read by many literature</u>
                                              24

<u>students today.</u>
        24

    [1] To protest slavery, Thoreau refused to pay his

taxes in 1846. [2] Thoreau was a firm believer in the

abolition of slavery, and he objected to the practice's

extension into the new territories of the West. [3] For

this act of rebellion, he was thrown in the Concord

jail. [25]

21. A.   NO CHANGE
     B.   was, in fact, a
     C.   was in fact a
     D.   was in fact, a

22. F.   NO CHANGE
     G.   uniquely
     H.   uniqueness
     J.   the most unique

23. A.   NO CHANGE
     B.   cabin. On
     C.   cabin, by
     D.   cabin near

24. F.   NO CHANGE
     G.   This book is read by many literature
          students today.
     H.   Today, many literature students read
          Walden.
     J.   OMIT the underlined portion.

25. What is the most logical order of sentences in
     this paragraph?
     A.   NO CHANGE
     B.   3, 2, 1
     C.   2, 1, 3
     D.   3, 1, 2

GO ON TO THE NEXT PAGE

Thoreau used his writing to spread his message of

resistance and <u>activism; he published</u> an essay entitled
26

Civil Disobedience (also known as *Resistance to Civil*

Government). In it, Thoreau laid out his argument for

refusing to obey unjust laws.

Although Thoreau's life was very brief, <u>his</u> works and
27

his ideas continue to touch and influence people.

Students all over the country—all over the world—

continue to read his essays and hear his unique voice,

urging them to lead lives of principle, individuality, and

freedom. 28

To be able to live out the ideas that burn in <u>the heart of</u>
29

<u>a person</u>—surely that is the meaning of success.
29

26. **F.** NO CHANGE
G. activism and he published
H. activism; which is why he published
J. activism to publish

27. **A.** NO CHANGE
B. he's
C. their
D. those

28. The purpose of this paragraph is to:
F. explain why Thoreau was put in jail.
G. prove a point about people's conception of success.
H. suggest that Thoreau may be misunderstood.
J. discuss Thoreau's importance in today's world.

29. A. NO CHANGE
B. one's heart
C. the heart and soul of a person
D. through the heart of a person

> Question 30 asks about the preceding passage as a whole.

30. By including questions throughout the entire first paragraph, the author allows the reader to:
F. answer each question as the passage proceeds.
G. think about the meaning of "success."
H. assess the quality of Thoreau's work.
J. form an opinion about greed in modern society.

GO ON TO THE NEXT PAGE

PASSAGE III

[1]

More than half of the world's <u>currently living plant</u> and
                                                31
animal species live in tropical rainforests. Four square

miles of a Central American rainforest can be home to

up to 1,500 different species of flowering plants, 700

species of trees, 400 species of birds, and 125 species of

mammals. Of these mammals, the sloth is one of the

most unusual.

[2]

Unlike most mammals, the sloth is usually upside

down. A sloth does just about everything upside down,

including sleeping, eating, mating, and giving birth. <u>Its'</u>
                                                        32
<u>unique</u> anatomy allows the sloth to spend most of the
 32
time hanging from one tree branch or another, high in

the canopy of a rainforest tree. About the size of a large

domestic <u>cat, the</u> sloth hangs from its unusually long
          33
limbs and long hook-like claws. <u>Specially designed for</u>
                                                      34
<u>limbs, the sloth's muscles seem to cling to things.</u>
                  34

31. A. NO CHANGE
    B. currently existing plant
    C. living plant
    D. plant

32. F. NO CHANGE
    G. It's unique
    H. Its unique
    J. Its uniquely

33. A. NO CHANGE
    B. cat; the
    C. cat. The
    D. cat, but the

34. F. NO CHANGE
    G. The sloth's muscles seem to cling to
        things for specially designed limbs.
    H. The muscles in a sloth's limbs seem to be
        specially designed for clinging to things.
    J. OMIT the underlined portion.

GO ON TO THE NEXT PAGE

[3]

In fact, a sloth's limbs are <u>so specific</u> adapted to upside-
                            35
down life that a sloth is essentially incapable of walking

on the ground. <u>Instead, they</u> must crawl or drag itself
                36
with its massive claws. This makes it easy to see why the

sloth rarely leaves its home in the trees. <u>Because</u> it can
                                            37
not move swiftly on the ground, the sloth is an

excellent swimmer.

[4]

[38] A sloth can hang upside down and, without moving

the rest of its <u>body turn</u> its face 180 degrees so that it
                 39
<u>was looking</u> at the ground. A sloth can rotate its
  40
forelimbs in all directions, so it can easily reach the

35. A. NO CHANGE
    B. so specific and
    C. so specified
    D. so specifically

36. F. NO CHANGE
    G. Instead, it
    H. However, they
    J. In addition, it

37. A. NO CHANGE
    B. Despite
    C. Similarly,
    D. Though

38. The author wants to insert a sentence here to
    help connect paragraph 3 and paragraph 4.
    Which of the following sentences would best
    serve that purpose?
    F. Of course, many other animals are also
        excellent swimmers.
    G. Another unique characteristic of the
        sloth is its flexibility.
    H. In addition to swimming, the sloth is an
        incredible climber.
    J. Flexibility is a trait that helps the sloth
        survive.

39. A. NO CHANGE
    B. body turns
    C. body, it has the capability of turning
    D. body, turn

40. F. NO CHANGE
    G. had been looking
    H. will have the ability to be looking
    J. can look

GO ON TO THE NEXT PAGE

leaves that make up its diet. The sloth can also roll itself

up into a ball in order to protect and defend itself from
41

predators. The howler monkey, another inhabitant of
42

the rainforest, is not as flexible as the sloth.
42

[5]

The best defense a sloth has from predators such as

jaguars and large snakes, though, is its camouflage.

During the rainy season, a sloth's thick brown or gray

fur is usually covered with a coat of blue-green algae.
43

Which helps it blend in with its forest surroundings.
43

Another type of camouflage is the sloth's incredibly

slow movement: it often moves less than 100 feet

during a 24-hour period.

[6]

It is this slow movement that earned the sloth its

name. *Sloth* is also a word for laziness or an aversion to

work. But even though it sleeps an average of 15 hours

a day, the sloth isn't necessarily lazy. It just moves,

upside down, at its own slow pace through its world of

rainforest trees. 44

41. A. NO CHANGE
    B. protect, and defend itself
    C. protects itself
    D. protect itself

42. F. NO CHANGE
    G. Another inhabitant of the rainforest, the howler monkey, is not as flexible as the sloth.
    H. Not as flexible as the sloth is the howler monkey, another inhabitant of the rainforest.
    J. OMIT the underlined portion.

43. A. NO CHANGE
    B. algae, which
    C. algae, being that it
    D. algae

44. The author is considering deleting the last sentence of paragraph 6. This change would:
    F. diminish the amount of information provided about the habits of the sloth.
    G. make the ending of the passage more abrupt.
    H. emphasize the slothful nature of the sloth.
    J. make the tone of the essay more consistent.

GO ON TO THE NEXT PAGE

Question 45 asks about the preceding
passage as a whole.

---

45. The author wants to insert the following
description:

An observer could easily be tricked into
thinking that a sloth was just a pile of
decaying leaves.

What would be the most appropriate placement for this sentence?

A.   After the last sentence of paragraph 1

B.   After the third sentence of paragraph 2

C.   Before the last sentence of paragraph 5

D.   Before the first sentence of paragraph 6

GO ON TO THE NEXT PAGE

PASSAGE IV

During the summer of 1988, I watched Yellowstone

National Park go up in flames. In June, <u>fires ignited by</u>
                                              46

<u>lightning</u> had been allowed to burn unsuppressed
   46

because park officials expected that the usual summer

rains would douse the flames. However, the rains never

<u>will have come.</u> A plentiful fuel supply of fallen logs
      47

and pine needles was available, and winds of up to

100 mph whipped the spreading fires along and carried

red-hot embers to other areas, creating new fires. By

the time park officials succumbed to the pressure of

public opinion and <u>decide</u> to try to extinguish the
                        48

<u>flames. It's</u> too late. The situation remained out of
      49

control in spite of the efforts of 9,000 fire fighters who

were using state-of-the-art equipment. By September,

more than 720,000 acres of Yellowstone had been

affected by fire. <u>Nature was only able to curb the</u>
                              50

<u>destruction;</u> the smoke did not begin to clear until the
      50

first snow arrived on September 11.

46. **F.** NO CHANGE
    G. fires having been ignited by lightning
    H. fires, the kind ignited by lightning,
    J. fires ignited and started by lightning

47. A. NO CHANGE
    B. came
    C. were coming
    D. have come

48. F. NO CHANGE
    G. are deciding
    H. decided
    J. OMIT the underlined portion.

49. A. NO CHANGE
    B. flames, it's
    C. flames, it was
    D. flames; it was

50. F. NO CHANGE
    G. Only curbing the destruction by able
       nature
    H. Only nature was able to curb the
       destruction
    J. Nature was able to curb only the
       destruction

 GO ON TO THE NEXT PAGE

Being that I was an ecologist who has studied forests
                51
for 20 years, I knew that this was not nearly the tragedy

it seemed to be. Large fires are, after all, necessary in
                                                      52
order that the continued health in the forest ecosystem
                52
be maintained. Fires thin out overcrowded areas and
  52
allow the sun to reach species of plants stunted by

shade. Ash fertilizes the soil, and fire smoke kills forest

bacteria. In the case of the lodgepole pine, fire is

essential to reproduction: the pines' cone open only
                                        53
when exposed to temperatures greater than 112 degrees.

The fires in Yellowstone did result in some loss of

wildlife, but overall, the region's animals proved to be

fire-tolerant and fire-adaptive. However, large animals
                                      54
such as bison were often seen grazing, and bedding
                                    55
down in meadows near burning forests. Also, the fire

posed little threat to the members of any endangered

animal species in the park.

My confidence in the natural resilience of the

forest has been borne out in the years since the fires

51. A. NO CHANGE
    B. Being that I am
    C. I'm
    D. As

52. F. NO CHANGE
    G. for the continued health of the forest
       ecosystem to be maintained.
    H. in order to continue the maintenance of
       the health of the forest ecosystem.
    J. for the continued health of the forest
       ecosystem.

53. A. NO CHANGE
    B. pines cones'
    C. pine's cones
    D. pine's cone

54. F. NO CHANGE
    G. Clearly,
    H. In fact,
    J. Instead,

55. A. NO CHANGE
    B. grazing; and bedding
    C. grazing: and bedding
    D. grazing and bedding

GO ON TO THE NEXT PAGE

ravaged Yellowstone. <u>Judged from recent pictures of the</u>
56

<u>park</u> the forest was not destroyed; <u>it</u> was rejuvenated.

56   57

56. A. NO CHANGE
    G. Recent pictures of the park show that
    H. Judging by the recent pictures of the park,
    J. As judged according to pictures taken of the park recently,

57. A. NO CHANGE
    B. they
    C. the fires
    D. I

Items 58–59 pose questions about the passage as a whole.

---

58. The writer is considering inserting the following true statement after the first sentence of the second paragraph:

> Many more acres of forest burned in Alaska in 1988 than in Yellowstone Park.

Would this addition be appropriate for the essay?

F. Yes, the statement would add important information about the effects of large-scale forest fires.

G. Yes, the statement would provide an informative contrast to the Yellowstone fire.

H. No, the statement would not provide any additional information about the effect of the 1988 fire in Yellowstone.

J. No, the statement would undermine the author's position as an authority on the subject of forest fires.

59. Suppose that the writer wishes to provide additional support for the claim that the fire posed little threat to the members of any endangered animal species in the park. Which of the following additions would be most effective?

A. A list of the endangered animals known to inhabit the park

B. A discussion of the particular vulnerability of endangered species of birds to forest fires

C. An explanation of the relative infrequency of such an extensive series of forest fires

D. A summary of reports of biologists who monitored the activity of endangered species in the park during the fire

GO ON TO THE NEXT PAGE

PASSAGE V

[1]

White water rafting <u>being</u> a favorite pastime of
 60
mine for several years. I have drifted down many

challenging North American rivers, including the

Snake, the Green, and the <u>Salmon, and there are many</u>
 61
<u>other rivers in America as well.</u> I have spent some of
 61
my best moments in dangerous rapids, yet nothing has

matched the thrill I experienced facing my first <u>rapids,</u>
 62
<u>on the Deschutes River.</u>
 62

[2]

My father and I spent the morning floating down a

calm and peaceful stretch of the Deschutes in his

wooden MacKenzie river boat. This trip <u>it being the</u>
 63
wooden boat's first time down rapids, as well as mine.

<u>Rapids are rated according to a uniform scale of</u>
 64
<u>relative difficulty.</u>
 64

[3]

<u>Roaring, I was in the boat approaching Whitehorse</u>
 65
<u>Rapids.</u> I felt much like a novice skier peering down her
 65
first steep slope: I was scared, but even more excited.

60. F.   NO CHANGE
    G.   have been
    H.   has been
    J.   was

61. A.   NO CHANGE
    B.   Salmon, just three of many rivers exist-
         ing in North America.
    C.   Salmon; many other rivers exist in North
         America.
    D.   Salmon.

62. F.   NO CHANGE
    G.   rapids: on Deschutes River.
    H.   rapids; on the Deschutes River.
    J.   rapids on the Deschutes River.

63. A.   NO CHANGE
    B.   it happened that it was
    C.   was
    D.   being

64. F.   NO CHANGE
    G.   Rated according to a uniform scale, rap-
         ids are relatively difficult.
    H.   (Rapids are rated according to a uniform
         scale of relative difficulty.)
    J.   OMIT the underlined portion.

65. A.   NO CHANGE
    B.   It roared, and the boat and I approached
         Whitehorse Rapids.
    C.   While the roaring boat was approaching
         Whitehorse Rapids, I could hear the water.
    D.   I could hear the water roar as we
         approached Whitehorse Rapids.

GO ON TO THE NEXT PAGE

The water churned and covering me with a refreshing

spray. My father, towards the stern, controlled the oars.

The carefree expression he usually wore on the river

had been replaced and instead he adopted a look of

intense concentration as he maneuvered around boulders

dotting our path. To release tension, we began to

holler like kids on a roller coaster, our voices echoing

across the water as we lurched violently about.

[4]

    Suddenly we came to a jarring halt and we

stopped; the left side of the bow was wedged on a large

rock. A whirlpool whirled around us; if we capsized we

would be sucked into the undertow. Instinctively, I

threw all of my weight towards the right side of the

tilting boat. Luckily, it was just enough force to

dislodge us, and we continued on down for about ten

more minutes of spectacular rapids.

[5]

    Later that day we went through Buckskin Mary

Rapids and Boxcar Rapids. When we pulled up on the

bank that evening, we saw that the boat had received its

first scar: that scar was a small hole on the upper bow

66. F. NO CHANGE
    G. churned, and covering me
    H. churning and covering me
    J. churned, covering me

67. A. NO CHANGE
    B. with
    C. by another countenance altogether:
    D. instead with some other expression;

68. F. NO CHANGE
    G. throughout
    H. around
    J. from

69. A. NO CHANGE
    B. which stopped us
    C. and stopped
    D. OMIT the underlined portion.

70. F. NO CHANGE
    G. it's
    H. it is
    J. its

71. A. NO CHANGE
    B. that was a
    C. which was a
    D. a

 GO ON TO THE NEXT PAGE

from the boulder we had wrestled with. In the years to

come, we went down many rapids and the boat

receiving many bruises, but Whitehorse is the most
    72
memorable rapids of all. 73

72. F. NO CHANGE
    G. received many
    H. received much
    J. receives many

73. Which of the following concluding sentences would most effectively emphasize the final point made in this paragraph while retaining the style and tone of the narrative as a whole?

    A. The brutal calamities that it presented the unwary rafter were more than offset by its beguiling excitement.

    B. Perhaps it is true that your first close encounter with white water is your most intense.

    C. Or, if not the most memorable, then at least a very memorable one!

    D. Call me crazy or weird if you want, but white water rafting is the sport for me.

Items 74–75 pose questions about the passage as a whole.

---

74. The writer has been assigned to write an essay that focuses on the techniques of white water rafting. Would this essay meet the requirements of that assignment?

    F. No, because the essay's main focus is on a particular experience, not on techniques.

    G. No, because the essay mostly deals with the relationship between father and daughter.

    H. Yes, because specific rafting techniques are the essay's main focus.

    J. Yes, because it presents a dramatic story of a day of white water rafting.

75. Suppose that the writer wants to add the following sentence to the essay:

    It was such a peaceful summer day that it was hard to believe dangerous rapids awaited us downstream.

    What would be the most logical placement of this sentence?

    A. After the last sentence of paragraph 1
    B. After the last sentence of paragraph 2
    C. Before the first sentence of paragraph 4
    D. After the last sentence of paragraph 4

MATH TEST

60 Minutes—60 Questions

> **Directions:** Solve each of the following problems, select the correct answer, and then fill in the corresponding space on your answer sheet.
>
> Don't linger over problems that are too time-consuming. Do as many as you can, then come back to the others in the time you have remaining.
>
> Calculator use is permitted, but some problems can best be solved without a calculator.
>
> **Note:** Unless otherwise noted, all of the following should be assumed.
>
> 1. Illustrative figures are *not* necessarily drawn to scale.
> 2. All geometric figures lie in a plane.
> 3. The term *line* indicates a straight line.
> 4. The term *average* indicates arithmetic mean.

1. In a recent survey, 14 people found their mayor to be "very competent." This number is exactly 20% of the people surveyed. How many people were surveyed?

    A. 28
    B. 35
    C. 56
    D. 70
    E. 84

DO YOUR FIGURING HERE.

2. A train traveled at a rate of 90 miles per hour for x hours and then at a rate of 60 miles per hour for y hours. Which expression represents the train's average rate in miles per hour for the entire distance traveled?

    F. $\dfrac{540}{xy}$

    G. $\dfrac{90}{x} \times \dfrac{60}{y}$

    H. $\dfrac{90}{x} + \dfrac{60}{y}$

    J. $\dfrac{90x + 60y}{x + y}$

    K. $\dfrac{150}{x + y}$

GO ON TO THE NEXT PAGE

3. In a certain string ensemble, the ratio of men to women is 5:3. If there are a total of 24 people in the ensemble, how many women are there?

A. 12
B. 11
C. 10
D. 9
E. 8

DO YOUR FIGURING HERE.

$5:3 = 8$

$\times 3$

4. If $x \neq 0$, and $x^2 - 3x = 6x$, then $x = ?$

F. -9
G. -3
H. $\sqrt{3}$
J. 3
K. 9

$x^2 3x - 6x$

$x(x-9)$

5. The two overlapping circles below form three regions, as shown:

What is the maximum number of regions that can be formed by three overlapping circles?

A. 5
B. 6
C. 7
D. 8
E. 9

6. If $x^2 + 6x + 8 = 4 + 10x$, then x equals which of the following?

F. -2
G. -1
H. 0
J. 1
K. 2

GO ON TO THE NEXT PAGE

7. Nine less than the number c is the same as the number d, and d less than twice c is 20. Which two equations could be used to determine the value of c and d?

DO YOUR FIGURING HERE.

A. $d - 9 = c$
   $d - 2c = 20$

B. $c - 9 = d$
   $2c - d = 20$

C. $c - 9 = d$
   $d - 2c = 20$

D. $9 - c = d$
   $2c - d = 20$

E. $9 - c = d$
   $2cd = 20$

8. An ice cream parlor offers 5 flavors of ice cream and 4 different toppings (sprinkles, hot fudge, whipped cream, and butterscotch). There is a special offer that includes one flavor of ice cream and one topping, served in a cup, sugar cone, or waffle cone. How many ways are there to order ice cream with the special offer?

F. 4

G. 5

H. 12

J. 23

K. 60

9. At a recent audition for a school play, 1 out of 3 students who auditioned were asked to come to a second audition. After the second audition, 75% of those asked to the second audition were offered parts. If 18 students were offered parts, how many students went to the first audition?

A. 18

B. 24

C. 48

D. 56

E. 72

GO ON TO THE NEXT PAGE

10. One number is 5 times another number and their sum is −60. What is the lesser of the two numbers?

    F. −5
    G. −10
    H. −12
    J. −48
    K. −50

DO YOUR FIGURING HERE.

11. In the figure below, which is composed of equilateral triangles, what is the greatest number of parallelograms that can be found?

    A. 6
    B. 9
    C. 12
    D. 15
    E. 18

12. The circle in the figure below is inscribed in a square with a perimeter of 16 inches. What is the area of the shaded region?

    F. 4π
    G. 16 − 2π
    H. 16 − 4π
    J. 8 − 2π
    K. 8 − 4π

GO ON TO THE NEXT PAGE

13. How many positive integers less than 50 are multiples of 4 but *not* multiples of 6?

   A. 4
   B. 6
   C. 8
   D. 10
   E. 12

DO YOUR FIGURING HERE.

14. What is the value of $f(3)$ where $f(x) = (8 - 3x)$ $(x^2 - 2x - 15)$?

   F. −30
   G. −18
   H. 12
   J. 24
   K. 30

15. A class contains five juniors and five seniors. If one member of the class is assigned at random to present a paper on a certain subject, and another member of the class is randomly assigned to assist him, what is the probability that both will be juniors?

   A. $\dfrac{1}{10}$

   B. $\dfrac{1}{5}$

   C. $\dfrac{2}{9}$

   D. $\dfrac{2}{5}$

   E. $\dfrac{1}{2}$

GO ON TO THE NEXT PAGE

16. In triangle XYZ below, $\overline{XS}$ and $\overline{SZ}$ are 3 and 12 units, respectively. If the area of triangle XYZ is 45 square units, how many units long is altitude $\overline{YS}$?

DO YOUR FIGURING HERE.

F.   3
G.   6
H.   9
J.   12
K.   15

17. At which y-coordinate does the line described by the equation $6y - 3x = 18$ intersect the y-axis?

A.   18
B.   9
C.   6
D.   3
E.   2

18. If $x^2 - y^2 = 12$ and $x - y = 4$, what is the value of $x^2 + 2xy + y^2$?

F.   3
G.   8
H.   9
J.   12
K.   16

GO ON TO THE NEXT PAGE

19. What is the area in square units of the figure
below?

A. 147
B. 108.5
C. 91
D. 60.5
E. $39 + 7\sqrt{2}$

DO YOUR FIGURING HERE.

20. A carpenter is cutting wood to make a new
bookcase with a board that is 12 feet long. If
the carpenter cuts off 3 pieces, each of which
is 17 inches long, how many inches long is
the remaining fourth and final board? (A foot
contains 12 inches.)

F.   36
G.   51
H.   93
J.   108
K.   144

21. If $x^2 - 4x - 6 = 6$, what are the possible values
for x?

A.   4, 12
B.   −6, 2
C.   −6, −2
D.   6, 2
E.   6, −2

22. If −3 is a solution for the equation $x^2 + kx - 15 = 0$, what is the value of k?

F.   5
G.   2
H.   −2
J.   −5
K.   Cannot be determined from the
information given.

GO ON TO THE NEXT PAGE

23. If the lengths, in inches, of all three sides of a triangle are integers, and one side is 7 inches long, what is the smallest possible perimeter of the triangle, in inches?

A.   9
B.   10
C.   12
D.   15
E.   18

DO YOUR FIGURING HERE.

24. If $0° < \theta < 90°$ and $\sin \theta = \dfrac{\sqrt{11}}{2\sqrt{3}}$, then $\cos \theta = ?$

F. $\dfrac{1}{2\sqrt{3}}$

G. $\dfrac{1}{\sqrt{11}}$

H. $\dfrac{2}{\sqrt{3}}$

J. $\dfrac{2\sqrt{3}}{\sqrt{11}}$

K. $\dfrac{11}{2\sqrt{3}}$

25. Which of the following expressions is equivalent to $\dfrac{\sqrt{3+x}}{\sqrt{3-x}}$ for all x such that $-3 < x < 3$?

A. $\dfrac{3-x}{3+x}$

B. $\dfrac{3+x}{3-x}$

C. $\dfrac{-3\sqrt{3+x}}{3-x}$

D. $\dfrac{\sqrt{9-x^2}}{3-x}$

E. $\dfrac{x^2-9}{3+x}$

GO ON TO THE NEXT PAGE

DO YOUR FIGURING HERE.

26. In a certain cookie jar containing only macaroons and gingersnaps, the ratio of macaroons to gingersnaps is 2 to 5. Which of the following could be the total number of cookies in the cookie jar?

   F.   24
   G.   35
   H.   39
   J.   48
   K.   52

27. What is the sum of $\frac{3}{16}$ and .175?

   A.   .3165
   B.   .3500
   C.   .3625
   D.   .3750
   E.   .3875

28. What is the maximum possible area, in square inches, of a rectangle with a perimeter of 20 inches?

   F.   15
   G.   20
   H.   25
   J.   30
   K.   40

29. $\dfrac{\dfrac{3}{2}+\dfrac{7}{4}}{\left(\dfrac{15}{8}-\dfrac{3}{4}\right)-\left(\dfrac{4+3}{-4+3}\right)}=?$

   A. $\dfrac{3}{8}$

   B. $\dfrac{2}{3}$

   C. $\dfrac{9}{13}$

   D. $\dfrac{5}{2}$

   E. $\dfrac{8}{3}$

GO ON TO THE NEXT PAGE →

30. If $x - 15 = 7 - 5(x - 4)$, then $x = ?$

    F. 0
    G. 2
    H. 4
    J. 5
    K. 7

    (handwritten: $-5x + 20$, $x = 15 \quad -5x + 27$, $6x = 12$)

DO YOUR FIGURING HERE.

31. The sketch below shows the dimensions of a
    flower garden. What is the area of this garden
    in square meters?

9 meters

9 meters

13 meters

    A. 31
    B. 85
    C. 99
    D. 101
    E. 117

32. What is the slope of the line described by the
    equation $6y - 3x = 18$?

    F. -2
    G. $-\dfrac{1}{2}$
    H. $\dfrac{1}{2}$
    J. 2
    K. 3

    (handwritten: $\dfrac{3x}{6}$)

GO ON TO THE NEXT PAGE

33. Line m passes through the point $(4, 3)$ in the standard (x, y) coordinate plane, and is perpendicular to the line described by the equation $y = -\frac{4}{5}x + 6$. Which of the following equations describes line m?

A. $y = \frac{5}{4}x + 2$

B. $y = -\frac{5}{4}x + 6$

C. $y = \frac{4}{5}x - 2$

D. $y = -\frac{4}{5}x + 2$

E. $y = \frac{5}{4}x - 2$

34. Line t in the standard (x, y) coordinate plane has a y-intercept of -3 and is parallel to the line having the equation $3x - 5y = 4$. Which of the following is an equation for line t?

F. $y = -\frac{3}{5}x + 3$

G. $y = -\frac{5}{3}x - 3$

H. $y = \frac{3}{5}x + 3$

J. $y = \frac{5}{3}x + 3$

K. $y = \frac{3}{5}x - 3$

35. If $y = mx + b$, which of the following equations expresses x in terms of y, m, and b?

A. $x = \frac{y - b}{m}$

B. $x = \frac{b - y}{m}$

C. $x = \frac{y + b}{m}$

D. $x = \frac{y}{m} - b$

E. $x = \frac{y}{m} + b$

GO ON TO THE NEXT PAGE

36. In the figure below, $\overline{AB} = 20$, $\overline{BC} = 15$, and $\angle ADB$ and $\angle ABC$ are right angles. What is the length of $\overline{AD}$?

DO YOUR FIGURING HERE.

F.   9
G. 12
H. 15
J. 16
K. 25

37. In the standard (x, y) coordinate plane shown in the figure below, points A and B lie on line m, and point C lies below it. The coordinates of points A, B, and C are $(0, 5)$, $(5, 5)$, and $(3, 3)$, respectively. What is the shortest possible distance from point C to a point on line m?

A. 2
B. $2\sqrt{2}$
C. 3
D. $\sqrt{13}$
E. 5

GO ON TO THE NEXT PAGE

DO YOUR FIGURING HERE.

38. For all $x \neq 8$, $\dfrac{x^2 - 11x + 24}{8 - x} = ?$

    F. $8 - x$

    G. $3 - x$

    H. $x - 3$

    J. $x - 8$

    K. $x - 11$

39. Points A and B lie in the standard (x, y) coordinate plane. The (x, y) coordinates of A are $(2, 1)$ and the (x, y) coordinates of B are $(-2, -2)$. What is the distance from A to B?

    A. $3\sqrt{2}$

    B. $3\sqrt{3}$

    C. 5

    D. 6

    E. 7

40. In the figure below, $\overline{AB}$ and $\overline{CD}$ are both tangent to the circle as shown, and $ABCD$ is a rectangle with side lengths $2x$ and $5x$ as shown. What is the area of the shaded region?

F. $10\pi x^2$

G. $10x^2 - \pi x^2$

H. $10x^2 - 2\pi x$

J. $9\pi x^2$

K. $6\pi x^2$

GO ON TO THE NEXT PAGE

DO YOUR FIGURING HERE.

41. If $0° < \theta < 90°$ and $\cos\theta = \dfrac{5\sqrt{2}}{8}$, then $\tan\theta = ?$

    A. $\dfrac{5}{\sqrt{7}}$

    B. $\dfrac{\sqrt{7}}{5}$

    C. $\dfrac{\sqrt{14}}{8}$

    D. $\dfrac{8}{\sqrt{14}}$

    E. $\dfrac{8}{5\sqrt{2}}$

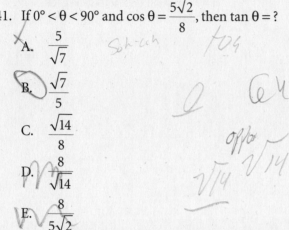

42. Consider fractions of the form $\dfrac{7}{n}$, where n is an integer. How many integer values of n make this fraction greater than .5 and less than .8?

    F. 3

    G. 4

    H. 5

    J. 6

    K. 7

43. The circumference of circle X is 12π and the circumference of circle Y is 8π. What is the greatest possible distance between two points, one of which lies on the circumference of circle X and one of which lies on the circumference of circle Y?

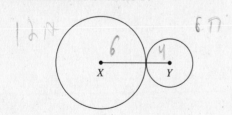

    A. 6

    B. 10

    C. 20

    D. 10π

    E. 20π

GO ON TO THE NEXT PAGE

44. $\sqrt{(x^2 + 4)^2} - (x + 2)(x - 2) = ?$

    F. $2x^2$

    G. $x^2 - 8$

    H. $2(x - 2)$

    J. 0

    K. 8

45. If $s = -3$, then $s^3 + 2s^2 + 2s = ?$

    A. -15

    B. -10

    C. -5

    D. 5

    E. 33

46. How many different numbers are solutions for the equation $2x + 6 = (x + 5)(x + 3)$?

    F. 0

    G. 1

    H. 2

    J. 3

    K. Infinitely many

47. In square $ABCD$ below, $\overline{AC} = 8$. What is the perimeter of $ABCD$?

    A. $4\sqrt{2}$

    B. 8

    C. $8\sqrt{2}$

    D. 16

    E. $16\sqrt{2}$

GO ON TO THE NEXT PAGE

48. The front surface of a fence panel is shown below with the lengths labeled representing inches. The panel is symmetrical along its center vertical axis. What is the surface area of the front surface of the panel in square inches?

DO YOUR FIGURING HERE.

F. 144
G. 132
H. 120
J. 80
K. $64 + 6\sqrt{5}$

49. In the figure below, O is the center of the circle, and C, D, and E are points on the circumference of the circle. If $\angle OCD$ measures 70° and $\angle OED$ measures 45°, what is the measure of $\angle CDE$?

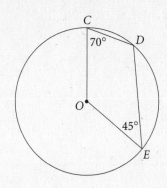

A. 25°
B. 45°
C. 70°
D. 90°
E. 115°

GO ON TO THE NEXT PAGE

50. Which of the following systems of equations does NOT have a solution?

DO YOUR FIGURING HERE.

   F. $x + 3y = 19$
        $3x + y = 6$

   G. $x + 3y = 19$
        $x - 3y = 13$

   H. $x - 3y = 19$
        $3x - y = 7$

   J. $x - 3y = 19$
        $3x + y = 6$

   K. $x + 3y = 6$
        $3x + 9y = 7$

51. What is the 46th digit to the right of the decimal point in the decimal equivalent of $\frac{1}{7}$?

   A.   1
   B.   2
   C.   4
   D.   7
   E.   8

52. Which of the following inequalities is equivalent to $-2 - 4x \le -6x$?

   F. $x \ge -2$
   G. $x \ge 1$
   H. $x \ge 2$
   J. $x \le -1$
   K. $x \le 1$

GO ON TO THE NEXT PAGE

53. If $x > 0$ and $y > 0$, $\dfrac{\sqrt{x}}{x} + \dfrac{\sqrt{y}}{y}$ is equivalent to which of the following?

   A. $\dfrac{2}{xy}$

   B. $\dfrac{\sqrt{x} + \sqrt{y}}{\sqrt{xy}}$

   C. $\dfrac{x + y}{xy}$

   D. $\dfrac{\sqrt{x} + \sqrt{y}}{\sqrt{x+y}}$

   E. $\dfrac{x + y}{\sqrt{xy}}$

DO YOUR FIGURING HERE.

54. In the diagram below, $\overline{CD}$, $\overline{BE}$, and $\overline{AF}$ are all parallel and are intersected by two transversals as shown. What is the length of $\overline{EF}$?

   F. 2
   G. 3
   H. 4
   J. 6
   K. 9

GO ON TO THE NEXT PAGE

55. What is the area, in square units, of the square whose vertices are located at the (x, y) coordinate points indicated in the figure below?

DO YOUR FIGURING HERE.

A. 9

B. 12

C. 16

D. 18

E. 24

56. Compared to the graph of $y = \cos \theta$, the graph of $y = 2 \cos \theta$ has:

F. twice the period and the same amplitude.

G. half the period and the same amplitude.

H. twice the period and half the amplitude.

J. half the amplitude and the same period.

K. twice the amplitude and the same period.

57. Brandy has a collection of comic books. If she adds 15 to the number of comic books in her collection and multiplies the sum by 3, the result will be 65 less than 4 times the number of comic books in her collection. How many comic books are in her collection?

A. 50

B. 85

C. 110

D. 145

E. 175

GO ON TO THE NEXT PAGE

58. One empty cylinder has three times the height and twice the diameter of another empty cylinder. How many fillings of the smaller cylinder would be equivalent to one filling of the larger cylinder?

   (Note: The volume of a cylinder of radius r and height h is $\pi r^2 h$.)

   F. 6
   G. $6\sqrt{2}$
   H. 12
   J. 18
   K. 24

DO YOUR FIGURING HERE.

59. What is the perimeter of a 30°-60°-90° triangle with a long leg of 12 inches?

   A. $6\sqrt{3}+12$
   B. $4\sqrt{3}+18$
   C. $8\sqrt{3}+18$
   D. $12\sqrt{3}+12$
   E. $12\sqrt{3}+18$

60. A baseball team scores an average of x points in its first n games and then scores y points in its next and final game of the season. Which of the following represents the team's average score for the entire season?

   F. $x+\dfrac{y}{n}$
   G. $x+\dfrac{y}{n+1}$
   H. $\dfrac{x+ny}{n+1}$
   J. $\dfrac{nx+y}{n+1}$
   K. $\dfrac{n(x+y)}{n+1}$

IF YOU FINISH BEFORE TIME IS CALLED, YOU MAY CHECK YOUR WORK ON THIS SECTION ONLY. DO NOT TURN TO ANY OTHER SECTION IN THE TEST.

STOP

READING TEST

35 Minutes—40 Questions

Directions: This test contains four passages, each followed by several questions. After reading a passage, select the best answer to each question and fill in the corresponding oval on your answer sheet. You are allowed to refer to the passages while answering the questions.

PASSAGE I

Emma Woodhouse, handsome, clever, and rich, with a comfortable home and happy disposition, seemed to unite some of the best blessings of exis-
Line tence. She had lived nearly twenty-one years in the
(5) world with very little to distress or vex her. She was the youngest of the two daughters of a most affectionate, indulgent father, and had, in conse-quence of her sister's marriage, been mistress of his house from a very early period. Her mother
(10) had died too long ago for her to have more than an indistinct remembrance of her caresses, and her place had been taken by an excellent governess who had fallen little short of a mother in affection.

Sixteen years had Miss Taylor been in Mr.
(15) Woodhouse's family, less as a governess than a friend, very fond of both daughters, but particu-larly of Emma. Between them it was more the inti-macy of sisters. Even before Miss Taylor had ceased to hold the nominal office of governess, the
(20) mildness of her temper had hardly allowed her to impose any restraint. The shadow of authority being now long passed away, they had been living together as friend and friend very mutually attached, and Emma doing just what she liked,
(25) highly esteeming Miss Taylor's judgment, but directed chiefly by her own. The real evils, indeed, of Emma's situation were the power of having rather too much her own way, and a disposition to think a little too well of herself; these were the dis-
(30) advantages which threatened alloy to her many enjoyments. The danger, however, was at present so unperceived, that they did not by any means rank as misfortunes with her.

Sorrow came—a gentle sorrow—but not at all
(35) in the shape of any disagreeable consciousness. Miss Taylor married. It was Miss Taylor's loss which first brought grief. It was on the wedding-day of this beloved friend that Emma first sat in mournful thought of any continuance. The wed-
(40) ding over, and the bride-people gone, she and her father were left to dine together, with no prospect of a third to cheer a long evening. Her father com-posed himself to sleep after dinner, as usual, and she had then only to sit and think of what she had
(45) lost.

The marriage had every promise of happiness for her friend. Mr. Weston was a man of unexcep-tionable character, easy fortune, suitable age, and pleasant manners. There was some satisfaction in
(50) considering with what self-denying, generous friendship she had always wished and promoted the match, but it was a black morning's work for her. The want of Miss Taylor would be felt every hour of every day. She recalled her past kind-
(55) ness—the kindness, the affection of sixteen years—how she had taught her and how she had played with her from five years old—how she had devoted all her powers to attach and amuse her in health—and how she had nursed her through the
(60) various illnesses of childhood. A large debt of gratitude was owing here, but the intercourse of the last seven years, the equal footing and perfect unreserve which had soon followed Isabella's mar-riage, on their being left to each other, was yet a
(65) dearer, tenderer recollection. She had been a friend and companion such as few possessed:

GO ON TO THE NEXT PAGE ⟹

intelligent, well-informed, useful, gentle, knowing all the ways of the family, interested in all its concerns, and peculiarly interested in her, in every
(70) pleasure, every scheme of hers—one to whom she could speak every thought as it arose, and who had such an affection for her as could never find fault.

How was she to bear the change? It was true
(75) that her friend was going only half a mile from them, but Emma was aware that great must be the difference between a Mrs. Weston, only half a mile from them, and a Miss Taylor in the house. With all her advantages, natural and domestic, she was
(80) now in great danger of suffering from intellectual solitude.

This passage is an adapted excerpt from Jane Austen's novel *Emma*. In this passage, Emma confronts a change in her previously happy life.

1. According to the passage, what are the greatest disadvantages facing Emma?

   A. Her father is not a stimulating conversationalist, and she is bored.
   B. She is lonely and afraid that Mrs. Weston will not have a happy marriage.
   C. She is used to having her way too much, and she thinks too highly of herself.
   D. She misses the companionship of her mother, her sister, and Miss Taylor.

2. The name of Emma's sister is:

   F. Mrs. Weston.
   G. Isabella.
   H. Miss Taylor.
   J. Mrs. Woodhouse.

3. As described in the passage, Emma's relationship with Miss Taylor can be characterized as:

   A. similar to a mother-daughter relationship.
   B. similar to the relationship of sisters or best friends.
   C. weaker than Emma's relationship with her sister.
   D. stronger than Miss Taylor's relationship with her new husband.

4. As used in line 28, *disposition* can most closely be defined as:

   F. a tendency.
   G. control.
   H. placement.
   J. transfer.

5. Which of the following are included in Emma's memories of her relationship with Miss Taylor?

   I. Miss Taylor taking care of Emma during childhood illnesses
   II. Miss Taylor's interest in all of the concerns of Emma's family
   III. Miss Taylor teaching her mathematics
   IV. Miss Taylor scolding her for being selfish

   A. I, III, and IV only
   B. I and III only
   C. II, III, and IV only
   D. I and II only

GO ON TO THE NEXT PAGE ⟩

6. It is most reasonable to infer from Emma's realization that "great must be the difference between a Mrs. Weston, only half a mile from them, and a Miss Taylor in the house" (lines 76–78) that:

    F. Miss Taylor will no longer be a part of Emma's life.

    G. Emma is happy about the marriage because now she will have more freedom.

    H. Emma regrets that her relationship with Miss Taylor will change.

    J. Emma believes that her relationship with Miss Taylor will become stronger.

7. Based on the passage, Emma could best be described as:

    A. sweet and naïve.

    B. self-centered and naïve.

    C. self-centered and headstrong.

    D. unappreciative and bitter.

8. The passage suggests that the quality Emma values most in a friend is:

    F. charisma.

    G. devotion.

    H. honesty.

    J. intelligence.

9. How does Emma view Mr. Weston?

    A. She thinks that he is an excellent match, and it required considerable self-sacrifice not to pursue him herself.

    B. She considers him to be a respectable if somewhat average match for her friend.

    C. She sees him as an intruder who has carried away her best friend in "a black morning's work" (line 52).

    D. She believes he is an indulgent, easily swayed man, reminiscent of her father.

10. From the passage, it can be inferred that Emma is accustomed to:

    F. behaving according to the wishes of her affectionate father.

    G. taking the advice of Miss Taylor when faced with deciding upon a course of action.

    H. doing as she pleases without permission from her father or governess.

    J. abiding by strict rules governing her behavior.

GO ON TO THE NEXT PAGE ⟹

Passage II

Learning and its result, memory, are processes by which we retain acquired information, emotions, and impressions that can influence our
Line behavior. At the psychological level, memory is
(5) not a single process. Sensory memory, the first of three main systems of memory, describes the momentary lingering of perceptual information as it is initially sensed and briefly recorded. When an image strikes the eyes it lingers in the visual sys-
(10) tem for an instant while the image is interpreted, and is quickly overwritten by new information. In the visual system this is called *iconic memory*, in the auditory system it is *echoic memory*, and in reference to touch it is *haptic memory*.
(15) If sensory information is processed it can move into the second main system of memory, working memory. This was once known as short-term memory (and that term is still popularly used). But working memory is viewed as a more accurate
(20) term, since this system not only stores information for short periods of time, but also enables the use and manipulation of information processed there. However, only a limited number of items can be held in working memory (the average for
(25) most people is seven), and decay of the memory occurs rapidly, although it can be held longer if the information is mentally or vocally repeated. Unless we make a conscious effort to retain it, a working memory may disappear forever.
(30) Long-term memory is the most comprehensive of the three, with apparently infinite capacity. Memories recorded in long-term memory are never lost, although at times there may be difficulty accessing them. There are three independent
(35) categories of long-term memory which interact extensively: *episodic* involves personal memories and details of daily life, and is closely identified with its time and place; *semantic* contains facts and general knowledge that are not tied to when
(40) or how they were learned; and *procedural* retains skills used to perform certain activities that eventually may not require conscious effort.

Although the main systems of memory are widely accepted, controversy continues about
(45) memory formation and retrieval. It was once believed that for a memory to enter long-term memory it must first be held in working memory. However, this idea has been challenged by an alternate theory suggesting that sensory memories
(50) can be directly entered into long-term memory through a pathway that runs parallel to, rather than in series with, working memory. Memories therefore can register simultaneously in both systems.
(55) Likewise, all agree that the retrieval of long-term memories is facilitated by repetition, but there is no agreement about the accuracy of these memories. For many years the scientific community viewed human memory as similar to
(60) computer memory, with the mind recording each detail just as it was presented. However, there is a growing consensus that our memory is sometimes flawed. An inference or assumption made by an individual when a memory is created may later be
(65) recalled as fact, or the mind may fill in details that were originally missing. Moreover, when we try to recall a particular memory, an unrelated memory may alter it through a process called interference. There is even evidence that an entirely false memory
(70) can be incorporated as a memory indistinguishable from true memories. Although for most purposes these discrepancies are harmless, concerns regarding the accuracy of human memory challenge the reliability of eyewitness testimony.

GO ON TO THE NEXT PAGE ⇨

11. The main purpose of the passage is to:

A. describe the main memory systems and why they are increasingly controversial.

B. describe the main memory systems and some views of memory formation and retrieval.

C. demonstrate that early ideas about memory formation and retrieval were incorrect.

D. demonstrate that theories about the main memory systems are incorrect.

12. Based on information in the passage, which of the following would be recalled from semantic long-term memory?

F. Ballet steps

G. A childhood birthday

H. Multiplication tables

J. Riding a bicycle

13. It can be reasonably inferred from the passage that, if a man in a car accident is unable to remember details of his life and family, but does remember how to perform his job, his:

A. episodic memories have been lost.

B. episodic memories have become inaccessible.

C. procedural memories have been lost.

D. procedural memories have become inaccessible.

14. The fact that the scientific community once viewed human memory as similar to computer memory is mentioned in the last paragraph in order to:

F. illustrate that memory is now viewed as complex rather than mechanical.

G. explain that memory is now viewed as an exact record of events.

H. illustrate that memory is always inaccurate.

J. explain that memories are formed the same way computers encode data.

15. If a person reads, "The baseball hit the window," and, when asked to recall the sentence, remembers "The baseball broke the window," according to the passage this is probably an example of:

A. interference altering a memory.

B. a memory that became inaccessible.

C. a reader's assumption altering a memory.

D. a completely false memory being created.

16. According to the passage, all the following are examples of episodic memory EXCEPT:

F. the meal you ate last night

G. the name of an old classmate

H. the year your class won a trophy

J. the face of a stranger passed on the street

GO ON TO THE NEXT PAGE ⟹

17. Based on information in the passage the term
    short-term memory was most likely replaced
    with *working memory* in order to:

    A. refute the idea that memories in this
        category degrade quickly.

    B. emphasize that memories in this category
        can be manipulated.

    C. show that memories in this category
        become long-term memories.

    D. demonstrate that echoic memories are
        held in the visual system.

18. As it is used in the passage, the word *iconic*
    (line 12) most nearly means relating to:

    F. something sacred.

    G. a symbolic representation.

    H. visual sensory memory.

    J. a picture that represents a computer
        command.

19. According to the passage, most of the scientific
    community now agrees that:

    A. there are really four main categories of
        memory, not three.

    B. memories held in long-term memory
        remain forever.

    C. memories must be held in working
        memory before long-term memory.

    D. repetition does not affect the duration of
        memory.

20. According to the passage, which of the
    following is a characteristic of working
    memory?

    F. A slight echo in the ear

    G. Quick replacement by new sensory
        information

    H. Rapid forgetting

    J. Infinite capacity

GO ON TO THE NEXT PAGE

Passage III

There can be little doubt that women artists
have been most prominent in photography and
that they have made their greatest contribution in
Line this field. One reason for this is not difficult to
(5) ascertain. As several historians of photography have
pointed out, photography, being a new medium
outside the traditional academic framework, was
wide open to women and offered them opportunities that the older fields did not….

(10)   All these observations apply to the first woman
to have achieved eminence in photography, and
that is Julia Margaret Cameron…. Born in 1815 in
Calcutta into an upper-middle-class family and
married to Charles Hay Cameron, a distinguished
(15) jurist and member of the Supreme Court of India,
Julia Cameron was well-known as a brilliant conversationalist and a woman of personality and
intellect who was unconventional to the point of
eccentricity. Although the mother of six children,
(20) she adopted several more and still found time to
be active in social causes and literary activities.
After the Camerons settled in England in 1848 at
Freshwater Bay on the Isle of Wight, she became
the center of an artistic and literary circle that
(25) included such notable figures as the poet Alfred
Lord Tennyson and the painter George Frederick
Watts. Pursuing numerous activities and taking
care of her large family, Mrs. Cameron might have
been remembered as still another rather remark-
(30) able and colorful Victorian lady had it not been
for the fact that, in 1863, her daughter presented
her with photographic equipment, thinking her
mother might enjoy taking pictures of her family
and friends. Although forty-eight years old, Mrs.
(35) Cameron took up this new hobby with enormous
enthusiasm and dedication. She was a complete
beginner, but within a very few years she developed into one of the greatest photographers of her
period and a giant in the history of photography.
(40) She worked ceaselessly as long as daylight lasted
and mastered the technical processes of photography, at that time far more cumbersome than

today, turning her coal house into a darkroom and
her chicken house into a studio. To her, photogra-
(45) phy was a "divine art," and in it she found her
vocation. In 1864, she wrote triumphantly under
one of her photographs, "My First Success," and
from then until her death in Ceylon in 1874, she
devoted herself wholly to this art.

(50)   Working in a large format (her portrait studies
are usually about 11 inches by 14 inches) and
requiring a long exposure (on the average five
minutes), she produced a large body of work that
stands up as one of the notable artistic achieve-
(55) ments of the Victorian period. The English art
critic Roger Fry believed that her portraits were
likely to outlive the works of artists who were her
contemporaries. Her friend Watts, then a very
celebrated portrait painter, inscribed on one of
(60) her photographs, "I wish I could paint such a
picture as this." …Her work was widely exhibited,
and she received gold, silver, and bronze medals in
England, America, Germany, and Austria. No
other female artist of the nineteenth century
(65) achieved such acclaim, and no other woman
photographer has ever enjoyed such success.

Her work falls into two main categories on
which her contemporaries and people today differ
sharply. Victorian critics were particularly
(70) impressed by her allegorical pictures, many of
them based on the poems of her friend and neighbor Tennyson…. Contemporary taste much prefers
her portraits and finds her narrative scenes sentimental and sometimes in bad taste. Yet, not only
(75) Julia Cameron, but also the painters of that time
loved to depict subjects such as *The Five Foolish
Virgins* or *Pray God, Bring Father Safely Home.*
Still, today her fame rests upon her portraits
for, as she herself said, she was intent upon
(80) representing not only the outer likeness but also
the inner greatness of the people she portrayed.
Working with the utmost dedication, she produced photographs of such eminent Victorians as
Tennyson, Browning, Carlyle, Trollope,

GO ON TO THE NEXT PAGE ⟶

(85) Longfellow, Watts, Darwin, Ellen Terry, Sir John
Herschel, who was a close friend of hers, and Mrs.
Duckworth, the mother of Virginia Woolf.

21. Which of the following conclusions can
    be reasonably drawn from the passage's
    discussion of Julia Margaret Cameron?

    A. She was a traditional homemaker until
        she discovered photography.

    B. Her work holds a significant place in the
        history of photography.

    C. She was unable to achieve in her lifetime
        the artistic recognition she deserved.

    D. Her eccentricity has kept her from being
        taken seriously by modern critics of
        photography.

22. According to the passage, Cameron is most
    respected by modern critics for her:

    F. portraits.

    G. allegorical pictures.

    H. use of a large format.

    J. service in recording the faces of so many
        twentieth century figures.

23. The author uses which of the following
    methods to develop the second paragraph
    (lines 10–49)?

    A. A series of anecdotes depicting Cam-
        eron's energy and unconventionality

    B. A presentation of factual data demon-
        strating Cameron's importance in the
        history of photography

    C. A description of the author's personal
        acquaintance with Cameron

    D. A chronological account of Cameron's
        background and artistic growth

24. As it is used in the passage, *cumbersome*
    (line 42) most closely means:

    F. difficult to manage.

    G. expensive.

    H. intense.

    J. enjoyable.

25. When the author says that Cameron had
    found "her vocation" (lines 45–46), his main
    point is that photography:

    A. offered Cameron an escape from the
        confines of conventional social life.

    B. became the main interest of her life.

    C. became her primary source of income.

    D. provided her with a way to express her
        religious beliefs.

26. The main point of the third paragraph is that
    Cameron:

    F. achieved great artistic success during her
        lifetime.

    G. is the greatest photographer who ever
        lived.

    H. was considered a more important artist
        during her lifetime than she is now.

    J. revolutionized photographic methods in
        the Victorian era.

27. According to the passage, the art of
    photography offered women artists more
    opportunities than did other art forms
    because it:

    A. did not require expensive materials.

    B. allowed the artist to use family and
        friends for subject matter.

    C. was nontraditional.

    D. required little artistic skill.

GO ON TO THE NEXT PAGE

28. *The Five Foolish Virgins* and *Pray God, Bring Father Safely Home* are examples of:

    F.   portraits of celebrated Victorians.

    G.   allegorical subjects of the sort that were popular during the Victorian era.

    H.   photographs in which Cameron sought to show a subject's outer likeness and inner greatness.

    J.   photographs by Cameron that were scoffed at by her contemporaries.

29. According to the passage, which of the following opinions of Cameron's work was held by Victorian critics but is NOT held by modern critics?

    A.   Photographs should be based on poems.

    B.   Her portraits are too sentimental.

    C.   Narrative scenes are often in bad taste.

    D.   Her allegorical pictures are her best work.

30. The author's treatment of Cameron's development as a photographer can best be described as:

    F.   admiring.

    G.   condescending.

    H.   neutral.

    J.   defensive.

GO ON TO THE NEXT PAGE

PASSAGE IV

The harbor seal, *Phoca vitulina*, lives amphibiously along the northern Atlantic and Pacific coasts. This extraordinary mammal, which does
Line most of its fishing at night when visibility is low
(5) and in places where noise levels are high, has developed several unique adaptations that have sharpened its acoustic and visual acuity. The need for such adaptations has been compounded by the varying behavior of sound and light in each of the
(10) two habitats of the harbor seal—land and water.

While the seal is on land, its ear operates much like the human ear, with sound waves traveling through air and entering the inner ear through the auditory canal. The directions from which sounds
(15) originate are distinguishable because the sound waves arrive at each inner ear at different times. In water, however, where sound waves travel faster than they do in air, the ability of the brain to differentiate arrival times between each ear is severely
(20) reduced. Yet it is crucial for the seal to be able to pinpoint the exact origins of sound in order to locate both its offspring and its prey. Therefore, the seal has developed an extremely sensitive quadraphonic hearing system, composed of a spe-
(25) cialized band of tissue that extends down from the ear to the inner ear. In water, sound is conducted to the seal's inner ear by this special band of tissue, making it possible for the seal to identify the exact origins of sounds.

(30) The eye of the seal is also uniquely adapted to operate in both air and water. The human eye, adapted to function primarily in air, is equipped with a cornea, which aids in the refraction and focusing of light onto the retina. As a result, when
(35) a human eye is submerged in water, light rays are further refracted and the image is blurry. The seal's cornea, however, refracts light as water does. Therefore, in water, light rays are transmitted by the cornea without distortion, and are clearly
(40) focused on the retina. In air, however, the cornea is astigmatic, resulting in a distortion of incoming light rays. The seal compensates for this by having a stenopaic pupil, which constricts into a vertical

slit. Since the astigmatism is most pronounced in
(45) the horizontal plane of the eye, the vertical pupil serves to minimize its effect on the seal's vision.

Since the harbor seal hunts for food under conditions of low visibility, some scientists believe it has echolocation systems akin to those of bats,
(50) porpoises, and dolphins. This kind of natural radar involves the emission of high frequency sound pulses that reflect off obstacles such as predators, prey, or natural barriers. The reflections are received as sensory signals by the brain, which
(55) processes them into an image. The animal, blinded by unfavorable lighting conditions, is thus able to perceive its surroundings. Such echolocation by harbor seals is suggested by the fact that they emit "clicks," high frequency sounds produced in short,
(60) fast bursts that occur mostly at night, when visibility is low.

Finally, there is speculation that the seal's whiskers, or vibrissae, which are unusually well developed and highly sensitive to vibrations, act as
(65) additional sensory receptors. Scientists speculate that the vibrissae may sense wave disturbances produced by nearby moving fish, allowing the seal to home in on and capture prey.

31. The harbor seal's eye compensates for the distortion of light rays on land by means of its:

A. vibrissae
B. cornea
C. stenopaic pupil
D. echolocation

32. The passage implies that a harbor seal's vision is:

F. inferior to a human's vision in the water, but superior to it on land.
G. superior to a human's vision in the water, but inferior to it on land.
H. inferior to a human's vision both in the water and on land.
J. equivalent to a human's vision both in the water and on land.

GO ON TO THE NEXT PAGE ⟶

33. According to the passage, scientists think vibrissae help harbor seals to catch prey by:

    A. improving underwater vision.
    B. sensing vibrations in the air.
    C. camouflaging predator seals.
    D. detecting underwater movement.

34. According to the passage, the speed of sound in water is:

    F. faster than the speed of sound in air.
    G. slower than the speed of sound in air.
    H. the same as the speed of sound in air.
    J. unable to be determined exactly.

35. According to the passage, which of the following have contributed to the harbor seal's need to adapt its visual and acoustic senses?

    I. Night hunting
    II. The need to operate in two habitats
    III. A noisy environment

    A. I and II only
    B. II and III only
    C. I and III only
    D. I, II, and III

36. Which of the following claims expresses the writer's opinion and not a fact?

    F. The human eye is adapted to function primarily in air.
    G. When the seal is on land, its ear operates like a human ear.
    H. The "clicks" emitted by the harbor seal mean it uses echolocation.
    J. The need for adaptation is increased if an animal lives in two habitats.

37. The passage suggests that the harbor seal lives in:

    A. cold ocean waters with accessible coasts.
    B. all areas with abundant fish populations.
    C. most island and coastal regions.
    D. warm coastlines with exceptionally clear waters.

38. According to the passage, a special band of tissue extending from the ear to the inner ear enables the harbor seal to:

    F. make its distinctive "clicking" sounds.
    G. find prey by echolocation.
    H. breathe underwater.
    J. determine where a sound originated.

39. The author compares harbor seal sensory organs to human sensory organs primarily in order to:

    A. point out similarities among mammals.
    B. explain how the seal's sensory organs function.
    C. prove that seals are more adaptively successful than humans.
    D. prove that humans are better adapted to their environment than seals.

40. According to the passage, one way in which seals differ from humans is:

    F. that sound waves enter the inner ear through the auditory canal.
    G. the degree of refraction of light by their corneas.
    H. they focus light rays on the retina.
    J. they have adapted to live in a certain environment.

IF YOU FINISH BEFORE TIME IS CALLED, YOU MAY CHECK YOUR WORK ON THIS SECTION ONLY. DO NOT TURN TO ANY OTHER SECTION IN THE TEST. STOP

SCIENCE TEST

35 Minutes—40 Questions

Directions: Each of the following seven passages is followed by several questions. After reading each passage, decide on the best answer to each question and fill in the corresponding oval on your answer sheet. You are allowed to refer to the passages while answering the questions. Calculator use is not allowed on this test.

PASSAGE I

The table below contains some physical properties of common optical materials. The refractive index of a material is a measure of the amount by which light is bent upon entering the material. The transmittance range is the range of wavelengths over which the material is transparent.

Table 1

Physical Properties of Optical Materials				
Material	Refractive index for light of 0.589 µm	Transmittance range (µm)	Useful range for prisms (µm)	Chemical resistance
Lithium fluoride	1.39	0.12–6	2.7–5.5	Poor
Calcium fluoride	1.43	0.12–12	5–9.4	Good
Sodium chloride	1.54	0.3–17	8–16	Poor
Quartz	1.54	0.20–3.3	0.20–2.7	Excellent
Potassium bromide	1.56	0.3–29	15–28	Poor
Flint glass*	1.66	0.35–2.2	0.35–2	Excellent
Cesium iodide	1.79	0.3–70	15–55	Poor

*Flint glass is lead oxide doped quartz

1. According to the table, which material(s) will transmit light at 25 µm?

    A. Potassium bromide only
    B. Potassium bromide and cesium iodide
    C. Lithium fluoride and cesium iodide
    D. Lithium fluoride and flint glass

2. A scientist hypothesizes that any material with poor chemical resistance would have a transmittance range wider than 10 µm. The properties of which of the following materials contradicts this hypothesis?

    F. Lithium fluoride
    G. Flint glass
    H. Cesium iodide
    J. Quartz

GO ON TO THE NEXT PAGE

3. When light travels from one medium to another, total internal reflection can occur if the first medium has a higher refractive index than the second. Total internal reflection could occur if light were travelling from:

A. lithium fluoride to flint glass.

B. potassium bromide to cesium iodide.

C. quartz to potassium bromide.

D. flint glass to calcium fluoride.

4. Based on the information in the table, how is the transmittance range related to the useful prism range?

F. The transmittance range is always narrower than the useful prism range.

G. The transmittance range is narrower than or equal to the useful prism range.

H. The transmittance range increases as the useful prism range decreases.

J. The transmittance range is wider than and includes within it the useful prism range.

5. The addition of lead oxide to pure quartz has the effect of:

A. decreasing the transmittance range and the refractive index.

B. decreasing the transmittance range and increasing the refractive index.

C. increasing the transmittance range and the useful prism range.

D. increasing the transmittance range and decreasing the useful prism range.

PASSAGE II

Osmosis is the diffusion of a solvent (often water) across a semipermeable membrane from the side of the membrane with a lower concentration of dissolved material to the side with a higher concentration of dissolved material. The result of osmosis is an equilibrium—an even distribution—on both sides of the membrane. In order to prevent osmosis, external pressure must be applied to the side with the higher concentration of dissolved material. *Osmotic pressure* is the external pressure required to prevent osmosis. The apparatus shown below was used to measure osmotic pressure in the following experiments.

semipermeable membrane

EXPERIMENT 1

Aqueous (water-based) solutions containing different concentrations of sucrose were placed in the closed side of the apparatus. The open side was filled with water. The sucrose solutions also contained a blue dye that binds to the sucrose. The osmotic pressure created by the piston was measured for each solution at various temperatures. The results are given in Table 1.

GO ON TO THE NEXT PAGE ⇨

Table 1

Concentration of sucrose solution (mol/L)	Temperature (K)	Osmotic pressure (atm)
1.00	298.0	24.47
0.50	298.0	12.23
0.10	298.0	2.45
0.05	298.0	1.22
1.00	348.0	28.57
0.50	348.0	14.29
0.10	348.0	2.86
0.05	348.0	1.43

EXPERIMENT 2

Sucrose solutions of 4 different organic solvents were investigated in the same manner as in Experiment 1 with all trials at 298 K. The results are shown in Table 2.

Table 2

Solvent	Concentration of sucrose solution (mol/L)	Osmotic pressure (atm)
Ethanol	0.50	12.23
Ethanol	0.10	2.45
Acetone	0.50	12.23
Acetone	0.10	2.45
Diethyl ether	0.50	12.23
Diethyl ether	0.10	2.45
Methanol	0.50	12.23
Methanol	0.10	2.45

6. According to the experimental results, osmotic pressure is dependent upon the:

   F. solvent and temperature only.

   G. solvent and concentration only.

   H. temperature and concentration only.

   J. solvent, temperature, and concentration.

7. According to Experiment 2, if methanol was used as a solvent, what pressure must be applied to a 0.5 mol/L solution of sucrose at 298 K to prevent osmosis?

   A. 24.46 atm

   B. 12.23 atm

   C. 2.45 atm

   D. 1.23 atm

8. A 0.10 mol/L aqueous sucrose solution is separated from an equal volume of pure water by a semipermeable membrane. If the solution is at a pressure of 1 atm and a temperature of 298 K, the sucrose solution:

   F. will diffuse across the semipermeable membrane from the sucrose solution side to the pure water side.

   G. will diffuse across the semipermeable membrane from the pure water side to the sucrose solution side.

   H. will not diffuse across the semipermeable membrane.

   J. will diffuse across the semipermeable membrane, but the direction of diffusion cannot be determined.

GO ON TO THE NEXT PAGE

9. In Experiment 1, the scientists investigated the effect of:

    A. solvent and concentration on osmotic pressure.

    B. volume and temperature on osmotic pressure.

    C. concentration and temperature on osmotic pressure.

    D. temperature on atmospheric pressure.

10. Which of the following conclusions can be drawn from the experimental results?

    I. Osmotic pressure is independent of the solvent used.

    II. Osmotic pressure is only dependent upon the temperature of the system.

    III. Osmosis occurs only when the osmotic pressure is exceeded.

    F. I only

    G. III only

    H. I and II only

    J. I and III only

11. What was the most likely purpose of the dye placed in the sucrose solutions in Experiments 1 and 2?

    A. The dye showed when osmosis was completed.

    B. The dye showed the presence of ions in the solutions.

    C. The dye was used to make the experiment more colorful.

    D. The dye was used to make the onset of osmosis visible.

PASSAGE III

A chemist investigating the influence of molecular weight and structure on the boiling point (transition from liquid to gaseous state) of different compounds recorded the data in the tables below. Two types of compounds were investigated: organic carbon compounds (shown in Table 1) and inorganic compounds (shown in Table 2).

Table 1

Straight-Chain Hydrocarbons		
Molecular formula	Molar weight* (g/mol)	Boiling point (°C)
CH_4	16	−162
C_2H_6	30	−88
C_3H_8	44	−42
C_4H_{10}	58	0
C_5H_{12}	72	36
C_8H_{18}	114	126
$C_{20}H_{42}$	282	345

*Molar weight is the weight of one mole, or an *Avogadro's Number* of molecules ($\approx 6 \times 10^{23}$), in grams.

Table 2

Other Substances (Polar and Non-Polar)		
Molecular formula	Molar weight (g/mol)	Boiling point (°C)
N_2*	28	−196
SiH_4*	32	−112
GeH_4*	77	−90
Br_2*	160	59
CO**	28	−192
PH_3**	34	−85
AsH_3**	78	−55
ICl**	162	97

* *Non-Polar*: molecule's charge is evenly distributed

**Polar: molecule's negative and positive charges are partially separated

GO ON TO THE NEXT PAGE ⟹

12. Which of the following straight-chain hydrocarbons would NOT be a gas at room temperature?

F. C_2H_6

G. C_3H_8

H. C_4H_{10}

J. C_5H_{12}

13. Which of the following conclusions is supported by the observed results?

   I. Boiling point varies directly with molecular weight.

  II. Boiling point varies inversely with molecular weight.

 III. Boiling point is affected by molecular structure.

A. I only

B. II only

C. I and III only

D. II and III only

14. Based on the data in Table 1, the boiling point of the straight-chain hydrocarbon C_6H_{14} (molecular weight 86 g/mol) is most likely:

F. 30° C.

G. 70° C.

H. 130° C.

J. impossible to predict.

15. Based on the data in Table 2, as molecular weight increases, the difference between the boiling points of polar and non-polar substances of similar molecular weight:

A. increases.

B. decreases.

C. remains constant.

D. varies randomly.

16. A polar substance with a boiling point of 0° C is likely to have a molar weight closest to which of the following:

F. 58

G. 80

H. 108

J. 132

GO ON TO THE NEXT PAGE

PASSAGE IV

A series of experiments was performed to study the environmental factors affecting the size and number of leaves on the *Cyas* plant.

EXPERIMENT 1

Five groups of 25 *Cyas* seedlings, all from 2–3 cm tall, were allowed to grow for 3 months, each group at a different humidity level. All of the groups were kept at 75° F and received 9 hours of sunlight a day. The average leaf lengths, widths, and densities are given in Table 1.

Table 1

% Humidity	Average length (cm)	Average width (cm)	Average density* (leaves/cm)
15	5.6	1.6	0.13
35	7.1	1.8	0.25
55	9.8	2.0	0.56
75	14.6	2.6	0.61
95	7.5	1.7	0.52

*Number of leaves per 1 cm of plant stalk

EXPERIMENT 2

Five new groups of 25 seedlings, all from 2–3 cm tall, were allowed to grow for 3 months, each group receiving different amounts of sunlight at a constant humidity of 55%. All other conditions were the same as in Experiment 1. The results are listed in Table 2.

Table 2

Sunlight (hrs/day)	Average length (cm)	Average width (cm)	Average density* (leaves/cm)
0	5.3	1.5	0.32
3	12.4	2.4	0.59
6	11.2	2.0	0.56
9	8.4	1.8	0.26
12	7.7	1.7	0.19

*Number of leaves per 1 cm of plant stalk

EXPERIMENT 3

Five new groups of 25 seedlings, all from 2–3 cm tall, were allowed to grow at a constant humidity of 55% for 3 months at different daytime and nighttime temperatures. All other conditions were the same as in Experiment 1. The results are shown in Table 3.

Table 3

Day/Night temperature (° F)	Average length (cm)	Average width (cm)	Average density* (leaves/cm)
85/85	6.8	1.5	0.28
85/65	12.3	2.1	0.53
65/85	8.1	1.7	0.33
75/75	7.1	1.9	0.45
65/65	8.3	1.7	0.39

*Number of leaves per 1 cm of plant stalk

17. Which of the following conclusions can be made based on the results of Experiment 2 alone?

    A. The seedlings do not require long daily periods of sunlight to grow.

    B. The average leaf density is independent of the humidity the seedlings receive.

    C. The seedlings need more water at night than during the day.

    D. The average length of the leaves increases as the amount of sunlight increases.

18. Seedlings grown at a 40% humidity level under the same conditions as in Experiment 1 would have average leaf widths closest to:

    F. 1.6 cm.

    G. 1.9 cm.

    H. 2.2 cm.

    J. 2.5 cm.

GO ON TO THE NEXT PAGE ⟩

19. According to the experimental results, under which set of conditions would a *Cyas* seedling be most likely to produce the largest leaves?

A. 95% humidity and 3 hours of sunlight

B. 75% humidity and 3 hours of sunlight

C. 95% humidity and 6 hours of sunlight

D. 75% humidity and 6 hours of sunlight

20. Which variable remained constant throughout all of the experiments?

F. The number of seedling groups

G. The percent of humidity

H. The daytime temperature

J. The nighttime temperature

21. It was assumed in the design of the 3 experiments that all of the *Cyas* seedlings were:

A. more than 5 cm tall.

B. equally capable of germinating.

C. equally capable of producing flowers.

D. equally capable of further growth.

22. As a continuation of the 3 experiments listed, it would be most appropriate to next investigate:

F. how many leaves over 6.0 cm long there are on each plant.

G. which animals consume *Cyas* seedlings.

H. how the mineral content of the soil affects the leaf size and density.

J. what time of year the seedlings have the darkest coloring.

PASSAGE V

The resistance (R) of a conductor is the extent to which it opposes the flow of electricity. Resistance depends not only on the conductor's resistivity (ρ), but also on the conductor's length (L) and cross-sectional area (A). The resistivity of a conductor is a physical property of the material that varies with temperature.

A research team designing a new appliance was researching the best type of wire to use in a particular circuit. The most important consideration was the wire's resistance. The team studied the resistance of wires made from four metals—gold (Au), aluminum (Al), tungsten (W), and iron (Fe). Two lengths and two gauges (diameters) of each type of wire were tested at 20° C. The results are recorded in the following table.

10-gauge wire
$A = 5.26$ mm^2

16-gauge wire
$A = 1.31$ mm^2

2.59 mm

1.29 mm

Note: area of circle = πr^2

GO ON TO THE NEXT PAGE

Table 1

Material	Resistivity (mV $ cm)	Length (cm)	Cross-sectional area (mm²)	Resistance (mV)
Au	2.44	1.0	5.26	46.4
Au	2.44	1.0	1.31	186.0
Au	2.44	2.0	5.26	92.8
Au	2.44	2.0	1.31	372.0
Al	2.83	1.0	5.26	53.8
Al	2.83	1.0	1.31	216.0
Al	2.83	2.0	5.26	107.6
Al	2.83	2.0	1.31	432.0
W	5.51	1.0	5.26	105.0
W	5.51	1.0	1.31	421.0
W	5.51	2.0	5.26	210.0
W	5.51	2.0	1.31	842.0
Fe	10.00	1.0	5.26	190.0
Fe	10.00	1.0	1.31	764.0
Fe	10.00	2.0	5.26	380.0
Fe	10.00	2.0	1.31	1,528.0

23. Of the wires tested, resistance increases for any given material as which parameter is decreased?

   A. Length
   B. Cross-sectional area
   C. Resistivity
   D. Gauge

24. Given the data in the table, which of the following best expresses resistance in terms of resistivity (ρ), cross-sectional area (A), and length (L)?

   F. $\dfrac{\rho A}{L}$
   G. $\dfrac{\rho L}{A}$
   H. $\rho A L$
   J. $\dfrac{AL}{\rho}$

   $P \, A \, L$

25. Which of the following wires would have the highest resistance?

   A. A 1-cm aluminum wire with a cross-sectional area of 3.31 mm²
   B. A 2-cm aluminum wire with a cross-sectional area of 3.31 mm²
   C. A 1-cm tungsten wire with a cross-sectional area of 0.33 mm²
   D. A 2-cm tungsten wire with a cross-sectional area of 0.33 mm²

26. According to the information given, which of the following statements is (are) correct?

   I. 10-gauge wire has a larger diameter than 16-gauge wire.
   II. Gold has a higher resistivity than tungsten.
   III. Aluminum conducts electricity better than iron.

   F. I only
   G. II only
   H. III only
   J. I and III only

GO ON TO THE NEXT PAGE

27. Which of the following graphs best represents the relationship between the resistivity of a tungsten wire and its length?

A.

B.

C.

D.

PASSAGE VI

How does evolution occur? Two views are presented below.

SCIENTIST 1

Evolution occurs by natural selection. Random mutations are continually occurring in a species as it propagates. A number of these mutations result in traits that help the species adapt to environmental changes. Because these mutant traits are advantageous, the members of the species who possess them tend to survive and pass on their genes more often than those who do not have these traits. Therefore, the percentage of the population with an advantageous trait increases over time. Long necks evolved in giraffes by natural selection. The ancestors of giraffes had necks of various sizes, however their average neck length was much shorter than the average neck length of modern-day giraffes. Since the food supply was limited, the individuals with necks on the long range of the spectrum had access to more food (the leaves of trees) and therefore were more likely to survive and pass on their traits than individuals with shorter necks. Therefore, the proportion of the individuals with long necks is slightly greater in each subsequent generation.

SCIENTIST 2

Evolution occurs by the inheritance of acquired characteristics. Characteristics that are acquired by an individual member of a species during its lifetime are passed on to its offspring. Therefore, each generation's traits are partially accounted for by all the changes that occurred in the individuals of the previous generation. This includes changes that occurred as a result of accidents, changes in the environment, overuse of muscles, etc. The evolution of long necks of giraffes is an example. Ancestors of giraffes had short necks and consequently had to stretch their necks to reach the leaves of trees that were their main source of food. This

GO ON TO THE NEXT PAGE

repeated stretching of their necks caused them to elongate slightly. This trait was passed on, so that the individuals of the next generation had slightly longer necks. Each subsequent generation also stretched their necks to feed; therefore, each generation had slightly longer necks than the previous generation.

28. Both scientists agree that:

   F.   the environment affects evolution.

   G.   the individuals of a generation have identical traits.

   H.   acquired characteristics are inherited.

   J.   random mutations occur.

29. How would the two hypotheses be affected if it were found that all of the offspring of an individual with a missing leg due to an accident were born with a missing leg?

   A.   It would support Scientist 1's hypothesis, because it is an example of random mutations occurring within a species.

   B.   It would refute Scientist 1's hypothesis, because it is an example of random mutations occurring within a species.

   C.   It would support Scientist 2's hypothesis, because it is an example of an acquired characteristic being passed on to the next generation.

   D.   It would support Scientist 2's hypothesis, because it is an example of random mutations occurring within a species.

30. Which of the following characteristics can be inherited according to Scientist 2?

   I.   Fur color

   II.   Bodily scars resulting from a fight with another animal

   III.   Poor vision

   F.   I only

   G.   II only

   H.   I and III only

   J.   I, II, and III

31. Scientist 1 believes that the evolution of the long neck of the giraffe:

   A.   is an advantageous trait which resulted from overuse of neck muscles over many generations.

   B.   is an advantageous trait that resulted from a random mutation.

   C.   is an advantageous trait that resulted from a mutation that occurred in response to a change in the environment.

   D.   is a disadvantageous trait that resulted from a random mutation.

32. The fundamental point of disagreement between the two scientists is whether:

   F.   giraffes' ancestors had short necks.

   G.   evolved traits come from random mutations or from the previous generation.

   H.   the environment affects the evolution of a species.

   J.   the extinction of a species could be the result of random mutations.

GO ON TO THE NEXT PAGE

33. Suppose evidence was found that suggested that before the discovery of fire, human skin lacked the nerve endings necessary to detect extreme heat. Which of the following pieces of information, if true, would most seriously weaken the hypothesis of Scientist 2?

   A. Human skin is capable of generating nerve endings with new functions during life.

   B. The total number of nerve endings in the skin of a human is determined at birth and remains constant until death.

   C. An excess of nerve endings that are sensitive to extreme heat is a relatively common human mutation.

   D. No evidence exists to suggest that an excess of nerve endings that are sensitive to heat could be acquired through mutation.

34. The average height of a full-grown person today is significantly greater than was the average height of a full-grown person 1,000 years ago. If it was proven that the increase in average height was due only to evolutionary changes, how would Scientist 1 most likely explain this increase?

   F. People genetically prone to growing taller have been more likely to produce offspring over the last 1,000 years.

   G. Over the last 1,000 years, improvements in nutrition and medicine have led to greater average growth over a person's lifetime, and this growth has been passed from one generation to the next.

   H. Increased height is not a trait that can be acquired through mutation.

   J. Measurements of average height were less accurate 1,000 years ago than they are today.

PASSAGE VII

Bovine spongiform encephalopathy (BSE) is caused by an unconventional pseudovirus that eventually kills infected cattle. BSE is diagnosed post mortem from the diseased cavities that appear in brain tissue, and is associated with the use in cattle feed of ground-up meat from scrapie-infected sheep. A series of experiments was performed to determine the mode of transmission of BSE. The results are given in the table below.

EXPERIMENT 1

Sixty healthy cows were divided into two equal groups. Group A's feed included meat from scrapie-free sheep; and Group B's feed included meat from scrapie-infected sheep. Eighteen months later, the two groups were slaughtered and their brains examined for BSE cavities.

EXPERIMENT 2

Researchers injected ground-up sheep brains directly into the brains of two groups of thirty healthy cows. The cows in Group C received brains from scrapie-free sheep. The cows in Group D received brains from scrapie-infected sheep. Eighteen months later, both groups were slaughtered and their brains examined for diseased cavities.

Table 1

Group	Mode of transmission	Scrapie present	Number of cows infected with BSE*
A	feed	no	1
B	feed	yes	12
C	injection	no	0
D	injection	yes	3

*As determined visually by presence/absence of spongiform encephalopathy

GO ON TO THE NEXT PAGE ⟹

35. Which of the following hypotheses was investigated in Experiment 1?

   A. The injection of scrapie-infected sheep brains into cows' brains causes BSE.

   B. The ingestion of wild grasses causes BSE.

   C. The ingestion of scrapie-infected sheep meat causes scrapie.

   D. The ingestion of scrapie-infected sheep meat causes BSE.

36. What is the purpose of Experiment 2?

   F. To determine whether BSE can be transmitted by injection

   G. To determine whether BSE can be transmitted by ingestion

   H. To determine whether ingestion or injection is the primary mode of BSE transmission

   J. To determine the healthiest diet for cows

37. Which of the following assumptions is made by the researchers in Experiments 1 and 2?

   A. Cows do not suffer from scrapie.

   B. A year and a half is a sufficient amount of time for BSE to develop in a cow.

   C. Cows and sheep suffer from the same diseases.

   D. Cows that eat scrapie-free sheep meat will not develop BSE.

38. A researcher wishes to determine whether BSE can be transmitted through scrapie-infected goats. Which of the following experiments would best test this?

   F. Repeating Experiment 1, using a mixture of sheep and goat meat in Group C's feed

   G. Repeating Experiments 1 and 2, replacing sheep with healthy goats

   H. Repeating Experiments 1 and 2, replacing healthy sheep with healthy goats and scrapie-infected sheep with scrapie-infected goats

   J. Repeating Experiment 2, replacing healthy cows with healthy goats

39. What is the control group in Experiment 1?

   A. Group A

   B. Group B

   C. Group C

   D. Group D

40. Which of the following conclusions is (are) supported by the experiments?

   I. Cows that are exposed to scrapie-infected sheep are more likely to develop BSE than cows that are not.

   II. BSE is only transmitted by eating scrapie-infected sheep meat.

   III. A cow that eats scrapie-infected sheep meat is more likely to develop BSE than a cow that is injected with scrapie-infected sheep brains.

   F. II only

   G. III only

   H. I and III only

   J. II and III only

IF YOU FINISH BEFORE TIME IS CALLED, YOU MAY CHECK YOUR WORK ON THIS SECTION ONLY. DO NOT TURN TO ANY OTHER SECTION IN THE TEST.

WRITING TEST

30 Minutes—1 Question

Directions: This section will test your writing ability. You will have thirty (30) minutes to compose an essay in English. Prior to planning your essay, pay close attention to the essay prompt so that you understand exactly what you are supposed to do. Your essay's grade will be based on how well it expresses an opinion on the question in the prompt, as well as its logical construction, supporting evidence, and clarity of expression based on the standards of written English.

You may use the unlined space on the next page to plan your essay. Anything written in this space will not be scored by the graders. Your essay must be written on the lined pages. While you may not need all the space to finish, you should not skip lines. Corrections and additions may be written neatly in between lines but not in the margins. Be sure to write clearly. Illegible work will not receive credit.

If you finish in under thirty minutes, you may review your essay. When time is called, lay your pencil down immediately.

DO NOT CONTINUE UNTIL TOLD TO DO SO.

While some high schools offer art and music courses to their students, these courses are not always mandatory. Some teachers, students, and parents think that schools should emphasize traditional academic subjects like math and science, as those skills will help the students more in the future when they join the workforce. Others feel that requiring all high school students to take classes in music or the visual arts would teach equally valuable skills that the students may not learn otherwise, and would also help them do better in traditional academic subject areas. In your opinion, should art or music classes be mandatory for all high school students?

In your essay, take a position on this question. You may write about either one of the two points of view given, or you may present a different point of view on this question. Use specific reasons and examples to support your position.

Use this space to *plan* your essay. Your work here will not be graded. Write your essay on the lined pages that follow.

_____

_____

_____

_____

_____

_____

_____

_____

_____

_____

_____

_____

_____

_____

_____

_____

_____

_____

_____

_____

_____

_____

_____

_____

_____

IF YOU FINISH BEFORE TIME IS CALLED, YOU MAY CHECK YOUR WORK ON THIS SECTION ONLY. DO NOT TURN TO ANY OTHER SECTION IN THE TEST. STOP

Practice Test One: **Answer Key**

ENGLISH TEST					
1. C	26. F	51. D
2. F	27. A	52. J
3. D	28. J	53. C
4. F	29. B	54. H
5. D	30. G	55. D
6. G	31. D	56. G
7. B	32. H	57. A
8. J	33. A	58. H
9. A	34. H	59. D
10. J	35. D	60. H
11. C	36. G	61. D
12. G	37. D	62. J
13. B	38. G	63. C
14. H	39. D	64. J
15. C	40. J	65. D
16. H	41. D	66. J
17. B	42. J	67. B
18. G	43. B	68. F
19. A	44. G	69. D
20. J	45. C	70. F
21. B	46. F	71. D
22. G	47. B	72. G
23. D	48. H	73. B
24. J	49. C	74. F
25. C	50. H	75. B

MATH TEST	
1. D	31. C
2. J	32. H
3. D	33. E
4. K	34. K
5. C	35. A
6. K	36. J
7. B	37. A
8. K	38. G
9. E	39. C
10. K	40. G
11. D	41. B
12. H	42. H
13. C	43. C
14. H	44. K
15. C	45. A
16. G	46. G
17. D	47. E
18. H	48. G
19. D	49. E
20. H	50. K
21. E	51. E
22. H	52. K
23. D	53. B
24. F	54. G
25. D	55. D
26. G	56. K
27. C	57. C
28. H	58. H
29. B	59. D
30. K	60. J

READING TEST	
1. C	21. B
2. G	22. F
3. B	23. D
4. F	24. F
5. D	25. B
6. H	26. F
7. C	27. C
8. G	28. G
9. B	29. D
10. H	30. F
11. B	31. C
12. H	32. G
13. B	33. D
14. F	34. F
15. C	35. D
16. J	36. H
17. B	37. A
18. H	38. J
19. B	39. B
20. H	40. G

SCIENCE TEST	
1. B	21. D
2. F	22. H
3. D	23. B
4. J	24. G
5. B	25. D
6. H	26. J
7. B	27. D
8. G	28. F
9. C	29. C
10. F	30. J
11. D	31. B
12. J	32. G
13. C	33. B
14. G	34. F
15. A	35. D
16. H	36. F
17. A	37. B
18. G	38. H
19. B	39. A
20. F	40. G

ANSWERS AND EXPLANATIONS

ENGLISH TEST

PASSAGE I

1. (C)

(C) is the most correct and concise answer choice. (A) uses an unnecessary comma. (B) is unnecessarily wordy. (D) is redundant—if the societies created the legends, there is no need to describe the legends as original.

2. (F)

The question stem gives an important clue to the best answer: the purpose of the inserted sentence is "to describe the different kinds" of stories. (F) is the only choice that does this. (G) explains how the stories were told. (H) explains why more is not known about the stories. (J) describes the length of some stories.

3. (D)

Answer choices (A), (B), and (C) create run-on sentences. (D) describes a relationship that makes sense between our "many more permanent ways of handing down our beliefs" and the fact that "we continue to create and tell legends." It also creates a complete sentence.

4. (F)

(H) and (J) are ungrammatical after a colon. Answer choices (G), (H), and (J) are unnecessarily wordy.

5. (D)

In addition to other problems, answer choices (A), (B), and (C) are redundant or unnecessarily wordy.

Because the contrasting word *but* is already used, *however* is repetitive and should be eliminated.

6. (G)

Answer choices (F), (H), and (J) are all redundant. The word *conclusion* is unnecessary because it expresses the same thing as the word *ending*, which has already been used.

7. (B)

(B) is the only choice that stays consistent with the verb tense established by *knew* and *decided*.

8. (J)

(F) creates a run-on sentence and also makes it seem that the hunter, not the deer, "was only temporarily knocked unconscious by the car." (G) and (H) use incorrect verb tenses.

9. (A)

(B) is incorrect because the words preceding the semicolon could not be a complete sentence on their own. (C) would create a sentence fragment. (D) would create a run-on sentence.

10. (J)

Regardless of the sequence of the words, the information provided in choices (F), (G), and (H) is irrelevant to the passage's topic of urban legends.

11. (C)

The subject of the sentence is *One*, so the verb must be singular. (B) and (D) use incorrect verb tenses.

12. (G)

(F) creates a sentence that does not make sense. (H) and (J) use the plural *women* instead of the singular *woman*.

13. (B)

(B) most clearly expresses the idea that several websites research "the validity of commonly told urban legends." Because this information is relevant to the topic of urban legends, "OMIT the underlined portion" is not the best answer.

14. (H)

Paragraph 3 describes an urban legend that is "humorous in nature." Paragraph 4 describes a rather frightening legend: alligators living underneath the city in the sewer system. The sentence "Other urban legends seem to be designed to instill fear" is an appropriate topic sentence for paragraph 4, and it also serves as a needed transition between paragraph 3 and paragraph 4.

15. (C)

Although the third and fourth sentences of paragraph 1 provide some general information about the purpose and topics of the myths and legends of primitive societies, no specifics are given. This makes (C) the best answer.

PASSAGE II

16. (H)

The choices here would be *do you* or *does one*. The latter appears as an answer choice.

17. (B)

(A) incorrectly uses a colon. (C) and (D) are grammatically incorrect.

18. (G)

Solitary and *alone* are redundant in the same sentence. (H) and (J) also have redundancy.

19. (A)

The underlined portion is clearest the way it is written.

20. (J)

The colon is incorrect, so eliminate (F) and (H). Because it is a compound sentence, a comma is needed before *and*.

21. (B)

In fact is nonessential—it should be set off by commas.

22. (G)

American (an adjective) is the word being modified. Therefore, the adverb form of *unique* is needed.

23. (D)

Near Walden Pond . . . is a long sentence fragment. The best way to fix the error is to simply combine the sentences.

24. (J)

This paragraph and the ones that immediately follow outline Thoreau's life. His influence on the people of today is not discussed until the end of the essay. Therefore, the underlined sentence does not belong.

25. (C)

Sentence 3 comes immediately after sentence 1. (C) is the only choice that lists it this way.

26. (F)

There is one independent clause on each side of the semicolon, so the sentence is punctuated correctly. (G) needs a comma before *and*. (H) is incorrect because the second half of the sentence is not an independent clause. (J) does not make sense.

27. (A)

A possessive pronoun is needed because the works belong to Thoreau. Eliminate (B) and (D). (C) relates to more than one person, so it is incorrect as well.

28. (J)

This paragraph is all about what Thoreau means to us today.

29. (B)

(A), (C), and (D) are excessively wordy.

30. (G)

The use of questions forces the reader to think about the answers. (F) is too literal, and (J) is too broad for the topic of the essay. (H) is incorrect because the author establishes the quality of Thoreau's work.

Passage III

31. (D)

Because the word live is used later in the sentence, (A), (B), and (C) contain redundant information.

32. (H)

In this sentence, the *its* must be possessive because the *unique anatomy* belongs to the sloth. The word describing *anatomy* must be an adjective, not an adverb.

33. (A)

The comma is correctly used in (A) to separate the nonessential descriptive phrase *about the size of a large domestic cat* from the rest of the sentence.

34. (H)

The information about the sloth's limbs is relevant to the topic, so it should not be omitted. (H) makes the most sense in the context of the passage.

35. (D)

Adapted needs to be modified by an adverb, so (D) is the best answer choice.

36. (G)

Instead describes the right relationship between the two sentences. The pronouns must be consistent, and since *its* is already used in the sentence, (G) is the best answer choice.

37. (D)

(D) is the only choice that correctly describes the relationship between the sloth's inability to "move swiftly on the ground" and its ability to swim.

38. (G)

(G) connects the sloth's unique characteristics discussed in paragraph 3 with the description of its flexibility in paragraph 4.

39. (D)

(D) correctly uses the second comma necessary to separate the phrase *without moving the rest of its body* from the rest of the sentence. (C) can be eliminated because it is unnecessarily wordy.

40. (J)

(J) is the only choice that contains a consistent verb tense.

41. (D)

(A) and (B) contain redundant information. (C) uses an incorrect form of the verb.

42. (J)

This information about the howler monkey is irrelevant to the topic of the passage.

43. (B)

(A) creates a sentence fragment. (C) is unnecessarily wordy and awkward. (D) creates a run-on sentence.

44. (G)

The last sentence serves as a conclusion for the entire passage, and removing it would make the ending more abrupt.

45. (C)

The description of the sloth's "camouflage" is in paragraph 5.

PASSAGE IV

46. (F)

The underlined portion is best left as is. The other answer choices make the sentence unnecessarily wordy.

47. (B)

The verb tense must agree with the tense that has been established up to this point. The passage is in past tense, so the past tense choice (B) is correct.

48. (H)

Like the previous question, the simple past tense is correct.

49. (C)

(A) creates a sentence fragment and uses an incorrect verb tense. (B) also uses the wrong verb tense. (D) incorrectly uses a semicolon, as the words preceding the semicolon do not constitute an independent clause.

50. (H)

In the context of the rest of the passage, only (H) makes sense. The fire fighters' attempts to extinguish the flames failed; only nature could stop the fire with the first snowfall.

51. (D)

(A) and (B) are unnecessarily wordy and awkward. (C) creates a run-on sentence.

52. (J)

All of the other answer choices are unnecessarily wordy and/or repetitive.

53. (C)

From the word *open*, you can determine that the best answer will contain *cones*. This makes (C) the only possible answer, as the apostrophe is incorrectly used in (B).

54. (H)

This is the only answer choice that makes sense in the context of the passage. The sighting of the large animals near burning forests is used as evidence that the animals of the region were "fire-tolerant and fire-adaptive."

55. (D)

The comma in (A) is unnecessary because the sentence has a list of only two examples, not three. The semicolon in (B) is incorrectly used because *and bedding down* does not begin an independent clause. The colon in (C) is incorrectly used because it is not being used to introduce or emphasize information.

56. (G)

The problem with *judging from the recent pictures of the park* is that the phrase is modifying *forest*, and a forest obviously can't judge anything. The phrase would have been okay if the sentence read "judging from the recent pictures of the park, I think that the forest was not destroyed." In this case the phrase modifies *I*, the author, who is capable of judging. Choice (G) takes care of the problem by rewriting the sentence so that the modifying phrase is gone.

57. (A)

The pronoun refers to *forest*.

58. (H)

The introduction of information about fires in Alaska is unwarranted, so (F) and (G) can be eliminated. (J) is incorrect because the additional information would actually uphold the author's position as an authority.

59. (D)

The reports mentioned in (D) would substantiate the author's claims much more so than any of the other answer choices.

PASSAGE V

60. (H)

(F) creates a sentence fragment, and (G) incorrectly uses a plural verb with a singular subject. The context of the paragraph makes (H) a better choice than (J).

61. (D)

The final part of the sentence, ". . . and there are many other rivers in America as well," is completely irrelevant to the rest of the sentence and the paragraph, in which the author discusses white water rafting and the rivers she's rafted.

62. (J)

The phrase *on the Deschutes River* is essential information and, therefore, should not be set off by a comma. (G) and (H) incorrectly use the colon and semicolon, respectively.

63. (C)

(A) and (D) create sentence fragments, and (B) is extremely awkward.

64. (J)

This sentence is irrelevant to the topic of the passage.

65. (D)

This sentence makes it sound as though the author were roaring, not the rapids; *roaring* is a misplaced modifier. (B) doesn't fix the problem because the reader has no idea what *it* refers to. (C) has *the boat* roaring. (D) is the clearest choice.

66. (J)

The word *cover* must either be in past tense, or the structure of the sentence must change. (J) does the latter.

67. (B)

(B) is the simplest, most concise way of expressing the idea. Replacing *and instead he adopted* with *with* makes the sentence much less awkward.

68. (F)

(G) and (J) make it sound as though the author were in the water. (F) expresses the idea better than (H).

69. (D)

The phrase *and we stopped* is redundant because *we came to a jarring halt* says the same thing much more expressively. Omit the underlined portion.

70. (F)

It was is fine here because the author is telling her story in the past tense. (G) and (H) are the present tense, and (J) incorrectly introduces the possessive form.

71. (D)

The other answer choices are unnecessarily wordy; the simplest choice is the best.

72. (G)

The participle *receiving* has to be changed into a verb in the past tense, *received*, in order to be consistent with *went*. (G) is correct as opposed to (H) because the number of bruises something has can be counted, which necessitates *many bruises*, not *much bruises*.

73. (B)

(A) wouldn't work as a concluding sentence because its style and tone are off; nowhere in the passage does the writer use language such as *brutal calamities* and *beguiling excitement*. Also, the writer and her father were not "unwary rafters." (C) contradicts the writer's main theme that nothing was as memorable as her first ride through the rapids. The tone in (D), "call me crazy or weird . . .," is much different from the writer's. (B) is the choice that closely matches the author's style and tone while restating the main theme of the passage.

74. (F)

This essay relates a personal experience of the writer: her first time rafting down the rapids. There is very little mention of the techniques of white water rafting, so the essay would not meet the requirements of the assignment. (G) is wrong because the essay does not focus on the relationship between father and daughter, but on their first rafting experience together.

75. (B)

The sentence is a preface of things to come, so it must appear towards the beginning of the essay.

That eliminates (C) and (D). The second paragraph is about the peaceful setting, so (B) is the most sensible answer.

MATH TEST

1. (D)

You know that 14 people are 20% of the total, and you need to find 100% of the total. You could set up an equation, or you could multiply 14 by 5, since 100% is 5 times as much as 20%. The number of people surveyed is 14×5, or 70.

2. (J)

One safe way to answer this question is by picking numbers. For instance, if you let $x = 2$ and $y = 3$, the train would have traveled $90 \times 2 + 60 \times 3 = 360$ miles in 5 hours, or $\frac{360}{5} = 72$ miles per hour. If you then plug $x = 2$ and $y = 3$ into the answer choices looking for 72, it's clear that the correct answer is (J). No other answer choice equals 72 when $x = 2$ and $y = 3$.

3. (D)

If the ratio of men to women is 5:3, then the ratio of women to the total is 3:8. Since you know the total number of string players is 24, you can set up the equation $\frac{3}{8} = \frac{x}{24}$ to find that $x = 9$. Also, without setting up the proportion, you could note that the total number of players is 3 times the ratio total, so the number of women will be 3 times the part of the ratio that represents women.

4. (K)

In a pinch you could back-solve on this question, but this one is fairly easy to solve algebraically, like so:

$$x^2 - 3x = 6x$$
$$x^2 = 9x$$

Now you can divide both sides by x because $x \neq 0$:

$$\frac{x^2}{x} = \frac{9x}{x}$$
$$x = 9$$

5. (C)

With visual perception problems such as this one, the key is to play around with possibilities as you try to draw a solution. Eventually, you should be able to come up with a picture like this:

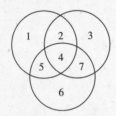

6. (K)

This problem could be solved algebraically, but look at the answer choices. They are all simple numbers, making this a great opportunity for back-solving. Begin with choice (H).

Plugging in 0, you get:

$$(0)^2 + 6(0) + 8 = 4 + 10(0)$$
$$8 = 4$$

Since 8 does not equal 4, you know this isn't the correct answer. But it is difficult to know which answer to try next. Should you aim higher or lower? If you're unsure of which direction to go, just try whatever looks easiest. Choice (J), 1, looks like a good candidate:

$$(1)^2 + 6(1) + 8 = 4 + 10(1)$$
$$1 + 6 + 8 = 4 + 10$$
$$15 = 14$$

So (J) doesn't work either, but it looks like the numbers are getting closer, so you're going in the right direction. Try out choice (K) just to be sure.

$$(2)^2 + 6(2) + 8 = 4 + 10(2)$$
$$4 + 12 + 8 = 4 + 20$$
$$24 = 24$$

Choice (K) is the correct answer.

7. (B)

Translate piece by piece:

"Nine less than c" indicates subtraction: $c - 9$.

"Nine less than c is the same as the number d": $c - 9 = d$. There's one equation.

"d less than" also indicates subtraction: $-d$.

"d less than twice c is 20": $2c - d = 20$. There's the second equation.

Choice (B) matches what we found.

8. (K)

To determine the total number of possible arrangements on a question like this one, simply determine the number of possibilities for each component, and then multiply them together. There are 3 ways of serving the ice cream, 5 flavors, and 4 toppings. Therefore there are $3 \times 5 \times 4 = 60$ ways to order ice cream, and choice (K) is correct.

9. (E)

Back-solving is a great technique to use for this problem. Start with (C). The director asked one out of 3 students to come to the second audition and $\frac{1}{3}$ of 48 is 16, so 16 students were invited to a second audition. Then 75% of 16, which is $\frac{3}{4}(16) = 12$

students were offered parts. The question states that 18 students were offered parts, so you already know that (C) is too small. You can also eliminate (A) and (B). Since the director invited $\frac{1}{3}$ of the students to a second audition, the number of students at the first audition must be divisible by 3. (You can't have a fraction of a student.) That eliminates (D), which leaves only (E).

10. (K)

Begin by translating the English into math: $x + 5x = -60$, $6x = -60$, so $x = -10$, and the two numbers are -10 and -50. Thus the lesser number is -50.

By the way, this is where most people mess up. They forget that the "lesser" of two negative numbers is the negative number with the larger absolute value (since *less* means *to the left of* on the number line):

11. (D)

You're looking for the total number of parallelograms that can be found among the triangles, and parallelograms could be formed two ways from these triangles, either from two adjacent triangles, or from four adjacent triangles, like so:

Begin by looking for the smaller parallelograms. If you look for parallelograms leaning in the same direction as the one we drew, you'll find three. But there are two other possible orientations for the smaller parallelogram; it could be flipped

horizontally, or it could be rotated 90 degrees so that one triangle sits atop the other in the form of a diamond; both of these orientations also have three parallelograms, for a total of nine smaller parallelograms.

Now look for larger parallelograms. Perhaps the easiest way to count these is to look along the sides of the larger composite triangle. You should be able to spot two of the larger parallelograms along each side, one originating at each vertex, for a total of six larger parallelograms. Thus there are a total of $9 + 6 = 15$ parallelograms in all.

12. (H)

The square has a perimeter of 16 inches, so each side of the square is 4 inches, and the area of the square is, therefore, 16 square inches. If the side of the square is 4 inches, then the diameter of the circle is also 4 inches. The radius of the circle is then 2 inches. The area of the circle is 4π square inches. The area of the shaded region is then $16 - 4\pi$ square inches.

13. (C)

The safest strategy is simply to list out the possibilities. It's also helpful to realize that multiples of both 4 and 6 are multiples of 12 (the least common multiple between the two), so skip over all multiples of 12:

4, 8, ~~12~~, 16, 20, ~~24~~, 28, 32, ~~36~~, 40, 44, ~~48~~

So there are 8 in all.

14. (H)

Don't be intimidated by the expression $f(x)$. In this case, that just means that you should plug in the number that appears in the parentheses for the x in the expression they have given you.

So, if $f(x) = (8 - 3x)(x^2 - 2x - 15)$, $f(3) =$ $[8 - 3(3)][(3)^2 - 2(3) - 15]$.

Once you get to this point, just remember PEMDAS. $[8 - 3(3)][(3)^2 - 2(3) - 15] = (8 - 9)(9 - 6 - 15) = (-1)(-12) = 12$, choice (H).

15. (C)

A class contains five juniors and five seniors. If one member of the class is assigned at random to present a paper on a certain subject, and another member of the class is randomly assigned to assist him, then:

The probability that the first student picked will be a junior $= \dfrac{\text{\# of Juniors}}{\text{Total \# of Students}} = \dfrac{5}{10} = \dfrac{1}{2}$.

The probability that the second student picked will be a junior, given that the first student picked was a junior $= \dfrac{\text{\# of Juniors Remaining}}{\text{Total \# of Students Remaining}}$

So the probability that both students will be juniors $= \dfrac{1}{2} \times \dfrac{4}{9} = \dfrac{2}{9}$.

16. (G)

Since the formula to find the area of a triangle is $\dfrac{1}{2}$ (*base*)(*height*), you can plug in the base and area to find the height. You know that the area of this triangle is 45 units and that the base is $3 + 12 = 15$. Let x be the length of altitude $\overline{YS}$. Plug these into the area formula to get $45 = \dfrac{15x}{2}$. Solve for x to get $x = 6$.

17. (D)

The y-coordinate is the point on which the x value is zero, so plug $x = 0$ into the equation:

$$6y - 3(0) = 18$$
$$6y = 18$$
$$y = 3$$

18. (H)

This question involves common quadratics, so the key is to write these quadratic expressions in their other forms. For instance $x^2 - y^2 = 12$, so $(x + y)(x - y) = 12$. Since $x - y = 4$, $(x + y)(4) = 12$, so $x + y = 3$. Finally, $x^2 + 2xy + y^2 = (x + y)^2 = (3)^2 = 9$.

19. (D)

This shape must be divided into 3 simple shapes. By drawing downward two perpendicular line segments from the endpoints of the side which is 10 units long, you are left with a 3×10 rectangle, a triangle with a base of 4 and a height of 3, and a triangle with a base of 7 and a hypotenuse of $7\sqrt{2}$. The rectangle has an area of $3 \times 10 = 30$ square units. The smaller triangle has an area of $\dfrac{4 \times 3}{2} = 6$ square units. The larger triangle is a 45°-45°-90° triangle, so the height must be 7. Therefore, it has an area of $\dfrac{7 \times 7}{2} = 24.5$ square units. The entire shape has an area of $6 + 30 + 24.5 = 60.5$ square units.

20. (H)

Although back-solving is certainly possible with this problem, it's probably quicker to solve with arithmetic. The board is 12 feet long, which means it is $12 \times 12 = 144$ inches. The carpenter cuts off $3 \times 17 = 51$ inches. That leaves $144 - 51 = 93$ inches.

21. (E)

To answer this question, begin by setting the right side of the equation to equal zero:

$$x^2 - 4x - 6 = 6$$
$$x^2 - 4x - 12 = 0$$

Now use reverse-FOIL to factor the left side of the equation:

$$(x - 6)(x + 2) = 0$$

Thus, either $x - 6 = 0$ or $x + 2 = 0$, so $x = 6$ or -2.

22. (H)

Here's another question that tests your understanding of FOIL, but you have to be careful. The question states that -3 is a possible solution for the equation $x^2 + kx - 15 = 0$, so in its factored form, one set of parentheses with a factor inside must be $(x + 3)$. Since the last term in the equation in its expanded form is -15, that means that the entire factored equation must read $(x + 3)(x - 5) = 0$, which in its expanded form is $x^2 - 2x - 15 = 0$. Thus $k = -2$.

23. (D)

To solve this problem you need to understand the triangle inequality theorem, which states: The sum of the lengths of any two sides of a triangle is always greater then the length of the third side. Therefore, the other sides of this triangle must add up to more than 7. You know from the problem that every side must be an integer. That means that the sides must add up to at least 8 inches (4 inches and 4 inches, or 7 inches and 1 inch, for example). The smallest possible perimeter is $7 + 8 = 15$.

24. (F)

It's time to use SOHCAHTOA, and drawing a triangle might help as well. If the sine of θ (opposite side over hypotenuse) is $\dfrac{\sqrt{11}}{2\sqrt{3}}$, then one of the legs of the right triangle is $\sqrt{11}$ and the hypotenuse is $2\sqrt{3}$. Now apply the Pythagorean theorem to come up with the other (adjacent) leg: $(\sqrt{11})^2 + (n)^2 = (2\sqrt{3})^2$,

so $11 + n^2 = 12$, which means that $n^2 = 1$, and $n = 1$. Thus cosine (adjacent side over hypotenuse) θ is $\dfrac{1}{2\sqrt{3}}$.

25. (D)

Take a quick look at the answer choices before simplifying an expression like this one. Notice that none of these choices contain a radical sign in their denominators. So when you simplify the expression, try to eliminate that radical sign. Your calculations should look something like this:

$$\frac{\sqrt{3 + x}}{\sqrt{3 - x}} \times \frac{\sqrt{3 - x}}{\sqrt{3 - x}} = \frac{\sqrt{(3 + x)(3 - x)}}{\sqrt{(3 - x)^2}} =$$

$$\frac{\sqrt{9 - 3x + 3x - x^2}}{3 - x} = \frac{\sqrt{9 - x^2}}{3 - x}.$$

So choice (D) is correct.

26. (G)

If the ratio of the parts is 2:5, then the ratio total is $2 + 5 = 7$. Thus the actual total number of cookies must be a multiple of 7. The only answer choice that's a multiple of 7 is (G), 35.

27. (C)

This question is a great opportunity to use your calculator. Notice that all your answer choices are decimals. In order to solve, convert $\dfrac{3}{16}$ into a decimal and add that to .175. $\dfrac{3}{16} = .1875$, so the sum equals $.1875 + .175 = .3625$. So choice (C) is correct.

28. (H)

Remember that if you are given a perimeter for a rectangle, the rectangle with the greatest area for that perimeter will be a square. So we are looking for the area of a square with a perimeter of 20.

The perimeter of a square equals $4s$, where s is the length of one side of the square. If $4s = 20$, then $s = 5$. The area of the square equals $s^2 = 5^2 = 25$, choice (H).

29. (B)

Be careful on this one. You can't start plugging numbers into your calculator without paying attention to the order of operations. This one is best solved on your own.

$$\frac{\frac{3}{2} + \frac{7}{4}}{\left(\frac{15}{8} - \frac{3}{4}\right) - \left(\frac{4+3}{-4+3}\right)} = \frac{\frac{3}{2} + \frac{7}{4}}{\left(\frac{9}{8}\right) - \left(\frac{7}{-1}\right)} = \frac{\frac{13}{4}}{\frac{9}{8} + \frac{7}{1}}$$

$$= \frac{\frac{13}{4}}{\frac{65}{8}} = \frac{13}{4} \times \frac{8}{65} = \frac{2}{5}$$

30. (K)

You could solve this algebraically for x as follows:

$$x - 15 = 7 - 5(x - 4)$$
$$x - 15 = 7 - 5x + 20$$
$$x - 15 = -5x + 27$$
$$6x = 42$$
$$x = 7$$

Remember also that if you are ever stuck, you can try to backsolve with the answer choices. Here if you try them all out, only 7 works:

$$7 - 15 = 7 - 5(7 - 4)$$
$$-8 = 7 - 5(3)$$
$$-8 = 7 - 15$$
$$-8 = -8$$

31. (C)

Break strange figures like this one up into shapes that are more familiar and easier to handle. In this case, the quadrilateral can be split into a square and a right triangle. The square is 9×9, so the area of that part of the figure is 81 square meters. The right triangle has a height of 9 and a base of 4, so the area of the triangle would be $\frac{1}{2}bh = \frac{1}{2}(4 \times 9) = \frac{1}{2}(36) = 18$ square meters. So the total area of the figure is $(81 + 18)$ square meters = 99 square meters, choice (C).

32. (H)

The easiest way to solve this question is to put it in the form $y = mx + b$, in which case m equals the slope. In other words, you want to isolate y:

$$6y - 3x = 18$$
$$6y = 3x + 18$$
$$y = \frac{3x + 18}{6}$$
$$y = \frac{1}{2}x + 3$$

So the slope equals $\frac{1}{2}$.

33. (E)

To answer this question you have to know that perpendicular lines on the standard (x, y) coordinate plane have slopes that are negative reciprocals of each other. In other words, the line described by the equation $y = -\frac{4}{5}x + 6$ has a slope of $-\frac{4}{5}$, so a line perpendicular to it has a slope of $\frac{4}{5}$. Looking at the answer choices, you can immediately eliminate (B), (C), and (D). Now just plug the coordinates you're given, $(4, 3)$, into one of the remaining equations. Let's try choice (A):

$$3 = \frac{5}{4}(4) + 2$$
$$3 = 5 + 2$$

This does not compute, so the answer must be (E). (Try it out if you're not convinced.)

34. (K)

Since the problem gives you the y-intercept, it is easy to look at the answer choices and rule out (F), (H), and (J). Put the equation from the question in slope-intercept form to find its slope:

$$3x - 5y = 4$$
$$-5y = -3x + 4$$
$$y = \frac{-3x + 4}{-5}$$
$$y = \frac{3}{5}x - \frac{4}{5}$$

Since line t is parallel, it has the same slope. This matches (K).

35. (A)

To solve for x in the equation $y = mx + b$, isolate x on one side of the equation. Begin by subtracting b from both sides. You will be left with $y - b = mx$. Then divide both sides by m, and you will be left with $x = \dfrac{y - b}{m}$, choice (A).

36. (J)

In this figure there are many right triangles, and many similar triangles. If you know to be on the lookout for 3-4-5 triangles, it should be easy to spot that triangle ABC has sides of 15-20-25, so $\overline{AC}$ is 25. Now turn your attention to triangle ABD. Since it's a right triangle that shares $\angle BAC$ with triangle ABC, it too must be a 3-4-5 triangle. So if the hypotenuse is 20, the shorter leg ($\overline{BD}$) must have a length of 12, and the longer leg ($\overline{AD}$) must have a length of 16.

37. (A)

The shortest distance to line m will be a line perpendicular to m. So, the distance will be the difference between the y-coordinates of point C and the nearest point on line m. Since every point

on m has a y-coordinate of 5, and point C has a y-coordinate of 3, the difference is 2.

38. (G)

Perhaps the easiest approach here is to pick numbers. Pick a simple number such as $x = 2$. Thus,
$$\frac{x^2 - 11x + 24}{8 - x} = \frac{(2)^2 - 11(2) + 24}{6} =$$
$$\frac{4 - 22 + 24}{6} = \frac{6}{6} = 1.$$ So 1 is your target number.
When you plug $x = 2$ into the answer choices, the only choice that gives you 1 is (G).

39. (C)

It may help you to draw a picture. Draw a right triangle into the coordinate plane as we've done above. Note that the distance between the two points represents the hypotenuse of the triangle. The legs of the triangle have lengths of 3 and 4, so the distance between the two points must be 5, choice (C).

40. (G)

To find the area of the shaded region, you must subtract the area of the circle from the area of the rectangle. Since the sides of the rectangle are $2x$ and $5x$, it has an area of $2x \times 5x = 10x^2$. By examining the diagram, you can see that the circle has a diameter of $2x$, so it has a radius of x. Its area is, therefore, πx^2. The shaded region, therefore, has an area of $10x^2 - \pi x^2$.

41. (B)

Since you are not given a diagram for this problem, it's best to draw a quick sketch of a right triangle to help keep the sides separate in your mind. Mark one of the acute angles θ. Since $\cos\theta = \dfrac{5\sqrt{2}}{8}$, mark the adjacent side $5\sqrt{2}$ and the hypotenuse as 8. (Remember SOHCAHTOA.) Use the Pythagorean theorem to find that the side opposite θ is $\sqrt{14}$. The problem asks you to find $\tan\theta$. Tangent $= \dfrac{\text{opposite}}{\text{adjacent}}$, so $\tan\theta = \dfrac{\sqrt{14}}{5\sqrt{2}}$, which can be simplified to $\dfrac{\sqrt{7}}{5}$.

42. (H)

This question is one where your calculator can come in handy. Divide 7 by integer values for n, and look for values between .5 and .8. Begin by looking for the integer values of n where $\dfrac{7}{n}$ is greater than .5. If $n = 14$, then $\dfrac{7}{n} = .5$, so n must be less than 14. Work through values of n until you get to the point where $\dfrac{7}{n} \geq .8$. When $n = 9$, $\dfrac{7}{n} = .778$, but when $n = 8$, $\dfrac{7}{n} = .875$. So the integer values that work for n in this case are $n = 9, 10, 11, 12,$ and 13. Five integer values work, so choice (H) is correct.

43. (C)

The points are as far apart as possible when separated by a diameter of X and a diameter of Y.

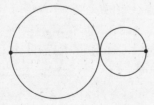

The circumference of a circle is $\pi \times$ (diameter), so the diameter of circle X is 12 and the diameter of

circle Y is 8. The greatest possible distance between points then is $12 + 8 = 20$.

44. (K)

Begin by getting rid of the square root sign. If $y \geq 0$, then $\sqrt{y^2} = y$, so $\sqrt{(x^2 + 4)^2} = x^2 + 4$. $(x + 2)(x - 2) = x^2 - 4$, so you now have $(x^2 + 4) - (x^2 - 4) = ?$ Get rid of the parentheses and you have $x^2 + 4 - x^2 + 4 = x^2 - x^2 + 4 + 4 = 8$.

45. (A)

Here you need to substitute -3 for s and solve. That gives you the expression $(-3)^3 + 2(-3)^2 + 2(-3)$, which equals $-27 + 18 - 6$, or -15. If you missed this problem, you probably made a mistake with the signs of the numbers.

46. (G)

Be careful on this one. Begin by simplifying the equation by FOILing one side:

$$2x + 6 = (x + 5)(x + 3)$$
$$2x + 6 = x^2 + 8x + 15$$

Then get the right side of the equation to equal zero: $x^2 + 6x + 9 = 0$.

The left side of this equation is the perfect square $(x + 3)^2$, so $(x + 3)^2 = 0$, which has only one solution, $x = -3$. Choice (G) is correct.

47. (E)

This is a great eyeballing question. The perimeter is greater than $\overline{AC}$, so you can get rid of choices (A) and (B). It appears to be quite a bit greater than $\overline{AC}$, more than twice as great, so choices (C) and (D) are out as well. That only leaves choice (E).

If you wanted to solve this the conventional way, since the perimeter is the sum of the lengths of all the sides of the square, you need to find the length of the square's sides. Let the length of each of the square's sides be x. $\overline{AC}$ divides the square into two right triangles, so we can apply the Pythagorean theorem: $\overline{AB}^2 + \overline{BC}^2 = \overline{AC}^2$. Since $\overline{AB}$ and $\overline{BC}$ are sides of the square they have the same length. We can write that as $x^2 + x^2 = \overline{AC}^2$. $\overline{AC} = 8$, so $2x^2 = 8^2$; $2x^2 = 64$; $x^2 = 32$; $x = \sqrt{32} = \sqrt{16 \times 2} = 4\sqrt{2}$. So each side of the square is $4\sqrt{2}$, and the perimeter of the square is $4 \times 4\sqrt{2} = 16\sqrt{2}$.

48. (G)

To find the area of this complex shape, you could divide it into 2 simple shapes by drawing a line 30 inches up, parallel to the horizontal base. This leaves you with a 4×30 rectangle and a triangle with height of 6 and a base of 4. The rectangle has an area of $4 \times 30 = 120$ square inches, and the triangle has an area of $\dfrac{4 \times 6}{2} = 12$ square inches. That makes a total of $120 + 12 = 132$ square inches.

49. (E)

Drawing $\overline{OD}$ divides quadrilateral $OCDE$ into two triangles, OCD and ODE. Both triangles are isosceles because $\overline{OC}$, $\overline{OD}$, and $\overline{OE}$ are all radii of circle O. Angles ODC and OCD have equal measures, since they're opposite equal sides, so $\angle ODC$ measures 70°. Similarly, $\angle ODE$ measures 45°. Together, angles ODC and ODE make up $\angle CDE$, so its measure is $70° + 45° = 115°$.

50. (K)

Remember that lines intersect at the point that is a solution to both equations. So, equations with no common solution don't intersect—they have the same slope and are parallel. To solve this problem,

search through the answer choices to find the pair of equations representing lines with the same slope. If you write the equations in (K) in slope-intercept form, you'll get $y = -\dfrac{1}{3}x + 2$, $y = -\dfrac{1}{3}x + \dfrac{7}{9}$, so the slope is clearly the same for both equations.

51. (E)

To solve a repeating decimal question, begin by determining the pattern of the decimal on your calculator. $\dfrac{1}{7} = 0.142857142857\ldots$, so you know that this fraction repeats every 6 decimal places. Since we are looking for the 46th decimal place, we need to determine where in the 6-term pattern we would be at the 46th place. Divide 46 by 6, and look for the remainder. The remainder in this case is 4, so we are looking for the fourth term in the sequence, which is 8, choice (E).

52. (K)

Remember that you treat an inequality exactly like an equality, except that you need to flip the sign when you multiply or divide by a negative number. In this problem, you start with the inequality $-2 - 4x \leq -6x$. Add $4x$ to both sides to get $-2 \leq -2x$. Divide by -2 and flip the sign to get $1 \geq x$, which matches (K).

53. (B)

For this problem, it would probably be easiest to pick numbers. Since you will be taking the square root of the numbers, it's easiest to pick perfect squares, like 4 and 9 $\dfrac{\sqrt{4}}{4} + \dfrac{\sqrt{9}}{9} = \dfrac{2}{4} + \dfrac{3}{9} = \dfrac{1}{2} + \dfrac{1}{3} = \dfrac{5}{6}$. When you plug 4 and 9 into the answer choices, only (B) gives you $\dfrac{5}{6}$.

54. (G)

When transversals intersect parallel lines, corresponding line segments on the transversals are proportional. In other words, $\dfrac{\overline{DE}}{\overline{CB}} = \dfrac{\overline{EF}}{\overline{BA}}$.
Thus $= \dfrac{6}{8} = \dfrac{\overline{EF}}{4}$, so $\overline{EF} = 3$.

55. (D)

Divide the square into two right triangles by drawing the diagonal from (2, 7) to (2, 1). Remember that the area of each triangle is half its base times its height. Treat the diagonal as the base of a triangle. Its length is the distance from (2, 7) to (2, 1). Since the x-coordinates are the same, that distance is simply the difference between the y-coordinates, $7 - 1$, or 6. The diagonal bisects the square, so the height of the triangle is half the distance from $(-1, 4)$ to $(5, 4)$. We already know that a diagonal of this square is 6, so half the distance is 3. Therefore, the base and height of either triangle are 6 and 3, so the area of each triangle is $\dfrac{6 \times 3}{2}$ or 9 square units. The square is made up of two such triangles and so has twice the area, or 18 square units.

56. (K)

Compared to the graph of $y = \cos \theta$, the graph of $y = 2 \cos \theta$ would have twice the amplitude and the same period, choice (K). Here you are doubling y, which represents the vertical coordinates, but the θ coordinates stay the same. The amplitude of a trigonometric equation refers to how high or low the curve moves from the horizontal axis. The period refers to the distance required to complete a single wave along the horizontal axis.

57. (C)

To solve this problem with algebra, you need to translate each phrase into mathematics. Translated, the problem is $3(x + 15) = 4x - 65$. Solve for x to get 110. Alternatively, you could back-solve.

58. (H)

The volume of a cylinder is $\pi r^2 h$, so pick numbers to make this question more concrete and plug them into this volume formula. Let's say the smaller cylinder has a height of 1 and a radius of 1 (diameter of 2), for a volume of $\pi(1)^2 \times 1 = \pi$. The larger cylinder would then have a height of 3 and a radius of 2 (diameter of 4), for a volume of $\pi(2)^2 \times 3 = 12\pi$. Thus, it would take 12 fillings of the smaller cylinder to fill the larger cylinder.

59. (D)

Draw a picture of the triangle, and carefully apply your knowledge of the ratio of the lengths of the sides of a 30°-60°-90° triangle ($x:x\sqrt{3}:2x$). So if the longer leg has a length of 12, the shorter leg has a length of $\dfrac{12}{\sqrt{3}} = \dfrac{12\sqrt{3}}{\sqrt{3} \times \sqrt{3}} = \dfrac{12\sqrt{3}}{3} = 4\sqrt{3}$.
Thus, the hypotenuse is twice this, or $8\sqrt{3}$. So the perimeter is the sum of the three sides, or $4\sqrt{3} + 12 + 8\sqrt{3} = 12\sqrt{3} + 12$.

60. (J)

Remember the average formula on this one. The average formula states, $\text{Average} = \dfrac{\text{Sum of the terms}}{\text{Number of the terms}}$.
So to find the total average, find the total sum and divide it by the total number of terms. If a team averages x points in n games, then it scored nx points in n games. In the final game of the season, it scored y points. So the total sum of points for the season is $nx + y$, and the total number of games is $n + 1$. So the team's average score for the entire season is $\dfrac{nx + y}{n + 1}$, choice (J).

READING TEST

PASSAGE I

1. (C)

The answer can be found in lines 26–31: "The real evils, indeed, of Emma's situation were the power of having rather too much her own way, and a disposition to think a little too well of herself; these were the disadvantages which threatened alloy to her many enjoyments."

2. (G)

Isabella's name is given in line 63.

3. (B)

The answer can be found in lines 17–18: "Between them it was more the intimacy of sisters."

4. (F)

As it is used in the sentence, *disposition* means "tendency" or "inclination." It would not make sense for Emma to have (G) control, (H) placement, or (J) transfer "to think a little too well of herself" (lines 28–29).

5. (D)

The answer can be found in lines 54–60: "She recalled her past kindness—the kindness, the affection of sixteen years—how she had taught her and…how she had devoted all her powers to attach and amuse her in health—and how she had nursed her through the various illnesses of childhood."

6. (H)

Miss Taylor will continue to be a part of Emma's life, but they will not be as close because Miss Taylor no longer lives with Emma and because Miss Taylor will be primarily concerned with her husband's, not Emma's, well-being.

7. (C)

Emma is self-centered, as evidenced by her description of her relationship with Miss Taylor. Among Miss Taylor's admirable qualities, Emma includes the fact that Miss Taylor was "interested in her, in every pleasure, every scheme of hers—one to whom she could speak every thought as it arose, and who had such an affection for her as could never find fault" (lines 69–73). Emma is also clearly headstrong. She is described as "having rather too much her own way" (lines 27–28).

8. (G)

Emma's description of her friendship with Miss Taylor suggests that Emma most highly values devotion in her friends.

9. (B)

The description of Mr. Weston is in lines 46–49: "The marriage had every promise of happiness for her friend. Mr. Weston was a man of unexceptionable character, easy fortune, suitable age, and pleasant manners." None of the other choices match this description.

10. (H)

The answer to the question is in lines 24–26: "Emma doing just what she liked, highly esteeming Miss Taylor's judgment, but directed chiefly by her own."

PASSAGE II

11. (B)

The passage presents the three main systems of memory and states that these systems are widely accepted—so eliminate (A)—but gives alternate theories about the way long-term memories are formed and possible flaws in the process. Although the passage mentions two early ideas about memory that were too simplistic (C) and (D), this is not the main focus of the passage.

12. (H)

Described in paragraph three, semantic memory holds facts and general knowledge, like the multiplication tables (H). Ballet steps (F) and riding a bicycle (J) would be in procedural memory, a childhood memory (G) would be in episodic.

13. (B)

All the information you need is in paragraph three. Memories of one's personal life would be held in episodic memory, therefore the man's episodic memory was affected. Eliminate (C) and (D). Long-term memories are "never lost," but they may become inaccessible, therefore the author would most likely agree that the man's episodic memories had become inaccessible to him.

14. (F)

While memory was once viewed as relatively simple and automatic with memories being held exactly as they were originally received, it is now believed that many factors alter the way memories are formed and retrieved. (G) and (J) contradict this. (H) is too extreme.

15. (C)

In the last paragraph the author states that assumptions and inferences can affect memory. A person might assume that if the ball hits a window the window will break. Interference (A) is when one, unrelated memory alters another. The memory described in the question is not inaccessible (B), but

wrong. And most of the memory was still correct, not false (D).

16. (J)

This detail question requires very careful reading. Refresh your memory by looking at *episodic* in paragraph three. It's in long-term memory, and involves personal events closely identified with a time and place. (F), (G), and (H) fit that idea closely. If you're unsure, look at the description of working (short-term) memory in paragraph two. You'll see that it includes those things briefly remembered and then lost forever—like the face of a stranger passed on the street.

17. (B)

Paragraph two describes this change in terminology. The term *short-term memory* did not accurately describe all the functions of this category of memory. *Working memory* is more accurate since, although these memories degrade quickly—eliminating (A)— these memories can also be used and manipulated as described in the second paragraph. (C) and (D) confuse information in other paragraphs.

18. (H)

Don't panic. All you have to do is look at the line where this term is defined for you. The term doesn't relate to any of the usual meanings of the word *icon*.

19. (B)

The second sentence in paragraph three states, "Memories recorded in long-term memory are never lost…." Although absolute statements are often too extreme to be correct in Reading, when the passage explicitly supports an absolute statement don't be afraid to choose it. You might choose (A) if you mistook "short-term" and "working" memory for two separate categories. (C) is contradicted in paragraph four, and (D) is contradicted at the end of paragraph two and again at the start of paragraph five.

20. (H)

Paragraph two states that working memories decay rapidly, which means that they are quickly forgotten. (F) and (G) relate to sensory memory. (J) is characteristic of long-term memory.

PASSAGE III

21. (B)

In lines 10–11 Julia Margaret Cameron is described as "the first woman to have achieved eminence in photography." The other answer choices contradict information supplied in the passage.

22. (F)

The answer to this question can be found in lines 72–73: "Contemporary taste much prefers her portraits…" and in line 78: "today her fame rests upon her portraits…"

23. (D)

The dates used in the passage tell you that this is a chronological account; the author begins with Cameron's birth in 1815, tells of her marriage and then her move to England in 1848, points out that she received her first photographic equipment in 1863, describes one of her photographs from 1864, and then concludes the paragraph with her death in 1874.

24. (F)

The dictionary definition of *cumbersome* is "difficult to handle because of weight or bulk." (F) most closely fits this definition, and it is the only answer choice that makes sense within the context of the sentence.

25. (B)

(A) contradicts information from the passage, which suggests that Cameron led anything but a conventional life. Neither the money that Cameron earned as a photographer nor her religious beliefs are discussed in the passage, making (C) and (D) incorrect answers.

26. (F)

Lines 53–55 say, "She produced a large body of work that stands up as one of the notable artistic achievements of the Victorian period." To say that she is "the greatest photographer who ever lived" goes beyond anything stated or implied in the passage. The third paragraph does not compare her importance as an artist during her lifetime to her importance today. The passage also does not state that she "revolutionized" any photographic methods.

27. (C)

The answer to this question can be found in lines 6–9: "photography, being a new medium outside the traditional academic framework, was wide open to women and offered them opportunities that the older fields did not…"

28. (G)

These titles refer to allegorical pictures, as described in lines 69–72: "Victorian critics were particularly impressed by her allegorical pictures, many of them based on the poems of her friend and neighbor Tennyson…"

29. (D)

The answer to this question can be found in lines 72–74: "Contemporary taste much prefers her portraits and finds her narrative scenes sentimental and sometimes in bad taste."

30. (F)

The author says that Cameron "achieved eminence" (line 11) in her field, that she "devoted herself wholly to this art" (line 49), and that "no other woman photographer has ever enjoyed such success" (lines 65–66). Only (F) fits these descriptions.

PASSAGE IV

31. (C)

For details about the eye, look at paragraph three. Only the cornea and stenopaic pupil are relevant, eliminating (A) and (D). But the cornea (B) is helpful underwater, not on land.

32. (G)

The eye is covered in paragraph three. The seal's cornea improves vision in the water (note the comparison to human underwater vision), but distorts light moving through the air. Another adaptation was then needed to "minimize" distortion, but that doesn't mean distortion is completely eliminated, so the seal's vision in the air is distorted, (G).

33. (D)

The vibrissae are discussed only in the last paragraph. They sense wave disturbances made by nearby moving fish, so (D) is correct.

34. (F)

This is stated in the second paragraph, where the seal's hearing is discussed.

35. (D)

This appears in the first paragraph, which introduces the influences on the seal's adaptations. They include that the seal "does most of its fishing at night," that "noise levels are high," and that these factors are compounded by the seal's "two habitats."

36. (H)

Locating each of these claims in the passage, we find that (H) is "suggested" and the subject of speculation, rather than stated as fact. All of the others are given in support of claims.

37. (A)

We find in the first paragraph that they live along the northern Atlantic and Pacific coasts. Since they live in both the land and water, the coastlines must be accessible. We can infer that the waters are cold rather than warm, eliminating (D). (B) and (C) are too broad.

38. (J)

This feature is mentioned at the end of paragraph two. It shouldn't be confused with echolocation, which is discussed in paragraph four, but not connected with any particular sensory organ.

39. (B)

The entire passage is about how the seal's sensory organs have adapted to life on land and in the water, making (B) the best choice. Generally, we are told about differences, not similarities, between the two, eliminating (A). The relative success of human and seal adaptation to their environments isn't discussed, (C) and (D).

40. (G)

In paragraph three, we see that human corneas refract light badly in water, and the seal's corneas perform well.

SCIENCE TEST

PASSAGE I

1. (B)

To answer this question, you have to examine the third column of the table, transmittance range. For a material to transmit light at a wavelength of 25 μm, its transmittance range—the range of wavelengths over which the material is transparent—must include 25 μm. Only potassium bromide (0.3–29 μm) and cesium iodide (0.3–70 μm) have transmittance ranges that include 25 μm, so (B) is correct.

2. (F)

The material that contradicts this hypothesis is going to have poor chemical resistance, but a transmittance range less than 10 μm. Lithium fluoride (F) fits the bill: its chemical resistance is poor, and its transmittance range is less than 6 μm wide. (G) and (J) are wrong because both flint glass and quartz have excellent chemical resistance. (H) is out because cesium iodide has a transmittance range nearly 70 μm wide.

3. (D)

The correct answer is a pair of materials in which the refractive index of the first material is greater than that of the second. In (A), (B), and (C), the refractive index of the first material is less than that of the second. In (D), however, flint glass has a refractive index of 1.66 while calcium fluoride's refractive index is only 1.43. That makes (D) the correct answer.

4. (J)

The easiest way to answer this question is to use the first couple of materials and test each hypothesis

on them. (F) and (G) are incorrect because the transmittance range of lithium fluoride is wider than its useful prism range. Comparing the data on lithium fluoride and calcium fluoride rules out (H) because transmittance range does NOT increase as useful prism range decreases. In fact, looking down the rest of the table, you see that transmittance range seems to decrease as useful prism range decreases. (J) is the only one left, and the data on lithium fluoride and calcium fluoride as well as all the other materials confirms that the transmittance range is always wider than, and includes within it, the useful prism range.

5. (B)

According to the footnote to the table, quartz infused with lead oxide is flint glass. A comparison of the properties of pure quartz and flint glass shows that the transmittance range of flint glass is narrower than that of quartz but that its refractive index is greater. This supports (B).

PASSAGE II

6. (H)

Use the results of both experiments to answer this question. The answer choices all involve temperature, concentration, and solvent in different combinations. To determine whether osmotic pressure is dependent upon a variable, look for a pair of trials in which all conditions except for that variable are identical. In doing so, you see that temperature and concentration affect osmotic pressure, but solvent does not.

7. (B)

Find methanol at 0.5 mol/L, which is in Table 2. The text above the table states that all the trials were conducted under the same temperature (298 K).

Therefore, simply look across the row that you identified. The osmotic pressure is 12.23, (B).

8. (G)

To figure out whether or not the sucrose solution will diffuse across the membrane under the conditions described in the question, go back to the definition of osmotic pressure given in the introduction. Once the external pressure reaches the osmotic pressure, osmosis will not occur. In order for osmosis to occur, the external pressure must be less than the osmotic pressure of the solution. The solution in this question is a 0.1 mol/L aqueous sucrose solution at 298 K; those conditions correspond to an osmotic pressure of 2.45 atm. Since the external pressure is 1 atm, which is less than the osmotic pressure, osmosis will occur. From the definition of osmosis in the passage, it is clear that the solution will diffuse from the side of the membrane with a lower concentration of dissolved material, in this case pure water, to the side with a higher concentration, in this case sucrose solution. (G) is correct.

9. (C)

To determine what the scientists investigated in Experiment 1, look at what they varied and what they measured. In Experiment 1, the scientists varied the concentration and the temperature of sucrose solutions, and they measured the osmotic pressure. Therefore, they were investigating the effect of concentration and temperature on osmotic pressure (C). Watch out for (A): it states what was investigated in Experiment 2, not Experiment 1.

10. (F)

The results in Table 2 indicate that osmotic pressure doesn't depend on the solvent, as discussed in the explanation to Question 1. So Statement I is a valid

conclusion, and (G) can be eliminated. Statement II is false. The results in Table 1 indicate that osmotic pressure is dependent on concentration as well as temperature. So (H) can be ruled out. Now consider Statement III. It is not a valid conclusion because osmotic pressure is the pressure required to prevent osmosis, so osmosis occurs only if the external pressure is less than the osmotic pressure.

11. (D)

To answer questions that ask about the design of an experiment, look at what the scientists are trying to measure. You're told that osmotic pressure is the pressure required to prevent osmosis. In order to measure the osmotic pressure of a solution, scientists need to be able to tell when osmosis begins. If you have two clear solutions with sucrose dissolved in one of them, how can you tell when there's any movement of solvent between the two of them? If the sucrose is dyed, the blue solution will become paler when osmosis starts, i.e., when solvent moves across the membrane to create an equilibrium. Therefore, (D) is correct.

PASSAGE III

12. (J)

Even if you do not know how many °C are equivalent to room temperature, you can eliminate all of the incorrect answer choices. Choices (F), (G), and (H) all reach a boiling point at low temperatures and, therefore, would all be gases at room temperature. (J), at 36° C, is the only logical choice.

13. (C)

To answer this question, you have to look for trends in each table and draw conclusions. This can be done by looking at the values in each category and seeing how they vary with respect to each other. If you look at Tables 1 and 2, you can see that there is a direct variation between boiling point and molecular weight: as one increases, the other increases. Therefore, Statement I is correct, Statement II is false, and you can eliminate (B) and (D). Now consider Statement III. To investigate the relationship between molecular structure and boiling point, you have to keep the third variable—molecular weight—constant. Look at the data for two compounds with different molecular structures but the same molecular weight: N_2 and CO; their boiling points differ. Therefore, Statement III is correct, and (C) is the correct response.

14. (G)

In order to answer this question, you need to establish where C_6H_{14} would fit in Table 1. It is clear from Table 1 that the boiling point increases as the molecular weight increases, so the boiling point of C_6H_{14} will be between the boiling points of molecules with greater and lesser molecular weights. The molecular weight of C_6H_{14} is 86 g/mol, so it will lie between those hydrocarbons with molecular weights of 72 g/mol and 114 g/mol. Therefore, its boiling point will be between 36° C and 126° C. (G), with a value of 70° C, is the only choice that lies between these two boiling points.

15. (A)

N_2, a non-polar molecule, and CO, a polar molecule, have identical molecular weights and their boiling points differ by only 4° C. SiH_4 (non-polar) and PH_3 (polar) have nearly identical molecular weights as well, but the difference between their boiling points is 27° C—much greater than the difference between the boiling points of N_2 and CO, which have lower molecular weights than SiH_4 and PH_3. The difference between the boiling points of

polar and non-polar substances of similar molecular weight increases as molecular weight increases, so (A) is correct.

16. (H)

If you refer to Table 2, you'll see that for polar substances, as the molar weight goes from 78 to 162, the boiling point goes from −55° C to 97° C. You know the molar weight has to be somewhere between 78 and 162, so (F) is clearly out, and (G), 80, is too close to 78 to be the answer. You would expect the molar weight to be closer to 78 than 162, since 0 is closer to −55 than 97. Therefore, (J), 132, is out, and (H) is the answer.

Passage IV

17. (A)

The question refers to Experiment 2 only, so the correct answer will involve sunlight. Table 2 shows that the average length of the leaves increased from 5.3 cm to 12.4 cm as the amount of sunlight increased from 0 to 3 hours per day. But as the amount of sunlight increased further, leaf size decreased. Therefore, (D) is incorrect. Neither humidity (B) nor water (C) is relevant to Experiment 2.

18. (G)

Table 1 gives leaf widths at 35% and 55% humidity as 1.8 cm and 2.0 cm, respectively. The leaf width at 40% humidity would most likely be between those two figures. (G) is the only choice within that range.

19. (B)

All the answer choices involve humidity and sunlight, which were investigated in Experiments 1 and 2, respectively. In Table 1, leaf length and width were greatest at 75% humidity. In Table 2, they were greatest at 3 hours per day of sunlight. Combining those two conditions, as in (B), would probably produce the largest leaves.

20. (F)

This question relates to the method of the study. Each experiment begins with a statement that 5 groups of seedlings were used. Therefore, (F) is correct. The other answer choices list variables that were manipulated.

21. (D)

(D) is an assumption that underlies the design of all three experiments. If the seedlings were not equally capable of further growth, then changes in leaf size and density could not be reliably attributed to researcher-controlled changes in humidity, sunlight, and temperature. (A) is wrong because all the seedlings were 2–3 cm tall. The seedlings' abilities to germinate (B) or to produce flowers (C) were not mentioned in the passage.

22. (H)

Each of the three experiments investigated a different factor. To produce the most useful new data, researchers would probably vary a fourth condition. Soil mineral content would be an appropriate factor to examine. None of the other choices relate directly to the purpose of the experiments as expressed in paragraph 1 of the passage.

PASSAGE V

23. (B)

According to the table, decreasing the cross-sectional area of a given wire always increases resistance, so (B) is correct. (C) is wrong because resistivity, displayed in the second column, is constant for each material and thus cannot be responsible for variations in resistance for any given material.

Gauge varies inversely with cross-sectional area, so (D) is incorrect.

24. (G)

Because resistance varies inversely with cross-sectional area A, as discussed in the previous explanation, the correct answer to this question must place A in the denominator. The only choice that does so is (G).

25. (D)

Compare the choices two at a time. The wires in (A) and (B) are made of the same material and have the same cross-sectional area; only their length is different. Doubling the length doubles the resistance, so (B) would have a higher resistance than (A). By similar reasoning, (D) would have a higher resistance than (C). The only difference between (B) and (D) is the material. Even though the research team didn't test wire with a 0.33 mm^2 crosssectional area, it's safe to assume that the tungsten wire would have a higher resistance than the aluminum one.

26. (J)

The larger circle represents 10-gauge wire; its diameter is 2.59 mm. The smaller circle has a diameter of only 1.29 mm, but it represents 16-gauge wire, so Statement I is true, and you can eliminate choices (G) and (H) without even checking Statements II or III. To check Statement III, the table shows that the resistance of an iron (Fe) wire is much higher than that of an aluminum (Al) wire with the same length and cross-sectional area. The first sentence of paragraph 1 defined the resistance of a conductor as "the extent to which it opposes the flow of electricity." Since iron has a higher resistance than aluminum, iron must not conduct electricity as well. Therefore, Statement III is true, and (J) is correct.

27. (D)

The data indicate that the resistivity of a material doesn't change when wire length changes. Therefore, the graph of resistivity versus length for tungsten (or any other) wire is a horizontal line.

PASSAGE VI

28. (F)

To answer this question, you have to refer to the examples presented by the scientists to find a point of agreement. Both use the example of giraffes to show how scarcity of food and the need to reach higher and higher branches led to the evolution of long necks; thus, they both agree that environment affects evolution.

29. (C)

This Principle question requires that you figure out how new evidence affects the two hypotheses. To answer it, all you have to consider are the hypotheses of the two scientists. Scientist 2 believes that characteristics acquired by an individual over a lifetime are passed on to its offspring, a theory that would be supported by this finding.

30. (J)

This question requires some reasoning. Scientist 2 states that all of the changes that occur in an individual's life can be passed on to offspring. Since he believes that any characteristic can undergo change, he must also believe that any characteristic can be inherited.

31. (B)

You don't need any information other than the hypotheses of Scientist 1 to answer this question. He believes that random mutations continually occur within a species as it propagates, and that advantageous mutations, such as long necks on giraffes, help the species adapt to environmental changes, and thus become more prevalent within the species, which is what (B) states.

32. (G)

Here you don't need any information other than the hypotheses of the two scientists. The crux of their disagreement is over how evolution occurs—whether through random mutations or through the inheritance of acquired characteristics.

33. (B)

Recall that Scientist 2 states that evolution occurs through the inheritance of acquired characteristics. In order to account for humans possessing nerve endings now that were not present before the discovery of fire, Scientist 2 would have to believe that new nerve endings could be acquired during a single lifetime. Choice (B) directly contradicts this idea and would therefore refute the hypothesis.

34. (F)

Recall that Scientist 1 explains that evolution occurs as a result of random mutation, while Scientist 2 credits the inheritance of acquired characteristics. Choice (G) can then be eliminated, since it is related to the explanation of the wrong scientist. Choice (H) would actually refute Scientist 1's hypothesis, and choice (J) is irrelevant. Only choice (F) provides a valid explanation for the increase in average height based on the random mutations described by Scientist 1.

PASSAGE VII

35 (D)

In Experiment 1, the researchers vary what is fed to the cows by giving them meat from scrapie-free sheep and from scrapie-infected sheep. The cows are later examined for signs of BSE. One common type of wrong answer choice for Experiment questions are choices, such as choice (B) for this question, that include factors that are outside the parameters of the experiment.

36. (F)

In Experiment 2, the researchers vary what is injected into cows' brains. Any answer choice that discusses ingestion as a focus of this experiment is wrong. This eliminates (G), (H), and (J). Often, wrong answer choices for Experiment questions, such as choice (G) for this question, will include the appropriate information from the wrong experiment.

37. (B)

By examining the method used in a given experiment, one can determine the assumptions the researchers made in carrying out the experiment and the sources of error. Often, an error enters the experiment because of the assumptions researchers make. In Experiments 1 and 2, the researchers examined the brains of cows a year and a half after the cows were fed scrapie-infected sheep meat or were injected with scrapie-infected sheep brains. If a year and a half is not a sufficient amount of time for BSE to develop, some of the cows that were counted as not infected might have developed BSE if they had been given more time.

38. (H)

To answer this question, you need to determine how to test whether BSE can be transmitted via scrapie-infected goats. To test this one would compare the effects of feeding cows scrapie-free goat meat with the effects of feeding cows scrapie-infected goat meat and compare the effects of injecting cows with scrapie-free goat brains with the effects of injecting them with scrapie-infected goat brains.

39. (A)

Remember that control groups are used as standards of comparison. The control group used in Experiment 1 is the group that is fed scrapie-free sheep meat. If the same proportion of Group A developed BSE as that of Group B, then the researchers would not have any evidence to support the hypothesis that the ingestion of scrapie-infected sheep meat causes BSE.

40. (G)

Since the proportion of the group of cows that ate scrapie-infected sheep meat and developed BSE was greater than the proportion of the group that were injected with scrapie-infected sheep brains and developed BSE, one can conclude that a cow that eats scrapie-infected sheep meat is more likely to develop BSE than a cow that is injected with scrapie-infected sheep brains. Mere exposure to scrapie-infected sheep, as opposed to ingestion thereof, is never studied in either experiment, so conclusion I can be eliminated.

WRITING TEST

MODEL ESSAY

Below is an example of what a high-scoring essay might look like. Notice the author states her position clearly in the introductory paragraph and supports that position with evidence in the following paragraphs. This essay also uses transitions, some advanced vocabulary, and an effective "hook" to draw in the reader.

When people think about what students should learn in high school, they often focus on "the three Rs": reading, writing, and arithmetic. It's true that in an increasingly competitive global economy, those skills are more important than ever. However, in our society's rush to make sure students are keeping up through required standardized testing and increased computer education, are we forgetting another important aspect of education? Are we forgetting to teach our students how to think creatively and express themselves artistically? I think that requiring all high school students to take music or visual arts classes would benefit our country's students in several ways.

Learning about art and music actually helps students do better in other subjects. People often forget that studying art or music isn't just about putting paint to canvas or lips to trumpet. There is a lot of background information that students learn as well. When students study music they also have to learn a lot of history: who was the composer, where was he or she from, what was happening politically and socially during the time the music was composed, and how does the work compare historically to music by other composers. The same holds true for the visual arts; students can learn a lot from art history, not just about the artist but also about different cultures and time periods. Studies have shown that students who take music classes do better at math, maybe because these classes emphasize dividing up measures of music and counting out times.

With so much focus on standardized test scores and grade point averages, schools today emphasize individual academic performance and overlook the teaching of teamwork skills. Through playing in my high school's band, I have learned that even though it is important for me to practice so that I can play my best (and maybe move up a chair), what really matters is how we sound as a group. My bandmates and I push each other to succeed, and we get together outside of school to practice for big games and competitions. Band is also where I have made most of my friends. Participation in the arts is a great way for students to build social skills and create school spirit. It teaches students to help one another so that going to school isn't just about getting good grades for one's own benefit.

Learning about art or music is also helpful to students because it teaches them how to think creatively. When you take a photograph or paint a portrait you have to look at things in a new way, and you must try to synthesize your perception into a medium that other people can relate to. Between all the pressure to do well academically and all the social pressure teenagers face to fit in, being a teenager can be really stressful. Art and music can allow students to express their feelings in a positive, constructive way. Such classes can give students who aren't good at traditional academic subjects like math or science a chance to shine.

In conclusion, I think requiring all high school students to take music or visual arts classes would help students not only academically but socially and emotionally as well. Studying the arts actually helps students succeed in traditional subject areas, builds their confidence and social skills, and gives them the opportunity to learn to think creatively, all skills that will help them once they reach the workforce.

You can evaluate your essay and the model essay based on the following criteria, covered in chapter 16.

- Does the author answer the question?

- Is the author's position clearly stated?

- Does the body of the essay support and develop the position taken?

- Are there at least three supporting paragraphs?

- Is the essay a reasonable length?

- Is the essay organized, with a clear introduction, middle, and end?

- Did the author use one paragraph for each new idea?

- Is each sentence in a paragraph relevant to the point made in that paragraph?

- Are transitions clear?

- Is the essay easy to read? Is it engaging?

- Are sentences varied?

- Is vocabulary used effectively? Is college-level vocabulary used?

PRACTICE TEST TWO

ACT Practice Test Two
Answer Sheet

English Test

10. Ⓕ Ⓖ Ⓗ Ⓙ   20. Ⓕ Ⓖ Ⓗ Ⓙ   30. Ⓕ Ⓖ Ⓗ Ⓙ   40. Ⓕ Ⓖ Ⓗ Ⓙ   50. Ⓕ Ⓖ Ⓗ Ⓙ   60. Ⓕ Ⓖ Ⓗ Ⓙ   70. Ⓕ Ⓖ Ⓗ Ⓙ
1. Ⓐ Ⓑ Ⓒ Ⓓ   11. Ⓐ Ⓑ Ⓒ Ⓓ   21. Ⓐ Ⓑ Ⓒ Ⓓ   31. Ⓐ Ⓑ Ⓒ Ⓓ   41. Ⓐ Ⓑ Ⓒ Ⓓ   51. Ⓐ Ⓑ Ⓒ Ⓓ   61. Ⓐ Ⓑ Ⓒ Ⓓ   71. Ⓐ Ⓑ Ⓒ Ⓓ
2. Ⓕ Ⓖ Ⓗ Ⓙ   12. Ⓕ Ⓖ Ⓗ Ⓙ   22. Ⓕ Ⓖ Ⓗ Ⓙ   32. Ⓕ Ⓖ Ⓗ Ⓙ   42. Ⓕ Ⓖ Ⓗ Ⓙ   52. Ⓕ Ⓖ Ⓗ Ⓙ   62. Ⓕ Ⓖ Ⓗ Ⓙ   72. Ⓕ Ⓖ Ⓗ Ⓙ
3. Ⓐ Ⓑ Ⓒ Ⓓ   13. Ⓐ Ⓑ Ⓒ Ⓓ   23. Ⓐ Ⓑ Ⓒ Ⓓ   33. Ⓐ Ⓑ Ⓒ Ⓓ   43. Ⓐ Ⓑ Ⓒ Ⓓ   53. Ⓐ Ⓑ Ⓒ Ⓓ   63. Ⓐ Ⓑ Ⓒ Ⓓ   73. Ⓐ Ⓑ Ⓒ Ⓓ
4. Ⓕ Ⓖ Ⓗ Ⓙ   14. Ⓕ Ⓖ Ⓗ Ⓙ   24. Ⓕ Ⓖ Ⓗ Ⓙ   34. Ⓕ Ⓖ Ⓗ Ⓙ   44. Ⓕ Ⓖ Ⓗ Ⓙ   54. Ⓕ Ⓖ Ⓗ Ⓙ   64. Ⓕ Ⓖ Ⓗ Ⓙ   74. Ⓕ Ⓖ Ⓗ Ⓙ
5. Ⓐ Ⓑ Ⓒ Ⓓ   15. Ⓐ Ⓑ Ⓒ Ⓓ   25. Ⓐ Ⓑ Ⓒ Ⓓ   35. Ⓐ Ⓑ Ⓒ Ⓓ   45. Ⓐ Ⓑ Ⓒ Ⓓ   55. Ⓐ Ⓑ Ⓒ Ⓓ   65. Ⓐ Ⓑ Ⓒ Ⓓ   75. Ⓐ Ⓑ Ⓒ Ⓓ
6. Ⓕ Ⓖ Ⓗ Ⓙ   16. Ⓕ Ⓖ Ⓗ Ⓙ   26. Ⓕ Ⓖ Ⓗ Ⓙ   36. Ⓕ Ⓖ Ⓗ Ⓙ   46. Ⓕ Ⓖ Ⓗ Ⓙ   56. Ⓕ Ⓖ Ⓗ Ⓙ   66. Ⓕ Ⓖ Ⓗ Ⓙ
7. Ⓐ Ⓑ Ⓒ Ⓓ   17. Ⓐ Ⓑ Ⓒ Ⓓ   27. Ⓐ Ⓑ Ⓒ Ⓓ   37. Ⓐ Ⓑ Ⓒ Ⓓ   47. Ⓐ Ⓑ Ⓒ Ⓓ   57. Ⓐ Ⓑ Ⓒ Ⓓ   67. Ⓐ Ⓑ Ⓒ Ⓓ
8. Ⓕ Ⓖ Ⓗ Ⓙ   18. Ⓕ Ⓖ Ⓗ Ⓙ   28. Ⓕ Ⓖ Ⓗ Ⓙ   38. Ⓕ Ⓖ Ⓗ Ⓙ   48. Ⓕ Ⓖ Ⓗ Ⓙ   58. Ⓕ Ⓖ Ⓗ Ⓙ   68. Ⓕ Ⓖ Ⓗ Ⓙ
9. Ⓐ Ⓑ Ⓒ Ⓓ   19. Ⓐ Ⓑ Ⓒ Ⓓ   29. Ⓐ Ⓑ Ⓒ Ⓓ   39. Ⓐ Ⓑ Ⓒ Ⓓ   49. Ⓐ Ⓑ Ⓒ Ⓓ   59. Ⓐ Ⓑ Ⓒ Ⓓ   69. Ⓐ Ⓑ Ⓒ Ⓓ

Math Test

9. Ⓐ Ⓑ Ⓒ Ⓓ Ⓔ   18. Ⓕ Ⓖ Ⓗ Ⓙ Ⓚ   27. Ⓐ Ⓑ Ⓒ Ⓓ Ⓔ   36. Ⓕ Ⓖ Ⓗ Ⓙ Ⓚ   45. Ⓐ Ⓑ Ⓒ Ⓓ Ⓔ   54. Ⓕ Ⓖ Ⓗ Ⓙ Ⓚ
1. Ⓐ Ⓑ Ⓒ Ⓓ Ⓔ   10. Ⓕ Ⓖ Ⓗ Ⓙ Ⓚ   19. Ⓐ Ⓑ Ⓒ Ⓓ Ⓔ   28. Ⓕ Ⓖ Ⓗ Ⓙ Ⓚ   37. Ⓐ Ⓑ Ⓒ Ⓓ Ⓔ   46. Ⓕ Ⓖ Ⓗ Ⓙ Ⓚ   55. Ⓐ Ⓑ Ⓒ Ⓓ Ⓔ
2. Ⓕ Ⓖ Ⓗ Ⓙ Ⓚ   11. Ⓐ Ⓑ Ⓒ Ⓓ Ⓔ   20. Ⓕ Ⓖ Ⓗ Ⓙ Ⓚ   29. Ⓐ Ⓑ Ⓒ Ⓓ Ⓔ   38. Ⓕ Ⓖ Ⓗ Ⓙ Ⓚ   47. Ⓐ Ⓑ Ⓒ Ⓓ Ⓔ   56. Ⓕ Ⓖ Ⓗ Ⓙ Ⓚ
3. Ⓐ Ⓑ Ⓒ Ⓓ Ⓔ   12. Ⓕ Ⓖ Ⓗ Ⓙ Ⓚ   21. Ⓐ Ⓑ Ⓒ Ⓓ Ⓔ   30. Ⓕ Ⓖ Ⓗ Ⓙ Ⓚ   39. Ⓐ Ⓑ Ⓒ Ⓓ Ⓔ   48. Ⓕ Ⓖ Ⓗ Ⓙ Ⓚ   57. Ⓐ Ⓑ Ⓒ Ⓓ Ⓔ
4. Ⓕ Ⓖ Ⓗ Ⓙ Ⓚ   13. Ⓐ Ⓑ Ⓒ Ⓓ Ⓔ   22. Ⓕ Ⓖ Ⓗ Ⓙ Ⓚ   31. Ⓐ Ⓑ Ⓒ Ⓓ Ⓔ   40. Ⓕ Ⓖ Ⓗ Ⓙ Ⓚ   49. Ⓐ Ⓑ Ⓒ Ⓓ Ⓔ   58. Ⓕ Ⓖ Ⓗ Ⓙ Ⓚ
5. Ⓐ Ⓑ Ⓒ Ⓓ Ⓔ   14. Ⓕ Ⓖ Ⓗ Ⓙ Ⓚ   23. Ⓐ Ⓑ Ⓒ Ⓓ Ⓔ   32. Ⓕ Ⓖ Ⓗ Ⓙ Ⓚ   41. Ⓐ Ⓑ Ⓒ Ⓓ Ⓔ   50. Ⓕ Ⓖ Ⓗ Ⓙ Ⓚ   59. Ⓐ Ⓑ Ⓒ Ⓓ Ⓔ
6. Ⓕ Ⓖ Ⓗ Ⓙ Ⓚ   15. Ⓐ Ⓑ Ⓒ Ⓓ Ⓔ   24. Ⓕ Ⓖ Ⓗ Ⓙ Ⓚ   33. Ⓐ Ⓑ Ⓒ Ⓓ Ⓔ   42. Ⓕ Ⓖ Ⓗ Ⓙ Ⓚ   51. Ⓐ Ⓑ Ⓒ Ⓓ Ⓔ   60. Ⓕ Ⓖ Ⓗ Ⓙ Ⓚ
7. Ⓐ Ⓑ Ⓒ Ⓓ Ⓔ   16. Ⓕ Ⓖ Ⓗ Ⓙ Ⓚ   25. Ⓐ Ⓑ Ⓒ Ⓓ Ⓔ   34. Ⓕ Ⓖ Ⓗ Ⓙ Ⓚ   43. Ⓐ Ⓑ Ⓒ Ⓓ Ⓔ   52. Ⓕ Ⓖ Ⓗ Ⓙ Ⓚ
8. Ⓕ Ⓖ Ⓗ Ⓙ Ⓚ   17. Ⓐ Ⓑ Ⓒ Ⓓ Ⓔ   26. Ⓕ Ⓖ Ⓗ Ⓙ Ⓚ   35. Ⓐ Ⓑ Ⓒ Ⓓ Ⓔ   44. Ⓕ Ⓖ Ⓗ Ⓙ Ⓚ   53. Ⓐ Ⓑ Ⓒ Ⓓ Ⓔ

Reading Test

6. Ⓕ Ⓖ Ⓗ Ⓙ   12. Ⓕ Ⓖ Ⓗ Ⓙ   18. Ⓕ Ⓖ Ⓗ Ⓙ   24. Ⓕ Ⓖ Ⓗ Ⓙ   30. Ⓕ Ⓖ Ⓗ Ⓙ   36. Ⓕ Ⓖ Ⓗ Ⓙ
1. Ⓐ Ⓑ Ⓒ Ⓓ   7. Ⓐ Ⓑ Ⓒ Ⓓ   13. Ⓐ Ⓑ Ⓒ Ⓓ   19. Ⓐ Ⓑ Ⓒ Ⓓ   25. Ⓐ Ⓑ Ⓒ Ⓓ   31. Ⓐ Ⓑ Ⓒ Ⓓ   37. Ⓐ Ⓑ Ⓒ Ⓓ
2. Ⓕ Ⓖ Ⓗ Ⓙ   8. Ⓕ Ⓖ Ⓗ Ⓙ   14. Ⓕ Ⓖ Ⓗ Ⓙ   20. Ⓕ Ⓖ Ⓗ Ⓙ   26. Ⓕ Ⓖ Ⓗ Ⓙ   32. Ⓕ Ⓖ Ⓗ Ⓙ   38. Ⓕ Ⓖ Ⓗ Ⓙ
3. Ⓐ Ⓑ Ⓒ Ⓓ   9. Ⓐ Ⓑ Ⓒ Ⓓ   15. Ⓐ Ⓑ Ⓒ Ⓓ   21. Ⓐ Ⓑ Ⓒ Ⓓ   27. Ⓐ Ⓑ Ⓒ Ⓓ   33. Ⓐ Ⓑ Ⓒ Ⓓ   39. Ⓐ Ⓑ Ⓒ Ⓓ
4. Ⓕ Ⓖ Ⓗ Ⓙ   10. Ⓕ Ⓖ Ⓗ Ⓙ   16. Ⓕ Ⓖ Ⓗ Ⓙ   22. Ⓕ Ⓖ Ⓗ Ⓙ   28. Ⓕ Ⓖ Ⓗ Ⓙ   34. Ⓕ Ⓖ Ⓗ Ⓙ   40. Ⓕ Ⓖ Ⓗ Ⓙ
5. Ⓐ Ⓑ Ⓒ Ⓓ   11. Ⓐ Ⓑ Ⓒ Ⓓ   17. Ⓐ Ⓑ Ⓒ Ⓓ   23. Ⓐ Ⓑ Ⓒ Ⓓ   29. Ⓐ Ⓑ Ⓒ Ⓓ   35. Ⓐ Ⓑ Ⓒ Ⓓ

Science Test

6. Ⓕ Ⓖ Ⓗ Ⓙ   12. Ⓕ Ⓖ Ⓗ Ⓙ   18. Ⓕ Ⓖ Ⓗ Ⓙ   24. Ⓕ Ⓖ Ⓗ Ⓙ   30. Ⓕ Ⓖ Ⓗ Ⓙ   36. Ⓕ Ⓖ Ⓗ Ⓙ
1. Ⓐ Ⓑ Ⓒ Ⓓ   7. Ⓐ Ⓑ Ⓒ Ⓓ   13. Ⓐ Ⓑ Ⓒ Ⓓ   19. Ⓐ Ⓑ Ⓒ Ⓓ   25. Ⓐ Ⓑ Ⓒ Ⓓ   31. Ⓐ Ⓑ Ⓒ Ⓓ   37. Ⓐ Ⓑ Ⓒ Ⓓ
2. Ⓕ Ⓖ Ⓗ Ⓙ   8. Ⓕ Ⓖ Ⓗ Ⓙ   14. Ⓕ Ⓖ Ⓗ Ⓙ   20. Ⓕ Ⓖ Ⓗ Ⓙ   26. Ⓕ Ⓖ Ⓗ Ⓙ   32. Ⓕ Ⓖ Ⓗ Ⓙ   38. Ⓕ Ⓖ Ⓗ Ⓙ
3. Ⓐ Ⓑ Ⓒ Ⓓ   9. Ⓐ Ⓑ Ⓒ Ⓓ   15. Ⓐ Ⓑ Ⓒ Ⓓ   21. Ⓐ Ⓑ Ⓒ Ⓓ   27. Ⓐ Ⓑ Ⓒ Ⓓ   33. Ⓐ Ⓑ Ⓒ Ⓓ   39. Ⓐ Ⓑ Ⓒ Ⓓ
4. Ⓕ Ⓖ Ⓗ Ⓙ   10. Ⓕ Ⓖ Ⓗ Ⓙ   16. Ⓕ Ⓖ Ⓗ Ⓙ   22. Ⓕ Ⓖ Ⓗ Ⓙ   28. Ⓕ Ⓖ Ⓗ Ⓙ   34. Ⓕ Ⓖ Ⓗ Ⓙ   40. Ⓕ Ⓖ Ⓗ Ⓙ
5. Ⓐ Ⓑ Ⓒ Ⓓ   11. Ⓐ Ⓑ Ⓒ Ⓓ   17. Ⓐ Ⓑ Ⓒ Ⓓ   23. Ⓐ Ⓑ Ⓒ Ⓓ   29. Ⓐ Ⓑ Ⓒ Ⓓ   35. Ⓐ Ⓑ Ⓒ Ⓓ

ENGLISH TEST
45 Minutes—75 Questions

Directions: In the following five passages, certain words and phrases have been underlined and numbered. You will find alternatives for each underlined portion in the right-hand column. Select the one that best expresses the idea, that makes the statement acceptable in standard written English, or that is phrased most consistently with the style and tone of the entire passage. If you feel that the original version is best, select "NO CHANGE." You will also find questions asking about a section of the passage or about the entire passage. For these questions, decide which choice gives the most appropriate response to the given question. For each question in the test, select the best choice, and fill in the corresponding space on the answer sheet. You may wish to read each passage through before you begin to answer the questions associated with it. Most answers cannot be determined without reading several sentences around the phrases in question. Make sure to read far enough ahead each time you choose an alternative.

PASSAGE I

[1]

By the time Duke Ellington published his autobiography, *Music is My Mistress* in 1973 he had traveled to
₁
dozens of countries and every continent. "I pay rent in
New York City," he answered when asked of his residence.

1. A. NO CHANGE
    B. 1973. He had
    C. 1973, it had
    D. 1973, he had

[2]

In the 1920s though, Ellington pays more than rent
₂
in New York; he paid his dues on the bandstand. Having
moved to Harlem from Washington, D.C., in 1923,
Ellington established: his own band and achieved critical
₃
recognition with a polished sound and appearance. The
first New York review of the Ellingtonians in 1923 com-
mented, "The boys look neat in dress suits and labor
hard but not in vain at their music." As Ellington made

2. F. NO CHANGE
    G. paid
    H. has to pay
    J. pay

3. A. NO CHANGE
    B. established the following: his own
    C. established his own
    D. took the time and effort to establish his own

GO ON TO THE NEXT PAGE →

a name for himself as a leader arranger and pianist, his
                              4
Harlem Renaissance compositions and recordings

highlighted two enduring characteristics of the man.

First, Ellington lived for jazz. Second, Harlem

sustained it, physically and spiritually.
            5

[3]

Ellington himself admitted he was not a very good
                                              6
pianist. As a teenager in Washington. He missed more
   6
piano lessons then he took with his teacher, Mrs.
         7
Clinkscales, and spent more time going to dances

than practicing the piano. Mrs. Clinkscales was really
                                    8
the name of his piano teacher! In the clubs,
   8
therefore, Ellington and his friends eventually caught
   9
word of New York and the opportunities that awaited
                                         10
and were there for young musicians. Ellington wrote,
   10
"Harlem, to our minds, did indeed have the world's most

4. F. NO CHANGE
    G. leader arranger, and pianist,
    H. leader, arranger, and pianist
    J. leader, arranger, and pianist,

5. A. NO CHANGE
    B. him,
    C. them,
    D. itself,

6. F. NO CHANGE
    G. good pianist as a teenager
    H. good pianist, a teenager
    J. good pianist, as a teenager

7. A. NO CHANGE
    B. lessons then he had taken
    C. lessons; he took
    D. lessons than he took

8. F. NO CHANGE
    G. That was really the name of his piano
        teacher: Mrs. Clinkscales!
    H. Mrs. Clinkscales was really the name of
        his piano teacher.
    J. OMIT the underlined portion.

9. A. NO CHANGE
    B. however
    C. despite
    D. then

10. F. NO CHANGE
    G. awaiting and being there for
    H. that awaited
    J. which were there for

GO ON TO THE NEXT PAGE

glamorous atmosphere. We had to go there." <u>He left</u>
<u>Washington with drummer Sonny Greer.</u> Before they
11

could even unpack in Harlem, though, they found them-

selves penniless. Not until Ellington was lucky enough

to find fifteen dollars on the street could he return to

Washington and recollect himself.

[4]

Ellington eventually did return to Harlem, and he

achieved great success as the bandleader at the Cotton

Club from 1927 to 1932. Located in the heart of Harlem

at 142nd Street and Lenox Avenue, <u>he played at the</u>
12
<u>Cotton Club, which was frequented</u> by top entertainers
12

and rich patrons. Harlem's nightlife, "cut out of a very

luxurious, royal-blue bolt of velvet," was an inspirational

backdrop, and Ellington composed, arranged, and

recorded prolifically to the rave of excited critical

acclaim. "Black and Tan Fantasy," "Hot and Bothered,"

and "Rockin' in Rhythm" were Ellington's early hits

during this period. [13] They exhibited his unique ability

to compose music that animated both dancers in search

of a good time and improvising musicians in search of

good music. Before long, the once fumbling pianist

from Washington, D.C., became the undisputed leader

of hot jazz in decadent Harlem. [14]

11. **A.** NO CHANGE
   B. With drummer Sonny Greer, it was Washington that he left.
   C. Leaving Washington, he, Ellington, left with drummer Sonny Greer.
   D. OMIT the underlined portion.

12. **F.** NO CHANGE
   G. he played at the Cotton Club, a club that was frequented
   H. the Cotton Club, which was frequented
   J. the Cotton Club was frequented

13. The purpose of including the names of Ellington's songs is to:
   A. provide some details about Ellington's early music.
   B. contradict an earlier point that Ellington did not create his own music.
   C. illustrate the complexity of Ellington's music.
   D. discuss the atmosphere at the Cotton Club.

14. The purpose of paragraph 4, as it relates to the previous paragraphs, is primarily to:
   F. demonstrate how accomplished Ellington had become.
   G. suggest that Ellington did not like living in New York.
   H. remind us how difficult it is to be a musician.
   J. make us skeptical of Ellington's abilities.

GO ON TO THE NEXT PAGE ⟶

Question 15 asks about the preceding passage as a whole.

15. The writer wishes to insert the following detail into the essay:

> The combination of fun and seriousness in his music led to critical acclaim and wide mass appeal.

The sentence would most logically be inserted into paragraph:

A. 1, after the last sentence.

B. 3, before the first sentence.

C. 4, after the first sentence.

D. 4, before the last sentence.

Passage II

The paragraphs in this passage may not be in the most logical order. Each paragraph is numbered in brackets, and question 29 will ask you to choose the appropriate order.

[1]

Some animals change <u>its</u> coloring with the seasons.
16

The ptarmigan sheds its brown plumage <u>in winter,</u>
17

<u>replacing</u> it with white feathers. The stoat, a member of
17

the <u>weasel family is known</u> as the *ermine* in winter
18

because its brown fur changes to white. The chameleon

is perhaps the most versatile of all animals <u>which change</u>
19

their protective coloration. The chameleon changes its

color in just a few minutes to whatever surface it

happens to be sitting on.

16. F. NO CHANGE

G. their

H. it's

J. there

17. A. NO CHANGE

B. winter and replacing

C. winter: replacing

D. winter replacing

18. F. NO CHANGE

G. weasel family known

H. weasel family, which is known

J. weasel family, is known

19. A. NO CHANGE

B. who changes

C. that change

D. that changed

GO ON TO THE NEXT PAGE

[2]

While animals like the chameleon use their coloring
                                                    20
as a way of hiding from predators, the skunk uses its

distinctive white stripe as a way of standing out from

its surroundings. Far from placing it in danger; the
                                                21
skunk's visibility actually protects it. By distinguishing
   21
itself from other animals. The skunk warns its
                      22
predators to avoid its infamous stink. Think about it:

the question is would your appetite be whetted by the
                                                23
skunk's odor?
   23

[3]

Researchers have been investigating how animal
                      24
species have come to use coloring as a means of protect-

ing themselves. One study has shown that certain animals

have glands that release special hormones, resulting in

the change of skin or fur color. Therefore, not all the
                                         25
 animals that camouflage themselves have these glands.

The topic remains and endures as one of the many
                  26
mysteries of the natural world.

20. F. NO CHANGE
    G. their use coloring
    H. use coloring their
    J. coloring their use

21. A. NO CHANGE
    B. danger, the skunk's
    C. danger; the skunks'
    D. danger, it is the skunk's

22. F. NO CHANGE
    G. animals, therefore, the
    H. animals because
    J. animals, the

23. A. NO CHANGE
    B. would your appetite be whetted by the
        skunk's odor?
    C. the question is as follows, would your
        appetite be whetted by the skunk's odor?
    D. the question is would your appetite be
        whetted by the odor of the skunk?

24. F. NO CHANGE
    G. investigated
    H. were investigating
    J. investigate

25. A. NO CHANGE
    B. Nevertheless,
    C. However,
    D. Finally,

26. F. NO CHANGE
    G. remaining and enduring as
    H   remains and endures
    J. remains

GO ON TO THE NEXT PAGE

[4]

Animals have a variety of ways of protecting themselves from enemies. Some animals adapt in shape and color to their environment. The tree frog, for example, blends perfectly into its surroundings. When it sits motionless, <u>a background of leaves completely hides</u>
27
<u>the tree frog.</u>
27
<u>This camouflage enables the tree frog to hide from other</u>
28
<u>animals that would be interested in eating the tree frog.</u>
28

27. A. NO CHANGE
    B. the tree frog is completely hidden in a background of leaves.
    C. completely hidden is the tree frog in a background of leaves.
    D. a background of leaves and the tree frog are completely hidden.

28. F. NO CHANGE
    G. This camouflage enables the tree frog to hide from predators.
    H. This camouflage enables the tree frog to hide from other animals interested in eating the tree frog.
    J. OMIT the underlined portion.

Items 29–30 ask about the passage as a whole.

---

29. What would be the most logical order of paragraphs for this essay?

    A. 3, 1, 4, 2
    B. 1, 2, 4, 3
    C. 4, 1, 2, 3
    D. 2, 1, 3, 4

30. Suppose the author had been asked to write an essay on how animals use their colorings to protect themselves in the wild. Would this essay meet the requirement?

    F. Yes, because the author covers several aspects of how animals use their colorings to protect themselves.
    G. Yes, because the author thoroughly investigates how one animal protects itself with its colorings.
    H. No, because the author does not consider animals that exist in the wild.
    J. No, because the author does not include information from research studies.

GO ON TO THE NEXT PAGE ⇒

PASSAGE III

The word *chocolate* is used to describe a variety of

<u>foods made</u> from the beans of the cacao tree. The first
  31

people known to have made chocolate were the <u>Aztecs, a</u>
                                                       32

<u>people who used</u> cacao seeds to make a bitter but tasty
    32

drink. However, it was not until Hernan Cortez's

exploration of Mexico in <u>1519. That</u> Europeans first
                   33

learned of chocolate.

Cortez came to the New World in search of gold,

but his interest was also fired by the Aztecs' strange drink.

When Cortez returned to Spain, his ship's cargo <u>included</u>
                                  34

<u>and held</u> three chests of cacao beans. It was from these
  34

beans that Europe experienced its first taste of what

<u>seemed to be</u> a very unusual beverage. The drink soon
  35

became popular among those people wealthy enough to

afford it. <u>Over the next century cafes specializing in</u>
          36

31. A. NO CHANGE
    B. foods, which are made
    C. foods and made
    D. foods and are

32. F. NO CHANGE
    G. Aztecs, and they used
    H. Aztecs a people that use
    J. Aztecs, who used

33. A. NO CHANGE
    B. 1519 that
    C. 1519, that
    D. 1519:

34. F. NO CHANGE
    G. included, held
    H. included
    J. including and holding

35. A. NO CHANGE
    B. seems to be
    C. seemingly is
    D. to seemed be

36. F. NO CHANGE
    G. Over the next century cafes specialize
    H. Over the next century, cafes specializing
    J. Over the next century, there were cafes
       specializing

GO ON TO THE NEXT PAGE ⟹

chocolate drinks began to appear throughout

Europe. [37]

   Of course, chocolate is very popular today. People all

over the world enjoy chocolate bars chocolate sprinkles
                                                    38
and even chocolate soda.
              38
In fact, Asia has cultivated the delicacy of chocolate-
  39
covered ants! People enjoy this food as a snack at the

movies or sporting events. The chocolate ant phenome-

non has yet to take over America, but enjoy their
                                              40
chocolate Americans do nonetheless.
              40
   Many chocolate lovers around the world were

ecstatic to hear that chocolate may actually be good for

you. Researchers say: chocolate contains a chemical that
                        41
could prevent cancer and heart disease. New research

measures the amount of catechins, the chemical thought

to be behind the benefits, in different types of chocolate.

37. The author is considering the addition of
    another sentence here that briefly describes
    one of the first European cafes to serve a
    chocolate drink. This addition would:

   A. weaken the author's argument.
   B. provide some interesting details.
   C. contradict the topic of the paragraph.
   D. highlight the author's opinion of
      chocolate.

38. F. NO CHANGE
    G. chocolate, bars, chocolate, sprinkles, and
        even chocolate soda.
    H. chocolate bars chocolate sprinkles—even
        chocolate soda.
    J. chocolate bars, chocolate sprinkles, and
        even chocolate soda.

39. A. NO CHANGE
    B. Unfortunately,
    C. In spite of this,
    D. The truth is,

40. F. NO CHANGE
    G. but Americans enjoy their chocolate
    H. but enjoy their chocolate is what
        Americans do
    J. but Americans do enjoy their chocolate

41. A. NO CHANGE
    B. have said the following: chocolate
        contains
    C. say that chocolate contains
    D. say: chocolate contained

GO ON TO THE NEXT PAGE ➔

The substance is also found in tea. The studies
42
show that chocolate is very high in catechins. The

research is likely to be welcomed by those with a sweet
43

tooth, although dentists may less be pleased.
44

Question 45 asks about the preceding passage
as a whole.

42. F.   NO CHANGE
    G.   Another place where the substance is
         found is tea.
    H.   Also, tea contains the substance.
    J.   OMIT the underlined portion.

43. A.   NO CHANGE
    B.   with them
    C.   by us
    D.   to those

44. F.   NO CHANGE
    G.   pleased less they will be.
    H.   may be pleased less.
    J.   may be less pleased.

45. Suppose the author had been given the
    assignment of writing about culinary trends
    in history. Would this essay satisfy the
    requirement?

    A.   Yes, because the essay discusses many
         culinary trends in history.
    B.   Yes, because the essay shows how choco-
         late has been used over time.
    C.   No, because the essay focuses too much
         on chocolate in present times.
    D.   No, because the essay only covers
         chocolate.

GO ON TO THE NEXT PAGE

PASSAGE IV

[1]

Scientists, in programs administers by the
46
United States Army, are experimenting to develop the

military uniform of the future. As imagined, it would
47
be light as silk, bulletproof, and able to rapidly
47
change at the molecular level to adapt to biological or

chemical threats. In response to a detected anthrax

threat, for example, it would become an impermeable

shield. The pant leg of a soldier who's leg had been
48
broken would have been able to morph into
49
a splint, or, even form an artificial muscle.
50
Nanosensors would transmit vital signs back to a

medical team, or monitor the breath for increased

nitric oxide, a sign of stress.

46. F.   NO CHANGE
    G.   administering by
    H.   administered by
    J.   administers with

47. A.   NO CHANGE
    B.   would: be light as silk, bulletproof, and able to
    C.   would be light as silk bulletproof and able to
    D.   light as silk, bulletproof, and was able to

48. F.   NO CHANGE
    G.   soldier whose
    H.   soldier, who's
    J.   soldier that's

49. A.   NO CHANGE
    B.   would be
    C.   will have been
    D.   is

50. F.   NO CHANGE
    G.   splint or even form
    H.   splint, or even, form
    J.   splint or, even, form

GO ON TO THE NEXT PAGE

[2]

The especially promising Invisible Soldier

program aims to make the long-held dream of human

invisibility a reality by using technology. To create
                                        _____
                                            51
a covering capable of concealing a soldier and
                       _____
                                    52
making him invisible from most wavelengths of
_____
        52
visible light. 53 54

[3]

A solution proposed in the early stages near the
                             _____
                                     55
beginning of the program's development would
_____
     55
construct a suit or cape from fabric linked to sensors

that can detect the coloring and pattern of the

background. The sensors would then send varying

intensities of electrical current to the appropriate areas

of the fabric, they would be impregnated with
              ____
               56
chemicals sensitive to electricity. The coveralls would

change colors continually as the soldier moved.

51. A. NO CHANGE
    B. technology to create
    C. technology, which were creating
    D. technology; create

52. F. NO CHANGE
    G. making a soldier invisible and concealing him
    H. concealing a soldier making that soldier invisible
    J. concealing a soldier

53. The writer's description of the U.S. Army's Invisible Soldier program seems to indicate that the army's opinion of the program is:
    A. skeptical
    B. curious
    C. enthusiastic
    D. detailed

54. What is the purpose of this paragraph, as it relate to the rest of the essay?
    F. To highlight one of the successes of the scientists' programs
    G. To predict the future of U.S. military uniforms
    H. To outline what will follow in the essay
    J. To introduce a specific example of the uniform of the future

55. A. NO CHANGE
    B. beginning and the early stages of
    C. early stages of
    D. OMIT the underlined portion.

56. F. NO CHANGE
    G. that
    H. it
    J. which

GO ON TO THE NEXT PAGE

[4]

The problem with this solution from a military

standpoint, you know, is power: the fact that the suit
                57   58

would require a continuous flow of electricity means

that a soldier would have to carry a large number of

batteries, which would hardly contribute to ease of

movement and camouflage.

[5]

[1] But army researchers have developed a new kind of

color-changing pixel, known as the intererometric

modulator or i-mod, that may successfully address this

problem. [2] The researchers hope that a flexible suit

made of i-mod pixels could completely blend into any

background. [3] In addition to matching a background,

the pixels could also be set to show other colors, for

example, a camouflage mode that would render a sol-

dier effectively invisible in the forest and a flash mode

that would enhance a soldier's visibility in a rescue sit-

uation. [4] Changing the distance between the mirrors

changes the color of the light that they reflect. [5] Each

i-mod pixel is made up of a pair of tiny mirrors. 59

57. A. NO CHANGE
    B. is, like,
    C. however, is
    D. therefore, is

58. F. NO CHANGE
    G. power; the fact that the suit
    H. power the fact that the suit
    J. power the fact that, the suit

59. Which of the following sequences will make
    paragraph 5 most logical?
    A. 2, 4, 5, 3, 1
    B. 2, 3, 1, 5, 4
    C. 1, 4, 5, 2, 3
    D. 1, 5, 4, 2, 3

Question 60 asks about the preceding passage
as a whole.

60. The writer wishes to insert the following
    material into the passage:
    "When H.G. Wells wrote *The Invisible Man*,
    there was no interest in camouflaging soldiers;
    the British army was garbed in bright red
    uniforms. Since that time, governments have
    learned the value of making soldiers difficult
    to see, first by using camouflage fabrics, and
    today by envisioning something even more
    effective that would change color to match the
    terrain."
    The new material would most logically be
    placed in paragraph:
    F. 2
    G. 3
    H. 4
    J. 5

GO ON TO THE NEXT PAGE

PASSAGE V

It lasted fewer than 10 years, but when it was over, the United States had been radically and forever changed. The population had exploded on the west coast of the country, fonts had been made and those same fortunes were lost, and a new state had entered the union—a state that would become a state of mind for all Americans: California.

The United States acquiring the territory that would later become California during the Mexican War (1846–1848). One of the many settlers who traveled to the new territory was John Sutter who was a shopkeeper from Switzerland who had left behind his wife, his children, and his debts, in search of a new life. Hired he did a carpenter named James Marshall to build a sawmill for him on the American River in the foothills of the Sierra Nevada mountains.

On January 24, 1848, while inspecting the mill's runoff into the river, Marshall saw two shiny objects below the surface of the water. He took the nuggets to

61. A. NO CHANGE
    B. fortunes had been made and lost,
    C. fortunes, which had been made, were then lost,
    D. made and lost were fortunes,

62. F. NO CHANGE
    G. Americans, and that place was called California.
    H. Americans, California.
    J. Americans. California.

63. A. NO CHANGE
    B. had acquired
    C. is acquiring
    D. acquired

64. F. NO CHANGE
    G. John Sutter, a shopkeeper
    H. John Sutter; a shopkeeper
    J. John Sutter, who was a shopkeeper

65. A. NO CHANGE
    B. He hired
    C. Hiring
    D. He did hire

66. F. NO CHANGE
    G. (he was inspecting the mill's runoff into the river)
    H. inspecting the mill's runoff into the river all the while,
    J. OMIT the underlined portion.

GO ON TO THE NEXT PAGE

Sutter, who was annoyed by the discovery; Sutter didn't

want them mill workers distracted by gold fever.
     67

Keeping the discovery quiet for a while, but then he
      68

couldn't resist bragging about it. Word got out, and

workers began quitting their jobs and heading into the

hills to look for the source of the gold that had washed

down the river.

    69 Thousands of people poured into California in

search of fortune and glory. This is similar to recent
                      70

stock market increases. During the two years after
   70

Marshall's discovery, more than 90,000 people made their

way to California, looking for gold. In fact, so many

people moved west in just singularly one of those years,
            71

1849, that all the prospectors, regardless of when they

arrived, became known as Forty-niners. By 1850, so

many people had moved to the California territory that

the United States Congress was forced to declare it a

new state. In 1854, the population had increased by

67. A. NO CHANGE
    B. this
    C. his
    D. there

68. F. NO CHANGE
    G. The discovery he was keeping
    H. He kept the discovery
    J. Keeps he the discovery

69. Which of the following would provide the best transition here, guiding the reader from the topic of the previous paragraph to the new topic of this paragraph?

    A. Sutter and Marshall did not make a profit.
    B. The Gold Rush had officially begun.
    C. Can you image how a small discovery led to such a large state?
    D. Most of the "gold" turned out to be a hoax.

70. F. NO CHANGE
    G. The rush for gold was similar to recent stock market increases.
    H. This was similar to recent stock market increases.
    J. OMIT the underlined portion.

71. A. NO CHANGE
    B. one
    C. one and only one
    D. singular

GO ON TO THE NEXT PAGE

another 300,000 people. In fact, one out of every 90
72

people then living in the United States was living in

California.

Even after all of the gold had been taken from the

ground, California remained a magical place in the

American imagination. The 31st state had become a

place that lives could change, fortunes could be made,
73

and dreams could come true. For many people, and
74

California is still such a place.
74

---

72. F.   NO CHANGE
    G.   In spite of this,
    H.   Believe it or not,
    J.   Therefore,

73. A.   NO CHANGE
    B.   where
    C.   through which
    D.   in

74. F.   NO CHANGE
    G.   Forty-niners, California
    H.   people and California
    J.   people, California

Question 75 asks about the preceding passage
as a whole.

75. Suppose the writer had been assigned to write
    a brief essay detailing the life of a Forty-niner
    during the California Gold Rush. Would this
    essay successfully fulfill the assignment?

    A.   Yes, because the essay tells about the lives
         of John Sutter and James Marshall.

    B.   No, because the essay covers a historical
         rather than biographical perspective of
         the Gold Rush.

    C.   Yes, because one can imagine the life of a
         Forty-niner from the details provided in
         the essay.

    D.   No, because the essay does not discuss
         Forty-niners.

IF YOU FINISH BEFORE TIME IS CALLED, YOU MAY CHECK YOUR WORK ON
THIS SECTION ONLY. DO NOT TURN TO ANY OTHER SECTION IN THE TEST.

STOP

MATH TEST

60 Minutes—60 Questions

Directions: Solve each of the following problems, select the correct answer, and then fill in the corresponding space on your answer sheet.

Don't linger over problems that are too time-consuming. Do as many as you can, then come back to the others in the time you have remaining.

Calculator use is permitted, but some problems can best be solved without a calculator.

Note: Unless otherwise noted, all of the following should be assumed.

1. Illustrative figures are *not* necessarily drawn to scale.

2. All geometric figures lie in a plane.

3. The term *line* indicates a straight line.

4. The term *average* indicates arithmetic mean.

---

1. The regular price for a certain bicycle is $125.00. If that price is reduced by 20%, what is the new price?

   A. $100.00
   B. $105.00
   C. $112.50
   D. $120.00
   E. $122.50

2. If $x = -5$, then $2x^2 - 6x + 5 = ?$

   F. -15
   G. 15
   H. 25
   J. 85
   K. 135

3. How many distinct prime factors does the number 36 have?

   A. 2
   B. 3
   C. 4
   D. 5
   E. 6

DO YOUR FIGURING HERE.

GO ON TO THE NEXT PAGE ⇨

4. In the figure below, what is the value of x?

DO YOUR FIGURING HERE.

F. 105°

G. 115°

H. 135°

J. 245°

K. 255°

5. What is the average of $\dfrac{1}{20}$ and $\dfrac{1}{30}$?

A. $\dfrac{1}{25}$

B. $\dfrac{1}{24}$

C. $\dfrac{2}{25}$

D. $\dfrac{1}{12}$

E. $\dfrac{1}{6}$

6. The toll for driving a segment of a certain freeway is $1.50 plus 25 cents for each mile traveled. Joy paid a $25.00 toll for driving a segment of the freeway. How many miles did she travel?

F. 10

G. 75

H. 94

J. 96

K. 100

7. For all x, $3x^2 \cdot 5x^3 = ?$

A. $8x^5$

B. $8x^6$

C. $15x^5$

D. $15x^6$

E. $15x^8$

GO ON TO THE NEXT PAGE

8. How many units apart are the points
   $P(-1, -2)$ and $Q(2, 2)$ in the standard (x, y)
   coordinate plane?

   F. 2

   G. 3

   H. 4

   J. 5

   K. 6

9. In a group of 25 students, 16 are female. What
   percentage of the group is female?

   A. 16%

   B. 40%

   C. 60%

   D. 64%

   E. 75%

10. For how many integer values of x will $\dfrac{7}{x}$ be
    greater than $\dfrac{1}{4}$ and less than $\dfrac{1}{3}$?

    F. 6

    G. 7

    H. 12

    J. 28

    K. Infinitely many

11. Which of the following is a polynomial factor
    of $6x^2 - 13x + 6$?

    A. $2x + 3$

    B. $3x - 2$

    C. $3x + 2$

    D. $6x - 2$

    E. $6x + 2$

DO YOUR FIGURING HERE.

GO ON TO THE NEXT PAGE ⟹

12. What is the value of a if $\dfrac{1}{a} + \dfrac{2}{a} + \dfrac{3}{a} + \dfrac{4}{a} = 5$?

   F. $\dfrac{1}{2}$

   G. 2

   H. 4

   J. $12\dfrac{1}{2}$

   K. 50

DO YOUR FIGURING HERE.

13. In the figure below, $\overline{AD}$, $\overline{BE}$, and $\overline{CF}$ all intersect at point G. If the measure of $\angle AGB$ is $40°$ and the measure of $\angle CGE$ is $105°$, what is the measure of $\angle AGF$?

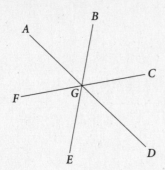

   A. $35°$

   B. $45°$

   C. $55°$

   D. $65°$

   E. $75°$

14. Which of the following is the solution statement for the inequality $-3 < 4x - 5$?

   F. $x > -2$

   G. $x > \dfrac{1}{2}$

   H. $x < -2$

   J. $x < \dfrac{1}{2}$

   K. $x < 2$

GO ON TO THE NEXT PAGE

15. In the figure below, $\overline{BD}$ bisects $\angle ABC$. The measure of $\angle ABC$ is $100°$ and the measure of $\angle BAD$ is $60°$. What is the measure of $\angle BDC$?

A. $80°$

B. $90°$

C. $100°$

D. $110°$

E. $120°$

16. If $x + 2y - 3 = xy$, where x and y are positive, then which of the following equations expresses y in terms of x?

F. $y = \dfrac{3 - x}{2 - x}$

G. $y = \dfrac{3 - x}{x - 2}$

H. $y = \dfrac{x - 3}{2 - x}$

J. $y = \dfrac{x - 2}{x - 3}$

K. $y = \dfrac{6 - x}{x - 2}$

17. In a group of 50 students, 28 speak English and 37 speak Spanish. If everyone in the group speaks at least one of the two languages, how many speak both English and Spanish?

A. 11

B. 12

C. 13

D. 14

E. 15

GO ON TO THE NEXT PAGE

18. A car travels 288 miles in 6 hours. At that rate, how many miles will it travel in 8 hours?

    F.   216
    G.   360
    H.   368
    J.   376
    K.   384

DO YOUR FIGURING HERE.

19. When $\dfrac{4}{11}$ is written as a decimal, what is the 100th digit after the decimal point?

    A.   3
    B.   4
    C.   5
    D.   6
    E.   7

20. What is the solution for x in the system of equations below?

    $$3x + 4y = 31$$
    $$3x - 4y = -1$$

    F.   4
    G.   5
    H.   6
    J.   9
    K.   10

21. In the standard (x, y) coordinate plane, points P and Q have coordinates $(2, 3)$ and $(12, -15)$, respectively. What are the coordinates of the midpoint of $\overline{PQ}$?

    A.   (6, -12)
    B.   (6, -9)
    C.   (6, -6)
    D.   (7, -9)
    E.   (7, -6)

GO ON TO THE NEXT PAGE

22. In the figure below, ∠B is a right angle, and the measure of ∠C is θ. What is the value of cos θ?

F. $\dfrac{3}{4}$

G. $\dfrac{3}{5}$

H. $\dfrac{4}{5}$

J. $\dfrac{5}{4}$

K. $\dfrac{4}{3}$

23. In the figure below, the circle centered at P is tangent to the circle centered at Q. Point Q is on the circumference of circle P. If the circumference of circle P is 6 inches, what is the circumference, in inches, of circle Q ?

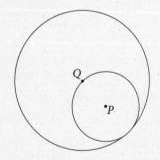

A. 12

B. 24

C. 36

D. 12π

E. 36π

GO ON TO THE NEXT PAGE

24. If $f(x) = x^3 - x^2 - x$, what is the value of $f(-3)$?

F. -39

G. -33

H. -21

J. -15

K. 0

25. If the lengths, in inches, of all three sides of a triangle are integers, and one side is 7 inches long, what is the least possible perimeter of the triangle, in inches?

A.   9

B.   10

C.   15

D.   21

E.   24

26. What is the complete factorization of $2x + 3x^2 + x^3$?

F. $x(x^2 + 2)$

G. $x(x - 2)(x + 3)$

H. $x(x - 1)(x + 2)$

J. $x(x + 1)(x + 2)$

K. $x(x + 2)(x + 3)$

27. If $xyz \neq 0$, which of the following is equivalent to $\dfrac{x^2 y^3 z^4}{(xyz^2)^2}$?

A. $\dfrac{1}{y}$

B. $\dfrac{1}{z}$

C. y

D. $\dfrac{x}{yz}$

E. xyz

DO YOUR FIGURING HERE.

GO ON TO THE NEXT PAGE

28. As a decimal, what is the sum of $\frac{2}{3}$ and $\frac{1}{12}$?

    F.   0.2

    G.   0.5

    H.   0.75

    J.   0.833

    K.   0.875

29. The formula for converting a Fahrenheit temperature reading to Celsius is $C = \frac{5}{9}(F - 32)$, where C is the reading in degrees Celsius and F is the reading in degrees Fahrenheit. Which of the following is the Fahrenheit equivalent to a reading of 95° Celsius?

    A.   35° F

    B.   53° F

    C.   63° F

    D.   203° F

    E.   207° F

30. A jar contains 4 green marbles, 5 red marbles, and 11 white marbles. If one marble is chosen at random, what is the probability that it will be green?

    F. $\frac{1}{3}$

    G. $\frac{1}{4}$

    H. $\frac{1}{5}$

    J. $\frac{1}{16}$

    K. $\frac{5}{15}$

DO YOUR FIGURING HERE.

GO ON TO THE NEXT PAGE

31. What is the average of the expressions $2x + 5$, $5x - 6$, and $-4x + 2$?

   A. $x + \dfrac{1}{3}$

   B. $x + 1$

   C. $3x + \dfrac{1}{3}$

   D. $3x + 3$

   E. $3x + 3\dfrac{1}{3}$

32. The line that passes through the points $(1, 1)$ and $(2, 16)$ in the standard (x, y) coordinate plane is parallel to the line that passes through the points $(-10, -5)$ and $(a, 25)$. What is the value of a?

   F. -8

   G.   3

   H.   5

   J.   15

   K.   20

33. In the figure below, $\overline{QS}$ and $\overline{PT}$ are parallel, and the lengths of $\overline{QR}$ and $\overline{PQ}$, in units, are as marked. If the perimeter of $\triangle QRS$ is 11 units, how many units long is the perimeter of $\triangle PRT$?

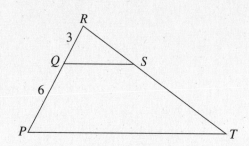

   A.   22

   B.   33

   C.   66

   D.   88

   E.   99

DO YOUR FIGURING HERE.

GO ON TO THE NEXT PAGE

34. The figure shown below belongs in which of
the following classifications?

DO YOUR FIGURING HERE.

  I.   Polygon
  II. Quadrilateral
  III. Rectangle
  IV. Trapezoid

  F. I only
  G. II only
  H. IV only
  J. I, II, and III only
  K. I, II, and IV only

35. If one solution to the equation $2x^2 + (a - 4)$
$x - 2a = 0$ is $x = -3$, what is the value of a?

  A. 0
  B. 2
  C. 4
  D. 6
  E. 12

36. A menu offers 4 choices for the first course,
5 choices for the second course, and 3 choices
for dessert. How many different meals,
consisting of a first course, a second course,
and a dessert, can one choose from this menu?

  F. 12
  G. 24
  H. 30
  J. 36
  K. 60

GO ON TO THE NEXT PAGE

37. If an integer is divisible by 6 and by 9, then the integer must be divisible by which of the following?

    I. 12

    II. 18

    III. 36

    A. I only

    B. II only

    C. I and II only

    D. I, II, and III

    E. None

38. For all $x \neq 0$, $\dfrac{x^2 + x^2 + x^2}{x^2} = ?$

    F. 3

    G. $3x$

    H. x^2

    J. x^3

    K. x^4

39. Joan has q quarters, d dimes, n nickels, and no other coins in her pocket. Which of the following represents the total number of coins in Joan's pocket?

    A. $q + d + n$

    B. $5q + 2d + n$

    C. $.25q + .10d + .05n$

    D. $(25 + 10 + 5)(q + d + n)$

    E. $25q + 10d + 5n$

DO YOUR FIGURING HERE.

GO ON TO THE NEXT PAGE

40. Which graph below represents the solutions for
x of the inequality $5x - 2(1 - x) \geq 4(x + 1)$?

    F.

    G.

    H.

    J.

    K.

41. In the standard (x, y) coordinate plane, line
m is perpendicular to the line containing the
points $(5, 6)$ and $(6, 10)$. What is the slope of
line m?

    A. -4

    B. $-\dfrac{1}{4}$

    C. $\dfrac{1}{4}$

    D. 4

    E. 8

DO YOUR FIGURING HERE.

GO ON TO THE NEXT PAGE

42. In the right triangle below, sin θ = ?

12 in   13 in

5 in

DO YOUR FIGURING HERE.

F. $\dfrac{5}{13}$

G. $\dfrac{5}{12}$

H. $\dfrac{12}{13}$

J. $\dfrac{13}{12}$

K. $\dfrac{13}{5}$

43. If $9^{2x-1} = 3^{3x+3}$, then $x = ?$

A. -4

B. $-\dfrac{7}{4}$

C. $-\dfrac{10}{7}$

D. 2

E. 5

44. From 1970 through 1980, the population of City Q increased by 20%. From 1980 through 1990, the population increased by 30%. What was the combined percent increase for the period 1970–1990?

F. 25%

G. 26%

H. 36%

J. 50%

K. 56%

GO ON TO THE NEXT PAGE

45. Martin's average score after 4 tests is 89. What score on the 5th test would bring Martin's average up to exactly 90?

A. 90
B. 91
C. 92
D. 93
E. 94

46. Which of the following is an equation for the circle in the standard (x, y) coordinate plane that has its center at $(-1, -1)$ and passes through the point $(7, 5)$?

F. $(x - 1)^2 + (y - 1)^2 = 10$
G. $(x + 1)^2 + (y + 1)^2 = 10$
H. $(x - 1)^2 + (y - 1)^2 = 12$
J. $(x - 1)^2 + (y - 1)^2 = 100$
K. $(x + 1)^2 + (y + 1)^2 = 100$

47. Which of the following is an equation for the graph in the standard (x, y) coordinate plane below?

A. $y = -2x + 1$
B. $y = x + 1$
C. $y = x + 2$
D. $y = 2x + 1$
E. $y = 2x + 2$

DO YOUR FIGURING HERE.

GO ON TO THE NEXT PAGE

48. What is $\frac{1}{4}$% of 16 ?

    F. 0.004

    G. 0.04

    H. 0.4

    J. 4

    K. 64

49. For all s, $(s+4)(s-4)+(2s+2)(s-2) = ?$

    A. $s^2 - 2s - 20$

    B. $3s^2 - 12$

    C. $3s^2 - 2s - 20$

    D. $3s^2 + 2s - 20$

    E. $5s^2 - 2s - 20$

50. Which of the following is an equation of the parabola graphed in the (x, y) coordinate plane below?

    F. $y = \dfrac{x^2}{3} - 3$

    G. $y = \dfrac{x^2 - 3}{3}$

    H. $y = \dfrac{x^2}{3} + 3$

    J. $y = \dfrac{x^2 + 3}{3}$

    K. $y = 3x^2 - 3$

DO YOUR FIGURING HERE.

GO ON TO THE NEXT PAGE

51. In the figure below, $\sin a = \dfrac{4}{5}$. What is $\cos b$?

DO YOUR FIGURING HERE.

A. $\dfrac{3}{4}$

B. $\dfrac{3}{5}$

C. $\dfrac{4}{5}$

D. $\dfrac{5}{4}$

E. $\dfrac{4}{3}$

52. For all $x \neq 0$, $\dfrac{x^2 + x^2 + x^2}{x} = ?$

F. $3x$

G. x^3

H. x^5

J. x^7

K. $2x^2 + x$

53. One can determine a student's score S on a certain test by dividing the number of wrong answers (w) by 4 and subtracting the result from the number of right answers (r). This relation is expressed by which of the following formulas?

A. $S = \dfrac{r-w}{4}$

B. $S = r - \dfrac{w}{4}$

C. $S = \dfrac{r}{4} - w$

D. $S = 4r - w$

E. $S = r - 4w$

GO ON TO THE NEXT PAGE

54. What is the volume, in cubic inches, of the cylinder shown in the figure below?

DO YOUR FIGURING HERE.

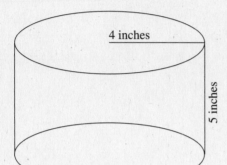

4 inches

5 inches

F. 20π

G. 40π

H. 60π

J. 80π

K. 100π

55. In the figure below, $\overline{AB}$ is perpendicular to $\overline{BC}$. The lengths of $\overline{AB}$ and $\overline{BC}$, in inches, are given in terms of x. Which of the following represents the area of $\triangle ABC$, in square inches, for all $x > 1$?

B

$x-1$ $x+1$

A   C

A. x

B. $2x$

C. x^2

D. $x^2 - 1$

E. $\dfrac{x^2 - 1}{2}$

GO ON TO THE NEXT PAGE

56. In 1990, the population of Town *A* was 9,400 and the population of Town *B* was 7,600. Since then, each year, the population of Town *A* has decreased by 100, and the population of Town *B* has increased by 100. Assuming that in each case the rate continues, in what year will the two populations be equal?

F.   1998

G.   1999

H.   2000

J.   2008

K.   2009

57. In a certain club, the average age of the male members is 35 and the average age of the female members is 25. If 20% of the members are male, what is the average age of all the club members?

A.   26

B.   27

C.   28

D.   29

E.   30

DO YOUR FIGURING HERE.

GO ON TO THE NEXT PAGE

58. To determine the height h of a tree, Roger stands b feet from the base of the tree and measures the angle of elevation to be θ, as shown in the figure below. Which of the following relates h and b ?

DO YOUR FIGURING HERE.

F. $\sin \theta = \dfrac{h}{b}$

G. $\sin \theta = \dfrac{b}{h}$

H. $\sin \theta = \dfrac{b}{\sqrt{b^2 + h^2}}$

J. $\sin \theta = \dfrac{h}{\sqrt{b^2 + h^2}}$

K. $\sin \theta = \dfrac{\sqrt{b^2 + h^2}}{b}$

59. The formula for the lateral surface area S of a right circular cone is $S = \pi r \sqrt{r^2 + h^2}$, where r is the radius of the base and h is the altitude. What is the lateral surface area, in square feet, of a right circular cone with base radius 3 feet and altitude 4 feet?

A. $3\pi\sqrt{5}$

B. $3\pi\sqrt{7}$

C. 15π

D. 21π

E. $\dfrac{75\pi}{2}$

GO ON TO THE NEXT PAGE

60. In the figure below, line *t* crosses parallel lines *m* and *n*. Which of the following statements must be true?

DO YOUR FIGURING HERE.

F. $a = b$
G. $a = d$
H. $b = e$
J. $c = g$
K. $d = g$

IF YOU FINISH BEFORE TIME IS CALLED, YOU MAY CHECK YOUR WORK ON THIS SECTION ONLY. DO NOT TURN TO ANY OTHER SECTION IN THE TEST.

STOP

READING TEST

35 Minutes—40 Questions

Directions: This test contains four passages, each followed by several questions. After reading a passage, select the best answer to each question and fill in the corresponding oval on your answer sheet. You are allowed to refer to the passages while answering the questions.

PASSAGE I

I can remember, when I was a very little girl indeed, I used to say to my doll when we were alone together, "Now, Dolly, I am not clever, you
Line know very well, and you must be patient with me,
(5) like a dear!"

…My dear old doll! I was such a shy little thing that I seldom dared to open my lips, and never dared to open my heart, to anybody else. It almost makes me cry to think what a relief it used to be
(10) to me when I came home from school of a day to run upstairs to my room and say, "Oh, you dear faithful Dolly, I knew you would be expecting me!" and then to sit down on the floor, leaning on the elbow of her great chair, and tell her all I had
(15) noticed since we parted….

I was brought up, from my earliest remembrance—like some of the princesses in the fairy stories, only I was not charming—by my godmother. At least, I only knew her as such. She was a
(20) good, good woman! She went to church three times every Sunday, and to morning prayers on Wednesdays and Fridays, and to lectures whenever there were lectures; and never missed. She was handsome; and if she had ever smiled, would
(25) have been (I used to think) like an angel—but she never smiled. She was always grave and strict. She was so very good herself, I thought, that the badness of other people made her frown all her life…. It made me very sorry to consider how good she
(30) was and how unworthy of her I was, and I used ardently to hope that I might have a better heart; and I talked it over very often with the dear old doll, but I never loved my godmother as I ought to

have loved her and as I felt I must have loved her
(35) if I had been a better girl….

I had never heard my mama spoken of…. I had never been shown my mama's grave. I had never been told where it was….

Although there were seven girls at the neigh-
(40) boring school where I was a day boarder, and although they called me little Esther Summerson, I knew none of them at home. All of them were older than I, to be sure (I was the youngest there by a good deal), but there seemed to be some
(45) other separation between us besides that, and besides their being far more clever than I was and knowing much more than I did. One of them in the first week of my going to the school (I remember it very well) invited me home to a little party,
(50) to my great joy. But my godmother wrote a stiff letter declining for me, and I never went. I never went out at all.

It was my birthday. There were holidays at school on other birthdays—none on mine. There
(55) were rejoicings at home on other birthdays, as I knew from what I heard the girls relate to one another—there were none on mine. My birthday was the most melancholy day at home in the whole year….

(60) Dinner was over, and my godmother and I were sitting at the table before the fire. The clock ticked, the fire clicked; not another sound had been heard in the room or in the house for I don't know how long. I happened to look timidly up from my
(65) stitching, across the table at my godmother, and I saw in her face, looking gloomily at me, "It would have been far better, little Esther, that you had had no birthday, that you had never been born!"

GO ON TO THE NEXT PAGE

I broke out crying and sobbing, and I said,
(70) "Oh, dear godmother, tell me, pray do tell me, did
Mama die on my birthday?"

"No," she returned. "Ask me no more, child!"

...I put up my trembling little hand to clasp
hers or to beg her pardon with what earnestness
(75) I might, but withdrew it as she looked at me, and
laid it on my fluttering heart. She...said slowly
in a cold, low voice—I see her knitted brow and
pointed finger—"The time will come—and soon
enough—when you will understand this better
(80) and will feel it too.... I have forgiven her"—but
her face did not relent—"the wrong she did to me,
and I say no more of it, though it was greater than
you will ever know.... Forget your mother and
leave all other people to forget her.... Now, go!"
(85) ...I went up to my room, and crept to bed, and
laid my doll's cheek against mine wet with tears,
and holding that solitary friend upon my bosom,
cried myself to sleep. Imperfect as my understanding of my sorrow was, I knew that I had brought
(90) no joy at any time to anybody's heart and that I
was to no one upon earth what Dolly was to me.

Dear, dear, to think how much time we passed
alone together afterwards, and how often I repeated
to the doll the story of my birthday and confided
(95) to her that I would try as hard as ever I could to
repair the fault I had been born with.... I hope it
is not self-indulgent to shed these tears
as I think of it.

Adapted excerpt from *Bleak House*, by Charles Dickens. In this
passage, Esther recounts some of her childhood experiences.

1. According to the passage, Esther only
remembers:

    A. being brought up by her parents for a
       short time.

    B. being brought up by her mother for a
       short time.

    C. being brought up by her godmother for
       a short time.

    D. being brought up by her godmother.

2. It is most likely that Esther thought of her
doll as:

    F. only an amusing plaything.

    G. her only friend and confidante.

    H. a princess in a fairy tale.

    J. a beautiful toy that was too fragile to
       touch.

3. As it is used in the passage, *stiff* (line 50) most
closely means:

    A. difficult to bend.

    B. rigidly formal.

    C. unchanging.

    D. not moving easily or freely.

4. Which of the following most likely
contributed to Esther's belief that she had
been born with a fault (line 96)?

    I. She had never heard anyone talk about
       her mother.

    II. Her birthday was never celebrated.

    III. Her godmother told her that she should
       never have been born.

    F. I and III only

    G. I and II only

    H. I only

    J. I, II, and III

5. Esther's godmother's words, actions, and facial
expression as described in paragraph 9 (lines
73–84) suggest that she:

    A. had a change of heart about celebrating
       Esther's birthday.

    B. did not know what had happened to
       Esther's mother.

    C. continued to resent Esther's mother.

    D. had truly forgiven Esther's mother.

GO ON TO THE NEXT PAGE ⟶

6. According to the passage, Esther's childhood could be most accurately characterized as:

    F.   an adventure.

    G.   a time of loneliness and confusion.

    H.   a period of dedication to education and self-improvement.

    J.   a period of attempting to become more like her godmother.

7. From Esther's statement, "I was to no one upon earth what Dolly was to me" (lines 90–91), it is reasonable to infer that Esther:

    A.   believed that her godmother loved her.

    B.   believed that she would be able to become friends with the girls at school.

    C.   believed that no one loved her.

    D.   believed that her mother was alive.

8. In the passage, it is implied that all of the following contributed to separating Esther from the other girls at her school EXCEPT:

    F.   the other girls were older than Esther.

    G.   Esther's godmother did not allow Esther to socialize with the other girls outside of school.

    H.   Esther believed that the other girls were much smarter.

    J.   Esther was self-indulgent.

9. According to the passage, one reason that Esther thinks of her godmother as a "good, good woman" (line 20) is:

    A.   that when she smiles, she looks like an angel.

    B.   that she forgave Esther's mother.

    C.   that she frequently attends church services.

    D.   that she gave Esther a doll.

10. In the passage, Esther describes herself as a child as:

    F.   self-indulgent and not very clever.

    G.   shy and not very clever.

    H.   shy and faithful.

    J.   self-indulgent and faithful.

GO ON TO THE NEXT PAGE

PASSAGE II

Marcos Nunes is not likely to forget his first holiday in Brazil's Pantanal wilderness. One afternoon last October he was coaxing his horse
Line through a lonely tuft of woods when he suddenly
(5) found himself staring down a fully grown spotted jaguar. He held his breath while the painted cat and her cub paraded silkily through the grove, not 10 meters away…. "Thank you," he wrote later in a hotel visitor's log, "for the wonderful fright!"

(10)   As Nunes and other ecotourists are discovering, these big, beautiful animals, once at the brink of extinction, are now staging a comeback. Exactly how dramatic a comeback is difficult to say because jaguars—*Panthera onca*, the largest feline
(15) in the New World—are solitary, secretive, nocturnal predators. Each cat needs to prowl at least 35 square kilometers by itself. Brazil's Pantanal, vast wetlands that spill over a 140,000-square-kilometer swath of South America the size of Germany, gives
(20) them plenty of room to roam. Nevertheless, scientists who have been tagging jaguars with radio transmitters for two decades have in recent years been reporting a big increase in sightings. Hotels, campgrounds, and bed-and-breakfasts have sprung
(25) up to accommodate the half-million tourists a year (twice the number of five years ago) bent on sampling the Pantanal's wildlife, of which the great cats must be the most magnificent example.

Most sightings come from local cattle herders—
(30) but their jaguar stories have a very different ring. One day last September, ranch hand Abel Monteiro was tending cattle near the Rio Vermelho, in the southern Pantanal, when, he says, a snarling jaguar leaped from the scrub and
(35) killed his two bloodhounds. Monteiro barely had time to grab his .38 revolver and kill the angry cat. Leonelson Ramos da Silva says last May he and a group of field hands had to throw flaming sticks all night to keep a prowling jaguar from invading
(40) their forest camp…. The Brazilian interior, famous for its generous spirit and cowboy *bonhomie*, is now the scene of a political cat fight between the scientists, environmentalists, and ecotourists who want to protect the jaguars and
(45) the embattled ranchers who want to protect themselves and their livelihood.

The ranchers, to be sure, have enough headaches coping with the harsh, sodden landscape without jaguars attacking their herds and
(50) threatening their livelihoods. Hard data on cattle losses due to jaguars in the Pantanal are nonexistent, but there are stories. In 1995, Joo Julio Dittmar bought a 6,200-hectare strip of ideal breeding ground, only to lose 152 of his 600 calves
(55) to jaguars, he claims. Ranchers chafe at laws that forbid them to kill the jaguars. "This is a question of democracy," says Dittmar. "We ranchers ought to be allowed to control our own environment."

Man and jaguar have been sparring for
(60) territory ever since 18th-century settlers, traders, and herdsmen began to move into this sparsely populated serto, or back lands. By the 1960s, the Pantanal was a vast, soggy canvas, white with gleaming herds of Nelore cattle. Game hunters
(65) were bagging 15,000 jaguars a year in the nearby Amazon Basin (no figures exist on the Pantanal) as the worldwide trade in pelts reached $30 million a year. As the jaguars grew scarce, their chief food staple, the capybaras—a meter-long rodent,
(70) the world's largest—overran farmers' fields and spread trichomoniasis, a livestock disease that renders cows sterile.

Then in 1967, Brazil outlawed jaguar hunting, and a world ban on selling pelts followed in 1973.
(75) Weather patterns also shifted radically—due most likely to global warming—and drove annual floods to near-Biblical proportions. The waters are only now retreating from some inundated pasturelands. As the Pantanal herds shrank from
(80) 6 million to about 3.5 million head, the jaguars advanced. Along the way they developed a taste for the bovine intruders.

The ranchers' fear of the big cats is partly cultural. The ancient Inca and Maya believed that

GO ON TO THE NEXT PAGE ⟩

(85) jaguars possessed supernatural powers. In Brazil, the most treacherous enemy is said to be *o amigo da onca*, a friend to the jaguar….

Some people believe there may be a way for ranchers and jaguars to coexist. Sports hunters on (90) "green safaris" might shoot jaguars with immobilizing drugs, allowing scientists to fit the cats with radio collars. Fees would help sustain jaguar research and compensate ranchers for livestock losses. (Many environmentalists, though, fear (95) fraudulent claims.) Scientists are setting up workshops to teach ranchers how to protect their herds with modern husbandry, pasture management, and such gadgets as blinking lights and electric fences.

(100) Like many rural folk, however, the wetland ranchers tend to bristle at bureaucrats and foreigners telling them what to do. When the scholars go home and the greens log off, the *pantaneiros* will still be there—left on their own to deal with (105) the jaguars as they see fit.

Excerpt from "The Return of the Big Cats" by Mac Margolis, *Newsweek*, December 11, 2000, copyright © 2000 by Newsweek, Inc. All rights reserved. Reprinted by permission.

11. As it is used in the passage, *canvas* (line 63) most closely means:

    A. a survey of public opinion.
    B. a background.
    C. a coarse cotton fabric.
    D. a painting.

12. According to the passage, one result of the decline of the jaguar population during the 1960s was:

    F. the increase in the population of the settlers.
    G. an increase in Brazil's ecotourist business.
    H. an increase in the price of a jaguar pelt.
    J. an increase in the population of their most common source of food, the capybaras.

13. According to the passage, it is difficult to determine the extent of the jaguar's comeback because:

    A. the area they inhabit is so large.
    B. the stories that the local ranchers tell about jaguars contradict the conclusions reached by scientists.
    C. jaguars are solitary, nocturnal animals that can have a territory of 35 square kilometers.
    D. scientists have only used radio transmitters to track the movements of the jaguar population.

14. The information about ecotourism in the first and second paragraphs of the passage (lines 1–28) suggests that:

    F. the jaguars are seen as a threat to the safety of tourists.
    G. the jaguars are important to the success of Brazil's growing ecotourism industry.
    H. the growth of the ecotourism industry is threatening the habitat of the jaguars.
    J. it is common for ecotourists to spot one or more jaguars.

15. According to the passage, which of the following is NOT a method for protecting cattle herds that scientists are teaching ranchers?

    A. "Green safaris"
    B. Pasture management
    C. The use of blinking lights and electric fences
    D. Modern husbandry

GO ON TO THE NEXT PAGE

16. It is most likely that the author of the passage included the jaguar stories of three ranchers (lines 29–40, 52–58) in order to:

   F. express more sympathy toward the ranchers than toward the environmentalists and scientists.

   G. illustrate the dangers and economic losses that the jaguars currently pose to ranchers.

   H. show the violent nature of the ranchers.

   J. provide a complete picture of the Pantanal landscape.

17. From information in the passage, it is most reasonable to infer that the cattle herds "shrank from 6 million to about 3.5 million head" (lines 79–80) because:

   A. the jaguars had killed so many cattle.

   B. environmentalists and scientists worked to convert pastureland into refuges for the jaguars.

   C. many cows had become sterile from trichomoniasis and annual floods submerged much of the pastureland used by ranchers.

   D. the cattle could not tolerate the increase in the average temperature caused by global warming.

18. The main conclusion reached about the future of the relationship between the people and the jaguars in the Pantanal is that:

   F. the increase in ecotourism will ensure the continued growth in the jaguar population.

   G. the ranchers themselves will ultimately determine how they will cope with the jaguars.

   H. the jaguar population will continue to fluctuate with the number of tourists coming into Pantanal.

   J. the scientists' new ranching methods will make it easy for the ranchers and jaguars to coexist.

19. According to the passage, which of the following groups want to protect the jaguar?

   I. Ecotourists
   II. Environmentalists
   III. Scientists

   A. I and II only

   B. I and III only

   C. II and III only

   D. I, II, and III

20. According to the passage, there is no accurate data available on:

   F. the number of cattle killed by jaguars.

   G. the number of ranchers attacked by jaguars.

   H. the growth rate of ecotourism in Brazil.

   J. the percentage of the Pantanal wetlands inhabited by jaguars.

GO ON TO THE NEXT PAGE

PASSAGE III

Greek instruments can be classified into two general categories—string and pipe, or lyre and aulos. Our knowledge of them comes from rep-
Line resentations on monuments, vases, statues, and
(5) friezes and from the testimony of Greek authors. The lyre was the national instrument and included a wide variety of types. In its most antique form, the chelys, it is traced back to the age of fable and allegedly owed its invention to Hermes. Easy to
(10) carry, this small lyre became the favorite instrument of the home, amateurs, and women, a popular accompaniment for drinking songs and love songs as well as more noble kinds of poetry…. Professional Homeric singers used a kithara, a
(15) larger, more powerful instrument, which probably came from Egypt. The kithara had a flat wooden sound box and an upper horizontal bar supported by two curving arms. Within this frame were stretched strings of equal length, at first but three
(20) or four in number. Fastened to the performer by means of a sling, the kithara was played with both hands. We are not sure in just what manner the instrument was used to accompany the epics. It may have been employed for a pitch-fixing pre-
(25) lude and for interludes, or it may have paralleled or decorated the vocal melody in more or less free fashion.

…Two types of tuning were used: the dynamic, or pitch method, naming the degrees "according
(30) to function"; and the thetic, or tablature, naming them "according to position" on the instrument.

As early as the eighth century b.c., lyres of five strings appeared. Terpander (fl. c. 675 B.C.), one of the first innovators, is said to have increased
(35) the number of strings to seven. He is also supposed to have completed the octave and created the Mixolydian scale. Aristoxenos claimed that the poetess Sappho, in the seventh century B.C., in addition to introducing a mode in which Dorian
(40) and Lydian characteristics were blended, initiated use of the plectrum or pick. At the time of

Sophocles (495–406 B.C.), the lyre had eleven strings.

Another harplike instrument was the magadis,
(45) whose tone was described as trumpetlike. Of foreign importation, it had twenty strings, which, by means of frets, played octaves. As some of the strings were tuned in quartertones, it was an instrument associated with the enharmonic mode.
(50) Smaller versions, the pectis and the barbitos, were also tuned in quartertones. Greek men and boys had a style of singing in octaves that was called magadizing, after the octave-playing instruments.

The kithara was identified with Apollo and the
(55) Apollonian cult, representing the intellectual and idealistic side of Greek art. The aulos or reed pipe was the instrument of Dionysians, who represented the unbridled, sensual and passionate aspect of Greek culture.
(60) Although translated as "flute," the aulos is more like our oboe. Usually found in double form, the pipes set at an angle, the aulos was imputed to have a far more exciting effect than that produced by the subdued lyre. About 600 B.C., the aulos was
(65) chosen as the official instrument of the Delphian and Pythian festivals. It was also used in performances of the Dionysian dithyramb as well as a supplement of the chorus in classic Greek tragedy and comedy.
(70) There was a complete family of auloi covering the same range as human voices. One authority names three species of simple pipes and five varieties of double pipes. (The double pipe was the professional instrument.) An early specimen
(75) was supposed to have been tuned to the chromatic tetrachord D, C sharp, B flat, A—a fact that points to Oriental origin. Elegiac songs called aulodia were composed in this mode to be accompanied by an aulos. Although the first wooden pipes had
(80) only three or four finger holes, the number later increased so that the Dorian, Phrygian and Lydian modes might be performed on a single pair. Pictures of auletes show them with a bandage or

GO ON TO THE NEXT PAGE

phorbeia over their faces; this might have been
(85) necessary to hold the two pipes in place, to
modulate the tone or, perhaps, to aid in storing
air in the cheeks for the purpose of sustained
performance.

21. The passage suggests that the aulos was
considered "the official instrument of the
Dionysians" (lines 56–59) because:

    A. it expressed the excitement and passion
    of that aspect of Greek culture.

    B. it was chosen as the official instrument
    of the Delphian and Pythian festivals.

    C. it represented the intellectual and idealis-
    tic side of Greek art.

    D. it was invented around the time that the
    Dionysian cult originated.

22. The statement that the chelys can be "traced
back to the age of fable" (line 8) implies that
the chelys:

    F. was invented by storytellers.

    G. was used to accompany the epics.

    H. probably existed in legend only.

    J. was a particularly ancient instrument.

23. The main purpose of the passage is to
describe the:

    A. use of the lyre in different musical settings.

    B. connection between the ancient Greek
    arts of music and drama.

    C. references to music in ancient Greek
    literature.

    D. origin and development of various Greek
    instruments.

24. According to the passage, the kithara was:

    F. most likely of Greek origin.

    G. played with one hand.

    H. used by professional musicians.

    J. less powerful than a chelys.

25. Which of the following is NOT cited as a
change that occurred to the lyre between the
eighth and fifth centuries B.C.?

    A. Musicians began to use a plectrum.

    B. Lyres featured increasing numbers of
    strings.

    C. Musicians began to use different scales
    and modes.

    D. Lyres were used to accompany dramatic
    productions.

26. It can be inferred from the passage that the
chromatic tetrachord D, C sharp, B flat, A
(lines 75–76) was:

    F. not appropriate for elegaic songs.

    G. only used by professional musicians.

    H. impossible on the first wooden pipes.

    J. present in ancient Oriental music.

27. According to the passage, the most ancient
form of the lyre was called a:

    A. magadis.

    B. kithara.

    C. chelys.

    D. barbitos.

GO ON TO THE NEXT PAGE

28. According to the passage, one of Sappho's contributions to ancient Greek music was that she:

    F. completed the octave and created the Mixolydian scale.

    G. introduced a mode blending Dorian and Lydian characteristics.

    H. incorporated poetry into recitals of lyre music.

    J. helped increase the number of strings on the lyre.

29. According to the passage, which of the following is/are characteristic of the aulos?

    I. It was used in performances of the Dionysian dithyramb.

    II. It sounded more exciting than the lyre.

    III. It resembles the modern-day flute more than it does the oboe.

    A. I only

    B. I and II only

    C. II and III only

    D. I, II, and III

30. Which of the following does the passage suggest is true about our knowledge of ancient Greek instruments?

    F. Our knowledge is dependent on secondary sources.

    G. Little is known about how instruments were tuned.

    H. Very few pictures of ancient Greek instruments have survived.

    J. More is known about string instruments than about pipe instruments.

GO ON TO THE NEXT PAGE ▷

PASSAGE IV

Astronomers noted more than 150 years ago that sunspots wax and wane in number in an 11-year cycle. Ever since, people have speculated
Line that the solar cycle might exert some influence on
(5) the Earth's weather. In this century, for example, scientists have linked the solar cycle to droughts in the American Midwest. Until recently, however, none of these correlations has held up under close scrutiny.
(10)   One problem is that sunspots themselves are so poorly understood. Observations have revealed that the swirly smudges represent areas of intense magnetic activity where the sun's radiative energy has been blocked and that they are considerably
(15) cooler than bright regions of the sun. Scientists have not been able, however, to determine just how sunspots are created or what effect they have on the solar constant (a misnomer that refers to the sun's total radiance at any instant).
(20)   The latter question, at least, now seems to have been resolved by data from the *Solar Maximum Mission* satellite, which has monitored the solar constant since 1980, the peak of the last solar cycle. As the number of sunspots decreased
(25) through 1986, the satellite recorded a gradual dimming of the sun. Over the past year, as sunspots have proliferated, the sun has brightened. The data suggest that the sun is 0.1 percent more luminous at the peak of the solar cycle, when
(30) the number of sunspots is greatest, than at its nadir, according to Richard C. Willson of the Jet Propulsion Laboratory and Hugh S. Hudson of the University of California at San Diego.
The data show that sunspots do not themselves
(35) make the sun shine brighter. Quite the contrary. When a sunspot appears, it initially causes the sun to dim slightly, but then after a period of weeks or months islands of brilliance called faculas usually emerge near the sunspot and more than
(40) compensate for its dimming effect. Willson says faculas may represent regions where energy that initially was blocked beneath a sunspot has finally breached the surface.

Does the subtle fluctuation in the solar constant
(45) manifest itself in the Earth's weather? Some recent reports offer statistical evidence that it does, albeit rather indirectly. The link seems to be mediated by a phenomenon known as the quasi-biennial oscillation (QBO), a 180-degree shift in the direc-
(50) tion of stratospheric winds above the Tropics that occurs about every two years.
Karin Labitzke of the Free University of Berlin and Harry van Loon of the National Center for Atmospheric Research in Boulder, Colorado, were
(55) the first to uncover the QBO link. They gathered temperature and air-pressure readings from vari- ous latitudes and altitudes over the past three solar cycles. They found no correlation between the solar cycle and their data until they sorted the
(60) data into two categories: those gathered during the QBO's west phase (when the stratospheric winds blow west) and those gathered during its east phase. A remarkable correlation appeared: temperatures and pressures coincident with the
(65) QBO's west phase rose and fell in accordance with the solar cycle.
Building on this finding, Brian A. Tinsley of the National Science Foundation discovered a statisti- cal correlation between the solar cycle and the
(70) position of storms in the North Atlantic. The lati- tude of storms during the west phase of the QBO, Tinsley found, varied with the solar cycle: storms occurring toward the peak of a solar cycle traveled at latitudes about six degrees nearer the Equator
(75) than storms during the cycle's nadir.
Labitzke, van Loon, and Tinsley acknowledge that their findings are still rather mysterious. Why does the solar cycle seem to exert more of an influence during the west phase of the QBO
(80) than it does during the east phase? How does the 0.1 percent variance in solar radiation trigger the much larger changes—up to six degrees Celsius in polar regions—observed by Labitzke and van Loon? Van Loon says simply, "We can't explain it."

GO ON TO THE NEXT PAGE ⇒

(85)   John A. Eddy of the National Center for Atmospheric Research, nonetheless, thinks these QBO findings as well as the *Solar Maximum Mission* data "look like breakthroughs" in the search for a link between the solar cycle and

(90) weather. With further research, for example, into how the oceans damp the effects of solar flux, these findings may lead to models that have some predictive value. The next few years may be particularly rich in solar flux.

Excerpt from "The Solar Inconstant," by John Horgan, *Scientific American*, September 1988, copyright © 1988 by *Scientific American*. Reprinted by permission of *Scientific American*. All rights reserved.

31. According to the passage, the main source of information about the effect of sunspots on the solar constant is provided by:

    A. studies of droughts in the Midwest.

    B. data from the *Solar Maximum Mission* satellite.

    C. temperature and air pressure readings taken in Colorado.

    D. discussions between various eminent astronomers.

32. As it is used in the passage, the term *solar constant* refers to:

    F. magnetic activity.

    G. the sun's total radiance.

    H. the sun's surface temperature.

    J. wind direction.

33. The main purpose of this passage is to:

    A. explain why scientists have failed to find any direct correlation between sunspots and the Earth's weather.

    B. describe a possible correlation between the solar cycle and the Earth's weather.

    C. describe the solar cycle and its relation to the solar constant.

    D. prove conclusively that sunspots dramatically influence the Earth's weather.

34. As it is used in line 27, the word *proliferated* means:

    F. grown in size.

    G. brightened.

    H. decreased in number.

    J. increased in number.

35. Which of the following explains why the sun appears brighter during periods of sunspot activity?

    A. Energy that has been blocked is finally released.

    B. The sun shines brighter when sunspots first appear.

    C. Magnetic activity increases the sun's temperature.

    D. Air pressure in the Earth's atmosphere falls.

36. The shift in the direction of stratospheric winds that occurs every two years is known as:

    F. a facula.

    G. the solar flux.

    H. North Atlantic storms.

    J. the quasi-biennial oscillation.

GO ON TO THE NEXT PAGE

37. Which of the following best summarizes the main point of the last paragraph?

    A. Scientists will soon be in a position to accurately predict the Earth's weather.

    B. Many findings of the *Solar Maximum Mission* cannot yet be explained.

    C. The relationship between the solar cycle and the Earth's weather may become clear with further research.

    D. Scientists disagree as to whether studying sunspots will ever have any practical value.

38. According to the passage, changes in the solar cycle may influence the Earth's weather in which of the following ways?

    I.   Changing the direction of stratospheric winds

    II. Altering temperature and pressure levels

    III. Influencing the latitude of storms

    F. I only

    G. I and II only

    H. II and III only

    J. I, II, and III

39. From the information in the first paragraph, it may be inferred that scientists now consider a correlation between the solar cycle and droughts in the American Midwest to be:

    A. probable.

    B. unlikely.

    C. confusing.

    D. useful.

40. According to the passage, which of the following statements best describes the current understanding of the relationship between sunspot activity and solar luminosity?

    F. At the peak of sunspot activity, the solar constant decreases in magnitude.

    G. At the peak of sunspot activity, the solar constant increases in magnitude.

    H. At the low point of sunspot activity, the sun is 0.1 percent brighter than it is at the peak of such activity.

    J. Scientists have yet to demonstrate a relationship between the two phenomena.

SCIENCE TEST
35 Minutes—40 Questions

Directions: Each of the following seven passages is followed by several questions. After reading each passage, decide on the best answer to each question and fill in the corresponding oval on your answer sheet. You are allowed to refer to the passages while answering the questions. Calculator use is not allowed on this test.

PASSAGE I

Acid-base indicators are used to determine changes in pH. The pH is a quantitative measure of the hydrogen ion concentration of a solution. For any solution, the pH ranges from 0 to 14. An acid-base indicator is a weak acid or base that is sensitive to the hydrogen ion concentration and changes color at a known pH. At any other pH, the acid-base indicator is clear.

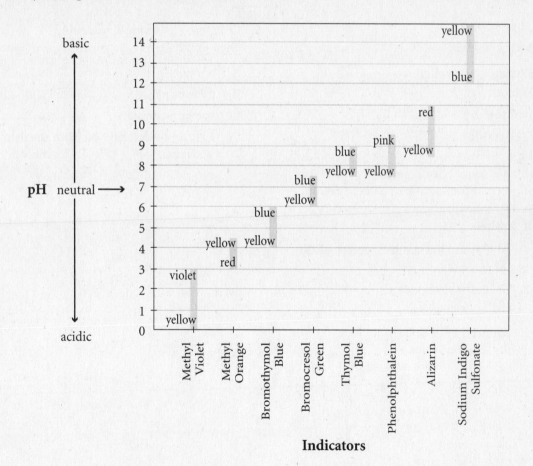

GO ON TO THE NEXT PAGE

1. Which indicators undergo a color change in the region from pH 8 to pH 12?

   A. Bromocresol green, bromothymol blue, and thymol blue

   B. Thymol blue, phenolphthalein, and alizarin

   C. Phenolphthalein, alizarin, and sodium indigo sulfonate

   D. Phenolphthalein and bromothymol blue

2. Which of the following indicators undergoes a red-to-yellow or yellow-to-red color change?

   I. Alizarin

   II. Thymol blue

   III. Methyl orange

   F. I only

   G. II only

   H. I and III only

   J. I, II, and III

3. A chemist is running an experiment in a solution that becomes basic upon completion. According to the diagram, the reaction is complete when:

   A. the addition of bromocresol green results in a blue color.

   B. any indicator turns violet.

   C. a white solid appears.

   D. the addition of bromothymol blue results in a blue color.

4. Which of the following hypotheses is consistent with the information in the passage and the diagram?

   F. Color changes for any given acid-base indicator occur in a solution with a pH less than 7.

   G. Color changes for any given acid-base indicator occur in a solution with a pH greater than 7.

   H. Color changes for acid-base indicators always occur within the same pH range.

   J. Color changes for acid-base indicators vary within the pH range.

5. Compared to bromothymol blue, phenolphthalein undergoes a color change at:

   A. a higher pH.

   B. a lower pH.

   C. the same pH.

   D. Cannot be determined from the data provided.

GO ON TO THE NEXT PAGE

Passage II

The Brazilian tree frog (*Hyla faber*) exchanges gases through both its skin and lungs. The exchange rate depends on the temperature of the frog's environment. A series of experiments was performed to investigate this dependence.

Experiment 1

Fifty frogs were placed in a controlled atmosphere that, with the exception of temperature, was designed to simulate their native habitat. The temperature was varied from 5° C to 25° C, and equilibrium was attained before each successive temperature change. The amount of oxygen absorbed by the frogs' lungs and skin per hour was measured, and the results for all the frogs were averaged. The results are shown in Table 1.

Table 1

Temperature (°C)	Moles O_2 absorbed/hr	
	Skin	Lungs
5	15.4	8.3
10	22.7	35.1
15	43.6	64.9
20	42.1	73.5
25	40.4	78.7

Experiment 2

The same frogs were placed under the same conditions as in Experiment 1. For this experiment, the amount of carbon dioxide eliminated through the skin and lungs was measured. The results are averaged and given in Table 2.

Table 2

Temperature (°C)	Moles CO_2 released/hr	
	Skin	Lungs
5	18.9	2.1
10	43.8	12.7
15	79.2	21.3
20	91.6	21.9
25	96.5	21.4

GO ON TO THE NEXT PAGE

6. The results of Experiment 1 suggest that the total amount of O_2 absorbed per hour is:

   F.   correlated to the temperature.

   G.   independent of the temperature.

   H.   an indication of how healthy a Brazilian tree frog is.

   J.   always less than the total amount of CO_2 eliminated per hour.

7. According to Experiment 2, the total amount of CO_2 eliminated per hour at 17° C is closest to:

   A.   21 mol/hr

   B.   85 mol/hr

   C.   106 mol/hr

   D.   115 mol/hr

8. Ectotherms are animals whose bodily functions are affected by the temperature of their environment. Which of the following results supports the conclusion that *Hyla fabers* is an ectotherm?

   F.   The oxygen absorbed at 25° C

   G.   The carbon dioxide released by the lungs

   H.   The oxygen absorbed over the entire temperature range

   J.   The results do not support this conclusion.

9. According to the results of Experiment 2, which of the following plots best represents the amount of carbon dioxide eliminated through the skin and lungs as a function of temperature?

   A.   B.

   C.   D.

10. On the basis of the experimental results, one could conclude that as temperature increases:

    F. O_2 absorbed by the lungs increases and CO_2 released by the skin decreases.

    G. O_2 absorbed by the lungs increases and CO_2 released by the skin increases.

    H. O_2 absorbed by the lungs decreases and CO_2 released by the lungs increases.

    J. O_2 absorbed by the lungs decreases and CO_2 released by the lungs decreases.

11. According to the results of these experiments, as the temperature rises above 15° C, which of the following phenomena can be observed?

    A.   The Brazilian tree frog's ability to absorb oxygen through the skin decreases, as does its ability to release carbon dioxide through the lungs.

    B.   The Brazilian tree frog's ability to absorb oxygen through the skin decreases, while its ability to release carbon dioxide through the lungs remains about the same.

    C.   The Brazilian tree frog's ability to absorb oxygen through the skin remains about the same, as does its ability to release carbon dioxide through the lungs.

    D.   The Brazilian tree frog's ability to absorb oxygen through the skin increases, while its ability to release carbon dioxide through the lungs remains about the same.

GO ON TO THE NEXT PAGE

PASSAGE III

A scientist wants to use a certain organic reagent to develop a means of extracting valuable elements from radioactive nuclear power plant effluent. Using the organic reagent, she measured extraction curves for six different elements: tungsten (W), molybdenum (Mo), ytterbium (Yb), erbium (Er), thulium (Tm), and europium (Eu).

12. At which pH level is the organic reagent most effective in extracting molybdenum?

    F.   3

    G.   4

    H.   5

    J.   6

13. The engineers who run a power plant that ejects waste with high levels of erbium and tungsten isotopes would like to extract as much of both elements as possible. Assuming a single-step extraction, this could be accomplished by using the organic reagent at a pH of:

    A.   less than 1.5 or greater than 5.5

    B.   4

    C.   4.6

    D.   It is impossible to extract large amounts of both elements using the reagent at any pH.

14. Based on the data given, which of the following conclusions can be drawn about the effect of pH on the percentage extracted?

    F.   The percentage of an element extracted increases as pH increases.

    G.   The percentage of an element extracted decreases as pH increases.

    H.   The percentage of an element extracted is independent of pH.

    J.   The effect of pH is different for different elements.

15. The researcher was able to extract 45% of the thulium from the plant's effluent. The pH level of the organic reagent was most likely between:

    A.   4 and 5

    B.   5 and 6

    C.   6 and 7

    D.   7 and 8

GO ON TO THE NEXT PAGE

16. If erbium is among the elements being extracted by the organic reagent at a certain pH, which of the following cannot be among the other elements being extracted?

   F. Europium

   G. Thulium

   H. Molybdenum

   J. Ytterbium

PASSAGE IV

While the focus (point of origin) of most earthquakes lies less than 20 km below the Earth's surface, certain unusual seismographic readings indicate that some activity originates at considerably greater depths. Below, two scientists discuss the possible causes of deep-focus earthquakes.

SCIENTIST 1

Surface earthquakes occur when rock in the Earth's crust fractures to relieve stress. However, below 50 km, rock is under too much pressure to fracture normally. Deep-focus earthquakes are caused by the pressure of fluids trapped in the Earth's tectonic plates. As a plate is forced down into the mantle by convection, increases in temperature and pressure cause changes in the crystalline structure of minerals such as serpentine. In adopting a denser configuration, the crystals dehydrate, releasing water. Other sources of fluid include water trapped in pockets of deep-sea trenches and carried down with the plates. Laboratory work has shown that fluids trapped in rock pores can cause rock to fail at lower shear stresses. In fact, at the Rocky Mountain Arsenal, the injection of fluid wastes into the ground accidentally induced a series of shallow-focus earthquakes.

SCIENTIST 2

Deep-focus earthquakes cannot result from normal fractures because rock becomes ductile at the temperatures and pressures that exist at depths greater than 50 km. Furthermore, mantle rock below 300 km is probably totally dehydrated because of the extreme pressure. Therefore, trapped fluids could not cause quakes below that depth. A better explanation is that deep-focus quakes result from the slippage that occurs when rock in a descending tectonic plate undergoes a phase change in its crystalline structure along a thin plane parallel to a stress. Just such a phase change and resultant slippage can be produced in the laboratory by compressing a slab of calcium magnesium silicate. The pattern of deep-quake activity supports this theory. In most seismic zones, the recorded incidence of deep-focus earthquakes corresponds to the depths at which phase changes are predicted to occur in mantle rock. For example, little or no phase change is thought to occur at 400 km, and indeed, earthquake activity at this level is negligible. Between 400 and 680 km, activity once again increases. Although seismologists initially believed that earthquakes could be generated at depths as low as 1,080 or 1,200 km, no foci have been confirmed below 700 km. No phase changes are predicted for mantle rock below 680 km.

GO ON TO THE NEXT PAGE ⟩

17. Scientists 1 and 2 agree on which point?

    A. Deep-earthquake activity does not occur below 400 km.

    B. Fluid allows tectonic plates to slip past one another.

    C. Water can penetrate mantle rock.

    D. Rock below 50 km will not fracture normally.

18. Which of the following is evidence that would support Scientists 1's hypothesis?

    F. The discovery that water can be extracted from mantle-like rock at temperatures and pressures similar to those found below 300 km

    G. Seismographic indications that earthquakes occur 300 km below the surface of the Earth

    H. The discovery that phase changes occur in the mantle rock at depths of 1,080 km

    J. An earthquake underneath Los Angeles that was shown to have been caused by water trapped in sewer lines

19. Both scientists assume that:

    A. deep-focus earthquakes are more common than surface earthquakes.

    B. trapped fluids cause surface earthquakes.

    C. the Earth's crust is composed of mobile tectonic plates.

    D. deep-focus earthquakes cannot be felt on the Earth's crust without special recording devices.

20. To best refute Scientist 2's hypothesis, Scientist 1 might:

    F. find evidence of other sources of underground water.

    G. record a deep-focus earthquake below 680 km.

    H. find a substance that doesn't undergo phase changes even at depths equivalent to 680 km.

    J. show that rock becomes ductile at depths of less than 50 km.

21. According to Scientist 1, the earthquake at Rocky Mountain Arsenal occurred because:

    A. serpentine or other minerals dehydrated and released water.

    B. fluid wastes injected into the ground compressed a thin slab of calcium magnesium silicate.

    C. fluid wastes injected into the ground flooded pockets of a deep-sea trench.

    D. fluid wastes injected into the ground lowered the shear stress failure point of the rock.

22. Scientist 2's hypothesis would be strengthened by evidence showing that:

    F. water evaporates at high temperatures and pressures.

    G. deep-focus earthquakes can occur at 680 km.

    H. stress has the same effect on mantle rock that it has on calcium magnesium silicate.

    J. water pockets exist at depths below 300 km.

GO ON TO THE NEXT PAGE

23. According to Scientist 2, phase changes in the crystalline structure of a descending tectonic plate:

A. occur only at the earth's surface.

B. are not possible.

C. cause certain minerals to release water, which exerts pressure within the plate.

D. cause slippage that directly results in an earthquake.

PASSAGE V

Astronomers want to know the effects of atmospheric conditions on the impact of an asteroid-to-Earth collision. The most common hypothesis is that the presence of moisture in the Earth's atmosphere significantly reduces the hazardous effects of such a collision. One researcher has decided to create a laboratory model of the Earth. The researcher has the ability to control the amount of moisture surrounding the model. The researcher has also created models of asteroids at various sizes. The researcher will use a collision indicator (see table below) based on the Torino Scale to measure the results of two experiments.

Collision Indicator	
0 to 0.9	A collision capable of little destruction
1 to 3.9	A collision capable of localized destruction
4 to 6.9	A collision capable of regional destruction
7 to 10	A collision capable of global catastrophe

EXPERIMENT 1

The researcher simulated collisions on the Earth model with asteroid models equivalent to mass ranging from 1,000 kg to 1,000,000 kg. The controlled moisture level of the model Earth's atmosphere was 86%. The effects of the collisions were recorded and rated according to the collision indicator.

GO ON TO THE NEXT PAGE

EXPERIMENT 2

The researcher simulated collisions on the Earth model with asteroid models equivalent to the same mass as in Experiment 1. The controlled moisture level of the model Earth's atmosphere in this experiment was 12%. The effects of the collisions were recorded and rated according to the collision indicator. The results of both experiments are shown in the graph.

24. How was the experimental design of Experiment 1 different from that of Experiment 2?

   F. The impacts of more asteroids were measured.

   G. The impacts of larger asteroids were measured.

   H. There was more moisture in the atmosphere.

   J. There was a different collision indicator.

25. If the atmospheric moisture in Experiment 2 was increased to 50%, the collision rating for an asteroid with a mass of 400,000 kg would most likely be between:

   A. 2 and 3.

   B. 4.5 and 5.5.

   C. 6 and 7.

   D. 9 and 10.

26. Based on the experimental results, one can generalize that an increase of moisture in the atmosphere would:

   F. decrease the impact of an asteroid-to-Earth collision, regardless of the size of the asteroid.

   G. decrease the impact of an asteroid-to-Earth collision with asteroids under 700,000 kg.

   H. increase the impact of an asteroid-to-Earth collision, regardless of the size of the asteroid.

   J. increase the impact of an asteroid-to-Earth collision with asteroids under 700,000 kg.

GO ON TO THE NEXT PAGE

27. In a simulated asteroid-to-Earth collision, a 400,000 kg asteroid received a collision rating of 4. The amount of moisture in the atmosphere was most likely closest to:

A.   0%

B.   12%

C.   86%

D.   100%

28. According to the researcher's model, a 100,000 kg asteroid colliding in an atmosphere with a moisture level of 12% would be likely to have the same impact as an asteroid colliding in an atmosphere with a moisture level of 86% with a size closest to which of the following?

F.   50,000 kg

G.   120,000 kg

H.   270,000 kg

J.   490,000 kg

29. To be minimally capable of regional destruction, an asteroid entering an atmosphere with a moisture level of 86% would have to be roughly what percent larger than an asteroid capable of the same level of destruction entering an atmosphere with a moisture level of 12%?

A.   20%

B.   70%

C.   150%

D.   220%

Passage VI

The electrical conductivity of a material determines how it will react to various temperature conditions in a consumer product. Product researchers need to know how a material will react in order to determine its safety for consumer use. The electrical conductivity of two different samples of a platinum dithiolate compound was measured from 10 K to 275 K. The results and general conductivity versus temperature plots for conductors and semiconductors are shown below.

GO ON TO THE NEXT PAGE

temperature
Conductor

temperature
Semiconductor

30. For Sample HST-52, which of the following describes its behavior when the temperature is dropped from 200 K to 100 K?

   F.   The sample remains a semiconductor.

   G.   The sample remains a conductor.

   H.   The sample undergoes a conductor to semiconductor transition.

   J.   The sample undergoes a semiconductor to conductor transition.

31. In a material exhibiting conductor-like behavior, the conductivity:

   A.   increases as the temperature increases.

   B.   decreases as the temperature increases.

   C.   decreases as the temperature decreases.

   D.   remains the same at all temperatures.

32. A newly developed material has a semiconductor to conductor transition at about 10 K as the temperature increases. Its conductivity versus temperature plot would resemble which of the following?

   F.   G.

   H.   J.

33. An industrial firm wishes to use HST-52 as a semiconductor in an assembly line component. The experimental results indicate that:

   A.   HST-52 is not a semiconductor; a new material will have to be chosen.

   B.   HST-52 is suitable for the planned application.

   C.   HST-52 is too brittle to be used in this manner.

   D.   HST-52 will be usable only if the assembly line is maintained at less than 150 K.

34. The temperature at which a compound's conductivity-versus-temperature plot declines most quickly is known as its "optimal conductor" temperature. Which of the following could be the optimal conductor temperature for Sample HST-52?

   F.   20 K

   G.   80 K

   H.   160 K

   J.   180 K

GO ON TO THE NEXT PAGE

PASSAGE VII

Siamese cats have a genotype for dark fur, but the enzymes that produce the dark coloring function best at temperatures below the cat's normal body temperature. A Siamese cat usually has darker fur on its ears, nose, paws, and tail, because these parts have a lower temperature than the rest of its body. If a Siamese cat spends more than one hour a day for six consecutive days outdoors (an "outdoor" cat) during very cold weather, darker fur grows in other places on its body. If a Siamese cat does not spend this amount of time outdoors, it is an "indoor" cat. The amount of dark fur on its body remains constant throughout the year.

35. According to the graph, if the average temperature outdoors drops from 2°C to 0°C over the course of a month, what will most likely happen to the fur of an outdoor Siamese cat during the same time period? Over that time, the percentage of the cat's body covered in dark fur will:

   A. increase.
   B. decrease.
   C. remain the same.
   D. increase, then decrease.

36. A particular Siamese cat goes outdoors a total of 3 hours per week during the coldest part of the year. One could predict that the percentage of its body covered by dark fur would be closest to:

   F. 0%
   G. 10%
   H. 40%
   J. 60%

37. According to the graph, what is the most likely temperature outside if outdoor Siamese cats have 45% of their bodies covered in dark fur?

   A. 0° C
   B. 3° C
   C. 6° C
   D. 9° C

GO ON TO THE NEXT PAGE ⇨

38. If a Siamese cat that lived indoors was lost and later found with dark fur over 30% of its body, which of the following could be inferred about the period during which it was missing:

    I. It was living in an area where temperatures fell below 5° C.

    II. It spent more time outdoors than indoors.

    III. It was missing for at least 6 days.

    F. I and II only

    G. I and III only

    H. II and III only

    J. I, II, and III

39. If a Siamese cat has dark fur over 10% of its body, which of the following must be true about the cat?

    A. It lives indoors.

    B. It lives in an area where the temperature outdoors is usually 7° C or higher.

    C. It either lives indoors or it lives in an area where the temperature outdoors is usually 7° C or higher.

    D. None of the above

40. If a researcher wants to find out how fur color is affected by the amount of time a Siamese cat spends outside in cold weather, which experiment would be the most helpful?

    F. The "indoor" cats in the original experiment should be used as the control group and their fur color should be compared to a group of Siamese cats spending six hours or more a day outside in cold weather for six consecutive days.

    G. A new group of Siamese cats should be formed and kept outside two or more hours a day at varying temperatures. Their fur color at different outdoor temperatures should be compared to the "outdoor" cats already charted.

    H. Siamese cats should be split into two groups, one group spending only one hour per day outside for six consecutive days in cold weather, and the other group spending at least two hours a day outside for six consecutive days in the same weather.

    J. No new experiment is needed. The data already gathered shows that the more time a Siamese cat spends outside in cold weather, the darker its fur will be.

IF YOU FINISH BEFORE TIME IS CALLED, YOU MAY CHECK YOUR WORK ON THIS SECTION ONLY. DO NOT TURN TO ANY OTHER SECTION IN THE TEST. STOP

WRITING TEST
30 Minutes—1 Question

Directions: This section will test your writing ability. You will have thirty (30) minutes to compose an essay in English. Prior to planning your essay, pay close attention to the essay prompt so that you understand exactly what you are supposed to do. Your essay's grade will be based on how well it expresses an opinion on the question in the prompt, as well as its logical construction, supporting evidence, and clarity of expression based on the standards of written English.

You may use the unlined space on the next page to plan your essay. Anything written in this space will not be scored by the graders. Your essay must be written on the lined pages. While you may not need all the space to finish, you should not skip lines. Corrections and additions may be written neatly in between lines but not in the margins. Be sure to write clearly. Illegible work will not receive credit.

If you finish in under thirty minutes, you may review your essay. When time is called, lay your pencil down immediately.

DO NOT CONTINUE UNTIL TOLD TO DO SO.

School athletics has become increasingly competitive in recent years, as professional athletes are drafted at younger ages and the money and fame that professional athletes enjoy has risen to astronomical levels. Some students and school administrators believe that all student athletes should be required to maintain a minimum grade point average or be barred from playing, to ensure that they still get a good education. Others believe this requirement would be unfair because athletics and academics are unrelated, and because such a rule would make it too difficult for coaches to do their jobs. In your opinion, should student athletes be required to maintain a minimum grade point average?

In your essay, take a position on this question. You may write about either one of the two points of view given, or you may present a different point of view on this question. Use specific reasons and examples to support your position.

Use this space to *plan* your essay. Your work here will not be graded. Write your essay on the lined pages that follow.

IF YOU FINISH BEFORE TIME IS CALLED, YOU MAY CHECK YOUR WORK ON THIS SECTION ONLY. DO NOT TURN TO ANY OTHER SECTION IN THE TEST.

Practice Test Two: **Answer Key**

ENGLISH TEST

1. D	26. J	51. B
2. G	27. B	52. J
3. C	28. G	53. C
4. J	29. C	54. J
5. B	30. F	55. C
6. G	31. A	56. J
7. D	32. J	57. C
8. J	33. B	58. F
9. B	34. H	59. D
10. H	35. A	60. F
11. A	36. H	61. B
12. J	37. B	62. F
13. A	38. J	63. D
14. F	39. A	64. G
15. D	40. G	65. B
16. G	41. C	66. F
17. A	42. J	67. C
18. J	43. A	68. H
19. C	44. J	69. B
20. F	45. D	70. J
21. B	46. H	71. B
22. J	47. A	72. F
23. B	48. G	73. B
24. F	49. B	74. J
25. C	50. G	75. B

MATH TEST

1. A	31. A
2. J	32. F
3. A	33. B
4. G	34. K
5. B	35. D
6. H	36. K
7. C	37. B
8. J	38. F
9. D	39. A
10. F	40. K
11. B	41. B
12. G	42. H
13. D	43. E
14. G	44. K
15. D	45. E
16. F	46. K
17. E	47. E
18. K	48. G
19. D	49. C
20. G	50. F
21. E	51. C
22. H	52. F
23. A	53. B
24. G	54. J
25. C	55. E
26. J	56. G
27. C	57. B
28. H	58. J
29. D	59. C
30. H	60. J

READING TEST

1. D	21. A
2. G	22. J
3. B	23. D
4. G	24. H
5. C	25. D
6. G	26. J
7. C	27. C
8. J	28. G
9. C	29. B
10. G	30. F
11. B	31. B
12. J	32. G
13. C	33. B
14. G	34. J
15. A	35. A
16. G	36. J
17. C	37. C
18. G	38. H
19. D	39. A
20. F	40. G

SCIENCE TEST

1. B	21. D
2. H	22. H
3. A	23. D
4. J	24. H
5. A	25. B
6. F	26. G
7. C	27. C
8. H	28. H
9. B	29. B
10. G	30. H
11. B	31. B
12. F	32. H
13. D	33. D
14. J	34. J
15. B	35. C
16. J	36. G
17. D	37. B
18. F	38. G
19. C	39. C
20. G	40. H

ANSWERS AND EXPLANATIONS

ENGLISH TEST

PASSAGE I

1. (D)

A comma is needed to set off the introductory phrase, so (A) cannot be correct. (B) creates a sentence fragment, and the pronoun *it* in (C) does not match the subject of the sentence—Duke Ellington.

2. (G)

The whole passage is in past tense, and there is no reason why this verb should not be in past tense as well. Also, the part of the sentence on the other side of the semicolon gives you a big clue by using *paid*.

3. (C)

The colon is used incorrectly in the original sentence, and (B) does not solve the problem. (D) is unnecessarily wordy.

4. (J)

Commas are needed between items in a series, so eliminate (F) and (G). A comma is also needed to set off the introductory phrase, so eliminate (H).

5. (B)

In order to figure out the appropriate pronoun, identify the noun to which the pronoun refers. The only possible corresponding noun is *Ellington*; therefore, (B) is the correct answer.

6. (G)

As a teenager in Washington is not a complete sentence. (H) does not make sense, and (J) is incorrect because the comma is unnecessary.

7. (D)

The word *then* should be *than*—(D) is the choice that makes this correction.

8. (J)

Even though the piano teacher's name is mentioned in the preceding sentence, more information about her name is unnecessary.

9. (B)

There is a contrast between Ellington's not being a good pianist and his hearing about the opportunities for musicians in New York. The best contrast is established by (B).

10. (H)

Awaited and *were there for* mean the same thing, so one part of the underlined portion should be deleted—that eliminates (F) and (G). (J) incorrectly uses *which* instead of *that*, so it too can be eliminated.

11. (A)

The sentence is logical in the flow of the paragraph, so eliminate (D). (A) is the simplest and most correct way to phrase the sentence.

12. (J)

The subject of the sentence is the Cotton Club, so answer choices with the pronoun *he*—(F) and (G)—should be eliminated. (H) creates a sentence fragment.

13. (A)

This list of songs simply provides some detail. The songs do not contradict anything, so eliminate (B). The names of the songs themselves do not illustrate complexity; therefore, (C) is incorrect. This part of the paragraph is no longer about the Cotton Club, so eliminate (D).

14. (F)

The last paragraph of the essay lists the accomplishments of Ellington. (F) is the only answer choice that makes sense.

15. (D)

Paragraph 4 is the only paragraph that covers elements of Ellington's music. The logical place for the insertion is before the last sentence of the essay.

PASSAGE II

16. (G)

The subject is *animals*, so a plural pronoun is needed. (F) is a singular pronoun, (H) is a contraction, and (J) uses *there* instead of *their*.

17. (A)

The comma is needed to set off the second clause from the first.

18. (J)

The phrase *a member of the weasel family* is a nonessential clause and should be set off by commas. Eliminate (G) and (H) because they create sentence fragments.

19. (C)

Which should be *that*—rule out (A) and (B). The whole passage is in present tense, so eliminate (D) because it is in past tense.

20. (F)

Choose the most logical order of the words. (F) is the choice that makes the most sense.

21. (B)

Far from placing it in danger is an introductory phrase and should be set off by a comma. Eliminate (A) and

(C). (D) is unnecessarily wordy and doesn't make sense with the rest of the sentence.

22. (J)

By distinguishing itself from other animals is a sentence fragment. These words make sense as an introductory phrase and should therefore be set off by a comma. (J) is the choice that accomplishes this.

23. (B)

(B) is the simplest and most correct way to phrase the question.

24. (F)

The investigating has occurred in the past, and it is still occurring. The tense of the answer choice should reflect this. (G) and (H) only refer to the past, and (J) refers only to the present.

25. (C)

The previous sentence speaks of special glands, but this sentence says that some animals do not have these glands. This is a contrast, and *however* sets it up best.

26. (J)

Remains and *endures as* are the same thing, so the correct choice will eliminate one of them. (J) does just that.

27. (B)

The pronoun *it* refers to the tree frog, not a background of leaves. (B) fixes the error.

28. (G)

The information is useful in the paragraph, so eliminate (J). (G) is a simple and logical way of rephrasing all of the excess words.

29. (C)

Paragraph 4 begins with an introduction, and Paragraph 3 ends with a conclusion. (C) is the only choice that reflects this.

30. (F)

The author covers a range of topics in the area and uses several animals as examples. All of the other answer choices are incorrect because they contradict things that the author does in the essay.

PASSAGE III

31. (A)

The other answer choices are unnecessarily wordy.

32. (J)

The other answer choices are unnecessarily wordy.

33. (B)

The sentences on both sides of the period are fragments. The best way to fix this mistake is to simply combine the sentences.

34. (H)

Included and *held* relay the same information. (H) deletes one of the unnecessary words.

35. (A)

The drink was unusual to the people who never experienced it before. In other words, the verb form should be past tense. Eliminate (B) and (C). (D) does not make sense, so eliminate it.

36. (H)

Over the next century is an introductory phrase and should be set off by a comma. (H) and (J) add the comma, but (J) also adds unnecessary words.

37. (B)

This description would provide some "color" to the essay. It would not weaken or contradict anything, so eliminate (A) and (C). It would not say anything about the author's opinion of chocolate either, so eliminate (D).

38. (J)

Commas are needed between items in a series. (G) is incorrect because there are too many commas.

39. (A)

The sentence provides an example of the uses of chocolate worldwide. (B) and (C) set up an unwarranted contrast. (D) is not a good transition between the two sentences.

40. (G)

The word *do* is unnecessary in the sentence, especially with the presence of *nonetheless*. (G) is the most concise statement of the information.

41. (C)

The colon is not used properly here, so eliminate (A), (B), and (D).

42. (J)

Tea has nothing to do with the topic, so the sentence should be eliminated.

43. (A)

The research will be welcomed "by" people, not "to" or "with" them. Therefore, eliminate (B) and (D). *Us with a sweet tooth* does not make sense, so (A) is the correct answer.

44. (J)

(F) and (G) do not make any sense at all. Between (H) and (J), the latter is the better sounding choice.

45. (D)

This essay is about only chocolate, and it does not cover any other culinary trends in history. Therefore, it would not meet the requirement.

Passage IV

46. (H)

Here, the verb is being used as part of a modifying phrase. Choice (H) is idiomatically correct.

47. (A)

Commas are needed in a series, so eliminate (C). A colon is not appropriate; eliminate (B). (D) incorrectly switches to the past tense.

48. (G)

The form needed is the possessive of *who,* so (G) is correct.

49. (B)

This sentence is part of a list of proposed *uniform of the future* developments. The other sentences in that list use the verbs *would be*, *would become*, and *would transmit*. So the correct form is (B).

50. (G)

No commas are needed in a list of only two items.

51. (B)

Be wary of sentences that begin with *to*; they are often fragments like the one here. (B) is the best way to combine the two parts of the sentence.

52. (J)

Two words in the underlined portion of the sentence telling what the proposed covering does to a soldier have closely related meanings: "concealing" means *keeping from being observed* or *hiding*, and "invisible" means *hidden* or *impossible to see*. Because these words convey the same idea, this is a simple redundancy that can be fixed by eliminating one of the two words. Therefore, we can eliminate choices (F), (G), and (H), and select (J) as the answer.

53. (C)

To determine the U.S. Army's opinion of the Invisible Soldier program, look at the words used to introduce and describe it: the army has dreamed of such a program and invested in it. So the army attitude is positive; we can eliminate the negative word *skeptical* in (A) and the neutral words *curious* and *detailed* in (B) and (D), leaving *enthusiastic*, (C).

54. (J)

In context, this paragraph offers a specific example of the more general issues raised in paragraph 1.

55. (C)

Having *beginning* and *early stages* is redundant. (C) is the most concise way to rephrase this.

56. (J)

As written, this is a run-on sentence, so eliminate (F). To correct it, the new clause should be made subordinate by replacing the pronoun with a relative pronoun, so eliminate (H). The correct form, since it follows a comma, is *which* rather than *that*, so eliminate (G).

57. (C)

The passage has a formal, technical tone. It would, therefore, be inappropriate for the author to use the highly informal expressions *you know, is* or *is, like*; eliminate (A) and (B). The choice *however, is* is appropriate since this paragraph contrasts with the preceding one. (D) would be appropriate if this paragraph drew a conclusion based on the prior paragraph, but it doesn't.

58. (F)

A colon is correct punctuation here because the material that follows it is an explanation of what precedes it.

59. (D)

Only sentence 2 and sentence 1 are choices for a first sentence. To put the sentences in logical order, first look for a good transition from paragraph 4, which discusses a problem. Sentence 1 explicitly refers to addressing the problem, so it's the better choice. Eliminate (A) and (B). The second sentence should follow logically from sentence 1's description of the new color-changing pixel, and our choices are sentences 4 and 5. Sentence 4 in (C) refers to mirrors, which we haven't encountered before in the passage, rather than pixels, so we can eliminate this choice. That leaves us with (D), sentence 5, which refers to the pixels introduced in the first sentence.

60. (F)

To answer this question, we need an idea of the purpose of each paragraph. Paragraph 1 introduces the *uniform of the future*, paragraph 2 the *Invisible Soldier* program, paragraph 3 the program's early-stage solution, paragraph 4 a problem with that solution, and paragraph 5 a new advance that may solve that problem. The new sentences to be inserted do not discuss a problem with such a program. We

can therefore eliminate choices (G), (H), and (J). The material properly belongs in paragraph 2, choice (G), because it introduces camouflage generally.

PASSAGE V

61. (B)

(A) and (C) are too wordy, and (D) does not continue the verb tense established in the series.

62. (F)

The colon is used here to dramatically introduce California. The commas in (G) and (H) do not do this well, and the separate sentence in (J) does not work either.

63. (D)

This paragraph is in the past tense, so the introductory sentence should be in the past tense as well.

64. (G)

This is a long nonessential clause that should be set off by a comma. (J) is incorrect because it unnecessarily adds more words.

65. (B)

The word order is incorrect in (A). (C) creates a sentence fragment, and *did* in (D) is unnecessary.

66. (F)

The information is pertinent to the topic, and (F) is the clearest statement.

67. (C)

The only choice that works here is (C). *Their* would have also worked, but it does not appear as one of the answer choices.

68. (H)

(F) is a sentence fragment. (G) and (J) are very awkward.

69. (B)

The last sentence of the previous paragraph talks about how workers began to quit their jobs to join the Gold Rush. The first sentence of this paragraph magnifies this point. (B) is the only logical transition.

70. (J)

This information is not pertinent to the Gold Rush back in 1849.

71. (B)

Singularly and *one* are redundant. (C) is too wordy, and (D) is incorrect within the context of the sentence.

72. (F)

This sentence is a more specific detail that illustrates the preceding sentence. (F) is the best transition between the two sentences.

73. (B)

(A) makes it sound as though lives are changing the place rather than the other way around. (C) does not make sense, and (D) is grammatically incorrect.

74. (J)

(H) and (F) do not make sense because of the word *and*. (G) is incorrect because the sentence is talking about people today, not the Forty-niners.

75. (B)

Though the Forty-niners are mentioned, the focus of the essay is on the history of the California Gold Rush. Therefore, the essay would not meet the requirements of the assignment.

MATH TEST

1. (A)—Percent Increase and Decrease

100 Key Math Concepts for the ACT, #33. To reduce a number by 20%, you could take 20% of the original number and subtract the result, or you could just take 80% of the original number:

$$
\begin{aligned}
\text{New price} &= 80\% \text{ of original price} \\
&= (.80)(\$125) \\
&= \$100
\end{aligned}
$$

2. (J)—Evaluating an Algebraic Expression

100 Key Math Concepts for the ACT, #52. Plug in $x = -5$ and see what you get:

$$
\begin{aligned}
2x^2 - 6x + 5 &= 2(-5)^2 - 6(-5) + 5 \\
&= 2 \times 25 - (-30) + 5 \\
&= 50 + 30 + 5 \\
&= 85
\end{aligned}
$$

3. (A)—Prime Factorization

100 Key Math Concepts for the ACT, #11. The prime factorization of 36 is $2 \times 2 \times 3 \times 3$. That factorization includes 2 distinct prime factors, 2 and 3.

4. (G)—Exterior Angles of a Triangle

100 Key Math Concepts for the ACT, #81. The exterior angles of a triangle (or any polygon, for that matter) add up to $360°$:

$$
\begin{aligned}
x + 85 + 160 &= 360 \\
x &= 115
\end{aligned}
$$

5. (B)—Average Formula, Adding/Subtracting Fractions

100 Key Math Concepts for the ACT, #41, #22. Don't jump to hasty conclusions—don't just average the denominators. Do it right—add the fractions and divide by 2:

$$\text{Average of 2 numbers} = \frac{\text{Sum}}{2}$$

$$\frac{\frac{1}{20} + \frac{1}{30}}{2} = \frac{\frac{3}{60} + \frac{2}{60}}{2} = \frac{\frac{5}{60}}{2} = \frac{\frac{1}{12}}{2} = \frac{1}{12} \times \frac{1}{2} = \frac{1}{24}$$

6. (H)—Rate

100 Key Math Concepts for the ACT, #39. Everyone pays $1.50, and the rest of the toll is based on the number of miles traveled. Subtract $1.50 from Joy's toll to see how much is based on distance traveled: $25.00 − $1.50 = $23.50. Then divide that amount by 25 cents per mile:

$$\frac{\$23.50}{\$0.25 \text{ per mile}} = 94 \text{ miles}$$

7. (C)—Multiplying and Dividing Powers, Multiplying Monomials

100 Key Math Concepts for the ACT, #47, #55. Multiply the coefficients and add the exponents:

$$3x^2 \times 5x^3 = 3 \times 5 \times x^{2+3} = 15x^5$$

8. (J)—Finding the Distance Between Two Points

100 Key Math Concepts for the ACT, #71. You could use the distance formula, but it's easier here to think about a right triangle. One leg is the difference between the xs, which is 3, and the other leg is the difference between the ys, which is 4, so you're looking at a 3-4-5 triangle, and the hypotenuse, which is the distance from P to Q, is 5.

9. (D)—Percent Formula

100 Key Math Concepts for the ACT, #32. Percent times Whole equals Part:

$$(\text{Percent}) \times 25 = 16$$
$$\text{Percent} = \frac{16}{25} = 0.64 = 64\%$$

10. (F)—Comparing Fractions

100 Key Math Concepts for the ACT, #28. For $\frac{7}{x}$ to be greater than $\frac{1}{4}$ the denominator x has to be less than 4 times the numerator, or 28. And for $\frac{7}{x}$ to be less than $\frac{1}{3}$, the denominator x has to be greater than 3 times the numerator, or 21. Thus, x could be any of the integers 22 through 27, of which there are 6.

11. (B)—Factoring Other Polynomials—FOIL in Reverse

100 Key Math Concepts for the ACT, #61. To factor $6x^2 - 13x + 6$, you need a pair of binomials whose "first" terms will give you a product of $6x^2$ and whose "last" terms will give you a product of 6. And since the middle term of the result is negative, the two last terms must both be negative. You know that one of the factors is among the answer choices, so you can use them in your trial-and-error effort to factor. You know you're looking for a factor with a minus sign in it, so the answer's either B or D.

Try B first: Its first term is $3x$, so the other factor's first term would have to be $2x$ (to get that $6x^2$ in the product). B's last term is −2, so the other factor's last term would have to be −3. Check to see if $(3x - 2)(2x - 3)$ works:

$$(3x - 2)(2x - 3)$$
$$= (3x \cdot 2x) + [3x(-3)] + [(-2)(2x)] + [(-2)(-3)]$$
$$= 6x^2 - 9x - 4x + 6$$
$$= 6x^2 - 13x + 6$$

It works. There's no need to check D.

12. (G)—Adding/Subtracting Fractions

100 Key Math Concepts for the ACT, #22. The four fractions on the left side of the equation are all ready to be added, because they already have a common denominator: a.

$$\frac{1}{a} + \frac{2}{a} + \frac{3}{a} + \frac{4}{a} = 5$$

$$\frac{1 + 2 + 3 + 4}{a} = 5$$

$$\frac{10}{a} = 5$$

$$10 = 5a$$

$$a = 2$$

13. (D)—Intersecting Lines

100 Key Math Concepts for the ACT, #78. $\angle CGE$ and $\angle BGF$ are vertical angles, so they're equal, and $\angle BGF$ measures 105°. If you subtract $\angle AGB$ from $\angle BGF$, you're left with $\angle AGF$, the angle you're looking for. So, $\angle AGF$ measures 105° − 40°, or 65°.

14. (G)—Solving an Inequality

100 Key Math Concepts for the ACT, #69. You solve an inequality much the way you solve an equation: Do the same things to both sides until you've isolated what you're solving for. (Just remember to flip the sign if you ever multiply or divide both sides by a negative number.) Here you want to isolate x:

$$-3 < 4x - 5$$

$$2 < 4x$$

$$\frac{2}{4} < x$$

$$x > \frac{1}{2}$$

15. (D)—Interior Angles of a Triangle, Exterior Angles of a Triangle

100 Key Math Concepts for the ACT, #80, #81. Because $\overline{BD}$ bisects $\angle ABC$, the measure of $\angle ABD$ is 50°. Now you know 2 of the 3 angles of $\triangle ABD$, so the third angle measures 180° − 60° − 50° = 70°.

$\angle BDC$, the angle you're looking for, is supplementary to the 70° angle, so $\angle BDC$ measures 180° − 70° = 110°.

16. (F)—Solving "In Terms Of," Factoring out a Common Divisor

100 Key Math Concepts for the ACT, #64, #58. To express y in terms of x, isolate y:

$$x + 2y - 3 = xy$$

$$2y - xy = -x + 3$$

$$y(2 - x) = 3 - x$$

$$y = \frac{3 - x}{2 - x}$$

17. (E)—Parts and Whole

If you add the number of English-speakers and the number of Spanish-speakers, you get 28 + 37 = 65. But there are only 50 students, so 65 − 50 = 15 of them are being counted twice—because those 15 speak both languages.

18. (K)—Rate

100 Key Math Concepts for the ACT, #39. Set up a proportion:

$$\frac{288 \text{ miles}}{6 \text{ hours}} = \frac{x \text{ miles}}{8 \text{ hours}}$$

$$6x = 288 \times 8$$

$$6x = 2{,}304$$

$$x = 384$$

19. (D)—Repeating Decimals

100 Key Math Concepts for the ACT, #30. To convert a fraction to a decimal, you divide the denominator into the numerator. Clearly you don't have time to take the division out to 100 places after the decimal point. There must be a pattern you can take advantage of. Start dividing and continue just until you see what the pattern is:

$$11\overline{)4.000000\ldots} = .363636\ldots$$

The 1st, 3rd, 5th, etc. digits are 3; and the 2nd, 4th, etc. digits are 6. In other words, every odd-numbered digit is a 3 and every even-numbered digit is a 6. The 100th digit is an even-numbered digit, so it's a 6.

20. (G)—Solving a System of Equations

100 Key Math Concepts for the ACT, #67. Since it's x you're looking for, eliminate y. Fortunately, the equations are all ready for you—just add them and the $+4y$ cancels with the $-4y$:

$$3x + 4y = 31$$
$$\underline{3x - 4y = -1}$$
$$6x \phantom{{}+ 4y} = 30$$
$$x = 5$$

21. (E)—Finding the Distance Between Two Points

100 Key Math Concepts for the ACT, #71. The coordinates of the midpoint are the averages of the coordinates of the endpoints. The average of the xs is $\frac{2 + 12}{2} = 7$, and the average of the ys is $\frac{3 + (-15)}{2} = -6$, so the coordinates of the midpoint are $(7, -6)$.

22. (H)—Sine, Cosine, and Tangent of Acute Angles

100 Key Math Concepts for the ACT, #96. Cosine is "adjacent over hypotenuse." Here the leg adjacent to θ is 4 and the hypotenuse is 5, so $\cos \theta = \frac{4}{5}$.

23. (A)—Circumference of a Circle

100 Key Math Concepts for the ACT, #89. The radius of circle Q is twice the radius of circle P. You could use the circumference of circle P to find the radius of circle P, then double that radius to get the radius of circle Q, and finally use that radius to calculate the circumference of circle Q. It's much easier and faster, however, if you realize that "double the radius means double the circumference." If the circumference of circle P is 6, then the circumference of circle Q is twice that, or 12.

24. (G)—Evaluating an Algebraic Expression

100 Key Math Concepts for the ACT, #52. This looks like a functions question, but in fact it's just a "plug-in-the-number-and-see-what-you-get" question.

$$f(x) = x^3 - x^2 - x$$
$$f(-3) = (-3)^3 - (-3)^2 - (-3)$$
$$= -27 - 9 + 3$$
$$= -33$$

25. (C)—Integer/Noninteger, Miscellaneous Triangles

100 Key Math Concepts for the ACT, #3. If the two unknown side lengths are integers, and the sum of the two lengths has to be greater than 7, then the least amount the two unknown sides could add up to would be 8, which would make the perimeter $7 + 8 = 15$.

26. (J)—Factoring Other Polynomials—FOIL in Reverse, Factoring out a Common Divisor

100 Key Math Concepts for the ACT, #61. First factor out an x from each term, then factor what's left:

$$2x + 3x^2 + x^3 = x(2 + 3x + x^2)$$
$$= x(x^2 + 3x + 2)$$
$$= x(x + 1)(x + 2)$$

27. (C)—Simplifying an Algebraic Fraction, Multiplying and Dividing Powers, Raising Powers to Powers

100 Key Math Concepts for the ACT, #62, #47, #48. Get rid of the parentheses in the denominator, and then cancel factors the numerator and denominator have in common:

$$\frac{x^2 y^3 z^4}{(xyz^2)^2} = \frac{x^2 y^3 z^4}{x^2 y^2 z^4} = \frac{x^2}{x^2} \times \frac{y^3}{y^2} \times \frac{z^4}{z^4} = y$$

28. (H)—Adding/Subtracting Fractions, Converting Fractions to Decimals

100 Key Math Concepts for the ACT, #22, #29. Normally you would have a choice: Either convert the fractions to decimals first and then add, or add the fractions first and then convert the sum to a decimal. In this case, however, both fractions would convert to endlessly repeating decimals, which might be a bit unwieldy when adding. In this case it seems to make sense to add first, then convert:

$$\frac{2}{3} + \frac{1}{12} = \frac{8}{12} + \frac{1}{12} = \frac{9}{12} = \frac{3}{4} = 0.75$$

29. (D)—Solving a Linear Equation

100 Key Math Concepts for the ACT, #63. This looks like a physics question, but in fact it's just a "plug-in-the-number-and-see-what-you-get" question. Be sure you plug 95 in for C (not F):

$$C = \frac{5}{9}(F - 32)$$
$$95 = \frac{5}{9}(F - 32)$$
$$\frac{9}{5} \times 95 = F - 32$$
$$F - 32 = 171$$
$$F = 171 + 32 = 203$$

30. (H)—Probability

100 Key Math Concepts for the ACT, #46. Probability equals the number of favorable outcomes divided by the total number of possible outcomes. In this problem, a "favorable outcome" is choosing a green marble—that's 4. The "total number of possible outcomes" is the total number of marbles, or 20:

$$\text{Probability} = \frac{\text{Favorable Outcomes}}{\text{Total Number of Possible Outcomes}}$$
$$= \frac{4}{20}$$
$$= \frac{1}{5}$$

31. (A)—Adding and Subtracting Polynomials, Average Formula

100 Key Math Concepts for the ACT, #54, #41. To find the average of three numbers—even if they're algebraic expressions—add them and divide by 3:

$$\begin{aligned}
\text{Average} &= \frac{\text{Sum of terms}}{\text{Number of terms}} \\
&= \frac{(2x + 5) + (5x - 6) + (-4x + 2)}{3} \\
&= \frac{3x + 1}{3} \\
&= x + \frac{1}{3}
\end{aligned}$$

32. (F)—Using Two Points to Find the Slope

100 Key Math Concepts for the ACT, #72. Parallel lines have the same slope. Use the first pair of points to figure out the slope:

$$\text{Slope} = \frac{y_2 - y_1}{x_2 - x_1} = \frac{16 - 1}{2 - 1} = 15$$

Then use the slope to figure out the missing coordinate in the second pair of points:

$$\begin{aligned}
\text{Slope} &= \frac{y^2 - y^1}{x^2 - x^1} \\
15 &= \frac{(25 - (-5))}{a - (-10))} \\
15 &= \frac{30}{a + 10} \\
15a + 150 &= 30 \\
15a &= -120 \\
a &= -8
\end{aligned}$$

33. (B)—Similar Triangles

100 Key Math Concepts for the ACT, #82. When parallel lines make a big triangle and a little triangle as they do here, the triangles are similar (because they have the same angle measurements). Side $\overline{PR}$ is three times the length of $\overline{QR}$, so each side of the big triangle is three times the length of the corresponding side of the smaller triangle, and therefore the ratio of the perimeters is also 3:1. So the perimeter of $\triangle PRT$ is 3 times 11, or 33.

34. (K)—Special Quadrilaterals

100 Key Math Concepts for the ACT, #86. It is a poly-gon because it's composed of straight line segments. It is a quadrilateral because it has four sides. It is not a rectangle because opposite sides are not equal. It is a trapezoid because it has one pair of parallel sides.

35. (D)—Evaluating an Algebraic Expression, Solving a Linear Equation

100 Key Math Concepts for the ACT, #52, #63.

Plug in $x = -3$ and solve for a:

$$\begin{aligned}
2x^2 + (a - 4)x - 2a &= 0 \\
2(-3)^2 + (a - 4)(-3) - 2a &= 0 \\
18 - 3a + 12 - 2a &= 0 \\
30 - 5a &= 0 \\
-5a &= -30 \\
a &= 6
\end{aligned}$$

36. (K)—Counting the Possibilities

100 Key Math Concepts for the ACT, #45. The total number of combinations of a first course, second course, and dessert is equal to the product of the 3 numbers:

$$\text{Total possibilities} = 4 \times 5 \times 3 = 60$$

37. (B)—Prime Factorization, Least Common Multiple

100 Key Math Concepts for the ACT, #11, #14. An integer that's divisible by 6 has at least one 2 and one 3 in its prime factorization. An integer that's divisible by 9 has at least two 3s in its prime factorization. Therefore, an integer that's divisible by both 6 and 9 has at least one 2 and two 3s in its prime factorization. That means it's divisible by 2, 3, $2 \times 3 = 6$, $3 \times 3 = 9$, and $2 \times 3 \times 3 = 18$. It's not necessarily divisible by 12 or 36, each of which includes two 2s in its prime factorization. You could also do this one by **picking numbers.** Think of a common multiple of 6 and 9 and use it to eliminate some options. $6 \times 9 = 54$ is an obvious common multiple—and it's not divisible by 12 or 36, but it is divisible by 18. The *least* common multiple of 6 and 9 is 18, which is also divisible by 18. It looks like every common multiple of 6 and 9 is also a multiple of 18.

38. (F)—Simplifying an Algebraic Fraction

100 Key Math Concepts for the ACT, #62.

$$\frac{x^2 + x^2 + x^2}{x^2} = \frac{3x^2}{x^2} = 3$$

39. (A)—Translating from English into Algebra

100 Key Math Concepts for the ACT, #65. Read carefully. This question's a lot easier than you might think. It's asking for the total number of coins, not the total value. q quarters, d dimes, and n nickels add up to a total of $q + d + n$ coins.

40. (K)—Solving an Inequality and Graphing Inequalities

100 Key Math Concepts for the ACT, #69, #70. You solve an inequality much the way you solve an equation: do the same things to both sides until you've isolated what you're solving for. (Just remember to flip the sign if you ever multiply or divide both sides by a negative number.)

$$5x - 2(1 - x) \geq 4(x + 1)$$
$$5x - 2 + 2x \geq 4x + 4$$
$$5x + 2x - 4x \geq 4 + 2$$
$$3x \geq 6$$
$$x \geq 2$$

The "greater-than-or-equal-to" symbol is graphed as a solid circle.

41. (B)—Using Two Points to Find the Slope

100 Key Math Concepts for the ACT, #72. First find the slope of the line that contains the given points:

$$\text{Slope} = \frac{y_2 - y_1}{x_2 - x_1} = \frac{10 - 6}{6 - 5} = 4$$

Line m is perpendicular to the above line, so the slope of m is the negative reciprocal of 4, or $-\frac{1}{4}$.

42. (H)—Sine, Cosine, and Tangent of Acute Angles

100 Key Math Concepts for the ACT, #96. Sine is "opposite over hypotenuse." Here the leg opposite θ is 12 and the hypotenuse is 13, so:

$$\sin \theta = \frac{12}{13}$$

43. (E)—Raising Powers to Powers, Solving a Linear Equation

100 Key Math Concepts for the ACT, #48, #63. Express the left side of the equation so that both sides have the same base:

$$9^{2x-1} = 3^{3x+3}$$
$$(3^2)^{2x-1} = 3^{3x+3}$$
$$3^{4x-2} = 3^{3x+3}$$

Now that the bases are the same, just set the exponents equal:

$$4x - 2 = 3x + 3$$
$$4x - 3x = 3 + 2$$
$$x = 5$$

44. (K)—Combined Percent Increase and Decrease

100 Key Math Concepts for the ACT, #35. Be careful with combined percent increase. You cannot just add the two percents, because they're generally percents of different wholes. In this instance, the 20% increase is based on the 1970 population, but the 30% increase is based on the larger 1980 population. If you just added 20% and 30% to get 50%, you fell into the test maker's trap.

The best way to do a problem like this one is to pick a number for the original whole and just see what happens. As usual, the best number to pick is 100. (That may be a small number for the population of a city, but verisimilitude is not important—all that matters is the math.)

If the 1970 population was 100, then a 20% increase would put the 1980 population at 120. Now, to figure the 30% increase, multiply 120 by 130%:

New # = (Original #) + (30% of Original #)
New # = 130% of Original #
$$x = 1.3(120)$$
$$= 156$$

Since the population went from 100 to 156, that's a 56% increase.

45. (E)—Finding the Missing Number

100 Key Math Concepts for the ACT, #44. The best way to deal with changing averages is go by way of the sums. Use the old average to figure out the total of the first 4 scores:

Sum of first 4 scores = $4 \times 89 = 356$

And use the new average to figure out the total he needs after the 5th score:

Sum of 5 scores = $5 \times 90 = 450$

To get his sum up from 356 to 450, Martin needs to score $450 - 356 = 94$.

46. (K)—Equation for a Circle

100 Key Math Concepts for the ACT, #75. If you find the distance from the center to the given point on the circle, you'll have the radius. The difference between the xs is 8, and the difference between the ys is 6. If 8 and 6 are the lengths of the legs of a right triangle, then the hypotenuse is 10. The radius, then, is 10. Now you can plug the radius and the coordinates of the center point into the general form of the equation of a circle:

$$(x - h)^2 + (y - k)^2 = r^2$$
$$(x + 1)^2 + (y + 1)^2 = 10^2$$
$$(x + 1)^2 + (y + 1)^2 = 100$$

47. (E)—Using Two Points to Find the Slope, Using an Equation to Find the Slope and the Intercept

100 Key Math Concepts for the ACT, #72, #73, #74. Use the points where the line crosses the axes— $(-1, 0)$ and $(0, 2)$—to find the slope:

$$\text{Slope} = \frac{y_2 - y_1}{x_2 - x_1} = \frac{2 - 0}{0(-1)} = 2$$

The y-intercept is 2. Now plug $m = 2$ and $b = 2$ into the slope-intercept equation form:

$$y = mx + b$$
$$y = 2x + 2$$

48. (G)—Percent Formula

100 Key Math Concepts for the ACT, #32. Be careful. The question is not asking, "What is $\frac{1}{4}$ of 16?" It's asking, "What is $\frac{1}{4}$ *percent* of 16?" One-fourth of 1 percent is 0.25%, or 0.0025:

$$\frac{1}{4}\% \text{ of } 16 = 0.0025 \times 16 = 0.04$$

49. (C)—Multiplying Binomials—FOIL

100 Key Math Concepts for the ACT, #56. Use FOIL to get rid of the parentheses, and then combine like terms:

$$(s + 4)(s - 4) + (2s + 2)(s - 2)$$
$$= (s^2 - 16) + (2s^2 - 2s - 4)$$
$$= s^2 + 2s^2 - 2s - 16 - 4$$
$$= 3s^2 - 2s - 20$$

50. (F)—Equation for a Parabola and Evaluating an Algebraic Expression

100 Key Math Concepts for the ACT, #76, #52. The easiest way to find the equation of a given parabola is to take a point or two from the graph and plug the coordinates into the answer choices, eliminating the choices that don't work. Start with a point with coordinates that are easy to work with. Here you could start with (3, 0). Plug $x = 3$ and $y = 0$ into each answer choice and you'll find that only F works.

51. (C)—Sine, Cosine, and Tangent of Acute Angles

100 Key Math Concepts for the ACT, #96. Since $\sin a = \frac{4}{5}$, you could think of this as a 3-4-5 triangle:

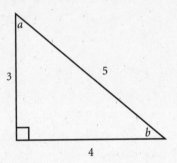

Cosine is "adjacent over hypotenuse." Here the leg adjacent to b is 4, and the hypotenuse is 5, so $\cos b = \frac{4}{5}$. (Notice that the sine of one acute angle in a right triangle is equal to the cosine of the other acute angle.)

52. (F)—Adding and Subtracting Monomials, Simplifying an Algebraic Fraction

100 Key Math Concepts for the ACT, #53, #62. Add the like terms in the numerator and then divide by the denominator:

$$\frac{x^2 + x^2 + x^2}{x} = \frac{3x^2}{x} = 3x$$

If you weren't careful, you might have confused this with problem 38 and missed the change in the denominator.

53. (B)—Translating from English into Algebra

100 Key Math Concepts for the ACT, #65. When you divide w by 4, you get $\frac{w}{4}$. When you subtract that result from r, you get $r - \frac{w}{4}$.

54. (J)—Volume of Other Solids

100 Key Math Concepts for the ACT, #95. The formula for the volume of a cylinder is $V = \pi r^2 h$, where r is the radius of the circular base and h is the height. Here $r = 4$ and $a = 5$, so:

$$\begin{aligned}
\text{Volume} &= \pi r^2 h \\
&= \pi(4)^2(5) \\
&= \pi(16)(5) \\
&= 80\pi
\end{aligned}$$

55. (E)—Area of a Triangle and Multiplying Binomials—FOIL

100 Key Math Concepts for the ACT, #83, #56. With a right triangle you can use the two legs as the base and the height to figure out the area. Here the leg lengths are expressed algebraically. Just plug the two expressions in for b and h in the triangle area formula:

$$\text{Area} = \frac{1}{2}(x-1)(x+1) = \frac{1}{2}(x^2-1) = \frac{x^2-1}{2}$$

56. (G)—Rate

100 Key Math Concepts for the ACT, #39. The difference between the populations in 1990 was $9,400 - 7,600 = 1,800$. Each year, as the larger population goes down by 100 and the smaller population goes up by 100, the difference decreases by 200. Thus it will take $1,800 \div 200 = 9$ years to erase the difference.

57. (B)—Miscellaneous Averages: Weighted Average

The overall average is not simply the average of the two average ages. Because there are a lot more women than men, women carry more weight, and the overall average will be closer to 25 than 35. Pick particular numbers for the females and males, say 4 females and 1 male. The ages of the 4 females total

4 times 25, or 100, and the age of the 1 male totals 35. The average, then, is $(100 + 35)$ divided by 5, or 27.

58. (J)—Sine, Cosine, and Tangent of Acute Angles and Pythagorean Theorem

100 Key Math Concepts for the ACT, #96, #84. The height h of the tree is the leg opposite θ. The distance b from the base of the tree is the leg adjacent to θ. "Opposite over adjacent" is tangent, but all the answer choices are in terms of the sine. Sine is "opposite over hypotenuse," so you're going to have to figure out the hypotenuse. Use the Pythagorean theorem:

$$\begin{aligned}
(\text{hypotenuse})^2 &= (\text{leg}_1)^2 + (\text{leg}_2)^2 \\
(\text{hypotenuse})^2 &= b^2 + h^2 \\
\text{hypotenuse} &= \sqrt{b^2 + h^2}
\end{aligned}$$

Now, to get the sine, put the opposite h over the hypotenuse $\sqrt{b^2 + h^2}$: $\sin\theta = \dfrac{h}{\sqrt{b^2 + h^2}}$

59. (C)—Evaluating an Algebraic Expression

100 Key Math Concepts for the ACT #52. This looks like a solid geometry question, but in fact it's just a "plug-in-the-numbers" question.

$$S = \pi r \sqrt{r^2 = h^2} = \pi(3)\sqrt{3^2 + 4^2} = 3\pi\sqrt{9+16}$$
$$3\pi\sqrt{25} = 3\pi \times 5 = 15\pi$$

60. (J)—Parallel Lines and Transversals

100 Key Math Concepts for the ACT #79. When a transversal crosses parallel lines, all the resulting acute angles are equal and all the resulting obtuse angles are equal. You can generally tell at sight which angles are equal. In this problem's figure, $a = c = e = g$, and $b = d = f = h$. Only J is true: c and g are both obtuse. In all the other choices you'll find an obtuse and an acute.

READING TEST

PASSAGE I

1. (D)

Lines 16–18 provide the answer: "I was brought up, from my earliest remembrance…by my godmother."

2. (G)

From the description of Dolly in the first two paragraphs, it is clear that Esther viewed her doll as her only friend. "I was such a shy little thing that I seldom dared to open my lips, and never dared to open my heart, to anybody else" (lines 6–8). This idea is repeated in lines 85–88: "I went up to my room, and crept to bed, and laid my doll's cheek against mine wet with tears, and holding that solitary friend upon my bosom, cried myself to sleep."

3. (B)

In this case, *stiff* is used to describe the tone of the letter that Esther's godmother wrote to decline the invitation to another student's birthday party. (B), "rigidly formal," is the most appropriate definition in this context.

4. (G)

Esther only *imagines* that her godmother tells her she should never have been born. "I saw in her face, looking gloomily at me, 'It would have been far better, little Esther, that you had no birthday, that you had never been born!' " (lines 66–68).

5. (C)

Although Esther's godmother says that she has forgiven Esther's mother, her facial expression directly contradicts this. "I see her knitted brow and pointed finger…her face did not relent…" (lines 77–81).

6. (G)

Esther is clearly lonely, as evidenced by her description of Dolly as her only friend and her explanation that there is a separation dividing her from the other girls at school. The birthday scene with her godmother also shows that Esther is quite confused about her own family past.

7. (C)

Her confrontation with her godmother gives Esther further reason to believe that no one loves her. The phrase before the cited line also points to (C) as the best answer: "I knew that I had brought no joy at any time to anybody's heart" (lines 89–90).

8. (J)

Answers (F), (G), and (H) are all mentioned in paragraph 5 (lines 39–52). At the end of the passage, Esther says, "I hope it is not self-indulgent to shed these tears as I think of it" (lines 96–98).

9. (C)

Esther's evidence that her godmother is a "good, good woman" is explained in lines 20–23: "She went to church three times every Sunday, and to morning prayers on Wednesdays and Fridays, and to lectures whenever there were lectures; and never missed."

10. (G)

In the first paragraph, Esther says, "Now, Dolly, I am not clever…" (line 3). In the second paragraph, Esther describes herself as "such a shy little thing" (line 6).

PASSAGE II

11. (B)

In the phrase "the Pantanal was a vast, soggy canvas, white with gleaming herds of Nelore cattle" (lines 62–64), *canvas* is used to mean "a background." None of the other choices makes sense.

12. (J)

The answer to this question can be found in lines 68–70: "As the jaguars grew scarce, their chief food staple, the capybaras—a meter-long rodent, the world's largest—overran farmers' fields…."

13. (C)

The answer to this question can be found in lines 12–17: "Exactly how dramatic a comeback is difficult to say because jaguars—*Panthera onca*, the largest feline in the New World—are solitary, secretive, nocturnal predators. Each cat needs to prowl at least 35 square kilometers by itself."

14. (G)

The last sentence of the second paragraph provides the answer. "Hotels, campgrounds, and bed-and-breakfasts have sprung up to accommodate the half-million tourists a year…bent on sampling the Pantanal's wildlife, of which the great cats must be the most magnificent example" (lines 23–28). Tourists want to see the jaguars, and not having the jaguars might negatively affect the booming ecotourist business.

15. (A)

The "green safari" example is mentioned as a way for "scientists to fit the cats with radio collars" (lines 89–92). The other three examples provided are listed in lines 95–99 as methods the scientists are teaching the ranchers.

16. (G)

In lines 50–51, the author says, "Hard data on cattle losses due to jaguars in the Pantanal are nonexistent…." One reason for providing anecdotal information, then, is to tell the story of the hardships faced by the ranchers due to the jaguars. The author does not suggest that he empathizes with the ranchers more than the jaguars—in fact, he refers to the jaguars as "magnificent." The only example that shows rancher violence is Abel Monteiro shooting an attacking jaguar who had killed his two dogs (lines 34–36), an act of self-defense. The landscape of the Pantanal is not the focus of these two paragraphs, so (J) can be eliminated.

17. (C)

The passage explains that because of the decrease in the jaguar population, the capybara population increased. These rodents "spread trichomoniasis, a livestock disease that renders cows sterile" (lines 71–72). Lines 75–79 describe the effect of weather patterns and floods on the ranchers' land. "Weather patterns also shifted radically—due most likely to global warming—and drove annual floods to near-Biblical proportions. The waters are only now retreating from some inundated pasturelands."

18. (G)

The last sentence of the paragraph reads, "When the scholars go home and the greens log off, the *pantaneiros* will still be there—left on their own to deal with the jaguars as they see fit" (lines 102–105).

19. (D)

Evidence is given throughout the passage that all three groups support protecting the jaguars. It is most concisely stated in lines 42–45: "a political cat fight between the scientists, environmentalists, and ecotourists who want to protect the jaguars and the embattled ranchers...."

20. (F)

The answer to this question can be found in lines 50–53: "Hard data on cattle losses due to jaguars in the Pantanal are nonexistent, but there are stories."

PASSAGE III

21. (A)

This Inference Question asks you why the aulos was considered "the instrument of the Dionysians." In the fifth paragraph, you find out that the Dionysians "represented the unbridled, sensual and passionate aspect of Greek culture" (lines 57–59). The passage also says that the aulos had a "far more exciting effect" (line 63) than the lyre. The suggestion here is clearly that the aulos must have been able to express the unbridled passion and excitement of the Dionysians, making (A) the best answer. (B) is out because the fact that the aulos was chosen as the official instrument of the Delphian and Pythian festivals doesn't explain why it was the instrument of the Dionysians. (C) contradicts the passage: the kithara, not the aulos, represented the intellectual, idealistic side of Greek art. Finally, the author never says when the Dionysian cult originated, so (D) is also out.

22. (J)

All the author means by saying that the chelys can be "traced back to the age of fable" is that it is an ancient instrument. The chelys was an actual, not an imaginary, instrument, so (H) is wrong. (G) is out because the kithara was used to accompany the epics, not the chelys.

23. (D)

(D) is the only answer choice to this Big Picture Question that adequately covers the entire passage. (A) focuses only on the lyre. The connection between Greek music and drama (B) is mentioned only in passing, as are the references to music in ancient Greek literature (C). The passage is really all about the "origin and development of various Greek instruments" (D).

24. (H)

The first thing the author says about the kithara is that it was used by professional Homeric singers. The kithara, according to the author, probably came from Egypt, so (F) is wrong. (G) and (J) contradict information in the paragraph to the effect that the kithara was more powerful than the chelys and was played with both hands.

25. (D)

Skim through the third paragraph to find the changes that occurred to the lyre between the eighth and fifth centuries B.C. Musicians began to use a plectrum in the seventh century B.C. (A), lyres featured an increasing number of strings (B) during this period, and musicians also began to use different scales and modes (C). That leaves (D). Nothing in the paragraph indicates that lyres were used to accompany dramatic productions.

26. (J)

The final paragraph says that "an early specimen" of the aulos was tuned to the chromatic tetrachord, "a fact that points to Oriental origin" (lines 74–77). From this you can infer that the chromatic tetrachord must have been used in ancient Oriental music (J). (F) is contradicted by the author's assertion that elegiac songs were composed in the mode of the chromatic tetrachord. There is no evidence to support either (G) or (H).

27. (C)

In the fourth sentence of the first paragraph (lines 7–9), the author indicates that the chelys is the most antique form of the lyre.

28. (G)

Sappho did two things that we know about from lines 39–41. She introduced a mode in which Dorian and Lydian characteristics were blended, and she initiated the use of the plectrum.

29. (B)

All of the details you need to answer this question are in the sixth paragraph (lines 60–69). The first sentence states that the aulos is more like our oboe than our flute, so Roman numeral III is false. This means (C) and (D) can be eliminated. The second sentence of the paragraph confirms that the aulos sounded more exciting than the lyre (Roman numeral II). Since (B) is the only remaining answer choice that includes II, you know it has to be the best answer.

30. (F)

Greek instruments are discussed as a whole at the very beginning of the passage. The author says that our knowledge of Greek instruments comes from "representations on monuments, vases, statues, and friezes and from the testimony of Greek authors" (lines 3–5). These are all "secondary sources" of information about the instruments, so (F) is the best answer. (G) is wrong because quite a bit is known about the tuning of the instruments, as represented

in the second paragraph. (H) is contradicted by the same sentence that supports (F). Finally, there is no evidence to suggest that more is known about one type of instrument than the other (J).

PASSAGE IV

31. (B)

Lines 15–18 state that "Scientists have not been able, however, to determine just how sunspots are created or what effect they have on the solar constant.…" This is followed by the statement that the question might be answered with "data from the *Solar Maximum Mission* satellite, which has monitored the solar constant since 1980" (lines 21–23).

32. (G)

The definition of *solar constant* is given in lines 18–19: "a misnomer that refers to the sun's total radiance at any instant."

33. (B)

The second sentence of the passage says, "People have speculated that the solar cycle might exert some influence on the earth's weather" (lines 3–5). The concluding paragraph suggests that the findings discussed in the passage point to "a link between the solar cycle and weather" (lines 89–90).

34. (J)

From the sentence alone, it may be difficult to determine the answer. But the preceding sentence clarifies that *proliferated* means "increased in number." Lines 24–25 read, "As the number of sunspots decreased through 1986.…"

35. (A)

The answer to this question can be found in lines 36–43: "When a sunspot appears, it initially causes the sun to dim slightly, but then after a period of weeks or months islands of brilliance called faculas usually emerge near the sunspot and more than compensate for its dimming effect. Wilson says faculas may represent regions where energy that initially was blocked beneath a sunspot has finally breached the surface."

36. (J)

The answer to this question is found in lines 48–51: "the quasi-biennial oscillation (QBO), a 180-degree shift in the direction of stratospheric winds above the Tropics that occurs about every two years."

37. (C)

The last paragraph quotes a scientist as believing that there will be "breakthroughs" in our understanding of the relationship between the solar cycle and the weather.

38. (H)

As described in the passage, the QBO changes directions every two years independently of the solar cycle. Lines 64–66 state that: "temperatures and pressures coincident with the QBO's west phase rose and fell in accordance with the solar cycle." Lines 70–72 state that: "The latitude of storms during the west phase of the QBO…varied with the solar cycle…"

39. (A)

Lines 7–9 read: "Until recently, however, none of these correlations has held up under close scrutiny." This suggests that recently they have begun to hold up under scrutiny.

40. (G)

The answer to this question can be found in lines 28–30: "The data suggest that the sun is 0.1 percent more luminous at the peak of the solar cycle, when the number of sunspots is greatest…."

SCIENCE TEST

PASSAGE I

1. (B)

Look at the *y*-axis of the graph between the region of pH 8 and pH 12 and then scan across at that level. The indicators that undergo color change at this pH range are thymol blue, phenolphthalein, and alizarin. These indicators correspond to (B).

2. (H)

Looking carefully at the graph, you can see that methyl orange changes from red to yellow between pH 3 and pH 5, and alizarin changes from yellow to red between pH 9 and pH 11. Thymol blue undergoes a yellow to blue color change, so it is not correct.

3. (A)

In order to determine when the reaction is complete and the solution is basic, the chemist should select an indicator that turns color when the pH has risen into the region of basicity (above 7). When bromocresol green inches above the pH of 7, it turns blue, so (A) is correct.

4. (J)

This question requires you to make a broad conclusion about acid-base indicators. (F) and (G) are incorrect because there are plenty of indicators that change colors above or below pH 7. (H) is incorrect because different indicators change colors at different pH levels, which explains why (J) is correct.

5. (A)

Compare the two indicators on the graph and you'll find that phenolphthalein undergoes a color change at a higher pH than bromothymol blue.

PASSAGE II

6. (F)

The quickest way to answer the question is to eliminate the wrong answer choices. A look at Table 1 rules out (G) because the total amount of oxygen absorbed is clearly affected by temperature. (H) is wrong because frog health is never an issue. The very mention of CO_2 makes (J) incorrect—Experiment 1 was only concerned with oxygen.

7. (C)

There is no data for 17° C, so an estimate is necessary. The total (skin plus lungs) amount of carbon dioxide released per hour was about 100 mol/hr at 15° C and about 110 mol/hr at 20° C. The only choice that falls between these is (C).

8. (H)

To show that *Hyla faber* is an ectotherm, one must find evidence demonstrating that changes in temperature cause changes in gas exchange. Table 1 demonstrates that as temperature increases, *Hyla faber*'s oxygen absorption increases, so (H) is correct. (F) is not good evidence because data for only one temperature does not give an idea of how temperature changes affect gas exchange. (G) is incorrect because the amount of carbon dioxide eliminated by the lungs is the same for 15° C, 20° C, and 25° C, which makes it look as though changes in temperature have little effect on gas exchange in the frog.

9. (B)

The amount of carbon dioxide eliminated by the skin increases over the range of temperatures; the increase levels off at the highest temperature. Carbon dioxide release by the lungs increases a bit over the lower temperatures and then levels off almost completely. The curve for skin release has to be much higher on the graph than the curve for lung release because the skin eliminated more carbon dioxide at each temperature than did the lungs. (B) is the only graph that fits these patterns.

10. (G)

When the answer choices all look similar like in this problem, find the differences between them and rule out the ones that cannot be correct. You can eliminate (H) and (J) right away because the results show that as temperature increases, O_2 absorbed by the lungs increases. (F) is not correct either—as temperature increases, CO_2 released by the skin increases, which is stated by (G).

11. (B)

Here again you want to be careful and refer to the answer choices as you review the tables to observe what happens as the temperature rises above 15° C. Since each of the answer choices refers to the tree frog's ability to absorb oxygen through the skin, start there. From Table 1 you can see that the skin's oxygen absorption rate goes down, so (C) and (D) are out. Now you need to refer to Table 2 to see what happens to the rate at which carbon dioxide is released from the lungs. It appears to remain about the same, so the correct answer is (B).

PASSAGE III

12. (F)

A good way to approach this question would be to draw a vertical line on the graph from 100% extraction of molybdenum (Mo) to the x-axis. This line lands closest to the pH of 3. Therefore, (F) is correct.

13. (D)

To answer this question, you need to look at the extraction curves for both erbium and tungsten and observe how they change with pH. For tungsten, the percentage extracted decreases from 100% to 0% as the pH increases from 1 to 2. The percentage of erbium extracted increases from 0% to 100% as the pH increases from 4 to 6. There is no overlap between the two ranges. "A single-step extraction" could not remove both at the same time.

14. (J)

In the graph, there are two types of slopes: one in which the percentage of an element extracted increases as the pH increases, and one in which the percentage of an element extracted decreases with increasing pH. Since there are two types of slopes, (J) is the correct response. (F) or (G) would be correct if the question pertained to a specific element, but the question asks you to consider the graph as a whole. If the percentage of an element extracted was independent of pH, you would expect to see the same percentage extracted at every pH. In other words, the graph for each element would be a horizontal line. This is not the case, so (H) is incorrect.

15. (B)

Draw a line on the graph from 45% to the line for thulium (Tm). Then draw a vertical line from that point to the *x*-axis. You should land on the *x*-axis between 5 and 6.

16. (J)

To answer this question, refer to the extraction curve for erbium. Erbium begins to be extracted when the pH level of the organic reagent is 4 or greater, and by a pH of 6 all of it is being extracted. Ytterbium (J) does not begin to be extracted until pH reaches approximately 9.

PASSAGE IV

17. (D)

Scientist 1 states that "below 50 km, rock is under too much pressure to fracture normally." Scientist 2 gives the fact that "rock becomes ductile at the temperatures and pressures that exist at depths greater than 50 km" as the reason that "deep-focus earthquakes cannot result from normal fractures."

18. (F)

Scientist 1's theory is invalid unless water can be shown to exist in mantle rock at the level of deep-focus earthquakes. If researchers could subject mantle-like rock to those temperatures and pressures, and then extract water from it (F), their experimental results would support the hypothesis of Scientist 1.

19. (C)

Both scientists believe that the Earth's crust (surface layer) is composed of mobile tectonic plates. In describing the plates as being "forced down into the mantle," Scientist 1 implies that they are normally in the crust and Scientist 2 makes reference to "a descending tectonic plate." The introductory paragraph says that "most" earthquakes originate less than 20 km below the Earth's surface, so (A) is wrong. Neither scientist assumes that surface quakes are caused by trapped fluids (B); both state that such quakes are caused by normal fractures in the Earth's crust. Neither scientist discusses how deep-focus earthquakes are detected, so (D) is not an assumption made by either scientist.

20. (G)

Scientist 2 believes that deep-focus quakes are the result of slippage caused by phase changes. Scientist 2 would, therefore, not expect deep quakes to occur below 680 km where, according to the last sentence of the passage, "no phase changes are predicted." Recording a quake with an origin below that depth would send Scientist 2 back to the drawing board, or at least in search of deeper phase changes.

21. (D)

The final sentence of Scientist 1's paragraph mentions that when fluids were injected into the ground at the Rocky Mountain Arsenal, the unintended result was "a series of shallow-focus earthquakes." The opening words *in fact* signal that this final sentence is meant to illustrate the previous sentence, which refers to experiments in which trapped fluids caused rock to fail at lower than normal shear stresses. The implication is that the quakes at the arsenal occurred because the fluid wastes lowered the shear stress failure point of the rock, (D). Dehydration (A) and the slab of calcium magnesium silicate (B) belong in Scientist 2's paragraph. (C) confuses the Rocky Mountain Arsenal incident with the deep-sea trenches that are mentioned in the previous two sentences.

22. (H)

Scientist 2 claims that the slippage involved in deep- focus quakes results from phase changes. To support this contention, she cites laboratory work that produced similar phase changes and slippage in a slab of calcium magnesium silicate. But neither scientist says that mantle rock is composed of calcium magnesium silicate. If the slippery slab is to serve as evidence for Scientist 2's theory, it must at least be similar to mantle rock, so (H) is correct. (F) might help refute Scientist 1's viewpoint, but would not strengthen Scientist 2's theory. (G) and (J) would tend to weaken Scientist 2's theory.

23. (D)

Phase changes are fundamental to the arguments of both scientists, and both agree that they occur deep beneath the earth's surface, so you can eliminate choices (A) and (B). The release of water from minerals is part of the explanation of Scientist 1, so choice (C) is out as well. Only choice (D) agrees with the logic of Scientist 2.

PASSAGE V

24. (H)

The one variable that changes is the amount of moisture. (G) cannot be correct because Experiment 2 says that the reseracher used models equivalent to the same mass as in Experiment 1. There is no evidence for (F) or (J).

25. (B)

The moisture in Experiment 1 is 86%, and the moisture in Experiment 2 is 12%. If the moisture was changed to 50%, the collision rating would fall between the lines of the two experiments on the graphs. At 400,000 kg, the collision rating would be between 4.5 and 5.5.

26. (G)

The collision ratings for Experiment 1, with a high percentage of moisture in the atmosphere, were mostly lower than those in Experiment 2. Therefore, an increase in moisture would decrease the impact of a collision. Eliminate (H) and (J). However, for asteroids over 700,000 kg, the lines on the graph meet—the presence of moisture loses its effect. (G) is correct.

27. (C)

Feel free to draw on the graph (you can write on your test booklet during the ACT). Draw a line from 4 on the x-axis straight up. Draw a line from the 4 on the y-axis straight across. Those two lines meet on the line for Experiment 1. The moisture level for Experiment 1 was 86%, so (C) is correct.

28. (H)

Again it might help to draw on the graph to answer this question. Draw a vertical line up from 1 (100,000 kg) on the horizontal scale to see where it hits the curve representing Experiment 2. Then draw a horizontal line from this curve to the curve representing Experiment 1 and draw from that point down to the horizontal scale once again. You'll see that the size is closest to (H), 270,000 kg.

29. (B)

To be minimally capable of regional destruction, an asteroid must have a collision rating of 4, so draw a horizontal line over from 4 on the vertical scale. If you do so you'll see that size of an asteroid capable of such destruction goes from roughly 250,000 kg at a 12% moisture level to about 400,000 kg at an 86% moisture level. 400,000 is roughly 70% larger than 250,000, so (B) is the correct answer.

Passage VI

30. (H)

Following HST-52 from right to left across the first figure (because the temperature is decreasing), conductivity increases and temperature decreases — just like the conductivity of a conductor—until 160 K, at which point HST-52's conductivity starts to decrease with decreasing temperature, like a semiconductor. With decreasing temperature, the sample undergoes a conductor to semiconductor transition (H).

31. (B)

The plot for conductor-like behavior indicates that as the temperature increases, its conductivity decreases. (A) and (C) describe the behavior of semiconductors, not conductors. (D) is incorrect: if the conductivity of conductors were the same at all temperatures, the plot of conductivity vs. temperature for conductors would be a horizontal line.

32. (H)

A material that has a semiconductor to conductor transition at 10 K will show a brief increase and then, starting at 10 K, a steady decrease as the temperature increases. (H) is the plot that shows this brief increase at low temperatures and then the decrease as the temperature rises.

33. (D)

The figure shows that HST-52 displays semiconductor behavior only up to about 150 K. Therefore, HST-52 will be usable as a semiconductor only at temperatures below about 150 K (D). (A) is wrong because HST-52 is a semiconductor at certain temperatures, and (B)

is wrong because HST-52 is not a semiconductor at all temperatures. The brittleness of HST-52 is never discussed in the passage, so (C) should be eliminated from the outset.

34. (J)

You are looking for the temperature at which the downward slope for Sample HST-52 is the steepest. This is somewhat difficult to determine, but this much is clear: the slope does not begin to go down until the temperature rises above 160 K. Thus the only answer that could make sense is (J), 180 K.

Passage VII

35. (C)

The graph shows no difference in the percentage of body covered in dark fur for outdoor temperatures less than or equal to 2°C, making choice (C) correct. The phrase "According to the graph" should remind you to extract data directly from the graph. Based on the passage alone you might incorrectly assume that since the temperature drops over that month the percentage of body covered in dark fur would increase as in choice (A). The graph shows, however, that is this is only true for outdoor temperatures between 2°C and 7°C.

36. (G)

The key to this question is determining whether the cat in question is an outdoor or indoor cat. This cat goes outdoors a total of three hours per week, whereas an outdoor cat would spend at least six hours outdoors per week. Therefore, this cat is an indoor cat, and the percentage of dark fur on its body would remain just above 10%.

37. (B)

You can draw a line from 45% dark fur across to the solid line representing outdoor cats. If you draw a line from that intersection straight down to the x-axis, you will hit 3° C.

38. (G)

If the cat grew dark fur over 30% of its body, it must have been an "outdoor" cat as defined in the passage, and, according to the table, been exposed to temperature below 5° C (Statement I). To be an outdoor cat, a cat does not have to spend more time outdoors than indoors (Statement II) but it has to spend time outdoors for 6 consecutive days (Statement III).

39. (C)

If a Siamese cat does not have dark fur over more than 10% of its body, then it must *either* be an indoor cat *or* live in an area where it is not regularly exposed to temperatures below 7° C.

40. (H)

Choice (F) is wrong because the "indoor" cats will not help us, since they don't go outside. (G) is not a good choice because the "outdoor" cats of the original experiment cannot be used as a control group: The time they spent outside was not monitored—we only know that they spent more than one hour outside a day. (J) is incorrect because the data already gathered only showed that outdoor cats turn darker in cold weather than indoor cats and doesn't provide any data about how varying the amount of time outdoors affects fur color. The correct answer is (H): a completely new experiment would have to be set up.

WRITING TEST

MODEL ESSAY

Below is an example of what a high-scoring essay might look like. Notice the author states her position clearly in the introductory paragraph and supports that position with evidence in the following paragraphs. This essay also uses transitions, some advanced vocabulary, and an effective "hook" to draw in the reader.

While some people believe academics and athletics are not related, I think it is important to hold student athletes responsible for earning a minimum grade point average. We live in a sports-obsessed world, where professional athletes receive multi-million dollar contracts and where highly paid athletes are becoming younger and younger. For example, LeBron James, still in high school, obtained a lucrative endorsement deal with Nike and was a highly sought-after NBA draft pick. Sadly, when teams are recruiting young athletes, the last thing they often look at is grades. It is also unfortunate that, feeling the pressure from alumni and fans to have successful teams, schools are often willing to overlook poor grades in their high-performing athletes. With so much money and fame at stake, and with so many institutions turning a blind eye, is it any wonder that many young athletes will sacrifice anything to get ahead, even their academic performance? Requiring student athletes to maintain a minimum grade point average is important for several reasons.

As an educational institution, a school's number-one priority should be the education of its students. The school does its student athletes a disservice when it doesn't push them to do their best at academics and learn as much as they can. It is unfair to hold other students, who may not be lucky enough to have the same natural athletic abilities, to a higher academic standard than athletes, and devalues any effort they make to get good grades by showing them in effect that what really matters in life is how good you are at sports. Also, since sports place so many demands on students' time and energy, what incentive do athletes have to take the extra time to keep up with schoolwork if they aren't required to do so?

When a school does not require student athletes to achieve a specified grade point average, it sets them up for failure later in life. The hard truth is that there are not enough jobs in professional sports for every student athlete. If students don't get drafted to play sports once they finish school, or if they do get chosen and then get injured and can no longer play the sport as well or at all, they only will have their grades and grade point average to show for their time in school. If their grades aren't good, they will have difficulty finding a job and starting a new career.

I am not trying to say that high-school sports are bad, or that they don't offer benefits to students involved in them. Not only do those students get in shape, but they also get to be on a team and feel like a part of something important. I think, however, that when schools treat academics as secondary they are taking the focus off all the positive things students get by participating in sports. When students think their athletic performance is their best chance for a post-high school career, they no longer think about accomplishments like learning discipline and improving self-esteem. They only focus on winning at all costs. Schools encourage this by making athletic performance more important than academics. If students know that they have a high enough grade point average to succeed if their sport doesn't become their career, maybe sports can go back to being fun again.

Participating in sports is a great thing for students to do. It builds self-confidence, fosters school spirit, and teaches determination. However, high schoolers should be students first. Requiring student athletes to maintain a certain grade point average would ensure that students get the education they need whether or not they go on to play professional sports. Schools' number-one priority should be making sure that all of their students, whether they are athletes or not, have the education required to succeed in life.

You can evaluate your essay and the model essay based on the following criteria, covered in chapter 16.

- Does the author answer the question?

- Is the author's position clearly stated?

- Does the body of the essay support and develop the position taken?

- Are there at least three supporting paragraphs?

- Is the relevance of each supporting paragraph clear?

- Is the essay a reasonable length?

- Is the essay organized, with a clear introduction, middle, and end?

- Did the author use one paragraph for each new idea?

- Is each sentence in a paragraph relevant to the point made in that paragraph?

- Are transitions clear?

- Is the essay easy to read? Is it engaging?

- Are sentences varied?

- Is vocabulary used effectively? Is college-level vocabulary used?

PRACTICE TEST THREE

ACT Practice Test Three
Answer Sheet

English Test

	10. Ⓕ Ⓖ Ⓗ Ⓙ	20. Ⓕ Ⓖ Ⓗ Ⓙ	30. Ⓕ Ⓖ Ⓗ Ⓙ	40. Ⓕ Ⓖ Ⓗ Ⓙ	50. Ⓕ Ⓖ Ⓗ Ⓙ	60. Ⓕ Ⓖ Ⓗ Ⓙ	70. Ⓕ Ⓖ Ⓗ Ⓙ
1. Ⓐ Ⓑ Ⓒ Ⓓ	11. Ⓐ Ⓑ Ⓒ Ⓓ	21. Ⓐ Ⓑ Ⓒ Ⓓ	31. Ⓐ Ⓑ Ⓒ Ⓓ	41. Ⓐ Ⓑ Ⓒ Ⓓ	51. Ⓐ Ⓑ Ⓒ Ⓓ	61. Ⓐ Ⓑ Ⓒ Ⓓ	71. Ⓐ Ⓑ Ⓒ Ⓓ
2. Ⓕ Ⓖ Ⓗ Ⓙ	12. Ⓕ Ⓖ Ⓗ Ⓙ	22. Ⓕ Ⓖ Ⓗ Ⓙ	32. Ⓕ Ⓖ Ⓗ Ⓙ	42. Ⓕ Ⓖ Ⓗ Ⓙ	52. Ⓕ Ⓖ Ⓗ Ⓙ	62. Ⓕ Ⓖ Ⓗ Ⓙ	72. Ⓕ Ⓖ Ⓗ Ⓙ
3. Ⓐ Ⓑ Ⓒ Ⓓ	13. Ⓐ Ⓑ Ⓒ Ⓓ	23. Ⓐ Ⓑ Ⓒ Ⓓ	33. Ⓐ Ⓑ Ⓒ Ⓓ	43. Ⓐ Ⓑ Ⓒ Ⓓ	53. Ⓐ Ⓑ Ⓒ Ⓓ	63. Ⓐ Ⓑ Ⓒ Ⓓ	73. Ⓐ Ⓑ Ⓒ Ⓓ
4. Ⓕ Ⓖ Ⓗ Ⓙ	14. Ⓕ Ⓖ Ⓗ Ⓙ	24. Ⓕ Ⓖ Ⓗ Ⓙ	34. Ⓕ Ⓖ Ⓗ Ⓙ	44. Ⓕ Ⓖ Ⓗ Ⓙ	54. Ⓕ Ⓖ Ⓗ Ⓙ	64. Ⓕ Ⓖ Ⓗ Ⓙ	74. Ⓕ Ⓖ Ⓗ Ⓙ
5. Ⓐ Ⓑ Ⓒ Ⓓ	15. Ⓐ Ⓑ Ⓒ Ⓓ	25. Ⓐ Ⓑ Ⓒ Ⓓ	35. Ⓐ Ⓑ Ⓒ Ⓓ	45. Ⓐ Ⓑ Ⓒ Ⓓ	55. Ⓐ Ⓑ Ⓒ Ⓓ	65. Ⓐ Ⓑ Ⓒ Ⓓ	75. Ⓐ Ⓑ Ⓒ Ⓓ
6. Ⓕ Ⓖ Ⓗ Ⓙ	16. Ⓕ Ⓖ Ⓗ Ⓙ	26. Ⓕ Ⓖ Ⓗ Ⓙ	36. Ⓕ Ⓖ Ⓗ Ⓙ	46. Ⓕ Ⓖ Ⓗ Ⓙ	56. Ⓕ Ⓖ Ⓗ Ⓙ	66. Ⓕ Ⓖ Ⓗ Ⓙ	
7. Ⓐ Ⓑ Ⓒ Ⓓ	17. Ⓐ Ⓑ Ⓒ Ⓓ	27. Ⓐ Ⓑ Ⓒ Ⓓ	37. Ⓐ Ⓑ Ⓒ Ⓓ	47. Ⓐ Ⓑ Ⓒ Ⓓ	57. Ⓐ Ⓑ Ⓒ Ⓓ	67. Ⓐ Ⓑ Ⓒ Ⓓ	
8. Ⓕ Ⓖ Ⓗ Ⓙ	18. Ⓕ Ⓖ Ⓗ Ⓙ	28. Ⓕ Ⓖ Ⓗ Ⓙ	38. Ⓕ Ⓖ Ⓗ Ⓙ	48. Ⓕ Ⓖ Ⓗ Ⓙ	58. Ⓕ Ⓖ Ⓗ Ⓙ	68. Ⓕ Ⓖ Ⓗ Ⓙ	
9. Ⓐ Ⓑ Ⓒ Ⓓ	19. Ⓐ Ⓑ Ⓒ Ⓓ	29. Ⓐ Ⓑ Ⓒ Ⓓ	39. Ⓐ Ⓑ Ⓒ Ⓓ	49. Ⓐ Ⓑ Ⓒ Ⓓ	59. Ⓐ Ⓑ Ⓒ Ⓓ	69. Ⓐ Ⓑ Ⓒ Ⓓ	

Math Test

	9. Ⓐ Ⓑ Ⓒ Ⓓ Ⓔ	18. Ⓕ Ⓖ Ⓗ Ⓙ Ⓚ	27. Ⓐ Ⓑ Ⓒ Ⓓ Ⓔ	36. Ⓕ Ⓖ Ⓗ Ⓙ Ⓚ	45. Ⓐ Ⓑ Ⓒ Ⓓ Ⓔ	54. Ⓕ Ⓖ Ⓗ Ⓙ Ⓚ
1. Ⓐ Ⓑ Ⓒ Ⓓ Ⓔ	10. Ⓕ Ⓖ Ⓗ Ⓙ Ⓚ	19. Ⓐ Ⓑ Ⓒ Ⓓ Ⓔ	28. Ⓕ Ⓖ Ⓗ Ⓙ Ⓚ	37. Ⓐ Ⓑ Ⓒ Ⓓ Ⓔ	46. Ⓕ Ⓖ Ⓗ Ⓙ Ⓚ	55. Ⓐ Ⓑ Ⓒ Ⓓ Ⓔ
2. Ⓕ Ⓖ Ⓗ Ⓙ Ⓚ	11. Ⓐ Ⓑ Ⓒ Ⓓ Ⓔ	20. Ⓕ Ⓖ Ⓗ Ⓙ Ⓚ	29. Ⓐ Ⓑ Ⓒ Ⓓ Ⓔ	38. Ⓕ Ⓖ Ⓗ Ⓙ Ⓚ	47. Ⓐ Ⓑ Ⓒ Ⓓ Ⓔ	56. Ⓕ Ⓖ Ⓗ Ⓙ Ⓚ
3. Ⓐ Ⓑ Ⓒ Ⓓ Ⓔ	12. Ⓕ Ⓖ Ⓗ Ⓙ Ⓚ	21. Ⓐ Ⓑ Ⓒ Ⓓ Ⓔ	30. Ⓕ Ⓖ Ⓗ Ⓙ Ⓚ	39. Ⓐ Ⓑ Ⓒ Ⓓ Ⓔ	48. Ⓕ Ⓖ Ⓗ Ⓙ Ⓚ	57. Ⓐ Ⓑ Ⓒ Ⓓ Ⓔ
4. Ⓕ Ⓖ Ⓗ Ⓙ Ⓚ	13. Ⓐ Ⓑ Ⓒ Ⓓ Ⓔ	22. Ⓕ Ⓖ Ⓗ Ⓙ Ⓚ	31. Ⓐ Ⓑ Ⓒ Ⓓ Ⓔ	40. Ⓕ Ⓖ Ⓗ Ⓙ Ⓚ	49. Ⓐ Ⓑ Ⓒ Ⓓ Ⓔ	58. Ⓕ Ⓖ Ⓗ Ⓙ Ⓚ
5. Ⓐ Ⓑ Ⓒ Ⓓ Ⓔ	14. Ⓕ Ⓖ Ⓗ Ⓙ Ⓚ	23. Ⓐ Ⓑ Ⓒ Ⓓ Ⓔ	32. Ⓕ Ⓖ Ⓗ Ⓙ Ⓚ	41. Ⓐ Ⓑ Ⓒ Ⓓ Ⓔ	50. Ⓕ Ⓖ Ⓗ Ⓙ Ⓚ	59. Ⓐ Ⓑ Ⓒ Ⓓ Ⓔ
6. Ⓕ Ⓖ Ⓗ Ⓙ Ⓚ	15. Ⓐ Ⓑ Ⓒ Ⓓ Ⓔ	24. Ⓕ Ⓖ Ⓗ Ⓙ Ⓚ	33. Ⓐ Ⓑ Ⓒ Ⓓ Ⓔ	42. Ⓕ Ⓖ Ⓗ Ⓙ Ⓚ	51. Ⓐ Ⓑ Ⓒ Ⓓ Ⓔ	60. Ⓕ Ⓖ Ⓗ Ⓙ Ⓚ
7. Ⓐ Ⓑ Ⓒ Ⓓ Ⓔ	16. Ⓕ Ⓖ Ⓗ Ⓙ Ⓚ	25. Ⓐ Ⓑ Ⓒ Ⓓ Ⓔ	34. Ⓕ Ⓖ Ⓗ Ⓙ Ⓚ	43. Ⓐ Ⓑ Ⓒ Ⓓ Ⓔ	52. Ⓕ Ⓖ Ⓗ Ⓙ Ⓚ	
8. Ⓕ Ⓖ Ⓗ Ⓙ Ⓚ	17. Ⓐ Ⓑ Ⓒ Ⓓ Ⓔ	26. Ⓕ Ⓖ Ⓗ Ⓙ Ⓚ	35. Ⓐ Ⓑ Ⓒ Ⓓ Ⓔ	44. Ⓕ Ⓖ Ⓗ Ⓙ Ⓚ	53. Ⓐ Ⓑ Ⓒ Ⓓ Ⓔ	

Reading Test

	6. Ⓕ Ⓖ Ⓗ Ⓙ	12. Ⓕ Ⓖ Ⓗ Ⓙ	18. Ⓕ Ⓖ Ⓗ Ⓙ	24. Ⓕ Ⓖ Ⓗ Ⓙ	30. Ⓕ Ⓖ Ⓗ Ⓙ	36 Ⓕ Ⓖ Ⓗ Ⓙ
1. Ⓐ Ⓑ Ⓒ Ⓓ	7. Ⓐ Ⓑ Ⓒ Ⓓ	13. Ⓐ Ⓑ Ⓒ Ⓓ	19. Ⓐ Ⓑ Ⓒ Ⓓ	25. Ⓐ Ⓑ Ⓒ Ⓓ	31. Ⓐ Ⓑ Ⓒ Ⓓ	37. Ⓐ Ⓑ Ⓒ Ⓓ
2. Ⓕ Ⓖ Ⓗ Ⓙ	8. Ⓕ Ⓖ Ⓗ Ⓙ	14. Ⓕ Ⓖ Ⓗ Ⓙ	20. Ⓕ Ⓖ Ⓗ Ⓙ	26. Ⓕ Ⓖ Ⓗ Ⓙ	32. Ⓕ Ⓖ Ⓗ Ⓙ	38. Ⓕ Ⓖ Ⓗ Ⓙ
3. Ⓐ Ⓑ Ⓒ Ⓓ	9. Ⓐ Ⓑ Ⓒ Ⓓ	15. Ⓐ Ⓑ Ⓒ Ⓓ	21. Ⓐ Ⓑ Ⓒ Ⓓ	27. Ⓐ Ⓑ Ⓒ Ⓓ	33. Ⓐ Ⓑ Ⓒ Ⓓ	39 Ⓐ Ⓑ Ⓒ Ⓓ
4. Ⓕ Ⓖ Ⓗ Ⓙ	10. Ⓕ Ⓖ Ⓗ Ⓙ	16. Ⓕ Ⓖ Ⓗ Ⓙ	22. Ⓕ Ⓖ Ⓗ Ⓙ	28. Ⓕ Ⓖ Ⓗ Ⓙ	34. Ⓕ Ⓖ Ⓗ Ⓙ	40. Ⓕ Ⓖ Ⓗ Ⓙ
5. Ⓐ Ⓑ Ⓒ Ⓓ	11. Ⓐ Ⓑ Ⓒ Ⓓ	17. Ⓐ Ⓑ Ⓒ Ⓓ	23. Ⓐ Ⓑ Ⓒ Ⓓ	29. Ⓐ Ⓑ Ⓒ Ⓓ	35. Ⓐ Ⓑ Ⓒ Ⓓ	

Science Test

	6. Ⓕ Ⓖ Ⓗ Ⓙ	12. Ⓕ Ⓖ Ⓗ Ⓙ	18. Ⓕ Ⓖ Ⓗ Ⓙ	24. Ⓕ Ⓖ Ⓗ Ⓙ	30. Ⓕ Ⓖ Ⓗ Ⓙ	36. Ⓕ Ⓖ Ⓗ Ⓙ
1. Ⓐ Ⓑ Ⓒ Ⓓ	7. Ⓐ Ⓑ Ⓒ Ⓓ	13. Ⓐ Ⓑ Ⓒ Ⓓ	19. Ⓐ Ⓑ Ⓒ Ⓓ	25. Ⓐ Ⓑ Ⓒ Ⓓ	31. Ⓐ Ⓑ Ⓒ Ⓓ	37. Ⓐ Ⓑ Ⓒ Ⓓ
2. Ⓕ Ⓖ Ⓗ Ⓙ	8. Ⓕ Ⓖ Ⓗ Ⓙ	14. Ⓕ Ⓖ Ⓗ Ⓙ	20. Ⓕ Ⓖ Ⓗ Ⓙ	26. Ⓕ Ⓖ Ⓗ Ⓙ	32. Ⓕ Ⓖ Ⓗ Ⓙ	38. Ⓕ Ⓖ Ⓗ Ⓙ
3. Ⓐ Ⓑ Ⓒ Ⓓ	9. Ⓐ Ⓑ Ⓒ Ⓓ	15. Ⓐ Ⓑ Ⓒ Ⓓ	21. Ⓐ Ⓑ Ⓒ Ⓓ	27. Ⓐ Ⓑ Ⓒ Ⓓ	33. Ⓐ Ⓑ Ⓒ Ⓓ	39 Ⓐ Ⓑ Ⓒ Ⓓ
4. Ⓕ Ⓖ Ⓗ Ⓙ	10. Ⓕ Ⓖ Ⓗ Ⓙ	16. Ⓕ Ⓖ Ⓗ Ⓙ	22. Ⓕ Ⓖ Ⓗ Ⓙ	28. Ⓕ Ⓖ Ⓗ Ⓙ	34. Ⓕ Ⓖ Ⓗ Ⓙ	40. Ⓕ Ⓖ Ⓗ Ⓙ
5. Ⓐ Ⓑ Ⓒ Ⓓ	11. Ⓐ Ⓑ Ⓒ Ⓓ	17. Ⓐ Ⓑ Ⓒ Ⓓ	23. Ⓐ Ⓑ Ⓒ Ⓓ	29. Ⓐ Ⓑ Ⓒ Ⓓ	35. Ⓐ Ⓑ Ⓒ Ⓓ	

ENGLISH TEST

45 Minutes—75 Questions

Directions: In the following passage, certain words and phrases have been underlined and numbered. You will find alternatives for each underlined portion in the corresponding questions and answer choices. Select the one that best expresses the idea, that makes the sentence acceptable in standard written English, or that is phrased most consistently with the style and tone of the entire passage. If you feel that the original version is best, select "NO CHANGE." You will also find questions asking about a section of the passage or the entire passage. For each question in the test, select the best choice. You may wish to read the passage through before you begin to answer questions associated with it. Most answers cannot be determined without reading several sentences around the phrases in question. Make sure to read far enough ahead each time you choose an alternative.

PASSAGE I

[1]

Until three years ago, I had never considered myself

to be athletically talented. I have never been able to hit,

catch, throw, or kick a ball with any degree of

confidence or accuracy. For years, physical

<u>education being</u> often the worst part of the school day
    1

for me. Units on tennis, touch football, volleyball, and

basketball were torturous. I not only dreaded fumbling

a pass, <u>so</u> I also feared being hit in the face by a ball.
    2

However, at the beginning of my freshman year of high

school, my attitude toward sports changed.

[2]

Somehow, my good friend Gretchen convinced me

to join <u>our schools</u> swim team. <u>Knowing that I enjoyed</u>
    3   4

1. A. NO CHANGE
   B. education, was
   C. education was
   D. education,

2. F. NO CHANGE
   G. and
   H. but
   J. though

3. A. NO CHANGE
   B. our schools'
   C. our school's
   D. ours school

4. F. NO CHANGE
   G. Because we had spent two summers practically living at the pool, it was Gretchen who knew that swimming was enjoyed by me.
   H. Having practically lived at the pool over two summers, the two of us, Gretchen knew it was swimming that I enjoyed.
   J. Gretchen knew I enjoyed swimming, as we had spent two summers practically living at the pool.

GO ON TO THE NEXT PAGE ⟶

swimming, over the course of two summers, it was
_____
                              4

with Gretchen that I practically had lived at the pool.
_____
                              4

My mother had insisted that I take swimming lessons
                 _____
                   5

every summer since I was seven, so I was entirely

comfortable in the water. I also was eager to start my

high school experience with a new challenge and a new

way to think of myself.

[3]

Of course, I had no idea what I was getting into when

Gretchen and I showed up for the first day of practice.

The team was made up of twenty young women, most
                                    _____
                                         6

of these swimmers had been participating in the
_____
       6

community swim team for years. I couldn't do a flip

turn at the end of the lane without getting water up my

nose. In contrast, most of the other swimmers, who

had been swimming competitively, since elementary
_____
                        7

school, were able to gracefully somersault and begin
_____
   7

the next lap. By the end of the first hour of practice, I

was exhausted and waterlogged.

[4]

However, I had no intention of giving up, which
                                _____
                                      8

would mean quitting. I came back the next day and the
_____
       8

next day for practice. Things begun to get serious in the
                               _____
                                 9

5. Of the four choices, which is the only one that
   does NOT indicate that the narrator's mother
   decided that the narrator must take swimming
   lessons?

   A. NO CHANGE
   B. suggested
   C. required
   D. demanded

6. F. NO CHANGE
   G. women, the majority of them
   H. women most of them
   J. women, most of whom

7. A. NO CHANGE
   B. had been swimming competitively since
       elementary school,
   C. had been swimming, competitively since
       elementary school,
   D. had been swimming competitively since
       elementary school

8. F. NO CHANGE
   G. giving up and resigning myself to failure.
   H. giving up and quitting what I had set out
       to do.
   J. giving up.

9. A. NO CHANGE
   B. had been begun
   C. had began
   D. began

GO ON TO THE NEXT PAGE

second week, when we started the regular schedule of

four early morning and five afternoon practices. Our

coach, <u>whom</u> had led the team to several state
                10
championships, demanded dedication from everyone

on the team. The hard work <u>eventually paid off. By</u>
                                        11
the end of the first month, I had discovered that I was

good at the butterfly, <u>a relatively new stroke that was</u>
                              12
<u>first introduced in the 1930s.</u> I rarely won individual
            12
races, but I made a solid member of our <u>team's medley</u>
                                                    13
<u>relay.</u>

    13

    After that intimidating first season, I continued

swimming. I even <u>will have earned</u> a varsity letter last
                          14
year. Now I'm hoping to earn a spot in the state

competition my senior year. [15]

10. F. NO CHANGE
    G. for whom
    H. who
    J. which

11. A. NO CHANGE
    B. eventually paid off, so, as a result
    C. paid off eventually, however, by
    D. paid off, eventually, by

12. Assuming each of the following creates a true statement, which provides the information most relevant to the narrator's experience on the swim team?

    F. NO CHANGE
    G. a difficult stroke that interested few other members of our team.
    H. which is faster than the backstroke but somewhat slower than the crawl.
    J. which is still sometimes called the dolphin because it incorporates a two-stroke dolphin kick.

13. A. NO CHANGE
    B. team's medley relay (it consists of four swimmers).
    C. team's medley relay, which the person swimming backstroke always begins.
    D. team.

14. F. NO CHANGE
    G. would have earned
    H. earned
    J. earn

15. If inserted here, which of the following would be the most appropriate sentence to conclude the essay?

    A. My coach continues to schedule demanding practices, but I have come to enjoy the early morning swims.
    B. For someone who thought she didn't have any athletic talent, I have come a long way.
    C. Gretchen is also still on the team, but she does not swim the medley relay.
    D. I've always enjoyed swimming, so I'm not all that surprised by my success as an athlete.

GO ON TO THE NEXT PAGE ⇨

Passage II

[1]

One lazy day last summer, my parents decided that my younger sister and I needed a break from our vacation from academics. They took us to the National Mississippi River Museum and Aquarium in Dubuque, Iowa. I was prepared to be bored by this family educational trip. However, from the first moment I walked through the museum's doors, I was captivated; by
<u>16</u>
all that there was to learn about life in the Mississippi.

[2]

[1] A large tank stocked with fish and turtles was there to greet us as we walked into the main hall.
<u>17</u>
[2] There were also animals I had never before glimpsed, such as a fish called the long-nosed gar. [3] I was amazed by this fish in particular. [4] Its long, tubular shape and distinctive rod-shaped nose that made it
<u>18</u>
appear like something that lived in the dark depths of the ocean. [5] This first of five freshwater aquariums offered a close-up view of familiar animals that I had
<u>19</u>
seen before, such as ducks. 20
19

[3]

In the next aquarium, I see a catfish bigger than I had
21

16. F. NO CHANGE
    G. captivated, by
    H. captivated by,
    J. captivated by

17. A. NO CHANGE
    B. is there
    C. are there
    D. were there

18. F. NO CHANGE
    G. nose, which
    H. nose, and this
    J. nose

19. A. NO CHANGE
    B. animals that were familiar sights to me,
    C. familiar animals to which I was no stranger,
    D. familiar animals,

20. To make Paragraph 2 coherent and logical, the best placement of Sentence 5 is:
    F. where it is now.
    G. before Sentence 1.
    H. after Sentence 1.
    J. after Sentence 2.

21. A. NO CHANGE
    B. had been seeing
    C. saw
    D. spot

GO ON TO THE NEXT PAGE

ever imagined this species could be. According to the posted information, this specimen weighed more than 100 pounds. With its long whiskers and slow, lazy movements, this catfish looked like the grandfather of all the other fish in the tank.

[4]

I couldn't decide which I liked better, the catfish or the
<u>   </u>
                          22
long-nosed gar. The next floor-to-ceiling tank, which
<u>   </u>
   22
represented the ecosystem of the Mississippi bayou, held an animal I had never seen: an alligator. At first, I had a hard time spotting the creature—it blended in almost completely with a half-submerged log. [23]

Suddenly, though, it <u>slides into the water and aims</u>
                                        24
itself right at the glass separating me from its ferocious claws and skin-tearing teeth. I had a <u>slightly moment</u>
                                                              25
of panic before I remembered that, try as it might, this alligator would never successfully hunt tourists like me.

As <u>much</u> of the on-lookers squealed in delight as the
      26
alligator moved through the tank, I noticed his companion. Far off in a corner slept an enormous snapping turtle. I could imagine no better roommate for the alligator than this hook-beaked turtle with rough ridges running along its shell.

22. Which sentence most effectively connects this paragraph to the preceding paragraph?

F. NO CHANGE

G. Although the catfish was impressive, it was not the biggest animal on display in the museum.

H. After seeing the catfish, I was interested in exhibits that were a bit more hands-on.

J. Until my visit to the museum, I had never really considered what the Mississippi River was like south of my home.

23. At this point, the writer is considering removing the following phrase:

—it blended in almost completely with a half-submerged log.

The primary effect of removing this phrase would be:

A. a smoother transition between sentences.

B. a greater contrast between images.

C. the loss of descriptive information.

D. an increased level of suspense.

24. F. NO CHANGE

G. slides into the water to aim

H. slid into the water and aiming

J. slid into the water and aimed

25. A. NO CHANGE

B. momentarily slight

C. slight moment

D. slight momentarily

26. F. NO CHANGE

G. a large amount

H. the many

J. many

GO ON TO THE NEXT PAGE

[5]

Despite my initial expectations, I happily spent the entire day soaking up information about creatures that live in the Mississippi River. In one section of the museum, I held a crayfish. [27] Later, I had the opportunity to touch the cool, sleek skin of a stingray, which can be found where the Mississippi empties into the Gulf of Mexico.

[6]

After seeing all, I could inside the museum, I
<u>   28</u>
wandered outside, only to find even more exhibits.

<u>Having just enough time, it was that I was able</u> to see
<u>   29</u>
the otters and watch a riverboat launching, but it was closing time before I was able to see the most impressive thing the museum had to offer. A football-field-sized steamboat from the 1930s is open to <u>tourists. And operates</u> as a "Boat and Breakfast" that
<u>   30</u>
hosts overnight guests. I'm hoping that my family will plan another educational trip to Dubuque soon so I can experience life on a steamboat.

27. The writer would like to insert a sentence describing the appearance of the crayfish at this point. Which sentence would best accomplish the writer's goal?

   A. Also know as crawdads, crayfish are close relatives of the lobsters that live in fresh water.

   B. At an average length of about three inches, the crayfish looks like a miniature lobster, complete with small but effective front pincers.

   C. Although they are found throughout the United States, crayfish populations are densest in Kentucky and Mississippi.

   D. At first I was a bit nervous to touch the small creature, but then I relaxed and enjoyed the opportunity to look at it so closely.

28. F. NO CHANGE
    G. all I could inside the museum,
    H. all, I could inside the museum
    J. all I could inside the museum

29. A. NO CHANGE
    B. It was that I had just enough time, so I was able
    C. Having just enough time, it was possible
    D. I had just enough time

30. F. NO CHANGE
    G. tourists and that operates
    H. tourists, it operates
    J. tourists and

GO ON TO THE NEXT PAGE

PASSAGE III

> The paragraphs in this essay may or may not follow the most logical order. Each paragraph is numbered, and question 45 will ask you to determine the best placement of Paragraph 6.

[1]

Although secret identities and elaborate disguises are typically associated with the world of spies and villains, it has other uses. For six years Ruth <u>Reichl the</u>
31   32
<u>restaurant critic for The New York Times,</u> used aliases
32
and costumes as a regular part of her job.

[2]

Dining is big business in New York City, from the neighborhood noodle shops and diners to the upscale steak houses and four-star French restaurants. 33

Many of the more than one million people who read The Times each day <u>look to</u> it for advice on where to
34

31. A. NO CHANGE
    B. it does have
    C. they do have
    D. and they have

32. F. NO CHANGE
    G. Reichl, the restaurant critic, for *The New York Times*,
    H. Reichl, the restaurant critic for *The New York Times*,
    J. Reichl the restaurant critic for *The New York Times*

33. Should the following sentence be inserted into the passage at this point?

    The legendary French restaurant Le Bernardin received a four-star rating from *The Times* shortly after opening in 1986, an honor it has maintained ever since.

    A. Yes, because the added sentence emphasizes how important a positive review from *The Times* can be.
    B. Yes, because the specific information helps the reader develop a clearer picture of the type of restaurant reviewed by *The Times*.
    C. No, because it is unclear whether Reichl was responsible for reviewing this specific restaurant.
    D. No, because the specific information about one restaurant leads the reader away from the main topic of the essay.

34. F. NO CHANGE
    G. look with
    H. look by
    J. looking to

GO ON TO THE NEXT PAGE

eat. A positive review from *The Times* <u>could have</u>
35

<u>brought</u> a restaurant unimagined success and
35

month-long waiting lists for reservations. A negative

review, on the other hand, can undermine a

restaurant's popularity and seriously cut into its profits.

Obviously, <u>restaurant owners and workers</u> have a lot at
36

stake when the restaurant critic for *The Times* walks in

the door. Waiters and chefs often pull out all of the

stops to impress the writer <u>that the</u> meal can make or
37

break a restaurant.

[3]

    Reichl was acutely aware that <u>she received special</u>
38

<u>treatment</u> once restaurant staff recognized her. She
38

would be graciously greeted and led to the best table in

the restaurant, offered dishes prepared specially by the

head chef, and given multiple courses of amazing

desserts. In other words, the dining experience of the

restaurant critic was nothing like that of the <u>commonly</u>
39

<u>ordinary</u> person walking in from the street.
39

35. A. NO CHANGE
    B. can bring
    C. will have brought
    D. will be bringing

36. F. NO CHANGE
    G. restaurant owners and workers;
    H. restaurant, owners and workers
    J. restaurant owners, and workers

37. A. NO CHANGE
    B. who's
    C. whose
    D. which

38. F. NO CHANGE
    G. special treatment was received by her
    H. she was the recipient of special treatment
    J. she was in the position of receiving special treatment

39. A. NO CHANGE
    B. common, representative, and average
    C. typical
    D. extravagant

GO ON TO THE NEXT PAGE →

[4]

To remedy this, Reichl decided a solution would be
                                            40
to become, for short periods of time, someone else.

Transforming herself into different personas, Reichl
                                            41
used wigs, special makeup, and carefully selected
                                            41
clothing, such as an attractive blonde named Chloe, a
   41
redhead named Brenda, and an older woman named

Betty. 42

40. F.   NO CHANGE

    G.   she created a solution to the problem by
         becoming

    H.   Reichl decided to become

    J.   Reichl found a way to fix the problem,
         which involved becoming

41. A.   NO CHANGE

    B.   With wigs, special makeup, and carefully
         selected clothing, Reichl transformed
         herself into different personas,

    C.   Transformed with wigs, special makeup,
         and carefully selected clothing, Reichl's
         different personas,

    D.   Reichl used wigs, special makeup, and
         carefully selected clothing, that trans-
         formed herself into different personas,

42. Which of the following true statements would
    make the most effective and logical conclusion
    for Paragraph 4?

    F.   Reichl found that she could quickly dis-
         guise herself as Betty, but it took more
         time to become Chloe.

    G.   Her true identity hidden, Reichl would
         then dine at a restaurant she was cur-
         rently evaluating.

    H.   After six years at *The Times*, Reichl
         moved on to become the editor of
         Gourmet magazine.

    J.   The former restaurant critic for *The
         Times* did not always agree with Reichl's
         methods or her selection of restaurants
         to review.

[5]

Sometimes, Reichl developed a different view about

the quality when she was not treated like a very important

person of a restaurant. Indeed, the difference between
                          43

the treatment she received as herself and as one of her

characters was occasionally so great that Reichl would

revise her initial impression of a restaurant and write a

more negative review. 44

[6]

By becoming an average customer, Reichl encouraged

even the most expensive and popular restaurants to

improve how they treated all of their customers. After

all, waiters could never be certain when they were

serving the powerful restaurant critic for *The New York*

Times.

43. For the sake of logic and coherence, the underlined portion should be placed:

A. where it is now.
B. after the word *developed*.
C. after the word *view*.
D. after the word *quality*.

44. Would deleting the word "occasionally" from the previous sentence change the meaning of the sentence?

F. Yes, because without this word the reader would not understand that Reichl had different experiences when she dined in disguise.
G. Yes, because without this word the reader would think that Reichl always changed her impression of restaurants when she received different treatment because she was not recognized.
H. No, because this word repeats an idea that is already presented in the sentence.
J. No, because this word is used only to show emphasis, and it does not contribute to the meaning of the sentence.

Question 45 asks about the passage as a whole.

45. To make the passage flow logically and smoothly, the best place for Paragraph 6 is:

A. where it is now.
B. after Paragraph 1.
C. after Paragraph 3.
D. after Paragraph 4.

GO ON TO THE NEXT PAGE

PASSAGE IV

[1]

[1] I used to start every spring with great hopes for my backyard vegetable garden. [2] After the last freeze in late March or early April, I devoted an entire weekend to preparing the soil in the garden. [3] I thinned out the rows that had too many plants and spent hours tugging out each weed that threatened to rob my little plants of the nutrients they needed to thrive. [4] Once spring truly arrived, I marked out my rows and scattered the packets of seeds that I hoped, would
                                                        46
develop into prize-winning vegetables. [5] In the first few weeks of the season, I was almost always in the garden. 47

[2]

Despite my best intentions, my garden never lived up to the vision I had for it. After I had devoted several weekends to watering and weeding, the garden always started to become more of a burden less of a hobby. By
                                                        48
July, the garden was usually in disarray, and I didn't have the energy or time to save it. July and August are
                                                        49
always the hottest parts of the year.
                49

46. F. NO CHANGE
    G. hoped, would,
    H. hoped would,
    J. hoped would

47. To make Paragraph 1 more logical and coherent, Sentence 3 should be placed:
    A. where it is now.
    B. before Sentence 1.
    C. after Sentence 1.
    D. after Sentence 4.

48. F. NO CHANGE
    G. burden:
    H. burden and
    J. burden, but,

49. A. NO CHANGE
    B. The hottest months are July and August.
    C. (July, along with August, provides the hottest temperatures of the year.)
    D. OMIT the underlined portion.

[3]

This past year, <u>however</u>, my garden was finally the
          50

success I had imagined it could be. Instead of planning

the traditional garden of closely planted <u>rows that is</u>
                              51

<u>modeled after large-scale farming,</u> I tried a new
          51

technique. My new approach is called square foot

gardening.

[4]

<u>A square foot garden is designed for efficiency.</u> In a
          52

<u>traditionally</u> garden, you scatter a packet of seeds down
  53

a row. When the plants emerge, <u>they spend</u> hours
               54

thinning each row by pulling out at least half of what

was planted. In a square foot garden, you plant each

seed individually, so there is never a need for thinning

50. Of the following choices, which would be the LEAST acceptable substitution for the underlined word?

  F. on the other hand

  G. indeed

  H. though

  J. in contrast

51. A. NO CHANGE

  B. rows, which is modeled after large-scale farming,

  C. rows, which is based on the techniques for large-scale farming,

  D. rows,

52. Which sentence most effectively links the topic of Paragraph 3 to the topic of Paragraph 4?

  F. NO CHANGE

  G. The technique of square foot gardening was pioneered by Mel Bartholomew.

  H. One of the benefits of a square foot garden is that it is less expensive to maintain than a traditional garden.

  J. My neighbor, who always has a beautiful garden, introduced me to the concept of square foot gardening, and I have been grateful ever since.

53. A. NO CHANGE

  B. conventionally

  C. traditional

  D. tradition

54. F. NO CHANGE

  G. he spends

  H. people spend

  J. you spend

GO ON TO THE NEXT PAGE ⟶

<u>in the garden</u>. You create the garden plan one square
55

foot at a time, until you have a block of sixteen squares.

Sturdy pieces of lumber <u>which could make</u> effective
56

borders for each square. Walking paths that are at least

two feet wide separate each sixteen-square-foot garden.

The design is clean and simple, and it eliminates the

problem of getting to the rows in the middle of a large

garden. In fact, <u>you can do</u> all the weeding, watering,
57

and harvesting from the walking paths.

[5]

In addition to being easier to weed and water, a

square foot garden takes up much less space than a regular

garden. I was able to grow <u>an increased number of more</u>
58

vegetables in two square foot gardens, which took up a

total of 32 square feet, than I ever had grown in my

traditional garden, which took up 84 square feet.

Preparing the soil for the smaller space only required a

few hours instead of a whole weekend. There was so

much less weeding to do that the task never felt

55. A. NO CHANGE
    B. out the garden
    C. in that garden
    D. OMIT the underlined portion.

56. F. NO CHANGE
    G. that make
    H. make
    J. OMIT the underlined portion.

57. A. NO CHANGE
    B. you could have done
    C. one can do
    D. one is able to do

58. F. NO CHANGE
    G. a larger quantity of more
    H. an increased, bigger quantity
    J. more

GO ON TO THE NEXT PAGE

overwhelming. One season of using the square garden

techniques <u>were all</u> it took for me to convert to a
                59
completely new outlook on backyard gardening.

59. A. NO CHANGE
    B. were just what
    C. was all
    D. could be

The following question asks about the passage in its entirety.

---

60. If the writer had intended to write an essay detailing how to plan, prepare, and care for a square garden, would this essay meet the writer's goal?

    F. No, because the writer relies on generalities rather than specifics when describing her square garden.

    G. No, because the writer focuses on comparing two different types of gardens instead of explaining how to begin and care for one type of garden.

    H. Yes, because the writer states specific measurements for her square garden.

    J. Yes, because the writer maintains that square gardens are superior to traditional gardens.

GO ON TO THE NEXT PAGE

PASSAGE V

[1]

Most new car owners glance briefly at the owner's manual before depositing it in the glove compartment of their new automobile. Owners may dig out their manuals when something goes <u>wrong, such as a flat tire</u>
                                                    61
<u>or a flashing engine light</u> but few car owners take the
          61
time to learn the basics about maintaining their new purchase. This is truly unfortunate, as a few simple and routine steps <u>improves the long-term performance of</u>
                                                    62
<u>an automobile and decreases</u> the possibility of a traffic
          62
accident.

[2]

One of the easiest and most overlooked maintenance steps is caring for a car's wiper blades. Most people don't <u>notice a problem</u> until the blades fail to clear the
          63
windshield during a rainstorm or heavy snowfall. When a driver's <u>vision being</u> obscured, an accident is
                    64
more likely to happen. Replacing the <u>set</u> blades at a
                                          65
time each year greatly reduces this risk. In addition, frequently refilling the windshield washer fluid reservoir guarantees that there will be always be enough fluid to wash away grime that accumulates on the windshield.

61. A. NO CHANGE
    B. wrong; such as a flat tire or a flashing engine light
    C. wrong, such as a flat tire, or a flashing engine light
    D. wrong, such as a flat tire or a flashing engine light,

62. F. NO CHANGE
    G. improve the long-term performance of an automobile and decreases
    H. improve the long-term performance of an automobile and decrease
    J. improves the long-term performance of an automobile and decrease

63. A. NO CHANGE
    B. notice a problem that causes trouble
    C. recognize that their wiper blades are the source of a problem
    D. realize that their blades are failing and will become a problem

64. F. NO CHANGE
    G. vision, has been
    H. vision is
    J. vision,

65. The underlined word would be most logically placed:
    A. where it is now.
    B. before the word *time*.
    C. before the word *year*.
    D. before the word *risk*.

GO ON TO THE NEXT PAGE

[3]

Much of car maintenance focuses on preventing

problems before they occur. For example, checking the

levels of coolant, oil, brake fluid, and transmission fluid

can avert serious malfunctions. <u>In general,</u> these fluids
                                        66

should be checked monthly and refilled whenever the

need is indicated.

[4]

<u>Cars are becoming more sophisticated every year, but</u>
                          67
<u>car owners without any expertise in mechanics can still</u>
                          67
<u>perform much of the basic upkeep of their vehicle.</u>
                          67
You should change the oil in most cars every 3,000 to

7,000 miles. This task requires a willingness to get a bit

dirty, <u>so</u> you don't have to be a mechanic to change a
        68

car's oil. Before you get started, read the oil change

<u>section, in your owner's manual</u> and collect all of the
                          69

66. F. NO CHANGE
    G. For generally,
    H. With usual
    J. By typically,

67. Which sentence is the most effective way to
    begin Paragraph 4?

    A. NO CHANGE
    B. Changing the oil and oil filter regularly is
        another key to keeping your car's engine
        performing at its best.
    C. An entire industry now focuses on pro-
        viding regular car maintenance, such as
        changing the oil and rotating the tires.
    D. Even if you haven't read your car owner's
        manual, you probably know that your
        car needs a tune-up every so often.

68. F. NO CHANGE
    G. but
    H. for
    J. because

69. A. NO CHANGE
    B. section, in your owner's manual,
    C. section in your owner's manual;
    D. section in your owner's manual

GO ON TO THE NEXT PAGE

tools you will need. You <u>won't need many tools, but</u>
70

<u>you will definitely need a car jack.</u> Never get under
70

a car that is supported only by car <u>jacks:</u> you do not
71

want to risk being crushed by a car. After you've secured

the car, changing the oil is as straightforward as sliding

under the car with a drain pan to catch the oil and a

wrench to loosen the oil drain plug. Then follow the

instructions for changing the oil filter and fill the oil

pan to the recommended level with fresh oil. 72

[5]

These simple steps to maintaining the health of a car

can be done by just about anyone. However,

successfully changing a car's oil does not turn a car

owner into a repair expert. More complicated tasks,

such as adjusting a carburetor or installing new brake

pads, should be <u>performed by a qualified</u> auto
73

mechanic.

70. In Paragraph 4, the writer wants to provide an explanation of how to change the oil in an automobile. Which of the following would most logically fit the writer's intention for this paragraph?

F. NO CHANGE

G. need to get under the car to open the oil drain, so use car jacks to raise the car and sturdy car jack stands to support it.

H. may find it helpful to watch someone else change the oil before you try to perform the job on your own.

J. only need to follow a few basic steps in order to successfully change your car's oil.

71. A. NO CHANGE

B. jacks, you

C. jacks you

D. jacks you,

72. Paragraph 4 of the essay uses the second person (*you*, *your*). Revising this paragraph to remove the second-person pronouns would have the primary effect of:

F. disrupting the logical flow of the essay.

G. making Paragraph 4 more consistent with the voice used in the rest of the essay.

H. underscoring the direct advice given to the reader.

J. lightening the essay's formal tone

73. A. NO CHANGE

B. professionally completed by a qualified

C. performed by a certifiably qualified

D. undertaken by qualifying

GO ON TO THE NEXT PAGE

Questions 74–75 ask about the passage in its entirety.

74. After reading back through the essay, the writer decided that the following sentence contains important information:

The owner's manual provides instructions on how to test the levels of these different fluids used to lubricate and cool the engine.

Logically, this sentence should be placed:

F. after the last sentence of Paragraph 2.

G. before the first sentence of Paragraph 3.

H. after the last sentence of Paragraph 3.

J. after the last sentence of Paragraph 4.

75. If the writer had intended to write an essay persuading readers to familiarize themselves with the basic safety features and maintenance needs of their cars, would this essay meet the writer's goal?

A. Yes, because the essay repeatedly encourages readers to refer to the owner's manual for their car.

B. Yes, because the essay lists many basic maintenance steps that owners can independently accomplish.

C. No, because the essay encourages readers to go beyond learning about the features of their car and actually perform some of the basic upkeep.

D. No, because the essay does not discuss a car's safety features in any detail.

IF YOU FINISH BEFORE TIME IS CALLED, YOU MAY CHECK YOUR WORK ON THIS SECTION ONLY. DO NOT TURN TO ANY OTHER SECTION IN THE TEST.

STOP

MATH TEST

60 Minutes—60 Questions

Directions: Solve each of the following problems, select the correct answer, and then fill in the corresponding space on your answer sheet.

Don't linger over problems that are too time-consuming. Do as many as you can, then come back to the others in the time you have remaining.

Calculator use is permitted, but some problems can best be solved without a calculator.

Note: Unless otherwise noted, all of the following should be assumed.

1. Illustrative figures are *not* necessarily drawn to scale.

2. All geometric figures lie in a plane.

3. The term *line* indicates a straight line.

4. The term *average* indicates arithmetic mean.

1. Tanya used $3\frac{3}{8}$ yards of fabric to make her dress and she used $1\frac{1}{3}$ yards of fabric to make her jacket. What was the total amount, in yards, that Tanya used for the complete outfit of dress and jacket?

   A. $4\frac{1}{8}$

   B. $4\frac{1}{6}$

   C. $4\frac{4}{11}$

   D. $4\frac{1}{2}$

   E. $4\frac{17}{24}$

DO YOUR FIGURING HERE.

2. $5x^3y^5 \times 6y^2 \times 2xy$ is equivalent to

   F. $13x^3y^7$

   G. $13x^4y^8$

   H. $60x^3y^7$

   J. $60\ x^3y^{10}$

   K. $60\ x^4y^8$

GO ON TO THE NEXT PAGE

3. Brandon puts 6 percent of his $36,000 yearly salary into savings, in 12 equal monthly installments. Jacqui deposits $200 every month into savings. At the end of one full year, what is the difference, in dollars, between the amount of money that Jacqui saved and the amount of money that Brandon saved?

A.   20

B.   24

C.   240

D.   1,960

E.   2,800

DO YOUR FIGURING HERE.

4. Mikhail has received bowling scores of 190, 200, 145, and 180 so far in the state bowling tournament. What score must he receive on the fifth game to earn an average score of 180 for his 5 games?

F.   179

G.   180

H.   185

J.   200

K.   Mikhail cannot earn an average of 180.

5. For steel to be considered stainless steel, it must have a minimum of 10.5 percent chromium in the metal alloy. If there is 262.5 pounds of chromium available, what is the maximum amount of stainless steel, in pounds, that can be manufactured?

A.   27.56

B.   252

C.   262.5

D.   2,500

E.   25,000

GO ON TO THE NEXT PAGE

6. A homeowner wants to put a wallpaper border on the top edge of all the walls of his kitchen. The kitchen measures 6.5 meters by 4 meters. What is the required length, in meters, of the border?

F.   8

G.   10.5

H.   13

J.   21

K.   26

DO YOUR FIGURING HERE.

7. Which expression below is equivalent to $w(x - (y + z))$?

A. $wx - wy - wz$

B. $wx - wy + wz$

C. $wx - y + z$

D. $wx - y - z$

E. $wxy + wxz$

8. Solve for n: $6n - 4 = 3n + 24$

F. 28

G. $\dfrac{28}{3}$

H. $\dfrac{28}{9}$

J. $\dfrac{20}{9}$

K. $\dfrac{3}{28}$

9. What two numbers should be placed in the blanks below so that the difference between successive entries is the same?

26, _____, _____, 53

A.   36, 43

B.   35, 44

C.   34, 45

D.   33, 46

E.   30, 49

GO ON TO THE NEXT PAGE

10. What is the real number value of $m^3 + \sqrt{12m}$ when $5m^2 = 45$?

    F.   15
    G.   27
    H.   33
    J.   38.09
    K.   739.39

11. The radius of a sphere is $3\frac{3}{5}$ meters. What is the volume of the sphere, to the nearest cubic meter? Use the formula $V = \frac{4}{3}\pi r^3$.

    A.   42
    B.   45
    C.   157
    D.   195
    E.   3,429

12. There are 10 peanuts, 6 cashews, and 8 almonds in a bag of mixed nuts. If a nut is chosen at random from the bag, what is the probability that the nut is NOT a peanut?

    F. $\frac{5}{12}$

    G. $\frac{7}{12}$

    H. $\frac{5}{7}$

    J.   10

    K.   14

DO YOUR FIGURING HERE.

GO ON TO THE NEXT PAGE

13. The number of people in the electronics store is shown in the matrix below.

Adolescents   Adults   Senior Citizens

$$[\quad 75 \qquad 100 \qquad 30 \qquad]$$

The ratio of people from each age group who will purchase a product to the number of people in that age group in the store is shown in the following matrix:

$$\begin{matrix} \text{Adolescents} \\ \text{Adults} \\ \text{Senior Citizens} \end{matrix} \begin{bmatrix} 0.20 \\ 0.35 \\ 0.10 \end{bmatrix}$$

Based on the matrices, how many people will make purchases?

A. 15
B. 41
C. 53
D. 133
E. 205

DO YOUR FIGURING HERE.

GO ON TO THE NEXT PAGE

Use the following table to answer questions 14 and 15:

The table below shows the genres of radio music, broken down by the medium, (AM, FM, or satellite) on which it is aired. In addition, the table shows the number of hours in which there is a "live" disc jockey.

Genre	Medium	# Of Hours Where There Is A "Live" Disc Jockey
Classical	AM	6
	FM	3
	Satellite	12
Country	AM	24
	FM	7
	Satellite	16
News	AM	24
	FM	24
	Satellite	24
Pop	AM	14
	Satellite	5
Rock	FM	12
	Satellite	24

DO YOUR FIGURING HERE.

14. What is the average number of hours, rounded to the nearest hour, that the Country genre has a "live" disc jockey?

F. 3
G. 7
H. 14
J. 16
K. 24

GO ON TO THE NEXT PAGE

15. The time of day in which there is a "live" disc jockey does not matter, as long as there is a "live" disc jockey for the number of hours listed in the table. Assume that a disc jockey can switch from any genre and medium to another with the flip of a switch. Based on the table above, what is the minimum number of disc jockeys needed, if each works an 8-hour shift?

    A.   5
    B.   13
    C.   24
    D.   25
    E.   195

16. In the table below, every row, column, and diagonal must have equivalent sums. What is the value of the lower left cell in order for this to be true?

m	$-4m$	$3m$
$2m$	0	$-2m$
	$4m$	$-m$

    F. $-4m$
    G. $-3m$
    H. -3
    J. 0
    K. m

DO YOUR FIGURING HERE.

GO ON TO THE NEXT PAGE

17. The standard coordinate plane is shown below, with the four quadrants labeled. Point R, denoted by R(x, y) is graphed on this plane, such that x ≠ 0 and y ≠ 0.

If the product xy is a positive number, then point R is located in:

A.   Quadrant I only

B.   Quadrant II only

C.   Quadrant III only

D.   Quadrant I or IV only

E.   Quadrant I or III only

18. The cafeteria offers 7 different sandwiches, 3 different soups, and 4 different drink choices on the luncheon menu. How many distinct meals are available if a meal consists of one sandwich, one soup, and one drink?

F.   7

G.   14

H.   21

J.   84

K.   Cannot be determined by the given information.

19. At the university there are 5 females for every 3 males. If there are 6,000 male students, how many students are female?

A.   10,000

B.   12,000

C.   16,000

D.   18,000

E.   30,000

DO YOUR FIGURING HERE.

GO ON TO THE NEXT PAGE

20. What is the length, in inches, of the diagonal of a rectangle whose dimensions are 16 inches by 30 inches?

    F.   25
    G.   23
    H.   34
    J.   578
    K.   1,156

21. Which of the following expressions is NOT equivalent to $5n + 1$?

    A. $\dfrac{1}{5n+1}$

    B. $5(n + 2) - 9$

    C. $\dfrac{1}{\dfrac{1}{5n+1}}$

    D. $\dfrac{5n^2 + n}{n}$

    E. $\dfrac{25n^2 - 1}{5n - 1}$

22. Which of the following equations is equivalent to $3x + 2y = 16$?

    F. $y = -\dfrac{3}{2}x + 16$

    G. $y = -\dfrac{2}{3}x + 8$

    H. $y = \dfrac{3}{2}x + 8$

    J. $y = -\dfrac{3}{2}x + 8$

    K. $y = -\dfrac{2}{3}x + 8$

23. A solution to the equation $x^2 - 20x + 75 = 0$ is:

    A. -15
    B. -5
    C. 0
    D. 3
    E. 5

DO YOUR FIGURING HERE.

GO ON TO THE NEXT PAGE

24. Given right triangle △*LMN* below, what is the value of cos *N*?

F. $\dfrac{5}{13}$

G. $\dfrac{5}{12}$

H. $\dfrac{12}{13}$

J. $\dfrac{13}{12}$

K. $\dfrac{12}{5}$

DO YOUR FIGURING HERE.

25. In the circle below, chord *AB* passes through the center of circle *O*. If the radius, *OC*, is perpendicular to chord *AB* and has length of 7 centimeters, what is the length of chord *BC*, to the nearest tenth of a centimeter?

A. 5.3

B. 7

C. 9.9

D. 12.1

E. 14.0

GO ON TO THE NEXT PAGE

26. To convert a temperature in degrees Celsius to degrees Fahrenheit, the formula is $F = \frac{9}{5}C + 32$, where C is the degrees in Celsius. What temperature, to the nearest degree Celsius, equals a temperature of 86 degrees Fahrenheit?

F. 30

G. 54

H. 80

J. 86

K. 187

27. The Olympic-sized pool is 50 meters long, 25 meters wide, and holds 14,375 cubic meters of water. If the pool is the same depth in all parts, about how many meters deep is the water in the pool?

A. Less than 9

B. Between 9 and 10

C. Between 10 and 11

D. Between 11 and 12

E. More than 12

28. In right triangle ΔDEF below, the measure of segment DE is 42 inches, and the tangent of angle D is $\frac{5}{8}$. What is the length of segment EF, to the nearest tenth of an inch?

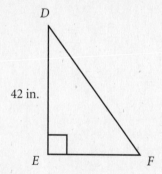

F. 26.3

G. 42.625

H. 49.6

J. 67.2

K. 210

DO YOUR FIGURING HERE.

GO ON TO THE NEXT PAGE

29. The bar graph below shows the number of people at the spring prom, according to their grade level at the high school. According to the graph, what fraction of the people at the prom were sophomores?

Number of Prom Attendees, by Grade Level

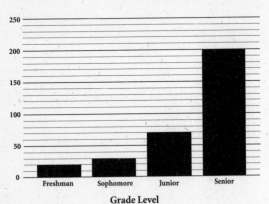

A. $\dfrac{1}{16}$

B. $\dfrac{3}{32}$

C. $\dfrac{3}{29}$

D. $\dfrac{3}{20}$

E. $\dfrac{3}{10}$

30. In the segment shown below, point X is the midpoint of segment WZ. If the measure of WY is 26 cm and the measure of WZ is 44 cm, what is the length, in centimeters, of segment XY?

F. 70

G. 22

H. 18

J. 13

K. 4

DO YOUR FIGURING HERE.

GO ON TO THE NEXT PAGE

31. What is the *x*-coordinate of the intersection point, in the (x, y) coordinate system, of the lines $2x + 3y = 8$ and $5x + y = 7$?

A.   −1

B. $\dfrac{1}{3}$

C.   1

D.   2

E.   3

DO YOUR FIGURING HERE.

32. For all pairs of real numbers *a* and *b*, where $a = 2b − 8$, $b = ?$

F. $a + 4$

G. $2a − 8$

H. $2a + 8$

J. $\dfrac{a − 8}{2}$

K. $\dfrac{a + 8}{2}$

33. What is the area, in square millimeters, of the parallelogram *RSTU* shown below?

A.   30

B.   39

C.   54

D.   168

E.   182

GO ON TO THE NEXT PAGE

34. If $x = -(y + 3)$, then $(x + y)^3 = ?$

    F. -27

    G. -9

    H. 9

    J. 27

    K.   Cannot be determined from the given
         information

DO YOUR FIGURING HERE.

35. Shown below is a partial map of Centerville,
    showing 80 square miles—a total of 8 miles
    of Main Street and a total of 10 miles of Front
    Street. There is a fire station at the corner of
    Main and Front St, shown as point F. The
    town wants to build a new fire station exactly
    halfway between the hospital, at H, and
    the school, at S. What would be the driving
    directions to get from the current fire station
    to the new fire station, by way of Main and
    Elm streets? All streets and avenues shown
    intersect at right angles.

    A.   2.5 miles east, 4 miles north

    B.   2.5 miles west, 4 miles north

    C.   2.5 miles east, 6 miles south

    D.   5.5 miles west, 4 miles south

    E.   5.5 miles west, 6 miles south

GO ON TO THE NEXT PAGE

36. There are two consecutive odd integers. The difference between four times the larger and twice the smaller is 36. If x represents the smaller integer, which equation below can be used to determine the smaller integer?

    F. $4x - 2x = 36$

    G. $4(x + 1) - 2x = 36$

    H. $4(x + 2) - 2x = 36$

    J. $4(x + 3) - 2x = 36$

    K. $36 - 4x = 2x$

37. A 15-foot supporting wire is attached to a telephone pole 12 feet from the ground. The wire is then anchored to the ground. The telephone pole stands perpendicular to the ground. How far, in feet, is the anchor of the supporting wire from the base of the telephone pole?

    A.   3

    B.   6

    C.   9

    D.   12

    E.   15

38. In the figure below, the sides of the square are tangent to the inner circle. If the area of the circle is 100π square units, what is the unit length of a side of the square?

    F.   400

    G.   100

    H.   20

    J.   10

    K. π

DO YOUR FIGURING HERE.

GO ON TO THE NEXT PAGE

39. The rectangles *ABCD* and *EFGH* shown below are similar. Using the given information, what is the length of side *EH*, to the nearest tenth of an inch?

3 in

8 in

2 in

A. 0.8

B. 1.3

C. 5.3

D. 7

E. 8

DO YOUR FIGURING HERE.

40. In the parallelogram *VWXY* below, points *U*, *V*, *Y* and *Z* form a straight line. Given the angle measures as shown in the figure, what is the measure of angle ∠*WYX*?

50°

150°

F. 25°

G. 30°

H. 50°

J. 100°

K. 150°

GO ON TO THE NEXT PAGE

41. In the figure below, all interior angles are 90°, and all dimension lengths are given in centimeters. What is the perimeter of this figure, in centimeters?

DO YOUR FIGURING HERE.

A.   40

B.   61

C.   82

D.   122

E.   Cannot be determined from the given information.

42. In the mayoral election, $\frac{3}{4}$ of the eligible voters at one site cast a vote. Three-fifths of the votes at this site were for candidate Martinez. If there are 3,500 eligible voters at this site, how many of them voted for Martinez?

F.   417

G.   1,575

H.   2,100

J.   2,625

K.   4,725

43. Given that a and b are positive integers, and the greatest common factor of a^4b^2 and a^3b is 54, what is a possible value for b?

A.   2

B.   3

C.   6

D.   9

E.   27

GO ON TO THE NEXT PAGE

44. If 40 percent of x is 70, then what is 160 percent of x?

    F.   28
    G.   45
    H.   112
    J.   175
    K.   280

DO YOUR FIGURING HERE.

45. Point M (2, 3) and point N (6, 5) are points on the coordinate plane. What is the length of the segment MN?

    A. $\sqrt{2}$ units
    B. $2\sqrt{3}$ units
    C. $2\sqrt{5}$ units
    D.   6 units
    E.   20 units

46. The ratio of the sides of two squares is 5:7. What is the ratio of the perimeters of these squares?

    F.   1:2
    G.   1:12
    H.   1:35
    J.   5:7
    K.   25:49

47. What is the equation of a circle in the coordinate plane with center $(-2, 3)$ and radius of 9 units?

    A. $(x - 2)^2 + (y + 3)^2 = 9$
    B. $(x + 2)^2 + (y - 3)^2 = 9$
    C. $(x - 2)^2 + (y + 3)^2 = 81$
    D. $(x + 2)^2 + (y - 3)^2 = 3$
    E. $(x + 2)^2 + (y - 3)^2 = 81$

GO ON TO THE NEXT PAGE

48. In the complex number system, $i^2 = -1$. Given that $\dfrac{3}{5-i}$ is a complex number, what is the result of $\dfrac{3}{5-i} \times \dfrac{5+i}{5+i}$?

DO YOUR FIGURING HERE.

F. $\dfrac{3}{5+i}$

G. $\dfrac{15+3i}{24}$

H. $\dfrac{15+3i}{26}$

J. $\dfrac{15+i}{26}$

K. $\dfrac{15+i}{24}$

49. The figures below show regular polygons and the sum of the degrees of the angles in each polygon. Based on these figures, what is the number of degrees in an n-sided regular polygon?

180°   360°   540°   720°

A. $60n$

B. $180n$

C. $180(n-2)$

D. $20n^2$

E. Cannot be determined.

GO ON TO THE NEXT PAGE

50. Fifty high school students were polled to see if they owned a cell phone and an mp3 player. A total of 35 of the students own a cell phone, and a total of 18 of the students own an mp3 player. What is the minimum number of students who own both a cell phone and an mp3 player?

F.   0
G.   3
H.   17
J.   32
K.   53

51. What is the solution set of all real numbers n such that $-4n + 3 > -4n + 1$?

A.   All real numbers
B.   All positive numbers
C.   All negative numbers
D.   All numbers such that $n > -\dfrac{1}{2}$
E.   All numbers such that $n < -\dfrac{1}{2}$

52. If 3 people all shake hands with each other, there are a total of 3 handshakes. If 4 people all shake hands with each other, there are a total of 6 handshakes. How many total handshakes will there be if 5 people all shake hands with each other?

F.   7
G.   9
H.   10
J.   11
K.   12

DO YOUR FIGURING HERE.

GO ON TO THE NEXT PAGE

53. The chart below shows the percentages of the county budget expenses by category. The remainder of the budget will be placed in the category Miscellaneous. If this data is to be put into a circle graph, what will be the degree measure of the Miscellaneous wedge, rounded to the nearest degree?

Budget Category	Percentage of Budget
Salaries	23
Road Repair	5
Employee Benefits	22
Building Maintenance/ Utilities	18

A. 32

B. 58

C. 68

D. 115

E. 245

54. If $\tan \theta = -\dfrac{4}{3}$, and $\dfrac{\pi}{2} < \theta < \pi$, then $\sin \theta = ?$

F. $-\dfrac{4}{5}$

G. $-\dfrac{3}{4}$

H. $-\dfrac{3}{5}$

J. $\dfrac{3}{5}$

K. $\dfrac{4}{5}$

DO YOUR FIGURING HERE.

GO ON TO THE NEXT PAGE

55. Which of the following systems of inequalities is represented by the shaded region on the coordinate plane below?

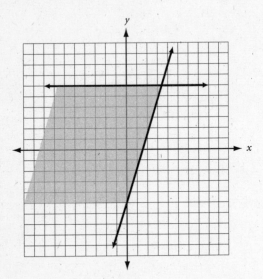

A. $y < 6$ and $y > 3x - 5$

B. $x < 6$ and $y > 3x - 5$

C. $y < 6$ and $y < 3x - 5$

D. $x < 6$ and $y < -3x - 5$

E. $y < 6$ and $y > \dfrac{1}{3}x - 5$

56. If $f(x) = 2(x + 7)$ then $f(x + c) = ?$

F. $2x + 2c + 7$

G. $2x + c + 7$

H. $2x + c + 14$

J. $2x + 2c + 14$

K. $2(x + 7) + c$

GO ON TO THE NEXT PAGE

57. Which graph below represents the solution set
for the equation $y = \dfrac{2x^2 - 8}{x - 2}$?

DO YOUR FIGURING HERE.

A.

B.

C.

D.

E.

GO ON TO THE NEXT PAGE

58. What are the coordinates of Q', the reflection of the point $Q(r, s)$ after a reflection over the y-axis?

F. $(-r, s)$

G. $(-r, -s)$

H. $(s, -r)$

J. $(r, -s)$

K. $(-s, r)$

59. If $g = 4q + 3$ and $h = 2q - 8$, what is g in terms of h?

A. $g = \dfrac{h + 8}{2}$

B. $g = \dfrac{4h + 11}{2}$

C. $2h + 19$

D. $2h + 11$

E. $h = \dfrac{g - 3}{4}$

DO YOUR FIGURING HERE.

GO ON TO THE NEXT PAGE

60. Find the $\cos(75°)$ knowing that $\cos(75°) = \cos(30° + 45°)$. Use the formula $\cos(\alpha + \beta) = \cos(\alpha)\cos(\beta) - \sin(\alpha)\sin(\beta)$ and the table of values below:

θ	sin θ	cos θ	tan θ
30°	$\dfrac{1}{2}$	$\dfrac{\sqrt{3}}{2}$	$\dfrac{\sqrt{3}}{3}$
45°	$\dfrac{\sqrt{2}}{2}$	$\dfrac{\sqrt{2}}{2}$	1
60°	$\dfrac{\sqrt{3}}{2}$	$\dfrac{1}{2}$	$\sqrt{3}$

F. $\dfrac{\sqrt{3} - \sqrt{2}}{4}$

G. $\dfrac{\sqrt{3} - \sqrt{2}}{2}$

H. $\dfrac{\sqrt{6} - \sqrt{2}}{4}$

J. $\dfrac{\sqrt{6} - \sqrt{2}}{2}$

K. $\dfrac{3 - \sqrt{2}}{4}$

DO YOUR FIGURING HERE.

READING TEST

35 Minutes—40 Questions

Directions: This test contains four passages, each followed by several questions. After reading a passage, select the best answer to each question and fill in the corresponding oval on your answer sheet. You are allowed to refer to the passages while answering the questions.

PASSAGE I

Emily couldn't help but grin broadly after answering the phone. She frequently called us "two peas in a pod," but I'd always felt like any

Line time we were mentioned outside of my presence
(5) he was "Bruce" and I was "Bruce's twin brother." Because of this, I wasn't surprised to hear my wife giggling uncontrollably and see her twirling the phone cord around her finger while talking to him. Despite the fact she was speaking to someone
(10) genetically identical to me, I couldn't help but wonder if she had ever responded so enthusiastically to one of my stories.

"Okay, I'll tell him. Talk to you soon." After Emily hung up, I watched her take a deep, almost
(15) wistful breath before walking over to me.

"Bruce seems well," I said, trying to sound casual. "He told me about the new job and everything. What did you guys talk about?"

"Not much." Emily replied. She walked behind
(20) my chair and patted my shoulder before sitting on the couch and opening her magazine. It didn't appear as if she was really reading. She seemed to stop and start, pausing and reflecting about something unrelated to the smiling celebrities featured
(25) in the article.

"It's funny to think that he knows some of these people," she said, pointing at her magazine.

I looked at the gleaming teeth and chiseled features of the actors, and then looked over at a
(30) picture of Bruce and me resting on the mantel. Looking closely at the photo always made my stomach turn; as with every picture of us, there was an unmistakable vitality in Bruce's face that

wasn't present in mine. It was as if I was wearing a
(35) "Bruce" costume; I was trying to mimic one of his trademark smiles, but always seemed to produce a different failed attempt.

"You all right?" Emily asked, noticing my expression.
(40) I grabbed the picture from the mantel and brought it to her. She looked at it, and looked up at me, quizzically.

"Can you tell which one is me?" I asked.

She looked back at the picture and pushed her
(45) lip out as she looked from one face to the next. After about five seconds she pointed to my face, then turned and looked at me confidently.

"How could you tell?" I asked.

"Well, it wasn't very hard," she responded. "You
(50) are my husband, and I love the way you smile. Bruce looks exactly the same in every picture, it looks practiced, but for you it always seems like you're thinking about something, even concentrating, to make sure you smile right."
(55) "Really?" I was surprised by how much thought she had put into this.

She took the picture and put it back on the mantel. I could still see the perfection in Bruce's smile and hesitation in mine, but at least Emily
(60) found a way to compliment my insecurities.

Emily went back to perusing her magazine.

"At least you ended up with a Fairholm," I said, "even if it wasn't the famous one."

"Oh, was I supposed to pursue the famous
(65) one?" she shot back.

She closed her magazine and put it down on the coffee table. There wasn't an argument coming, but I saw her disappointment. The problem

GO ON TO THE NEXT PAGE

was not that she actually would have married my
(70) brother before me; it was the simple fact that I
couldn't help but believe that to be the case. I saw
myself as second to him and always had. With
embarrassing relatives, people will always point
out that one can't choose his or her family, but
(75) when you're a twin, it's not the association that
you fear, it's the comparison.

"Do you want to be where he is?" she inquired,
with an empty tone.

"This is exactly where I want to be." I replied.
(80) "I just never know how to explain to people that
I'm an insurance adjuster, not a Hollywood agent.
They always want to know how it happened when
we had the same upbringing and education. They
look at me as if I did something wrong."
(85) "Do you ever call him?" she asked.

"I figure he's busy, and he calls enough," I said.

She cradled her chin in her hand, and looked at
me in mild disbelief. "You realize that by not calling and turning down his invitations to visit you
(90) make him feel rejected, right?"

"Come on, Emily. He's surrounded by famous
people, he doesn't need my approval."

"Maybe not," she sighed, "but his favorite stories
to tell me aren't about Hollywood, they're about
(95) you two growing up."

"Well, he was popular then, too," I said, shrug-
ging.

"He doesn't look at it that way," she responded.
"He would give up a lot to have your approval, Dave.
(100) He wants to be your brother, not a competitor."

"It's okay, Emily. I'll call him soon, but I think
that he'll be okay either way."

1. Dave would probably agree with which
   of the following statements regarding his
   relationship with Bruce?

   A. They would be better off not talking at all.

   B. Their phone conversations are vital to
   their relationship.

   C. Their bond as twins is stronger due to
   Emily's effort.

   D. Their competition makes it harder for
   them to get along.

2. Emily is best described as:

   F. aloof and ineffectual.

   G. needling and meddlesome.

   H. caring and diplomatic.

   J. pained and inconsolable.

3. Which of the following statements does NOT
   describe a feeling Dave has toward his brother?

   A. He is jealous of the reaction his brother
   gets from Emily during their phone
   conversation.

   B. He believes he would be better suited for
   his brother's type of work.

   C. He is resentful of his brother's superior
   social skills.

   D. He is skeptical of his brother's desire for
   his approval.

4. The primary focus of the first paragraph is:

   F. Emily's attempt to make her husband
   jealous.

   G. Emily's desire for the brothers to resolve
   their differences.

   H. Dave's hope to distance himself from his
   twin brother.

   J. Dave's feelings of inferiority to his twin
   brother.

GO ON TO THE NEXT PAGE ⇨

5. Lines 85–102 ("Do you ever… either way.") suggest that Dave does not contact Bruce because Dave:

   A. believes that Bruce has great need for him, but does not want to admit to Emily that she is right.

   B. feels guilty about being distant toward Bruce, and worries that he will have to explain himself.

   C. wants to prove to Emily that he is not impressed by Bruce's high profile job.

   D. still harbors resentment over Bruce getting preferential treatment during their childhood.

6. According to the passage, when Dave looks at the photograph, he sees:

   F. his brother being cruel to him.

   G. two indistinguishable faces.

   H. a comparison unfavorable to him.

   J. his wife paying more attention to Bruce.

7. Which of the following best summarizes Dave's feelings when he asks Emily to pick him out in the picture?

   A. Dave is confident that Emily will prefer his image to Bruce's.

   B. Dave is insecure; he feels the picture compares him unfavorably to Bruce.

   C. Dave is worried, because he thinks Emily will want to talk more about Bruce after seeing a picture of him.

   D. Dave is angry, because he did not want to talk about the picture in the first place.

8. It can be logically deduced from the passage that Dave and Bruce:

   F. tell Emily different sounding stories about their shared childhood.

   G. are frequently at odds regarding their different professions.

   H. have often fought over Emily's attention.

   J. were much closer shortly before Bruce moved.

9. Both Emily and Dave conclude that when pictures are taken of the brothers:

   A. Bruce looks much better than Dave.

   B. Dave appears angry at Bruce.

   C. Pictures of Bruce are more consistent than those of Dave.

   D. Dave's expression makes a greater impression on the viewer than Bruce's.

10. According to the passage, the reason Emily tells Dave about the content of Bruce's stories is because Emily:

    F. wants to convince Dave that Bruce does not see himself as better than Dave.

    G. wishes to hear Dave's version of the stories.

    H. sees this as a way to make Dave more impressed with his brother.

    J. thinks that this will make Dave sympathetic to Bruce's loneliness.

GO ON TO THE NEXT PAGE

PASSAGE II

Large-scale media would likely be traced back to ancient tribes sharing information about the edibility of berries or the aggressiveness of ani-
Line mals. Despite constant evolution, the information
(5) most sought after is that regarding personal safety, personal opportunity, and the triumphs and misdeeds of others—the larger the persona and more laudatory or despicable the act, the better. When a story is of continued national interest, however,
(10) the focus shifts even further from facts and more to theater. To step back and compose an objective plot of goings on is a distant possibility, but establishing the hero or villain of the day is paramount. Ultimately, the public's desire to have cold, dry
(15) and correct facts is virtually nonexistent.

Current newscasts exacerbate this by delivering an assault on the senses with meaningless graphics and theatrical music; meanwhile the monotone newscaster reads, verbatim from a teleprompter,
(20) often using identical phrases to those on other networks. Additionally, the viewer has probably already read the same story on the Internet earlier. When television was limited to three networks, rather than ubiquitous news-only channels, the
(25) newscaster was a national figure, audience members would eagerly await information that was new to them, and would expect a relatively thorough explanation of any complicated goings on. For example, to this day many people, in explain-
(30) ing the Watergate scandal to those too young to know of it, use Walter Cronkite's delineation as the basis for their understanding.

The objective, trustworthy anchorperson has also given way to vociferous demagogues promis-
(35) ing truth but delivering oversimplified, bias-driven sound bites. The idea of allowing individuals to draw their own conclusions is notably absent; in fact, many personalities mock those with opinions differing from those presented. The availability of
(40) neutral online sources mitigates this slightly, but not to any large degree. While the actual article may be impartial, electronic periodicals will still sensationalize headlines in order to attract casual readers, and those very headlines sway many
(45) readers to certain opinions before the article is even read. For example, if a headline mentions an "enraged public," the reader is far more likely to both read and take umbrage with the information than he or she would if the article mentioned a
(50) subject that "irked locals."

In truth, though, the public is as desirous for dry and objective facts as finicky children are for brussels sprouts. The personalities willing to shrug off accountability in favor of wild accusations and
(55) bombastic slogans captivate a large demographic, while one would be generous by saying that objective fact-based programs occupy even a niche market. This not only damages the general accuracy of so-called "news," but further polarizes the
(60) public. People now have the option to receive their news from hosts with a variety of political leanings, and one almost invariably chooses to watch the personality closest to one's own personal opinions. This is more harmful than convenient,
(65) because it allows viewers to simply parrot information they are given, eliminating any thought or scrutiny. It is this intellectual laziness that aids in distancing the general public from factual information: as a growing number become resigned to
(70) accept whatever their favorite host tells them, the more freedom networks have in passing sensationalist entertainment as news. It boils down to the unfortunate truth that most are far more likely to accept inaccurate information as fact rather than
(75) question the legitimacy of something that seems to fit with opinions a particular audience member holds.

Those who make the news also obfuscate objective facts. A legion of employees is designated
(80) solely for the purpose of making the decisions of political figures sound flawless. Oftentimes, important decisions are made, and throughout a lengthy press conference, not a single factual implication is discussed. The meeting becomes

GO ON TO THE NEXT PAGE ▷

(85) nothing more than an opportunity for political
employees to test their infallible sounding slogans,
while the media dissects the semantics rather than
the facts. Semantics, however, are all the media is
presented with.

(90)   Despite all these methods of prevarication,
people still are better informed than they were in
the past. Public knowledge of events often occurs
minutes after the fact, rather than days or weeks.
The populace has a strong desire for news in gen-

(95) eral, and amid all the unscrupulous presentation
methods, facts do exist. However, the profitability
of news has made presentation premium, not
trustworthiness. Complicating matters further is
the populace's impatience; the standard consumer

(100) would rather be presented with a minute and
potentially inaccurate statement—one that may
or may not be retracted the following day—than
suffer through a lengthy treatise comprised of all
the known facts and nuances of a particular event.

(105) The desire to know still exists, however; it just
happens to be overshadowed by the public's desire
for personal consensus and the media's desire to
reel in the public.

11. One of the primary points the author attempts
to make regarding the current news media is
that:

A. the media passes off made-up stories as
facts.

B. the news anchors are not as opinionated
as they were in decades past.

C. the media focuses more on presentation
than substance.

D. the media goes directly against what
news audiences truly desire to see.

12. The author makes what claim about impartial
news stories?

F. They no longer exist.

G. They can be sensationalized in ways
other than article content.

H. They often have headlines that correctly
reflect the emotional level of the story.

J. They all have headlines that attempt
to make the reader feel involved in the
story.

13. The author brings up Walter Cronkite's
coverage of Watergate in order to assert that:

A. Walter Cronkite was a particularly adept
newsperson.

B. a previous standard for news rightly
included clarification of complex issues.

C. current newscasters are far more forget-
table than those before them.

D. the expanding number of television
channels has made individual newscasters less famous.

14. By stating that "personal consensus" is of great
importance to the public (line 107), the author
is probably suggesting that members of the
public:

F. do not want information that contradicts
their own beliefs.

G. work hard to find the source closest to
truth, despite the difficulties present.

H. wish to resolve any moral conflicts
they may have with practices in news
reporting.

J. have difficulty finding news sources
reflecting their personal views.

GO ON TO THE NEXT PAGE

15. According to the passage, what type of news stories are sensationalized the most?

    A. Those with a fairly clear chain of events.

    B. Those that stay in the public's consciousness for long periods of time.

    C. Those that clearly support one political view.

    D. Those with the most scandalous information.

16. As used in line 12 (paragraph 1), the word *distant* most nearly means:

    F. separated

    G. different

    H. reserved

    J. unlikely

17. Based on the passage, which of the following headlines would the author be most likely to criticize?

    A. Earthquake Rocks Small Community, Arouses Questions Regarding Preparedness

    B. New Tax Protested by Idaho Farmers

    C. Parents Across Country Outraged at Offensive Song

    D. Governor Describes Proposed Legislation as "Monstrous"

18. The author asserts that individuals will often accept potentially inaccurate information because they:

    F. believe that most newscasters are honest.

    G. have no way to research correct facts.

    H. are forced to translate the guarded words of political employees.

    J. have similar political beliefs to specific personalities.

19. In the fourth paragraph, the phrase "even a niche market" (lines 57–58) expresses the author's feeling that:

    A. media companies are influenced greatly by public demand.

    B. cable television networks are unwilling to present objective facts.

    C. factual news media should look into better marketing practices.

    D. factual news would be profitable with greater exposure.

20. The author argues that in searching for a news source audience members are most likely to choose the source that:

    F. features the most entertaining newscaster.

    G. validates the audience member's opinion.

    H. presents the shortest and simplest explanation for goings on.

    J. focus on big stories rather than local ones.

GO ON TO THE NEXT PAGE

PASSAGE III

My grandfather was born in a turbulent time
in Russia. His non-communist lineage made him
unwelcome, before he had left the womb. His
Line father, an officer in the Russian army, was consid-
(5) ered an enemy of the communist Bolsheviks, so
my grandfather lived less than a year in what was
his native Moscow, and spent most of his younger
years moving across Asia. Despite this, he had
pride in being Russian, associated with Russians
(10) throughout his life, and would frequently quiz me
on Russian history. This all in tribute to a country
that ended up under different rule during the time
his mother was pregnant with him.

As a child, exiled to Siberia, my great grandfa-
(15) ther told his son of the greatness that existed within
the country that had forced the family into exile.
It was known that, first as a family, and later as an
adult, my grandfather was going to have to seek
a new place to call home, but despite this fore-
(20) gone conclusion, Russia was still romanticized,
and my grandfather learned to treat the country
with reverence. This was in contrast to the sentiments found in other recently exiled Russians,
who would not simply lament the actions taken by
(25) the country, but disparage all eight million square
miles. In my family's search for a place to settle,
attempting to forge a consistent identity was nearly
impossible, as no one knew if the next location
would hold for a month, let alone a year, all hoped
(30) for an unattainable "new Moscow."

The first elongated refuge was found, ironically,
in China, which would later have its own communist revolution. After several years of relative
stability, the revolution precipitated the move to
(35) the United States. Upon arrival in San Francisco,
my grandfather, along with my grandmother and
their young son, my father, found other Russian
immigrants who were also new to the country.
"*Ya amerikanets*" people would say, and despite
(40) the fact that they were recent immigrants who
associated primarily with those of shared ethnicity

and circumstance, they would play the role they
desired, and repeat "*ya amerikanets*"—"I am
American." They would share many stories about
(45) their native land, but did not repeat "*ya russkiy*,"
because being Russian went without saying.

While it was clear that this would be the last
country my grandfather would reside in, and that
he wished to become more American, it was per-
(50) haps the most confusing of times. It was less of
a problem in acclimating to an adopted setting;
the problem was dealing with a permanent setting at all. The only consistency throughout the
first thirty years of my grandfather's life was the
(55) knowledge that every "home" was temporary, and
now this was no longer the case. I often wonder if
his successful career in the real estate business had
anything to do with what must have been a rare
transformation of circumstance.

(60) Not only was my grandfather interested in real
estate, he was ardent about the importance of
ownership, a naturally discordant view to that of
the then Soviet Union, and thus selling homes
became a purpose in addition to an occupation.

(65) Part of his success in real estate was owed to
strategic compromise. Considering American
sentiments regarding Russia during the Cold War,
there were times that he was sure he lost certain house sales due to his last name and accent.
(70) However, to those willing to listen, he found
advantages informing people that he was an exiled
Russian, and ardently disagreed with the communist government. He would also point out his
pride in being a new American, and allow a poten-
(75) tial buyer to degrade Russia without blinking.

Fortunately, the 1950s were a time of settling
across the country, and this made real estate a
very lucrative profession. It wasn't just this that
attracted my grandfather, though; he also saw it as
(80) an opportunity to give tiny parts of the country to
other people, returning the favor, in a way.

Yet, it always seemed that something vital
still rested in the opposite hemisphere. Once

GO ON TO THE NEXT PAGE

communism fell, he began returning to Russia yearly,
(85) and while he and my grandmother never showed the
family pictures from Russia the way they would
from the various cruise ships they traveled on, it
could be deduced that returning to Russia was
analogous to an adopted child traveling to meet his
(90) or her birth-parents: the journey is one of personal
necessity rather than pleasure, and the encounter
is one that elucidates one's very existence. In selling real estate, my grandfather had worked to make
this unnecessary. I believe that he wished for people
(95) to keep those houses, and pass them down to later
generations, giving the space a sort of familial permanence, rather than a fleeting stay.

For most, the thought of real estate agents
conjures up images of smiling advertisements on
(100) benches and buses, and the skill of selling something so important. Many are wary of salespeople
in general, questioning the practice of convincing
people something is in their best interest when
the salesperson stands to personally benefit. My
(105) grandfather did financially benefit from sales,
but there was more to it; his realization of the
American dream only made him want to be a part
of others reaching for the same thing, whether
their native home was around the block or thou-
(110) sands of miles away.

21. One of the main points the author attempts to
convey in the passage is that:

A. immigrants would often rather live in
their native land.

B. American-born people tend not to be
able to understand how displacement
affects immigrants.

C. immigrants that acclimate well to
America still may have indelible ties to
their native land.

D. immigrants are often shocked by the stability offered to them in America.

22. Based on the first three paragraphs, which of
the following best describes the movements
of the author's grandfather, prior to his
emigration to America?

F. He grew up primarily in Siberia and
then moved to China during the Russian
revolution.

G. He grew up in Moscow, was exiled as an
adult, and rapidly moved through Asia.

H. He was born in Moscow, moved rapidly
through Asia, and settled for a while in
communist China.

J. He was born in Moscow, exiled to Siberia
with his family, and moved frequently
before settling for a somewhat longer
period in China.

23. The author's grandfather's "purpose" (line 64)
and desire to return "the favor" (line 81) are
best described as:

A. providing others with a sense of pride in
being American.

B. shedding light on injustices carried out
by other countries.

C. facilitating a stable situation for others.

D. providing well for his family.

GO ON TO THE NEXT PAGE

24. Which of the following actions contradicts a general attitude held by the author's grandfather?

    F. "He would also point out his pride in being a new American, and allow a potential buyer to degrade Russia without blinking" (lines 73–75)

    G. "They would share many stories about their native land, but did not repeat "*ya russkiy*," because being Russian went without saying" (lines 44–46)

    H. "he was ardent about the importance of ownership, a naturally discordant view to that of the then Soviet Union" (lines 61–63)

    J. "Once communism fell, he began returning to Russia yearly" (lines 83–84)

25. The author classifies a "new Moscow" as "unattainable" (line 30) because:

    A. the family believed Moscow to be the most desirable city in the world.

    B. it was unlikely that communism would fall shortly after the revolution.

    C. cities in other countries are entirely unlike those in Russia.

    D. it would not be possible to find a new home that could still be considered a native home.

26. When the author refers to Russians "playing the role" (line 42), he most likely means that the Russians were:

    F. convincing themselves that they were ready to acclimate.

    G. joking with each other.

    H. naïve to the way Americans tend to act with each other.

    J. still hopeful that they would see Russia again.

27. The "strategic compromise" applied by the author's grandfather (line 66) would most likely involve:

    A. agreeing with the potential buyer, no matter what.

    B. ignoring offensive statements.

    C. acting as American as possible.

    D. taking America's side in international disputes.

28. According to the passage, the grandfather's trip back to his native Russia provided him with:

    F. a greater understanding of the inner workings of his native land.

    G. greater motivation to sell homes in America.

    H. a greater sense of personal understanding.

    J. a necessary visit with estranged family members.

29. According to the first paragraph, the author's grandfather's birth happened:

    A. during the communist revolution.

    B. under communist rule.

    C. prior to the communist revolution.

    D. after the fall of communism.

30. When the author states that his grandfather "worked to make this unnecessary" (lines 93–94), he is suggesting that his grandfather's occupation could potentially:

    F. help his grandfather feel more connected to America through his success.

    G. oversee a transaction that could give others a sense belonging.

    H. sell houses that would allow other recent immigrants stability.

    J. help others realize the American dream.

GO ON TO THE NEXT PAGE

PASSAGE IV

In both recorded and oral history, the rattlesnakes are categorized as malevolent beings.
Their lance-shaped heads and angular brow-lines
Line make them look the perfect villain, and their
(5) venom cements this classification. Publicized
reports of bite victims seem to prove their nefari-
ous nature.

Unlike mammalian predators like bears, rattlesnakes are not given the classification of an animal
(10) deserving human respect. One imagines the rattlesnake hiding in our backyards, waiting to strike.

In recent long-term studies, however, the
social behavior of rattlesnakes has been found
to be quite different than many would expect.
(15) Herpetologists, scientists who study snakes, had
long suspected a more complex and thoughtful existence for the reptiles, and now have hard
information to back up their theories. When
examined, the sinister opportunist lurking in
(20) the shadows better resembles a mild-mannered
domestic. Unlike the non-venomous kingsnake,
rattlesnakes are entirely non-cannibalistic, and
tend to spend their entire lives with a single mate.
The mating ritual in which two males will extend
(25) almost half of their bodies off the ground to
wrestle is not lethal, and, once bested, a rattlesnake
peacefully retreats to find a new den of eligible
mates. Female rattlesnakes give birth to live young,
and rattlesnakes often share their dens, even
(30) hibernating with tortoises without incident.

Sadly, it seems that only those with an existing
fascination with snakes are aware of this socially
functional rattlesnake. Another discovery that
made little stir in the public consciousness is an
(35) experiment in which herpetologists tracked snakes
with radio transmitters, and saw their behavior
when humans entered their habitat. While a few
snakes did hold their ground and rattle, most saw
or sensed a disturbance (snakes cannot hear) and
(40) immediately headed in the opposite direction.
Many of the snakes that were handled by herpetologists did not coil or strike. This is not to say that

a snake will not bite a human if disturbed, but the
tendency is to retreat first and give warning sec-
(45) ond, before striking becomes a possibility.

Describing a more docile nature does not
imply that rattlesnakes would make good pets
for children, but considering the aggressiveness
often displayed by a South American pit viper, the
(50) fer-de-lance, one familiar with both would have
far fewer trepidations in passing by a rattlesnake.
For one thing, rattlesnakes do coil and rattle, giving humans an opportunity to move away, while
fer-de-lances will often strike at passersby without
(55) warning. Furthermore, when it comes down to
statistics, American hospitals report an average
of 7,000 snakebite patients a year, generally more
than half are actually from non-venomous snakes
mistook by victims as venomous. On average,
(60) fewer than six people die of snake envenomation
annually, and the vast majority of the serious bites
are due to either handling the snake or stepping
on it; most people bitten by snakes they were not
engaging end up with very mild bites. Compare
(65) this with an average of over one million hospital
visits for dog bites and twenty annual deaths at
the jaws of man's best friend. With such miniscule
statistics regarding snakebites, it is curious why
they are still viewed as unfathomably dangerous,
(70) when bees, lightning—and yes, dogs—are far
more responsible for human fatalities. The fer-
de-lance, however, is responsible for thousands of
annual deaths in Central and South America.

If one is looking for proof that rattlesnakes do
(75) not intend to harm humans, one should consider
perhaps the most stunning evidence regarding bite
behavior. Over half of the bites rattlesnakes admin-
ister to humans are "dry," meaning the rattlesnake
purposely does not release venom. While I will
(80) not posit that this is due to rattlesnakes possessing awareness for the well-being of its non-food
source bite victim, there is a great deal of thought
present. The snake acknowledges that venom
is needed for immobilizing and digesting prey
(85) (venom is actually saliva), producing venom

GO ON TO THE NEXT PAGE

takes time, and the human is not a food source. Therefore, if the snake is not surprised or fearing death, the damage of a rattlesnake bite will likely be far less severe than if the snake used all its

(90) venom. This has been known for some time, but in many cases, it is probably better for humans to believe that the snakes are more liberal with venom than they are, simply because a frightened and cornered rattlesnake is very dangerous.

(95) Unfortunately, some take the traditional role of the rattlesnake and use it as an excuse to harm the animals. People in various areas use the fearsome reputation of rattlesnakes, along with the more docile reality, for profit. Rattlesnake "round-ups"

(100) are held, where people collect snakes beforehand and join in a festival celebrating their conquest. The events are billed as both entertainment and as making surrounding residential areas safer for children, however the vast majority of snakes are

(105) collected from uninhabited areas, and people are frequently bitten at the festivals while handling the snakes for the audience. Eventually, the snakes are killed to make clothing or trophies, and these events are estimated to be responsible for 100,000

(110) rattlesnake deaths annually, in comparison to fewer than six for humans.

Behavior like this provides a better reason for *crotalid* mythology. With statistics categorically showing a low level of danger from rattlesnakes to

(115) humans, and an extremely high level vice-versa, it would be a wonder to see what human-related folklore would be like if rattlesnakes were able to speak or write.

31. In relation to the entire passage, the phrase "the sinister opportunist lurking in the shadows better resembles a mild-mannered domestic" (lines 19–21) most likely implies that:

A. adult rattlesnakes are considerable less aggressive than juveniles.

B. recent studies regarding rattlesnakes found few incidents of aggressive behavior.

C. rattlesnakes are more similar to mammals than once thought.

D. rattlesnakes are entirely predictable in behavior.

32. The passage implies that the rattlesnakes fearsome reputation can be beneficial because:

F. it influences people to avoid or move away from rattlesnakes.

G. it protects the lives of rattlesnakes.

H. it inspires medical advancement in treating snakebites, despite a low mortality rate.

J. adventurous people may seek rattlesnakes as pets.

33. What evidence does the passage give regarding the social ability of rattlesnakes?

A. Rattlesnakes are aware of the uses of their venom.

B. Wrestling between males establishes a social hierarchy.

C. Rattlesnakes can share their habitat with other species.

D. Rattlesnakes rarely eat other snakes.

GO ON TO THE NEXT PAGE

34. The statement "it would be a wonder to see what human-related folklore would be like if rattlesnakes were able to speak or write" (lines 115–118) means that:

   F. humans and rattlesnakes both present great risks to each other's safety.

   G. humans and rattlesnakes behave in many similar ways.

   H. humans are a much greater threat to rattlesnakes than rattlesnakes are to humans.

   J. humans have traditionally assigned human emotions to rattlesnakes in folklore.

35. According to the passage, what is the correlation between human behavior and serious rattlesnake bites?

   A. There is no statistical relationship.

   B. Humans that move in quick motions attract strikes.

   C. Humans that actively seek interaction with snakes are less likely to receive a "dry" bite.

   D. Rattlesnakes deliver a variable amount of venom based on how threatening humans act.

36. What is suggested by lines 46–48 when the author states that the new evidence "does not imply that rattlesnakes would make good pets for children"?

   F. Only professional herpetologists should keep rattlesnakes.

   G. Dogs can also be dangerous pets.

   H. Non-aggressive behavior does not make a venomous animal harmless.

   J. Rattlesnakes in the wild are more docile than those in captivity.

37. The passage states that the relative likelihood of a human being killed by a rattlesnake bite is:

   A. greater than that of a dog bite.

   B. less than that of a bee sting.

   C. equal to that of a lightning strike.

   D. comparable to that of the South American fer-de-lance.

38. Which of the following correctly categorizes a rattlesnake's strategy in venom usage?

   F. The larger the prey or predator, the more venom is used.

   G. Even when threatened, a rattlesnake reserves venom to use on prey.

   H. Rattlesnakes are aware that they will wound larger animals.

   J. Rattlesnakes would rather use venom solely for prey.

GO ON TO THE NEXT PAGE

39. The author states rattlesnake "round-ups" use contradictory logic because:

    A. children are rarely bit by rattlesnakes.

    B. the rattlesnakes that bite people at "round-ups" would have been far less likely to bite someone in their natural habitat.

    C. organizers use erroneous statistics to make the rattlesnakes seem more dangerous and the events more impressive.

    D. many that go to the events are unaware how many snakes are killed.

40. As used in line 113, the term *crotalid* is most likely:

    F. an unfavorable characterization of humans.

    G. a scientific word meaning "rattlesnakes."

    H. a word describing a herpetologist that specializes in rattlesnakes.

    J. a general word for a group unfairly accused of wrongdoing.

IF YOU FINISH BEFORE TIME IS CALLED, YOU MAY CHECK YOUR WORK ON THIS SECTION ONLY. DO NOT TURN TO ANY OTHER SECTION IN THE TEST.

STOP

SCIENCE TEST

35 Minutes—40 Questions

> **Directions:** Each of the following seven passages is followed by several questions. After reading each passage, decide on the best answer to each question and fill in the corresponding oval on your answer sheet. You are allowed to refer to the passages while answering the questions. Calculator use is not allowed on this test.

PASSAGE I

Glaciers are large masses of ice that move slowly over the earth's surface due to the force of gravity and changes in elevation. Glacial *calving* occurs when one edge of a glacier borders a body of water. A calving glacier's *terminus* (the lower edge) periodically produces icebergs as they break away from the glacier and into the water.

STUDY 1

A computer was used to create a model of a typical calving glacier. It was hypothesized that a primary factor determining the calving rate is the glacier's velocity at its terminus. Figure 1 shows the calving rate, in meters per year, and length of the computer-generated glacier over a period of 2,000 years.

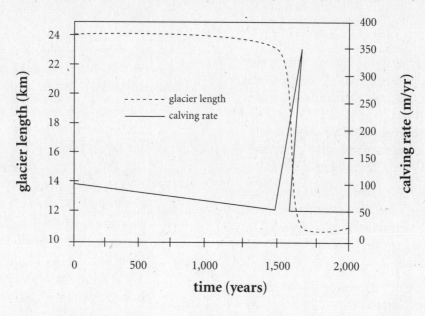

Figure 1

GO ON TO THE NEXT PAGE ⇒

STUDY 2

Four calving glaciers (A–D) were studied over a period of 10 years. The average velocity at the terminus of each glacier was recorded for years 1–5, and again for years 6–10. The calving rate of each glacier was estimated for the same time periods. The results are recorded in Table 1.

Table 1

| | Years 1–5 | | Years 6–10 | |
Glacier	Average velocity (m/yr)	Calving rate (m/yr)	Average velocity (m/yr)	Calving rate (m/yr)
A	72	72	63	64
B	51	52	45	47
C	98	106	256	312
D	160	189	53	54

STUDY 3

Meteorologists reported unusually high average temperatures in the regions of Glacier C and Glacier D during the same 10-year period examined in Study 2. It was hypothesized that the high temperatures were responsible for the relatively rapid variations in velocity and calving rate evident for Glacier C and Glacier D in Table 1.

1. If the glacier model used in Study 1 is typical of all calving glaciers, the scientists would draw which of the following conclusions about the relationship between glacier length and calving rate?

    A. As calving rate decreases, glacier length always increases.

    B. As glacier length decreases, calving rate always decreases.

    C. A sharp increase in calving rate results in a sharp decrease in glacier length.

    D. A sharp increase in calving rate results in a sharp increase in glacier length.

2. The meteorologists in Study 3 hypothesized that the faster the calving rate, the faster the sea level at a calving glacier's terminus would rise. If this hypothesis is correct, which of the following glaciers resulted in the fastest rise in sea level during years 6–10?

    F. Glacier A

    G. Glacier B

    H. Glacier C

    J. Glacier D

3. Based on the results of Study 2, a calving glacier traveling at a velocity of 80 m/yr would most likely have a calving rate:

    A. between 72 m/yr and 106 m/yr.

    B. between 106 m/yr and 189 m/yr.

    C. between 189 m/yr and 312 m/yr.

    D. over 312 m/yr.

4. Which of the following statements best describes the behavior of the glaciers observed during Study 2?

    F. All of the glaciers observed traveled faster during the first five years than during the last five years.

    G. All of the glaciers observed traveled faster during the last five years than during the first five years.

    H. The calving rate is always less than the average velocity for all of the glaciers observed.

    J. The calving rate is always greater than or equal to the average velocity for all of the glaciers observed.

GO ON TO THE NEXT PAGE

5. Which of the following graphs best represents the relationship between the calving rate and the average velocity of the glaciers observed in Study 2 for years 6–10?

A.

B.

C.

D.

6. If the hypothesis made by the meteorologists in Study 3 is correct, the glacier modeled in Study 1 most likely experienced unusually high temperatures at approximately what time during the simulated 2,000-year study?

F.   500 years

G.   1,000 years

H.   1,500 years

J.   2,000 years

GO ON TO THE NEXT PAGE

PASSAGE II

Allergic rhinitis refers to a person's nasal reaction to small airborne particles called *allergens*.

Table 1 shows the specific allergen, its type, and the approximate number of reported cases of allergic symptoms for a population of 1,000 people living in northern Kentucky during a single year.

Table 1

Month	Allergen type — Specific allergen	Pollen — Trees	Pollen — Grass	Pollen — Weeds	Mold — Alternaraa	Mold — Cladosporium	Mold — Aspergillus
January					⊛	⊛	⊛
February		⊛			⊛	⊛	⊛
March		⊛⊛			⊛	⊛	⊛
April		⊛⊛⊛⊛			⊛	⊛	⊛
May		⊛⊛⊛	⊛⊛⊛		⊛	⊛	⊛
June			⊛⊛⊛⊛		⊛	⊛	⊛
July			⊛⊛	⊛	⊛⊛	⊛	⊛
August				⊛⊛⊛	⊛⊛⊛⊛	⊛⊛⊛	⊛⊛⊛⊛
September				⊛⊛	⊛⊛⊛	⊛⊛⊛⊛	⊛⊛⊛⊛
October				⊛⊛	⊛⊛⊛	⊛⊛	⊛⊛
November					⊛⊛	⊛	⊛
December					⊛	⊛	⊛

Note: Each ⊛ equals 100 reported cases of allergic rhinitis.

Weekly tree pollen and total mold spore concentrations were measured in grains per cubic meter (gr/m³) for samples of air taken in southern Iowa for eight weeks. The pollen and mold spore counts are shown in Figures 1 and 2, respectively.

Figure 1

Figure 2

GO ON TO THE NEXT PAGE ⟹

7. Based on Figure 1, the tree pollen count on March 2 was closest to:

   A. 75 gr/m³.

   B. 150 gr/m³.

   C. 1,500 gr/m³.

   D. 1,900 gr/m³.

8. According to Figure 2, the mold spore count in the weeks after November 5:

   F. increased.

   G. decreased.

   H. varied between 1,000 gr/m³ and 2,000 gr/m³.

   J. remained above 2,000 gr/m³.

9. Based on the data in Figure 1, the tree pollen count increased the most between which two dates?

   A. February 9 to February 16

   B. February 23 to March 2

   C. March 2 to March 9

   D. October 29 to November 5

10. According to Figure 1, which of the following conclusions about the tree pollen count is most valid?

    F. The tree pollen count was highest on March 9.

    G. The tree pollen count was highest on March 16.

    H. The tree pollen count was lowest on February 23.

    J. The tree pollen count was lowest on March 16.

11. Based on Table 1, most of the cases of allergic rhinitis in May in northern Kentucky were caused by which of the following allergens?

    A. Tree and grass pollen

    B. Grass and weed pollen

    C. Alternaria

    D. Aspergillus

PASSAGE III

Simple harmonic motion (SHM) is motion that is *periodic*, or repetitive, and can be described by a frequency of oscillation. Students performed three experiments to study SHM.

EXPERIMENT 1

The students assembled the pendulum shown in Diagram 1. The mass at the end of the arm was raised to a small height, h, and released. The frequency of oscillation was measured in oscillations per second, or Hertz (Hz), and the process was repeated for several different arm lengths. The results are shown in Figure 1.

Diagram 1

GO ON TO THE NEXT PAGE

Figure 1

Figure 2

EXPERIMENT 2

A spring was suspended vertically from a hook, and a mass was connected to the bottom of the spring, as shown in Diagram 2. The mass was pulled downward a short distance and released, and the frequency of the resulting oscillation was measured. The procedure was repeated with 4 different springs and 4 different masses, and the results are shown in Figure 2.

Diagram 2

EXPERIMENT 3

Using the apparatus from Experiment 2, the mass-spring system was allowed to come to rest, and the *equilibrium length* of the spring was measured. The same 4 masses and 4 springs were used, and the results are shown in Figure 3.

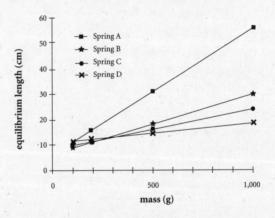

Figure 3

12. In Experiment 3, for which of the following masses would Spring B, Spring C, and Spring D have closest to the same equilibrium lengths?

F.   100 g

G.   270 g

H.   500 g

J.   1,000 g

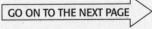
GO ON TO THE NEXT PAGE

13. A student has hypothesized that as the length of the arm of a pendulum increases, the oscillation frequency of the pendulum during SHM will decrease. Do the results of Experiment 1 support her hypothesis?

    A. Yes; the oscillation frequency of the pendulum observed in Experiment 1 decreased as the arm length increased.

    B. Yes; although the longest pendulum arm resulted in the highest oscillation frequency, the frequency decreased with increasing arm length for the other 3 lengths tested.

    C. No; the oscillation frequency of the pendulum observed in Experiment 1 increased as the arm length increased.

    D. No; although the longest pendulum arm resulted in the lowest oscillation frequency, the frequency increased with increasing arm length for the other 3 lengths tested.

14. Based on the results of Experiment 2, if an engineer needs a spring that oscillates most slowly after being stretched and released, which of the following springs should be chosen?

    F. Spring A
    G. Spring B
    H. Spring C
    J. Spring D

15. Based on the results of Experiment 3, if a 700 g mass was suspended from Spring A, at what equilibrium length would the system come to rest?

    A. Less than 20 cm
    B. Between 20 cm and 30 cm
    C. Between 30 cm and 50 cm
    D. Greater than 50 cm

16. The students tested a fifth spring, Spring E, in the same manner as in Experiment 2. With a 100 g mass suspended from Spring E, the oscillation frequency was 1.4 Hz. Based on the results of Experiment 2, which of the following correctly lists the 5 springs by their oscillation frequency with a 100 g mass suspended from *fastest* to *slowest*?

    F. Spring E, Spring B, Spring C, Spring A, Spring D

    G. Spring D, Spring A, Spring C, Spring B, Spring E

    H. Spring A, Spring B, Spring C, Spring E, Spring D

    J. Spring D, Spring E, Spring C, Spring B, Spring A

17. Experiment 1 was repeated using a larger pendulum mass. Which of the following figures best expresses the comparison between the results found using the larger pendulum mass and using the original mass?

GO ON TO THE NEXT PAGE

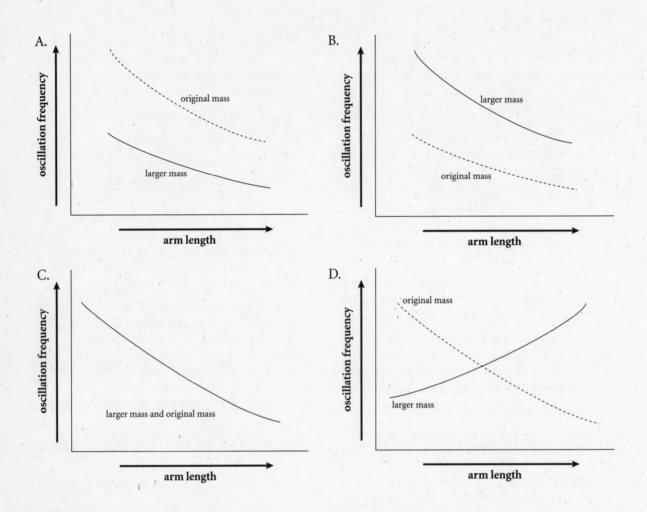

PASSAGE IV

An *alloy* is a uniform mixture of two or more metals. When the melting point of an alloy is lower than the melting point of any of its metal components, the alloy is referred to as a *eutectic* system. Figure 1 is a *phase diagram* that illustrates the states of matter of the gold-silicon (Au-Si) eutectic system over a range of temperatures and alloy compositions. For the Au-Si system, 0 percent Si means pure Au, and 100 percent Si means pure Si.

Note: (Au) and (Si) represent the solid forms of gold and silicon, respectively.

GO ON TO THE NEXT PAGE ⇨

Figure 1

18. According to Figure 1, at what temperature will Au begin to boil?

    F. 363°C

    G. 1063°C

    H. 1412°C

    J. The boiling point of Au is not included on the figure.

19. Based on Figure 1, an alloy that is atomically 50% Si and 50% Au will be in what state at a temperature of 600°C?

    A. Completely liquid

    B. Liquid with some amount of solid Si

    C. Liquid with some amount of solid Au

    D. Completely solid

20. A *solder* is a metallic material designed specifically to have a very low melting point. To make a solder out of a Au-Si alloy, what atomic percentages of Au and Si would be most appropriate?

    F. 0% Si, 100% Au

    G. 19.5% Si, 80.5% Au

    H. 80.5% Si, 19.5% Au

    J. 100% Si, 0% Au

GO ON TO THE NEXT PAGE

21. Based on the information in Figure 1, one could generalize that for Au-Si alloy compositions containing atomically less than 10 percent Si, the temperature at which the alloy becomes completely liquid decreases with:

    A. increasing Si atomic percentage.

    B. decreasing Si atomic percentage.

    C. increasing Au atomic percentage.

    D. neither increasing nor decreasing Si atomic percentage. The melting point is constant for all alloy compositions.

22. A liquid Au-Si alloy of unknown composition is gradually cooled from an initial temperature of 1,500°C. Solid particles are observed to begin forming as the temperature drops to 1,200°C. The particles must consist of which material, and what must be the approximate atomic composition of the alloy?

    F. The particles are Au, and the atomic composition of the alloy is 10% Si, 90% Au.

    G. The particles are Au, and the atomic composition of the alloy is 19.5% Si, 80.5% Au.

    H. The particles are Si, and the atomic composition of the alloy is 73% Si, 27% Au.

    J. The particles are Si, and the atomic composition of the alloy is 90% Si, 10% Au.

GO ON TO THE NEXT PAGE

PASSAGE V

A person requires a certain percentage of oxygen in the blood for proper respiratory function. The amount of oxygen in the air varies enough with altitude that people normally accustomed to breathing near sea level may experience respiratory problems at significantly higher altitudes. Table 1 shows the average percentage of oxygen saturation in the blood, as well as the blood concentrations of 3 enzymes, GST, ECH, and CR, for 3 populations of high altitude (ha) dwellers and 3 populations of sea level (sl) dwellers. Enzyme concentrations are given in arbitrary units (a.u.). Figure 1 shows average oxygen partial pressure and average temperature at various altitudes.

Table 1

Population	Altitude range (m)	Oxygen saturation (%)	Enzyme concentration (a.u.)		
			GST	ECH	CR
ha1	3,500–4,000	98.1	121.0	89.2	48.8
ha2	3,300–3,700	99.0	108.3	93.5	45.6
ha3	3,900–4,200	97.9	111.6	91.9	52.3
sl1	0–300	98.5	86.7	57.1	44.9
sl2	0–150	99.2	79.8	65.8	53.1
sl3	0–200	98.7	82.5	61.4	47.0

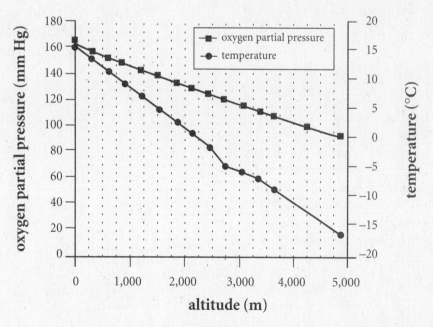

Figure 1

GO ON TO THE NEXT PAGE

23. Based on the data in Table 1, one would conclude that the blood of high altitude dwellers contains a higher concentration of:

    A. CR than ECH.

    B. CR than GST.

    C. ECH than GST.

    D. GST than CR.

24. Based on the information given, one would expect that, compared to the high altitude dwellers, the sea level dwellers:

    F. have blood with a lower percentage oxygen saturation.

    G. have blood with a lower GST concentration.

    H. can tolerate lower oxygen partial pressures.

    J. can tolerate lower temperatures.

25. According to Figure 1, an atmospheric sample found at an oxygen partial pressure of 110 mm Hg was most likely found at a temperature of about:

    A. 8.1°C.

    B. 0°C.

    C. −5.4°C.

    D. −12.5°C.

26. ECH is an enzyme that improves the efficiency of cellular energy production. Assume that people with higher ECH concentrations in the blood can function normally at higher altitudes without any respiratory difficulties. Based on Table 1, people from which population can function normally at the highest altitude?

    F. sl 1

    G. sl 2

    H. ha 2

    J. ha 3

27. Assume that a person's blood oxygen saturation percentage is determined only by the oxygen partial pressure at the location at which they live and the efficiency of the person's respiratory system at incorporating oxygen into the blood. Which of the following pieces of information supports the hypothesis that people from population ha 2 can incorporate oxygen into their blood more efficiently than people from population sl 1?

    A. Population ha 2 lives where the oxygen partial pressure is lower than that of where population sl 1 lives, yet population ha 2 has a higher blood oxygen saturation percentage than does population ha 1.

    B. Population ha 2 lives where the oxygen partial pressure is higher than that of where population sl 1 lives, yet population ha 2 has a lower blood oxygen saturation percentage than does population ha 1.

    C. Population ha 2 has a higher CR concentration than does population sl 1.

    D. Population ha 2 has an unusually high GST concentration.

GO ON TO THE NEXT PAGE ⟶

PASSAGE VI

Two students explain why lakes freeze from the surface downward. They also discuss the phenomena of the melting of ice under the blades of an ice skater's skates.

STUDENT 1

Water freezes first at the surface of lakes because the freezing point of water decreases with increasing pressure. Under the surface, *hydrostatic pressure* causes the freezing point of water to be slightly lower than it is at the surface. Thus, as the air temperature drops, it reaches the freezing point of water at the surface before reaching that of the water beneath it. Only as the temperature becomes even colder will the layer of ice at the surface become thicker.

Pressure is defined as *force* divided by the *surface area* over which the force is exerted. An ice skater exerts the entire force of her body weight over the tiny surface area of two very thin blades. This results in a very large pressure, which quickly melts a small amount of ice directly under the blades.

STUDENT 2

Water freezes first at the surface of lakes because the density of ice is less than that of liquid water. Unlike most liquids, the volume of a given mass of water expands upon freezing, and the density therefore decreases. As a result, the *buoyant force* of water acting upward is greater than the force of gravity exerted downward by any mass of ice, and all ice particles float to the surface upon freezing.

Ice melts under an ice skater's skates because of friction. The energy used to overcome the force of friction is converted to heat, which melts the ice under the skates. The greater the weight of the skater, the greater the force of friction, and the faster the ice melts.

28. According to Student 1, which of the following quantities is *greater* for water molecules beneath a lake's surface than for water molecules at the surface?

    F. Temperature
    G. Density
    H. Buoyant force
    J. Hydrostatic pressure

29. When two ice skaters, wearing identical skates, skated across a frozen lake at the same speed, the ice under the blades of Skater B was found to melt faster than the ice under the blades of Skater A. What conclusion would each student draw about which skater is heavier?

    A. Both Student 1 and Student 2 would conclude that Skater A is heavier.
    B. Both Student 1 and Student 2 would conclude that Skater B is heavier.
    C. Student 1 would conclude that Skater A is heavier; Student 2 would conclude that Skater B is heavier.
    D. Student 1 would conclude that Skater B is heavier; Student 2 would conclude that Skater A is heavier.

30. Which student(s), if either, would predict that ice will melt under the blades of an ice skater who is NOT moving?

    F. Student 1 only
    G. Student 2 only
    H. Both Student 1 and Student 2
    J. Neither Student 1 nor Student 2

GO ON TO THE NEXT PAGE

31. A beaker of ethanol is found to freeze from the bottom upward, instead of from the surface downward. Student 2 would most likely argue that the density of frozen ethanol is:

 A. greater than the density of water.

 B. less than the density of ice.

 C. greater than the density of liquid ethanol.

 D. less than the density of liquid ethanol.

32. A toy boat was placed on the surface of a small pool of water, and the boat was gradually filled with sand. After a certain amount of sand had been added, the boat began to sink. Based on Student 2's explanation, the boat began to sink because:

 F. hydrostatic pressure became greater than the buoyant force of the water on the boat.

 G. atmospheric pressure became greater than the buoyant force of the water on the boat.

 H. the force of gravity of the boat on the water became greater than the buoyant force of the water on the boat.

 J. the force of gravity of the boat on the water became less than the buoyant force of the water on the boat.

33. According to Student 2, if friction between the ice and the blades of an ice skater's skates is reduced, which of the following quantities simultaneously decreases at the point where the blades and the ice are in contact?

 A. Pressure exerted by the blades on the ice

 B. Heat produced

 C. Force of gravity of the blades on the ice

 D. Freezing point of water

34. Based on Student 2's explanation, the reason a hot air balloon is able to rise above the ground is that the balloon and the air inside it are:

 F. less dense than the air outside the balloon.

 G. more dense than the air outside the balloon.

 H. at a higher pressure than the air outside the balloon.

 J. less buoyant than the air outside the balloon.

GO ON TO THE NEXT PAGE

PASSAGE VII

In many communities, chemicals containing fluoride ions (F^-) are added to the drinking water supply to help prevent tooth decay. Use of F^- is controversial because studies have linked F^- with bone disease. Students performed 2 experiments to measure F^- levels.

EXPERIMENT I

Five solutions, each containing a different amount of Na_2SiF_6 (sodium silicofluoride) in H_2O were prepared. Five identical *electrodynamic cells* were filled with equal volumes of each of the five solutions, and a sixth identical cell was filled with a *blank* solution (one containing no added Na_2SiF_6). The cells were activated to measure the electrical *conductivity* for each. The conductivities were then corrected by subtracting the conductivity of the blank solution from each value (see Table 1 and Figure 1).

Table 1

Concentration of F^- (mg/L*)	Measured conductivity ($\mu S/cm$**)	Corrected conductivity ($\mu S/cm$**)
0.0	15.96	0.00
0.1	16.13	0.17
0.5	16.80	.084
1.0	17.63	1.67
2.0	19.30	3.34
4.0	22.64	6.68

* mg/L is milligrams per Liter

** $\mu S/cm$ is microSeimens per centimer

Figure 1

GO ON TO THE NEXT PAGE

EXPERIMENT 2

A water sample was taken directly from the drinking water supply of one community. An electrodynamic cell identical to those used in Experiment 1 was filled with water from this sample, and the cell was activated. The procedure was repeated for water samples from several communities, and the conductivities were measured (Table 2).

Table 2

Community	Measured conductivity ($\mu S/cm**$)	Concentration of F^- (mg/L)
Newtown	22.31	3.8
Springfield	16.46	0.3
Lakewood	18.63	1.6
Reading	19.47	2.1

35. Based on the results of Experiment 1, if the concentration of F^- in a solution is doubled, then the corrected conductivity of the solution will approximately:

    A. remain the same.

    B. halve.

    C. double.

    D. quadruple.

36. A sample was also taken from the drinking water supply of the community of Bluewater in Experiment 2 and its conductivity was measured to be 20.69 $\mu S/cm$. Which of the following correctly lists the drinking water supplies of Newtown, Lakewood, and Bluewater in *increasing* order of F^- concentration?

    F. Lakewood, Newtown, Bluewater

    G. Bluewater, Newtown, Lakewood

    H. Newtown, Bluewater, Lakewood

    J. Lakewood, Bluewater, Newtown

37. Based on the results of Experiment 1, if a solution with a concentration of 3.0 mg/L F^- had been tested, the corrected conductivity would have been closest to which of the following values?

    A. 1.3 $\mu S/cm$

    B. 3.3 $\mu S/cm$

    C. 5.0 $\mu S/cm$

    D. 6.5 $\mu S/cm$

38. If Experiments 1 and 2 were repeated to measure the concentration of chloride ions (Cl^-) in drinking water, then which of the following changes in procedure would be necessary?

    F. The solutions in Experiment 1 should be prepared by adding different concentrations of NaCl (or another chemical containing Cl^-) to H_2O.

    G. The conductivity of the blank solution should be added to the measured conductivities.

    H. The electrodynamic cells should be set to measure resistivity instead of conductivity.

    J. Both NaCl and Na_2SiF_6 should be added to all of the samples.

GO ON TO THE NEXT PAGE

39. Based on the results of Experiments 1 and 2, if the measured conductivities for the samples tested in Experiment 2 were compared with their corrected conductivities, the measured conductivities would be:

    A. lower for all of the samples tested.

    B. higher for all of the samples tested.

    C. lower for some of the samples tested, higher for others.

    D. the same for all of the samples tested.

40. The presence of other negative ions, such as Cl^-, results in an increase in the electrical conductivity of a solution. If all of the samples tested in Experiment 2 contained trace concentrations of Cl^-, how would the measurements have been affected? Compared to the actual F^- concentrations, the F^- concentrations apparently measured would be:

    F. higher.

    G. lower.

    H. the same.

    J. higher for some of the samples, lower for others.

IF YOU FINISH BEFORE TIME IS CALLED, YOU MAY CHECK YOUR WORK ON THIS SECTION ONLY. DO NOT TURN TO ANY OTHER SECTION IN THE TEST.

STOP

WRITING TEST
30 Minutes—1 Question

Directions: This section will test your writing ability. You will have thirty (30) minutes to compose an essay in English. Prior to planning your essay, pay close attention to the essay prompt so that you understand exactly what you are supposed to do. Your essay's grade will be based on how well it expresses an opinion on the question in the prompt, as well as its logical construction, supporting evidence, and clarity of expression based on the standards of written English.

You may use the unlined space on the next page to plan your essay. Anything written in this space will not be scored by the graders. Your essay must be written on the lined pages. While you may not need all the space to finish, you should not skip lines. Corrections and additions may be written neatly in between lines but not in the margins. Be sure to write clearly. Illegible work will not receive credit.

If you finish in under thirty minutes, you may review your essay. When time is called, lay your pencil down immediately.

DO NOT CONTINUE UNTIL TOLD TO DO SO.

In some cities, laws have been proposed that would restrict licensed drivers under 18 to driving alone or with an adult in the car. Parents and lawmakers who favor such laws point to the high incidence of car accidents with 16- and 17-year old drivers, and claim that not allowing teenagers under 18 to ride together will help newer drivers to focus on driving safely. Teenagers and parents who are against the restriction argue that teenagers riding together isn't necessarily the cause of accidents and that more comprehensive driver training is a better way to reduce accidents. In your opinion, should cities pass laws that ban teenagers from riding in a car that is driven by a driver under 18?

In your essay, take a position on this question. You may write about either one of the two points of view given, or you may present a different point of view on this question. Use specific reasons and examples to support your position.

Use this space to *plan* your essay. Your work here will not be graded. Write your essay on the lined pages that follow.

Practice Test Three: **Answer Key**

ENGLISH TEST			MATH TEST		READING TEST		SCIENCE TEST	
1. C	26. J	51. D	1. E	31. C	1. D	21. C	1. C	21. A
2. H	27. B	52. F	2. K	32. K	2. H	22. J	2. H	22. H
3. C	28. G	53. C	3. C	33. D	3. B	23. C	3. A	23. D
4. J	29. D	54. J	4. H	34. F	4. J	24. F	4. J	24. G
5. B	30. J	55. D	5. D	35. E	5. D	25. D	5. B	25. C
6. J	31. C	56. H	6. J	36. H	6. H	26. F	6. H	26. H
7. B	32. H	57. A	7. A	37. C	7. B	27. B	7. C	27. A
8. J	33. D	58. J	8. G	38. H	8. F	28. H	8. H	28. J
9. D	34. F	59. C	9. B	39. C	9. C	29. B	9. B	29. B
10. H	35. B	60. G	10. H	40. J	10. F	30. G	10. F	30. F
11. A	36. F	61. D	11. D	41. D	11. C	31. B	11. A	31. C
12. G	37. C	62. H	12. G	42. G	12. G	32. F	12. G	32. H
13. A	38. F	63. A	13. C	43. A	13. B	33. C	13. A	33. B
14. H	39. C	64. H	14. J	44. K	14. F	34. H	14. F	34. F
15. B	40. H	65. B	15. D	45. C	15. B	35. C	15. C	35. C
16. J	41. B	66. F	16. G	46. J	16. J	36. H	16. J	36. J
17. A	42. G	67. B	17. E	47. E	17. C	37. B	17. C	37. C
18. J	43. D	68. G	18. J	48. H	18. J	38. J	18. J	38. F
19. D	44. G	69. D	19. A	49. C	19. A	39. B	19. B	39. B
20. H	45. A	70. G	20. H	50. G	20. G	40. G	20. G	40. F
21. C	46. J	71. A	21. A	51. A				
22. G	47. D	72. G	22. J	52. H				
23. C	48. H	73. A	23. E	53. D				
24. J	49. D	74. H	24. H	54. K				
25. C	50. G	75. D	25. C	55. A				
			26. F	56. J				
			27. D	57. B				
			28. F	58. F				
			29. B	59. C				
			30. K	60. H				

ANSWERS AND EXPLANATIONS

ENGLISH TEST

PASSAGE I

1. (C)

Choice (C) forms a complete sentence by using the simple past tense *was*. Choice (A) creates a sentence fragment; an *-ing* verb needs a helping verb, such as *was* or *is*, to be the main verb in a sentence. Choice (B) incorrectly uses a comma to separate the subject from the main verb. Choice (D) omits the verb entirely, creating a sentence fragment.

2. (H)

The phrase *not only* in the beginning of the sentence is your clue to the correct answer. Logically, the phrase *not only* is always followed by *but also*. Here's another example: I *not only* studied math, *but* I *also* studied science. The other choices neither complete the idiom correctly nor convey the necessary contrast between the ideas in the two clauses.

3. (C)

Add an apostrophe and an *s* to a singular noun to show possession. The narrator and Gretchen attend one school, so choice (C) is correct. Choice (A) omits the apostrophe needed to show that the *swim team* belongs to the *school*. Choice (B) incorrectly treats *school* as a plural, placing the apostrophe after the *s*. Choice (D) incorrectly uses *ours* and does not make *school* possessive.

4. (J)

The test makers value simple and direct prose, so change passive constructions such as *it was with Gretchen that I* when you're given the opportunity. As is often the case on the English section of the

ACT, the shortest answer—choice (J)—is correct. In addition to being verbose, choice (F) contains a sentence structure error: It is not clear who knows that the writer enjoyed swimming. Choices (G) and (H) are both also verbose.

5. (B)

Slow down and carefully read the Nonstandard-Format questions. You just may see a question such as this that tests vocabulary. Choice (B) indicates that the narrator's mother recommended swimming lessons but did not decide that the narrator *must* take them. Choices (A), (C), and (D) all indicate that the mother's mind was made up.

6. (J)

If a sentence seems to have too many ideas, then it is probably a run-on. By itself, a comma cannot separate two clauses that could be independent sentences, as in choice (F). Choice (G) replaces *swimmers* with a pronoun but does not correct the run-on. Similarly, choice (H) removes the comma but does not address the problem of two complete thoughts that are incorrectly joined. Choice (J) solves the problem by using *whom*, which turns the second half of the sentence into a dependent clause that describes the *women*.

7. (B)

This sentence contains a parenthetical phrase. If you omitted *who had been swimming competitively since elementary school*, you would still have a complete sentence. Like all parenthetical phrases, this needs to be set off from the rest of the sentence. A comma is used at the beginning of the phrase, so a comma must also be used at the end of the phrase. This makes choice (D) incorrect. Choices (A) and (C) insert unnecessary commas within the parenthetical phrase.

8. (J)

When in doubt, take it out. *Giving up*, by definition, means *quitting* or *failing*. Choices (F), (G), and (H) create redundancies.

9. (D)

Trust your ear. *Begin* is an irregular verb; the simple past tense *began* can be used by itself, but the past participle *begun* cannot. Instead, *begun* always appears with *has*, *have*, or *had*, as in "I *have begun* to prepare for the ACT." Choice (D) correctly uses the simple past tense *began*. Choice (B) creates another verb usage error by inserting *been*. Choice (C) incorrectly uses *began* with *had*.

10. (H)

Don't panic if you see a question that tests the use of *who* and *whom*. The pronoun *who* refers to a subject, just like the pronouns *he* and *she* replace subjects. The pronoun *whom* refers to an object, just like the pronouns *him* and *her* replace objects. Here, *coach* is the subject of the sentence, so *who* (choice H) is correct. Never refer to a person as *which* (choice J).

11. (A)

Don't force a change where one isn't needed. The correct answer for some of the underlined portions will be NO CHANGE. The sentence *The hard work eventually paid off* is correct and concise as it is written. Choice (B) is verbose, and choices (C) and (D) create run-on sentences.

12. (G)

Start by asking yourself, "Does this stuff belong here?" The question asks for a sentence that is relevant to the narrator's experience on the swim team. Only choice (G) is connected to the narrator and the swim team; the sentence explains that the narrator was one of the only swimmers on the team to be interested in the butterfly. The history of the stroke (F), the relative speed of the stroke (H), and an alternative name for the stroke (J) are not as related to the narrator's personal experience.

13. (A)

The shortest answer is often, but not always, correct. Don't omit portions that add relevant information to the sentence. The sentence is about the narrator's swimming, so her participation in the medley relay is relevant. Choices (B) and (C) add descriptions of the medley relay that are not relevant to the topic.

14. (H)

The four choices offer different tenses of the same verb. The clue *last year* indicates that the narrator earned the varsity letter in the past. Choice (H), the simple past tense, is correct. Neither the future tense (F) nor the present tense (J) makes sense with the clue *last year*. Choice (G) would only make sense if something had prevented the narrator from earning the varsity letter.

15. (B)

Keep the main point of the passage in mind. Before beginning high school, the narrator had never thought of herself as an athlete. Then she joined the swim team and became successful at the sport. Choice (B) is most relevant to the central ideas of the passage. Choices (A) and (C) focus too narrowly on details in the passage, while choice (D) contradicts the main point of the passage.

PASSAGE II

16. (J)

Don't assume that a comma or semicolon is needed just because a sentence is long. Read the sentence aloud to yourself, and you should be able to hear that a comma is not needed in the underlined portion. A semicolon would only be correct if the second half of the sentence expressed a complete thought (choice (F)). Choices (G) and (H) both use an unnecessary comma.

17. (A)

When a verb is underlined, check to see if it agrees with its noun. Watch out for descriptive phrases that separate a verb from its noun. Here, the verb *was* agrees with the singular noun *tank*. NO CHANGE is needed. Choice (B) uses the present tense, but the surrounding sentences use the past tense. Choices (C) and (D) incorrectly use a verb in the plural form.

18. (J)

When the word *that* or *which* is underlined, watch out for an incomplete sentence. As it is written, this is a sentence fragment; a complete verb is missing. Removing *that*, as in choice (J), turns *made* into the main verb of a complete and correct sentence. Choice (G) does not address the sentence fragment error, and choice (H) also fails to provide a clear and appropriate sentence.

19. (D)

If you are *familiar* with a type of animal, then you have almost certainly *seen it before*. Choice (D) creates a concise sentence that does not lose any of the original meaning. The other choices are redundant. Choice (B) repeats *sights* when *view* has already been used, and Choice (C) uses the unnecessarily repetitive phrase *to which I was no stranger*.

20. (H)

Scan the paragraph for connecting words and phrases that you can use as clues to determine the most logical order of sentences. In Sentence 5, the word *first* suggests that the sentence should be placed close to the beginning of the paragraph. Sentence 2 says "There were *also* animals I had never before glimpsed," which indicates that a preceding sentence discusses animals the writer had glimpsed. Sentence 5, which describes the writer's view of familiar animals, most logically belongs immediately after Sentence 1.

21. (C)

If an underlined verb agrees with its noun, then determine whether the verb's tense makes sense in the context of the passage. The surrounding verbs are in the past tense, so this sentence should use the simple past tense *saw* (choice C). Choices (A) and (D) use the present tense, and choice (B) illogically uses the past progressive *had been seeing*.

22. (G)

An effective first sentence for a paragraph will introduce the topic of the paragraph and connect that topic to ideas that have come before. Paragraph 3 focuses on the catfish, while Paragraph 4 describes the large alligator and snapping turtle in the bayou tank. Choice (G) is an effective connection between these paragraphs, referring to the catfish and introducing the idea that there were even bigger animals on display. Neither choice (A) nor choice (H) leads into the topic of Paragraph 4. Choice (J) doesn't provide a transition from the discussion of the catfish in Paragraph 3.

23. (C)

The phrase in question provides a visual image; deleting the phrase would mean losing a description (choice C). The removal of the phrase would not affect the transition between sentences (choice (A)). Contrary to choice (B), the contrast between images would be decreased. The level of suspense may be somewhat decreased by the loss of the description, but it would not be increased (choice (D)).

24. (J)

The verbs *slides* and *aims* agree with the singular subject *it*, but they are in the wrong tense. The rest of the paragraph describes actions that took place in the past. For the sentence to make sense in context, these verbs should also be in the past tense (choice (J)). Choices (F) and (G) use present-tense verbs. Choice (H) creates a logically incomplete sentence.

25. (C)

Ask yourself, "Does this stuff sound like English?" If something sounds awkward or unusual, there is probably an error. Most words that end in *-ly* are adverbs; they are used to modify verbs, adjectives, or other adverbs. Adverbs cannot be used to describe nouns, such as *moment* (choice A). Choice (C) correctly uses the adjective *slight* to modify *moment*. The sentences formed by choices (B) and (D) don't make sense.

26. (J)

The phrase *much of the onlookers* probably sounds strange to you. That's because *much* is used with non-countable things or concepts (as in "There isn't much time") or quantities (as in "There isn't much pizza left"). You could count the number of *onlookers*, so *many*, choice (J), is correct. Choices (G) and (H) also create idiomatic errors.

27. (B)

The question tells you that the writer's goal is to describe the appearance of the crayfish, so eliminate any sentences that do not have details about how crayfish look (choice (C)). Choice (A) suggests that crayfish look like lobsters, and choice (D) describes the crayfish as small. Neither of these sentences offers the descriptive detail that is given in choice (B).

28. (G)

Trust your ear. You naturally pause when a comma or semicolon is needed in a sentence. A pause between *all* and *I* just doesn't sound right; that's because the full introductory phrase *After seeing all I could inside the museum* should not be interrupted. A comma should not separate a verb ("seeing") from its object ("museum"). This eliminates choices (F) and (H). A comma is needed between an introductory phrase and the complete thought that follows, making choice (G) correct and choice (J) incorrect.

29. (D)

Say it simply. The shortest answer here is correct: it turns the passive construction *it was that* in choices (A) and (B) into the active *I had*. Choice (C) is unnecessarily wordy.

30. (J)

A sentence must have a subject and verb and express a complete thought. The sentence that begins *And operates* does not have a subject. Removing the period (choice J) creates a grammatically incorrect sentence. Choice (G) is awkwardly worded. Choice (H) creates a run-on sentence; a coordinating conjunction such as *and* needs to be used along with a comma to link two complete thoughts.

PASSAGE III

31. (C)

When a pronoun is underlined, check to see that it agrees in number with the noun it replaces or refers to. In this sentence, the underlined pronoun refers back to the plural *secret identities and elaborate disguises*. Choice (C) uses the correct plural pronoun *they*. Choices (A) and (B) create pronoun agreement errors by using the singular pronoun *it*. Choice (D) creates a sentence fragment, since it makes the sentence into a dependent clause.

32. (H)

Many English questions will focus on the correct use of commas. Commas should be used to separate an appositive or descriptive phrase from the main part of the sentence. The phrase *the restaurant critic for The New York Times* describes the noun *Ruth Reichl*, so the phrase should be set off with commas (choice H). Choices (F) and (J) fail to use both necessary commas. On the other hand, choice (G) incorrectly inserts a third comma.

33. (D)

Only add sentences that are directly connected to the topic of a paragraph. Paragraph 2 discusses the importance of a *Times* review to restaurants in New York City. The suggested sentence provides a specific detail about one restaurant without explaining how the review from *The Times* affected business. Choice (D) best explains why the sentence should not be added.

34. (F)

Trust your ear. We look *to* someone or something for advice. No change is needed. Choice (G) suggests

that the paper is looking *along with* its readers, while choice (H) suggests that the readers are looking *near* the newspaper. Choice (J) uses an *-ing* verb without a helping verb, which creates a sentence fragment.

35. (B)

Verbs must make sense in the context of the passage. The next sentence says that a negative review *can undermine* a restaurant. Because the two sentences discuss possible results of a review, the underlined verb in this sentence should be in the same tense—*can bring* (choice (B)). Choice (A) illogically uses the conditional in the past tense, while choices (C) and (D) do not use the conditional at all.

36. (F)

The subject of the sentence is *restaurant owners and workers*, and the verb is *have*. There isn't a descriptive phrase or clause separating the subject and verb, so no comma is needed. A semicolon should be used to connect two complete thoughts (choice (G)). Choice (H) incorrectly treats *restaurant* as the first item in a list; instead, *restaurant* identifies the type of *owners* and *workers*.

37. (C)

To whom does the meal belong? It belongs to the *writer*, so the possessive pronoun *whose* is correct. *Who's* is always a contraction for who is or who has (choice (B)). Choices (A) and (D) introduce sentence structure errors.

38. (F)

The shortest answer is often correct. The sentence is concise and direct as it is written. Each of the other choices adds unnecessary words to the underlined portion.

39. (C)

On the ACT, there's no need to say the same thing twice. *Common*, *ordinary*, *representative*, and *average* all have very similar meanings; choices (A) and (B) use redundant language. Choice (C) makes the sentence concise by using only *typical*. Choice (D) uses a word that does not make sense in the context of the sentence.

40. (H)

If you have *decided* to do something to solve a problem, you have found a *solution*—there's no need to use both words. Choice (H) eliminates the redundancy and verbosity errors of the other choices.

41. (B)

As a rule, modifying words, phrases, and clauses should be as close as possible to the things or actions they describe. For instance, the list beginning *such as an attractive blonde named Chloe* describes the *different personas*. Therefore, *different personas* should come right before the list. This eliminates choice (A). Choice (B) correctly uses an introductory phrase and makes *Reichl* the subject of the sentence. Choice (C) is a sentence fragment; a complete verb is missing. Choice (D) inserts an unnecessary comma between *clothing* and *that*, and the pronoun *herself* is incorrect in context.

42. (G)

The most logical and effective sentence will be connected to the main topic of the paragraph and make a transition to the following sentence. Paragraph 4 describes how Reichl turned herself into different characters, and Paragraph 5 describes the result of reviewing a restaurant while in disguise. The best link between these ideas is choice (G). Choice (F) is a narrow detail that does not connect

the two paragraphs, while choices (H) and (J) move completely away from the topic of Reichl's disguises.

43. (D)

Sometimes it helps to rephrase a question in your own words. For example, how this question could be rewritten: "What does the phrase *of a restaurant* describe?" Reichl focuses on the quality of a restaurant, so the best placement is (D). The phrase does not describe *developed*, *view*, or *person*.

44. (G)

The word *occasionally* means sometimes; its placement in this sentence indicates that sometimes Reichl was sometimes treated very differently when she was in disguise, and sometimes she wasn't. Removing the word *occasionally* would indicate that Reichl always or typically had a different experience as one of her personas (choice (G)).

45. (A)

Paragraph 6 describes the effect of Reichl's use of disguises when she reviewed restaurants. Logically, this effect should follow the explanation of why and how Ruth dined as different people, the topics of Paragraphs 3 and 4. Paragraph 6 should remain where it is.

PASSAGE IV

46. (J)

Trust your ear. A comma indicates a short pause, which you won't hear when you read this part of the sentence aloud. No comma is needed (choice (J)). A comma can be used to separate a descriptive phrase from the rest of the sentence (choices F and H), but neither *would develop into prize-winning vegetables* nor d*evelop into prize-winning vegetables* is a descriptive phrase. Choice (G) incorrectly treats the underlined portion of the sentence as part of a list.

47. (D)

The paragraph describes events in chronological order, from the last freeze of the year to the time that spring *truly arrived*. Sentence 3 describes thinning out the plants and pulling weeds so the new plants would grow; it would only make sense to do this *after* the seeds have been planted and have started to grow. Sentence 4 is about planting seeds, so Sentence 3 must come after Sentence 4 (choice (D)).

48. (H)

When you read this sentence aloud, you should be able to hear a short pause between *burden* and *less*. This pause indicates that the conjunction *and* is needed to separate the two descriptions (choice H). Choice (G) is wrong because a colon is used to introduce a brief definition, explanation, or list. Choice (J) uses the inappropriate conjunction but, which doesn't make sense in context.

49. (D)

When *OMIT the underlined portion* is an option, consider whether the underlined portion is relevant to the topic of the sentence or paragraph. Paragraph 2 is about the writer's failure to maintain her garden, not about the weather in July and August. Choice (D) is correct.

50. (G)

Always read the questions carefully! This one asks for the choice that would NOT work in the sentence. In other words, three of the answer choices would make sense in the sentence. The first sentence of Paragraph 3 contrasts with Paragraph 2, so the contrasting transitions in (F), (H), and (J) are all

possible substitutions for the underlined word. *Indeed*, (choice (G)), however, is a word used to show emphasis, not contrast.

51. (D)

The shortest answer is often correct. Choices (A), (B), and (C) all refer to large-scale farming, which is only loosely related to the topic of gardening. Choice (D) keeps the sentence focused on the topic of Paragraph 3.

52. (F)

Before you answer this question, read enough of Paragraph 4 to identify its main idea. Paragraph 3 introduces the topic of square foot gardening, and Paragraph 4 describes several of its advantages. The best link between these ideas is the original sentence (choice (F)). Paragraph 4 doesn't mention the history of square foot gardening or the writer's neighbor, so choices (G) and (J) don't make sense. Choice (H) is a detail about square foot gardening, but it does not function as a topic sentence for the paragraph.

53. (C)

If an underlined word ends in *-ly*, you can be pretty sure that it is an adverb. Remember that adverbs can be used to describe verbs, adjectives, and other adverbs, but not nouns. The word *garden* is a noun, so choices (A) and (B) are incorrect. The adjective *traditional* (choice (C)) is correct. The phrase *tradition garden* (choice (D)) does not make sense.

54. (J)

Who spends hours thinning each row? From this sentence it's unclear: you have no idea who *they* are. Other sentences in Paragraph 4 use the pronoun *you*, so it makes sense to use *you* here.

55. (D)

OMIT the underlined portion is an option, so check to see if the information is irrelevant to the topic or repetitive. This sentence begins with the phrase *In a square foot garden*, so it is unnecessary to repeat *in the garden*. Choice (D) is correct.

56. (H)

OMIT the underlined portion isn't always the correct answer. As it is written, the sentence does not express a complete thought. To correct the error, remove *which could* so that *make* becomes the main verb of the sentence. Choices (G) and (J) create sentence fragments.

57. (A)

Don't look too hard for an error—many of the English questions will require NO CHANGE. The present tense and the pronoun *you* is used throughout Paragraph 4, so this sentence is correct as it is written.

58. (J)

Remember that the ACT values economy. If you can express an underlined portion in fewer words without changing or losing the original meaning, then the shortest answer is probably correct. The only choice that does not use redundant language is (J).

59. (C)

The verb in this sentence is separated from its singular subject *One season* by the phrase *of using the square garden techniques*. Choice (C) corrects the subject-verb agreement error of the original sentence. Incorrect choices use the plural form of the verb (A and B) or the future tense (D), which does not make sense in the context of the sentence.

60. (G)

This question asks about the passage as a whole, so take a moment to think about the main idea of the passage. Paragraphs 1 and 2 describe the writer's failed attempts at a traditional garden, while Paragraphs 3, 4, and 5 focus on the writer's success with a square foot garden. The essay is not instructive; instead, it compares two types of gardens, choice (G).

PASSAGE V

61. (D)

When a coordinating conjunction such as *but* or *and* combines two independent clauses (complete thoughts), a comma must come before it. In this sentence a comma should be inserted after *light* (choice D). Choice (C) incorrectly places a comma in a compound and fails to add one before the coordinating conjunction, and choice (B) incorrectly uses a semicolon between an independent and a dependent clause. You'll likely see at least one semicolon question on the ACT, so remember that a semicolon is used to separate two complete thoughts or to separate items in a series or list when one or more of those items already contains commas.

62. (H)

The answer choices present different forms of the verbs *improves* and *decreases*, so you know the issue is subject-verb agreement. The two underlined verbs need to agree with the plural subject *steps*; only choice (H) puts both *improve* and *decrease* in the correct form.

63. (A)

The simplest way to say something is often the most correct way to say something. The original sentence is the most concise and correct version. Choice (B) is redundant, using both *problem* and *trouble*. Choices (C) and (D) are both unnecessarily wordy in comparison to (A), which expresses the same meaning.

64. (H)

An *-ing* verb needs a helping verb, such as *is*, to function as the main verb in a clause or sentence. Changing *being* to *is*, as in choice (H), corrects the sentence structure error. Choice (G) inserts an incorrect comma between *vision* and *has*, while choice (J) creates a new sentence structure error by omitting the verb *being*.

65. (B)

Something that is *set* is established or predetermined. For the sentence to make sense, *set* should describe *time*; the wiper blades should be replaced at an *established* time each year. Choice (B) is correct. It does not make sense for the *blades* (choice (A)), the *year* (choice (C)) or the *risk* to be *set* or established.

66. (F)

Trust your ear. With some idiom questions, you have to rely on your ear to hear what sounds correct. *In general* is an introductory phrase used to mean usually or typically. Choice (F) provides the correct idiom for this context. The other choices contain idioms that are not typical of spoken English and do not fit this context.

67. (B)

To pick the best first sentence for Paragraph 4, you must be able to identify the main idea of the paragraph. If you scan a few sentences of Paragraph 4 before you answer the question, you'll see that the topic of the paragraph is changing a car's oil and oil filter. Only choice (B) introduces this topic. Choice (A) is too general, while choices (C) and (D) refer to car maintenance procedures that are not discussed in Paragraph 4.

68. (G)

The connecting word *so* is underlined, so consider the relationship between the two parts of the sentence. There is a slight contrast—the first part of the sentence explains what you *do* need, while the second part identifies what you *don't* need. The contrasting conjunction *but* (choice (G)) makes the most sense in context. The other choices indicate a cause-and-effect relationship that is not present in the sentence.

69. (D)

Information that is key to the main idea of a sentence should not be set off by commas. Here, it's important to know that the *section* is *in your owner's manual*, so commas are incorrect. Choice (D) is correct. Choice (C) incorrectly uses a semicolon; a complete thought is not expressed by *and collect all of the tools you need*.

70. (G)

Carefully read the question so that you understand the writer's purpose. If the writer wants to explain how to change oil, then the sentence should explain at least one specific step in the process. Choice (G) provides the most detailed information about how to go about changing oil.

71. (A)

Use a semicolon to introduce or emphasize what follows. The warning *you do not want to risk being crushed by a car* is certainly worthy of emphasis, so the sentence is correct as it is written. The other choices create run-ons, as the sentence expresses two complete thoughts; additionally, (D) incorrectly separates a subject noun from its verb with a comma.

72. (G)

Paragraph 4 uses the informal *you* and *your*, while the rest of the essay uses the more formal third person. Therefore, eliminating the second-person pronouns from Paragraph 4 would make the paragraph match the tone and voice of the rest of the essay (choice (G)). Choices (H) and (J) are opposite answers: eliminating *you* and *your* would make the advice less direct and would make the essay more formal.

73. (A)

Watch out for redundant language! A *qualified mechanic* will do a *professional* job, just as a *qualified mechanic* is likely *certified*; choices (B) and (C) use repetitive language. Choice (D) introduces a sentence structure error. The best version of the underlined portion is choice (A).

74. (H)

Knowing the general topic of each paragraph will help you quickly answer a question like this one. The sentence refers to *these different fluids*, so look for a part of the passage that discusses fluids. The second and third sentences of Paragraph 3 refer to different fluids (*coolant, oil, brake fluid*, and *transmission fluid*), so the most logical placement for the sentence is at the end of Paragraph 3 (choice (H)). Paragraph 2 and Paragraph 4 each only refer to one fluid, so choices (F) and (J) are incorrect.

75. (D)

Use your Reading Comp skills to answer this question. Does the main idea of the passage fit with this purpose? Not really, as the passage focuses solely on basic maintenance that car owners can do themselves. The passage doesn't discuss the need to learn about a car's safety features. Choice (D) is correct.

MATH TEST

1. (E)—Adding/Subtracting Fractions

100 Key Math Concepts for the ACT, #22. To determine the total amount of fabric used, add the mixed numbers. To add mixed numbers, add the whole number parts, and then add the fractions. The whole number parts add to 4. To add the fractions, find the least common denominator of 8 and 3, which is 24. Convert each fraction to an equivalent fraction with a denominator of 24: $\frac{3 \times 3}{8 \times 3} = \frac{9}{24}$, and $\frac{1 \times 8}{3 \times 8} = \frac{8}{24}$.

Now, add the numerators, and keep the denominator: $\frac{9}{24} + \frac{8}{24} = \frac{17}{24}$. The total fabric used is $4\frac{17}{24}$.

If you chose (B), you found a common denominator, but you did not add the numerators to get a total numerator of 4. A common error when adding fractions would result in choice (C). This fraction was obtained by the incorrect procedure of adding the numerators, and then adding the denominators.

2. (K)—Multiplying and Dividing Powers/ Multiplying Monomials

100 Key Math Concepts for the ACT #47, #55. To simplify this expression, first multiply the numerical coefficients to get $5 \times 6 \times 2 = 60$. To multiply the variable terms, keep the base of the variable and

add the exponents. Remember that x denotes x^1. Multiply the x variable terms: $x^3 \times x = x^{3+1} = x^4$. Multiply the y variable terms: $y^5 \times y^2 \times y = y^{5+2+1} = y^8$. The resultant expression is $60x^4y^8$.

If your answer was (J), you fell into the common trap of multiplying the exponents instead of the correct method of adding the exponents. If your answer was either (F) or (G), you added the numerical coefficients instead of multiplying. If your answer was (H), you did not include the exponents of 1 for the single terms of x and y.

3. (C)—Percent Formula

100 Key Math Concepts for the ACT, #32. First, find the amount each person saves yearly. Brandon puts 6% of his $36,000 salary, or $0.06 \times 36,000 = \$2,160$ each year. Jacqui puts $200 every month, or $12 \times 200 = \$2,400$ each year. The difference, in dollars, of their savings is therefore $2,400 - 2,160 = \$240$.

Answer choice (A) reflects the *monthly* difference in their savings. If you chose answer choice (D), you incorrectly found the difference between Brandon's yearly savings and Jacqui's *monthly* savings. Choice (E) indicates Brandon's monthly *salary*, minus Jacqui's monthly savings.

4. (H)—Average Formula/Using the Average to Find the Sum/Find the Missing Number

100 Key Math Concepts for the ACT, #41, #43, #44. An average is found by taking the total sum of the terms and dividing it by the total number of terms. Therefore, the sum = (average) × (number of terms). For Mikhail to have an average for the 5 games to be 180, the sum = $180 \times 5 = 900$. The first four scores total $190 + 200 + 145 + 180 = 715$. Therefore, his score for the 5th game must be $900 - 715 = 185$.

Answer choice (F) is just the average of the first four scores. Choice (G) is the average of the first four scores added and averaged with 180.

5. (D)—Percent Formula

100 Key Math Concepts for the ACT, #32. The amount of chromium is a part of the whole alloy. Use the formula Part = Percent × Whole. There are 262.5 pounds of chromium available, which must reflect at least 10.5% of the whole. Let w represent the whole amount of alloy that can be manufactured and write the algebraic equation: $262.5 = 10.5\%$ w or $262.5 = 0.105w$. Divide both sides of the equation by 0.105: $w = \dfrac{262.5}{0.105}$ pounds of steel.

Choice (A) represents 10.5% of 262.5. If you chose answer choice (B), you simply subtracted 10.5 from 262.5, without regard to the percent or the whole amount. Answer choice (C) is simply the amount of chromium. If you chose answer choice (E), you set up the problem correctly, but incorrectly converted 10.5% to the decimal 0.0105.

6. (J)—Special Quadrilaterals

100 Key Math Concepts for the ACT, #86. A wallpaper border is a strip that surrounds the perimeter of the kitchen. The perimeter of a rectangle = 2(length + width). The kitchen has a length of 6.5 meters and a width of 4 meters, so the amount of border needed is $2(6.5 + 4) = 2(10.5) = 21$ meters.

Answer choice (G) is a common mistake made when calculating perimeter. This answer would result from just adding the two dimensions, and not multiplying by 2. Answer choice (K) is the area, not the perimeter, of the kitchen.

7. (A)—PEMDAS

100 Key Math Concepts for the ACT, #7. To find an equivalent for the given expression, use the distributive property. First, evaluate the inner parentheses according to the order of operations, or PEMDAS. Distribute the negative sign to $(y + z)$ to get $w(x - y - z)$. Next, distribute the variable w to all terms in parentheses to get $wx - wy - wz$.

Answer choice (B) fails to distribute the negative sign to the z term. Answer choices (C) and (D) only distribute the w to the first term. Choice (E) incorrectly distributes wx to the $(y + z)$ term.

8. (G)—Solving a Linear Equation

100 Key Math Concepts for the ACT, #63. This is an equation with a variable on both sides. To solve, work to get the n terms isolated on one side of the equation, and the numerical terms on the other side. Subtract $3n$ from both sides to get $6n - 3n - 4 = 3n - 3n + 24$. Combine like terms: $3n - 4 = 24$. Now, add 4 to both sides: $3n - 4 + 4 = 24 + 4$, or $3n = 28$. Finally, divide both sides by 3: $n = \dfrac{28}{3}$. Answer choice (F) reflects a common trap: forgetting to divide by 3. If you chose answer choice (H) or (J), you incorrectly added $6n$ and $3n$, and possibly subtracted 4 from 24 instead of adding 4. Dividing incorrectly at the last step would have led you to answer choice (K).

9. (B)—Translating from English into Algebra/ Solving a Linear Equation

100 Key Math Concepts for the ACT, #63, #65. In this arithmetic sequence, you can think of the terms as 26, $26 + s$, $26 + s + s$, and $26 + s + s + s$. In this example, s represents the difference between successive terms. The final term is 53, so set up an algebraic equation: $26 + s + s + s = 53$. Solve this equation for s, by first combining like terms: $26 + 3s = 53$. Subtract 26 from both sides to get $26 - 26 + 3s = 53 - 26$, or $3s = 27$. Divide both sides by 3 to find that s, the difference between terms, is 9. Therefore the terms are 26, $26 + 9$, $26 + 9 + 9$, 53, or 26, 35, 44, 53.

Answer choice (D) results from taking $53 - 26$, dividing by 4, adding this value to each term, and rounding. In answer choices (A), (C), and (E), there is a common difference between second − first and then fourth − third, but it is different than the difference between the third and the second terms.

10. (H)—Evaluating an Expression/Solving a Linear Equation

100 Key Math Concepts for the ACT, #52, #63. First, solve the equation $5m^2 = 45$ for m. Once a value is obtained for m, substitute this into the expression to evaluate and find the answer. To solve the equation, divide both sides of the equation by 5 to get $m^2 = 9$. Take the square root of each side to get $m = 3$, or $m = -3$. Now, evaluate the expression. Because the expression contains the radical $\sqrt{12m}$, and the expression must be a real number, reject the value of $m = -3$. When a radicand, the expression under the radical sign, is negative, the number does not have a value in the set of real numbers. Substitute 3 for m in the expression:

$$(3)^3 + \sqrt{12(3)} = 27 + \sqrt{36} = 27 + 6 = 33.$$

If you chose answer choice (G), you just found the value of m^3. You might have selected answer choice (J) if you interpreted the $12m$ under the radical sign as the number 123 instead of 12×3. If you chose answer choice (K), you probably failed to take the square root of 9 when solving the equation and used the value of 9 for *m*.

11. (D)—Converting Fractions to Decimals/Volume of Other Solids

100 Key Math Concepts for the ACT, #29, #95. First, convert the mixed number radius to a decimal: $3\frac{3}{5} = 3.6$. Substitute 3.6 into the formula to get $V = \frac{4}{3} \times \pi \times (3.6)^3$. Use the π key on your calculator. If your calculator has fractional capability and follows the correct order of operations, type the entry in as listed above. Otherwise, first find 3.6 to the third power. Multiply the result by 4, and then divide by 3. Finally, multiply by π. In either case, the result is approximately 195.43, or 195 to the nearest cubic meter.

If you chose answer choices (A) or (B), you multiplied the radius by 3, instead of taking the radius to the third power. For choice (C), as well as choice (A), you incorrectly converted $3\frac{3}{5}$ to 3.35, a common trap. If you arrived at answer choice (E), you first multiplied $\frac{4}{3} \times \pi \times (3.6)$, and then raised this value the third power.

12. (G)—Probability

100 Key Math Concepts for the ACT, #46. Probability is a ratio that compares the number of favorable, or desired, outcomes to the total number of outcomes. Probability is always a number between 0 and 1, and is never greater than 1. In this question, the favorable outcome is the number of nuts that are NOT peanuts, or $6 + 8 = 14$. The total number of outcomes is $10 + 6 + 8 = 24$. The probability that the nut is NOT a peanut is $\frac{14}{24} = \frac{7}{12}$, in lowest terms.

Choice (F) is the probability that the nut IS a peanut. Choice (H) is the ratio that compares peanuts to other nuts.

13. (C)—Percent Formula

100 Key Math Concepts for the ACT, #32. The matrices outline the corresponding number of people in the store to the ratio, written as a decimal, of the number of people making purchases, *with reference to their age group*. A ratio written as a decimal is essentially a percentage. So following the correspondence yields $75 \times 0.20 = 15$ adolescent purchases, $100 \times 0.35 = 35$ adult purchases, and $30 \times 0.10 = 3$ senior-citizen purchases. This is a total of $15 + 35 + 3 = 53$ people making purchases.

Answer choice (A) represents the adolescent purchases. If you chose choice (B), you took the total number of people in the store, 205, and multiplied by the ratio for adolescents, 0.20. Choice (D) adds vthe total number of people, 205, multiplies by the sum of the ratios, 0.65, and then rounds. Choice (E) is the total number of people in the store, not the total number of purchases.

14. (J)—Average Formula

100 Key Math Concepts for the ACT, #41. To find an average, calculate the sum of the data and then divide by the total number of data items. According to the table, the number of hours that the Country genre has a "live" disc jockey is 24, 7, and 16. $24 + 7 + 16 = 47$. Divide: $47 \div 3 = 15.67$, which is 16 to the nearest hour.

Answer choice (F) is the number of *entries*, not hours, for the Country genre. Choice (G) is the average number of hours for the Classical genre. Answer choice (K) is the average number of hours for the News genre.

15. (D)

This problem tests your ability to read a table of information. You must study the wording in the problem and study the table to understand its structure. To determine the minimum number of disc jockeys needed given the information in the problem, add up all of the hours (the last column) and then divide by 8 (the number of hours a disc jockey works). From the table, the number of hours is: $6 + 3 + 12 + 24 + 7 + 16 + 24 + 24 + 24 + 14 + 5 + 12 + 24 = 195$ total hours. $195 \div 8 = 24.375$, which means you must have 25 disc jockeys, because you cannot have a fraction of a person.

A common trap would be answer choice (C), because the answer would round down to 24 disc jockeys, but this would fall short of the requirement to fulfill all of the hours.

Choice (E) reflects the total number of hours needed. Answer choice (A) is the number of 24-hour segments that require a "live" disc jockey.

16. (G)—Adding and Subtracting Signed Numbers/ Adding and Subtracting Monomials

100 Key Math Concepts for the ACT, #5, #53. To find the missing value, add the monomials in the first row: $m + -4m + 3m = 0$. This first row sums to zero. To be sure, check the rightmost column: $3m + -2m + -m = 0$. Every row, column, and diagonal must sum to 0, The first column must therefore be $m + 2m + \square = 0$, or $3m + \square = 0$. Isolate the missing term on one side of the equation by subtracting $3m$ from both sides: $\square = -3m$.

If your choice was (H), you ignored the m variable in the term. If your choice was (F), (J), or (K), you may have just looked at the first column and the last row and found a value that would work with those, without considering the other rows, columns, and diagonals.

17. (E)—Multiplying/Dividing Signed Numbers

100 Key Math Concepts for the ACT, #6. The algebraic expression xy means to multiply the point's x value by its y value. If the product is positive, then the x and y factors are either both positive or both negative, according to the rules for multiplying signed numbers. Positive x-coordinates are to the right of the origin. Positive y-coordinates are above the origin. In quadrant I, both coordinates are positive, and in quadrant III, both coordinates are negative. In quadrant II, the x-coordinate is negative (to the left of the origin) and the y-coordinate is positive (above the origin). In quadrant IV, the x-coordinate is positive (to the right of the origin), and the y-coordinate is negative (below the origin).

18. (J)—Counting the Possibilities

100 Key Math Concepts for the ACT, #45. The number of distinct lunches is determined by the fundamental counting principle. The counting principle directs you to multiply the different choices together to find the total number of combinations: $7 \times 3 \times 4 = 84$. If you consider just the sandwiches and soups alone, each sandwich can be paired with one of three soups, so there would be $7 \times 3 = 21$ different alternatives. These 21 alternatives would then become $21 \times 4 = 84$ different meals, because each of these 21 meals could be combined with 4 different drink choices.

A common trap answer is choice (G), where the numbers are added together, instead of multiplied. Choice (F) is the number of sandwiches available, not the number of distinct meals. Choice (H) reflects the number of distinct choices of just sandwich and soup.

19. (A)—Setting up a Ratio/Solving a Proportion

100 Key Math Concepts for the ACT, #36, #38. The question describes a comparison of the number of female to male students. This is a ratio—the ratio of female to male students is 5 to 3, or $\frac{5}{3}$. Let n represent the number of female students. Set up the proportion $\frac{5}{3} = \frac{n}{6,000}$ and cross multiply to get $3n = 5 \times 6,000$, or $3n = 30,000$. Divide both sides by 3 to get $n = 10,000$ females.

If you chose answer choice (B), you may have used rounding and incorrectly considered the ratio to be twice as many females as males. Answer choice (C) represents the total number of students at the university. If you chose choice (D) or choice (E), you may have stopped after multiplying 6,000 by 3 or by 5, respectively.

20. (H)—Pythagorean Theorem/Special Quadrilaterals

100 Key Math Concepts for the ACT, #84, #86. Draw a diagram of a rectangle:

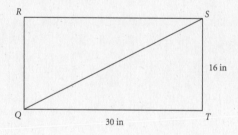

Because a rectangle has 4 right angles, you can treat the diagonal, QS, as the hypotenuse of a right triangle with legs of 16 and 30 inches. Use the Pythagorean theorem to solve for the length of the hypotenuse. If c represents the length of the hypotenuse and a and b represent the length of the legs, then $a^2 + b^2 = c^2$. Substitute into the formula:

$$c^2 = 16^2 + 30^2$$
$$c^2 = 256 + 900$$
$$c^2 = 1,156$$

Take the square root of both sides of the equation to find that $c = 34$ inches.

If you chose (F), you used 30 inches for c (the hypotenuse) in the formula, and then solved for one of the legs. Choice (G) adds the two dimensions and divides by 2. If you chose choice (J), you incorrectly divided by 2 instead of taking the square root; for choice (K) you added the squares but did not take the square root of the sum.

21. (A)—Simplifying an Algebraic Fraction

100 Key Math Concepts for the ACT, #62. Answer choice (A) is not equivalent to $5n + 1$—it is the reciprocal. If you chose answer choice (B), you may have incorrectly simplified by not multiplying 5×2. The expression simplifies as $5n + 10 - 9$, or $5n + 1$. Answer choice (C) is also equivalent to $5n + 1$— when you divide fractions, you multiply by the reciprocal of the denominator, and $\frac{1}{1} \div \frac{1}{5n-1} = \frac{1}{1} \times \frac{5n+1}{1} = 5n + 1$. If you chose either choice (D) or (E), you may have thought that they could not be equivalent because they have a squared variable. But when choice (D) is factored and simplified, you can see it is equivalent: $\frac{n(5n+1)}{n} = 5n + 1$. The same is true for choice (E): $\frac{(5n+1)(5n-1)}{5n-1} = 5n + 1$.

22. (J)—Solve "In Terms Of"

100 Key Math Concepts for the ACT, #64. Each of the answer choices is in the form "$y = ...$", so solve for y in terms of x. Isolate y on one side of the equation. First, subtract $3x$ from both sides: $3x - 3x + 2y = -3x + 16$. Combine like terms to get $2y = -3x + 16$. Now, divide all terms on both sides by 2: $y = -\frac{3}{2}x + 8$.

In answer choice (F) the numeric term 16 is not divided by 2. Answer choices (G) and (K) have the reciprocal of the coefficient of x. In answer choice (H), $3x$ was added to both sides of the equation instead of subtracted, to get the incorrect term of $+\frac{3}{2}x$.

23. (E)—Factoring Other Polynomials/Solving a Quadratic Equation

100 Key Math Concepts for the ACT, #61, #66. To solve a quadratic equation, first factor the trinomial in the form $ax^2 + bx + c$. Since the "c" term is positive, and the "b" term is negative, the factors will be $(x - \#)(x - \#)$. Look for factors of 75 that when added together will equal 20, the "b" coefficient. Some factor possibilities for 75 are 1 and 75, 3 and 25, and 5 and 15. Only the factors 5 and 15 will add to 20. The equation, after factoring, becomes $(x - 5)(x - 15) = 0$. The solutions are the values of x that result in either of the factors equaling 0: $x = 5$ or $x = 15$.

The common error traps are choices (A) or (B), where you might have quickly looked at the factors and thought the answers were either −5 or −15. If you chose choice (D), you may have thought the only factors of 75 were 3 and 25, and therefore chose 3 as a solution. If you chose answer choice (C), you may have ignored the term of 75, and found a solution of 0.

24. (H)—Sine, Cosine, and Tangent of Acute Angles

100 Key Math Concepts for the ACT, #96. The cosine (cos) ratio is the ratio of the side adjacent to angle N, to the hypotenuse of the right triangle. The $\cos N = \frac{12}{13}$.

Answer choice (F) is the sine (sin) ratio of angle N. Choice (G) is the tangent (tan) ratio of angle N. Choice (J) is the secant (sec), or the reciprocal of the cos to angle N. Choice (K) is the cosecant (csc), or the reciprocal of the sin to angle N.

25. (C)—Special Right Triangles

100 Key Math Concepts for the ACT, #85. Since chord AB passes through the center, it is a diameter of the circle, and segment OB is a radius, equal to 7 cm. Because OC is perpendicular to AB, a right angle is formed. To find the length of chord CB, note that it is the hypotenuse of right triangle $\triangle COB$, with legs that each measure 7 cm. Because the legs have the same measure, this is a special right triangle, the 45°-45°-90° right triangle, and the sides are in the ratio of $n:n:n\sqrt{2}$. Chord BC is therefore $7\sqrt{2} \approx 9.899$, or 9.9 to the nearest tenth of a centimeter. Alternately, you could have used the Pythagorean theorem, $a^2 + b^2 = c^2$, where $a = b = 7$:

$$7^2 + 7^2 = c^2$$
$$49 + 49 = c^2$$
$$c = \sqrt{98} \approx 9.9 \text{cm}.$$

If your answer was choice (A), you used the Pythagorean theorem, but evaluated 7^2 as 7×2, instead of 7×7. This is a common trap. Choice (B) is the length of the legs, not the hypotenuse. Choice (D) is $7\sqrt{3}$. Answer choice (E) is the length of the diameter of the circle.

26. (F)—Solving a Linear Equation

100 Key Math Concepts for the ACT, #63.
Substitute the value of 86 into the formula for F, the degrees in Fahrenheit, to get $86 = \frac{9}{5}C + 32$. Subtract 32 from both sides:

$$86 - 32 = \frac{9}{5}C + 32 - 32$$
$$54 = \frac{9}{5}C$$

Now, multiply both sides by the reciprocal of $\frac{9}{5}$ to isolate C:

$$\frac{5}{9} \times 54 = \frac{5}{9} \times \frac{9}{5} \times C$$
$$30 = C$$

If you chose answer choice (G), you forgot to multiply by the reciprocal to get rid of the fraction on the right side of the equation. Choice (H) makes the same error, but adds 32. Choice (J) is the degrees in Fahrenheit. Choice (K) would be the degrees in Fahrenheit of 86 degrees Celsius.

27. (D)—Volume of a Rectangular Solid

100 Key Math Concepts for the ACT, #94. A swimming pool that is the same depth in all parts is a rectangular solid. The amount of water in the pool is the volume of the water. Use the formula $V = lwh$, and substitute in the volume, length, and width given in the problem. $14,375 = 50 \times 25 \times h$, or $14,375 = 1,250h$. Divide both sides of the equation by 1,250, to get $11.5 = h$. The depth is between 11 and 12 meters.

28. (F)—Sine, Cosine, and Tangent of Acute Angles

100 Key Math Concepts for the ACT, #96. The tangent is the ratio of the side opposite to the given angle over the side adjacent to the given angle. Segment EF is the side opposite to angle D, so call

this side m. Segment DE, the adjacent side to angle D, equals 42 inches. Set up the equation:

$$\frac{5}{8} = \frac{m}{42}$$
$$(42)(5) = 8m$$
$$210 = 8m$$
$$m = 26.3$$

If your chose (G), you added 42 and $\frac{5}{8}$. Answer choice (H) reflects the length of side DF, the hypotenuse of the right triangle. Answer choice (J) incorrectly uses 42 as the opposite side and side EF as the adjacent side.

29. (B)—Setting Up a Ratio

100 Key Math Concepts for the ACT, #36. The fraction of the people who were sophomores would be the ratio of the number of sophomores to the total number of people at the prom. There were 30 sophomores, and a total of $20 + 30 + 70 + 200 = 320$ people at the prom. The fraction is $\frac{30}{320} = \frac{3}{32}$.

Answer choice (A) is the fraction of the attendees who were freshman. Answer choice (C) is the ratio of sophomores to those who are NOT sophomores. Answer choice (D) is the ratio of sophomores to seniors. Answer choice (E) is a common trap—it compares the number of sophomores to 100, instead of to the total number of students in attendance.

30. (K)

This problem requires you to understand that the sum of the parts of a segment is equal to the whole segment. It is given that X is the midpoint of segment WZ. Because the length of $WZ = 44$ cm, the length of WX is one half of this or 22 cm. From the relative positions of the points in the segment,

$WX + XY = WY$, or alternately, $WY - WX = XY$. It is given that $WY = 26$ and calculated that WX is 22. Therefore $XY = 26 - 22$, or 4 centimeters.

If you chose choice (F), you just added the two numbers given in the problem. Answer choice (G) is the length of one half of segment WZ, or the length of WX. If you answer was choice (H), you subtracted the two numbers given in the problem. Choice (J) is one half of segment WY.

31. (C)—Solving a System of Equations

100 Key Math Concepts for the ACT, #67. Find the point of intersection of two lines by solving the system of equations. Use the elimination method, by lining up the equations by like terms:

$$5x + y = 7$$
$$2x + 3y = 8$$

The problem asks for the x-coordinate, so look at the equations, and multiply one of them so that when the equations are combined, the y values are eliminated. If you multiply all terms in the top equation by -3, when you combine them, the y values will be eliminated:

$$-3(5x + y = 7) \Rightarrow -15x - 3y = -21$$
$$2x + 3y = 8 \Rightarrow 2x + 3y = 8$$

Combine like terms in the resulting equations: $(-15x + 2x) + (-3y + 3y) = -21 + 8$, or $-13x = -13$. Now, divide both sides of this simpler equation by -13 to get $x = 1$.

If you chose answer (A), you probably divided the negative numbers incorrectly to get -1. Answer choice (B) may have resulted from only multiplying the y by 3 and not multiplying the terms of $5x$ and 7,

and getting the result of $3x = 1$, or $x = \dfrac{1}{3}$. Answer choice (D) is the y-coordinate of the intersection of the two lines.

32. (K)—Solving "In Terms Of"

100 Key Math Concepts for the ACT, #64. To solve the equation for b, isolate b on one side of the equation. First, add 8 to both sides of the equation: $a + 8 = 2b - 8 + 8$, or $a + 8 = 2b$. Now, divide both sides by 2 to get $b = \dfrac{a + 8}{2}$.

If your answer was choice (F), you forgot to divide a by 2. In choice (G), you exchanged the variable a for the variable b, instead of solving for b. Answer choice (H) is similar to choice (G), but the subtraction was changed to addition. In choice (J), you may have subtracted 8 from both sides instead of adding 8.

33. (D)—Areas of Special Quadrilaterals

100 Key Math Concepts for the ACT, #87. The area of a parallelogram is $A = bh$, where height is the h is the length of the perpendicular segment to one of the sides of the parallelogram. In the figure, segment RT, of length $9 + 5$, or 14 mm, is the base and the dotted segment, of length 12 mm, is the height. The area is $14 \times 12 = 168$ mm^2.

Answer choice (A) is the area of the little triangle at the top, not the parallelogram. If you chose answer choice (B), you added the given numbers, without recognizing that the problem is asking for area. Answer choice (C) is the perimeter of the parallelogram. Answer choice (E) reflects a common error, where you multiplied the sides together, instead of the base times the height.

34. (F)—Evaluating an Expression/Solving an Equation

100 Key Math Concepts for the ACT, #52, #63. The problem asks for you to evaluate $(x + y)^3$, so manipulate the given equation to isolate $x + y$ on one side of the equation. Once you have this value, cube it to find the answer to the problem. For the given equation $x = -(y + 3)$, first distribute the negative sign on the right hand side to get $x = -y - 3$. Now, add y to both sides of the equation: $x + y = -y + y - 3$. Combine like terms to arrive at $x + y = -3$. Now substitute -3 for $(x + y)$ in the expression to get $(-3)^3 = -3 \times -3 \times -3 = -27$.

Answer choice (G) is a common trap: evaluating $(-3)^3$ as $-3 \times 3 = -9$. Answer choices (H) and (J) result from not applying integer multiplication rules for negative numbers.

35. (E)—Special Quadrilaterals

100 Key Math Concepts for the ACT, #86. Because all streets and avenues shown intersect at right angles, the map is a rectangle in which opposite sides have the same measures. To find the location halfway from H and S, first think of the corner of Oak and 10th to be the origin, or (0,0). Just as in coordinate geometry, the first ordered pair represents the east-west direction and the second ordered pair represents the north-south direction. The distance from the origin at Oak Street to the school is 5 miles east. The distance from the origin at 10th Avenue to the hospital is 8 miles north. The new station will be halfway between these coordinates, or $\frac{5}{2} = 2.5$ miles east of the origin and $\frac{8}{2} = 4$ miles north of the origin.

To drive from F to the new fire station, you would have to drive $8 - 2.5 = 5.5$ miles west on Main Street, and then $10 - 4 = 6$ miles south on Elm Street (the first two miles south to get to 2nd Avenue, and then the 4 more miles south to be halfway from the hospital and the school). Choice (A) is the directions of the new fire station starting from the origin at Oak and 10th. Choice (B) is the directions of the new fire station starting from the school. Choice (C) is the directions from the corner of Main and Oak to the new station. If your answered choice (D), you forgot to add in the 2 miles on Elm Street to get from Main to 2nd Avenue.

36. (H)—Translating from English into Algebra

100 Key Math Concepts for the ACT, #65. Consecutive integers are integers that differ by 1, such as 3, 4, 5... Consecutive odd integers are odd integers that differ by 2, such as 7, 9, 11, 13... Because the answer choices use the variable x, let x represent the smaller of the consecutive odd integers, so $(x + 2)$ would be the larger of the integers. Four times the larger is represented by $4(x + 2)$, and twice the smaller by $2x$. The key word "difference" means to subtract the smaller from the larger, and the key word "is" means equals. The equation is $4(x + 2) - 2x = 36$.

Choice (F) represents four times a number, minus twice the same number. Even though answer choices (G) and (J) are odd integers, they differ by an odd number, which would make the next number even. Choice (K) is an equation for the difference between 36 and four times the smaller integer.

37. (C)—Pythagorean Theorem

100 Key Math Concepts for the ACT, #84.
The question states that the telephone pole is perpendicular to the ground and a wire is attached to the pole. This will result in a right triangle. It helps to draw a quick figure to represent the situation. The thicker side of the triangle represents the telephone pole, and the hypotenuse is the wire:

To find out how far the anchor of the supporting wire is from the base of the telephone pole, solve for the length of the missing leg. Use the Pythagorean theorem, which is $a^2 + b^2 = hypotenuse^2$. Let b represent the missing leg and substitute in the given values to get $12^2 + b^2 = 15^2$, or $144 + b^2 = 225$. Subtract 144 from both sides: $b^2 = 81$. To solve for b, take the square root of both sides: $\sqrt{b^2} = \sqrt{81}$, so $b = 9$ or -9. A length cannot be negative, so the length is 9 ft.

Answer choice (A) subtracts $15 - 12$ to get 3. If you chose answer (B), you may have thought that 15^2 meant 15×2, and calculated $30 - 24 = 6$. Choice (D) is the length up the pole, and choice (E) is the length of the wire.

38. (H)—Area of a Circle

100 Key Math Concepts for the ACT, #91. The area of a circle is $A = \pi r^2$, where r is the radius of the circle. Use the equation $100\pi = \pi r^2$ and solve for r by dividing both sides by π: $100 = r^2$. If you take the square root of both sides then $r = 10$ or -10. Reject the -10 value, because a radius length cannot be negative. The radius of the circle is 10, so the diameter of the circle, which is the same as the length of a side of the square, is $2 \times 10 = 20$ units.

Answer choice (F) is the area of the square. Choice (G) is r^2. Choosing choice (J) is a common error that mistakes the radius of the circle for the side of the square.

39. (C)—Setting up a Ratio/Solving a Proportion

100 Key Math Concepts for the ACT, #36, #38. When figures are similar, the side lengths are in proportion. Let x represent the missing side length and set up the proportion of shorter side to longer side: $\dfrac{3}{8} = \dfrac{2}{x}$.

Cross-multiply to get $3x = 16$. Divide both sides by 3 to get $x = 16 \div 3 \approx 5.3$, to the nearest tenth of an inch.

If you chose answer choices (A) or (B), you set up the proportion incorrectly—make sure to match up the long sides and the short sides on the same side of the fraction. Answer choice (D) is the most common error made with similar figures, by assuming that since $3 - 1 = 2$ the missing side would be $8 - 1 = 7$. Similar figures have sides that are in proportion, which is not an additive relationship.

40. (J)—Parallel Lines and Transversals

100 Key Math Concepts for the ACT, #79. The figure shown is a parallelogram. Extend the top side out to make a parallel line to line *UZ*. Line *WY* is a transversal to the parallel lines, forming alternate interior angles, ∠*XWY* and ∠*WYV*, which have the same measures of 50°. Line *WV* is another transversal line to the parallel lines, forming alternate interior angles ∠*UVW* and ∠*VWX*. Because they have the same measure, ∠*VWX* = 150°. In addition, ∠*VWX* and ∠*VYX* have the same measure—they are opposite angles in a parallelogram. Now, ∠*VYX* − ∠*WYV* = ∠*WYX*, or 150 − 50 = 100°.

If your answer was choice (H), you incorrectly thought that ∠*WYX* had the same measure as ∠*XWY*. Answer choice (K) is the measure of ∠*VYX*, not ∠*WYX*.

41. (D)—Special Quadrilaterals

100 Key Math Concepts for the ACT, #86. The key to solving this problem is to simplify the drawing, knowing that you are looking for the perimeter. This figure, for perimeter purposes, can be thought of as a rectangle—just "lower" all the bottom pieces and move all left pieces to the right and you have a rectangle, with side lengths of 40 centimeters, and top/bottom lengths of 12 + 5 + 4 = 21 centimeters:

The perimeter is two times the length plus two times the width, or 2(40) + 2(21) = 80 + 42 = 122 centimeters.

Choice (A) is the measure of the length. Choice (B) is just the measure of two sides of the figure (just the numbers that are shown).

42. (G)—Convert Fractions to Decimals/Translating from English into Algebra

100 Key Math Concepts for the ACT, #29, #65. Convert the fractions into decimal equivalents, and remember that the key word *of* means to multiply. Because $\frac{3}{4}$ of the 3,500 eligible voters cast a vote, this is 0.75 · 3,500 = 2,625 votes that were cast at the site. Three-fifths of these votes were for Martinez, or 0.6 · 2,625 = 1,575 votes for Martinez.

If you answered choice (F), you followed the correct procedure, but incorrectly converted the fractions. Choice (H) is $\frac{3}{5}$ of all the eligible voters. Choice (J) is $\frac{3}{4}$ of the eligible voters. Answer (K) is the sum of choices (H) and (J).

43. (A)—Greatest Common Factor/Evaluating an Expression

100 Key Math Concepts for the ACT, #15, #52. To find the greatest common factor, find all factor pieces that the two expressions have in common. In this case, the factors in common are *a*, *a*, *a*, and *b*, or a^3b. It is given that the greatest common factor is 54, so think of a cubic number that is a factor of 54. The first cubic numbers are 1^3 (1), 2^3 (8), and 3^3 (27). Twenty seven is a factor of 54: 27 × 2 = 54, so a possible value for *b* is 2.

Answer choice (B) is the value of the variable *a*. Answer choice (C), 6, is a factor of 54, but that leaves the value of 9 for a, and 9 is not a perfect cube. The same reasoning would eliminate choice (D). Choice (E) is the value of a^3.

44. (K)—Percent Formula

100 Key Math Concepts for the ACT, #32. To tackle this problem, break it up into its parts. First, find the value of x, given that 40 percent of x is 70. The key word "of" means to multiply. Write this as the equation $0.40x = 70$; divide both sides by 0.4 to get $x = 175$. Now find 160 percent of x, or $1.60 \times 175 = 280$.

Answer choice (F) is 40% of 70. Choice (G) is 160% of 28, the incorrect value from choice (F). Answer choice (H) is 160% of 70. A common trap is answer choice (J), which is the value of the variable x.

45. (C)—Simplifying Square Roots/Finding the Distance Between Two Points

100 Key Math Concepts for the ACT, #49, #71. To find the length of segment MN, use the distance formula: $d = \sqrt{(x_2 - x_1)^2 + (y_2 - y_1)^2}$. Substitute in the point values:

$$d = \sqrt{(6 - 2)^2 + (5 - 3)^2}$$
$$d = \sqrt{4^2 + 2^2}$$
$$d = \sqrt{20} = \sqrt{4} \times \sqrt{5} + 2\sqrt{5}$$

If you chose answer choice (A), you may have used the distance formula incorrectly, using $(y_1 - x_1)$ and $(y_2 - x_2)$ instead of finding the difference between the x and y coordinates. Answer choice (B) multiplies by 2 instead of raising to the second power in the formula. Choice (D) is just the sum of the differences between the x and y coordinates. If your answer was choice (E), you forgot to take the square root of 20, as indicated by the distance formula.

46. (J)—Setting up a Ratio/Special Quadrilaterals

100 Key Math Concepts for the ACT, #36, #86. If the sides are in the ratio of 5:7, the perimeter will also be in this exact same ratio. When finding a perimeter, you add up the sides. Perimeter is measured in single units, just as is the side length. Therefore, the ratio will not change. If you are unsure about this fact, assign values and actually calculate the perimeters. Consider the smaller square to have sides $5s$ in length and the larger square to have sides $7s$ in length. The smaller square has a perimeter of $4 \times 5s = 20s$, and the larger $4 \times 7s = 28s$. The ratio $20s:28s$ is equivalent to 5:7, after dividing both terms of the ratio by $4s$.

If you chose answer (F), you may have thought you needed to subtract $7 - 5 = 2$, to get the (incorrect) ratio 1:2. Likewise, answer (G) adds $7 + 5 = 12$. Answer choice (H) multiplies $7 \times 5 = 35$. Answer choice (K) confuses area and perimeter—the ratio of the *areas* is 25:49.

47. (E)—Equation for a Circle

100 Key Math Concepts for the ACT, #75. The equation of a circle, when given the coordinates of the center (h, k) and the radius (r) is obtained by $(x - h)^2 + (y - k)^2 = r^2$. Substitute in the given values to get $(x - (-2))^2 + (y - 3)^2 = 9^2$. This simplifies to $(x + 2)^2 + (y - 3)^2 = 81$.

There are two common traps when finding the equation of a circle. One trap is to forget to square the radius, as in answer choice (B). The other common trap is adding h and k to x and y, instead of subtracting, as in answer choice (C). Answer choice (A) is both of these traps together.

Choice (D) incorrectly takes the square root of the radius, instead of squaring the radius.

48. (H)—Adding and Subtracting Signed Numbers/ Multiplying Fractions

100 Key Math Concepts for the ACT, #5, #23. In the complex number system, i^2 is defined to be equal to -1, as you are told in the question stem. Use the distributive property to multiply the fraction:

$$\frac{3}{5-i} \times \frac{5+i}{5+i} = \frac{(3 \times 5) + 3i}{5^2 + 5i - 5i - i^2}$$

$$= \frac{15 + 3i}{25 - (-1)} = \frac{15 + 3i}{26}$$

If your answer was choice (F), you may have cancelled incorrectly to simplify. Answer choice (G) reflects a common error when multiplying complex numbers— $25 - i^2$ was incorrectly interpreted to be $25 - 1 = 24$. In choice (J), the 3 in the numerator was not distributed to the i term. Choice (K) is the result of two errors—the common error described in choice (G), and the error in choice (J).

49. (C)—Interior Angles of a Polygon

100 Key Math Concepts for the ACT, #88. One way to solve this problem is to make a table. Each time the number of sides goes up by 1, the sum of the angles goes up by 180°. Make a third column in the table to discover a relationship.

Number of Sides	Sum of the Angles	
3	180°	180° × 1
4	360°	180° × 2
5	540°	180° × 3
6	720°	180° × 4

Notice that to find the sum of the angles, you can multiply 180 times 2 less than the number of sides of the polygon. This is choice (C).

If you chose choice (A), you may have just considered the triangle, and assumed that the relationship was $60n$. If your answer was choice (B), you may have noticed that the number of degrees rose by 180°, but did not consider the sides of the polygons. Choice (D) is a relationship that works for the 3-sided and 6-sided polygons, but not the other two.

50. (G)

This problem is a method of logical thinking. The key to solving this problem is to first assume that there are no students who have both a cell phone and an mp3 player. If this were the case, then there would be $35 + 18 = 53$ students polled. The problem states that 50 students were polled, so therefore at least 3 students have both electronic devices. This is the minimum number of students who own both.

If you chose answer choice (F), you may have ignored the fact that 50 students were polled. Choice (H) is the difference between the number of cell phone owners and mp3 owners. Answer choice (J) is a possible number of students who own *only* a cell phone. Choice (K) is the sum of 35 and 18.

51. (A)—Solving an Inequality

100 Key Math Concepts for the ACT, #69. To solve this inequality, attempt to get the variable on one side of the inequality by adding $4n$ to both sides: $-4n + 4n + 3 > -4n + 4n + 1$. Combine like terms to get $3 > 1$. This inequality is always true for the set of real numbers.

If you chose answer (B) or (C), you may have thought that the term $-4n$ would limit the set of solutions. If your answer was choice (D) or choice (E) you may have mistakenly added $-4n$ to both sides and added 3 to both sides to get $-8n > 4$, and then solved for n.

52. (H)

This question tests your problem solving strategies. Make a diagram of the situation in order to understand. In the diagram, the people are represented as diamonds, and the handshakes as connecting lines:

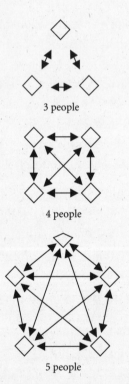

3 people

4 people

5 people

From the diagram, there are 10 total lines for 5 people, which represent 10 handshakes.

If you chose answer (F), you may have considered that 4 people have 2 more handshakes than people, and assumed this was the pattern for more people.

If your answer was (G), you may have incorrectly thought that the pattern in handshakes was multiples of 3. The key to the correct solution is to draw the picture.

53. (D)—Setting up a Ratio/Solving a Proportion

100 Key Math Concepts for the ACT, #36, #38. First, determine the percentage in the category Miscellaneous. The total percentage must sum to 100%, so the percentage for Miscellaneous is $100 - 23 - 5 - 22 - 18 = 32\%$. To find the number of degrees in a circle graph that corresponds with 32%, set up the ratio, where x represents the number of degrees for the Miscellaneous category. Recall that there are 360° in a circle: $\dfrac{32}{100} = \dfrac{x}{360}$. Cross multiply to get $32 \times 360 = 100x$, or $11{,}520 = 100x$. Divide both sides by 100 to get $x = 115°$, rounded to the nearest degree.

Choice (A) is a common trap that represents the percentage, not the number of degrees in a circle graph. If your answer was choice (B), you thought that there were 180° in a circle. Answer choice (C) is the percentage categories that are *not* Miscellaneous, and choice (E) is the number of degrees that are *not* Miscellaneous.

54. (K)—Special Right Triangles/Sine, Cosine, and Tangent of Acute Angles

100 Key Math Concepts for the ACT, #85, #96. The information that $\dfrac{\pi}{2} < \theta < \pi$ tells you that the angle is in quadrant II of the coordinate plane. In quadrant II, the sin values are positive. So the answer must be positive. Eliminate (F), (G), and (H). You are given the value of tan θ, which is the ratio of the opposite side to the adjacent side of a right triangle. Sketch this triangle, using leg lengths of 4 and 3:

This is a special right triangle, the 3-4-5 Pythagorean triple, so the hypotenuse is 5 units in length. The sin of an angle is the ratio of the length of the opposite side to the length of the hypotenuse, or $\frac{4}{5}$.

If you chose choice (F), you may have ignored the fact that the angle is in quadrant II, and thought that the sin value would be negative. Choice (G) is the cotangent of the angle. Choices (H) and (J) are cosine values for the angle for quadrants II and I, respectively.

55. (A)—Using an Equation to Find the Slope/ Using an Equation to Find an Intercept

100 Key Math Concepts for the ACT, #73, #74. Look at the graphed boundary lines for the inequalities. Find the equation for these boundary lines and then determine if the shading represents less than or greater than these boundary lines. The horizontal line has a slope of 0 and a y-intercept (where the line crosses the y-axis) of 6, so the equation of this boundary line is $y = 6$. It is shaded below this line, so the inequality is $y < 6$. The slanted line has a slope with a change in y values of 3 and a change in x values of 1, so the slope is $\frac{3}{1} = 3$. The y-intercept is −5. The line is increasing, so the slope is positive. The shading is greater than, or above, this boundary line, so the inequality is $y > 3x - 5$. If you chose answer choice (B), you fell into a common trap of interpreting the horizontal boundary line

equation to be $x < 6$. Answer choice (C) is another common error, thinking that the shading represents less than, or below, the slanted line. Answer choice (D) interprets the slope as −3. Negative slopes decrease, or slant downwards, when going from left to right. Answer choice (E) represents a slope of $\frac{1}{3}$, not the correct slope of 3. A slope of $\frac{1}{3}$ would mean for every change of 1 in the y values, the x values would change by 3.

56. (J)—Evaluating an Expression

100 Key Math Concepts for the ACT, #52. The question asks you to evaluate the function f(x), replacing x with ($x + c$). Replace any instance of x in the function definition with $x + c$: $2(x + 7)$ will be $2(x + c + 7)$. Use the distributive property and multiply each term in parentheses by 2 to get $2x + 2c + 2 \times 7$, or $2x + 2c + 14$.

In choice (F), the 2 was not distributed to the constant term 7. Choice (G) only multiplies the 2 by the first term in the parentheses. In choices (H) and (K), the c term was just added onto the end of the function definition, instead of replacing the x with ($x + c$).

57. (B)—Simplifying an Algebraic Fraction/Using an Equation to Find the Slope/Using an Equation to Find an Intercept

100 Key Math Concepts for the ACT, #62, #73, #74. First, simplify the equation by simplifying the fraction on the right hand side. Factor the numerator and then cancel the ($x - 2$) factor from the numerator and denominator:

$$\frac{2x^2 - 8}{x - 2} = \frac{2(x^2 - 4)}{x - 2} = \frac{2(x + 2)(x - 2)}{x - 2} = 2(x + 2)$$

The simplified equation is $y = 2(x + 2)$, or $y = 2x + 4$. This equation is now in slope-intercept form, where the y-intercept is 4 and the slope is $\frac{2}{1}$. Choice (B) is the correct graph that has a slope of 2 and crosses the y-axis at 4.

If you ignored the denominator in the given equation, then you would have incorrectly chosen answer choice (A), the graph of the quadratic $y = 2x^2 - 8$.

Answer choice (C) is the graph of the equation $y = \frac{1}{2}x + 4$. If this was your choice, you may have misinterpreted the slope of a line. Choice (D) is the graph of a quadratic function, not the correct linear function. You cannot assume a function is a quadratic just because you see a variable that is squared; you must first try to simplify the equation. Choice (E) is the graph of the linear function $y = -2x + 4$.

58. (F)

This problem tests your knowledge of line reflections in the coordinate plane.

When you reflect a point or a figure over the y-axis, the x-coordinate of each point is the opposite sign and the y-coordinate stays the same. The reflection of the point $Q(r, s)$ after a reflection over the y-axis is therefore $Q'(-r, s)$.

Answer choice (G) would be the result of a reflection over the y-axis, followed by a reflection over the x-axis. Choice (H) is incorrect—the x and y coordinates were switched. Answer choice (J) is a common trap that represents a reflection over the x-axis.

59. (C)—Solving "In Terms Of"

100 Key Math Concepts for the ACT, #64. The problem is asking what is the value of g in terms of h. The two given equations do not show a direct relationship between g and h, so you must solve for q in the second equation, to get q in terms of h, and then substitute this value in for q in the first equation. To solve for q in the second equation, isolate q by first adding 8 to both sides of the equation: $h + 8 = 2q - 8 + 8$, or $h + 8 = 2q$. Divide both sides by 2 to get $\frac{h + 8}{2} = q$. Use this value of q in the first equation: $g = 4q + 3$ becomes $g = \frac{4(h + 8)}{2} + 3$.

Factor out a 2 from the numerator and the denominator of the first term to get $g = 2(h + 8) + 3$. Multiply the terms in parentheses by 2, or $g = 2h + 16 + 3$, or $g = 2h + 19$.

Answer choice (A) is the value of q in terms of h, from the second equation. In choice (B) the constant term 3 in the first equation was incorrectly added to the numerator of the transformed first equation, and the 4 was not distributed to both terms of h and 8. In answer choice (D), the 2 was factored out correctly, but the remaining 2 was not distributed to the constant term of 8. Choice (E) is the value of q, not h, in terms of g from the first equation.

60. (H)—Evaluating an Expression/Trigonometric Functions of Other Angles

100 Key Math Concepts for the ACT, #52, #98. In this problem, you are asked to use the formula $\cos(\alpha + \beta) = \cos(\alpha)\cos(\beta) - \sin(\alpha)\sin(\beta)$ and the table of values, to find the value of $\cos(75°) = \cos(30° + 45°)$. Substitute in 30° for α and 45° for β to get: $\cos(30°)\cos(45°) - \sin(30°)\sin(45°)$. Now, use the table to replace each sin or cos with the corresponding values in the table:

$\dfrac{\sqrt{3}}{2} \times \dfrac{\sqrt{2}}{2} - \dfrac{1}{2} \times \dfrac{\sqrt{2}}{2}$. Using order of operations, multiply and then add the numerators and keep the denominator:

$\dfrac{\sqrt{6}}{4} - \dfrac{\sqrt{2}}{4} = \dfrac{\sqrt{6} - \sqrt{2}}{4}$. Alternately, you could use your calculator to find the value of the $\cos(75°) \approx 0.2588$, and then test each answer choice to find the answer closest to this value. Choice (H) will be the only value to equal the $\cos(75°)$.

If you chose answer choice (F) or choice (K), you probably used the wrong values in the table. In answer choice (G), you used the wrong values in the table, and also forgot to multiply the denominators, resulting in a denominator of 2 instead of 4. Answer choice (J) is the common trap—you correctly used the table, but did not multiply the denominators to get a denominator of 4.

READING TEST

PASSAGE I

1. (D)

The question is asking about Dave's opinion specifically. Throughout the passage Dave describes the problems with comparison between twins, and many of his comments to Emily are also focused on comparing himself to his twin. Choice (D) is correct because it mentions this competition and implies that it makes their relationship more difficult. Choice (A) is extreme, choice (B) implies that their relationship is stronger than it is, and choice (C) is not supported by the text, because Emily doesn't seem to be able to convince Dave to make more of an effort.

2. (H)

Emily has a good relationship with both brothers; she has an enjoyable conversation with Bruce and works to make Dave feel better. Also, she wants the brothers to be closer than they are. Because it reflects these details, choice (H) is the correct answer. Choice (F) is the opposite; Emily is very attentive, and choices (G) and (J) are both extreme and negative distortions of Emily's desire to help relations between the brothers.

3. (B)

This question is asking for an answer that is not found in the passage, so the first step is to eliminate choices that are contained in the passage. In the first paragraph, Dave is envious of the reaction his wife has when talking to Bruce, eliminating choice (A). The paragraph about Dave's reaction to the picture captures his negative feelings regarding the difference in their popularity, eliminating choice (C). The final conversation shows Dave as doubtful of Bruce's need for his approval, eliminating choice (D). This leaves choice (B), which is not found in the passage, and is therefore the correct answer.

4. (J)

The first paragraph starts with a description of Emily on the phone, but the focus quickly shifts to Dave's reaction. It then moves to Dave making some points about his brother's popularity and questioning if his own wife ever reacted so favorably to him. Choice (J) summarizes this well. Choices (F) and (H) are not found in the passage, and choice (G) occurs much later.

5. (D)

Emily attempts to make Dave believe that he is important to Bruce, but Dave still feels he is in Bruce's shadow. It is unclear whether or not Dave entirely believes Emily, but when she brings up Bruce's desire to talk about the brothers' childhood, Dave's response suggests that he does not want to talk about it because it again reminds him of how Bruce has always been the more popular of the two. This makes choice (D) the correct answer. Choice (A) is out of scope; the passage does not suggest that Dave does anything to spite Emily. Choice (B) is incorrect because Dave does not feel guilty; he sees Bruce's success as proof that it doesn't matter whether he calls Bruce or not. Choice (C) is out of scope; Dave's reasons for not calling Bruce have to do with his feelings towards his brother, not any feelings related to Emily.

6. (H)

In lines 32–34, Dave explicitly talks about how Bruce's image has positive aspects (vitality) that his image lacks. This is a perfect match for choice (H), which restates this generally. Choices (F) and (J) are not found in the passage, and choice (G) is contradicted by the fact that both Dave and Emily can tell the difference between the twins.

7. (B)

Dave is uncomfortable at this point, because Emily is clearly thinking about Bruce. The previous paragraph describes the picture as a source of insecurity for Dave, suggesting that he is nervous and seeking reassurance that Emily is with him for reasons other than his connection to Bruce. Only choice (B) describes these feelings. Choice (A) is the opposite of what Dave is feeling, and neither choice (C) nor (D) can be deduced from the information in the passage.

8. (F)

With an open-ended question like this, the answer choices must be individually tested. Choice (F) can be logically deduced, especially from the last exchange: Emily mentions that Bruce tells her stories about their childhood, and when Dave makes a comment about Bruce's popularity, Emily responds that "[Bruce] doesn't look at it that way" (line 98). This suggests that there is a difference between each brother's childhood stories. Choice (G) is too extreme and better describes the reaction other people have to the different professions of Bruce and Dave. Choice (H) is also too extreme: Dave feels competitive with Bruce, but that does not imply that they have fought. Choice (J) is not supported by the text; their childhood is the only time where it is stated that they spent time together.

9. (C)

Dave and Emily have different opinions regarding the picture. Dave is displeased with his image, while Emily professes to like his smile. However, Dave describes Bruce's smile as "trademark" and Emily says that Bruce looks "exactly the same" in every picture. This makes choice (C) correct. Choices (A) and (D) depict opinions that are strictly Dave's and Emily's, respectively, and choice (B) is not supported by the passage at all.

10. (F)

Emily follows her comment about Bruce's stories by dismissing Dave's comment about Bruce's popularity, saying that Bruce "doesn't look at it that way" (line 98). This is in reaction to Dave's frequent comments suggesting that Bruce has been more successful socially, and Dave's implication that Bruce feels superior to Dave. This matches choice (F), which correctly restates this idea. Choice (G) is not supported by the passage; choice (H) is opposite, because Emily wants Dave to focus less on his brother's successes; and choice (J) is extreme, since Bruce wants more attention from his brother but is not necessarily lonely.

PASSAGE II

11. (C)

The author is critical of the media throughout the passage, and focuses mostly on ways in which the current media is not concerned enough with factual accuracy. Choice (C) matches this nicely. Choice (A) is too extreme; the author talks about distorting facts, not making them up. Choice (B) contradicts paragraph 2, which characterizes some news personalities as "demagogues" with biased views. Choice (D) contradicts paragraph 4; the public's desire for this type of news is one of the reasons for its existence.

12. (G)

In paragraph 3, the author mentions how impartial stories can sway the opinions of readers through headlines rather than content. Choices (H) and (J) both mention headlines, but choice (H) makes the opposite point, and (J) is far too specific, using the example as a basis for a point that the author does not explicitly make. Choice (F) is contradicted by the passage. Choice (G) is general, but correct; the headline is another method used to sensationalize the story, as illustrated by the example of the "enraged public" versus the "irked locals."

13. (B)

The sentence preceding the Walter Cronkite example states that audience members expected to have complicated events explained to them; the Cronkite example follows this logic. Choice (B) matches this perfectly. Choice (A) may be inferred, but it is not the point the author is making—the author's concern is the treatment of the news, not specific news personalities. This reasoning also eliminates choice (C). Choice (D) is never mentioned in or suggested by the passage.

14. (F)

In order to research this statement, it is a good idea to look back at paragraph 3, because it details the public. "Personal consensus" applies to the author's point about people looking for news reported with a political opinion similar to their own. Choice (F) matches this. Choices (G) and (J) are both contradicted by information given in paragraph 3. Choice (H) is not supported by the passage, and contradicts the author's main point.

15. (B)

In paragraph 1, the author states that in stories of "continued national interest" the focus shifts from facts to "theater." Choice (B) is the best match. Choices (A), (C), and (D) are not explicitly mentioned as more or less likely to be sensationalized.

16. (J)

The sentence describes objective reporting as a "distant possibility." Questions like this are made easier if you pick a word that means the same thing in context. In this case, you can predict "improbable" or something similar. This matches choice (J) perfectly. Choices (F), (G), and (H) do not address the likelihood of objective reporting.

17. (C)

The author is most likely to criticize a headline that sensationalizes or makes a value judgment, and the end of paragraph 3 gives an example. Choices (A), (B), and (D) are all basically factual, and specific. Choice (C) is correct, because it uses a very inclusive group, like the example in paragraph 3 does, makes

a value judgment by calling the song offensive, and uses emotional language.

18. (J)

The fourth paragraph focuses on the flaws of the public, and states that individuals who agree with certain politically biased hosts are unlikely to question the validity of the "facts" presented. This matches choice (J) perfectly. Choices (F) and (G) are not explicitly stated by the author. Choice (H) describes accuracy problems for the media, not the public.

19. (A)

The author makes the point that fact-based news only captures a small minority of the news audience. Also, the beginning of paragraph 4 states that the public is not interested in dry facts. Choice (A) can be inferred, because the media companies are providing the type of programs that the public seems to want. Choice (B) is extreme—in fact, it could be inferred that if the greater public was interested in objective facts, the media (including cable) would provide programs of that sort. Choices (C) and (D) cannot be deduced from the passage; the author seems to believe that factual news will not draw a large audience no matter what.

20. (G)

Because this question deals with the audience, paragraph 4 is a good place to look. The author states that audience members look for hosts who share their political opinions. Choice (G) is a general restatement of this idea, so it is correct. Choice (F) is not stated in the passage. Choice (H) distorts a detail from the last paragraph; audience members prefer short to lengthy, but there is no statement about audience members gravitating toward the shortest or most simple stories. Choice (J) misuses the detail about headlines from paragraph 3.

PASSAGE III

21. (C)

The author frequently describes his grandfather's actions and describes their relationship to his heritage. Choice (C) fits this, as the other Russians in paragraph 3 are also characterized as being naturally tied to Russia. Choice (A) distorts the grandfather's later visits to Russia; the passage does not imply that immigrants would prefer to be elsewhere. Choice (B) cites the opinions of American-born people, while the passage does not focus on those opinions. Choice (D) refers only to the grandfather, who was perpetually displaced; his story is addressed as being unique.

22. (J)

The three specific locations mentioned are Moscow, Siberia, and China, in that order. Also, the author mentions that that China was the longest stay. Choices (F), (G), and (H) all have errors: (F) puts the Russian revolution in the wrong time period, (G) says he was exiled from Russia as an adult, and (H) says he settled in communist China, when he left during the revolution.

23. (C)

These line references both have to do with his work in real estate. You can deduce that he sees real estate as providing stability for people, something he did not have earlier in his life. Choice (C) matches this very well. Choice (A) is part of his sales strategy, not his purpose. Choices (B) and (D) are never discussed as tasks he specifically attempts.

24. (F)

The grandfather is proud to be Russian, and deeply influenced by his heritage, but is also proud to do his job and be a successful American. Choice (F) contradicts the grandfather's attitude, because while he criticizes the government, he loves the country itself. Choice (G) suggests an unspoken pride between Russians, which is in line with the grandfather's characterization. Choices (H) and (J) both fit, because he is critical of the communist government but still reverent regarding the country.

25. (D)

The passage deals heavily with displacement, and its implications, along with its effects on people. Since Moscow was where the family was originally from, you can deduce that the answer will have something to do with belonging. Choice (D) fits this classification well; Moscow is the family's native home, and all feel tied to Russia, but are searching for places to live outside of Russia. Choices (A) and (C) are not implied at all in the passage. Choice (B) may be factually true, but does not apply to the desires of the family.

26. (F)

This selection refers to Russians saying, "I am American" in Russian. It is contrasted with points about the fact that they are speaking Russian with other Russians, therefore suggesting that "playing the role" must mean becoming more accustomed to their new country. Choice (F) matches this perfectly. Choices (G) and (H) cannot be deduced from the information given, and choice (J) may be true, but does not apply to "playing the role."

27. (B)

"Strategic compromise" applies to the grandfather's desire to sell homes, in spite of the current stigma against Russians. The tactics mentioned by the author are informing the customer he was exiled and disagreed with the current Russian government, and not responding to negative remarks regarding the entire country of Russia. Choice (B) fits this final part, as negative statements about Russia as a whole would offend the grandfather. Choices (A) and (D) are too extreme and specific. Choice (C) is not mentioned.

28. (H)

According to the passage this sort of trip "elucidates one's very existence." This is the only result given; the rest of the details apply to the emotional strain involved. Choice (H) is the only choice that applies to this. Choices (F) and (G) are not even implied by the text, and choice (J) applies to the adoption analogy rather than the grandfather.

29. (B)

The last sentence in the first paragraph states that the country came under new rule during the time his mother was pregnant with him. He was therefore born after the revolution, and under communist rule. Choice (B) is correct. The other choices contradict that factual sentence.

30. (G)

The need to rediscover a lost native land is what would be made unnecessary, so the correct answer would have to describe the opposite situation. Choice (G) fits this very well; having a sense of belonging would alleviate the need to search for

it. Choice (F) is incorrect because the grandfather embodies the feelings he is potentially making "unnecessary." Choice (H) describes people that may still desire to revisit their roots. Choice (J) describes a totally unrelated achievement possible in real estate.

PASSAGE IV

31. (B)

The passage is most concerned with discrediting the myth that rattlesnakes are aggressive and very dangerous, and the selection refers to exactly that: the "sinister opportunist" is the myth, while the "mild-mannered domestic" is closer to fact. Choice (B) can be deduced from this. Choice (A) is incorrect, as juvenile snakes are not even mentioned. Choice (C) misuses the detail about rattlesnakes giving live birth, which is not treated as a recent discovery. Choice (D) is too extreme; the author describes rattlesnakes as fairly docile, but not entirely predictable.

32. (F)

At the end of paragraph 6, the author states that the reputation is good because a frightened and cornered rattlesnake is dangerous. Choice (F) fits this, because if people did not avoid or move away from rattlesnakes, there would be more dangerous interaction between humans and snakes. Choices (G) and (J) are contradicted by the passage; in rattlesnake round-ups their reputation costs the snakes their lives, and the author, who is aware of their docile nature, would certainly never believe a rattlesnake should be a pet. Choice (H) misuses the detail about snakebite deaths.

33. (C)

The passage gives quite a few examples of the social behavior of rattlesnakes, so be prepared to find a restated fact among the answer choices. Choice (C) fits this nicely, because the passage states that rattlesnakes have been known to hibernate with tortoises. Choice (A) is not a social behavior. Choice (B) goes beyond the text; the wrestling is used to claim a mate, but the losing snake will leave, rather than take a place within a hierarchy. Choice (D) also misuses a detail; rattlesnakes are described as "entirely" non-cannibalistic, meaning they never eat other snakes.

34. (H)—Inference Question

The mythology referred to is that of the heartless, aggressive rattlesnake. This relates to rattlesnake "round-ups" to which the author clearly objects, so it would follow that the author sees this particular human behavior as heartless and aggressive. Choice (H) matches this perfectly, and the statistical comparison in paragraph 8 supports this. Choice (F) contradicts the author's belief that rattlesnakes are not as dangerous as commonly thought. Choices (G) and (J) do not relate to the point the author is making.

35. (C)

It is stated that serious bites can usually be traced to people that either handle or step on snakes, in contrast to those who were not engaging the snakes. Choice (C) fits this nicely, specifically focusing on those handling snakes, an example of individuals purposefully seeking interaction. Choice (A) is incorrect because a relationship is mentioned. Choice (B) is not mentioned in the text. Choice (D) is a distortion, because rattlesnakes deliver venom based on how threatened they feel, not necessarily based on how threatening humans act.

36. (H)

The selection's sentence starts with describing the docile behavior of rattlesnakes, as a follow up to scientific findings in the previous paragraph. The implication is that snakes, while not as dangerous as often thought, can still be dangerous. Choice (H) matches this perfectly. Choice (F) is outside the scope of the passage; there is no mention of herpetologists keeping snakes. Choice (G) misuses a later detail; the author is not comparing the rattlesnake as a pet to dogs. Choice (J) states a comparison that is never made.

37. (B)

In paragraph 5, the author lists various statistics, and states that dogs, bees, and lightning are all responsible for more annual deaths, and that the fer-de-lance is responsible for substantially more. Choice (B) is the only answer that fits; every other choice is contradicted by the facts given.

38. (J)

In paragraph six, the author explains that the rattlesnakes knows that it needs its venom for food, and goes on to state that the only situations in which a rattlesnake would release all of its venom is when it feels threatened. Choice (J) fits with this; the rattlesnake wishes to conserve its venom, specifically for prey. Choice (F) is incorrect because humans are large in comparison, and receive mostly "dry" bites. Choice (G) contradicts the statement about rattlesnakes potentially using all their venom if threatened. Choice (H) contradicts the statement that rattlesnakes are not aware of the well-being of nonfood sources.

39. (B)

The author examines two pieces of contradictory logic. The first is that the organizers use the reputation of the rattlesnake to promote interest, but rely on the more docile nature of the snakes. The second is the fact that most of the snakes are taken from areas without people, and put into contact with people, thus making for a more dangerous situation. Choice (B) matches the second piece of information. Choice (A) is not stated as fact in the text. Choice (C) brings up erroneous statistics, when really it is the rattlesnake's erroneous reputation that is used. Choice (D) is not mentioned in the passage.

40. (G)

The answer lies in the last sentence, which speculates on the status of humans in rattlesnake folklore "if rattlesnakes were able to speak or write." This makes it clear that *crotalid* must have something to do with actual rattlesnakes. Choice (G) is the only choice that fits, because the sentence is mocking the way that humans have characterized rattlesnakes within human mythology. Choices (F), (G), and (H) all are incorrect, because they mention groups that are not specifically rattlesnakes.

SCIENCE TEST

PASSAGE 1

The first passage requires a little basic understanding of the scientific method and a lot of figure interpretation. You don't need to grasp all of the details of the passage or the diagrams, but do take note of obvious trends or extremes in the given data. For example, the large changes in the data in Figure 1 at around 1,500 years are particularly worth noting.

1. (C)

Be careful of extreme language, such as the use of "always" in choices (A) and (B). While the general trend is that decreasing glacier length corresponds to decreasing calving rate, the opposite is true at the sharp peak in calving rate at around 1,500 years, which choice (C) correctly describes.

2. (H)

This question asks you to find the glacier with the largest calving rate for years 6–10 in Table 1. Make sure you are looking in the right place, which in this case is the far right column of Table 1.

3. (A)

This question requires a little deeper understanding of the data presented Table 1. For all 4 glaciers during both time periods, the calving rate is slightly greater than or equal to the average velocity. To predict the calving rate of a glacier with a velocity of 80 m/yr, you must look for glaciers traveling at similar velocities. The closest values come from glaciers A and C during years 1–5, which had velocities of 72 m/yr and 98 m/yr, respectively.

The corresponding calving rates for these two glaciers are 72 m/yr and 106 m/yr. The correct answer should fall within this range, as described by choice (A).

4. (J)

With open-ended questions like this one, simple process of elimination is usually most efficient. Comparison of each choice with the data in Table 1 reveals that only choice (J) accurately reflects the "behavior of the glaciers."

5. (B)

Don't be too concerned with the strange scale of the horizontal axis of each choice. The values on the axis correspond exactly to the calving rates for years 6–10 given in Table 1. Simply find the graph that correctly plots the four points given by the data in the last two columns of Table 1.

6. (H)

The meteorologists in Study 3 hypothesized that high temperatures cause rapid variations in velocity and calving rate. Figure 1 shows a rapid change in calving rate at around 1,500 years. If the hypothesis is true, then the glacier modeled in Study 1 experienced a rapid change in temperature approximately 1,500 years ago, and choice (H) is correct.

PASSAGE II

This passage is consists almost entirely of Table 1 and Figures 1 and 2, with very little descriptive language. Fortunately, the more complicated the diagram, the more likely the questions referring to that diagram will be straightforward. In other words, don't waste too much time trying to interpret Table 1 right away. As it turns out, only one question requires you to refer to Table 1.

7. (C)

Sometimes, you will be asked to simply read information directly from a graph. If you are careful to refer to the right part of the right graph, you will find correct answers to these kinds of questions very quickly. The bar for March 2 on Figure 1 rises to approximately 1,500 gr/m3, as in choice (C).

8. (H)

You are asked to describe a trend in the data in Figure 1 beyond the high value given for November 5. After this value, the data maintains no discernable trend, but does stay within a relatively small range of values, as is correctly described in choice (H).

9. (B)

Be careful to answer the correct question. "Increased the most," doesn't necessarily mean the count increased to its largest value, which is the trap set in choice (C). Choice (D) is also a trap, set for those who refer to the wrong figure.

10. (F)

This question asks about the tree pollen count, so you should refer to Figure 1. Process of elimination reveals that only choice (F) correctly reflects the data shown in the figure.

11. (A)

You are finally asked to refer to the rather complicated Table 1. Find the row for the month of May, and look for the corresponding column(s) containing the most reported cases of allergic rhinitis. In this case, that means the most { symbols. Tree and grass pollens account for 6 of the 9 total { symbols in the May row, which indeed constitute "most" of the cases.

PASSAGE III

When a passage includes multiple experiments designed to study the same topic, look for key similarities and differences between the experiments. In Experiment 1, oscillation frequency of a pendulum is measured, and the only variable is the length of the pendulum arm. In Experiment 2, the oscillation frequencies of several springs are measured, and there are two variables: the spring and the suspended mass. Experiment 3 involves the same springs as does Experiment 2, but measures equilibrium length instead of oscillation frequency.

12. (G)

Notice that in Figure 3, the lines plotted for Springs B, C, and D intersect at approximately the same mass. The exact mass value is not completely clear from the figure, but it is definitely larger than choice (F) and smaller than choice (H), which leaves choice (G) as the only possibility.

13. (A)

According to Figure 1, oscillation frequency does indeed decrease with increasing arm length, so you can eliminate choices (C) and (D). The second part of choice (B) is simply false, which leaves only choice (A).

14. (F)

This question requires a couple of steps of logic. First, you must realize what "slowly" means in terms of oscillation frequency. Recall from the passage that oscillation frequency is measured in "oscillations per second." The faster the spring oscillates, the more oscillations it will complete per second. Therefore, you are looking for the spring with the lowest value for oscillation frequency, which is Spring A.

15. (C)

Refer to the line plotted for Spring A in Figure 3. On that line, a mass of 700 g corresponds to an equilibrium length of just less than 40 cm. Only choice (C) includes this estimate.

16. (J)

According to Figure 2, an oscillation frequency of 1.4 Hz at a mass of 100 g would be represented by a data point that would fall in between the frequency values for Spring C and Spring D at that mass. Only choices (H) and (J) place Spring E correctly between Springs C and D, and only choice (J) correctly lists the springs in order of *decreasing* oscillation frequency.

17. (C)

The effects of mass are not mentioned in Experiment 1. Only the pendulum arm length affects the oscillation frequency, so the plots for the original mass and the larger mass should be identical, as in choice (C).

PASSAGE IV

This passage is based almost entirely on Figure 1, which contains a great deal of information and deserves a few moments of your attention before attacking the questions. As always, it is important to understand what is represented on each axis. In this case, the vertical axis is straightforward, but the horizontal axis is a bit unconventional. The last sentence in the passage should help you to grasp that the horizontal axis represents the composition of the alloy, where the value (0–100%) is the atomic percentage of Si in the alloy. The further to the right on the Figure, the more Si and less Au there is in the alloy. The lines on the graph separate the different phases of the alloy, from completely solid at the bottom of the graph to completely liquid at the top. Play close attention to any notes included to help describe a figure. The note in this case tells you that parentheses around an element indicate that element's solid state.

18. (J)

Be careful to not confuse melting point with boiling point. Only the melting points are shown in Figure 1, so choice (J) is correct.

19. (B)

Draw a vertical line from the 50% mark on the horizontal axis and a horizontal line from the 600°C mark on the vertical axis. These lines intersect in the region of the diagram labeled "liquid + (Si)," which the note tells you means liquid plus Si in its solid state.

20. (G)

The lowest melting point is indicated by the section of the graph labeled "liquid" that reaches the furthest down on the graph. An arrow on the graph labels this point the "eutectic point" and gives the exact alloy composition there, which is reproduced correctly in choice (G).

21. (A)

The question asks you to look at compositions with less than 10% Si, which means you can draw a vertical line from the 10% mark on the horizontal axis and ignore everything to the right of that line. In the portion of the graph to the left of this line, the temperature required for the alloy to become completely liquid decreases with increasing Si atomic percentage. Choice (D) is a trap set for those drawn to the wrong line on the figure. The horizontal line

at a temperature of 363°C indicates the temperature at which the alloy becomes completely solid, not liquid.

22. (H)

Draw a horizontal line from 1,200°C on the *y*-axis to where it intersects the plot. Draw a line down from that point to the *x*-axis. It intersects somewhere between 70 and 80% Si. According to the figure, solid Si particles would also begin to form at this temperature. Choice (H) encompasses this information and is correct.

PASSAGE V

Don't be intimidated by unfamiliar language like the biological terms in this passage. Remember that no advanced scientific knowledge is assumed. As usual, here the important task is to be able to locate the appropriate information from the given figures. Note the trends in both figures, namely the decreases in temperature and oxygen partial pressure with increasing altitude in Figure 1 and the elevated GST and ECH concentrations of the high altitude dwellers in Table 1.

23. (D)

Make sure you refer to the correct part of Table 1 for the enzyme concentration values of populations ha 1, ha 2, and ha 3. The table shows that for all three high altitude populations, GST levels are highest, CR levels are lowest, and ECH levels are intermediate. Only choice (D) does not violate this relationship.

24. (G)

The process of elimination works best here. Choice (F) is not universally true; the oxygen saturation percentages are pretty similar for high altitude and sea level dwellers. Neither Table 1 nor Figure 1 show a comparison between high or low altitude populations and temperature or partial oxygen pressure, so choices (H) and (J) cannot be correct. Only choice (G) is directly supported by the values in the table.

25. (C)

The answer to this question comes directly from Figure 1, but you must be careful to not confuse the two data sets. You can draw a horizontal line from 110 mm Hg on the left vertical axis until it intersects with the oxygen partial pressure data (open squares). That intersection happens at about 3,200 m. To find the temperature at this altitude, draw a horizontal line from the temperature plot (closed circles) at 3,200 m to the right axis. It intersects at just under $-5°C$, choice (C). Accidentally reversing the two data sets likely results in selecting trap answer (A).

26. (H)

You are asked to find the highest ECH concentration for any of the six populations, which occurs for population ha 2.

27. (A)

Only choices (A) and (C) agree with the information in Table 1. You can eliminate choice (C), though, because nothing in the passage or data suggests that CR concentration has anything to do with efficiency at incorporating oxygen into the blood.

PASSAGE VI

On passages that present two conflicting viewpoints, make sure you read the first passage and answer the questions associated with it before reading the second passage and answering the remaining questions. Note the fundamental similarities and differences between the two viewpoints. In this case, Student 1 attributes the fact that lakes freeze from the surface downwards to the effects of pressure, while Student 2 credits a change in density. Both students are able to apply their explanations to the ice skating situation as well. You are not asked to determine the validity of either viewpoint, but instead to follow each argument separately and be able to apply each student's reasoning.

28. (J)

Recall that Student 1 credits pressure with the freezing phenomenon. Choices (G) and (H) reflect elements of the viewpoint of Student 2, and can therefore be eliminated. If choice (F) were true, the temperature and pressure effects would work against each other, so only choice (J) makes sense.

29. (B)

According to Student 1, pressure causes the ice to melt, and pressure increases with increasing weight. Student 2 states that friction causes the ice to melt, and that the force of friction increases with increasing weight. Therefore, the students would agree that ice would melt faster under the heavier skater, as in choice (B).

30. (F)

In the explanation of Student 2, ice melts when heat is generated as the skater overcomes the force of friction by *moving* across the ice. If the skater is not moving, then, no heat should be generated. Student 1, though, explains that ice melts due to pressure, which is present whether or not the skater is moving, making choice (F) correct.

31. (C)

Student 2 explains that less dense materials float above more dense materials. Since the frozen ethanol remains below the liquid ethanol, choice (C) must be true.

32. (H)

You can eliminate choices (F) and (G) due to the mention of pressure in both, which is a concept only Student 1 contemplates. Student 2 describes floating as the case in which the buoyant force exceeds the force of gravity, so the sinking boat is evidence of the opposite situation described in choice (H).

33. (B)

Eliminate choice (A), because only Student 1 considers pressure, and eliminate choice (D), because the only possible support for this explanation also comes from Student 1. Eliminate choice (C), because the force of gravity will only change as the mass of the skater changes. Student 2 states that heat is produced by overcoming friction, so less friction would mean less heat, as in choice (B).

34. (F)

Recall that the viewpoint of Student 2 focuses on a difference in *density*, and eliminate choice (H). Choices (G) and (J) both actually mean the same thing, but the term "buoyant" is included in choice (J) to entice the unwary test taker. In either case, the balloon would remain on the ground. The less dense balloon described in choice (F) would indeed rise above the ground.

Passage VII

The first paragraph of this research summary passage explains that the experiments were conducted to study F^- concentrations in water. Experiment 1 tested solutions prepared by the students to have specific F^- concentrations, and the solutions' electrical conductivities were measured. Table 1 shows a direct relationship between F^- concentration and conductivity, and Figure 1 further emphasizes the linearity of this relationship. Be careful to notice the difference between *measured* and *corrected* conductivities and that it is the corrected conductivities that are plotted in Figure 1. Don't worry if you don't recognize the units given for conductivity; knowledge of these units is not required to answer the questions.

Experiment 2 tested solutions taken from various communities' drinking water supplies. The direct relationship between F^- concentration and conductivity seen in Experiment 1 is confirmed.

35. (C)

Either Table 1 or Figure 1 can provide the answer here. Table 1 contains numerical examples of cases where the F^- concentration is indeed doubled (from 0.5 mg/L to 1 mg/L, for example), and gives the corresponding change in conductivity. Taking care to look the *corrected* conductivity column, you can see that 2 times the concentration results in 2 times the corrected conductivity. Likewise, Figure 1 makes it clear that relationship between the two quantities is linear, which means that any multiplication of the concentration results in the same multiplication of the conductivity.

36. (J)

Compare the new conductivity value to those given in Table 2, specifically those for Newtown and Lakewood, and recall the direct relationship between conductivity and F^- concentration. Noticing that Bluewater's conductivity value lies between the values for Newtown and Lakewood allows you to eliminate choices (F) and (G). Taking care to list the towns in order of *increasing* F^- leads you to choice (J).

37. (C)

Refer to Table 1 to see where a value of 3.0 mg/L would fit in. This new concentration is between the 2.0 mg/L and 4.0 mg/L values given in the table, so the corrected conductivity should lie between 3.34 µS/cm and 6.68 µS/cm. Choices (B) and (D) are too close to the extremes of this range, but choice (C) is exactly in the middle as it should be. Alternatively, you could read the corrected conductivity for a concentration of 3.0 mg/L directly from Figure 1.

38. (F)

Questions that ask you to change the procedure of an experiment usually require you to review the original experiment before answering. In this case, the description of Experiment 1 tells you that F^- is added in the form of dissolved Na_2SiF_6. To study Cl^- concentrations, the students must use a chemical that contains Cl^- when preparing the solutions, as in choice (F).

39. (B)

Experimental data is not required to answer this question. The last sentence of the description of Experiment 1 explains that the corrected conductivity is calculated by *subtracting* the measured conductivity of the blank solution. This always results in the corrected conductivity being less than the measured conductivity, as in choice (B).

40. (F)

You are told that Cl^- results in an increase in conductivity, and the data shows that F^- results in an increase in conductivity. Therefore, in a solution containing both F^- and Cl^-, it would be impossible to distinguish the contributions to conductivity from each ion given only conductivity measurements. Conductivity would be increased by the presence of Cl^-, and the apparent values for F^- concentration would be falsely high, as in choice (F). If you miss this point, you could at least eliminate choice (J), since the question asks only about the case where *all* of the samples have Cl^- concentrations. The effect of the Cl^- should not be different for different solutions.

WRITING TEST

MODEL ESSAY

Below is an example of what a high-scoring essay might look like. Notice the author states her position clearly in the introductory paragraph and supports that position with evidence in the following paragraphs. The essay also uses transitions, some advanced vocabulary, and an effective "hook" to draw in the reader.

The elevated rate of automobile accidents that occur when teenaged drivers are behind the wheel has driven some parents and legislators to lobby for laws that would ban drivers under 18 from driving with other teenagers in the car. Those who support these laws believe that driving alone or with an adult would minimize distraction for new drivers, helping them to drive more safely. Others disagree, pointing to the lack of evidence that groups of teenagers riding together are actually the cause of these accidents.

Everyone benefits from having more safe drivers on the road, but efforts to curb the freedoms of drivers under 18 are misguided and unfair. For example, elderly drivers may have impaired vision or motor skills, but are not subject to additional restrictions based only on their age. Male drivers are more prone to car accidents than female drivers, but one can only imagine the outcry if a restriction on the driving privileges of all men were proposed! A driver's license should provide the same responsibilities and freedoms to each person who receives one. If we don't believe that 16-year-olds are as capable of operating a car safely as 18-year-olds, we should not issue them driver's licenses at all.

If we want to promote safe driving, there are more evenhanded methods of doing so. In our state, all drivers who take their license exam must have completed 40 hours of classroom training, regardless of age. These classes are an effective way to ensure that everyone who takes the driver's exam has the same base level of knowledge about traffic laws, operation of a motor vehicle, and the importance of driving safely. This information is important for all new drivers. A requirement for licensed drivers to take a refresher course every five years could help to ensure that more drivers remain aware of new laws and safety issues.

Proponents of this law claim that preventing teenagers from riding in cars together will help to lower the number of accidents. However, no studies have been released that can isolate the presence of other teenagers in the car as a cause of accidents. Having a conversation with a friend in the passenger seat could certainly be distracting, but talking on a cell phone, or listening to loud music, might be equally or even more distracting—and again, all of these distractions can occur when an older person is driving, as well.

Safety and responsibility are important for drivers of all ages. The proposed laws target younger drivers unfairly, and there is no evidence that they would prevent accidents. Measures that attempt to promote safe driving should be aimed at all drivers, not the small percentage of them who are under 18 years old.

You can evaluate your essay and the model essay based on the following criteria, covered in chapter 16.

- Does the author answer the question?

- Is the author's position clearly stated?

- Does the body of the essay support and develop the position taken?

- Are there at least three supporting paragraphs?

- Is the relevance of each supporting paragraph clear?

- Is the essay a reasonable length?

- Is the essay organized, with a clear introduction, middle, and end?

- Did the author use one paragraph for each new idea?

- Is each sentence in a paragraph relevant to the point made in that paragraph?

- Are transitions clear?

- Is the essay easy to read? Is it engaging?

- Are sentences varied?

- Is vocabulary used effectively? Is college-level vocabulary used?

PRACTICE TEST FOUR

ACT Practice Test Four
Answer Sheet

English Test

10. Ⓕ Ⓖ Ⓗ Ⓙ   20. Ⓕ Ⓖ Ⓗ Ⓙ   30. Ⓕ Ⓖ Ⓗ Ⓙ   40. Ⓕ Ⓖ Ⓗ Ⓙ   50. Ⓕ Ⓖ Ⓗ Ⓙ   60. Ⓕ Ⓖ Ⓗ Ⓙ   70. Ⓕ Ⓖ Ⓗ Ⓙ
1. Ⓐ Ⓑ Ⓒ Ⓓ   11. Ⓐ Ⓑ Ⓒ Ⓓ   21. Ⓐ Ⓑ Ⓒ Ⓓ   31. Ⓐ Ⓑ Ⓒ Ⓓ   41. Ⓐ Ⓑ Ⓒ Ⓓ   51. Ⓐ Ⓑ Ⓒ Ⓓ   61. Ⓐ Ⓑ Ⓒ Ⓓ   71. Ⓐ Ⓑ Ⓒ Ⓓ
2. Ⓕ Ⓖ Ⓗ Ⓙ   12. Ⓕ Ⓖ Ⓗ Ⓙ   22. Ⓕ Ⓖ Ⓗ Ⓙ   32. Ⓕ Ⓖ Ⓗ Ⓙ   42. Ⓕ Ⓖ Ⓗ Ⓙ   52. Ⓕ Ⓖ Ⓗ Ⓙ   62. Ⓕ Ⓖ Ⓗ Ⓙ   72. Ⓕ Ⓖ Ⓗ Ⓙ
3. Ⓐ Ⓑ Ⓒ Ⓓ   13. Ⓐ Ⓑ Ⓒ Ⓓ   23. Ⓐ Ⓑ Ⓒ Ⓓ   33. Ⓐ Ⓑ Ⓒ Ⓓ   43. Ⓐ Ⓑ Ⓒ Ⓓ   53. Ⓐ Ⓑ Ⓒ Ⓓ   63. Ⓐ Ⓑ Ⓒ Ⓓ   73. Ⓐ Ⓑ Ⓒ Ⓓ
4. Ⓕ Ⓖ Ⓗ Ⓙ   14. Ⓕ Ⓖ Ⓗ Ⓙ   24. Ⓕ Ⓖ Ⓗ Ⓙ   34. Ⓕ Ⓖ Ⓗ Ⓙ   44. Ⓕ Ⓖ Ⓗ Ⓙ   54. Ⓕ Ⓖ Ⓗ Ⓙ   64. Ⓕ Ⓖ Ⓗ Ⓙ   74. Ⓕ Ⓖ Ⓗ Ⓙ
5. Ⓐ Ⓑ Ⓒ Ⓓ   15. Ⓐ Ⓑ Ⓒ Ⓓ   25. Ⓐ Ⓑ Ⓒ Ⓓ   35. Ⓐ Ⓑ Ⓒ Ⓓ   45. Ⓐ Ⓑ Ⓒ Ⓓ   55. Ⓐ Ⓑ Ⓒ Ⓓ   65. Ⓐ Ⓑ Ⓒ Ⓓ   75. Ⓐ Ⓑ Ⓒ Ⓓ
6. Ⓕ Ⓖ Ⓗ Ⓙ   16. Ⓕ Ⓖ Ⓗ Ⓙ   26. Ⓕ Ⓖ Ⓗ Ⓙ   36. Ⓕ Ⓖ Ⓗ Ⓙ   46. Ⓕ Ⓖ Ⓗ Ⓙ   56. Ⓕ Ⓖ Ⓗ Ⓙ   66. Ⓕ Ⓖ Ⓗ Ⓙ
7. Ⓐ Ⓑ Ⓒ Ⓓ   17. Ⓐ Ⓑ Ⓒ Ⓓ   27. Ⓐ Ⓑ Ⓒ Ⓓ   37. Ⓐ Ⓑ Ⓒ Ⓓ   47. Ⓐ Ⓑ Ⓒ Ⓓ   57. Ⓐ Ⓑ Ⓒ Ⓓ   67. Ⓐ Ⓑ Ⓒ Ⓓ
8. Ⓕ Ⓖ Ⓗ Ⓙ   18. Ⓕ Ⓖ Ⓗ Ⓙ   28. Ⓕ Ⓖ Ⓗ Ⓙ   38. Ⓕ Ⓖ Ⓗ Ⓙ   48. Ⓕ Ⓖ Ⓗ Ⓙ   58. Ⓕ Ⓖ Ⓗ Ⓙ   68. Ⓕ Ⓖ Ⓗ Ⓙ
9. Ⓐ Ⓑ Ⓒ Ⓓ   19. Ⓐ Ⓑ Ⓒ Ⓓ   29. Ⓐ Ⓑ Ⓒ Ⓓ   39. Ⓐ Ⓑ Ⓒ Ⓓ   49. Ⓐ Ⓑ Ⓒ Ⓓ   59. Ⓐ Ⓑ Ⓒ Ⓓ   69. Ⓐ Ⓑ Ⓒ Ⓓ

Math Test

9. Ⓐ Ⓑ Ⓒ Ⓓ Ⓔ   18. Ⓕ Ⓖ Ⓗ Ⓙ Ⓚ   27. Ⓐ Ⓑ Ⓒ Ⓓ Ⓔ   36. Ⓕ Ⓖ Ⓗ Ⓙ Ⓚ   45. Ⓐ Ⓑ Ⓒ Ⓓ Ⓔ   54. Ⓕ Ⓖ Ⓗ Ⓙ Ⓚ
1. Ⓐ Ⓑ Ⓒ Ⓓ Ⓔ   10. Ⓕ Ⓖ Ⓗ Ⓙ Ⓚ   19. Ⓐ Ⓑ Ⓒ Ⓓ Ⓔ   28. Ⓕ Ⓖ Ⓗ Ⓙ Ⓚ   37. Ⓐ Ⓑ Ⓒ Ⓓ Ⓔ   46. Ⓕ Ⓖ Ⓗ Ⓙ Ⓚ   55. Ⓐ Ⓑ Ⓒ Ⓓ Ⓔ
2. Ⓕ Ⓖ Ⓗ Ⓙ Ⓚ   11. Ⓐ Ⓑ Ⓒ Ⓓ Ⓔ   20. Ⓕ Ⓖ Ⓗ Ⓙ Ⓚ   29. Ⓐ Ⓑ Ⓒ Ⓓ Ⓔ   38. Ⓕ Ⓖ Ⓗ Ⓙ Ⓚ   47. Ⓐ Ⓑ Ⓒ Ⓓ Ⓔ   56. Ⓕ Ⓖ Ⓗ Ⓙ Ⓚ
3. Ⓐ Ⓑ Ⓒ Ⓓ Ⓔ   12. Ⓕ Ⓖ Ⓗ Ⓙ Ⓚ   21. Ⓐ Ⓑ Ⓒ Ⓓ Ⓔ   30. Ⓕ Ⓖ Ⓗ Ⓙ Ⓚ   39. Ⓐ Ⓑ Ⓒ Ⓓ Ⓔ   48. Ⓕ Ⓖ Ⓗ Ⓙ Ⓚ   57. Ⓐ Ⓑ Ⓒ Ⓓ Ⓔ
4. Ⓕ Ⓖ Ⓗ Ⓙ Ⓚ   13. Ⓐ Ⓑ Ⓒ Ⓓ Ⓔ   22. Ⓕ Ⓖ Ⓗ Ⓙ Ⓚ   31. Ⓐ Ⓑ Ⓒ Ⓓ Ⓔ   40. Ⓕ Ⓖ Ⓗ Ⓙ Ⓚ   49. Ⓐ Ⓑ Ⓒ Ⓓ Ⓔ   58. Ⓕ Ⓖ Ⓗ Ⓙ Ⓚ
5. Ⓐ Ⓑ Ⓒ Ⓓ Ⓔ   14. Ⓕ Ⓖ Ⓗ Ⓙ Ⓚ   23. Ⓐ Ⓑ Ⓒ Ⓓ Ⓔ   32. Ⓕ Ⓖ Ⓗ Ⓙ Ⓚ   41. Ⓐ Ⓑ Ⓒ Ⓓ Ⓔ   50. Ⓕ Ⓖ Ⓗ Ⓙ Ⓚ   59. Ⓐ Ⓑ Ⓒ Ⓓ Ⓔ
6. Ⓕ Ⓖ Ⓗ Ⓙ Ⓚ   15. Ⓐ Ⓑ Ⓒ Ⓓ Ⓔ   24. Ⓕ Ⓖ Ⓗ Ⓙ Ⓚ   33. Ⓐ Ⓑ Ⓒ Ⓓ Ⓔ   42. Ⓕ Ⓖ Ⓗ Ⓙ Ⓚ   51. Ⓐ Ⓑ Ⓒ Ⓓ Ⓔ   60. Ⓕ Ⓖ Ⓗ Ⓙ Ⓚ
7. Ⓐ Ⓑ Ⓒ Ⓓ Ⓔ   16. Ⓕ Ⓖ Ⓗ Ⓙ Ⓚ   25. Ⓐ Ⓑ Ⓒ Ⓓ Ⓔ   34. Ⓕ Ⓖ Ⓗ Ⓙ Ⓚ   43. Ⓐ Ⓑ Ⓒ Ⓓ Ⓔ   52. Ⓕ Ⓖ Ⓗ Ⓙ Ⓚ
8. Ⓕ Ⓖ Ⓗ Ⓙ Ⓚ   17. Ⓐ Ⓑ Ⓒ Ⓓ Ⓔ   26. Ⓕ Ⓖ Ⓗ Ⓙ Ⓚ   35. Ⓐ Ⓑ Ⓒ Ⓓ Ⓔ   44. Ⓕ Ⓖ Ⓗ Ⓙ Ⓚ   53. Ⓐ Ⓑ Ⓒ Ⓓ Ⓔ

Reading Test

6. Ⓕ Ⓖ Ⓗ Ⓙ   12. Ⓕ Ⓖ Ⓗ Ⓙ   18. Ⓕ Ⓖ Ⓗ Ⓙ   24. Ⓕ Ⓖ Ⓗ Ⓙ   30. Ⓕ Ⓖ Ⓗ Ⓙ   36. Ⓕ Ⓖ Ⓗ Ⓙ
1. Ⓐ Ⓑ Ⓒ Ⓓ   7. Ⓐ Ⓑ Ⓒ Ⓓ   13. Ⓐ Ⓑ Ⓒ Ⓓ   19. Ⓐ Ⓑ Ⓒ Ⓓ   25. Ⓐ Ⓑ Ⓒ Ⓓ   31. Ⓐ Ⓑ Ⓒ Ⓓ   37. Ⓐ Ⓑ Ⓒ Ⓓ
2. Ⓕ Ⓖ Ⓗ Ⓙ   8. Ⓕ Ⓖ Ⓗ Ⓙ   14. Ⓕ Ⓖ Ⓗ Ⓙ   20. Ⓕ Ⓖ Ⓗ Ⓙ   26. Ⓕ Ⓖ Ⓗ Ⓙ   32. Ⓕ Ⓖ Ⓗ Ⓙ   38. Ⓕ Ⓖ Ⓗ Ⓙ
3. Ⓐ Ⓑ Ⓒ Ⓓ   9. Ⓐ Ⓑ Ⓒ Ⓓ   15. Ⓐ Ⓑ Ⓒ Ⓓ   21. Ⓐ Ⓑ Ⓒ Ⓓ   27. Ⓐ Ⓑ Ⓒ Ⓓ   33. Ⓐ Ⓑ Ⓒ Ⓓ   39. Ⓐ Ⓑ Ⓒ Ⓓ
4. Ⓕ Ⓖ Ⓗ Ⓙ   10. Ⓕ Ⓖ Ⓗ Ⓙ   16. Ⓕ Ⓖ Ⓗ Ⓙ   22. Ⓕ Ⓖ Ⓗ Ⓙ   28. Ⓕ Ⓖ Ⓗ Ⓙ   34. Ⓕ Ⓖ Ⓗ Ⓙ   40. Ⓕ Ⓖ Ⓗ Ⓙ
5. Ⓐ Ⓑ Ⓒ Ⓓ   11. Ⓐ Ⓑ Ⓒ Ⓓ   17. Ⓐ Ⓑ Ⓒ Ⓓ   23. Ⓐ Ⓑ Ⓒ Ⓓ   29. Ⓐ Ⓑ Ⓒ Ⓓ   35. Ⓐ Ⓑ Ⓒ Ⓓ

Science Test

6. Ⓕ Ⓖ Ⓗ Ⓙ   12. Ⓕ Ⓖ Ⓗ Ⓙ   18. Ⓕ Ⓖ Ⓗ Ⓙ   24. Ⓕ Ⓖ Ⓗ Ⓙ   30. Ⓕ Ⓖ Ⓗ Ⓙ   36. Ⓕ Ⓖ Ⓗ Ⓙ
1. Ⓐ Ⓑ Ⓒ Ⓓ   7. Ⓐ Ⓑ Ⓒ Ⓓ   13. Ⓐ Ⓑ Ⓒ Ⓓ   19. Ⓐ Ⓑ Ⓒ Ⓓ   25. Ⓐ Ⓑ Ⓒ Ⓓ   31. Ⓐ Ⓑ Ⓒ Ⓓ   37. Ⓐ Ⓑ Ⓒ Ⓓ
2. Ⓕ Ⓖ Ⓗ Ⓙ   8. Ⓕ Ⓖ Ⓗ Ⓙ   14. Ⓕ Ⓖ Ⓗ Ⓙ   20. Ⓕ Ⓖ Ⓗ Ⓙ   26. Ⓕ Ⓖ Ⓗ Ⓙ   32. Ⓕ Ⓖ Ⓗ Ⓙ   38. Ⓕ Ⓖ Ⓗ Ⓙ
3. Ⓐ Ⓑ Ⓒ Ⓓ   9. Ⓐ Ⓑ Ⓒ Ⓓ   15. Ⓐ Ⓑ Ⓒ Ⓓ   21. Ⓐ Ⓑ Ⓒ Ⓓ   27. Ⓐ Ⓑ Ⓒ Ⓓ   33. Ⓐ Ⓑ Ⓒ Ⓓ   39. Ⓐ Ⓑ Ⓒ Ⓓ
4. Ⓕ Ⓖ Ⓗ Ⓙ   10. Ⓕ Ⓖ Ⓗ Ⓙ   16. Ⓕ Ⓖ Ⓗ Ⓙ   22. Ⓕ Ⓖ Ⓗ Ⓙ   28. Ⓕ Ⓖ Ⓗ Ⓙ   34. Ⓕ Ⓖ Ⓗ Ⓙ   40. Ⓕ Ⓖ Ⓗ Ⓙ
5. Ⓐ Ⓑ Ⓒ Ⓓ   11. Ⓐ Ⓑ Ⓒ Ⓓ   17. Ⓐ Ⓑ Ⓒ Ⓓ   23. Ⓐ Ⓑ Ⓒ Ⓓ   29. Ⓐ Ⓑ Ⓒ Ⓓ   35. Ⓐ Ⓑ Ⓒ Ⓓ

ENGLISH TEST
45 Minutes—75 Questions

> **Directions:** In the following five passages, certain words and phrases have been underlined and numbered. You will find alternatives for each underlined portion in the right-hand column. Select the one that best expresses the idea, that makes the statement acceptable in standard written English, or that is phrased most consistently with the style and tone of the entire passage. If you feel that the original version is best, select "NO CHANGE." You will also find questions asking about a section of the passage or about the entire passage. For these questions, decide which choice gives the most appropriate response to the given question. For each question in the test, select the best choice, and fill in the corresponding space on the answer folder. You may wish to read each passage through before you begin to answer the questions associated with it. Most answers cannot be determined without reading several sentences around the phrases in question. Make sure to read far enough ahead each time you choose an alternative.

PASSAGE I

[1]

If you are like most visitors to Athens, you will

make your way to the Acropolis, the hill that once
                          1

served as a fortified, strategic position overlooking the

Aegean Sea—to see the Parthenon. This celebrated

temple was dedicated in the fifth century B.C. to the

goddess Athena. There is no more famous building in

all of Greece; to climb up its marble steps is to have
                                            2

beheld a human creation that has attained the stature
2

of a natural phenomenon like the Grand Canyon. You
                                                3

should also make an attempt to sample Athenian
                    3

cuisine while you're there.
          3

1. A. NO CHANGE
    B. Acropolis. The hill
    C. Acropolis—the hill
    D. Acropolis

2. F. NO CHANGE
    G. to behold
    H. beholding
    J. to be holding

3. A. NO CHANGE
    B. Also make an attempt to sample
        Athenian cuisine while you're there.
    C. While you're there, you should also make
        an attempt to sample Athenian cuisine.
    D. OMIT the underlined portion.

GO ON TO THE NEXT PAGE

[2]

Generations of architects <u>have proclaimed</u> the
                               4

Parthenon to be the most brilliantly conceived

structure in the Western world. The genius of its

construction is <u>subtle for example</u> the temple's
                   5

columns were made to bulge outward slightly in order

to compensate for the <u>fact, viewed from distance, that</u>
                                 6

<u>straight columns appear concave.</u>
             6

Using this and other techniques, the architects strove to

create an optical <u>illusion of; uprightness,</u> solidity and
                      7

permanence.

[3]

<u>Because of this,</u> the overall impression you'll get
          8

of the Parthenon will be far different from the one the

ancient Athenians had. Only by standing on the marble

steps of the Parthenon and allowing your imagination

to transport you back to the Golden Age of <u>Athens.</u>
                                     9

<u>You will</u> be able to see the temple's main attraction,
 9

the legendary statue of Athena Parthenos. It was 38 feet

high and made of ivory and over a ton of pure gold.

4. F.   NO CHANGE
     G.   has proclaimed
     H.   proclaims
     J.   are proclaiming

5. A.   NO CHANGE
     B.   subtle; for example
     C.   subtle. For example
     D.   subtle. For example,

6. F.   NO CHANGE
     G.   fact that straight columns, viewed from a
          distance, appear concave.
     H.   view from a distance: straight columns
          appearing concave.
     J.   fact, when viewed from far away, that
          straight columns appear concave.

7. A.   NO CHANGE
     B.   illusion of: uprightness
     C.   illusion of, uprightness
     D.   illusion of uprightness

8. F.   NO CHANGE
     G.   Thus
     H.   Rather
     J.   Of course

9. A.   NO CHANGE
     B.   Athens; you will
     C.   Athens will you
     D.   Athens. You may

GO ON TO THE NEXT PAGE ⇨

Removed from the temple in the fifth century CE,
                    10
all that remains is the slight rectangular depression on

the floor where it stood.

[4]

Many of the ornate carvings and sculptures that

adorned the walls of the Acropolis is no longer there,
                                   11
either. In the early nineteenth century, the British

diplomat Lord Elgins decision to "protect" the ones
                   12
that survived by removing them from the Parthenon

and carrying them back to Britain (he had the

permission of the Ottoman Turks, who controlled

Greece at the time, to do so).

[5]

After they gained independence from the Turks,

they began to demand the sculptures and carvings back
13
from the British, to no avail. Thus, if you want to gain

a complete picture of what the Parthenon once looked

like, you'll have to visit not only the Acropolis of

Athens, but the British Museum in London as well.

10. F. NO CHANGE
    G. Having been removed from the temple
        in the fifth century CE,
    H. Given its removal from the temple in the
        fifth century CE,
    J. The statue was removed from the temple
        in the fifth century CE;

11. A. NO CHANGE
    B. will be
    C. have been
    D. are

12. F. NO CHANGE
    G. Elgin's deciding that
    H. Elgin decided to
    J. Elgin's decision to

13. A. NO CHANGE
    B. the Turks
    C. the Greeks
    D. who

GO ON TO THE NEXT PAGE

Items 14–15 ask about the passage as a whole.

---

14. The writer wishes to insert the following material into the essay:

    "Some of them were destroyed in 1687 when attacking Venetians bombarded the Acropolis, setting off explosives that had been stored in the Parthenon."

    The new material best supports, and therefore would most logically be placed in Paragraph:

    F. 1
    G. 2
    H. 3
    J. 4

15. Suppose the editor of an architecture journal had requested that the writer focus primarily on the techniques the ancient Greek architects used in constructing the Parthenon. Does the essay fulfill this request?

    A. Yes, because the essay makes it clear that the Parthenon was an amazing architectural achievement.

    B. Yes, because the essay explains in the second paragraph the reason the temple's columns bulge outward slightly.

    C. No, because the Parthenon's construction is only one of several topics covered in the essay.

    D. No, because the author never explains what the architects who designed the Parthenon were trying to accomplish.

GO ON TO THE NEXT PAGE

PASSAGE II

Although there is no conclusive evidence that a

man named Robin Hood ever actually existed, the story

of Robin Hood and his band of merry men has become

one of the most popular traditional tales in English

literature. Robin is the hero in a series of ballads dating

from at least the fourteenth century. These ballads are

            16

telling of discontent among the lower classes in the
  16

north of England during a turbulent era culminating

in the Peasants' Revolt of 1381. A good deal of the

rebellion against authority stemmed from restriction of

hunting rights. These early ballads reveal the cruelty

that was a part of medieval life. Robin Hood was a

rebel, and many of the most striking episodes depict

him and his companions robbing and killing represen-

tatives of authority, and they gave the gains to the poor.
                        17

Their most frequentest enemy was the Sheriff of
        18

Nottingham, a local agent of the central government.

Other enemies included wealthy ecclesiastical

landowners.

16. F. NO CHANGE
    G. telling
    H. tell
    J. they are telling

17. A. NO CHANGE
    B. they were giving
    C. giving
    D. gave

18. F. NO CHANGE
    G. even more frequenter
    H. frequent
    J. frequently

GO ON TO THE NEXT PAGE

While Robin could be ruthless with those who abused their power, he was kind to the oppressed. He was a people's hero as King Arthur was a noble's.

(The Broadway musical *Camelot* and Walt Disney's
 19
The Sword in the Stone are based on the legend of
 19
King Arthur.)
 19

Some scholars have sought to prove that there was an actual Robin Hood. However, references to the Robin Hood legends by medieval writers make it clear that the ballads were the only evidence for Robin's existence available to them. A popular modern belief
 20
that Robin was of the time of Richard I probably stems from the antiquary Richard Stukely's fabrication of a
 21
"pedigree." 22

19. A. NO CHANGE
    B. (The Broadway musical and the movie, respectively, *Camelot* and Walt Disney's *The Sword in the Stone*, are based on the legend of King Arthur.)
    C. (Movies and musicals, including *The Sword in the Stone* and *Camelot*, are derived from the legend of King Arthur.)
    D. OMIT the underlined portion.

20. F. NO CHANGE
    G. him.
    H. it.
    J. those writing ballads about him.

21. A. NO CHANGE
    B. Stukelys fabrication
    C. Stukelys fabrication,
    D. Stukely's, fabrication

22. Suppose that at this point in the passage the writer wanted to add more information about Richard Stukely. Which of the following additions would be most relevant to the passage as a whole?

    F. A discussion of relevant books on England during the realm of Richard I
    G. A definition of the term *antiquary*
    H. An example of Stukely's interest in King Arthur
    J. A description of the influence Stukely's fabricated pedigree has had on later versions of the Robin Hood tale

GO ON TO THE NEXT PAGE

In the eighteenth century, the nature of the legend
was distorted by the suggestion that Robin <u>was as a</u>
                                            23
fallen nobleman. Writers adopted this new element <u>as</u>
                                                   24
<u>eagerly as puppies.</u> Robin was also given a love <u>interest;</u>
      24   25
<u>Maid</u> Marian. Some critics say that these ballads lost
 25
much of their vitality and poetic value by losing

the social impulse that prompted their creation.

    <u>Consequently, in the twentieth century,</u> the legend
                        26
of Robin Hood has inspired several movies and a

television series. Even a Broadway musical <u>basing</u> on
                                            27
the tale. So, whether or not a Robin Hood actually

lived in ancient <u>Britain, and</u> the legendary Robin has
                       28
lived in the popular imagination for more than six

hundred years.

23. A. NO CHANGE
    B. was like as if he was
    C. was a
    D. is as a

24. F. NO CHANGE
    G. eagerly.
    H. eagerly, like a puppy.
    J. like a puppy's eagerness.

25. A. NO CHANGE
    B. interests—Maid
    C. interest: Maid,
    D. interest—Maid

26. F. NO CHANGE
    G. (Do NOT begin new paragraph) In the
        twentieth century, on the one hand,
    H. (Begin new paragraph) In the twentieth
        century,
    J. (Begin new paragraph) In the twentieth
        century, therefore,

27. A. NO CHANGE
    B. has been based
    C. to base
    D. OMIT the underlined portion.

28. F. NO CHANGE
    G. Britain,
    H. Britain, therefore
    J. Britain;

GO ON TO THE NEXT PAGE

Items 29–30 ask about the passage as a whole.

29. Suppose this passage were written for an audience that was unfamiliar with the legend of Robin Hood. The writer could most effectively strengthen the passage by:

   A. citing examples of legendary rebels from Spanish and French literature.

   B. including further evidence of Robin Hood's actual existence.

   C. quoting a few lines from a Broadway musical about ancient Britain.

   D. including a brief summary of the Robin Hood legend.

30. This passage was probably written for readers who:

   F. are experts on how legends are handed down.

   G. are authorities on ancient British civilization and culture.

   H. are convinced that Robin Hood was an actual historical personage.

   J. have some familiarity with the Robin Hood legends.

GO ON TO THE NEXT PAGE

PASSAGE III

[1]

When Mt. St. Helens erupted, my training as a private pilot paid off. My editor asked me to write a feature story on the volcano. Only scientists and reporters were allowed within a <u>ten-mile radius of the</u>
   31
mountain. Eager to see Mt. St. Helens for himself, my brother Jeff volunteered to accompany me as an assistant on the flight. He had never flown with me before, <u>and I looked forward at the opportunity to</u>
   32
<u>show off my skills.</u>
   32

[2]

<u>If I could read a newspaper,</u> I entertained thoughts
   33
of becoming a photo journalist. I always envisioned
<u>myself</u> in some faraway exotic place performing
   34
dangerous deeds as a foreign correspondent. I was thrilled when I was hired for my first job as a cub reporter for the local newspaper in my rural home town. However, some of the glamour began to fade after covering the umpteenth garden party. Then one day Mother Nature <u>intervened,</u> giving me the
   35
opportunity to cover an international event.

31. A. NO CHANGE
    B. radius, consisting of ten miles,
    C. measurement of a ten mile radius
    D. radius, measuring ten miles,

32. F. NO CHANGE
    G. but looked forward to the opportunity of showing off my skills.
    H. and I looked forward to the opportunity to show off my skills.
    J. nevertheless I anticipated being able to show off my skills.

33. A. NO CHANGE
    B. Since I found it easy to read a newspaper,
    C. Although I could read a newspaper,
    D. Ever since I could read a newspaper,

34. F. NO CHANGE
    G. I
    H. me
    J. it

35. A. NO CHANGE
    B. intervened:
    C. intervened;
    D. —intervened—

GO ON TO THE NEXT PAGE

[3]

When we arrived at the airport <u>filing my flight</u>
                                    36
<u>plan; giving</u> my credentials as a reporter for the
    36
Gresham *Outlook*. As we departed Troutdale airport,

my Cessna 152 ascended slowly on its way towards Mt.

St. Helens. As we neared the crater, I kept a <u>careful</u>
                                                37
watch for other airplanes in the vicinity. A few other

pilots were also circling around the crater. I had to

maintain a high enough altitude to avoid both the

smoke being emitted <u>from: the crater</u> and the ashen
                            38
residue already in the atmosphere. Too much exposure

to the volcanic particles could put my plane out of

service. This element of danger served to increase not

only my awareness, but also my excitement.

[4]

Jeff and I were at first speechless <u>and mute</u> at the
                                        39
awesome sight below us as we circled the crater. It was

as if the spectacular beauty of a Fourth of July celebra-

tion were contained in one natural phenomenon. Jeff

helped me, <u>steadying the plane and took notes</u>, while
                        40
I shot pictures and dictated story ideas to him. [41]

36. F. NO CHANGE
    G. I filed my flight plan and gave
    H. filing my flight plan, giving
    J. my flight plan was filed by me, and I gave

37. A. NO CHANGE
    B. (place before *airplanes*)
    C. (place before *neared*)
    D. (place before *crater*)

38. F. NO CHANGE
    G. (from: the crater)
    H. from, the crater,
    J. from the crater

39. A. NO CHANGE
    B. and also mute
    C. —and mute—
    D. OMIT the underlined portion.

40. F. NO CHANGE
    G. steadying the plane and taking notes,
    H. steadied the plane and taking notes,
    J. steadies the plane and takes notes

41. The writer could most effectively strengthen
    the passage at this point by adding which of
    the following?

    A. A description of Mt. St. Helens
    B. The sentence, "Jeff, take this plane
        lower!" to add excitement
    C. The statement, "A volcano is a vent in
        the earth's crust through which lava is
        expelled," to inform the reader
    D. A discussion of other recent volcanic
        eruptions to provide a contrast

GO ON TO THE NEXT PAGE ⇨

[5]

My story appeared as the front-page feature the

following day. <u>However,</u> I have realized many of my
　　　　　　 42

early dreams, working as a foreign correspondent in

many different countries. And yet none of my

experiences has surpassed that special pride and excite-

ment I felt covering my first "international" story.

42. F.　NO CHANGE
　　 G.　Since that time,
　　 H.　Furthermore,
　　 J.　Nevertheless,

Items 43–45 ask about the passage as a whole.

---

43. Readers are likely to regard the passage as best
　　 described by which of the following terms?

　　 A.　Optimistic
　　 B.　Bitter
　　 C.　Nostalgic
　　 D.　Exhausted

44. Is the author's use of the pronoun *I*
　　 appropriate in the passage?

　　 F.　No, because, as a rule, one avoids *I* in formal
　　　　 writing.
　　 G.　No, because it weakens the passage's
　　　　 focus on volcanoes.
　　 H.　Yes, because it gives immediacy to the
　　　　 story told in the passage.
　　 J.　Yes, because *I* is, as a rule, appropriate in
　　　　 writing.

45. Choose the sequence of paragraph numbers
　　 that will make the passage's structure most
　　 logical.

　　 A.　NO CHANGE
　　 B.　2, 1, 3, 4, 5
　　 C.　3, 4, 5, 1, 2
　　 D.　4, 5, 1, 2, 3

GO ON TO THE NEXT PAGE

PASSAGE IV

[1]

Sherlock Holmes, the ingenious and extremely
                                          46
clever detective with the deer-stalker hat, pipe and
46
magnifying glass, is a universally recognizable

character. Everyone knows of Holmes's ability to solve

even the most bizarre mysteries through the

application of cold logic. Therefore, everyone is
                          47
familiar with the phrase "elementary, my dear Watson,"

Holmes's perennial response to the requests of his

baffled sidekick, Dr. Watson, for an explanation of his

amazing deductions. Strictly speaking, of course,
                    48
Holmes's "deductions" were not deductions at all, but
                          48
inductive inferences.
       48

[2]

But how many people know anything about the

creator of Sherlock Holmes, Sir Arthur Conan Doyle?

Fans of Holmes might be surprised to discover that

he did not want to be engraved forever in the memory
49   50
of the people as the author of the Sherlock Holmes
      50
stories.

46. F. NO CHANGE
    G. ingenious
    H. ingenious, extremely clever
    J. cleverly ingenious

47. A. NO CHANGE
    B. Although everyone
    C. For this reason, everyone
    D. Everyone

48. F. NO CHANGE
    G. (Strictly speaking, of course, Holmes's
        "deductions" were not deductions at all,
        but inductive inferences.)
    H. Holmes's "deductions" were, strictly
        speaking, not deductions at all, but
        inductive inferences.
    J. OMIT the underlined portion.

49. A. NO CHANGE
    B. Conan Doyle
    C. they
    D. the detective

50. F. NO CHANGE
    G. to go down in the annals of history
    H. to be permanently thought of forever
    J. to be remembered

GO ON TO THE NEXT PAGE

<u>In fact,</u> Conan Doyle sent Holmes to his death at
51

the end of the second book of short stories and

subsequently felt a great sense of relief. Having had

enough of his famous character by that time, <u>Sherlock</u>
52

<u>Holmes would never divert him again from more</u>
52

<u>serious writing, he promised himself.</u> It took eight
52

years and the offer of a princely sum of money before

Conan Doyle could be persuaded to revive the

detective. <u>Soap opera characters are sometimes brought</u>
53

<u>back to life after they've been pronounced dead, too.</u>
53

[1] Admirers of Holmes's coldly scientific approach to

his detective work may also be taken aback when they

learn that Conan Doyle <u>has been deeply immersed in</u>
54

spiritualism. [2] Convinced by these experiences of the

validity of paranormal <u>phenomena, that he lectured</u> on
55

spiritualism in towns and villages throughout Britain.

[3] For example, he and his family attempted to

communicate with the dead by automatic writing,

51. A. NO CHANGE
    B. Despite this,
    C. Regardless,
    D. Yet

52. F. NO CHANGE
    G. the diversion of Sherlock Holmes, he promised himself, would never again keep him from more serious writing.
    H. more serious writing consumed all his time from then on.
    J. he promised himself that Sherlock Holmes would never again divert him from more serious writing.

53. A. NO CHANGE
    B. (Soap opera characters are sometimes brought back to life after they've been pronounced dead, too.)
    C. Sometimes you'll see soap opera characters who were dead being brought back to life, just like Holmes.
    D. OMIT the underlined portion.

54. F. NO CHANGE
    G. is deeply immersed
    H. was deeply immersed
    J. has been immersed deeply

55. A. NO CHANGE
    B. phenomena, he lectured
    C. phenomena was he that he lectured
    D. phenomena. He lectured

GO ON TO THE NEXT PAGE ⟹

thought to be a method of talking with those no longer
                                    56
among the living, and through a spiritual medium,
        56
an individual who supposedly could contact those in

the world beyond. [4] Conan Doyle claimed to have

grasped materialized hands and watched heavy articles

swimming through the air during sessions led by the

medium. 57

[3]

Doyle seems never to have asked himself: why they
                                    58
would manifest themselves in such curious ways, or to

have reflected on the fact that many of these effects are

the standard trappings of cheating mediums. One has to

wonder, what would Sherlock Holmes have to say? 60
                59

56. F.   NO CHANGE
    G.   a means of getting in touch with those
         beyond the grave
    H.   thought to be a method of talking with the
         dead
    J.   OMIT the underlined portion.

57. For the sake of unity and coherence, sentence
    2 should be placed:
    A.   where it is now.
    B.   before sentence 1.
    C.   after sentence 3.
    D.   after sentence 4.

58. F.   NO CHANGE
    G.   himself—why they
    H.   himself why those in the other world
    J.   himself why they

59. A.   NO CHANGE
    B.   what would Sherlock Holmes have said?
    C.   what is Sherlock Holmes going to say?
    D.   what had Sherlock Holmes said?

60. Which of the following would be the best title
    for the passage?
    F.   Cheating Mediums: The Truth about
         Spiritualists
    G.   Conan Doyle and Spiritualism
    H.   The Secret Life of Sherlock Holmes
    J.   Writers and Their Religious Beliefs

GO ON TO THE NEXT PAGE

PASSAGE V

[1]

During the summer of 1988, I watched

Yellowstone National Park go up in flames. Fires
                                            61
ignited by lightning, in June, had been allowed to
   61
burn unsuppressed because park officials expected that

the usual summer rains would douse them. But the

rains never came, a more plentiful supply of fuel
             62
(fallen logs, branches, and pine needles were
              63
available, and winds of up to 100 mph whipped the

spreading fires along and carried red-hot embers to

other areas, creating new fires.

[2]

By the time park officials succumbed to the

pressure of public opinion and decided to try to

extinguish the flames. Its too late. The situation
                        64
remained out of control in spite of the efforts of 9,000
                   65
firefighters employed state-of-the-art equipment. By
             66
September, more than 720,000 acres of Yellowstone had

been affected by fire. Nature was only able to curb the
                        67
destruction; the smoke did not begin to clear until the
   67
first snow arrived on September 11.

61. A. NO CHANGE
    B. Fires having been ignited by lightning, in June,
    C. Fires ignited by lightning in June
    D. Fires ignited by lightning in June,

62. F. NO CHANGE
    G. very much
    H. much more
    J. OMIT the underlined portion.

63. A. NO CHANGE
    B. (fallen logs, branches, and pine needles) was
    C. (fallen logs, branches, and pine needles) were
    D. (fallen logs, branches, and pine needles had been

64. F. NO CHANGE
    G. flames. It's
    H. flames, it's
    J. flames, it was

65. A. NO CHANGE
    B. control. In spite of
    C. control; despite
    D. control; in spite of

66. F. NO CHANGE
    G. who were employing
    H. which were employing
    J. which employed

67. A. NO CHANGE
    B. Nature able only to curb the destruction;
    C. Nature was able to curb only the destruction;
    D. Only nature was able to curb the destruction;

GO ON TO THE NEXT PAGE

[3]

Having been an ecologist who has studied forests
68
for 20 years, I knew that this was not nearly the tragedy

it seemed to be. Many more acres of forest burned in
69
Alaska in 1988 than in Yellowstone Park. Large fires are,
69
after all, necessary in order that the continued health in
70
the forest ecosystem be maintained. Fires thin out over-
70
crowded areas and allow the sun to reach species of

plants stunted by shade. Ash fertilizes the soil, and fire

smoke kills forest bacteria. In the case of the lodgepole

pine, fire is essential to reproduction: the pines' cone
71
has only opened when exposed to temperatures greater
71
than 112 degrees.

[4]

The fires in Yellowstone did result in some loss of

wildlife, but overall the region's animals proved to be

fire-tolerant and fire-adaptive. However large animals
72
such as bison were often seen grazing and bedding

down in meadows near burning forests. Also, the fire

posed little threat to the members of any endangered

animal species in the park. [73]

68. F.   NO CHANGE
    G.   As an ecologist
    H.   I'm an ecologist
    J.   Being an ecologist,

69. A.   NO CHANGE
    B.   The amount of acreage that burned in
         Yellowstone in 1988 was nowhere near as
         great as in Alaska.
    C.   Many more acres of forest burned in
         Alaska in 1988, than in Yellowstone Park.
    D.   OMIT the underlined portion

70. F.   NO CHANGE
    G.   for the continued health of the forest
         ecosystem to be maintained.
    H.   in order that the continued health of the
         forest ecosystem can persevere.
    J.   for the continued health of the forest
         ecosystem.

71. A.   NO CHANGE
    B.   pine's cone has only opened
    C.   pine's cone opens only
    D.   pines' cones have only opened

72. F.   NO CHANGE
    G.   Clearly,
    H.   In fact,
    J.   Instead,

GO ON TO THE NEXT PAGE

[5]

My confidence in the natural resilience of the

forest has been borne out in the years since the fires

ravaged Yellowstone. <u>Judging from the recent pictures</u>
                                                74

<u>of the park,</u> the forest was not destroyed; it was
       74

rejuvenated.

73. The writer has decided that a better transition is needed between the previous paragraph and this one. Which of the following sentences could be added at the beginning of this paragraph to do that best?

A. Although fire is an integral part of the long-term life of the forest, animals suffer in the short term.

B. Since forest fires play such a natural role, I expected the impact on animal life to be minimal.

C. One never knows what toll a fire will take on the wildlife, though.

D. Temperatures greater than 112 degrees is indeed rather hot.

74. F. NO CHANGE

G. Recent pictures of the park show that

H. Judging by the recent pictures of the park,

J. As judged according to pictures taken of the park recently,

Item 75 asks about the passage as a whole.

75. If the writer wished to provide support for the claim that the fire posed little threat to the members of any endangered animal species in the park, he or she would most likely:

A. list the endangered animal species known to inhabit the park.

B. discuss the particular vulnerability of endangered species of birds to forest fires.

C. cite the reports of biologists who monitored animal activity in the park during the fire.

D. explain how infrequent such an extensive series of forest fires really is.

IF YOU FINISH BEFORE TIME IS CALLED, YOU MAY CHECK YOUR WORK ON THIS SECTION ONLY. DO NOT TURN TO ANY OTHER SECTION IN THE TEST.

STOP

MATH TEST

60 Minutes—60 Questions

Directions: Solve each of the following problems, select the correct answer, and then fill in the corresponding space on your answer sheet.

Don't linger over problems that are too time-consuming. Do as many as you can, then come back to the others in the time you have remaining.

Calculator use is permitted, but some problems can best be solved without a calculator.

Note: Unless otherwise noted, all of the following should be assumed.

1. Illustrative figures are *not* necessarily drawn to scale.
2. All geometric figures lie in a plane.
3. The term *line* indicates a straight line.
4. The term *average* indicates arithmetic mean.

---

1. The regular price for a certain bicycle is $125.00. If that price is reduced by 20%, what is the new price?

    A. $100.00
    B. $105.00
    C. $112.50
    D. $120.00
    E. $122.50

DO YOUR FIGURING HERE.

2. If $x = -5$, then $2x^2 - 6x + 5 =$?

    F. -15
    G. 15
    H. 25
    J. 85
    K. 135

GO ON TO THE NEXT PAGE

3. How many distinct prime factors does the number 36 have?

    A. 2

    B. 3

    C. 4

    D. 5

    E. 6

DO YOUR FIGURING HERE.

4. In the figure below, what is the value of x?

    F. 105°

    G. 115°

    H. 135°

    J. 245°

    K. 255°

5. What is the average of $\dfrac{1}{20}$ and $\dfrac{1}{30}$?

    A. $\dfrac{1}{25}$

    B. $\dfrac{1}{24}$

    C. $\dfrac{2}{25}$

    D. $\dfrac{1}{12}$

    E. $\dfrac{1}{6}$

GO ON TO THE NEXT PAGE

6. The toll for driving a segment of a certain freeway is $1.50 plus 25 cents for each mile traveled. Joy paid a $25.00 toll for driving a segment of the freeway. How many miles did she travel?

F. 10
G. 75
H. 94
J. 96
K. 100

7. For all x, $3x^2 \times 5x^3 = ?$

A. $8x^5$
B. $8x^6$
C. $15x^5$
D. $15x^6$
E. $15x^8$

8. How many units apart are the points $P(-1, -2)$ and $Q(2, 2)$ in the standard (x, y) coordinate plane?

F. 2
G. 3
H. 4
J. 5
K. 6

9. In a group of 25 students, 16 are female. What percentage of the group is female?

A. 16%
B. 40%
C. 60%
D. 64%
E. 75%

DO YOUR FIGURING HERE.

GO ON TO THE NEXT PAGE

10. For how many integer values of x will $\dfrac{7}{x}$ be greater than $\dfrac{1}{4}$ and less than $\dfrac{1}{3}$?

   F.   6

   G. 7

   H. 12

   J.   28

   K. Infinitely many

11. Which of the following is a polynomial factor of $6x^2 - 13x + 6$?

   A. $2x + 3$

   B. $3x - 2$

   C. $3x + 2$

   D. $6x - 2$

   E. $6x + 2$

12. What is the value of a if $\dfrac{1}{a} + \dfrac{2}{a} + \dfrac{3}{a} + \dfrac{4}{a} = 5$?

   F. $\dfrac{1}{2}$

   G. 2

   H. 4

   J. $12\dfrac{1}{2}$

   K. 50

DO YOUR FIGURING HERE.

GO ON TO THE NEXT PAGE

13. In the figure below, $\overline{AD}$, $\overline{BE}$, and $\overline{CF}$ all intersect at point G. If the measure of $\angle AGB$ is 40° and the measure of $\angle CGE$ is 105°, what is the measure of $\angle AGF$?

DO YOUR FIGURING HERE.

- A. 35°
- B. 45°
- C. 55°
- D. 65°
- E. 75°

14. Which of the following is the solution statement for the inequality $-3 < 4x - 5$?

- F. $x > -2$
- G. $x > \dfrac{1}{2}$
- H. $x < -2$
- J. $x < \dfrac{1}{2}$
- K. $x < 2$

GO ON TO THE NEXT PAGE

15. In the figure below, $\overline{BD}$ bisects $\angle ABC$. The measure of $\angle ABC$ is 100° and the measure of $\angle BAD$ is 60°. What is the measure of $\angle BDC$?

DO YOUR FIGURING HERE.

A.   80°

B.   90°

C.   100°

D.   110°

E.   120°

16. If $x + 2y - 3 = xy$, where x and y are positive, then which of the following equations expresses y in terms of x?

F. $y = \dfrac{3 - x}{2 - x}$

G. $y = \dfrac{3 - x}{x - 2}$

H. $y = \dfrac{x - 3}{2 - x}$

J. $y = \dfrac{x - 2}{x - 3}$

K. $y = \dfrac{6 - x}{x - 2}$

17. In a group of 50 students, 28 speak English and 37 speak Spanish. If everyone in the group speaks at least one of the two languages, how many speak both English and Spanish?

A.   11

B.   12

C.   13

D.   14

E.   15

GO ON TO THE NEXT PAGE

18. A car travels 288 miles in 6 hours. At that rate, how many miles will it travel in 8 hours?

F. 216

G. 360

H. 368

J. 376

K. 384

19. When $\dfrac{4}{11}$ is written as a decimal, what is the 100th digit after the decimal point?

A. 3

B. 4

C. 5

D. 6

E. 7

20. What is the solution for x in the system of equations below?

$$3x + 4y = 31$$

$$3x - 4y = -1$$

F. 4

G. 5

H. 6

J. 9

K. 10

21. In the standard (x, y) coordinate plane, points P and Q have coordinates $(2, 3)$ and $(12, -15)$, respectively. What are the coordinates of the midpoint of $\overline{PQ}$?

A. $(6, -12)$

B. $(6, -9)$

C. $(6, -6)$

D. $(7, -9)$

E. $(7, -6)$

DO YOUR FIGURING HERE.

GO ON TO THE NEXT PAGE

22. In the figure below, $\angle B$ is a right angle, and the measure of $\angle C$ is θ. What is the value of $\cos\theta$?

DO YOUR FIGURING HERE.

F. $\dfrac{3}{4}$

G. $\dfrac{3}{5}$

H. $\dfrac{4}{5}$

J. $\dfrac{5}{4}$

K. $\dfrac{4}{3}$

23. In the figure below, the circle centered at P is tangent to the circle centered at Q. Point Q is on the circumference of circle P. If the circumference of circle P is 6 inches, what is the circumference, in inches, of circle Q?

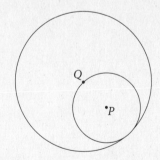

A. 12

B. 24

C. 36

D. 12π

E. 36π

GO ON TO THE NEXT PAGE

24. If $f(x) = x^3 - x^2 - x$, what is the value of $f(-3)$?

    F. -39

    G. -33

    H. -21

    J. -15

    K. 0

25. If the lengths, in inches, of all three sides of a triangle are integers, and one side is 7 inches long, what is the least possible perimeter of the triangle, in inches?

    A.   9

    B. 10

    C. 15

    D. 21

    E. 24

26. What is the complete factorization of $2x + 3x^2 + x^3$?

    F. $x(x^2 + 2)$

    G. $x(x - 2)(x + 3)$

    H. $x(x - 1)(x + 2)$

    J. $x(x + 1)(x + 2)$

    K. $x(x + 2)(x + 3)$

27. If $xyz \neq 0$, which of the following is equivalent to $\dfrac{x^2 y^3 z^4}{(xyz^2)^2}$?

    A. $\dfrac{1}{y}$

    B. $\dfrac{1}{z}$

    C. y

    D. $\dfrac{x}{yz}$

    E. xyz

DO YOUR FIGURING HERE.

GO ON TO THE NEXT PAGE

28. As a decimal, what is the sum of $\frac{2}{3}$ and $\frac{1}{12}$?

    F. 0.2

    G. 0.5

    H. 0.75

    J. 0.833

    K. 0.875

DO YOUR FIGURING HERE.

29. The formula for converting a Fahrenheit temperature reading to Celsius is $C = \frac{5}{9}(F - 32)$, where C is the reading in degrees Celsius and F is the reading in degrees Fahrenheit. Which of the following is the Fahrenheit equivalent to a reading of 95° Celsius?

    A. 35° F

    B. 53° F

    C. 63° F

    D. 203° F

    E. 207° F

30. A jar contains 4 green marbles, 5 red marbles, and 11 white marbles. If one marble is chosen at random, what is the probability that it will be green?

    F. $\frac{1}{3}$

    G. $\frac{1}{4}$

    H. $\frac{1}{5}$

    J. $\frac{1}{16}$

    K. $\frac{5}{15}$

GO ON TO THE NEXT PAGE

31. What is the average of the expressions $2x + 5$, $5x - 6$, and $-4x + 2$?

    A. $x + \dfrac{1}{3}$

    B. $x + 1$

    C. $3x + \dfrac{1}{3}$

    D. $3x + 3$

    E. $3x + 3\dfrac{1}{3}$

DO YOUR FIGURING HERE.

32. The line that passes through the points $(1, 1)$ and $(2, 16)$ in the standard (x, y) coordinate plane is parallel to the line that passes through the points $(-10, -5)$ and $(a, 25)$. What is the value of a?

    F. -8

    G. 3

    H. 5

    J. 15

    K. 20

33. In the figure below, $\overline{QS}$ and $\overline{PT}$ are parallel, and the lengths of $\overline{QR}$ and $\overline{PQ}$, in units, are as marked. If the perimeter of $\triangle QRS$ is 11 units, how many units long is the perimeter of $\triangle PRT$?

    A. 22

    B. 33

    C. 66

    D. 88

    E. 99

GO ON TO THE NEXT PAGE

34. The figure shown below belongs in which of the following classifications?

DO YOUR FIGURING HERE.

   I. Polygon

  II. Quadrilateral

 III. Rectangle

 IV. Trapezoid

  F.   I only

  G. II only

  H. IV only

  J.   I, II, and III only

  K. I, II, and IV only

35. If one solution to the equation $2x^2 + (a - 4)$ $x - 2a = 0$ is $x = -3$, what is the value of a?

  A.   0

  B.   2

  C.   4

  D.   6

  E. 12

36. A menu offers 4 choices for the first course, 5 choices for the second course, and 3 choices for dessert. How many different meals, consisting of a first course, a second course, and a dessert, can one choose from this menu?

  F.   12

  G. 24

  H. 30

  J.   36

  K. 60

GO ON TO THE NEXT PAGE

37. If an integer is divisible by 6 and by 9, then the integer must be divisible by which of the following?

   I. 12

  II. 18

 III. 36

  A. I only

  B. II only

  C. I and II only

  D. I, II, and III

  E. None

38. For all $x \neq 0$, $\dfrac{x^2 + x^2 + x^2}{x^2} = ?$

  F. 3

  G. $3x$

  H. x^2

  J. x^3

  K. x^4

39. Joan has q quarters, d dimes, n nickels, and no other coins in her pocket. Which of the following represents the total number of coins in Joan's pocket?

  A. $q + d + n$

  B. $5q + 2d + n$

  C. $.25q + .10d + .05n$

  D. $(25 + 10 + 5)(q + d + n)$

  E. $25q + 10d + 5n$

DO YOUR FIGURING HERE.

GO ON TO THE NEXT PAGE

40. Which graph below represents the solutions for
    x of the inequality $5x - 2(1 - x) \geq 4(x + 1)$?

    F.

    G. ![G number line with filled dot at -2]
       -4 -3 -2 -1 0 1 2 3 4

    H. ![H number line with filled dot at -2]
       -4 -3 -2 -1 0 1 2 3 4

    J. ![J number line with open circle at 2]
       -4 -3 -2 -1 0 1 2 3 4

    K. ![K number line with filled dot at 2]
       -4 -3 -2 -1 0 1 2 3 4

DO YOUR FIGURING HERE.

41. In the standard (x, y) coordinate plane, line m is
    perpendicular to the line containing the points
    $(5, 6)$ and $(6, 10)$. What is the slope of line m?

    A. -4

    B. $-\dfrac{1}{4}$

    C. $\dfrac{1}{4}$

    D. 4

    E. 8

GO ON TO THE NEXT PAGE

42. In the right triangle below, $\sin \theta = ?$

DO YOUR FIGURING HERE.

F. $\dfrac{5}{13}$

G. $\dfrac{5}{12}$

H. $\dfrac{12}{13}$

J. $\dfrac{13}{12}$

K. $\dfrac{13}{5}$

43. If $9^{2x-1} = 3^{3x+3}$, then $x = ?$

A. -4

B. $-\dfrac{7}{4}$

C. $-\dfrac{10}{7}$

D. 2

E. 5

44. From 1970 through 1980, the population of City Q increased by 20%. From 1980 through 1990, the population increased by 30%. What was the combined percent increase for the period 1970–1990?

F. 25%

G. 26%

H. 36%

J. 50%

K. 56%

GO ON TO THE NEXT PAGE

45. Martin's average score after 4 tests is 89. What score on the 5th test would bring Martin's average up to exactly 90?

   A. 90
   B. 91
   C. 92
   D. 93
   E. 94

46. Which of the following is an equation for the circle in the standard (x, y) coordinate plane that has its center at $(-1, -1)$ and passes through the point $(7, 5)$?

   F. $(x - 1)^2 + (y - 1)^2 = 10$
   G. $(x + 1)^2 + (y + 1)^2 = 10$
   H. $(x - 1)^2 + (y - 1)^2 = 12$
   J. $(x - 1)^2 + (y - 1)^2 = 100$
   K. $(x + 1)^2 + (y + 1)^2 = 100$

47. Which of the following is an equation for the graph in the standard (x, y) coordinate plane below?

   A. $y = -2x + 1$
   B. $y = x + 1$
   C. $y = x + 2$
   D. $y = 2x + 1$
   E. $y = 2x + 2$

DO YOUR FIGURING HERE.

GO ON TO THE NEXT PAGE

DO YOUR FIGURING HERE.

48. What is $\frac{1}{4}$% of 16?

    F.   0.004

    G.   0.04

    H.   0.4

    J.   4

    K.   64

49. For all s, $(s+4)(s-4)+(2s+2)(s-2) = ?$

    A. $s^2 - 2s - 20$

    B. $3s^2 - 12$

    C. $3s^2 - 2s - 20$

    D. $3s^2 + 2s - 20$

    E. $5s^2 - 2s - 20$

50. Which of the following is an equation of the parabola graphed in the (x, y) coordinate plane below?

    F. $y = \dfrac{x^2}{3} - 3$

    G. $y = \dfrac{x^2 - 3}{3}$

    H. $y = \dfrac{x^2}{3} + 3$

    J. $y = \dfrac{x^2 + 3}{3}$

    K. $y = 3x^2 - 3$

GO ON TO THE NEXT PAGE

51. In the figure below, $\sin a = \dfrac{4}{5}$. What is $\cos b$?

DO YOUR FIGURING HERE.

   A. $\dfrac{3}{4}$

   B. $\dfrac{3}{5}$

   C. $\dfrac{4}{5}$

   D. $\dfrac{5}{4}$

   E. $\dfrac{4}{3}$

52. For all $x \neq 0$, $\dfrac{x^2 + x^2 + x^2}{x} = ?$

   F. $3x$

   G. x^3

   H. x^5

   J. x^7

   K. $2x^2 + x$

53. One can determine a student's score S on a certain test by dividing the number of wrong answers (w) by 4 and subtracting the result from the number of right answers (r). This relation is expressed by which of the following formulas?

   A. $S = \dfrac{r - w}{4}$

   B. $S = r - \dfrac{w}{4}$

   C. $S = \dfrac{r}{4} - w$

   D. $S = 4r - w$

   E. $S = r - 4w$

GO ON TO THE NEXT PAGE

54. What is the volume, in cubic inches, of the cylinder shown in the figure below?

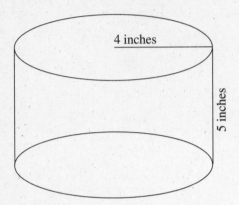

4 inches

5 inches

F. 20π

G. 40π

H. 60π

J. 80π

K. 100π

55. In the figure below, $\overline{AB}$ is perpendicular to $\overline{BC}$. The lengths of $\overline{AB}$ and $\overline{BC}$, in inches, are given in terms of x. Which of the following represents the area of $\triangle ABC$, in square inches, for all $x > 1$?

B

$x-1$

$x+1$

A C

A. x

B. $2x$

C. x^2

D. $x^2 - 1$

E. $\dfrac{x^2 - 1}{2}$

DO YOUR FIGURING HERE.

GO ON TO THE NEXT PAGE

56. In 1990, the population of Town *A* was 9,400 and the population of Town *B* was 7,600. Since then, each year, the population of Town *A* has decreased by 100, and the population of Town *B* has increased by 100. Assuming that in each case the rate continues, in what year will the two populations be equal?

F. 1998
G. 1999
H. 2000
J. 2008
K. 2009

57. In a certain club, the average age of the male members is 35 and the average age of the female members is 25. If 20% of the members are male, what is the average age of all the club members?

A. 26
B. 27
C. 28
D. 29
E. 30

DO YOUR FIGURING HERE.

GO ON TO THE NEXT PAGE

58. To determine the height h of a tree, Roger stands b feet from the base of the tree and measures the angle of elevation to be θ, as shown in the figure below. Which of the following relates h and b ?

F. $\sin\theta = \dfrac{h}{b}$

G. $\sin\theta = \dfrac{b}{h}$

H. $\sin\theta = \dfrac{b}{\sqrt{b^2+h^2}}$

J. $\sin\theta = \dfrac{h}{\sqrt{b^2+h^2}}$

K. $\sin\theta = \dfrac{\sqrt{b^2+h^2}}{b}$

59. The formula for the lateral surface area S of a right circular cone is $S = \pi r\sqrt{r^2+h^2}$, where r is the radius of the base and h is the altitude. What is the lateral surface area, in square feet, of a right circular cone with base radius 3 feet and altitude 4 feet?

A. $3\pi\sqrt{5}$

B. $3\pi\sqrt{7}$

C. 15π

D. 21π

E. $\dfrac{75\pi}{2}$

DO YOUR FIGURING HERE.

GO ON TO THE NEXT PAGE

60. In the figure below, line t crosses parallel lines m and n. Which of the following statements must be true?

DO YOUR FIGURING HERE.

F. $a = b$

G. $a = d$

H. $b = e$

J. $c = g$

K. $d = g$

READING TEST

35 Minutes—40 Questions

Directions: This test contains four passages, each followed by several questions. After reading a passage, select the best answer to each question and fill in the corresponding oval on your answer sheet. You are allowed to refer to the passages while answering the questions.

PASSAGE I

Men and women for whom economic security is the prime consideration do not usually choose a career in architecture. College graduates who
Line focus on the issue of opportunity are more likely
(5) to get an MBA or a law or medical degree. The image of these other professions and how much better their members fare financially haunts architects. Not only do architects generally have lower incomes than those in other professions, but the
(10) demand for services of lawyers and physicians is more stable, and they are able to exercise more control over the domains in which they work. The differences are very apparent now as the privileged position of lawyers and physicians has come under
(15) scrutiny. Critics, however, are finding it difficult to reduce the autonomy of these professions, while architects are continually losing out to clients and other parties in the building industry in the battle for hegemony.
(20) The use of these other professions as a reference group for architects in judging their own status in the hierarchy of social influence is a relatively new development. It begins in the middle of the nineteenth century, when a large number of middle-
(25) class occupations in Europe and America pressed governments to grant them special protected status, through a system of licensing. As a way of making sure they would be included under the licensing umbrella, architects began emphasizing
(30) those aspects of their work that most nearly resembled the thinking and skills of other fields. For example, architects, like physicians, argued that their work affected public health and safety. The result was a shift in the definition of architecture

(35) from a focus on artistic accomplishment to expertise in dealing with the structural integrity of buildings, ventilation requirements, and the ability to interpret building and housing codes. The registration examinations still emphasize this compo-
(40) nent of architecture, even though this emphasis defines architecture in a way that parallels what others in the building industry are better at handling than architects.

Should architects keep berating themselves
(45) because they do not enjoy many of the social and economic rewards of the other major professions? It might be worthwhile if there were a good chance that architecture could become more like law or medicine, that is, more science-based and
(50) more fully in control of its domain. A great deal of effort continues to go into programs intended to achieve these objectives, but I am doubtful that they can have much effect in transforming the fundamental existential condition of architecture. For
(55) example, even when architecture emphasizes its regard for the pragmatics of building, it still remains linked to the fate of the construction industry. Yet, as the current condition of the industry indicates, construction is notoriously
(60) volatile. Physicians face a much different situation, since illness and disease do not diminish during economic depression; indeed there is reason to believe that morbidity increases. And lawyers, like accountants, provide service to a wide range of
(65) industries, so that when business diminishes in one sector, they are supported by others.

At the same time, however, the attributes that first earned architecture its place as "the mother of

GO ON TO THE NEXT PAGE ⟶

all arts" are those that continue to set it apart
(70) today. There is no other profession that is able to
achieve what architects have historically accomplished in the realm of building. No other building profession is so learned about how to relate
light, mass and structure to produce memorable
(75) visual and spatial experiences. Rare is the building
not produced by an architect, that represents the
supreme values of civilization. The design of the
great seminal monumental buildings is the unique
province of architecture, its "natural market."
(80)   But many practitioners seem embarrassed to
present themselves as artists. They seem to fear it
may encourage clients to regard them as no different from painters, sculptors, and other visual
artists. They also appear worried that to promote
(85) this image will create the impression that architecture is a luxury service, which, as the history of the
profession's achievement shows, it usually is.
Routine, ordinary buildings can be constructed
without the benefit of architects. But instead of
(90) trying to compete in this market, where it is not
particularly successful anyway, the profession
should be making more effort to broaden what I
have called its natural market. The question is
how to stretch the profession's capacity, without at
(95) the same time injuring its fundamental strengths
and its acknowledged cultural role. The strategy of
emphasizing their skills in building, which so
many firms have adopted, puts architects in competition with other professions and parties that
(100) can do it just as well, if not better. It also just dis-
courages clients and the profession itself from rec-
ollecting the primary skill of the architect for
which there is no peer; the design of buildings
that have some value as art. This is the direction
(105) in which the profession must move if it is going to
find greater employment in the decades ahead.

Excerpt from "Architects and Power: The Natural Market
for Architecture," by Robert Gutman, *Progressive Architecture*,
December 1992. Reprinted by permission of Penton Publishing.

1. According to the passage, architects do not like
being regarded as:

A.   doctors.

B.   artists.

C.   builders.

D.   accountants.

2. As it is used in the passage, the word *privileged*
(line 13) most likely means:

F.   authorized.

G.   confidential.

H.   superior.

J.   aristocratic.

3. The passage suggests that architects were
granted special protected status through a
system of licensing partly because:

A.   their market was threatened by other
workers in the construction industry.

B.   their work affected public health and
safety.

C.   many other middle-class occupations
enjoyed similar protection.

D.   fewer great monumental buildings were
being designed.

4. According to the passage, doctors and lawyers
fare better financially than architects because:

I.   the demand for architects' services is
less stable.

II. doctors and lawyers are more able to
exercise control over their fields.

III. architects are forced to compete with
other parties in building industry.

F.   I and II

G.   II and III

H.   I and III

J.   I, II, and III   GO ON TO THE NEXT PAGE ⇨

5. The main point the passage makes about architecture is that:

   A. architects should focus on designing buildings that have some artistic value.

   B. architects should possess as much economic security as doctors and lawyers do.

   C. architects should work to abolish the traditional system of licensing.

   D. architects should work to compete more with other building professions.

6. According to the passage, architecture is described as the "mother of all arts" (line 68–69) because:

   F. architects have been designing buildings since the beginnings of civilization.

   G. architecture is similar in nature to painting, sculpture and other visual arts.

   H. architects relate light, mass and structure to produce memorable artistic effects.

   J. architecture has survived the passage of time better than other art forms.

7. According to the passage, all of the following professionals thrive during periods of economic depressions EXCEPT:

   A. physicians.

   B. architects.

   C. lawyers.

   D. accountants.

8. Which of the following statements is best supported by the fifth paragraph?

   F. Architects want their clients to acknowledge their status as artists.

   G. Routine, ordinary buildings don't necessarily need the help of architects.

   H. Architects would like their profession to be regarded as a luxury service.

   J. Architects have been most successful in the housing market.

9. According to the passage, college graduates are unlikely to choose a career in architecture because:

   A. there are fewer degrees offered in architecture than in other professions.

   B. architects are lower paid than those in other professions.

   C. rising costs in education make architecture a less practical choice.

   D. other professions have a more glamorous image.

10. According to the passage, law and medicine are different from architecture in that they are:

    F. less based on scientific knowledge.

    G. more dependent on economic conditions.

    H. better protected by a licensing system.

    J. more fully in control of their domain.

GO ON TO THE NEXT PAGE

PASSAGE II

Enlightenment ideas were put forth by a variety of intellectuals who in France came to be known as the *philosophes. Philosophes* is French for
Line philosophers, and in a sense these thinkers were
(5) rightly considered philosophers, for the questions they dealt with were philosophical: How do we discover truth? How should life be lived? What is the nature of God? But on the whole the term has a meaning different from the usual meaning of
(10) "philosopher." The *philosophes* were intellectuals, often not formally trained or associated with a university. They were usually more literary than scientific. They generally extended, applied, popularized, or propagandized ideas of others rather
(15) than originating those ideas themselves. The *philosophes* were more likely to write plays, satires, pamphlets or simply participate in verbal exchanges at select gatherings than to write formal philosophical books.
(20) It was the *philosophes* who developed the philosophy of the Enlightenment and spread it to much of the educated elite in Western Europe (and the American colonies). Although the sources for their philosophy can be traced to the Scientific
(25) Revolution in general, the *philosophes* were most influenced by their understanding of Newton, Locke, and English institutions.

The *philosophes* saw Newton as the great synthesizer of the Scientific Revolution who rightly
(30) described the universe as ordered, mechanical, material, and only originally set in motion by God, who since then has remained relatively inactive. Newton's synthesis showed to the *philosophes* that reason and nature were compatible: Nature
(35) functioned logically and discernibly, and what was natural was also reasonable. Newton exemplified the value of reasoning based on concrete experience. The *philosophes* felt that his empirical methodology was the correct path to discovering
(40) truth.

John Locke (1632–1704) agreed with Newton but went further. This English thinker would not exempt even the mind from the mechanical laws of the material universe. In his *Essay Concerning*
(45) *Human Understanding* (1691), Locke pictured the human brain at birth as a blank sheet of paper on which nothing would ever be written except sense perception and reason. What human beings become depends on their experiences—on the
(50) information received through the senses. Schools and social institutions could therefore play a great role in molding the individual from childhood to adulthood. Human beings were thus by nature far more malleable than had been assumed. This
(55) empirical psychology of Locke rejected the notion that human beings were born with innate ideas or that revelation was a reliable source of truth. Locke also enunciated liberal and reformist political ideas in his *Second Treatise of Civil Government*
(60) (1690), which influenced the *philosophes.* On the whole Locke's empiricism, psychology and politics were appealing to the *philosophes.*

England, not coincidentally the country of Newton and Locke, became the admired model
(65) for many of the *philosophes.* They tended to idealize it, but England did seem to allow greater individual freedom, tolerate religious differences, and evidence greater political reform than other countries, especially France. England seemed to have
(70) gone furthest in freeing itself from traditional institutions and accepting the new science of the seventeenth century. Moreover, England's approach seemed to work, for England was experiencing relative political stability and prosperity.
(75) The *philosophes* wanted to see in their own countries much of what England already seemed to have.

Many *philosophes* reflected the influence of Newton, Locke, and English institutions, but per-
(80) haps the most representative in his views was Voltaire (1694–1778). Of all leading figures of the Enlightenment, he was the most influential. Voltaire, the son of a Paris lawyer, became the idol of the French intelligentsia while still in his early
(85) twenties. His versatile mind was sparkling; his wit

GO ON TO THE NEXT PAGE ▷

was mordant. An outspoken critic, he soon ran afoul of both church and state authorities. First he was imprisoned in the Bastille; later he was exiled to England. There he encountered the ideas of
(90) Newton and Locke and came to admire English parliamentary government and tolerance. In *Letters on the English* (1732), *Elements of the Philosophy of Newton* (1738), and other writings, he popularized the ideas of Newton and Locke,
(95) extolled the virtues of English society, and indirectly criticized French society. Slipping back into France, he was hidden for a time and protected by a wealthy woman who became his mistress. Voltaire's facile mind and pen were never idle. He
(100) wrote poetry, drama, history, essays, letters, and scientific treatises—ninety volumes in all. The special targets of his cynical wit were the Catholic church and Christian institutions. Few people in history have dominated their age intellectually as
(105) did Voltaire.

Excerpt from *A Short History of Western Civilization, Volume 1* by John B. Harrison, Richard E. Sullivan, and Dennis Sherman. Copyright © 1990 by McGraw-Hill, Inc. Reprinted by permission of McGraw-Hill, Inc.

11. The *philosophes* can best be described as:

A. writers swept up by their mutual admiration of John Locke.

B. professors who lectured in philosophy at French universities.

C. intellectuals responsible for popularizing Enlightenment ideas.

D. scientists who furthered the work of the Scientific Revolution.

12. Which of the following would most likely have been written by Voltaire?

F. A treatise criticizing basic concepts of the Scientific Revolution.

G. A play satirizing religious institutions in France.

H. A collection of letters mocking the English Parliament.

J. A sentimental poem expounding the virtues of courtly love.

13. According to the passage, Locke felt that schools and social institutions could "play a great role in molding the individual" (lines 51–52) primarily because:

A. human beings were born with certain innate ideas.

B. human nature becomes more malleable with age.

C. society owes each individual the right to an education.

D. the human mind is chiefly influenced by experience.

14. Based on the information in the passage, which of the following best describes Newton's view of the universe?

I. The universe was initially set in motion by God.

II. Human reason is insufficient to understand the laws of nature.

III. The universe operates in a mechanical and orderly fashion.

F. I only

G. I and II only

H. I and III only

J. II and III only

GO ON TO THE NEXT PAGE

15. According to the passage, which of the following works questioned the idea that revelation was a reliable source of truth?

   A. *Letters on the English*
   B. *Second Treatise of Civil Government*
   C. *Elements of the Philosophy of Newton*
   D. *Essay Concerning Human Understanding*

16. The passage supports which of the following statements concerning the relationship between Newton and Locke?

   F. Locke's psychology contradicted Newton's belief in an orderly universe.
   G. Locke maintained that Newton's laws of the material universe also applied to the human mind.
   H. Newton eventually came to accept Locke's revolutionary ideas about the human mind.
   J. Newton's political ideas were the basis of Locke's liberal and reformist politics.

17. According to the passage, the *philosophes* believed that society should:

   I.   allow individuals greater freedom.
   II. free itself from traditional institutions.
   III. tolerate religious differences.

   A. I only
   B. I and II only
   C. II and III only
   D. I, II, and III

18. It can be inferred from the passage that the author regards England's political stability and economic prosperity as:

   F. the reason why the *philosophes* did not idealize England's achievement.
   G. evidence that political reforms could bring about a better way of life.
   H. the result of Voltaire's activities after he was exiled to England.
   J. an indication that the Scientific Revolution had not yet started there.

19. The passage suggests that the French political and religious authorities during the time of Voltaire:

   A. allowed little in the way of free speech.
   B. overreacted to Voltaire's mild satires.
   C. regarded the *philosophes* with indifference.
   D. accepted the model of English parliamentary government.

20. How does the passage support the point that the *philosophes* were "more literary than scientific" (line 12–13)?

   F. It demonstrates how the *philosophes'* writings contributed to the political change.
   G. It compares the number of works that Voltaire authored to Newton's output.
   H. It traces the influences of English literary works on French scientists.
   J. It describes the kinds of literary activities the *philosophes* commonly engaged in.

GO ON TO THE NEXT PAGE

Passage III

Rosemary sat at her kitchen table, working at a
crossword puzzle. Crosswords were nice; they
filled the time, and kept the mind active. She
Line needed just one word to complete this morning's
(5) puzzle; the clue was "a Swiss river," and the first of
its three letters was "A." Unfortunately, Rosemary
had no idea what the name of the river was, and
could not look it up. Her atlas was on the desk,
and the desk was in the guest room, currently
(10) being occupied by her grandson Victor. Looking
up over the tops of her bifocals, Rosemary glanced
at the kitchen clock: it was almost 10 A.M. *Land
sakes*! Did the boy intend to sleep all day? She
noticed that the arthritis in her wrist was throb-
(15) bing, and put down her pen. At eighty-seven years
of age, she was glad she could still write at all. She
had decided long ago that growing old was like
slowly turning to stone; you couldn't take anything for granted. She stood up slowly, painfully,
(20) and started walking to the guest room.

The trip, though only a distance of about
twenty-five feet, seemed to take a long while. Late
in her ninth decade now, Rosemary often experienced an expanded sense of time, with present
(25) and past tense intermingling in her mind. One
minute she was padding in her slippers across the
living room carpet, the next she was back on the
farm where she'd grown up, a sturdy little girl
treading the path behind the barn just before
(30) dawn. In her mind's eye, she could still pick her
way among the stones in the darkness, more than
seventy years later . . . Rosemary arrived at the door
to the guest room. It stood slightly ajar, and she
peered through the opening. Victor lay sleeping
(35) on his side, his arms bent, his expression slightly
pained. *Get up, lazy bones*, she wanted to say. Even
in childhood, Rosemary had never slept past
4 A.M.; there were too many chores to do. How different things were for Victor's generation! Her
(40) youngest grandson behaved as if he had never
done a chore in his life. Twenty-one years old, he

had driven down to Florida to visit Rosemary in
his shiny new car, a gift from his doting parents.
Victor would finish college soon, and his future
(45) appeared bright—if he ever got out of bed, that is.

Something Victor had said last night over dinner had disturbed her. Now what was it? Oh yes;
he had been talking about one of his college
courses—a "gut," he had called it. When she had
(50) asked him to explain the term, Victor had said it
was a course that you took simply because it was
easy to pass. Rosemary, who had not even had a
high school education, found the term repellent. If
she had been allowed to continue her studies, she
(55) would never have taken a "gut". . . . The memory
flooded back then, still painful as an open wound
all these years later. It was the first day of high
school. She had graduated from grammar school
the previous year, but her father had forbidden
(60) her to go on to high school that fall, saying
that she was needed on the farm. After much tearful
pleading, she had gotten him to promise that next
year, she could start high school. She had endured
a whole year of chores instead of books, with ani-
(65) mals and rough farmhands for company instead
of people her own age. Now, at last, the glorious
day was at hand. She had put on her best dress
(she owned two), her heart racing in anticipation.
But her father was waiting for her as she came
(70) downstairs.

"Where do you think you're going?" he asked.

"To high school, Papa."

"No you're not. Take that thing off and get back
to work."

(75) "But Papa, you promised!"

"*Do as I say*!" he thundered.

There was no arguing with Papa when he spoke
that way. Tearfully, she had trudged upstairs to
change clothes. Rosemary still wondered what life
(80) would have been like if her father had not been
waiting at the bottom of the stairs that day, or if
somehow she had found the strength to defy
him . . .

GO ON TO THE NEXT PAGE ⟶

Suddenly, Victor stirred, without waking, and
(85) mumbled something unintelligible. Jarred from
her reverie, Rosemary stared at Victor. She wondered if he were having a nightmare.

From "Graduation," by Jon Krupp.

21. According to the passage, Victor is Rosemary's:

A. nephew.

B. son.

C. grandson.

D. great grandson.

22. It can be inferred from the passage that
Rosemary is disturbed by Victor's:

F. intention to drop out of college.

G. disregard of her harsh upbringing.

H. willingness to take courses that are easy
to pass.

J. inability to get out of bed in the
morning.

23. The passage suggests that in the year after she
finished grammar school, Rosemary most
wanted:

A. an escape from her father's company.

B. the opportunity to go to college.

C. the chance to study challenging subjects.

D. the company of people her own age.

24. The passage suggests that Rosemary's attitude
towards the physical afflictions of old age is
generally one of:

F. sadness.

G. acceptance.

H. resentment.

J. optimism.

25. According to the passage, Rosemary does
crossword puzzles in order to:

A. keep her mind active.

B. practice her handwriting.

C. learn new geographical facts.

D. make her more aware of time.

26. The focus of the passage as a whole is on:

F. Rosemary's concern at Victor's lack of
motivation.

G. the harsh treatment Victor received from
his father.

H. the contrast between Victor's and
Rosemary's attitudes towards education.

J. Rosemary's struggle to suppress painful
memories.

27. It can be inferred from the passage that
Victor's "shiny new car" (line 43) is mentioned
in order to illustrate:

A. the excessive generosity of Rosemary's
parents.

B. the contrast between Rosemary's generation and his.

C. the strength of Victor's prospects for
the future.

D. the lack of physical hardship in
Victor's life.

28. The third paragraph (lines 46–70) primarily
portrays Rosemary in her youth as:

F. resentful of her father's conduct.

G. eager to continue her education.

H. undecided about her future career.

J. proud of her appearance.

GO ON TO THE NEXT PAGE

29. Rosemary's recollection of growing up on the farm (lines 25–32) is mentioned as an example of her:

A. nostalgia for her childhood experiences.

B. determination to overcome her physical disabilities.

C. ability to recall past and present events at the same time.

D. disappointment at being denied an education.

30. The statement that Victor's "future appeared bright" (lines 44–45) most likely reflects the opinion of:

F. Rosemary.

G. Victor.

H. Victor's parents.

J. Rosemary's father.

GO ON TO THE NEXT PAGE

PASSAGE IV

Sixty-five million years ago, something triggered mass extinctions so profound that they define the geological boundary between the
Line Cretaceous and Tertiary periods (the K-T
(5) Boundary). Approximately 75 percent of all animal species, including every species of dinosaur, were killed off; those that survived lost the vast majority of their numbers. The Earth exists in a region of space teeming with asteroids
(10) and comets, which on collision have frequently caused enormous environmental devastation, including extinctions of animal species. Yet few traditional geologists or biologists considered the effect such impacts may have had on the geologic
(15) and biologic history of the Earth. Since gradual geologic processes like erosion or repeated volcanic eruptions can explain the topographical development of the Earth, they felt that there was no need to resort to extraterrestrial explanations.

(20) An important theory proposed in 1980 by physicists Luis and Walter Alvarez challenged this view. The Alvarezes argued that an asteroid roughly 6 miles in diameter collided with the Earth in the K-T Boundary. Although the damage
(25) caused by the meteorite's impact would have been great, the dust cloud that subsequently would have enveloped the planet, completely blotting out the sun for up to a year—the result of soil displacement—would have done most of the harm,
(30) according to this theory. Plunged into darkness—and the resulting drastically reduced temperatures—plant growth would have been interrupted, cutting off the food supply to herbivorous species, the loss of which in turn would have starved car-
(35) nivores. Additional species would have perished as a result of prolonged atmospheric poisoning, acid rain, forest fires, and tidal waves, all initiated by the asteroid's impact.

Some subsequent research not only tended to
(40) support the Alvarez theory, but suggested that similar impacts may have caused other sharp breaks in Earth's geologic and biologic history.

Research in the composition of the Earth revealed a 160-fold enrichment of iridium all over the
(45) world in a thin layer of sediments formed at the K-T Boundary. The presence of this element, which is extremely uncommon in the Earth's crust but very common in asteroids and comets, suggested that a meteorite must have struck Earth at
(50) that time. Additional physical evidence of such a strike was found in rock samples, which contained shocked quartz crystals and microtektites (small glass spheres)—both byproducts of massive collisions.

(55) Observation of the lunar surface provided further evidence of the likelihood of a massive strike. Since the moon and the Earth lie within the same swarm of asteroids and comets, their impact histories should be parallel. Although some lunar
(60) craters were of volcanic origin, over the last 4 billion years at least five impact craters ranging from 31 to 58 miles in diameter have marred the lunar surface. Therefore, over the same time span Earth must have experienced some 400 collisions
(65) of similar magnitude. Although such an impact crater had not been found, Alvarez supporters didn't consider finding it necessary or likely. They reasoned that geologic processes over 65 million years, like erosion and volcanic eruptions, would
(70) have obscured the crater, which in any case probably occurred on the ocean floor.

Traditional biologists and geologists resisted the Alvarez theory. They pointed to the absence of any impact crater; to the fact that iridium, while rare
(75) at the Earth's surface, was common at its core and could be transported to the surface by volcanic activity; and to the fact that the Alvarezes, though eminent physicists, were not biologists, geologists, or paleontologists.

GO ON TO THE NEXT PAGE ⟹

31. According to the Alvarez theory, the mass extinctions of animal species at the end of the Cretaceous period were caused by:

    A. animals being crushed by an enormous asteroid.

    B. processes like erosion and repeated volcanic eruptions.

    C. extreme global warming causing a global firestorm.

    D. environmental conditions following a meteorite impact.

32. Based on the information in the passage, the author probably believes that those who held the traditional views about the topographical development of the Earth were:

    F. proven incorrect by the Alvarezes

    G. unrivaled at the present time.

    H. correct in challenging alternative views.

    J. unreceptive to new evidence.

33. As it is used in line 44, the word *enrichment* most nearly means:

    A. wealth.

    B. improvement.

    C. increase in amount.

    D. reward.

34. The views of scientists who opposed the Alvarez theory would have been strengthened if:

    F. major deposits of iridium were found in the lava flows of active Earth volcanoes.

    G. iridium were absent in sediments corresponding to several episodes of mass extinction.

    H. iridium were absent in fragments of several recently recovered meteorites.

    J. the Alvarezes were biologists as well as physicists.

35. The author's attitude toward the Alvarezes' theory is best characterized as:

    A. dismissive.

    B. neutral.

    C. skeptical.

    D. supportive.

36. According to the passage, which of the following is the correct order of events in the Alvarez theory explaining the mass extinction of species at the end of the Cretaceous period?

    F. Soil displacement, disappearance of the sun, decline of plant life, fall in temperature

    G. Soil displacement, disappearance of the sun, fall in temperature, decline of plant life

    H. Fall in temperature, decline of plant life, soil displacement, disappearance of the sun

    J. Disappearance of the sun, fall in temperature, decline of plant life, soil displacement

37. It can be inferred from paragraph 2 that the author discusses the Alvarezes' description of environmental conditions at the end of the Cretaceous period in order to:

    A. demonstrate that an immense meteorite hit the Earth.

    B. explain why no trace of an impact crater has yet been found.

    C. show that Earth is vulnerable to meteorite collisions.

    D. clarify how a meteorite may account for mass extinctions.

GO ON TO THE NEXT PAGE

38. The author's statement (lines 8–10) that "Earth exists in a region of space teeming with asteroids and comets" is important to:

   F. the Alvarezes' claim that an asteroid's impact caused atmospheric poisoning, acid rain, forest fires, and tidal waves.

   G. the Alvarezes' view that the resulting dust cloud, rather than the impact of the meteorite, did most of the harm.

   H. Alvarez supporters' argument based on the numbers of impact craters on the surface of the moon.

   J. traditionalists' view that topographical development of the Earth can be explained by gradual geologic processes.

39. Supporters of the Alvarezes's theory believe finding the impact crater is not necessary because:

   I. the crater probably is on the ocean floor.

   II. iridium occurs at the earth's core.

   III. processes like erosion and volcanic eruptions obscured the crater.

   A. I only

   B. I and II only

   C. I and III only

   D. II and III only

40. According to the passage, species died in mass extinctions as a result of all of the following EXCEPT:

   F. shocked quartz crystals and microtektites.

   G. reduced sunlight for up to a year.

   H. loss of food supplies.

   J. prolonged atmospheric poisoning.

IF YOU FINISH BEFORE TIME IS CALLED, YOU MAY CHECK YOUR WORK ON THIS SECTION ONLY. DO NOT TURN TO ANY OTHER SECTION IN THE TEST.

STOP

SCIENCE TEST

35 Minutes—40 Questions

Directions: Each of the following seven passages is followed by several questions. After reading each passage, decide on the best answer to each question and fill in the corresponding oval on your answer sheet. You are allowed to refer to the passages while answering the questions. Calculator use is not allowed on this test.

PASSAGE I

Optical fibers are strands of highly transparent glass used for communication transmissions. When light is transmitted through optical fibers, power is lost along the way. The power lost depends on the distance travelled, the wavelength of the light transmitted, the glass used, and any impurities present. The following attenuation (power loss in db/km) curve, which was recorded for a fluoride glass optical fiber, includes the attenuation caused by three different impurities commonly present in fluoride glass fibers.

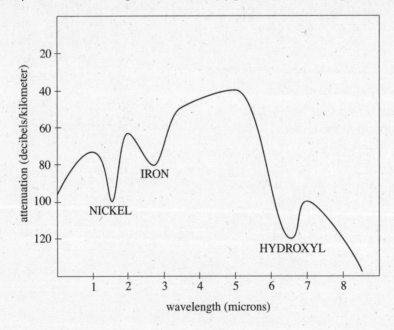

GO ON TO THE NEXT PAGE

1. In this fiber, copper impurities can lead to an attenuation of roughly 95 decibels per kilometer at wavelengths near 1.6 microns. Such impurities, if graphed as above, would produce an attenuation response similar to that of:

    A. nickel.

    B. iron.

    C. hydroxyl.

    D. none of the impurities in the graph.

2. According to the graph, in a fiber without any impurities, as wavelength increases, power loss will:

    F. decrease then increase.

    G. increase then decrease.

    H. remain the same.

    J. fluctuate randomly.

3. If a researcher using a 6.6 micron laser wished to limit power loss, this fluoride glass fiber would be:

    A. ideal, because attenuation is at a minimum at this wavelength.

    B. impossible, because the fiber does not conduct light at this wavelength.

    C. inefficient, because of interference from hydroxyl groups at this wavelength.

    D. unaffected by the laser's wavelength.

4. Suppose a scientist were able to develop a fluoride glass fiber without any hydroxyl impurities. Which of the following predictions would most likely be true?

    I. There will be less power lost in the range between six and seven microns.

    II. The attenuation due to iron impurities would increase.

    III. The fiber's overall power loss would decrease.

    F. I only

    G. I and III only

    H. II and III only

    J. I, II, and III

5. A certain computer communications system requires a cable five kilometers long. Based on the data in the graph, what is the minimum power loss that can be achieved using a fluoride glass fiber?

    A. 5 decibels

    B. 20 decibels

    C. 40 decibels

    D. 200 decibels

GO ON TO THE NEXT PAGE

PASSAGE II

A *binary star system* consists of two stars that are gravitationally bound to each other. If two stars that orbit each other are viewed along a line of sight that is not perpendicular to the orbital plane, they will alternately appear to eclipse each other. The orbit of *eclipsing binary* system Q is shown in Figure 1 below.

Astronomers deduce that a given "star" is an eclipsing binary from its *light curve*—the plot of its surface brightness (observed from a fixed position) against time. The light curve of an eclipsing binary typically displays a deep primary minimum and a shallower secondary minimum. Figure 2 shows the light curve of System Q.

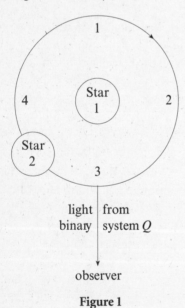

light   from
binary   system Q

observer

Figure 1

Notes: Diagram is not drawn to scale. Star 1 is brighter than Star 2.

Figure 2

6. The point on the light curve labeled c corresponds to the position in Figure 1 labeled:

   F.   1.
   G.   2.
   H.   3.
   J.   4.

7. The period of revolution for eclipsing binary Q is about:

   A.   4 days.
   B.   10 days.
   C.   12 days.
   D.   20 days.

8. The stars in eclipsing binary Q alternately eclipse each other for periods of approximately:

   F.   2 days and 4 days.
   G.   2 days and 5 days.
   H.   2 days and 8 days.
   J.   5 days each.

GO ON TO THE NEXT PAGE

Light Curve of System *X*

Light Curve of System *Z*

9. The light curves for two eclipsing binaries, Systems *X* and *Z*, are shown. Which of the following hypotheses would account for the deeper primary minimum of System *Z*?

A. There is a more extreme difference between the magnitudes of the two stars of System *X* than between those of the two stars of System *Z*.

B. There is a more extreme difference between the magnitudes of the two stars of System *Z* than between those of the two stars of System *X*.

C. System *X* has a longer period of revolution than does System *Z*.

D. System *Z* has a longer period of revolution than does System *X*.

10. The greatest total brightness shown on the light curve of an eclipsing binary system corresponds to the point in the orbit when:

F. the brighter star in the binary pair is directly in front of the darker star.

G. the larger star in the binary pair is directly in front of the smaller star.

H. the brighter star in the binary pair is directly in front of the smaller star.

J. both stars are visible.

GO ON TO THE NEXT PAGE

PASSAGE III

The utilization and replenishing of the Earth's carbon supply is a cyclic process involving all living matter. This cycle is shown below.

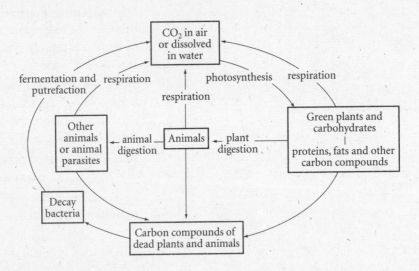

11. What effect would a sudden drop in the amount of the Earth's decay bacteria have on the amount of carbon dioxide in the atmosphere?

    A. The CO_2 level will drop to a life-threatening level since the bacteria is the sole source of CO_2.

    B. The CO_2 level will rise because the bacteria usually consume CO_2.

    C. The CO_2 level may decrease slightly, but there are other sources of CO_2.

    D. The CO_2 level will increase slightly due to an imbalance in the carbon cycle.

12. Which of the following statements are consistent with the carbon cycle as presented in the diagram?

    I. A non-plant-eating animal does not participate in the carbon cycle.

    II. Both plant and animal respiration contribute CO_2 to the earth's atmosphere.

    III. All CO_2 is released into the air by respiration.

    F. I only

    G. II only

    H. I and II only

    J. II and III only

GO ON TO THE NEXT PAGE

13. A direct source of CO_2 in the atmosphere is:

    A. the fermentation of green-plant carbohydrates.

    B. the photosynthesis of tropical plants.

    C. the digestion of plant matter by animals.

    D. the respiration of animal parasites.

14. Which of the following best describes the relationship between animal respiration and photosynthesis?

    F. Respiration and photosynthesis serve the same function in the carbon cycle.

    G. Animal respiration provides vital gases for green plants.

    H. Animal respiration prohibits photosynthesis.

    J. There is no relationship between respiration and photosynthesis.

15. The elimination of which of the following would cause the earth's carbon cycle to grind to a complete halt?

    A. Green plants

    B. Animals

    C. Animal predation

    D. Decay bacteria

PASSAGE IV

Microbiologists have observed that certain species of bacteria are magnetotactic, i.e., sensitive to magnetic fields. Several species found in the bottom of swamps in the Northern Hemisphere tend to orient themselves towards magnetic north (the northern pole of the earth's magnetic field). Researchers conducted the following series of experiments on magnetotactic bacteria.

STUDY 1

A drop of water filled with magnetotactic bacteria was observed under high magnification. The direction of the first 500 bacterial migrations across the field of view was observed for each of 5 trials and the tally for each trial recorded in Table 1. Trial 1 was conducted under standard laboratory conditions. In Trial 2, the microscope was shielded from all external light and electric fields. In Trials 3 and 4, the microscope was rotated clockwise 90° and 180°, respectively. For Trial 5, the microscope was moved to another laboratory at the same latitude.

Table 1

Trial #	Direction			
	North	East	South	West
1	474	7	13	6
2	481	3	11	5
3	479	4	12	5
4	465	9	19	7
5	484	3	11	6

GO ON TO THE NEXT PAGE

16. The theory that light was not the primary stimulus affecting the direction of bacterial migration is:

    F. supported by a comparison of the results of Studies 1 and 2.

    G. supported by a comparison of the results of Trials 1 and 2 of Study 1.

    H. supported by a comparison of the results of Trials 3 and 4 of Study 1.

    J. not supported by any of the results noted in the passage.

STUDY 2

The north pole of a permanent magnet was positioned near the microscope slide The magnet was at the 12:00 position for Trial 1 and was moved 90° clockwise for each of 3 successive trials All other conditions were as in Trial 1 of Study 1. The results were tallied and recorded in Table 2.

Table 2

Trial #	Direction			
	12:00	3:00	6:00	9:00
1	472	6	15	9
2	8	483	3	6
3	17	4	474	5
4	5	19	9	467

17. If the south pole of the permanent magnet used in Study 2 had been placed near the microscope slide, what would the most likely result have been?

    A. The figures for each trial would have remained approximately the same, since the strength of the magnetic field would be unchanged.

    B. The bacteria would have become disoriented, with approximately equal numbers moving in each direction.

    C. The major direction of travel would have shifted by 180° because of the reversed direction of the magnetic field.

    D. The bacteria would still have tended to migrate towards Earth's magnetic north, but would have taken longer to orient themselves.

18. It has been suggested that magnetic sensitivity helps magnetotactic bacteria orient themselves downwards. Such an orientation would be most advantageous from an evolutionary standpoint if:

    F. organisms that consume magnetotactic bacteria were mostly bottom-dwellers.

    G. the bacteria could only reproduce by migrating upwards to the water's surface.

    H. bacteria that stayed in the top layers of water tended to be dispersed by currents.

    J. the nutrients necessary for the bacteria's survival were more abundant in bottom sediments.

GO ON TO THE NEXT PAGE

19. Researchers could gain the most useful new information about the relationship between magnetic field strength and bacterial migration by repeating Study 2 with:

    A. incremental position changes of less than 90°.

    B. a magnet that rotated slowly around the slide in a counterclockwise direction.

    C. more and less powerful magnets.

    D. larger and smaller samples of bacteria.

20. Which of the following statements is supported by the results of Study 1?

    F. The majority of magnetotactic bacteria migrate toward the earth's magnetic north pole.

    G. The majority of magnetotactic bacteria migrate toward the north pole of the nearest magnet.

    H. The majority of magnetotactic bacteria migrate toward the 12:00 position.

    J. The effect of the earth's magnetic field on magnetotactic bacteria is counteracted by electric fields.

21. What is the control in Study 1?

    A. Trial 1

    B. Trial 2

    C. Trial 3

    D. Trial 5

PASSAGE V

A process has been developed by which plastic bottles can be recycled into a clear, colorless material. This material, called *nu-PVC*, can be used to form park benches and other similar structures. A series of experiments was performed to determine the weathering abilities of *nu-PVC*.

EXPERIMENT 1

Fifteen boards of *nu-PVC*, each $150 \times 25 \times 8$ cm in size, were sprayed with distilled water for ten hours a day for 32 weeks. All fifteen boards remained within 0.1 cm of their original dimensions. The surfaces of the boards displayed no signs of cracking, bubbling, or other degradation.

EXPERIMENT 2

Fifteen sheets of *nu-PVC*, each $2 \text{ m} \times 2 \text{ m} \times 5$ cm, were hung in a chamber in which the humidity and temperature were held constant. The sheets were irradiated with ultraviolet light for 12 hours a day for 32 weeks. At the end of the experiment, the sheets' flexibility had decreased by an average of 17.5%. The surface of the sheets showed no signs of degradation, but they had all become milky white in color.

EXPERIMENT 3

Fifteen boards, as in Experiment 1, were each found to be capable of supporting an average of 963 pounds for 15 days without breaking or bending. These same boards were then kept for 32 weeks at temperatures ranging from 5° C to −15° C. At the end of the experiment, the boards were able to support an average of only 400 pounds without bending or breaking.

GO ON TO THE NEXT PAGE

22. Based on the results of Experiment 1, which of the following conclusions concerning the effect of rain on *nu-PVC* is valid?

    F. The material absorbs water over time causing it to permanently swell.

    G. The material will be useful only in areas where there is no acid rain.

    H. The material's surface does not appear to require a protective coating to avoid water damage.

    J. The material loses flexibility after prolonged exposure to precipitation.

23. Park benches in an often snow-covered region of Minnesota are to be replaced with new ones, made of *nu-PVC*. The experimental results indicate that:

    A. the benches will suffer little degradation due to weathering.

    B. the benches would have to be stored indoors during the winter to remain usable.

    C. the benches should be varnished to prevent rain from seeping into the material.

    D. the benches will lose flexibility.

24. A reasonable control for Experiment 1 would be:

    F. a *nu-PVC* board submerged in distilled water.

    G. a *nu-PVC* board stored in a dry warehouse.

    H. a wooden board subjected to the same conditions.

    J. a wooden board stored in a dry warehouse.

25. The purpose of the ultraviolet radiation used in Experiment 2 was to:

    A. simulate the effects of sunlight.

    B. avoid damage to the material's finish.

    C. turn the boards a uniform color.

    D. test the strength of the *nu-PVC*.

26. From the information given, it can be inferred that *nu-PVC's* advantage over standard building materials such as wood is that it:

    F. is heavier and denser than other materials.

    G. can be developed in different colors and textures.

    H. is less subject to structural cracking and failure.

    J. is made from recycled plastic wastes.

27. Which of the following experiments would be the most likely to provide useful information concerning the weathering of *nu-PVC*?

    I.   Repeating Experiment 1, increasing the length of the experiment from 32 weeks to 64 weeks

    II. Investigating of the effects of sea water and salt-rich air on the material

    III. Repeating Experiment 3, decreasing the minimum temperature from −15° C to −40° C

    A. II only

    B. III only

    C. I and II only

    D. I, II, and III

GO ON TO THE NEXT PAGE

PASSAGE VI

Preliminary research indicates that dietary sugar may react with proteins in the body, damaging the proteins and perhaps contributing to the aging process. The chemical effects of glucose on lens proteins in the eye were investigated in the following experiments.

EXPERIMENT 1

A human tissue protein sample was dissolved in a glucose and water solution, resulting in a clear yellow solution. After 30 minutes, the solution became opaque. Spectrographic analysis revealed that an *Amadori product* had formed on the protein. It was determined that the Amadori products on one protein had combined with free amino groups on nearby proteins, forming brown pigmented cross-links between the two proteins. The cross-links are termed *Advanced Glycosylation End products (AGE)*.

EXPERIMENT 2

Forty-six samples of human lens proteins taken from subjects ranging in age from 12–80 years were studied under an electron microscope. The lens proteins in the samples from older subjects occured much more often in aggregates formed by cross-linked bonds than did the lens proteins in the samples from younger subjects. Fluorescent characteristics revealed the cross-links to be of two types: di-sulfide bonds and an indeterminate formation with brownish pigmentation.

EXPERIMENT 3

Two solutions containing lens proteins from cow lenses were prepared, one with glucose and one without. Only the glucose solution turned opaque. Analysis revealed that the lens proteins in the glucose solution had formed pigmented cross-links with the brownish color and fluorescence characteristics of those observed in Experiment 2.

28. It was assumed in the design of Experiment 3 that cow lens proteins:

F. have a brownish pigment.

G. react with sulfides.

H. remain insoluble in water.

J. react similarly to human lens proteins.

29. Based on the results in Experiment 1 only, it can be concluded that:

A. proteins can form di-sulfide cross-links.

B. glucose dissolved in water forms AGE.

C. glucose can react with proteins to form cross-links.

D. Amadori products are a result of glucose metabolism.

30. As people age, the lenses in their eyes sometimes turn brown and cloudy (known as senile cataracts). Based on this information and the results of Experiment 2, which of the following hypotheses is the most likely to be valid?

F. As people age, the amount of sulfur contained in lens proteins increases.

G. Senile cataracts are caused by cross-linked bonds between lens proteins.

H. Lens proteins turn brown with age.

J. Older lens proteins are more fluorescent than younger lens proteins.

GO ON TO THE NEXT PAGE

31. Which of the following hypotheses about the brown pigmented cross-links observed in Experiment 2 is best supported by the results of the three experiments?

    A. Their brownish color is caused by di-sulfide bonds.

    B. They are a natural formation which can be found at birth.

    C. They are caused by glucose in the diet reacting with lens proteins.

    D. They form when proteins are dissolved in water.

32. Based on the experimental results, lens proteins from a 32-year-old man would most likely have:

    F. more cross-links than lens proteins from a 32-year-old woman.

    G. more cross-links than lens proteins from an 18-year-old cow.

    H. more cross-links than lens proteins from an 18-year-old man.

    J. fewer cross-links than lens proteins from an 80-year-old man.

33. People with uncontrolled diabetes have excess levels of blood glucose. Based on this information and the results of the experiments, a likely symptom of advanced diabetes would be:

    A. senile cataracts, due to an increase of free amino groups in the urine.

    B. senile cataracts, due to glucose interacting with di-sulfide cross-links on lens proteins.

    C. senile cataracts, due to AGE cross-links of lens proteins.

    D. kidney failure, due to high levels of free amino groups in the urine.

PASSAGE VII

Two scientists discuss their views about the Quark Model.

SCIENTIST 1

According to the Quark Model, each proton consists of three quarks: two up quarks, which carry a charge of +2/3 each, and one down quark, which carries a charge of −1/3. All mesons, one of which is the p+ particle, are composed of one quark and one antiquark, and all baryons, one of which is the proton, are composed of three quarks. The Quark Model explains the numerous different types of mesons that have been observed. It also successfully predicted the essential properties of the Y meson. Individual quarks have not been observed because they are absolutely confined within baryons and mesons. However, the results of deep inelastic scattering experiments indicate that the proton has a substructure. In these experiments, high-energy electron beams were fired into protons. While most of the electrons incident on the proton passed right through, a few bounced back. The number of electrons scattered through large angles indicated that there are three distinct lumps within the proton.

SCIENTIST 2

The Quark Model is seriously flawed. Conventional scattering experiments should be able to split the proton into its constituent quarks, if they existed. Once the quarks were free, it would be easy to distinguish quarks from other particles using something as simple as the Millikan oil drop experiment, because they would be the only particles that carry fractional charge. Furthermore, the lightest quark would be stable because there is no lighter particle for it to decay into. Quarks would be so easy to produce, identify, and store that they would have been detected if they truly existed. In addition, the Quark Model

GO ON TO THE NEXT PAGE →

violates the Pauli exclusion principle which originally was believed to hold for electrons, but was found to hold for all particles of half-integer spin. The Pauli exclusion principle states that no two particles of half-integer spin can occupy the same state. The Δ^{++} baryon which supposedly has three up quarks violates the Pauli exclusion principle because two of those quarks would be in the same state. Therefore, the Quark Model must be replaced.

34. Which of the following would most clearly strengthen Scientist 1's hypothesis?

    F. Detection of the Δ^{++} baryon

    G. Detection of a particle with fractional charge

    H. Detection of mesons

    J. Detection of baryons

35. Which of the following are reasons why Scientist 2 claims quarks should have been detected, if they existed?

    I.   They have a unique charge.

    II. They are confined within mesons and baryons.

    III. They are supposedly fundamental particles, and so could not decay into any other particle.

    A. I only

    B. II only

    C. I and III only

    D. I, II, and III

36. Which of the following could Scientist 1 use to counter Scientist 2's point about the Pauli exclusion principle?

    F. Evidence that quarks do not have half-integer spin

    G. Evidence that the Δ^{++} baryon exists

    H. Evidence that quarks have fractional charge

    J. Evidence that quarks have the same spin as electrons

37. If Scientist 1's hypothesis is correct, the Δ^{++} baryon should have a charge of:

    A. −1

    B. 0

    C. 1

    D. 2

38. Scientist 2 says the Quark Model is flawed because:

    F. the existence of individual baryons cannot be experimentally verified.

    G. the existence of individual quarks cannot be experimentally verified.

    H. particles cannot have fractional charge.

    J. it doesn't include electrons as elementary particles.

GO ON TO THE NEXT PAGE

39. Scientist 1 says that some high-energy electrons that were aimed into the proton in the deep inelastic scattering experiments bounced back because they:

A. hit quarks.

B. hit other electrons.

C. were repelled by the positive charge on the proton.

D. hit baryons.

40. The fact that deep inelastic scattering experiments revealed a proton substructure of three lumps supports the Quark Model because:

F. protons are mesons, and mesons supposedly consist of three quarks.

G. protons are mesons, and mesons supposedly consist of a quark and an antiquark.

H. protons are baryons, and baryons supposedly consist of three quarks.

J. protons are baryons, and baryons supposedly consist of one quark and one antiquark.

IF YOU FINISH BEFORE TIME IS CALLED, YOU MAY CHECK YOUR WORK ON THIS SECTION ONLY. DO NOT TURN TO ANY OTHER SECTION IN THE TEST.

STOP

WRITING TEST
30 Minutes—1 Question

Directions: This section will test your writing ability. You will have thirty (30) minutes to compose an essay in English. Prior to planning your essay, pay close attention to the essay prompt so that you understand exactly what you are supposed to do. Your essay's grade will be based on how well it expresses an opinion on the question in the prompt, as well as its logical construction, supporting evidence, and clarity of expression based on the standards of written English.

You may use the unlined space on the next page to plan your essay. Anything written in this space will not be scored by the graders. Your essay must be written on the lined pages. While you may not need all the space to finish, you should not skip lines. Corrections and additions may be written neatly in between lines but not in the margins. Be sure to write clearly. Illegible work will not receive credit.

If you finish in under thirty minutes, you may review your essay. When time is called, lay your pencil down immediately.

DO NOT CONTINUE UNTIL TOLD TO DO SO.

School athletics have become increasingly competitive in recent years, as professional athletes are drafted at younger ages and the money and fame that professional athletes enjoy has risen to astronomical levels. Some students and school administrators believe that all student athletes should be required to maintain a minimum grade point average or be barred from playing, to ensure that they still get a good education. Others believe this requirement would be unfair because athletics and academics are unrelated, and because such a rule would make it too difficult for coaches to do their jobs. In your opinion, should student athletes be required to maintain a minimum grade point average?

In your essay, take a position on this question. You may write about either one of the two points of view given, or you may present a different point of view on this question. Use specific reasons and examples to support your position.

Use this space to *plan* your essay. Your work here will not be graded. Write your essay on the lined pages that follow.

PART FOUR: PRACTICE TESTS AND EXPLANATIONS
PRACTICE TEST FOUR

Practice Test Four: **Answer Key**

ENGLISH TEST			MATH TEST		READING TEST		SCIENCE TEST	
1. C	26. H	51. A	1. A	31. A	1. B	21. C	1. A	21. A
2. G	27. B	52. J	2. J	32. F	2. H	22. H	2. F	22. H
3. D	28. G	53. D	3. A	33. B	3. B	23. D	3. C	23. B
4. F	29. D	54. H	4. G	34. K	4. J	24. G	4. G	24. G
5. D	30. J	55. B	5. B	35. D	5. A	25. A	5. D	25. A
6. G	31. A	56. J	6. H	36. K	6. H	26. H	6. H	26. J
7. D	32. H	57. D	7. C	37. B	7. B	27. B	7. D	27. A
8. J	33. D	58. H	8. J	38. F	8. G	28. G	8. H	28. J
9. C	34. F	59. B	9. D	39. A	9. B	29. C	9. B	29. C
10. J	35. A	60. G	10. F	40. K	10. J	30. F	10. J	30. G
11. D	36. G	61. C	11. B	41. B	11. C	31. D	11. C	31. C
12. H	37. A	62. J	12. G	42. H	12. G	32. H	12. G	32. J
13. C	38. J	63. B	13. D	43. E	13. D	33. C	13. D	33. C
14. J	39. D	64. J	14. G	44. K	14. H	34. F	14. G	34. G
15. C	40. G	65. A	15. D	45. E	15. D	35. D	15. A	35. C
16. H	41. A	66. G	16. F	46. K	16. G	36. G	16. G	36. F
17. C	42. G	67. D	17. E	47. E	17. D	37. D	17. C	37. D
18. H	43. C	68. G	18. K	48. G	18. G	38. H	18. J	38. G
19. D	44. H	69. D	19. D	49. C	19. A	39. C	19. C	39. A
20. F	45. B	70. J	20. G	50. F	20. J	40. F	20. F	40. H
21. A	46. G	71. C	21. E	51. C				
22. J	47. D	72. H	22. H	52. F				
23. C	48. J	73. B	23. A	53. B				
24. G	49. B	74. G	24. G	54. J				
25. D	50. J	75. C	25. C	55. E				
			26. J	56. G				
			27. C	57. B				
			28. H	58. J				
			29. D	59. C				
			30. H	60. J				

ANSWERS AND EXPLANATIONS

ENGLISH TEST

The questions fall into the following categories, according to the skills they test. If you notice that you're having trouble with particular categories, review the following:

1. REDUNDANCY—English Workout 1

2. RELEVANCE—English Workout 1

3. VERBOSITY—English Workout 1

4. JUDGING THE PASSAGE—English Workout 2

5. LOGIC—English Workout 2

6. MODIFIERS—English Workout 2

7. READING-TYPE QUESTIONS—English Workout 2

8. STRUCTURE AND PURPOSE—English Workout 2

9. TONE—English Workout 2

10. VERB USAGE—English Workout 2

11. COMPLETENESS—English Workouts 2 and 3

12. IDIOM—English Workouts 2 and 3

13. PRONOUNS—English Workouts 2 and 3

14. SENTENCE STRUCTURE—English Workouts 2 and 3

15. PUNCTUATION—English Workout 3

PASSAGE I

1. (C)—Punctuation

At first glance, there may not seem to be anything wrong here. However, the dash after *Aegean Sea* alerts you that the writer has chosen to set off the parenthetical phrase describing *Acropolis* with dashes instead of commas. This means that you have to replace the comma after *Acropolis* with a dash, in order to have a matching pair. If there were a comma after *Aegean Sea*, this underlined part of the sentence would not need to be changed. Knowing that you need to "make it all match" will help you score points on ACT English.

2. (G)—Sentence Structure

This question tests your sense of parallelism. Your ear can often help you identify unparallel constructions. *To climb…is to have beheld* is unparallel. They should be in the same form: *to climb…is to behold.*

3. (D)—Relevance

You have the option to OMIT in this question, an option that you should definitely take. Athenian cuisine has nothing to do with the subject of the paragraph or the passage, which is the Parthenon.

4. (F)—Verb Usage

This verb is appropriately plural—the subject, *generations*, is plural—and in the present perfect tense. Choices (G) and (H) are singular verbs, while (J) is wrong because generations of architects can't all be proclaiming at the present time.

5. (D)—Sentence Structure

Run-on sentences are common in the English section. There are a couple of ways to deal with this run-on sentence. You could put a semicolon after *subtle* to separate the clauses, or you could put a period after *subtle* and make the clauses into separate sentences. Since the choices offer you both options, there must be something more. And there is: you need a comma after *For example* to set it off from the rest of the sentence. Choice (D) fixes both errors.

6. (G)—Modification

This part of the sentence sounds strange; it seems that the fact is what is being *viewed from a distance*, not the *straight columns. Viewed from a distance* is a misplaced modifier that has to be moved to a position where it clearly modifies *columns*. Choice (G) accomplishes this.

7. (D)—Punctuation

Read the sentence out loud and you'll hear that it has punctuation problems. There is no need for a semicolon or any other kind of punctuation mark between *of* and *uprightness*. Don't place a comma before the first element of a series (C), and don't place a colon between a preposition and its objects (B).

8. (J)—Logic

The phrase *because of this* doesn't make sense here. The optical illusion the architects created is not the reason you'll get a different impression of the Parthenon from the one the ancient Athenians had; the reason is that the statue of Athena Parthenos isn't there anymore. The introductory phrase that makes sense is *Of course* (J).

9. (C)—Completeness

Only by standing…Golden Age of Athens is a sentence fragment that has to be hooked up somehow to the sentence after it. You can't just use a semicolon to join the two (B) because then the first clause of the new sentence will still be only a fragment. You have to reverse the subject and verb of the second sentence to attach the fragment to it, as (C) does.

10. (J)—Modification

What was removed from the Temple? The underlined part of the sentence is an introductory modifying phrase that you know describes the statue, but the word *statue* isn't anywhere in the sentence. As a result, the sentence doesn't make sense at all; it's impossible that *all that remains* in the temple was removed in the fifth century A.D. Choice (J) makes the sentence make sense.

11. (D)—Verb Usage

Quite a few words come between the subject and the verb of this sentence. You shouldn't be fooled, though; *many* is the subject of the sentence, not *carvings, walls*, or Acropolis. Since *many* is plural, the verb of the sentence has to be plural as well. *Is* has to be changed to *are*.

12. (H)—Completeness

This sentence is really only a sentence fragment; it has a subject, *decision*, but no verb. Choice (H) rewords the underlined portion to make *Lord Elgin* the subject and *decided* the verb.

13. (C)—Pronouns

They is an ambiguous pronoun because it's not immediately clear what group *they* refers to. You can figure out from the context that *they* is the Greeks; no other group could have won independence from the Turks and demanded the carvings back from the British. To make the first sentence clear, you have to replace *they* with the Greeks.

14. (J)—Reading-Type

What could have been destroyed by explosions in the Parthenon? Carvings. The fact that some of the carvings were destroyed during a war is another good reason that many of them can no longer be found in the Parthenon, as Paragraph 4 states. Therefore, the new material belongs in Paragraph 4.

15. (C)—Judging the Passage

The answer to the question is clearly "no," the writer did not fulfill the request, because only the second paragraph discusses techniques of construction at all; even then, only one technique, the bulging of the columns, is described in any detail. The author covers several topics in the essay in addition to construction techniques, including the statue of Athena Parthenos and the fate of the carvings.

PASSAGE II

16. (H)—Verb Usage

The previous sentence tells you that "Robin is the hero"; look for a verb form that matches the present tense *is*, since the sentence continues the discussion of the ballads. (H)'s *tell* is in the right tense. (F) switches to another tense, the present progressive, which makes it sound as if the ballads were literally speaking. (G) lacks a main verb, creating a sentence fragment. (J) has the same tense problem as (F), and compounds it by adding an extra, unnecessary subject, *they*.

17. (C)—Verb Usage

Make it all match. You need a verb that is parallel to *robbing* and *killing*, so *giving* (C) is the correct choice.

18. (H)—Modification

The adjective *frequent* is the correct choice to modify *enemy*. The underlined choice uses the both the word *most* and the suffix *-est* to indicate the highest degree, or superlative form. Use one or the other, but not both. Likewise, (G) incorrectly uses "more" and the suffix *-er* together. Both of these express the comparative form—but again, you'd use one or the other, not both at once. In (J), *frequently* is an adverb and so can't describe a noun.

19. (D)—Relevance

When you see the OMIT option, ask yourself if the underlined portion is really necessary. The parentheses were a clue that the underlined part wasn't really essential. It goes off on a tangent about modern adaptations of the King Arthur legend whereas Robin Hood is the focus of the passage. (A), (B), and (C) all reword the irrelevant sentence.

20. (F)—Pronouns

This is correct as is. *Them* matches the plural noun it's standing in for: *writers*. (G) *him* and (H) *it* are singular, so they don't.

21. (A)—Punctuation

This is correct because we want the possessive apostrophe. (B) and (C) are wrong because they are the plural, not the possessive, form of Stukely. And there obviously aren't a lot of Stukelys running around. (D) is wrong because if you read it out loud you can tell that no pause—and so no comma—is called for.

22. (J)—Reading-Type

Since this passage is aimed at discussing the historical development of the Robin Hood legend, choice (J) would be most in keeping with the subject matter. (A) goes way off track; you're asked to add more information on Stukely, not on English history. (G) and (H) do relate their points to Stukely but they pursue details. The main topic of the passage is Robin Hood, not antiquaries (G). (Remember, you want a choice that is most relevant to the passage as a whole.) As for (H), King Arthur was mentioned earlier in the passage, but then only to make a point about Robin Hood. A discussion of Stukely's interest in King Arthur would stray from the topic of the passage.

23. (C)—Logic

The shortest answer is the best choice. Choices (A) and (D) wrongly imply a comparison between Robin and a nobleman, when the claim was that Robin was a nobleman. (B) is incoherent.

24. (G)—Tone

The comparison with a puppy is silly in this context since it jars with the matter-of-fact tone of this passage; all choices except (G) can be eliminated. The ACT will often try to fool you like this by sticking in a phrase that simply doesn't go with the passage's tone.

25. (D)—Punctuation

The only choice that will tie in both parts of the sentence is (D). A dash in this context correctly makes an emphatic pause between *love interest* and its appositive, *Maid Marian*. All the rest of the choices have punctuation errors. Semicolons are used between independent clauses, and the part that would follow the semicolon in (A) isn't a clause. The plural form of the noun, *interests* (B), doesn't agree with the singular article. (C) can be ruled out because there is no reason to pause in the middle of a name, and so the comma is incorrectly placed.

26. (H)—Logic

All the choices, with the exception of (H), have inappropriate connecting words. Since the passage moves to a discussion of a new time period, you should begin a new paragraph, ruling out (G). In addition, *on the one hand* should be followed by *on the other hand*. *Consequently* (F) and *therefore*

(J) wrongly imply that what follows is a result of something in the previous sentence.

27. (B)—Verb Usage

The correct verb tense, and the only choice that doesn't create a sentence fragment, is (B). *Basing* (A) and *to base* (C) create sentence fragments. Of course the omission of the verb would also result in a sentence fragment, so (D) is incorrect.

28. (G)—Logic

(G) is the only choice that fits the rest of the sentence both logically and grammatically. *And* doesn't make sense as a connecting word in the original. (H) also uses a connecting word that doesn't logically fit; *therefore* inaccurately suggests a cause and effect relationship. (J) is wrong because a semicolon should be used between independent clauses, and the first clause can't stand alone.

29. (D)—Reading-Type

Since we're told that the audience is unfamiliar with the story, it would make sense to include a summary of the Robin Hood legend (D), something the passage lacks. (A) and (C) would do nothing for a reader curious about Robin Hood, since they go off on tangents about other issues. As the passage states that Robin Hood's existence is questionable (*legendary*), (B) doesn't fit in with the stance of the writer.

30. (J)—Reading-Type

Rarely are ACT English passages written for authorities or experts; they're usually written for the general public, as (J) correctly states in this question. If the passage were directed towards "experts" (F) or "authorities" (G), much of the basic information it presents would be unnecessary and not included. Since the passage states that the existence of

Robin Hood is legendary, the passage can't be aimed at readers craving confirmation that he "was an actual historical personage," so (H) is wrong.

PASSAGE III

31. (A)—Verbosity

The shortest answer is correct. *Ten-mile* is correctly punctuated: The hyphen makes it an adjective modifying *radius*. The other answers are wordy and awkward.

32. (H)—Idiom

You don't look forward *at* something. You look forward *to* something. (G) wrongly implies that it is the brother who looks forward to the opportunity to show off the narrator's skills. (J) wrongly implies a contrast between the two parts of the sentence. Actually, it is precisely because she hasn't flown with her brother that the writer anticipates showing off her skills to him. In addition, (J) is punctuated incorrectly: you need a semicolon or a period before *nevertheless*.

33. (D)—Logic

Ever since means from the time the narrator first could read to the present time of the narrative. This span of time makes sense, since the writer is telling us how long she had planned on a journalism career. *If* in (A) signals a hypothetical situation, rather than a period of time. *Since* in (B) implies a cause and effect relationship that doesn't hold up. Why would her ability to easily read a newspaper be a reason for her career decision? *Although* in (C) signals a contrast, but there isn't one.

34. (F)—Pronouns

It's true that you use *I* and *me*, in (G) and (H), when you're writing about yourself. However, you can't say

"I always envisioned I," or "I always envisioned me." You have to say "I always envisioned myself."

35. (A)—Punctuation

(A) is correct because all you need to do is pause before the word "giving," and this pause is signaled by the comma. You don't need a colon, in (B). Colons signal lists or definitions. You don't need a semicolon in (C) either—a semicolon should be placed between clauses that could stand alone as sentences, but the second part of this sentence can't. (D) creates a sentence with no verb.

36. (G)—Modification

This is an example of a misplaced modifier. (F) and (H) make it sound as if it is the airport, and not the pilot, that is filing the flight plan. (J) is awkward (it uses a passive construction) and wordy. (G) is concise, and the verbs *filed* and *gave* are parallel.

37. (A)—Modification

The adjective *careful* should be placed next to *watch*, the noun it modifies. (B) is wrong because the reference is not to *careful airplanes*. *Neared* requires an adverb such as *carefully* before it, not an adjective. (D) is wrong because it is the people, not the crater, that are *careful*.

38. (J)—Punctuation

The colon in the original interrupts the flow of the sentence. Colons often function like equal signs. ("Here's what we need for the picnic: salami, ham, cheese, and bread.") Colons signal lists or definitions, but nothing needs to be equated in this sentence.

39. (D)—Redundancy

Since *speechless* and *mute* mean the same thing, it's redundant to use both of them.

40. (G)—Verb Usage

Steadying and *took* should be in parallel form. This makes (G) right. The verbs in (J) are parallel but they're in the present tense, which doesn't fit with the past tense verbs *shot* and *dictated* in the nonunderlined part of the sentence.

41. (A)—Tone

Since Jeff and the narrator are circling the mountain, "a description of Mt. St. Helens" would be appropriate. (B) contradicts the information in the passage; we're told that the plane must stay high enough to avoid smoke and ash. In any case, the tone of (B) doesn't suit the calm tone of the rest of the passage. (C) sounds as if it belongs in a science textbook rather than in a story. (D) wanders too far from the direct observation of the Mt. St. Helens volcano, which is the paragraph's focus.

42. (G)—Logic

Since that time is an appropriate transition. It makes clear the time shift between the day at Mt. St. Helens and the present. The other choices contain inappropriate connecting words. *However* in (F) and *nevertheless* in (J) signal contrasts, but there isn't one in the passage. *Furthermore* suggests an elaboration of what came before, but there is none in the passage.

43. (C)—Reading-Type Question

Since the author is favorably recalling a memorable past experience, *nostalgic* in (C) is the best choice. The passage is positive in tone. It's definitely not "bitter," (B), or "exhausted," (D). *Optimistic* is close but wrong. *Optimistic* means "hopeful." The passage focuses on the excitement of the past, not on the good things that might happen.

44. (H)—Judging the Passage

The use of *I* is appropriate because this is a firsthand account. First-person narratives do tend to draw the reader in. (J) is not true, since *I* is not appropriate in all types of writing. The passage is personal and chatty; it's not an example of "formal writing." The passage isn't focused on "volcanoes" in general, as (G) says, but on the Mt. St. Helens eruption, the narrator's first international story.

45. (B)—Structure and Purpose

The passage reads best if the first and second paragraphs are switched. (A), (C), and (D) confuse the time sequence of the narrative, which follows the narrator from her early dreams of becoming a photojournalist, to the memorable Mt. St. Helens story, to her present experience as a foreign correspondent.

PASSAGE IV

46. (G)—Redundancy

The description of Sherlock Holmes as "*ingenious and extremely clever*" is redundant because ingenious and extremely clever mean the same thing. You need to use only one of the two to get the point across.

47. (D)—Logic

Therefore is supposed to be a signal that the sentence that follows is a logical conclusion based on information from the preceding sentence or sentences. The use of *therefore* doesn't make any sense here because you can't conclude that everyone knows the phrase *elementary, my dear Watson* just because everyone knows of Holmes's detective abilities. Choice (C) is wrong for the same reason—*for this reason* and *therefore* mean the same thing in this context. *Although* (choice (B)) indicates some sort of contrast; this would be wrong because there is no contrast within this sentence or between this sentence and the previous one. Really, there is no need for a structural signal here at all. Choice (D) is correct.

48. (J)—Relevance

Note that this question has an OMIT option—a strong clue that the underlined portion is irrelevant to the paragraph. The theme of the first paragraph is "everyone knows who Sherlock Holmes is (or was)." The last sentence has absolutely nothing to do with this main idea, so it should be omitted. Putting parentheses around the sentence (choice (G)) will not make it more relevant, so that is not the way to solve the problem.

49. (B)—Pronouns

He is an ambiguous pronoun because it's unclear whether *he* refers to Conan Doyle or to Sherlock Holmes. You know after reading the entire sentence that "he" is Conan Doyle, so you have to replace *he* with "Conan Doyle" for the sake of clarity.

50. (J)—Verbosity

From a grammatical point of view, there is nothing wrong here; it's just unnecessarily wordy. The ACT prizes clarity and simplicity in style, which often means that the shortest answer is the best one. *To be remembered* is the most concise, and therefore the correct, answer.

51. (A)—Logic

In fact is the appropriate signal phrase here. *Despite this*, *regardless*, and *yet* would all indicate a contrast between this sentence and the previous one. There is no contrast, however; Conan Doyle did not want to be remembered as the author of Sherlock Holmes

stories, so he killed the detective off (at least for a while).

52. (J)—Modification

A modifying phrase that begins a sentence refers to the noun or pronoun immediately following the phrase. According to that rule, the phrase *having had enough of his famous character by that time* modifies *Sherlock Holmes*, which doesn't make sense at all. The sentence has to be rearranged so that the introductory phrase describes Conan Doyle. (J) is the choice that accomplishes this.

53. (D)—Relevance

Once again, take note of the OMIT choice. What do soap opera characters have to do with Arthur Conan Doyle and Sherlock Holmes? Nothing. This sentence disrupts the flow of the paragraph by being almost completely irrelevant, so it has to be omitted.

54. (H)—Verb Usage

The verb is in the wrong tense. *Has been deeply immersed* is in the present perfect tense, which is used to describe an action that started in the past and continues to the present or that happened a number of times in the past and may happen again in the future. Since Conan Doyle's immersion in spiritualism is over and done with, you have to use the simple past: *was deeply immersed*.

55. (B)—Completeness

This is a sentence fragment because there is no subject and verb; all you have is an introductory phrase and a subordinate clause starting with *that*. By omitting "that," you can turn the subordinate clause into a main clause, making "he lectured" the subject and verb (choice (B)). Choice (C) would work if the sentence began with "so convinced."

(D) is wrong because the introductory phrase can't stand alone as a sentence.

56. (J)—Redundancy

Since this sentence says that Conan Doyle and his family attempted to communicate with the dead by automatic writing, it's redundant to explain that automatic writing was thought to be a means of communicating with "those no longer among the living." Omit the underlined portion of the sentence.

57. (D)—Structure and Purpose

The second sentence refers to "these experiences," so it should come directly after the sentence that describes the paranormal experiences Conan Doyle seemed to have had. The fourth sentence is the one that talks about materialized hands and heavy articles swimming through the air, so the second sentence should come after the fourth.

58. (H)—Pronouns

There are two problems with the underlined portion of the sentence: the colon does not belong there, and the pronoun *they* is ambiguous because it doesn't refer to anything in particular in the previous sentence. Choice (H) takes care of both of these problems by dropping the colon and by spelling out what the pronoun was supposed to refer to.

59. (B)—Logic

Here you just have to pick the choice that makes sense. Sherlock Holmes is only a fictional character, so choices (A), (C), and (D) are wrong; Holmes could not possibly have said anything about Conan Doyle's spiritualism, nor will he ever. You can still wonder, however, what the esteemed detective would have said, if he were real. This is the idea behind the last sentence.

60. (G)—Reading-Type

The focus is on Conan Doyle's spirituality. Choice (G) does this; no other choice captures the scope of the passage.

PASSAGE V

61. (C)—Punctuation

Read this sentence to yourself, pausing whenever you hit a comma. It doesn't sound right, does it? Now read the sentence again without pausing for the two commas. It should sound as though it flows a lot more smoothly and naturally. There is no reason to set off *in June* from the rest of the sentence, because it is not a parenthetical phrase. The commas should be omitted.

62. (J)—Modification

There is no reason to use the comparative form of *plentiful* ("more plentiful") because nothing is being compared here. In fact, no sort of adjective is needed in front of *plentiful* at all, so the OMIT choice is the correct one.

63. (B)—Verb Usage

A look at the answer choices would have helped you spot the errors in this part of the sentence. There is no parenthesis after *needles* to match the parenthesis in front of *fallen*. Once you put the second parenthesis where it belongs, you can see that the subject of this clause is not *fallen logs, branches, and pine needles*, but rather *supply*. Since supply is singular, the verb should be singular also—*were* has to be changed to *was*.

64. (J)—Completeness

There are two problems here. One, the first "sentence" of this paragraph is really just a fragment because it doesn't have a subject or a verb. It should be the introductory phrase for the second sentence. Two, the second sentence uses *its*, the possessive form of *it*, when it should use *it was*. Merely adding an apostrophe to *its* (as choices (G) and (H) do) would be wrong because *it's* means *it is*, not *it was*; you have to have the past tense here. Choice (J) takes care of both of these problems.

65. (A)—Punctuation

This part of the sentence is okay. No punctuation is necessary. It would be a mistake to try to break the sentence up into two parts with a period or semicolon after *control* because the part that started with *in spite of* would only be a fragment. Likewise, choice (C) creates a fragment.

66. (G)—Pronoun

The phrase of *9,000 firefighters employed state-of-the-art equipment* doesn't make sense at all. You need a relative clause after *firefighters*, for example, *who employed state-of-the-art equipment*. It is not correct to use the relative pronoun *which* when referring to a person or a group of people, so choice (G) is correct.

67. (D)—Modification

As you can see from the choices, the question here is where to put the modifier *only* so that the sentence makes sense. Since the fires did not stop until the first snow, you can infer that "only nature" was able to curb the destruction (choice (D)). All of the other choices state that nature had just a limited ability to curb the destruction, which is not what the writer means to say.

68. (G)—Sentence Structure

The introductory modifying phrase is unnecessarily wordy; drop the *having been* and the phrase becomes clearer and more concise. Choice (H) is wrong

because it would produce a run-on sentence. Choice (J) is out because there is no reason to put a comma between *ecologist* and *who*.

69. (D)—Relevance

It seems at first that this sentence belongs in the paragraph because it follows the first sentence pretty naturally. Read further in the paragraph, however, and you realize that the fact that more acres burned in Alaska than in Yellowstone in 1988 is really irrelevant to the writer's argument in this paragraph. The writer is explaining that forest fires can be good for a forest, and that's why the Yellowstone fires were not such a great tragedy.

70. (J)—Redundancy

It's redundant to say *in order that continued health… be maintained*; if the health of the forest is maintained, obviously it will continue. (J) is the choice that avoids redundancy. Remember, the shortest choice is often the correct one.

71. (C)—Verb Usage

Use the present tense to describe things that are always true—"the sun comes up in the morning," "the cone only opens when exposed to great heat." Also, since the writer is talking about the cone of the lodgepole pine (which is singular), the possessive should be *pine's*, not *pines'*.

72. (H)—Logic

However is the wrong transition signal to use here because there is no contrast between this sentence and the previous one. This sentence actually supports the previous one. The fact that large animals were grazing and bedding down near the fire shows that they were indeed fire-tolerant and fire-adaptive so the appropriate signal phrase would be *in fact*.

73. (B)—Sentence Structure and Purpose

The third paragraph describes how the plant life of a forest benefits from a forest fire, while the fourth paragraph explains that the wildlife of Yellowstone survived the 1988 fires relatively well, as expected. A transition sentence between the two paragraphs is not going to say that "animals suffer" from a forest fire or that "one never knows what toll a fire will take"; these choices contradict the author's tone and opinion. (D) is an irrelevant statement. This leaves (B), which is correct because it reflects the author's opinion in both paragraphs and provides a good introduction to the fourth.

74. (G)—Modification

The problem with *judging from the recent pictures of the park* is that the phrase is modifying *forest*, and a forest obviously can't judge anything. The phrase would have been okay if the sentence read "judging from the recent pictures of the park, I think that the forest was not destroyed." In this case the phrase modifies *I*, the author, who is capable of judging. Choice (G) takes care of the problem by rewriting the sentence so that the modifying phrase is gone.

75. (C)—Reading-Type

Simply listing the endangered animal species in the park (A) would not show the fire to be relatively harmless to those species. Discussing the vulnerability of endangered birds to forest fires (B) would make the fire seem dangerous, so it's out, too. (D) may seem like an attractive choice, but it's not correct: even if the fires are infrequent, they could still be harmful to the endangered animals. (C) is the correct answer. Reports of park biologists that the endangered animals were okay during the fire would be good evidence that they were not significantly threatened.

MATH TEST

1. (A)—Percent Increase and Decrease

100 Key Math Concepts for the ACT, #33. To reduce a number by 20%, you could take 20% of the original number and subtract the result, or you could just take 80% of the original number:

New price = 80% of original price
$$= (.80)(\$125)$$
$$= \$100$$

2. (J)—Evaluating an Algebraic Expression

100 Key Math Concepts for the ACT, #52. Plug in $x = -5$ and see what you get:

$$2x^2 - 6x + 5 = 2(-5)^2 - 6(-5) + 5$$
$$= 2 \times 25 - (-30) + 5$$
$$= 50 + 30 + 5$$
$$= 85$$

3. (A)—Prime Factorization

100 Key Math Concepts for the ACT, #11. The prime factorization of 36 is $2 \times 2 \times 3 \times 3$. That factorization includes 2 distinct prime factors, 2 and 3.

4. (G)—Exterior Angles of a Triangle

100 Key Math Concepts for the ACT, #81. The exterior angles of a triangle (or any polygon, for that matter) add up to 360°:

$$x + 85 + 160 = 360$$
$$x = 115$$

5. (B)—Average Formula, Adding/Subtracting Fractions

100 Key Math Concepts for the ACT, #41, #22. Don't jump to hasty conclusions—don't just average

the denominators. Do it right—add the fractions and divide by 2:

$$\text{Average of 2 numbers} = \frac{\text{Sum}}{2}$$

$$\frac{\frac{1}{20} + \frac{1}{30}}{2} = \frac{\frac{3}{60} + \frac{2}{60}}{2} = \frac{\frac{5}{60}}{2} = \frac{\frac{1}{12}}{2} = \frac{1}{12} \times \frac{1}{2} = \frac{1}{24}$$

6. (H)—Rate

100 Key Math Concepts for the ACT, #39. Everyone pays $1.50, and the rest of the toll is based on the number of miles traveled. Subtract $1.50 from Joy's toll to see how much is based on distance traveled: $25.00 − $1.50 = $23.50. Then divide that amount by 25 cents per mile:

$$\frac{\$23.50}{\$0.25 \text{ per mile}} = 94 \text{ miles}$$

7. (C)—Multiplying and Dividing Powers, Multiplying Monomials

100 Key Math Concepts for the ACT, #47, #55. Multiply the coefficients and add the exponents:

$$3x^2 \times 5x^3 = 3 \times 5 \times x^{2+3} = 15x^5$$

8. (J)—Finding the Distance Between Two Points

100 Key Math Concepts for the ACT, #71. You could use the distance formula, but it's easier here to think about a right triangle. One leg is the difference between the xs, which is 3, and the other leg is the difference between the ys, which is 4, so you're looking at a 3-4-5 triangle, and the hypotenuse, which is the distance from P to Q, is 5.

9. (D)—Percent Formula

100 Key Math Concepts for the ACT, #32. Percent times Whole equals Part:

$$(\text{Percent}) \times 25 = 16$$

$$\text{Percent} = \frac{16}{25} = 0.64 = 64\%$$

10. (F)—Comparing Fractions

100 Key Math Concepts for the ACT, #28. For $\frac{7}{x}$ to be greater than $\frac{1}{4}$, the denominator x has to be less than 4 times the numerator, or 28. And for $\frac{7}{x}$ to be less than $\frac{1}{3}$, the denominator x has to be greater than 3 times the numerator, or 21. Thus x could be any of the integers 22 through 27, of which there are 6.

11. (B)—Factoring Other Polynomials–FOIL in Reverse

100 Key Math Concepts for the ACT, #61. To factor $6x^2 - 13x + 6$, you need a pair of binomials whose "first" terms will give you a product of $6x^2$ and whose "last" terms will give you a product of 6. And since the middle term of the result is negative, the two last terms must both be negative. You know that one of the factors is among the answer choices, so you can use them in your trial-and-error effort to factor. You know you're looking for a factor with a minus sign in it, so the answer's either B or D.

Try B first: Its first term is $3x$, so the other factor's first term would have to be $2x$ (to get that $6x^2$ in the product). B's last term is -2, so the other factor's last term would have to be -3. Check to see if $(3x - 2)(2x - 3)$ works:

$$(3x - 2)(2x - 3)$$
$$= (3x \times 2x) + [3x(-3)] + [(-2)(2x)] + [(-2)(-3)]$$
$$= 6x^2 - 9x - 4x + 6$$
$$= 6x^2 - 13x + 6$$

It works. There's no need to check D.

12. (G)—Adding/Subtracting Fractions

100 Key Math Concepts for the ACT, #22. The four fractions on the left side of the equation are all ready to be added, because they already have a common denominator: *a*.

$$\frac{1}{a} + \frac{2}{a} + \frac{3}{a} + \frac{4}{a} = 5$$

$$\frac{1 + 2 + 3 + 4}{a} = 5$$

$$\frac{10}{a} = 5$$

$$10 = 5a$$

$$a = 2$$

13. (D)—Intersecting Lines

100 Key Math Concepts for the ACT, #78. $\angle CGE$ and $\angle BGF$ are vertical angles, so they're equal, and $\angle BGF$ measures 105°. If you subtract $\angle AGB$ from $\angle BGF$, you're left with $\angle AGF$, the angle you're looking for. So, $\angle AGF$ measures 105° − 40°, or 65°.

14. (G)—Solving an Inequality

100 Key Math Concepts for the ACT, #69. You solve an inequality much the way you solve an equation: Do the same things to both sides until you've isolated what you're solving for. (Just remember to flip the sign if you ever multiply or divide both sides by a negative number.) Here you want to isolate *x*:

$$-3 < 4x - 5$$

$$2 < 4x$$

$$\frac{2}{4} < x$$

$$x > \frac{1}{2}$$

15. (D)—Interior Angles of a Triangle, Exterior Angles of a Triangle

100 Key Math Concepts for the ACT, #80, #81. Because $\overline{BD}$ bisects $\angle ABC$, the measure of $\angle ABD$ is 50°. Now you know 2 of the 3 angles of $\triangle ABD$, so the third angle measures 180° − 60° − 50° = 70°.

$\angle BDC$, the angle you're looking for, is supplementary to the 70° angle, so $\angle BDC$ measures 180° − 70° = 110°.

16. (F)—Solving "In Terms Of," Factoring out a Common Divisor

100 Key Math Concepts for the ACT, #64, #58. To express *y* in terms of *x*, isolate *y*:

$$x + 2y - 3 = xy$$

$$2y - xy = -x + 3$$

$$y(2 - x) = 3 - x$$

$$y = \frac{3 - x}{2 - x}$$

17. (E)—Parts and Whole

If you add the number of English-speakers and the number of Spanish-speakers, you get 28 + 37 = 65. But there are only 50 students, so 65 − 50 = 15 of them are being counted twice—because those 15 speak both languages.

18. (K)—Rate

100 Key Math Concepts for the ACT, #39. Set up a proportion:

$$\frac{288 \text{ miles}}{6 \text{ hours}} = \frac{x \text{ miles}}{8 \text{ hours}}$$
$$6x = 288 \times 8$$
$$6x = 2,304$$
$$x = 384$$

19. (D)—Repeating Decimals

100 Key Math Concepts for the ACT, #30. To convert a fraction to a decimal, you divide the denominator into the numerator. Clearly you don't have time to take the division out to 100 places after the decimal point. There must be a pattern you can take advantage of. Start dividing and continue just until you see what the pattern is:

$$11\overline{)4.000000...} \quad .363636...$$

The 1st, 3rd, 5th, etc. digits are 3; and the 2nd, 4th, etc. digits are 6. In other words, every odd-numbered digit is a 3 and every even-numbered digit is a 6. The 100th digit is an even-numbered digit, so it's a 6.

20. (G)—Solving a System of Equations

100 Key Math Concepts for the ACT, #67. Since it's x you're looking for, eliminate y. Fortunately, the equations are all ready for you—just add them and the $+4y$ cancels with the $-4y$:

$$
\begin{array}{r}
3x + 4y = 31 \\
3x - 4y = -1 \\
\hline
6x \quad\quad = 30 \\
x = 5
\end{array}
$$

21. (E)—Finding the Distance between Two Points

100 Key Math Concepts for the ACT, #71. The coordinates of the midpoint are the averages of the coordinates of the endpoints. The average of the x's is $\frac{2 + 12}{2} = 7$, and the average of the ys is $\frac{3 + (-15)}{2} = -6$, so the coordinates of the midpoint are $(7, -6)$.

22. (H)—Sine, Cosine, and Tangent of Acute Angles

100 Key Math Concepts for the ACT, #96. Cosine is "adjacent over hypotenuse." Here the leg adjacent to θ is 4 and the hypotenuse is 5, so $\cos \theta = \frac{4}{5}$.

23. (A)—Circumference of a Circle

100 Key Math Concepts for the ACT, #89. The radius of circle Q is twice the radius of circle P. You could use the circumference of circle P to find the radius of circle P, then double that radius to get the radius of circle Q, and finally use that radius to calculate the circumference of circle Q. It's much easier and faster, however, if you realize that "double the radius means double the circumference." If the circumference of circle P is 6, then the circumference of circle Q is twice that, or 12.

24. (G)—Evaluating an Algebraic Expression

100 Key Math Concepts for the ACT, #52. This looks like a functions question, but in fact it's just a "plug-in-the-number-and-see-what-you-get" question.

$$f(x) = x^3 - x^2 - x$$
$$f(-3) = (-3)^3 - (-3)^2 - (-3)$$
$$= -27 - 9 + 3$$
$$= -33$$

25. (C)–Integer/Noninteger, Miscellaneous Triangles

100 Key Math Concepts for the ACT, #3. If the two unknown side lengths are integers, and the sum of the two lengths has to be greater than 7, then the least amount the two unknown sides could add up to would be 8, which would make the perimeter $7 + 8 = 15$.

26. (J)–Factoring Other Polynomials–FOIL in Reverse, Factoring Out a Common Divisor

100 Key Math Concepts for the ACT, #61. First factor out an x from each term, then factor what's left:

$$2x + 3x^2 + x^3 = x(2 + 3x + x^2)$$
$$= x(x^2 + 3x + 2)$$
$$= x(x + 1)(x + 2)$$

27. (C)–Simplifying an Algebraic Fraction, Multiplying and Dividing Powers, Raising Powers to Powers

100 Key Math Concepts for the ACT, #62, #47, #48. Get rid of the parentheses in the denominator, and then cancel factors the numerator and denominator have in common:

$$\frac{x^2 y^3 z^4}{(xyz^2)^2} = \frac{x^2 y^3 z^4}{x^2 y^2 z^4} = \frac{x^2}{y^2} \times \frac{y^3}{y^2} \times \frac{z^4}{z^4} = y$$

28. (H)–Adding/Subtracting Fractions, Converting Fractions to Decimals

100 Key Math Concepts for the ACT, #22, #29. Normally you would have a choice: Either convert the fractions to decimals first and then add, or add the fractions first and then convert the sum to a decimal. In this case, however, both fractions would convert to endlessly repeating decimals, which might be a bit unwieldy when adding. In this case it seems to make sense to add first, then convert:

$$\frac{2}{3} + \frac{1}{12} = \frac{8}{12} + \frac{1}{12} = \frac{9}{12} = \frac{3}{4} = 0.75$$

29. (D)–Solving a Linear Equation

100 Key Math Concepts for the ACT, #63. This looks like a physics question, but in fact it's just a "plug-in-the-number-and-see-what-you-get" question. Be sure you plug 95 in for C (not F):

$$C = \frac{5}{9}(F - 32)$$
$$95 = \frac{5}{9}(F - 32)$$
$$\frac{9}{5} \times 95 = F - 32$$
$$F - 32 = 171$$
$$F = 171 + 32 = 203$$

30. (H)–Probability

100 Key Math Concepts for the ACT, #46. Probability equals the number of favorable outcomes divided by the total number of possible outcomes. In this problem, a "favorable outcome" is choosing a green marble—that's 4. The "total number of possible outcomes" is the total number of marbles, or 20:

$$\text{Probability} = \frac{\text{Favorable Outcomes}}{\text{Total Number of Possible Outcomes}}$$
$$= \frac{4}{20}$$
$$= \frac{1}{15}$$

31. (A)—Adding and Subtracting Polynomials, Average Formula

100 Key Math Concepts for the ACT, #54, #41. To find the average of three numbers—even if they're algebraic expressions—add them and divide by 3:

$$\begin{aligned} \text{Average} &= \frac{\text{Sum of terms}}{\text{Number of terms}} \\ &= \frac{(2x + 5) + (5x - 6) + (-4x + 2)}{3} \\ &= \frac{3x + 1}{3} \\ &= x + \frac{1}{3} \end{aligned}$$

32. (F)—Using Two Points to Find the Slope

100 Key Math Concepts for the ACT, #72. Parallel lines have the same slope. Use the first pair of points to figure out the slope:

$$\text{Slope} = \frac{y_2 - y_1}{x_2 - x_1} = \frac{16 - 1}{2 - 1} = 15$$

Then use the slope to figure out the missing coordinate in the second pair of points:

$$\begin{aligned} \text{Slope} &= \frac{y^2 - y^1}{x^2 - x^1} \\ 15 &= \frac{(25 - (-5))}{a - (-10)} \\ 15 &= \frac{30}{a + 10} \\ 15a + 150 &= 30 \\ 15a &= -120 \\ a &= -8 \end{aligned}$$

33. (B)—Similar Triangles

100 Key Math Concepts for the ACT, #82. When parallel lines make a big triangle and a little triangle

as they do here, the triangles are similar (because they have the same angle measurements). Side $\overline{PR}$ is three times the length of $\overline{QR}$, so each side of the big triangle is three times the length of the corresponding side of the smaller triangle, and therefore the ratio of the perimeters is also 3:1. So the perimeter of $\triangle PRT$ is 3 times 11, or 33.

34. (K)—Special Quadrilaterals

100 Key Math Concepts for the ACT, #86. It is a polygon because it's composed of straight line segments. It is a quadrilateral because it has four sides. It is not a rectangle because opposite sides are not equal. It is a trapezoid because it has one pair of parallel sides.

35. (D)—Evaluating an Algebraic Expression, Solving a Linear Equation

100 Key Math Concepts for the ACT, #52, #63.

Plug in $x = -3$ and solve for a:

$$\begin{aligned} 2x^2 + (a - 4)x - 2a &= 0 \\ 2(-3)^2 + (a - 4)(-3) - 2a &= 0 \\ 18 - 3a + 12 - 2a &= 0 \\ 30 - 5a &= 0 \\ -5a &= -30 \\ a &= 6 \end{aligned}$$

36. (K)—Counting the Possibilities

100 Key Math Concepts for the ACT, #45. The total number of combinations of a first course, second course, and dessert is equal to the product of the 3 numbers:

$$\text{Total possibilities} = 4 \times 5 \times 3 = 60$$

37. (B)—Prime Factorization, Least Common Multiple

100 Key Math Concepts for the ACT, #11, #14. An integer that's divisible by 6 has at least one 2

and one 3 in its prime factorization. An integer that's divisible by 9 has at least two 3s in its prime factorization. Therefore, an integer that's divisible by both 6 and 9 has at least one 2 and two 3s in its prime factorization. That means it's divisible by 2, 3, $2 \times 3 = 6$, $3 \times 3 = 9$, and $2 \times 3 \times 3 = 18$. It's not necessarily divisible by 12 or 36, each of which includes two 2s in its prime factorization.

You could also do this one by **picking numbers**. Think of a common multiple of 6 and 9 and use it to eliminate some options. $6 \times 9 = 54$ is an obvious common multiple—and it's not divisible by 12 or 36, but it is divisible by 18. The *least* common multiple of 6 and 9 is 18, which is also divisible by 18. It looks like every common multiple of 6 and 9 is also a multiple of 18.

38. (F)—Simplifying an Algebraic Fraction

100 Key Math Concepts for the ACT, #62.

$$\frac{x^2 + x^2 + x^2}{x^2} = \frac{3x^2}{x^2} = 3$$

39. (A)—Translating from English into Algebra

100 Key Math Concepts for the ACT, #65. Read carefully. This question's a lot easier than you might think. It's asking for the total number of coins, not the total value. q quarters, d dimes, and n nickels add up to a total of $q + d + n$ coins.

40. (K)—Solving an Inequality and Graphing Inequalities

100 Key Math Concepts for the ACT, #69, #70. You solve an inequality much the way you solve an equation: Do the same things to both sides until you've isolated what you're solving for.

(Just remember to flip the sign if you ever multiply or divide both sides by a negative number.)

$$5x - 2(1 - x) \geq 4(x + 1)$$
$$5x - 2 + 2x \geq 4x + 4$$
$$5x + 2x - 4x \geq 4 + 2$$
$$3x \geq 6$$
$$x \geq 2$$

The "greater-than-or-equal-to" symbol is graphed as a solid circle.

41. (B)—Using Two Points to Find the Slope

100 Key Math Concepts for the ACT, #72. First find the slope of the line that contains the given points:

$$\text{Slope} = \frac{y_2 - y_1}{x_2 - x_1} = \frac{10 - 6}{6 - 5} = 4$$

Line m is perpendicular to the above line, so the slope of m is the negative reciprocal of 4, or $-\frac{1}{4}$.

42. (H)—Sine, Cosine, and Tangent of Acute Angles

100 Key Math Concepts for the ACT, #96. Sine is "opposite over hypotenuse." Here the leg opposite θ is 12 and the hypotenuse is 13, so:

$$\sin \theta = \frac{12}{13}$$

43. (E)—Raising Powers to Powers, Solving a Linear Equation

100 Key Math Concepts for the ACT, #48, #63. Express the left side of the equation so that both sides have the same base:

$$9^{2x-1} = 3^{3x-3}$$
$$(3^2)^{2x-1} = 3^{3x-3}$$
$$3^{4x-2} = 3^{3x-3}$$

Now that the bases are the same, just set the exponents equal:

$$4x - 2 = 3x + 3$$
$$4x - 3x = 3 + 2$$
$$x = 5$$

44. (K)—Combined Percent Increase and Decrease

100 Key Math Concepts for the ACT, #35. Be careful with combined percent increase. You cannot just add the two percents, because they're generally percents of different wholes. In this instance, the 20% increase is based on the 1970 population, but the 30% increase is based on the larger 1980 population. If you just added 20% and 30% to get 50%, you fell into the test maker's trap.

The best way to do a problem like this one is to pick a number for the original whole and just see what happens. As usual, the best number to pick is 100. (That may be a small number for the population of a city, but verisimilitude is not important—all that matters is the math.)

If the 1970 population was 100, then a 20% increase would put the 1980 population at 120. Now, to figure the 30% increase, multiply 120 by 130%:

New # = (Original #) + (30% of Original #)

New # = 130% of Original #

$$x = 1.3(120)$$
$$= 156$$

Since the population went from 100 to 156, that's a 56% increase.

45. (E)—Finding the Missing Number

100 Key Math Concepts for the ACT, #44. The best way to deal with changing averages is go by way of the sums. Use the old average to figure out the total of the first 4 scores:

Sum of first 4 scores = $4 \times 89 = 356$

And use the new average to figure out the total he needs after the 5th score:

Sum of 5 scores = $5 \times 90 = 450$

To get his sum up from 356 to 450, Martin needs to score $450 - 356 = 94$.

46. (K)—Equation for a Circle

100 Key Math Concepts for the ACT, #75. If you find the distance from the center to the given point on the circle, you'll have the radius. The difference between the xs is 8, and the difference between the ys is 6. If 8 and 6 are the lengths of the legs of a right triangle, then the hypotenuse is 10. The radius, then, is 10. Now you can plug the radius and the coordinates of the center point into the general form of the equation of a circle:

$$(x - h)^2 + (y - k)^2 = r^2$$
$$(x + 1)^2 + (y + 1)^2 = 10^2$$
$$(x + 1)^2 + (y + 1)^2 = 100$$

47. (E)—Using Two Points to Find the Slope, Using an Equation to Find the Slope and the Intercept

100 Key Math Concepts for the ACT, #72, #73, #74. Use the points where the line crosses the axes—$(-1, 0)$ and $(0, 2)$—to find the slope:

$$\text{Slope} = \frac{y_2 - y_1}{x_2 - x_1} = \frac{2 - 0}{0 - (-1)} = 2$$

The y-intercept is 2. Now plug $m = 2$ and $b = 2$ into the slope-intercept equation form:

$$y = mx + b$$

$$y = 2x + 2$$

48. (G)—Percent Formula

100 Key Math Concepts for the ACT, #32. Be careful. The question is not asking, "What is $\frac{1}{4}$ of 16?" It's asking, "What is $\frac{1}{4}$ *percent* of 16?" One-fourth of 1 percent is 0.25%, or 0.0025: $\frac{1}{4}$% of 16 = $0.0025 \times 16 = 0.04$.

49. (C)—Multiplying Binomials—FOIL

100 Key Math Concepts for the ACT, #56. Use FOIL to get rid of the parentheses, and then combine like terms:

$$(s + 4)(s - 4) + (2s + 2)(s - 2)$$

$$= (s^2 - 16) + (2s^2 - 2s - 4)$$

$$= s^2 + 2s^2 - 2s - 16 - 4$$

$$= 3s^2 - 2s - 20$$

50. (F)—Equation for a Parabola and Evaluating an Algebraic Expression

100 Key Math Concepts for the ACT, #76, #52. The easiest way to find the equation of a given parabola is to take a point or two from the graph and plug the coordinates into the answer choices, eliminating the choices that don't work. Start with a point with coordinates that are easy to work with. Here you could start with (3, 0). Plug $x = 3$ and $y = 0$ into each answer choice and you'll find that only (F) works.

51. (C)—Sine, Cosine, and Tangent of Acute Angles

100 Key Math Concepts for the ACT, #96. Since $\sin a = \frac{4}{5}$, you could think of this as a 3-4-5 triangle:

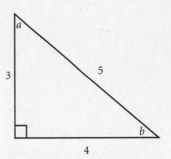

Cosine is "adjacent over hypotenuse." Here the leg adjacent to b is 4, and the hypotenuse is 5, so $\cos b = \frac{4}{5}$. (Notice that the sine of one acute angle in a right triangle is equal to the cosine of the other acute angle.)

52. (F)—Adding and Subtracting Monomials, Simplifying an Algebraic Fraction

100 Key Math Concepts for the ACT, #53, #62. Add the like terms in the numerator and then divide by the denominator:

$$\frac{x^2 + x^2 + x^2}{x} = \frac{3x^2}{x} = 3x$$

If you weren't careful, you might have confused this with problem 38 and missed the change in the denominator.

53. (B)—Translating from English into Algebra

100 Key Math Concepts for the ACT, #65. When you divide w by 4, you get $\frac{w}{4}$. When you subtract that result from r, you get $r - \frac{w}{4}$.

54. (J)—Volume of Other Solids

100 Key Math Concepts for the ACT, #95. The formula for the volume of a cylinder is $V = \pi r^2 h$, where r is the radius of the circular base and h is the height. Here $r = 4$ and $a = 5$, so:

$$\begin{aligned} \text{Volume} &= \pi r^2 h \\ &= \pi(4)^2(5) \\ &= \pi(16)(5) \\ &= 80\pi \end{aligned}$$

55. (E)—Area of a Triangle and Multiplying Binomials—FOIL

100 Key Math Concepts for the ACT, #83, #56. With a right triangle you can use the two legs as the base and the height to figure out the area. Here the leg lengths are expressed algebraically. Just plug the two expressions in for b and h in the triangle area formula:

$$\text{Area} = \frac{1}{2}(x-1)(x+1) = \frac{1}{2}(x^2 - 1) = \frac{x^2 - 1}{2}$$

56. (G)—Rate

100 Key Math Concepts for the ACT, #39. The difference between the populations in 1990 was $9{,}400 - 7{,}600 = 1{,}800$. Each year, as the larger population goes down by 100 and the smaller population goes up by 100, the difference decreases by 200. Thus it will take $1{,}800 \div 200 = 9$ years to erase the difference.

57. (B)—Miscellaneous Averages: Weighted Average

The overall average is not simply the average of the two average ages. Because there are a lot more women than men, women carry more weight, and the overall average will be closer to 25 than 35. Pick particular numbers for the females and males, say

4 females and 1 male. The ages of the 4 females total 4 times 25, or 100, and the age of the 1 male totals 35. The average, then, is $(100 + 35)$ divided by 5, or 27.

58. (J)—Sine, Cosine, and Tangent of Acute Angles and Pythagorean Theorem

100 Key Math Concepts for the ACT, #96, #84. The height h of the tree is the leg opposite θ. The distance b from the base of the tree is the leg adjacent to θ. "Opposite over adjacent" is tangent, but all the answer choices are in terms of the sine. Sine is "opposite over hypotenuse," so you're going to have to figure out the hypotenuse. Use the Pythagorean theorem:

$$(\text{hypotenuse})^2 = (\text{leg}_1)^2 + (\text{leg}_2)^2$$

$$(\text{hypotenuse})^2 = b^2 + h^2$$

$$\text{hypotenuse} = \sqrt{b^2 + h^2}$$

Now, to get the sine, put the opposite h over the hypotenuse $\sqrt{b^2 + h^2}$: $\sin \theta = \dfrac{h}{\sqrt{b^2 + h^2}}$

59. (C)—Evaluating an Algebraic Expression

Math Appendix #52. This looks like a solid geometry question, but in fact it's just a "plug-in-the-numbers" question.

$$S = \pi r \sqrt{r^2 = h^2} = \pi(3)\sqrt{3^2 + 4^2} = 3\pi\sqrt{9 + 16}$$
$$3\pi\sqrt{25} = 3\pi \times 5 = 15\pi$$

60. (J)—Parallel Lines and Transversals

Math Appendix #79. When a transversal crosses parallel lines, all the resulting acute angles are equal and all the resulting obtuse angles are equal. You can generally tell at sight which angles are equal. In this problem's figure, $a = c = e = g$, and $b = d = f = h$. Only J is true: c and g are both obtuse. In all the other choices you'll find an obtuse and an acute.

READING TEST

PASSAGE I—SOCIAL STUDIES

Here's a road map to this social studies passage on architecture:

Paragraph 1 compares architects to other professionals, noting that in an economic and social sense they are worse off than doctors and lawyers.

Paragraph 2 goes into the historical background of architecture as a profession.

Paragraphs 3, 4, and 5 discuss the passage's big idea—whether architects should try to improve their professional status. This question is posed in paragraph 3, while in paragraphs 4 and 5, the author argues that architects should emphasize the artistic value of their profession (rather than try to improve their economic and social standing).

1. (B)—Detail Question

The first sentence in paragraph 5 says that architects "seem embarrassed to present themselves as artists," choice (B). Choice (A) is wrong because paragraphs 1 and 2 show that architects want to be thought of in the same way as doctors. Although the passage mentions both builders (C) and accountants (D), there is no information that indicates that architects resent comparisons to them.

2. (H)—Detail Question

To determine the meaning of a word in the passage, it's necessary to understand the context in which that word appears. The word *privileged* comes up in the context of the author's point that doctors and lawyers, professionally speaking, are in a stronger position than architects. Thus, *privileged* in this case means "superior," choice (H).

3. (B)—Inference Question

Since the question asks about how architects came to be regarded as professionals, your mental road map of the passage should have sent you to paragraph 2, the only paragraph that discusses historical matters. Lines 27–33 say that architects convinced governments to grant them a professional license by emphasizing architecture's affect on "public health and safety," choice (B). Choices (A), (C), and (D) play on details that aren't linked to the licensing process.

4. (J)—Detail Question

The question asks why doctors and lawyers are in a better economic position than architects, so it's back to paragraph 1, where this issue is examined. The second half of the paragraph brings up three reasons why doctors and lawyers are better off: The demand for their services is "more stable," option I; they have more control over their fields, option II; and they aren't forced to deal with competitors, option III. Thus, (J) is correct.

5. (A)—Big Picture Question

The first part of the passage argues that architects are worse off economically and socially than other professionals. The second part of the passage argues that architects should concentrate on their art rather than try to improve their status. Choice (A), therefore, is correct. Choice (B), in contrast, goes against the spirit of the passage, which says that it isn't likely that architects will be able to achieve the status of doctors and lawyers. Choices (C) and (D), finally, distort details in the passage.

6. (H)—Detail Question

Architecture is described as the "mother of all arts" because of the "attributes" that "set it apart." These attributes include its unrivaled ability to "relate light, mass, and structure to produce memorable visual and spatial experiences," choice (H). Choice (G) runs counter to the thrust of the passage, which indicates that architecture is different from other arts. And choices (F) and (J) introduce issues not taken up in the text.

7. (B)—Detail Question

The effect of economic downturns on professionals is brought up towards the end of paragraph 3. Lines 59–60 note that the construction industry is "notoriously volatile," a clear indication that architects (B) face trouble in times of economic hardship. To the contrary, lines 60–66 say that doctors (A), lawyers (C), and accountants (D) are all assured of business in hard times.

8. (G)—Inference Question

Lines 88–89 state explicitly that architects aren't needed in the construction of routine, ordinary buildings, choice (G). Choices (F) and (H) are flatly contradicted in the text; and choice (J) is not dealt with in the passage at all.

9. (B)—Detail Question

The information you need is in the first two sentences of the passage. These sentences say that college students who are interested in economic prosperity are probably not going to seek a career in architecture because other professions offer more opportunity for advancement. In other words, these professions pay better than architecture. So, choice (B) is correct. Choice (D) distorts a detail in paragraph 1, while choices (A) and (C) bring up issues that the passage does not deal with at all.

10. (J)—Detail Question

Lines 49–50 indicate that law and medicine are "more fully in control of [their] domain" than

architecture, choice (J). Choices (F) and (G) are flatly contradicted by paragraph 3, which says that law and medicine are more science-based and less dependent on economic conditions than architecture. Choice (H) is contradicted by paragraph 2, which strongly implies that law, medicine, and architecture are all protected by a licensing system.

PASSAGE II—HUMANITIES

This passage tackles the *philosophes*, a group of mainly French intellectuals. Here's a road map:

Paragraph 1 defines the term *philosophes*—they were a group of thinkers who took the ideas of others and spread them through literary works.

Paragraph 2 says that the *philosophes* developed and spread the philosophy of the Enlightenment throughout Western Europe and the American colonies.

Paragraphs 3, 4, and 5 discuss the influence of Newton, Locke, and English institutions on the *philosophes*' thinking.

Paragraph 6 describes the ideas and career of perhaps the most famous *philosophe*, Voltaire.

11. (C)—Detail Question

This question asks for a description of the *philosophes*, so it's back to the first two paragraphs. Lines 13–15 say that they took the ideas of others and popularized them. The first sentence of paragraph 2 goes on to state that they "developed the philosophy of the Enlightenment and spread it to much of the educated elite in Western Europe (and the American colonies)." Thus, choice (C) is correct. Choices (B) and (D) are contradicted by information in the first paragraph, which states that the *philosophes* were generally neither professors nor scientists. Choice (A), on the other hand, is too narrow in scope: true, the *philosophes* were influenced by Locke, but they were also influenced by Newton and English institutions.

12. (G)—Inference Question

Your mental road map of the passage should have sent you directly to the last paragraph, where Voltaire is discussed. This paragraph says that Voltaire criticized both French society and religious institutions, so you can infer that he might have attacked French religious institutions, choice (G). Choice (H) is contradicted by information in the paragraph, which states that Voltaire "came to admire" English government. It's unlikely that he would have criticized the Scientific Revolution (F) because the *philosophes* were disciples of this revolution. Finally, the passage says nothing about Voltaire's views of "courtly love" (J), so you can't infer what his position on this issue would have been.

13. (D)—Detail Question

The answer to a question that contains a line reference is found in the lines around that reference. Locke's idea that "schools and social institutions could . . . play a great role in molding the individual" comes up right after his belief that humans are shaped by their experiences, choice (D). Choice (A) is contradicted by lines 45–48, while choices (B) and (C) distort details in paragraph 4.

14. (H)—Inference Question

Your mental road map should have pointed you to paragraph 3, where Newton is discussed. This paragraph says that Newton believed that "the universe [was] . . . originally set in motion by God," option I, and that "the universe operates in

a mechanical and orderly fashion," option III. But this paragraph doesn't say that Newton believed that "human reason is insufficient to understand the laws of nature," option II; if anything, it implies just the opposite. Choice (H), options I and III only, is correct.

15. (D)—Detail Question

Line 58 reveals that it was Locke who questioned the notion that "revelation was a reliable source of truth." Thus, you're looking for a work written by him, so you can immediately eliminate choices (A), *Letters on the English*, and (C), *Elements of the Philosophy of Newton*, both of which were authored by Voltaire. The remaining two works, *Second Treatise of Civil Government* (B) and *Essay Concerning Human Understanding* (D) were both written by Locke; but *Second Treatise of Civil Government* (B) is a political, not a philosophical, work, so it can be eliminated as well. That leaves choice (D) as the correct answer.

16. (G)—Inference Question

The first sentence of paragraph 4 states that Locke "agreed with Newton but went further." Specifically, Locke also thought that the human mind was subject to "the mechanical laws of the material universe," choice (G). The other choices distort details in paragraphs 3 and 4.

17. (D)—Big Picture Question

The philosophes—as paragraph 5 shows—were greatly influenced by an England that allowed more individual freedom, was more tolerant of religious differences, and was freer of traditional political institutions than other countries, particularly France. Indeed, the philosophes wanted other countries to adopt the English model. Thus, choice (D), options I, II, and III, is correct.

PART FOUR: PRACTICE AND EXPLANATIONS
ANSWERS AND EXPLANATIONS

18. (G)—Big Picture Question

Since this question also asks about England, it's right back to paragraph 5. In the second-to-last sentence of the paragraph, the *philosophes* cite England's political stability and prosperity as evidence that England's system worked. The last sentence of the paragraph goes on to say that the *philosophes* "wanted to see in their own countries much of what England already seemed to have." Choice (G), therefore, is correct. Choice (F), on the other hand, flatly contradicts the gist of paragraph 5. Finally, choices (H) and (J) distort details from the wrong part of the passage.

19. (A)—Inference Question

The French political and religious authorities during the time of Voltaire are discussed in paragraph 6. Voltaire got in hot water with the authorities over his outspoken views, so it's safe to assume that they weren't advocates of free speech, choice (A). Since they first imprisoned and then exiled him, they clearly didn't regard the *philosophes* with indifference, choice (C). The passage doesn't say precisely what Voltaire was imprisoned and exiled for, so you can't infer that the authorities "overreacted to Voltaire's mild satires" (B), which, in any case, weren't that mild. Finally, since Voltaire was an advocate of the English system of government, it's also safe to assume that the French hadn't accepted this model. So (D)'s out as well.

20. (J)—Big Picture Question

The notion that the *philosophes* were "more literary than scientific" appears in the middle of paragraph 1. A few lines further down, the paragraph furnishes a list of the types of literary works produced by the *philosophes*, so choice (J) is correct. The passage never mentions any "political change" (F). Nor

does it compare the literary outputs of Newton and Voltaire (G). Finally, choice (H) is out because the *philosophes* were not scientists.

PASSAGE III—PROSE FICTION

This passage, about an older woman called Rosemary and her grandson Victor, is essentially a story about the generation gap. Here's a road map:

In paragraph 1, Rosemary's awareness of the easy life Victor seems to be leading spurs a series of flashbacks in which she remembers her childhood experiences growing up on a farm.

Paragraph 2 relates her memories of getting up early in the morning.

In paragraph 3, Rosemary remembers her father preventing her from going to high school because he needed help on the farm. The author contrasts Rosemary's painful recollections with Victor's casual attitude towards education.

21. (C)—Detail Question

Line 10 explicitly states that Victor is Rosemary's grandson (C).

22. (H)—Inference Question

Rosemary's unease with Victor's behavior is the topic of paragraph 3. She is disturbed by his willingness to take a college course simply because it's "easy to pass," choice (H). Choices (G) and (J) distort details from the wrong paragraph, while choice (F) brings up an idea that's not in the passage.

23. (D)—Inference Question

The answer is strongly implied in the passage. Paragraph 3 notes that Rosemary wanted to go to high school after finishing grammar school.

Her father would not permit her to go, so she had to spend time "with animals and rough farmhands for company instead of people her own age" (D). Choice (B) is flatly contradicted by paragraph 3, which indicates that Rosemary wanted to go to high school, not college. Choices (A) and (C) make inferences that are not supported by the passage.

24. (G)—Inference Question

Lines 17–18 say that Rosemary "had decided long ago that growing old was like slowly turning to stone." This sentiment suggests that she is resigned to the physical problems that accompany old age. "Acceptance" (G), therefore, is correct. "Sadness" (F) and "resentment" (H) are too negative in tone, while "optimism" (J) is too positive: Rosemary, in short, isn't at all emotional about the aging process.

25. (A)—Detail Question

Rosemary's interest in crossword puzzles is discussed in the opening sentences of paragraph 1. She does them for two reasons: to pass the time and to keep her mind active, choice (A). The other choices distort details in paragraphs 1 and 2. Choice (B) plays on Rosemary's happiness at still being able to write at 87; choice (C) plays on her need to consult an atlas to look up the Swiss river; and choice (D) plays on her experience of "an expanded sense of time" as she grows older.

26. (H)—Big Picture Question

Most of the passage is about the different attitudes of Rosemary and Victor towards education (H). The first two paragraphs serve as a lead-in to this topic, while the remainder of the passage concentrates on Rosemary's thoughts and memories about education. Rosemary mentions Victor's laziness (F), but this isn't the main focus of the passage. Education is

the primary focus. There's no information at all to suggest that Victor's father has mistreated him (G). Indeed, just the opposite is implied: Victor's "doting parents," after all, have given him a new car. Finally, choice (J) doesn't mention education. Moreover, Rosemary doesn't try to suppress her memories.

27. (B)—Inference Question

The answer to a question that contains a line reference requires you to understand the context in which the reference appears. In the lines that precede the mention of Victor's "shiny new car," Rosemary considers his easy upbringing, how he looks as if he's never done a chore. In other words, Victor's car is a symbol of his generation, which has had a much easier time of it than Rosemary's. So (B) is correct. Rosemary's parents (A)—her father anyway—can't be described as generous. Besides, her parents have nothing to do with Victor's car. Similarly, while Rosemary seems to feel that Victor's future prospects are bright (C), and that his life lacks hardship (D), neither has anything to do with his car.

28. (G)—Detail Question

Paragraph 3 says that Rosemary is disturbed by Victor's dismissive attitude towards his education. She doesn't like the idea that his only reason for taking a course is that he can pass it. In contrast to Victor's attitude, in other words, Rosemary, in her youth, was eager to continue her education (G). Choices (F) and (J) refer to details from the wrong paragraphs, while choice (H) introduces an issue that the passage never tackles.

29. (C)—Detail Question

A few lines before Rosemary recalls what it was like growing up on the farm, the passage says that "Rosemary often experienced an expanded sense of time, with present and past tense intermingling in her mind." (C). Choice (D), on the other hand, alludes to recollections from the wrong paragraphs. Choices (A) and (B) distort details in paragraph 2.

30. (F)—Inference Question

The reference to Victor's bright future comes at the end of paragraph 2. It's clear from the text that it's Rosemary (F) who thinks that he has a good future. The passage never says what Victor thought about his own future (G). Nor does it say what his parents thought about his future (H). And it's extremely unlikely that Victor and Rosemary's father (J) were even alive at the same time.

PASSAGE IV—NATURAL SCIENCES

31. (D)—Detail Question

This question emphasizes the importance of reading all the choices before selecting one. The second paragraph tells us that the Alvarezes believe conditions created by the impact of a meteorite led to mass extinctions. The impact of the asteroid (A) caused great damage, but it didn't do "most of the harm"—see the third sentence. Processes like (B) and (C) are the explanations of the "traditional" scientists.

32. (H)—Inference Question

This isn't easy, but (H) is the only possible choice. The author is an objective scientist or science journalist who wouldn't want "opponents" to give up their view until the new theory has been fully tested against all their criticisms. The traditionalists' arguments are given only briefly, and the author clearly believes the Alvarezes have added something valuable to the study of mass extinctions; but the traditional view has not proven wrong

conclusively (F). And as the last paragraph indicates, traditionalists have produced their own theories to account for new evidence, such as iridium reaching the Earth's surface via volcanic activity (J). (G) is clearly not true; the author believes the new theory challenged the old one.

33. (C)—Detail Question

As it is used in the sentence, enrichment means "increase in amount." It wouldn't make sense for the earth to have (A) wealth, (B) improvement, or (D) reward of iridium.

34. (F)—Big Picture Question

The arguments of Alvarez-theory opponents are given in the last paragraph: no crater, iridium comes from the Earth's core, and the Alvarezes are only physicists. If sufficient iridium deposits come from the earth's core in lava flows (F), Alvarez supporters can't rely on them as evidence of impact. The Alvarezes didn't say extinctions never occurred without asteroid impact (G) or that all meteorites contain iridium (H). (J) contradicts one of the opponents' arguments.

35. (D)—Big Picture Question

In the first sentence of paragraph 2 the author calls the Alvarez theory important. The bulk of the passage explains and supports this theory. The implication is that the author believes the Alvarezes were on the right track. So we want a positive answer. Choices (A) and (C) are negative, and (B) is neutral.

36. (G)—Detail Question

According to the information in the second paragraph, soil displacement was the immediate result of a meteorite's impact; it "blotted out" the sun, which reduced temperatures and caused plants to die.

37. (D)—Inference Question

Look back at the second paragraph; these details clarify how the impact led to extinctions—the crater didn't simply smash all species into extinction. (A) is the wrong verb; this isn't offered as proof of the meteorite's impact, or of anything else. The lack of a known crater site (B) is mentioned at the end of paragraph 4, but that's not relevant to the discussion in paragraph 2. The conditions that result from meteorite collisions aren't evidence that the Earth is vulnerable to such collisions (C).

38. (H)—Big Picture Question

The large number of asteroids implied by "teeming" in paragraph 1 explains why Alvarez supporters believe frequent collisions must have occurred in Earth's history (paragraph 4). The fact that impact would result in certain effects (F), or the idea that the dust cloud would do more harm than the impact itself (G), or the traditional view about gradual processes (J) are not related to the number of impacts that are likely.

39. (C)—Detail Question

The two sentences at the end of paragraph 4 offer the answer; only I and III explain this position. Iridium relates to a different argument entirely.

40. (F)—Detail Question

As we've seen, the disastrous consequences of an asteroid's impact are covered in paragraph 2, where (G), (H), and (J) are mentioned. (F) is evidence of impact from paragraph 3.

SCIENCE

PASSAGE I

The first passage describes the power loss (attenuation) in optical fibers due to impurities. The graph shows the attenuation curve for fluoride glass fibers. At certain ranges in wavelength, as you can see, impurities cause a sharp increase in attenuation; for example, nickel causes a power loss of about 95 db/km at 1.5 microns. The thing to note about this graph is that attenuation in db/km (the y-axis) increases as you move downward. This means, for example, that hydroxyl causes greater power loss than either of the other two impurities.

1. (A)

Take a look at the graph and locate the point that corresponds to 1.6 microns and 95 db/km. As it turns out, this is precisely where the line dips—and attenuation sharply increases—due to the presence of nickel impurities. Therefore, copper impurities have an attenuation response similar to that of nickel (A).

2. (F)

In order to answer this question, you have to envision what the attenuation curve would look like without the sharp dips due to the impurities. It looks as though the curve would rise steadily going from left to right until it reached 5 microns and 20 db/km, at which point it would start to fall. Once you saw this, you might have been tempted to answer that power loss will "increase then decrease," but remember that the power loss increases as you go down the y-axis. This means that power loss is actually decreasing and then increasing (F) as you move along the curve from left to right.

3. (C)

At 6.6 microns, according to the graph, hydroxyl impurities in a fluoride glass fiber cause an attenuation of nearly 120 db/km. That's quite a considerable loss of power. Someone who wished to limit power loss at this wavelength would not choose to use fluoride glass fiber because of "the interference from the hydroxyl groups at this wavelength" (C). This does not mean, though, that a fluoride glass fiber does not conduct any light at this wavelength at all, as (B) suggests; it's just that a lot of power is lost.

4. (G)

This question is a follow-up to the last one. You already know that hydroxyl impurities in fluoride glass fibers cause power loss in the range between six and seven microns. It stands to reason, then, that if you could get rid of these impurities there would be less power loss both in the range of six to seven microns (Statement I) and in the fiber overall (Statement III). There is no reason to think that the attenuation due to iron impurities would increase, however, so Statement II is false. That makes (G) correct.

5. (D)

There are two steps to solving this problem. First, you have to figure out from the graph what the lowest attenuation could be for a fluoride glass fiber. The highest point on the curve—and the point of least power loss—is in the range of 5 microns, where the power loss is roughly 40 db/km. You could therefore transmit light at a wavelength of 5 microns and lose only 40 db/km. The second step to the problem is to multiply the power loss per kilometer (40 db/km) by 5 kilometers to determine what the power loss would be for a five-kilometer cable. The answer is 200 db (D).

PASSAGE II

This Data Representation passage is about binary star systems. Figure 1 shows how one star orbits around the other so that each appears to eclipse the other to the observer. The diagram is drawn so that you, the reader, are looking "down" on the system from "above"—from this vantage point you wouldn't see an eclipse. But the "observer" in the diagram is looking at the system "from the side"; from the observer's vantage point, one star can get in the way of the other and cause an eclipse.

Figure 2 is a light curve of the system. Note that the beginning and end points of the graph are the same point. In other words, when the system reaches the twentieth day it is right back where it started from, and it embarks on the cycle all over again. You can ignore the numbers on the y-axis; all you have to know is that as you go up the y-axis, brightness increases. The sharp drop in brightness between the ninth and eleventh days is what the text refers to as a deep primary minimum. The secondary minimum is the shallower dip in brightness that goes from the sixteenth day all the way around to the fourth day of the cycle.

6. (H)

Point c is the point on the light curve at which the eclipsing binary is the darkest. Take a look at Figure 1. From the point of view of the observer, System Q is going to be darkest when the light from the brighter star, Star 1, is being blocked by the light from the less bright Star 2. Star 2 interposes itself between Star 1 and the observer when Star 2 is in position 3 (H).

7. (D)

According to the x-axis of the light curve, the complete cycle of changes in the system's surface brightness (from point *a* through points *b*, *c*, and *d*, and back to point *a* again) lasts twenty days. This means that it takes Star 2 twenty days to complete its orbit around Star 1 (it is this orbit, after all, that is causing the changes in the system's brightness). (D) is the correct answer.

8. (H)

The drops in brightness on the light curve (Figure 2) indicate when one star is eclipsing the other. The sharp drop known as the primary minimum—when the darker star eclipses the brighter star—lasts approximately 2 days. The secondary minimum— when the brighter star eclipses the darker star—goes from day 16 through day 20 to day 4, a total of 8 days.

9. (B)

This question introduces two new light curve graphs. What gives System *Z* a deeper primary minimum than *X*? Well, the reason *Q* had a deep primary minimum was that one star was brighter than the other; during the time that the brighter star's light was eclipsed by the darker star, the whole system became much darker. You can safely assume that this is the reason *Z* has a deep primary minimum as well. *X*'s lack of a deep primary minimum must mean, then, that neither of its stars is significantly brighter than the other. As you can see from *X*'s light curve, the drop in brightness of the system is about the same no matter which star is being eclipsed, so the two stars must be equally bright. Since the more extreme difference in the magnitudes of System *Z*'s stars is the reason for *Z*'s deeper primary minimum, (B) is correct.

10. (J)

If either star in an eclipsing binary system is in front of the other, the brightness of the system is going to be reduced. The only time the system

reaches maximum brightness is when both stars are completely visible—when the full brightness of one star is added to the full brightness of the other (J).

PASSAGE III

This is a passage with practically no text and one diagram that illustrates the carbon cycle. Each box of the diagram is a state in which naturally occurring carbon can be found (e.g., in carbon dioxide in air or in animals) and the arrows show how carbon can move from one state to another. For example, the carbon found in carbon dioxide can, through the process of photosynthesis, be taken up by green plants and incorporated into various carbon compounds (in fact, according to the diagram, this is the only way that the carbon in carbon dioxide can enter the carbon cycle). Pay attention to the direction of the arrows.

11. (C)

Decay bacteria, according to the diagram, get carbon from the carbon compounds of dead plants and animals and add to the supply of carbon dioxide in air and water through fermentation and putrefaction. Since there is no other way to get carbon from dead plants and animals back to carbon dioxide, you know that a drop in decay bacteria will reduce the amount of carbon available for forming carbon dioxide. The carbon dioxide level will not be greatly affected, though, because there are three other sources of carbon for carbon dioxide. (C) is correct.

12. (G)

Let's take each of the statements one by one. Statement I is false because the diagram shows that the carbon in "animals" can move to "other animals" through the process of "animal digestion."

An animal that only eats other animals is participating in the carbon cycle when it digests its prey. Statement II is clearly true; there are arrows labeled "respiration" going from the "green plants," the "animals," and the "other animals" stages back to the carbon dioxide stage. Statement III, however, is not true, because some carbon dioxide is released into the air by fermentation and putrefaction. Since only Statement II is true, (G) is correct.

13. (D)

There are four direct sources of atmospheric carbon dioxide, according to the diagram: fermentation by decay bacteria and respiration by green plants, by animals, and by "other animals or animal parasites." (D) correctly cites the respiration of animal parasites. If you were tempted by (B), note the direction of the arrow for photosynthesis. Photosynthesis removes atmospheric carbon dioxide, using it as a source for carbon.

14. (G)

The arrow signifying animal respiration and the arrow signifying photosynthesis are linked in the diagram by the "carbon dioxide in air or dissolved in water" box. Animal respiration is one of the sources of carbon for carbon dioxide, and the carbon dioxide in turn provides carbon for the process of photosynthesis. In this sense, "animal respiration provides vital gases for green plants" (G).

15. (A)

Look closely at the diagram. The only way that carbon dioxide can enter the carbon cycle is through the process of photosynthesis in which it is taken up by green plants. Note that green plants also emit carbon dioxide back into the air via the process of respiration. Therefore, if green plants

were eliminated the carbon cycle would come to a complete stop and (A) is correct.

PASSAGE IV

The first paragraph of this Research Summary passage explains that the experiments were conducted on bacteria that are sensitive to magnetic fields. Study 1 tested to see whether these bacteria will migrate in the direction of magnetic north in various experimental conditions. The table of results indicates that the vast majority of bacterial migrations were in the direction of magnetic north no matter whether the microscope was in standard lab conditions, shielded, rotated, or moved to another laboratory.

Study 2 was conducted to determine whether the position of a nearby magnet would affect the direction of bacterial migration. In each experimental condition, according to the data, most of the bacterial migrations were in the direction of the north pole of the magnet. Clearly, you can conclude based on the evidence from this study and the previous one that the bacteria are sensitive to magnetic fields and tend to migrate in the direction of a magnet's north pole.

16. (G)

In order to be able to tell whether light was the stimulus affecting the direction of bacterial migration, you have to compare two trials, one with the light on and one with the light off. If there is no difference in the direction of bacterial migration in the two trials, then light does not have an effect and is not the primary stimulus. The two trials you need to compare are Trial 1 and Trial 2 of Study 1, because Trial 1 was conducted under standard lab conditions (with the light on) and in Trial 2 the microscope was shielded from all external light. Since the results of the trials differed only minimally, they support the theory that light was not the primary stimulus. (G) is correct.

17. (C)

As we saw from the data, the bacteria are sensitive to magnetic fields and tend to migrate in the direction of magnetic north. In Study 2 this meant that the bacteria moved toward the magnet because the magnet's north pole was near the slide. If the magnet's south pole were placed near the slide, the magnetic field would be reversed and the bacteria would migrate in exactly the opposite direction, away from the magnet. That makes (C) the correct answer.

18. (J)

You don't need experimental data to answer this question; you just have to figure out which answer choice provides the best reason a bacteria should be able to move downward. (F) and (G) are out immediately because both are good reasons a bacteria should move upward, not downward. While it may have been somewhat advantageous for bacteria not to be dispersed by currents (H), it would have been much more important for them to move downward to find food, so (J) is the best answer.

19. (C)

Here you have to determine which new study would yield new and useful information about the relationship between magnetic field strength and bacterial migrations. You should try to determine the experimental condition that the researchers should vary before you look at the answer choices. To gain new information about magnetic field strength and bacterial migrations, the researchers should vary the magnetic field strength and observe the effect on

bacterial migrations. (C) is correct because it suggests using more and less powerful magnets which would produce stronger and weaker magnetic fields than that of the magnet in Study 2.

20. (F)

In each of the trials of Study 1, bacterial migrations were largely found to be in the direction of magnetic north. Shielding from light and electric fields, rotation of the microscope, and movement of the microscope to another lab all had no distinct effect on the direction of migration. It is fairly easy to conclude from Study 1 that "the majority of magnetotactic bacteria migrate toward the earth's magnetic north pole" (F).

21. (A)

In any experiment, the control condition is the one used as a standard of comparison in judging the experimental effects of the other conditions. In Study 1, there would be no way to know what the effect of, say, rotating the microscope was on bacterial migration if you didn't know how the bacteria migrated before you rotated the microscope. The control condition is the trial that is run without any experimental manipulations: in this case, Trial 1 (A).

PASSAGE V

This Research Summary presents the results of three experiments that were done on the material *nu-PVC*. The purpose of the experiments was to "determine the weathering abilities of *nu-PVC*," so you can assume that each of the experimental conditions was designed to simulate some aspect of extreme weather. The method in Experiment 1 was to spray 15 boards of *nu-PVC* with distilled water 14 hours a day for 32 weeks; the boards were unaffected. The second experiment tested the ability of *nu-PVC* sheets to withstand ultraviolet light. Sheet flexibility decreased by 17.5% on average, and the sheets also turned white. In the third experiment, *nu-PVC* boards were tested for their ability to support weight before and after they were exposed for 32 weeks to cold temperatures. More than half of the boards' strength was lost as a result of this exposure.

22. (H)

According to the results of Experiment 1, *nu-PVC* does not suffer any kind of damage when exposed to water for a long period of time. It seems safe to say, then, that *nu-PVC* would not need a protective coating to avoid water damage (H).

23. (B)

The results that are relevant here are those from Experiment 3, in which *nu-PVC's* ability to withstand cold temperatures was tested. The *nu-PVC* boards did not fare well during this experiment; they lost more than half of their capacity to support weight without bending or breaking. In a cold environment, the benches could not be kept outside during the winter without sustaining damage. (B) is correct.

24. (G)

Remember that a control is an experimental condition in which nothing special is done to the thing being tested. The control serves as a standard of comparison for the experimental effects found in other conditions. In Experiment 1, the *nu-PVC* boards were sprayed with distilled water for a long period of time to see what effect the water would have. In order to assess the water's effects accurately, though, you have to compare the results of Experiment 1 to the results of a condition in which *nu-PVC* boards are not exposed to water (G).

25. (A)

Although at first this question seems to require outside knowledge, it can be answered by the process of elimination using the information in the introduction. The introduction of the passage states that the series of experiments was performed to test the weathering abilities of *nu-PVC*. The only weather phenomenon in the answer choices is sunlight (A).

26. (J)

You know nothing in particular about standard building materials from the passage—you don't know how well they stand up to rain or ultraviolet radiation or how well they support weight after exposure to cold weather. This means you cannot compare *nu-PVC* to other materials at all, which rules out (F) and (H). (G) is out because there is no information in the passage about the "different colors and textures" of *nu-PVC*. That leaves (J). (J) is correct because it is an advantage of *nu-PVC* (perhaps the only one) that it is made of recycled plastic wastes. *Nu-PVC* helps to solve the garbage problem at the same time that it fills the need for building materials; wood and other standard building materials don't do that.

27. (A)

The conditions of the original experiments were clearly chosen so that *nu-PVC* would be subjected to extremes of water, radiation and cold. There is little point in making the conditions even more extreme when a park bench would never have to survive such weather. It is unlikely, for example, that a park bench will be exposed to 32 weeks of continuous rain, much less 64 weeks, or that a bench will have to endure 8 months of −40° C temperature. Thus Statements I and III are not going to provide useful information. Statement II, on the other hand, is an important experiment, because sea water and salt-rich air may well have a corrosive effect on *nu-PVC* whereas distilled water did not. (A) is correct.

Passage VI

The purpose of the three experiments described in this Research Summary was to investigate the effect of glucose on lens proteins in the eye. You should expect, after reading the first paragraph, that glucose would be found to react adversely with the lens proteins and damage them.

Experiment 1 showed that when human tissue protein is dissolved in glucose, an Amadori product forms that causes one protein to bind with another in a brown pigmented cross-link called an Advanced Glycosylation End product. Experiment 2 demonstrated that the lens proteins in older subjects are often bound to each other by cross-links; the cross-links are either di-sulfide bonds or "an indeterminate formation with brownish pigmentation" (you can guess from the color that it is the same type of cross-link as was found in Experiment 1). In Experiment 3, it was found that the lens proteins of cow lenses form brown cross-links when dissolved in glucose—the same type of brown cross-links found in Experiment 2 (and, you can infer, in Experiment 1).

28. (J)

The researcher who designed the experiments was interested in the effect of dietary glucose on lens proteins in the human eye, not the cow eye. There would be no reason to use cow lens proteins in Experiment 3 if cow lens proteins were expected to react any differently from human lens proteins, especially when human lens proteins were readily

available for use—they were used, after all, for Experiment 1. Therefore, you know that the researcher assumed that cow lens proteins would react the same as human lens proteins (J).

29. (C)

Make sure that you stick to the results of Experiment 1 only when you answer this question. All you know from Experiment 1 is that when a human tissue protein was dissolved in a glucose and water solution, the proteins formed Amadori products that combined with other proteins to make brown cross-links. You can conclude from this that the glucose reacted with the proteins to form cross-links (C). Based on Experiment 1, though, you know nothing about di-sulfide cross links (A) or glucose metabolism (D). (B) contradicts the results of Experiment 1 because it is protein, not glucose, that forms AGE.

30. (G)

Take another look at the results of Experiment 2. It was found that in the samples from older subjects the lens proteins often formed cross-linked bonds, some of which were brown. The senile cataracts in the lenses of older people are also brown. The conclusion suggested by the identical colors of the cataracts and the cross-linked bonds is that the senile cataracts are made up of, or caused by, cross-linked bonds (G).

31. (C)

You don't know from the results of Experiment 2 how the brown pigmented cross-links developed among the lens proteins of older humans. Experiments 1 and 3 indicate, however, that glucose reacts with lens proteins in such a way that brown pigmented cross-links form among the proteins. And remember the main purpose of the experiments: the researcher is investigating the effects of glucose on lens proteins in order to see whether dietary sugar (glucose) damages proteins. The hypothesis that dietary sugar reacted with lens proteins to cause the brown pigmented cross-links found in older subjects would seem to be supported by the results of the three experiments (C).

32. (J)

The relevant results are those from Experiment 2: the lens proteins of younger subjects were found to have formed cross-linked aggregates much less frequently than the lens proteins of older subjects were. So you would expect that the lens proteins of a 32-year-old man would have fewer cross-links than the lens proteins of an 80-year-old man (J).

33. (C)

String together the hypotheses that were the correct answers from questions 30 and 31, and you have the following overall hypothesis: dietary glucose causes brown pigmented (AGE) cross-links to form among lens proteins, and these brown cross-links in turn cause the formation of brown senile cataracts. According to this hypothesis, the excess glucose in an uncontrolled diabetic's blood should cause the formation of AGE cross-links among lens proteins and subsequently the development of senile cataracts (C).

PASSAGE VII

This passage contains a lot of scientific information and terms that you probably have never seen before. Just remember that you are not expected to recognize or understand everything in the passage. Your job is to answer questions, not to learn particle physics.

Scientist 1 explains the Quark Model—the structure of the proton, the structure of mesons and baryons

in general—and then proceeds to give the reasons she thinks the Quark Model is correct. It explains the existence of the many different types of mesons, and it predicted the properties of at least one meson. Although individual quarks have not been observed, the deep inelastic scattering experiments indicated that the proton did indeed have a substructure of "three distinct lumps," which agrees with the Quark Model.

Scientist 2 asserts, however, that the Quark Model is flawed. He argues that if quarks really existed, they would have been found already; since they haven't been found, they don't exist. In addition, he says, the Quark Model violates the Pauli exclusion principle, which states that no two identical particles of half-integer spin can occupy the same state. The Δ^{++} baryon is cited as an example of a particle predicted by the Quark Model that violates the Pauli exclusion principle.

34. (G)

Scientist 1 is a proponent of the Quark Model, which says that baryons (including the proton) and mesons are made up of quarks, which have fractional charge. Quarks have never been observed, however. You find out from Scientist 2 that quarks should be easy to distinguish from other particles because they would be the only ones with fractional charge. If a particle with fractional charge was detected, then, it would most likely be a quark, and this would strengthen Scientist 1's hypothesis that the Quark Model is correct. Mesons, baryons and the Δ++ baryon have all been detected, but mere detection of them does not tell us anything about their substructure, so it cannot be used to support the Quark Model.

35. (C)

Scientist 2 says that it should be easy to split the proton into quarks; that the quarks should be easy to distinguish because of their unique charge (Statement I); and that they should be stable, because they can't decay into lighter particles (Statement III). Statement II is wrong because it is Scientist 1's explanation of why quarks cannot be detected. Therefore, (C) is correct.

36. (F)

Scientist 2 says that the Quark Model is wrong because it violates the Pauli exclusion principle, which states that no two particles of half-integer spin can occupy the same state. He says that in the Δ^{++} baryon, for example, the presence of two up quarks in the same state would violate the principle, so the model must be incorrect. If Scientist 1 were able to show, however, that quarks do not have half-integer spin (F), she could argue that the Pauli exclusion principle does not apply to quarks and thus counter Scientist 2's objections. Evidence that the Δ^{++} baryon exists (G) or that quarks have fractional charge (H) isn't going to help Scientist 1 because neither has anything to do with the Pauli exclusion principle. Evidence that quarks have the same spin as electrons (J) would only support Scientist 2's position.

37. (D)

According to Scientist 2, the Δ^{++} baryon has three up quarks. Each up quark has a charge of +2/3 each, so the three quarks together have a total charge of 2 (D).

38. (G)

Scientist 2 thinks that the Quark Model is flawed for two reasons: 1) quarks have not been detected experimentally, and they would have been if they existed, and 2) the Quark Model violates the Pauli exclusion principle. The first reason is paraphrased in (G), the correct answer. (F) is wrong because the existence of individual baryons, including protons, has been verified experimentally. Scientist 2 never says that he thinks particles cannot have fractional charge, nor does he complain that the Quark Model doesn't include electrons as elementary particles, so (H) and (J) are wrong as well.

39. (A)

The deep inelastic scattering experiments, according to Scientist 1, showed that the proton has a substructure. The three distinct lumps that were found to bounce high-energy electrons back and scatter them through large angles were the three quarks that make up the proton (at least in Scientist 1's view), so (A) is correct.

40. (H)

This question is a follow-up of the last one. If the three lumps were indeed quarks, then this supports the Quark Model because in the Quark Model the proton consists of three quarks. "Protons supposedly consist of three quarks" is not one of the choices, though, so you have to look for a paraphrase of this idea. Protons are baryons and not mesons, so (F) and (G) are out. Baryons, like the proton, are all supposed to consist of three quarks, so this rules out (J) and makes (H) the correct answer.

WRITING TEST

MODEL ESSAY

Below is an example of what a high-scoring essay might look like. Notice the author states her position clearly in the introductory paragraph and supports that position with evidence in the following paragraphs. This essay also uses transitions, some advanced vocabulary, and an effective "hook" to draw in the reader.

While some people believe academics and athletics are not related, I think it is important to hold student athletes responsible for earning a minimum grade point average. We live in a sports-obsessed world, where professional athletes receive multi-million dollar contracts and where highly paid athletes are becoming younger and younger. For example, LeBron James, still in high school, obtained a lucrative endorsement deal with Nike and was a highly sought-after NBA draft pick. Sadly, when teams are recruiting young athletes, the last thing they often look at is grades. It is also unfortunate that, feeling the pressure from alumni and fans to have successful teams, schools are often willing to overlook poor grades in their high-performing athletes. With so much money and fame at stake, and with so many institutions turning a blind eye, is it any wonder that many young athletes will sacrifice anything to get ahead, even their academic performance? Requiring student athletes to maintain a minimum grade point average is important for several reasons.

As an educational institution, a school's number-one priority should be the education of its students. The school does its student athletes a disservice when it doesn't push them to do their best at academics and learn as much as they can. It is unfair to hold other students, who may not be lucky enough to have the same natural athletic abilities, to a higher academic standard than athletes, and devalues any effort they make to get good grades by showing them in effect that what really matters in life is how good you are at sports. Also, since sports place so many demands on students' time and energy, what incentive do athletes have to take the extra time to keep up with schoolwork if they aren't required to do so?

When a school does not require student athletes to achieve a specified grade point average, it sets them up for failure later in life. The hard truth is that there are not enough jobs in professional sports for every student athlete. If students don't get drafted to play sports once they finish school, or if they do get chosen and then get injured and can no longer play the sport as well or at all, they only will have their grades and grade point average to show for their time in school. If their grades aren't good, they will have difficulty finding a job and starting a new career.

I am not trying to say that high-school sports are bad, or that they don't offer benefits to students involved in them. Not only do those students get in shape, but they also get to be on a team and feel like a part of something important. I think, however, that when schools treat academics as secondary they are taking the focus off all the positive things students get by participating in sports. When students think their athletic performance is their best chance for a post-high school career, they no longer think about accomplishments like learning discipline and improving self-esteem. They only focus on winning at all costs. Schools encourage this by making athletic performance more important than academics. If students know that they have a high enough grade point average to succeed if their sport doesn't become their career, maybe sports can go back to being fun again.

Participating in sports is a great thing for students to do. It builds self-confidence, fosters school spirit, and teaches determination. However, high schoolers should be students first. Requiring student athletes to maintain a certain grade point average would ensure that students get the education they need whether or not they go on to play professional sports. Schools' number-one priority should be making sure that all of their students, whether they are athletes or not, have the education required to succeed in life.

You can evaluate your essay and the model essay based on the following criteria, covered in chapter 16.

- Does the author answer the question?

- Is the author's position clearly stated?

- Does the body of the essay support and develop the position taken?

- Are there at least three supporting paragraphs?

- Is the relevance of each supporting paragraph clear?

- Is the essay a reasonable length?

- Is the essay organized, with a clear introduction, middle, and end?

- Did the author use one paragraph for each new idea?

- Is each sentence in a paragraph relevant to the point made in that paragraph?

- Are transitions clear?

- Is the essay easy to read? Is it engaging?

- Are sentences varied?

- Is vocabulary used effectively? Is college-level vocabulary used?

Compute Your Score

1 Figure out your score in each section. Refer to the answer keys to figure out the number right in each test section. Enter the results below:

Raw Scores

	TEST 1	TEST 2	TEST 3	TEST 4
English:				
Math:				

	TEST 1	TEST 2	TEST 3	TEST 4
Reading:				
Science:				

2 Find your Practice Test scores. Find your raw score on each section in the table below. The score in the far left column indicates your estimated scaled score if this were an actual ACT.

SCALED SCORE	RAW SCORES			
	Test 1 English	Test 2 Mathematics	Test 3 Reading	Test 4 Science
36	75	60	40	40
35	74	60	40	40
34	73	59	39	39
33	72	58	39	39
32	71	57	38	38
31	70	55–56	37	37
30	69	53–54	36	36
29	68	50–52	35	35
28	67	48–49	34	34
27	65–66	45–47	33	33
26	63–64	43–44	32	32
25	61–62	40–42	31	30–31
24	58–60	38–39	30	28–29
23	56–57	35–37	29	26–27
22	53–55	33–34	28	24–25
21	49–52	31–32	27	21–23
20	46–48	28–30	25–26	19–20
19	44–45	26–27	23–24	17–18
18	41–43	23–25	21–22	16
17	39–40	20–22	19–20	15
16	36–38	17–19	17–18	14
15	34–35	15–16	15–16	13
14	30–33	13–14	13–14	12
13	28–29	11–12	12–13	11
12	25–27	9–10	10–11	10
11	23–24	8	9	9
10	20–22	7	8	8
9	17–19	6	7	7
8	14–16	5	6	6
7	12–13	4	5	5
6	9–11	3	4	4
5	7–8	2	3	3
4	4–6	1	2	2
3	3	1	1	1
2	2	0	0	0
1	1	0	0	0

		TEST 1	TEST 2	TEST 3	TEST 4		TEST 1	TEST 2	TEST 3	TEST 4
Scaled Scores	English:					Reading:				
	Math:					Science:				

3 **Find your estimated composite score.** To calculate your estimated composite score, simply add together your scaled scores on each subsection and divide by four.

Composite Score:

TEST 1	TEST 2	TEST 3

100 KEY MATH CONCEPTS FOR THE ACT

NUMBER PROPERTIES

1. UNDEFINED

On the ACT, *undefined* almost always means **division by zero.** The expression $\frac{a}{bc}$ is undefined if either b or c equals 0.

2. REAL/IMAGINARY

A real number is a number that has a **location on the number line.** On the ACT, imaginary numbers are numbers that involve the square root of a negative number. $\sqrt{-4}$ is an imaginary number.

3. INTEGER/NONINTEGER

Integers are **whole numbers;** they include negative whole numbers and zero.

4. RATIONAL/IRRATIONAL

A **rational number** is a number that can be expressed as a **ratio of two integers. Irrational numbers** are real numbers—they have locations on the number line—they just **can't be expressed precisely as a fraction or decimal.** For the purposes of the ACT, the most important **irrational numbers** are $\sqrt{2}$, $\sqrt{3}$, and π.

5. ADDING/SUBTRACTING SIGNED NUMBERS

To **add a positive and a negative,** first ignore the signs and find the positive difference between the number parts. Then attach the sign of the original number to the larger number part. For example, to add 23 and −34, first we ignore the minus sign and find the positive difference between 23 and 34—that's 11. Then we attach the sign of the number with the larger number part—in this case it's the minus sign from the −34. So, 23 + (−34) = −11.

Make **subtraction** situations simpler by turning them into addition. For example, think of −17 − (−21) as −17 + (+21).

To **add or subtract a string of positives and negatives,** first turn everything into addition. Then combine the positives and negatives so that the string is reduced to the sum of a single positive number and a single negative number.

6. MULTIPLYING/DIVIDING SIGNED NUMBERS

To multiply and/or divide positives and negatives, treat the number parts as usual and **attach a negative sign if there were originally an odd number of negatives.** To multiply

−2, −3, and −5, first multiply the number parts: $2 \times 3 \times 5 = 30$. Then go back and note that there were three—an odd number—negatives, so the product is negative: $(−2) \times (−3) \times (−5) = −30$.

7. PEMDAS

When performing multiple operations, remember **PEMDAS,** which means **Parentheses** first, then **Exponents,** then **Multiplication** and **Division** (left to right), then **Addition** and **Subtraction** (left to right).

In the expression $9 − 2 \times (5 − 3)^2 + 6 \div 3$, begin with the parentheses: $(5 − 3) = 2$. Then do the exponent: $2^2 = 4$. Now the expression is: $9 − 2 \times 4 + 6 \div 3$. Next do the multiplication and division to get $9 − 8 + 2$, which equals 3.

8. ABSOLUTE VALUE

Treat absolute value signs a lot like **parentheses.** Do what's inside them first and then take the absolute value of the result. Don't take the absolute value of each piece between the bars before calculating. In order to calculate $|(−12) + 5 − (−4)| − |5 + (−10)|$, first do what's inside the bars to get: $|−3| − |−5|$, which is $3 − 5$, or −2.

9. COUNTING CONSECUTIVE INTEGERS

To count consecutive integers, **subtract the smallest from the largest and add 1.** To count the integers from 13 through 31, subtract: $31 − 13 = 18$. Then add 1: $18 + 1 = 19$.

DIVISIBILITY

10. FACTOR/MULTIPLE

The **factors** of integer n are the positive integers that divide into n with no remainder. The **multiples** of n are the integers that n divides into with no remainder. 6 is a factor of 12, and 24 is a multiple of 12. 12 is both a factor and a multiple of itself.

11. PRIME FACTORIZATION

A **prime number** is a positive integer that has exactly two positive integer factors: 1 and the integer itself. The first eight prime numbers are 2, 3, 5, 7, 11, 13, 17, and 19.

To find the prime factorization of an integer, just keep breaking it up into factors until **all the factors are prime.** To find the prime factorization of 36, for example, you could begin by breaking it into 4×9:

$$36 = 4 \times 9 = 2 \times 2 \times 3 \times 3$$

12. RELATIVE PRIMES

To determine whether two integers are relative primes, break them both down to their prime factorizations. For example: $35 = 5 \times 7$, and $54 = 2 \times 3 \times 3 \times 3$. They have **no prime factors in common**, so 35 and 54 are relative primes.

13. COMMON MULTIPLE

You can always get a common multiple of two numbers by **multiplying** them, but, unless the two numbers are relative primes, the product will not be the least common multiple. For example, to find a common multiple for 12 and 15, you could just multiply: $12 \times 15 = 180$.

14. LEAST COMMON MULTIPLE (LCM)

To find the least common multiple, check out the **multiples of the larger number** until you find one that's **also a multiple of the smaller.** To find the LCM of 12 and 15, begin by taking the multiples of 15: 15 is not divisible by 12; 30's not; nor is 45. But the next multiple of 15, 60, is divisible by 12, so it's the LCM.

15. GREATEST COMMON FACTOR (GCF)

To find the greatest common factor, break down both numbers into their prime factorizations and take **all the prime factors they have in common.** $36 = 2 \times 2 \times 3 \times 3$, and $48 = 2 \times 2 \times 2 \times 2 \times 3$. What they have in common is two 2s and one 3, so the GCF is $= 2 \times 2 \times 3 = 12$.

16. EVEN/ODD

To predict whether a sum, difference, or product will be even or odd, just **take simple numbers like 1 and 2 and see what happens.** There are rules—"odd times even is even," for example—but there's no need to memorize them. What happens with one set of numbers generally happens with all similar sets.

17. MULTIPLES OF 2 AND 4

An integer is divisible by 2 if the **last digit is even**. An integer is divisible by 4 if the **last two digits form a multiple of 4.** The last digit of 562 is 2, which is even, so 562 is a multiple of 2. The last two digits make 62, which is not divisible by 4, so 562 is not a multiple of 4.

18. MULTIPLES OF 3 AND 9

An integer is divisible by 3 if the s**um of its digits is divisible by 3.** An integer is divisible by 9 if the **sum of its digits is divisible by 9.**

The sum of the digits in 957 is 21, which is divisible by 3 but not by 9, so 957 is divisible by 3 but not 9.

19. MULTIPLES OF 5 AND 10

An integer is divisible by 5 if the **last digit is 5 or 0.** An integer is divisible by 10 if the **last digit is 0.** The last digit of 665 is 5, so 665 is a multiple of 5 but not a multiple of 10.

20. REMAINDERS

The remainder is the whole number left over after division. 487 is 2 more than 485, which is a multiple of 5, so when 487 is divided by 5, the remainder will be 2.

FRACTIONS AND DECIMALS

21. REDUCING FRACTIONS

To reduce a fraction to lowest terms, **factor out and cancel** all factors the numerator and denominator have in common.

$$\frac{28}{36} = \frac{4 \times 7}{4 \times 9} = \frac{7}{9}$$

22. ADDING/SUBTRACTING FRACTIONS

To add or subtract fractions, first find a **common denominator**, and then add or subtract the numerators.

$$\frac{2}{15} + \frac{3}{10} = \frac{4}{30} + \frac{9}{30} = \frac{4+9}{30} = \frac{13}{30}$$

23. MULTIPLYING FRACTIONS

To multiply fractions, **multiply** the numerators and **multiply** the denominators.

$$\frac{5}{7} \times \frac{3}{4} = \frac{5 \times 3}{7 \times 4} = \frac{15}{28}$$

24. DIVIDING FRACTIONS

To divide fractions, **invert** the second one and **multiply.**

$$\frac{1}{2} \div \frac{3}{5} = \frac{1}{2} \times \frac{5}{3} = \frac{1 \times 5}{2 \times 3} = \frac{5}{6}$$

25. CONVERTING A MIXED NUMBER TO AN IMPROPER FRACTION

To convert a mixed number to an improper fraction, **multiply** the whole number part by the denominator, then **add** the numerator. The result is the new numerator (over the same denominator). To convert $7\frac{1}{3}$, first multiply 7 by 3, then add 1, to get the new numerator of 22. Put that over the same denominator, 3, to get $\frac{22}{3}$.

26. CONVERTING AN IMPROPER FRACTION TO A MIXED NUMBER

To convert an improper fraction to a mixed number, **divide** the denominator into the numerator to get a **whole number quotient with a remainder.** The quotient becomes the whole number part of the mixed number, and the remainder becomes the new numerator—with the same denominator. For example, to convert $\frac{108}{5}$, first divide 5 into 108, which yields 21 with a remainder of 3. Therefore, $\frac{108}{5} = 21\frac{3}{5}$.

27. RECIPROCAL

To find the reciprocal of a fraction, switch the numer-ator and the denominator. The reciprocal of $\frac{3}{7}$ is $\frac{7}{3}$. The reciprocal of 5 is $\frac{1}{5}$. The product of reciprocals is 1.

28. COMPARING FRACTIONS

One way to compare fractions is to re-express them with a **common denominator.**

$\frac{3}{4} = \frac{21}{28}$ and $\frac{5}{7} = \frac{20}{28}$, $\frac{21}{28}$ is greater than $\frac{20}{28}$, so $\frac{3}{4}$ is greater than $\frac{5}{7}$.

Another way to compare fractions is to convert them both to **decimals.** $\frac{3}{4}$ converts to .75, and $\frac{5}{7}$ converts to approximately .714.

29. CONVERTING FRACTIONS TO DECIMALS

To convert a fraction to a decimal, **divide the bottom into the top.** To convert $\frac{5}{8}$, divide 8 into 5, yielding .625.

30. REPEATING DECIMAL

To find a particular digit in a repeating decimal, note the **number of digits in the cluster that repeats.** If there are 2 digits in that cluster, then every 2nd digit is the same. If there are 3 digits in that cluster, then every 3rd digit is the same. And so on. For example, the decimal equivalent of $\frac{1}{27}$ is .037037037 . . ., which is best written .037.

There are 3 digits in the repeating cluster, so every 3rd digit is the same: 7. To find the 50th digit, look for the multiple of 3 just less than 50—that's 48. The 48th digit is 7, and with the 49th digit the pattern repeats with 0. The 50th digit is 3.

31. IDENTIFYING THE PARTS AND THE WHOLE

The key to solving most fractions and percents story problems is to identify the part and the whole. Usually you'll find the **part** associated with the verb *is/are* and the **whole** associated with the word *of*. In the sentence, "Half of the boys are blonds," the whole is the boys ("*of* the boys"), and the part is the blonds ("*are* blonds").

PERCENTS

32. PERCENT FORMULA

Whether you need to find the part, the whole, or the percent, use the same formula:

$$Part = Percent \times Whole$$

Example: What is 12% of 25?
Setup: Part = .12 × 25

Example: 15 is 3% of what number?
Setup: 15 = .03 × Whole

Example: 45 is what percent of 9?
Setup: 45 = Percent × 9

33. PERCENT INCREASE AND DECREASE

To increase a number by a percent, **add the percent to 100%,** convert to a decimal, and multiply. To increase 40 by 25%, add 25% to 100%, convert 125% to 1.25, and multiply by 40. 1.25 × 40 = 50.

34. FINDING THE ORIGINAL WHOLE

To find the **original whole before a percent increase or decrease,** set up an equation. Think of a 15% increase over x as $1.15x$.

Example: After a 5% increase, the population was 59,346. What was the population *before* the increase?

Setup: $1.05x = 59,346$

35. COMBINED PERCENT INCREASE AND DECREASE

To determine the combined effect of multiple percents increase and/or decrease, **start with 100 and see what happens.**

Example: A price went up 10% one year, and the new price went up 20% the next year. What was the combined percent increase?

Setup: First year: 100 + (10% of 100) = 110. Second year: 110 + (20% of 110) = 132. That's a combined 32% increase.

RATIOS, PROPORTIONS, AND RATES

36. SETTING UP A RATIO

To find a ratio, put the number associated with the word *of* **on top** and the quantity associated with the word *to* **on the bottom** and reduce. The ratio of 20 oranges to 12 apples is $\frac{20}{12}$ which reduces to $\frac{5}{3}$.

37. PART-TO-PART AND PART-TO-WHOLE RATIOS

If the parts add up to the whole, a part-to-part ratio can be turned into two part-to-whole ratios by putting **each number in the original ratio over the sum of the numbers.** If the ratio of males to females is 1 to 2, then the males-to-people ratio is $\frac{1}{1+2} = \frac{1}{3}$ and the females-to-people ratio is $\frac{2}{1+2} = \frac{2}{3}$. Or, $\frac{2}{3}$ of all the people are female.

38. SOLVING A PROPORTION

To solve a proportion, **cross multiply:**

$$\frac{x}{5} = \frac{3}{4}$$

$$4x = 5 \times 3$$

$$x = \frac{15}{4} = 3.75$$

39. RATE

To solve a rates problem, **use the units** to keep things straight.

Example: If snow is falling at the rate of 1 foot every 4 hours, how many inches of snow will fall in 7 hours?

Setup:

$$\frac{1 \text{ foot}}{4 \text{ hours}} = \frac{x \text{ inches}}{7 \text{ hours}}$$

$$\frac{12 \text{ inches}}{4 \text{ hours}} = \frac{x \text{ inches}}{7 \text{ hours}}$$

$$4x = 12 \times 7$$

$$x = 21$$

40. AVERAGE RATE

Average rate is *not* simply the average of the rates.

$$\text{Average } A \text{ per } B = \frac{\text{Total } A}{\text{Total } B}$$

$$\text{Average Speed} = \frac{\text{Total distance}}{\text{Total time}}$$

To find the average speed for 120 miles at 40 mph and 120 miles at 60 mph, **don't just average the two speeds.** First figure out the total distance and the total time. The total distance is 120 + 120 = 240 miles. The times are 3 hours for the first leg and 2 hours for the second leg, or

5 hours total. The average speed, then, is $\frac{240}{5} =$ 48 miles per hour.

AVERAGES

41. AVERAGE FORMULA

To find the average of a set of numbers, **add them up and divide by the number of numbers.**

$$\text{Average} = \frac{\text{Sum of the terms}}{\text{Number of the terms}}$$

To find the average of the five numbers 12, 15, 23, 40, and 40, first add them: 12 + 15 + 23 + 40 + 40 = 130. Then divide the sum by 5: 130 ÷ 5 = 26.

42. AVERAGE OF EVENLY SPACED NUMBERS

To find the average of evenly spaced numbers, just **average the smallest and the largest.** The average of all the integers from 13 through 77 is the same as the average of 13 and 77: $\frac{13 + 77}{2} = \frac{90}{2} = 45$.

43. USING THE AVERAGE TO FIND THE SUM

$$\text{Sum} = (\text{Average}) \times (\text{Number of terms})$$

If the average of ten numbers is 50, then they add up to 10 × 50, or 500.

44. FINDING THE MISSING NUMBER

To find a missing number when you're given the average, **use the sum.** If the average of four numbers is 7, then the sum of those four numbers is 4 × 7, or 28. Suppose that three of the numbers are 3, 5, and 8. These numbers add up to 16 of that 28, which leaves 12 for the fourth number.

POSSIBILITIES AND PROBABILITY

45. COUNTING THE POSSIBILITIES

The fundamental counting principle: if there are **m ways** one event can happen and **n ways** a second event can happen, then there are **m × n ways** for the two events to happen. For example, with 5 shirts and 7 pairs of pants to choose from, you can put together $5 \times 7 = 35$ different outfits.

46. PROBABILITY

$$\text{Probability} = \frac{\text{Favorable outcomes}}{\text{Total possible outcomes}}$$

If you have 12 shirts in a drawer and 9 of them are white, the probability of picking a white shirt at random is $\frac{9}{12} = \frac{3}{4}$. This probability can also be expressed as .75 or 75%.

POWERS AND ROOTS

47. MULTIPLYING AND DIVIDING POWERS

To multiply powers with the same base, **add the exponents:** $x^3 \times x^4 = x^{3+4} = x^7$. To divide powers with the same base, **subtract the exponents:**
$y^{13} \div y^8 = y^{13-8} = y^5$

48. RAISING POWERS TO POWERS

To raise a power to an exponent, **multiply the exponents:** $(x^3)^4 = x^{3 \times 4} = x^{12}$

49. SIMPLIFYING SQUARE ROOTS

To simplify a square root, **factor out the perfect squares** under the radical, unsquare them and put the result in front: $\sqrt{12} = \sqrt{4 \times 3} = \sqrt{4} \times \sqrt{3} = 2\sqrt{3}$

50. ADDING AND SUBTRACTING ROOTS

You can add or subtract radical expressions only if the part under the radicals is the same:

$$2\sqrt{3} + 3\sqrt{3} = 5\sqrt{3}$$

51. MULTIPLYING AND DIVIDING ROOTS

The product of square roots is equal to the square root of the product:

$\sqrt{3} \times \sqrt{5} = \sqrt{3 \times 5} = \sqrt{15}$. The quotient of square roots is equal to the **square root of the quotient:**

$$\frac{\sqrt{6}}{\sqrt{3}} = \sqrt{\frac{6}{3}} = \sqrt{2}$$

ALGEBRAIC EXPRESSIONS

52. EVALUATING AN EXPRESSION

To evaluate an algebraic expression, **plug in** the given values for the unknowns and calculate according to PEMDAS. To find the value of $x^2 + 5x - 6$ when $x = -2$, plug in −2 for x:

$$(-2)^2 + 5(-2) - 6 = 4 - 10 - 6 = -12$$

53. ADDING AND SUBTRACTING MONOMIALS

To combine like terms, **keep the variable part unchanged while adding or subtracting the coefficients:** $2a + 3a = (2 + 3)a = 5a$

54. ADDING AND SUBTRACTING POLYNOMIALS

To add or subtract polynomials, **combine like terms:**

$(3x^2 + 5x - 7) - (x^2 + 12) =$
$(3x^2 - x^2) + 5x + (-7 - 12) = 2x^2 + 5x - 19$

55. MULTIPLYING MONOMIALS

To multiply monomials, **multiply the coefficients and the variables separately:**

$$2a \times 3a = (2 \times 3)(a \times a) = 6a^2$$

56. MULTIPLYING BINOMIALS—FOIL

To multiply binomials, use **FOIL**. To multiply $(x + 3)$ by $(x + 4)$, first multiply the **F**irst terms: $x \times x = x^2$. Next the **O**uter terms: $x \times 4 = 4x$. Then the **I**nner terms: $3 \times x = 3x$. And finally the **L**ast terms: $3 \times 4 = 12$. Then add and combine like terms: $x^2 + 4x + 3x + 12 = x^2 + 7x + 12$.

57. MULTIPLYING OTHER POLYNOMIALS

FOIL works only when you want to multiply two binomials. If you want to multiply polynomials with more than two terms, make sure you **multiply each term in the first polynomial by each term in the second.**

$$(x^2 + 3x + 4)(x + 5) =$$
$$x^2(x + 5) + 3x(x + 5) + 4(x + 5) =$$
$$x^3 + 5x^2 + 3x^2 + 15x + 4x + 20 =$$
$$x^3 + 8x^2 + 19x + 20$$

FACTORING ALGEBRAIC EXPRESSIONS

58. FACTORING OUT A COMMON DIVISOR

A factor common to all terms of a polynomial can be **factored out.** All three terms in the polynomial $3x^3 + 12x^2 - 6x$ contain a factor of $3x$. Pulling out the common factor yields $3x(x^2 + 4x - 2)$.

59. FACTORING THE DIFFERENCE OF SQUARES

One of the test maker's favorite factorables is the **difference of squares.**

$$a^2 - b^2 = (a - b)(a + b)$$

$x^2 - 9$, for example, factors to $(x - 3)(x + 3)$.

60. FACTORING THE SQUARE OF A BINOMIAL

Learn to recognize polynomials that are squares of binomials:

$$a^2 + 2ab + b^2 = (a + b)^2$$
$$a^2 - 2ab + b^2 = (a - b)^2$$

For example, $4x^2 + 12x + 9$ factors to $(2x + 3)^2$, and $n^2 - 10n + 25$ factors to $(n - 5)^2$.

61. FACTORING OTHER POLYNOMIALS— FOIL IN REVERSE

To factor a quadratic expression, **think about what binomials you could use FOIL on to get that quadratic expression.** To factor $x^2 - 5x + 6$, think about what **F**irst terms will produce x^2, what **L**ast terms will produce $+6$, and what **O**uter and **I**nner terms will produce $-5x$. Common sense—and trial and error—lead you to $(x - 2)(x - 3)$.

62. SIMPLIFYING AN ALGEBRAIC FRACTION

Simplifying an algebraic fraction is a lot like simplifying a numerical fraction. The general idea is to **find factors common to the numerator and denominator and cancel them.** Thus, simplifying an algebraic fraction begins with factoring.

To simplify $\dfrac{x^2 - x - 12}{x^2 - 9}$ first factor the numerator and denominator:

$$\frac{x^2 - x - 12}{x^2 - 9} = \frac{(x - 4)(x + 3)}{(x - 3)(x + 3)}$$

Canceling $x + 3$ from the numerator and denominator leaves you with $\dfrac{x - 4}{x - 3}$.

SOLVING EQUATIONS

63. SOLVING A LINEAR EQUATION

To solve an equation, do whatever is necessary to both sides to **isolate the variable.** To solve $5x - 12 = -2x + 9$, first get all the x's on one side by adding $2x$ to both sides: $7x - 12 = 9$. Then add 12 to both sides: $7x = 21$, then divide both sides by 7 to get: $x = 3$.

64. SOLVING "IN TERMS OF"

To solve an equation for one variable **in terms of** another means to **isolate the one variable on one side of the equation,** leaving an expression containing the other variable on the other side. To solve $3x - 10y = -5x + 6y$ for x in terms of y, isolate x:

$$3x - 10y = -5x + 6y$$
$$3x + 5x = 6y + 10y$$
$$8x = 16y$$
$$x = 2y$$

65. TRANSLATING FROM ENGLISH INTO ALGEBRA

To translate from English into algebra, look for the key words and systematically turn phrases into algebraic expressions and sentences into equations. Be careful about order, especially when subtraction is called for.

Example: The charge for a phone call is r cents for the first 3 minutes and s cents for each minute thereafter. What is the cost, in cents, of a call lasting exactly t minutes? ($t > 3$)

Setup: The charge begins with r, and then something more is added, depending on the length of the call. The amount added is s times the number of minutes past 3 minutes. If the total number of minutes is t, then the number of minutes past 3 is $t - 3$. So the charge is $r + s(t - 3)$.

INTERMEDIATE ALGEBRA

66. SOLVING A QUADRATIC EQUATION

To solve a quadratic equation, put it in the $ax^2 + bx + c = 0$ form, **factor** the left side (if you can), and set each factor equal to 0 separately to get the two solutions. To solve $x^2 + 12 = 7x$, first rewrite it as $x^2 - 7x + 12 = 0$. Then factor the left side:

$$(x - 3)(x - 4) = 0$$
$$x - 3 = 0 \text{ or } x - 4 = 0$$
$$x = 3 \text{ or } 4$$

Sometimes the left side might not be obviously factorable. You can always use the **quadratic formula.** Just plug in the coefficients a, b, and c from $ax^2 + bx + c = 0$ into the formula:

$$\frac{-b \pm \sqrt{b^2 - 4ac}}{2a}$$

To solve $x^2 + 4x + 2 = 0$, plug $a = 1$, $b = 4$, and $c = 2$ into the formula:

$$x = \frac{-4 \pm \sqrt{4^2 - 4 \times 1 \times 2}}{2 \times 1}$$

$$= \frac{-4 \pm \sqrt{8}}{2} = -2 \pm \sqrt{2}$$

67. SOLVING A SYSTEM OF EQUATIONS

You can solve for two variables only if you have two distinct equations. Two forms of the same equation will not be adequate. **Combine the equations in such a way that one of the variables cancels out.** To solve the two equations $4x + 3y = 8$ and $x + y = 3$, multiply both sides of the second equation by -3 to get: $-3x - 3y = -9$. Now add the equations; the $3y$ and the $-3y$ cancel out, leaving: $x = -1$. Plug that back into either one of the original equations and you'll find that $y = 4$.

68. SOLVING AN EQUATION THAT INCLUDES ABSOLUTE VALUE SIGNS

To solve an equation that includes absolute value signs, **think about the two different cases.** For example, to solve the equation $|x-12| = 3$, think of it as two equations:

$$x - 12 = 3 \text{ or } x - 12 = -3$$

$$x = 15 \text{ or } 9$$

69. SOLVING AN INEQUALITY

To solve an inequality, do whatever is necessary to both sides to **isolate the variable.** Just remember that when you **multiply or divide both sides by a negative number,** you must **reverse the sign.** To solve $-5x + 7 < -3$, subtract 7 from both sides to get: $-5x < -10$. Now divide both sides by -5, remembering to reverse the sign: $x > 2$.

70. GRAPHING INEQUALITIES

To graph a range of values, use a thick, black line over the number line, and at the end(s) of the range, use a **solid circle** if the point *is* included or an **open circle** if the point is ***not*** included. The figure here shows the graph of $-3 < x \leq 5$.

COORDINATE GEOMETRY

71. FINDING THE DISTANCE BETWEEN TWO POINTS

To find the distance between points, **use the Pythagorean theorem or special right triangles.** The difference between the xs is one leg and the difference between the ys is the other leg.

In the figure above, $\overline{PQ}$ is the hypotenuse of a 3-4-5 triangle, so $PQ = 5$.

You can also use the **distance formula:**

$$d = \sqrt{(x_2 - x_1)^2 + (y_2 - y_1)^2}$$

To find the distance between $R(3, 6)$ and $S(5, -2)$:

$$d = \sqrt{(5-3)^2 + (-2-6)^2}$$
$$= \sqrt{(2)^2 + (-8)^2}$$
$$= \sqrt{68} = 2\sqrt{7}$$

72. USING TWO POINTS TO FIND THE SLOPE

In mathematics, the slope of a line is often called m.

$$\text{Slope } = m = \frac{\text{Change in } y}{\text{Change in } x} = \frac{\text{Rise}}{\text{Run}}$$

The slope of the line that contains the points $A(2, 3)$ and $B(0, -1)$ is:

$$\frac{y_2 - y_1}{x_2 - x_1} = \frac{-1 - 3}{0 - 2} = \frac{-4}{-2} = 2$$

73. USING AN EQUATION TO FIND THE SLOPE

To find the slope of a line from an equation, put the equation into the **slope-intercept** form:

$$y = mx + b$$

The slope is m. To find the slope of the equation $3x + 2y = 4$, reexpress it:

$$3x + 2y = 4$$
$$2y = -3x + 4$$
$$y = -\frac{3}{2}x + 2$$

The slope is $-\frac{3}{2}$.

74. USING AN EQUATION TO FIND AN INTERCEPT

To find the y-intercept, you can either put the equation into $y = mx + b$ (**slope-intercept**) form—in which case b is the y-intercept—or you can just plug $x = 0$ into the equation and

solve for y. To find the x-intercept, plug $y = 0$ into the equation and solve for x.

75. EQUATION FOR A CIRCLE

The equation for a circle of radius r and centered at (h, k) is

$$(x - h)^2 + (y - k)^2 = r^2$$

The figure below shows the graph of the equation

$$(x - 2)^2 + (y + 1)^2 = 25:$$

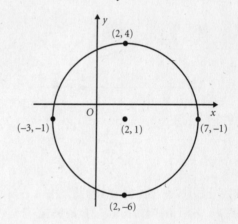

76. EQUATION FOR A PARABOLA

The graph of an equation in the form $y = ax^2 + bx + c$ is a parabola. The figure below shows the graph of seven pairs of numbers that satisfy the equation $y = x^2 - 4x + 3$:

77. EQUATION FOR AN ELLIPSE

The graph of an equation in the form

$$\frac{x^2}{a^2} + \frac{y^2}{b^2} = 1$$

is an ellipse with $2a$ as the sum of the focal radii and with foci on the x-axis at $(0, -c)$ and $(0, c)$, where $c = \sqrt{a^2 - b^2}$. The following figure shows the graph of $\frac{x^2}{25} + \frac{y^2}{16} = 1$:

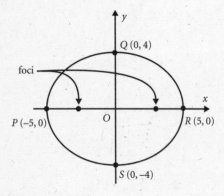

The foci are at $(-3, 0)$ and $(3, 0)$. $\overline{PR}$ is the **major axis**, and $\overline{QS}$ is the **minor axis.** This ellipse is symmetrical about both the x- and y-axes.

LINES AND ANGLES

78. INTERSECTING LINES

When two lines intersect, **adjacent angles are supplementary** and **vertical angles are equal.**

In the figure above, the angles marked $a°$ and $b°$ are adjacent and supplementary, so $a + b = 180$. Furthermore, the angles marked $a°$ and $60°$ are vertical and equal, so $a = 60$.

79. PARALLEL LINES AND TRANSVERSALS

A transversal across parallel lines forms **four equal acute angles and four equal obtuse angles.**

Here, line 1 is parallel to line 2. Angles a, c, e, and g are obtuse, so they are all equal. Angles b, d, f, and h are acute, so they are all equal.

Furthermore, **any of the acute angles is supplementary to any of the obtuse angles.** Angles a and h are supplementary, as are b and e, c and f, and so on.

TRIANGLES—GENERAL

80. INTERIOR ANGLES OF A TRIANGLE

The three angles of any triangle **add up to 180°.**

In the figure above, $x + 50 + 100 = 180$, so $x = 30$.

81. EXTERIOR ANGLES OF A TRIANGLE

An exterior angle of a triangle is equal to the **sum of the remote interior angles.**

In the figure above, the exterior angle labeled $x°$ is equal to the sum of the remote interior angles:

$$x = 50 + 100 = 150$$

The three exterior angles of any triangle add up to 360°.

In the figure above, $a + b + c = 360$.

82. SIMILAR TRIANGLES

Similar triangles have the same shape: **corresponding angles are equal and corresponding sides are proportional.**

The triangles above are similar because they have the same angles. The 3 corresponds to the 4 and the 6 corresponds to the s.

$$\frac{3}{4} = \frac{6}{s}$$
$$3s = 24$$
$$s = 8$$

83. AREA OF A TRIANGLE

Area of Triangle $= \frac{1}{2}$ (base)(height)

The height is the perpendicular distance between the side that's chosen as the base and the opposite vertex.

In the triangle above, 4 is the height when the 7 is chosen as the base.

$$\text{Area} = \frac{1}{2} bh = \frac{1}{2} (7)(4) = 14$$

RIGHT TRIANGLES

84. PYTHAGOREAN THEOREM

For all right triangles:

$$(\text{leg}_1)^2 + (\text{leg}_2)^2 = (\text{hypotenuse})^2$$

If one leg is 2 and the other leg is 3, then:

$$2^2 + 3^2 = c^2$$
$$c^2 = 4 + 9$$
$$c = \sqrt{13}$$

85. SPECIAL RIGHT TRIANGLES

• 3-4-5

If a right triangle's leg-to-leg ratio is 3:4, or if the leg-to-hypotenuse ratio is 3:5 or 4:5, then it's a 3-4-5 triangle and you don't need to use the Pythagorean theorem to find the third side. Just figure out what multiple of 3-4-5 it is.

In the right triangle above, one leg is 30 and the hypotenuse is 50. This is 10 times 3-4-5. The other leg is 40.

• 5-12-13

If a right triangle's leg-to-leg ratio is 5:12, or if the leg-to-hypotenuse ratio is 5:13 or 12:13, then it's a 5-12-13 triangle and you don't need to use the Pythagorean theorem to find the third side. Just figure out what multiple of 5-12-13 it is.

Here one leg is 36 and the hypotenuse is 39. This is 3 times 5-12-13. The other leg is 15.

• 30°-60°-90°

The sides of a 30°-60°-90° triangle are in a ratio of $1:\sqrt{3}:2$. You don't need to use the Pythagorean theorem.

If the hypotenuse is 6, then the shorter leg is half that, or 3; and then the longer leg is equal to the short leg times $\sqrt{3}$, or $3\sqrt{3}$.

• 45°-45°-90°

The sides of a 45°-45°-90° triangle are in a ratio of $1:1:\sqrt{2}$.

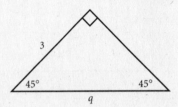

If one leg is 3, then the other leg is also 3, and the hypotenuse is equal to a leg times $\sqrt{2}$, or $3\sqrt{2}$.

OTHER POLYGONS

86. SPECIAL QUADRILATERALS

• Rectangle

A rectangle is a **four-sided figure with four right angles.** Opposite sides are equal. Diagonals are equal.

Quadrilateral *ABCD* above is shown to have three right angles. The fourth angle therefore also measures 90°, and *ABCD* is a rectangle. The perimeter of a rectangle is equal to the sum of the lengths of the four sides, which is equivalent to 2(length + width).

• Parallelogram

A parallelogram has **two pairs of parallel sides.** Opposite sides are equal. Opposite angles are equal. Consecutive angles add up to 180°.

In the figure above, *s* is the length of the side opposite the 3, so *s* = 3.

• Square

A square is a **rectangle with 4 equal sides.**

If *PQRS* is a square, all sides are the same length as *QR*. The perimeter of a square is equal to four times the length of one side.

• Trapezoid

A **trapezoid** is a quadrilateral with one pair of parallel sides and one pair of nonparallel sides.

In the quadrilateral above, sides $\overline{EF}$ and $\overline{GH}$ are parallel, while sides $\overline{EH}$ and $\overline{FG}$ are not parallel. *EFGH* is therefore a trapezoid.

87. AREAS OF SPECIAL QUADRILATERALS

Area of Rectangle = Length × Width

The area of a 7-by-3 rectangle is $7 \times 3 = 21$.

Area of Parallelogram = Base × Height

The area of a parallelogram with a height of 4 and a base of 6 is $4 \times 6 = 24$.

Area of Square = (Side)^2

The area of a square with sides of length 5 is $5^2 = 25$.

Area of Trapezoid = $\left(\dfrac{\text{base}_1 + \text{base}_2}{2} \right) \times$ Height

Think of it as the average of the bases (the two parallel sides) times the height (the length of the perpendicular altitude).

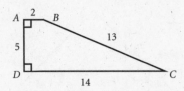

In the trapezoid $ABCD$ above, you can use side $\overline{AD}$ for the height. The average of the bases is $\dfrac{2 + 14}{2} = 8$, so the area is 5×8, or 40.

88. INTERIOR ANGLES OF A POLYGON

The sum of the measures of the interior angles of a polygon is $(n - 2) \times 180$, where n is the number of sides.

Sum of the Angles = $(n - 2) \times 180$ Degrees

The eight angles of an octagon, for example, add up to $(8 - 2) \times 180 = 1{,}080$.

To find **one angle of a regular polygon,** divide the sum of the angles by the number of angles (which is the same as the number of sides). The formula, therefore, is:

Interior Angle = $\dfrac{(n - 2) \times 180}{n}$

Angle A of the regular octagon above measures $\dfrac{1{,}080}{8} = 135$ degrees.

CIRCLES

89. CIRCUMFERENCE OF A CIRCLE

$$\text{Circumference of a Circle} = 2\pi r$$

Here, the radius is 3, and so the circumference is $2\pi(3) = 6\pi$.

90. LENGTH OF AN ARC

An **arc** is a piece of the circumference. If n is the measure of the arc's central angle, then the formula is:

$$\text{Length of an Arc} = \frac{n}{360}(2\pi r)$$

In the figure above, the radius is 5 and the measure of the central angle is 72°. The arc length is $\frac{72}{360}$ or $\frac{1}{5}$ of the circumference:

$$\left(\frac{72}{360}\right)2\pi(5) = \left(\frac{1}{5}\right)10\pi = 2\pi$$

91. AREA OF A CIRCLE

$$\text{Area of a Circle} = \pi r^2$$

The area of the circle above is $\pi(4)^2 = 16\pi$.

92. AREA OF A SECTOR

A **sector** is a piece of the area of a circle. If n is the measure of the sector's central angle, then the formula is:

$$\text{Area of a Sector} = \frac{n}{360}(\pi r^2)$$

In the figure above, the radius is 6 and the measure of the sector's central angle is 30°. The sector has $\frac{30}{360}$ or $\frac{1}{12}$ of the area of the circle:

$$\left(\frac{30}{360}\right)(\pi)(6^2) = \left(\frac{1}{12}\right)(36\pi) = 3\pi$$

SOLIDS

93. SURFACE AREA OF A RECTANGULAR SOLID

The surface of a rectangular solid consists of 3 pairs of identical faces. To find the surface area, find the area of each face and add them up.

If the length is *l*, the width is *w*, and the height is *h*, the formula is:

Surface Area = $2lw + 2wh + 2lh$

The surface area of the box above is:

$2 \times 7 \times 3 + 2 \times 3 \times 4 + 2 \times 7 \times 4 = 42 + 24 + 56 = 122$

94. VOLUME OF A RECTANGULAR SOLID

Volume of a Rectangular Solid = lwh

The volume of a 4-by-5-by-6 box is $4 \times 5 \times 6 = 120$.

A cube is a rectangular solid with length, width, and height all equal. The volume formula if *e* is the length of an edge of the cube is:

Volume of a Cube = e^3

The volume of the cube above is $2^3 = 8$.

95. VOLUME OF OTHER SOLIDS

Volume of a Cylinder = $\pi r^2 h$

The volume of a cylinder where $r = 2$, and $h = 5$ is $\pi(2^2)(5) = 20\pi$.

Volume of a Cone = $\frac{1}{3}\pi r^2 h$

The volume of a cone where $r = 3$, and $h = 6$ is:

Volume $= \frac{1}{3}\pi(3^2)(6) = 18$

Volume of a Sphere $= \dfrac{4}{3}\pi r^3$

If the radius of a sphere is 3, then:

Volume $= \dfrac{4}{3}\pi(3^3) = 36\pi$

TRIGONOMETRY

96. SINE, COSINE, AND TANGENT OF ACUTE ANGLES

To find the sine, cosine, or tangent of an acute angle, use SOHCAHTOA, which is an abbreviation for the following definitions:

$$Sine = \frac{Opposite}{Hypotenuse}$$

$$Cosine = \frac{Adjacent}{Hypotenuse}$$

$$Tangent = \frac{Opposite}{Adjacent}$$

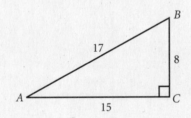

In the figure above:

$$\sin A = \frac{8}{17}$$

$$\cos A = \frac{15}{17}$$

$$\tan A = \frac{8}{15}$$

97. COTANGENT, SECANT, AND COSECANT OF ACUTE ANGLES

Think of the cotangent, secant, and cosecant as the reciprocals of the SOHCAHTOA functions:

$$Cotangent = \frac{1}{Tangent} = \frac{Adjacent}{Opposite}$$

$$Secant = \frac{1}{Cosine} = \frac{Hypotenuse}{Adjacent}$$

$$Cosecant = \frac{1}{Sine} = \frac{Hypotenuse}{Opposite}$$

In the preceeding figure:

$$\cot D = \frac{2}{3}$$

$$\sec D = \frac{\sqrt{13}}{2}$$

$$\csc D = \frac{\sqrt{13}}{3}$$

98. TRIGONOMETRIC FUNCTIONS OF OTHER ANGLES

To find a trigonometric function of an angle greater than 90°, sketch a circle of radius 1 and centered at the origin of the coordinate grid. Start from the point (1, 0) and rotate the appropriate number of degrees counterclockwise.

In the "unit circle" setup above, the basic trigonometric functions are defined in terms of the coordinates a and b:

$$\sin \theta = b$$

$$\cos \theta = a$$

$$\tan \theta = \frac{b}{a}$$

Example: $\sin 210° = ?$

Setup: Sketch a 210° angle in the coordinate plane:

Because the triangle shown in the figure above is a 30°-60°-90° right triangle, we can determine that the coordinates of point P are $-\frac{\sqrt{3}}{2}, -\frac{1}{2}$. The sine is therefore $-\frac{1}{2}$.

99. SIMPLIFYING TRIGONOMETRIC EXPRESSIONS

To simplify trigonometric expressions, use the inverse function definitions along with the fundamental trigonometric identity:
$$\sin^2 x + \cos^2 x = 1$$

Example: $\dfrac{\sin^2 \theta + \cos^2 \theta}{\cos \theta} = ?$

Setup: The numerator equals 1, so:

$$\frac{\sin^2 \theta + \cos^2 \theta}{\cos \theta} = \frac{1}{\cos \theta} = \sec \theta$$

100. GRAPHING TRIGONOMETRIC FUNCTIONS

To graph trigonometric functions, use the x-axis for the angle and the y-axis for the value of the trigonometric function. Use special angles—0°, 30°, 45°, 60°, 90°, 120°, 135°, 150°, 180°, etc.—to plot key points.

The figure above shows a portion of the graph of $y = \sin x$.

NOTES

NOTES

NOTES

NOTES

NOTES

NOTES

NOTES

NOTES

NOTES

Minimum System Requirements*

	Windows®	Macintosh®
Operating System:	Windows, 98SE, NT 4.0 (with Service Pack 6), 2000, ME, XP	Macintosh OS 8.6, OS 9, OS 10.1.3, 10.1.5, 10.2.4, 10.2.8, 10.3, 10.3.7, 10.3.8, 10.4
CPU Type and Speed:	Pentium II® 300 MHz or higher	400 MHz Power PC®, G3, G4, or higher
Hard Drive Space:	15 MB	15 MB
Graphics:	640x 480 thousands of colors (millions recommended)	640x 480 thousands of colors (millions recommended)
CD-ROM Speed:	4x CD-ROM or higher	4x CD-ROM or higher
	SoundBlaster compatible soundcard	Note: An Internet connection is required for the web features of this program.
	Note: An Internet connection is required for the web features of this program.	

Installation instructions are in the User's Guide.

SOFTWARE LICENSE/DISCLAIMER OF WARRANTIES

1. ACCEPTANCE. By using this compact disc you hereby accept the terms and provisions of this license and agree to be bound hereby.
2. OWNERSHIP. The software contained on these compact discs, all content, related documentation and fonts (collectively, the "Software") are all proprietary copyrighted materials owned by =licensors.
3. LICENSE. You are granted a limited license to use the Software. This License allows you to use the Software on a single computer only. You may not copy, distribute, modify, network, rent, lease, loan, or create derivative works based upon the Software in whole or in part. The Software is intended for personal usage only. Your rights to use the Software shall terminate immediately without notice upon your failure to comply with any of the terms hereof.
4. RESTRICTIONS. The Software contains copyrighted material, trade secrets and other proprietary material. In order to protect them, and except as permitted by applicable legislation, you may not decompile, reverse engineer, disassemble or otherwise reduce the Software to human-perceivable form.
5. LIMITED WARRANTY; DISCLAIMER. Kaplan warrants the compact discs on which the Software is recorded to be free from defects in materials and workmanship under normal use for a period of ninety (90) days from the date of purchase as evidenced by a copy of the receipt. Kaplan's entire liability and your exclusive remedy will be replacement of the compact discs not meeting this warranty. The Software is provided "AS IS" and without warranty of any kind and Kaplan and Kaplan's licensors EXPRESSLY DISCLAIM ALL WARRANTIES, EXPRESS OR IMPLIED, INCLUDING THE IMPLIED WARRANTIES OF MERCHANTABILITY OR FITNESS FOR A PARTICULAR PURPOSE. FURTHERMORE, KAPLAN DOES NOT WARRANT THAT THE FUNCTIONS CONTAINED IN THE SOFTWARE WILL MEET YOUR REQUIREMENTS, OR THAT THE OPERATION OF THE SOFTWARE WILL BE UNINTERRUPTED OR ERROR-FREE, OR THAT DEFECTS IN THE SOFTWARE WILL BE CORRECTED. KAPLAN DOES NOT WARRANT OR MAKE ANY REPRESENTATIONS REGARDING THE USE OR THE RESULTS OF THE USE OF THE SOFTWARE IN TERMS OF THEIR CORRECTNESS, ACCURACY, RELIABILITY OR OTHERWISE. UNDER NO CIRCUMSTANCES, INCLUDING NEGLIGENCE, SHALL KAPLAN BE LIABLE FOR ANY DIRECT, INDIRECT, PUNITIVE, INCIDENTAL, SPECIAL OR CONSEQUENTIAL DAMAGES, INCLUDING, BUT NOT LIMITED TO, LOST PROFITS OR WAGES, IN CONNECTION WITH THE SOFTWARE EVEN IF KAPLAN HAS BEEN ADVISED OF THE POSSIBILITY OF SUCH DAMAGES. CERTAIN OF THE LIMITATIONS HEREIN PROVIDED MAY BE PRECLUDED BY LAW.
6. EXPORT LAW ASSURANCES. You agree and certify that you will not export the Software outside of the United States except as authorized and as permitted by the laws and regulations of the United States. If the Software has been rightfully obtained by you outside of the United States, you agree that you will not re-export the Software except as permitted by the laws and regulations of the United States and the laws and regulations of the jurisdiction in which you obtained the Software.
7. MISCELLANEOUS. This license represents the entire understanding of the parties, may only be modified in writing and shall be governed by the laws of the State of New York.

If you need assistance with installations, need to request a replacement disk, or have any other software questions, please visit the "customer service" area of our website at www.kaptest.com.